SQL & PL/SQL for Oracle

Black Book™

Dr. P.S. Deshpande

AF632417

Published by:

dreamtech PRESS

©Copyright 2016 by Dreamtech Press, 19-A, Ansari Road, Daryaganj, New Delhi-110002

Black Book is a trademark of Paraglyph Press Inc., 2246 E. Myrtle Avenue, Phoenix Arizona 85202, USA exclusively licensed in Indian, Asian and African continent to Dreamtech Press, India.

This book may not be duplicated in any way without the express written consent of the publisher, except in the form of brief excerpts or quotations for the purposes of review. The information contained herein is for the personal use of the reader and may not be incorporated in any commercial programs, other books, databases, or any kind of software without written consent of the publisher. Making copies of this book or any portion for any purpose other than your own is a violation of copyright laws.

Limits of Liability/disclaimer of Warranty: The author and publisher have used their best efforts in preparing this book. The author make no representation or warranties with respect to the accuracy or completeness of the contents of this book, and specifically disclaim any implied warranties of merchantability or fitness of any particular purpose. There are no warranties which extend beyond the descriptions contained in this paragraph. No warranty may be created or extended by sales representatives or written sales materials. The accuracy and completeness of the information provided herein and the opinions stated herein are not guaranteed or warranted to produce any particulars results, and the advice and strategies contained herein may not be suitable for every individual. Neither Dreamtech Press nor author shall be liable for any loss of profit or any other commercial damages, including but not limited to special, incidental, consequential, or other damages.

Trademarks: All brand names and product names used in this book are trademarks, registered trademarks, or trade names of their respective holders. Dreamtech Press is not associated with any product or vendor mentioned in this book.

ISBN: 978-81-7722-940-0

Reprint Edition: 2026

Printed at: Nisha Enterprises.

Preface

After getting a good response to my earlier book on Oracle 10g, I started upgrading it for Oracle 11g.

Since Oracle 11g has introduced a large number of new features, I have rewritten almost the complete book. My teaching and consultancy experience is reflected in the book. I have given practical as well as theoretical concepts in Oracle 11g programming to help students prepare for OCP exams and be ready to face interviews.

The book covers all advanced features in Oracle 11g—SQL features, Views, Hierarchical queries, Integrity constraints, Analytical queries Rollup, Cube, Joins, Scalar Subquery, Multitable inserts, Merge statement, Statistical functions, Model queries, Collections, Dynamic SQL, Object and Object types, Error handling, Subprograms, Packages, Triggers, Transaction processing, ACID, Locking, Rollback Segments, UNDO Tablespace, Dependency tracking, Flashback Query, Expression Filter, Security, Auditing,...and more

To help students in understanding concepts better, the source code is also available on our website. This can encourage students to perform some experimentation.

I would appreciate your valuable suggestions/comments to help me in, further, improving this book.

P.S. Deshpande

psdesh@bsnlgp.com

Contents at Glance

UNIT - II: PL/SQL

Table of Contents

UNIT - II: PL/SQL

Unit I
SQL

1

Introduction to SQL

Structured Query Language (SQL) is the heart of Relational Database Management System (RDBMS). It is the language used to perform all the operations in a relational database. The operations that are required for handling a database are creating tables, inserting data in tables, updating data in tables, deleting data from the tables, and retrieving data from the tables. In addition to these operations, sometimes we may also require a control to access data in a multi-user database. In a multi-user database, users may want to secure their data from other users; therefore, adequate security should be provided. In most of the RDBMSs, the common operations, such as changing and retrieving data from the tables are specified using SQL, since it is the only language interpreted by the RDBMS.

This chapter introduces you to SQL and its various components, such as Data Definition Language (DDL), Data Manipulation Language (DML), and Data Control Language (DCL), in detail. Next, you learn to insert and modify data in tables and write queries to retrieve the required data from the database. You also learn about various datatypes used in SQL.

Describing the Importance of SQL in RDBMS

When you issue a command to the RDBMS in SQL, the RDBMS interprets your command and takes necessary actions. Figure 1.1 shows how SQL commands are interpreted by RDBMS:

USER → SQL → RDBMS

Figure 1.1: Displaying the Role of SQL in RDBMS

SQL is a very powerful language and most of the RDBMSs use SQL as their language for specifying operations. It is also a standardized language, similar to C, i.e. the syntax of SQL changes very little from one RDBMS to another. Therefore, SQL for Oracle is similar to SQL for Ingress or Sybase.

An important feature of SQL is that it is a non-procedural language. In a non-procedural language, you have to describe what to do, rather than how to do a job. How the job should be done is the responsibility of the underlying system, such as RDBMS. On the contrary, in the procedural way, you have to give the complete procedure of doing the job.

Suppose you ask your friend to reserve a railway ticket. The procedural way to do this is to give your friend complete stepwise instructions as follows:

- Take a bus
- Buy ticket for traveling in bus
- Go to the railway station
- Fill the reservation form
- Make the reservation
- Take a bus
- Buy ticket for traveling in bus
- Come back home

In this case, you are specifying a complete set of instructions. However, in a non-procedural way, you just need to specify your requirement to your friend as: make a railway reservation.

After you specify this, it becomes the responsibility of your friend to find out how to do it, i.e. how to go to the railway station and how to make the reservation.

The following are the advantages of using the non-procedural way:

- **Smaller code snippets**—Refers that the non-procedural way allows you to use smaller code snippets to perform a task.
- **Simplicity**—Refers to the simplicity of code. In this method, you need not remember lengthy code to perform a task.

- **Easy code writing**—Refers to the ease required in writing the code. This means that in a non-procedural way, you do not have to write complex programs to do the given task.
- **Reduction in the cost of maintaining a software**—Reduces the cost of maintaining a software. Though all the other advantages definitely reduce the time and effort you put in to perform a task, this is the most important advantage in real life. Let's first describe the meaning of maintenance.

Software industry is often referred to as a service industry. Therefore, developing a product and delivering it does not end your job. For example, you have developed a payroll software application in three months. The customer wants that the software should consider three late marks in a month as one leave. Suppose the rules regarding the number of late marks are changed and the new rule is to consider five late marks for one leave. To incorporate this change in the software, you will have to modify your software. The overhead expenditure in changing the software is called maintenance overhead. This maintenance overhead is directly proportional to the number of lines of codes in the software.

Exploring the Components of SQL

As already discussed, you can perform almost every database operation using SQL, such as creating a table, inserting data in the table, and manipulating the data. Since many things could be done using SQL, these things are grouped into different components according to their usage. The main components of SQL are DDL, DML, DCL, Query Language (QL), and Transaction Control Language (TCL).

Let's now discuss each of these components in detail.

Data Definition Language

In Oracle, tables are the only way to store data; therefore, all the information has to be arranged in the form of tables. Suppose you want to store some information about a company in the database.

Table 1.1 lists the data that you want to store in the Oracle database:

Table 1.1: Data for the Company Table

Cname	City
ACC	NAGPUR
TATA	DELHI

To store this data, you first need to create a table. You can create a table by using the create table command, as shown in the following code snippet:

```
create table company(cname char(10), city char(10));
```

This statement is a part of DDL. You can also create other objects, such as index and views by using a DDL statement. Using DDL, you can also drop or alter objects.

Data Manipulation Language

DML, as the name suggests, allows you to manipulate data in an existing table. Using DML, you can carry out various operations, such as insertion, updation, and deletion, on a table. Let's now learn how to add a row in an existing table.

Listing 1.1 shows the syntax to add a row in a table:

Listing 1.1: Adding a Row to a Table

```
insert into company values ('ACC','NAGPUR');
```

Listing 1.2 shows the syntax to update a record in an existing table:

Listing 1.2: Updating Data in an Existing Table

```
update company
set city = 'MUMBAI'
where cname = 'ACC';
```

Listing 1.3 shows the syntax to delete a record from an existing table:

Listing 1.3: Deleting Rows Using the delete Statement

```
delete company where cname = 'ACC';
```

In the preceding listings, you can see that any type of data manipulation can be carried out using insert, delete, and update statements. Other statements, which are included in this category, are merge, lock, and explain plan statements.

Query Language

The query language is also a part of DML and is used to retrieve data from a table. Now, let's learn how to retrieve data from a table.

Listing 1.4 shows the syntax to retrieve data from a table:

Listing 1.4: Retrieving Data from a Table

```
select * from company;
```

Listing 1.5 shows how to retrieve location of the ACC company:

Listing 1.5: Retrieving the Location of the ACC Company

```
select city
from company
where cname = 'ACC';
```

Listing 1.6 shows how to retrieve information about a company from a database table:

Listing 1.6: Retrieving Information about the Company, its employee, and company location

```
select emp_company.ename,company.cname,company.city
from emp_company,company
where emp_company.cname = company.cname;
```

You can also do set operations or group operations on the data that is retrieved using a query language.

Data Control Language

DCL allows you to control access to the data. In other words, it grants permissions to a user to access and manipulate data. The following are the statements of DCL:

- **GRANT**—Grants permissions to one or more users to perform an operation or a set of operations on an object
- **REVOKE**—Withdraws the access permissions given by the GRANT statement

Let's now learn how to grant access permissions to a user with the help of an example. Suppose, a table is owned by user U1, who wishes to give access of the table to another user, named U2. The user U1 can do so by using the GRANT statement.

Listing 1.7 shows the syntax to use the GRANT statement:

Listing 1.7: Granting Access of the Company Table to User **U2**

```
grant select on company to U2;
```

Now, user U2 can access data from the Company table, which is owned by user U1, by using the following statement:

```
select * from u1.company;
```

Apart from these four components—DDL, DML, query language, and DCL—that allow you to process data, another product of Oracle, called SQLPLUS gives additional facilities to carry out various operations, such as formatting an output and converting data in a table.

Transaction Control, Session Control, and System Control

Transaction control statements include commit (for saving changes or ending transaction), rollback (for undoing changes upto last commit), and savepoint (for storing state of database at particular point). The session control statement is used to change session level parameters, like default date formats and numeric formats. The session is created when the user logs in to Oracle and terminated, when the user exits from Oracle. The system control statements are used to change system-wide parameters, like memory allocation. Generally, they are used by a database administrator (DBA).

Starting SQLPLUS

The SQLPLUS command allows you to perform all the operations of SQL by executing various SQL commands. This command can be started only after starting Oracle database engine. The following code snippet shows the syntax to start Oracle database engine:

```
$sqldba startup
```

or

```
$svrmgrl startup (in 8i)
```

In the preceding code snippet, $ is the operating system Command Prompt. You can start Oracle server in Oracle 9i/10g/11g by using the following commands:

```
$sqlplus / as sysdba
startup
```

The following code snippet shows the command to start SQLPLUS:

```
$sqlplus
```

Now, give a valid username and password, and the following prompt gets displayed:

```
SQL>
```

Now, issue the sample command:

```
select * from company;
```

In the preceding code snippet, the semicolon ; is the terminator. An SQLPLUS command should be terminated by a semicolon ;.

You can write commands in a file by using a text editor. You need to invoke the editor before working with SQL files. The following code snippet shows the command to invoke an editor:

```
edit a
```

The preceding command invokes the operating system editor.

NOTE

If you write a command in the a.sql file, you can execute the command as SQL>@a.

To use vi editor in Unix, you can give the command as:

```
define _editor=/user/bin/vi
```

In the preceding code snippet:

- _editor is the name of the editor, as specified in the environment variable
- /user/bin/vi is the path of vi in Unix

If you are working in windows, then give the editor name as:

```
define _editor=notepad;
```

TIP

An editor can also be defined in Windows by opening the SQLPLUS and clicking the Edit|Editor|Define Editor menu option.

You can write the preceding command in the login.sql file and keep this file in a directory. The commands in the login.sql file are executed when SQLPLUS is invoked. The output of queries can be directed to a certain file, as shown in the following code snippet:

```
spool op_txt
select * from company;
spool off
```

In this case, the output of the query, select * from company, goes to the op_txt file. To close the file, the spool off command is used. By default, the spool file has the .lst extension. The file created, in this case, will be op_txt.lst present in the BIN directory.

NOTE

The path for the bin directory is ORACLE_HOME\BIN\. The environment variable ORACLE_HOME defines location of Oracle software.

Working with Data Definition Language

DDL allows you to define and manage the structure of tables and indexes in a database. The most-commonly used DDL statements are CREATE, ALTER, RENAME, DROP, and TRUNCATE. Let's now learn how to define the structure of a table with the help of an example. Suppose you want to store the following information:

- Employee name and his living city
- Employee name and his working company
- Company information
- Employee shift information
- Employee and his/her manager

The preceding information can be stored in the following tables:

Name of Employee	:	ename
Name of Company	:	cname
Date of Joining	:	jdate
Name of Manager	:	mname

Table 1.2 lists the data for the Employee table:

Table 1.2: Data for the Employee Table

	ename	city
1	ANIL	NAGPUR
2	SHANKAR	MUMBAI
3	JAYA	CHENNAI
4	SUNIL	MUMBAI
5	VIJAY	DELHI
6	PRAKASH	KOLKATA
7	AJAY	CHENNAI

Table 1.3 lists the data for the Emp_company table:

Table 1.3: Data for the Emp_company Table

ename	cname	salary	jdate
ANIL	ACC	1500.00	1-MAY-89
SHANKAR	TATA	2000.00	10-JUL-90
JAYA	CMC	1800.00	7-JUN-91
SUNIL	CMC	1700.00	1-JAN-88
VIJAY	TATA	5000.00	3-JAN-88
PRAKASH	TATA	3000.00	27-MAY-89
AJAY	ACC	8000.00	30-APR-95
AMOL	ACC	1000.00	17-MAR-95

Table 1.4 lists the data for the Company table:

Table 1.4: Data for the Company Table

cname	city
ACC	CHENNAI
TATA	MUMBAI
ACC	NAGPUR
CMC	MUMBAI
CMC	CHENNAI
TATA	DELHI

Table 1.5 lists the data for the Manager table:

Table 1.5: Data for the Manager Table

ename	mname
ANIL	AJAY
SHANKAR	VIJAY
JAYA	–
SUNIL	JAYA
VIJAY	–
PRAKASH	SHANKAR
AJAY	–

Table 1.6 lists the data for the Emp_shift table:

Table 1.6: Data for the Emp_shift Table

Ename	shift
ANIL	A
SUNIL	B
VIJAY	B
PRAKASH	C

Now, to store all this data, you have to create tables in the database, and for that, you first need to create the following columns:

- **Table Name**—Refers to the name of the table (already known here)
- **Column Name**—Refers to the name of the column (already known here)
- **Column Type**—Refers to the column type, which decides the type of data that can be stored in the column. If you want to store amount, you need to use the number datatype. To store joining date, you have to use the date datatype.

The syntax of the create table command is as follows:

```
create table <table name> (<column1><type>, <column2><type>,...);
```

NOTE

The character ; is the terminator for the SQL statement.

Listing 1.8 shows how to create a table:

Listing 1.8: Creating a Table

```
create table employee
(ename varchar2 (10),city varchar2 (10));
```

If the command runs successfully, the Table created message gets displayed.

The following code snippet shows the syntax to create the Emp_company table:

```
create table emp_company
(ename varchar2 (10),
cname varchar2 (10),
salary number (7,2),
jdate date);
```

To create the Company table, write the following create statement:

```
create table company
(cname varchar2 (10),
city varchar2 (10));
```

To create the Manager table, write the following create statement:

```
create table manager
(ename varchar2 (10),
mname varchar2 (10));
```

To create the Emp_shift table, write the following create statement:

```
create table emp_shift
(ename varchar2(10),
shift varchar2(1));
```

NOTE

The object names are not case sensitive. Therefore, ename and ENAME refer to the same column name.

The describe command displays the structure of a table.

Listing 1.9 shows the use of the describe command:

Listing 1.9: Using the describe Command

```
describe employee;
```

The output of Listing 1.9 is as follows:

```
Name                                    Null?          Type
--------------------------------      -------      ------------
ENAME                                                  VARCHAR2(10)
CITY                                                   VARCHAR2(10)
```

Working with Data Manipulation Language

DML is used for modifying the data in a table. Modification can be made by using insertion, updation, or deletion operations.

Inserting Data in Table

A row is inserted into the table by using the insert command. The syntax of the insert statement is as follows:

```
INSERT [INTO] {table_name} [(column_list)]
VALUES (expression [ ,...n])
```

Listing 1.10 shows how to insert data into the company table:

Listing 1.10: Inserting Data into the Company Table

```
insert into company values ('ACC','CHENNAI');
```

In this case, the first value, ACC, is inserted into the first column, while the second value, CHENNAI, is inserted into the second column of the table.

NOTE

As you cannot change the order in which data is inserted, you have to be careful while writing the insert statement. Suppose, you are not specifying a proper order, as shown in this code snippet:

```
insert into company  values ('CHENNAI', 'ACC');
```

In this case, CHENNAI will be inserted in the cname column, and ACC will be inserted in the column city. This is because we had already defined our table with cname as the first column and city as the second column.

If you want to change the order in which the data is inserted, then you can specify explicitly where the first and the second value should be inserted.

Listing 1.11 shows how to specify the locations where the values should be inserted:

Listing 1.11: Specifying the Locations

```
insert into company(city,cname) values
('CHENNAI', 'ACC');
```

In this case, CHENNAI gets inserted under the column city, while ACC under cname.

NOTE

As an exercise, you can insert all records of the tables given in Appendix A.

Inserting Null Values

Null represents the information that is not available. Nulls cannot be inserted in ways, shown in the following listings:

Listing 1.12: Inserting a Row When You Know the Salary of ANIL but Not the Joining Date

```
Insert into emp_company values
('ANIL', 'ACC', 1500.00);
```

The command, shown in Listing 1.12, will give an error because the emp_company table has four columns, while only three values are specified. By default, it expects data for all the columns.

This problem can be solved by using null values. You can insert null values in the following ways:

- Specifying null explicitly in values by using the word null:

```
insert into emp_company values
('ANIL','ACC',1500.00,null);
```

The preceding command will insert null value into the jdate column. Another way of inserting null value is by specifying the columns explicitly in the insert command:

```
insert into emp_company (ename, cname, salary)
values ('ANIL','ACC',1500.00);
```

One record is inserted for each execution of the insert statement. Suppose you write two statements—one for inserting a value under the cname column and the other for inserting a value, Nagpur, under the city column—then two rows are inserted as follows:

```
insert into company values (cname) values ('ACC', '');
insert into company (City) values ('', 'NAGPUR');
```

Table 1.7 lists the records to be inserted in the Company table:

Table 1.7: Records of the Company Table

cname	city
ACC	
-	NAGPUR

Earlier, in order to enter 50 records, you need to write the insert statement 50 times. However, now you can use the substitution variable to insert a large number of records. Use of substitution variable enables users to insert large data in less time.

Listing 1.13: Using the Substitution Variable

```
insert into company values (&cname,&city);
```

The statement prompts for values of cname and city.

The output of Listing 1.13 is as follows:

```
Enter the value of cname: 'ACC'
Enter the value of city: 'NAGPUR'
```

Enter the values of cname and city, shown in the preceding code snippet, and press the ENTER key. The message row is created. You can insert another record into the same table just by typing run at the SQL prompt, as follows:

```
run;
```

or

```
SQL>/
```

The run command is used for executing a previous command.

TIP

The combination of `&` and `run` can be used for repeating similar operations.

Listing 1.14: Inserting Rows into the Emp_company Table

```
insert into emp_company values(&ename,&cname,&sal,&jdate);
```

In Listing 1.14, & indicates a substitution variable. If the value of the variable is not defined, then it will ask for the value. You can use any names for variables, such as:

```
insert into company values (&cn1, &ct1);
```

This will prompt you to give values of cn1 and ct1 as:

```
Enter value of cn1 : 'TATA'
Enter value of ct1 : 'MUMBAI'
```

It will prepare and execute an insert statement as:

```
insert into company
```

and execute the statement as:

```
insert into company values ('TATA', 'MUMBAI');
```

Retrieving Data

The select statement is used to retrieve data from the existing tables. Using the select statement, you can get data from single as well as multiple tables.

Let's first understand how data is retrieved from a single table.

NOTE

You are advised to create tables and insert data into them like the one given in Appendix A, before you start reading further.

Retrieving Data from a Single Table

The following code snippet shows the syntax to retrieve data from the employee table:

```
select ename,city from employee;
```

In the preceding code snippet:

- The columns from which data has to be retrieved are to be mentioned after the select clause
- The name of the table has to be mentioned after the clause

NOTE

*If you want to get data of all the columns, then you can mention * after the select clause.*

Listing 1.15 shows how to get data from the Emp_company table:

Listing 1.15: Getting Data from the Emp_company Table

```
select * from emp_company;
```

The output of Listing 1.15 is as follows:

```
ENAME          CNAME        SALARY       JDATE
----------     --------     -------      ----------
ANIL           ACC          1500         01-MAY-89
SHANKAR        TATA         2000         10-JUL-90
JAYA           CMC          1800         07-JUNE-91
SUNIL          CMC          1700         01-JAN-89
VIJAY          TATA         5000         03-JAN-88
PRAKASH        TATA         3000         27-MAR-95
AJAY           ACC          8000         30-APR-95
AMOL           ACC          1000         17-MAY-95
```

You can also retrieve data by writing the alternative SQL statement and mentioning all columns in the select statement as:

```
select ename, cname, salary, jdate from emp_company;
```

The output of the preceding code snippet is as follows:

```
ENAME         CNAME        SALARY      JDATE
----------    ---------    -------     ----------
ANIL          ACC          1500        01-MAY-89
SHANKAR       TATA         2000        10-JUL-90
JAYA          CMC          1800        07-JUNE-91
SUNIL         CMC          1700        01-JAN-89
VIJAY         TATA         5000        03-JAN-88
PRAKASH       TATA         3000        27-MAR-95
AJAY          ACC          8000        30-APR-95
AMOL          ACC          1000        17-MAY-95

8 rows selected
```

The output is based on the order of columns in the statement. Listing 1.16 shows how to change the order of columns:

Listing 1.16: Changing the Order of the Columns

```
select cname, ename, jdate, salary from emp_company;
```

The output of Listing 1.16 is as follows:

```
CNAME        ENAME        JDATE        SALARY
-------      -------      ----------   -------
ACC          ANIL         01-MAY-89    1500
TATA         SHANKAR      10-JUL-90    2000
CMC          JAYA         07-JUN-91    1800
CMC          SUNIL        01-JAN-89    1700
TATA         VIJAY        03-JAN-88    5000
TATA         PRAKASH      27-MAR-89    3000
ACC          AJAY         30-APR-95    8000
ACC          AMOL         17-MAY-95    1000

8 rows selected
```

Retrieving Data from Selected Columns

If you want to get information on certain columns of the table, then you can mention those columns in the SELECT clause.

Listing 1.17 shows how to get information only on ename and salary:

Listing 1.17: Getting Information Only on ename and salary

```
select ename, salary from emp_company;
```

The output of Listing 1.17 is as follows:

```
ENAME        SALARY
--------     -------
ANIL         1500
SHANKAR      2000
JAYA         1800
SUNIL        1700
VIJAY        5000
PRAKASH      3000
```

```
AJAY        8000
AMOL        1000

8 rows selected
```

Listing 1.18 shows the code to display the names of the companies and the cities in which they are located:

Listing 1.18: Displaying Company Names and Their Cities

```
select cname, city from company;
```

The output of Listing 1.18 is as follows:

```
CNAME    CITY
ACC      CHENNAI
TATA     MUMBAI
ACC      NAGPUR
CMC      MUMBAI
CMC      CHENNAI
TATA     DELHI

6 rows selected
```

Let's take another example.

Suppose you want to get the name of a company located in the city MUMBAI. This is a slightly complex statement. So, let's first understand the syntax of the statement to be used.

Listing 1.19 shows the syntax of the select statement with condition:

Listing 1.19: Syntax of the select Statement with Condition

```
select col1, col2
from T1, T2......
where<condition>
```

In Listing 1.19:

- The tables T1, T2... indicate the name of the tables from which data is to be retrieved.
- The col1 and col2 indicate the name of the columns.
- The where condition indicates rows that are going to be selected. The where condition should be a Boolean expression that returns TRUE or FALSE. You can combine multiple conditions using AND, OR, and NOT operators.

You can write the query of retrieving the name of the company located in the city MUMBAI as:

```
select cname from company where city = 'MUMBAI';
```

NOTE

The select, from, and where components of the SELECT statement are capable of getting data from a single table in all possible ways.

Using Column Alias Names

You can use column alias names to have meaningful names in a query. The column alias is specified after the column name with space in between or with the AS keyword, as shown in the following code snippet:

```
select cname companyname from company;
```

or

```
select cname as companyname from company;
```

The output of the preceding code snippet is as follows:

```
COMPANYNAME
----------
ACC
```

```
TATA
ACC
CMC
CMC
TATA
```

Using Table Alias

You can use table alias similar to column alias. The table alias is mentioned after the table name. The column name can be mentioned as tablename.columnname, if alias is not mentioned and aliasname.columnname, if alias is mentioned. In the following example, c1 is the table alias:

```
select c1.cname as companyname from company c1;
```

Using Dual Table

The dual table is a single row, single column dummy table available to all users. In other words, it is a special one-row table that is present by default in all Oracle database installations. Listing 1.20 shows how to retrieve values of system variable in SQL format:

Listing 1.20: Retrieving Values of System Variable in SQL Format

```
select sysdate from dual;
```

The output of Listing 1.20 is as follows:

```
SYSDATE
---------
17-AUG-06
```

Listing 1.21 shows how to evaluate expressions in the SQL format:

Listing 1.21: Evaluating Expression in the SQL Format

```
select 3*4+2 from dual;
```

The output of Listing 1.21 is as follows:

```
    3*4+2
 --------
       14
```

Now, let's learn how to write a query.

Writing a Query

Prior to writing a query, you need to decide on the table from which you want to retrieve data, the columns that are required for output, and conditions for filtering rows.

Listing 1.22 shows how to display the names of companies located in MUMBAI:

Listing 1.22: Displaying the Names of Companies Located in MUMBAI

```
select cname from company where city ='MUMBAI';
```

The output of Listing 1.22 is as follows:

```
CNAME
TATA
CMC
```

Listing 1.23 shows how to display the names of employees living in a city:

Listing 1.23: Displaying the Names of Employees Living in the NAGPUR City

```
select ename from employee
where city = 'NAGPUR';
```

The output of Listing 1.23 is as follows:

```
ENAME
ANIL
```

Listing 1.24 shows how to display the names of employees based upon their salary:

Listing 1.24: Displaying the Names of Employees Working with the ACC Company and Receiving a Salary Greater than 1000.00

```
select ename from emp_company where cname = 'ACC' and salary > 1000;
```

The output of Listing 1.24 is as follows:

```
ENAME
--------
ANIL
AJAY
```

In this case, the AND operator is used to connect two conditions.

Listing 1.25 shows how to display the names of the persons who are not employees of the ACC company (notice that the condition is negative here and such conditions can be written by using the NOT operators):

Listing 1.25: Displaying the Names of the Persons who are not Employees of the ACC Company

```
select ename from emp_company where not (cname='ACC');
```

The output of Listing 1.25 is as follows:

```
ENAME
---------
SHANKAR
JAYA
SUNIL
VIJAY
PRAKASH
```

Alternatively, you can write the code, shown in Listing 1.25, as shown in the following code snippet:

```
select ename from emp_company where cname<>'ACC';
```

The output of the preceding code snippet is given as follows:

```
ENAME
SHANKAR
JAYA
SUNIL
VIJAY
PRAKASH
```

NOTE

<> is used for 'not equal', the alternative sign is != .

Listing 1.26 shows how to display the names of employees from the ACC or TATA company:

Listing 1.26: Displaying the Names of Employees from the ACC or TATA Company

```
select ename from emp_company where cname ='ACC' or cname = 'TATA';
```

The output of Listing 1.26 is as follows:

```
ENAME
-------
ANIL
SHANKAR
VIJAY
PRAKASH
AJAY
AMOL
```

Understanding Datatypes

Oracle provides different datatypes for storing various types of information, such as text, numeric, date, images, and sound files.

Table 1.8 lists the datatypes provided by Oracle:

Table 1.8: Datatypes Provided by Oracle

Datatype	Specification	Description
char	CHAR (size)	char data with size is specified in number, such as char(10). Maximum size is 2000 bytes. Minimum and default size is 1 byte.
varchar2	VARCHAR2 (size)	varchar data with size is specified in number, such as varchar2(10) (Recommended for less storage). Maximum size is 4000 bytes and minimum size is 1 byte. You have to specify the size; otherwise, error is returned.
date	DATE	Used for specifying dates. Date stores century, year, month, day, hour, minute, and seconds. The range is between January 1, 4712 BC and December 31, 9999 AD.
TIMESTAMP	[(fractional_seconds_precision)]	Used for fractional seconds. The fractional seconds precision is from 0 to 9, while default is 6.
number	NUMBER	Used to specify numeric data: • NUMBER (precision) or • NUMBER (precision, scale) • Number has digits equal to the specified size. It occupies 1 to 22 bytes. The range is 10^{126} to 10^{-130}. The maximum value of precision is 38. The scale can be between –84 to 127. If scale is negative, then data is rounded to scale digits to the left of decimal points. This implies that for specification number (10,-3) for number 123456, the storage is 123000,i.e. the number is rounded upto three places before decimal digits. If scale is more than precision, then maximum number of digits to the right of decimal point is equal to precision. If the input number is more than scale, then the rounding is done up to scale. For example, if you specify Number(3,4), then it is stored in the form 0.0xxx. If the number is 0.02345, then it is stored as it is. If the number is 0.023457, then it is stored as 0.02346. If you specify 0.2345, then an error is returned.
DEC		Indicates decimal digits.
DECIMAL		Similar to number.
BINARY_FLOAT		Similar to number, 32 bit single precision.

Table 1.8: Datatypes Provided by Oracle

Datatype	Specification	Description
BINARY_DOUBLE		Similar to number, 64 bit double precision.
INTEGER		Same as number but without decimal digit.
SMALLINT		Same as integer.
Raw	RAW (size)	Raw binary data. Maximum size is 2000 bytes.
Long raw	LONG RAW	Raw large binary data. Stores 2 GB data.
Blob		Large binary and character data. Maximum size is (4GB-1)*database block size.
Clob		Large binary and character data containing single-byte or multibyte characters Maximum size is (4GB-1)*database block size. It stores national character set data.
Bfile		External files. Maximum size of BFILE data is 4 GB.

Oracle provides char and varchar2 for storing text data. If you define char(10) and insert 4 char, then internal space allocation will be of 10 bytes. However, for varchar2 datatype, the allocation is 4 bytes only. When char and varchar2 data are compared, then nulls are padded to smaller data. The trailing blanks are ignored in the char comparison, as shown in Listing 1.27:

Listing 1.27: Creating Table ztemp5

```
SQL> create table ztemp5(a char(10), b varchar2(10));
```

The output of Listing 1.27 is as follows:

```
Table created.
```

Listing 1.28 shows how to insert values:

Listing 1.28: Inserting Values

```
SQL> insert into ztemp5 values('anil','anil');
```

The output of Listing 1.28 is as follows:

```
1 row created.
```

Listing 1.29 shows how to commit a transaction:

Listing 1.29: Committing a Transaction

```
SQL> commit;
```

The output of Listing 1.29 is as follows:

```
Commit complete.
```

Listing 1.30 shows how to display data where a = 'anil':

Listing 1.30: Displaying Data where a = 'anil'

```
SQL> select a from ztemp5 where a='anil ' --with blank;char data is compared even if blank
   is present;
```

The output of Listing 1.30 is as follows:

```
A
----------
ANIL
```

Listing 1.31 shows how to display data where b = 'anil':

Listing 1.31: Displaying Data where b = 'anil'

```
SQL> select b from ztemp5 where b='anil ' -- with blank;varchar2 data does not ignore
blanks
```

The output of Listing 1.31 is as follows:

```
no rows selected
```

Listing 1.32 shows the code to display data:

Listing 1.32: Displaying Data

```
SQL> select b from ztemp5 where b='anil' --without blank;
```

The output of Listing 1.32 is as follows:

```
B
----------
ANIL
```

Oracle has recommended to use BINARY_FLOAT and BINARY_DOUBLE instead of NUMBER for the following reasons:

- These datatypes are used for storing floating point number based on IEEE standards. BINARY_FLOAT is used to store 32-floating point number while BINARY_DOUBLE is used to store 64_bit floating point number.
- These datatypes make computations much faster than NUMBER because these operations are done primarily using hardware.
- BINARY_FLOAT requires 5 bytes while BINARY_DOUBLE requires 9 bytes. NUMBER may take 22 bytes.
- These datatypes support numbers that are smaller and larger than the numbers supported by NUMBER.
- Oracle recommends using Large Objects (LOB) datatype instead of the LONG datatype. You can specify maximum one long column in one table. The LONG column can appear only in the SET clause of the UPDATE statement, INSERT statement, and SELECT clause. You cannot use the LONG column in other clauses, such as the where clause.

Intervals are datatypes provided by Oracle, such as INTERVAL YEAR TO MONTH and INTERVAL DAY TO SECOND, to measure time intervals.

To measure a time interval, you need to create a table using interval datatypes. The first column stores data of interval in terms of year and month, while the second stores data in day and seconds. You can specify the maximum value of year as 99 and maximum value of days as 99 because both are having a precision of 2 digits.

Listing 1.33 shows how to create a table using the INTERVAL YEAR TO MONTH and INTERVAL DAY TO SECOND:

Listing 1.33: Creating Table Using INTERVAL YEAR TO MONTH and INTERVAL DAY TO SECOND

```
create table ztemp6(a  INTERVAL YEAR(2) TO MONTH, b  INTERVAL DAY(2) TO
  SECOND(6));
desc ztemp6;
```

The output of Listing 1.33 is as follows:

```
Name                            Null?    Type
------------------------------- -------- ----------------------------
A                                        INTERVAL YEAR(2) TO MONTH
B                                        INTERVAL DAY(2) TO SECOND(6)
```

Listing 1.34 shows how to add a row of data into a table:

Listing 1.34: Adding a Row of Data into the Table

```
insert into ztemp6 values (NUMTOYMINTERVAL(2,'year'),NUMTODSINTERVAL(2,'day'));
```

The output of Listing 1.34 is as follows:

```
1 row created
```

In Listing 1.34:

- The function NUMTOYMINTERVAL(2,'year') converts number 2 into an interval year to month literal of 2 years
- The function NUMTODSINTERVAL(99,'year') converts number 99 into an interval day to second literal of 99 days

Listing 1.35 shows how to list data of the ztemp6 table:

Listing 1.35: Listing Data of the ztemp6 Table

```
select * from ztemp6;
```

The output of Listing 1.35 is as follows:

```
A                B
--------         --------
+02-00           +02 00:00:00.000000
SQL> select numtoyminterval('3.5','year') from dual;

NUMTOYMINTERVAL('3.5','YEAR')
---------------------------------------------------------------------------
+000000003-06

SQL> select numtoyminterval('3.9','year') from dual;

NUMTOYMINTERVAL('3.9','YEAR')
---------------------------------------------------------------------------
+000000003-10
```

The value 3.5 indicates 3 years and 5 months. The value 3.9 is converted to 3 years and 9 months by rounding value 9 to 10 months.

The following code snippet generates an error because the value 100 is out of range:

```
insert into ztemp6 values (NUMTOYMINTERVAL(2,'year'),NUMTODSINTERVAL(100,        'day'));
insert into ztemp6 values (NUMTOYMINTERVAL(2,'year'),NUMTODSINTERVAL(100,        'day'));
```

The output of the preceding code snippet is as follows:

```
ERROR at line 1:
ORA-01873: the leading precision of the interval is too small
```

Listing 1.36 shows how to use the sysdate function to return the current system date:

Listing 1.36: Using the sysdate Function to Return the Current System Date

```
select sysdate from dual;
```

The output of Listing 1.36 is as follows:

```
SYSDATE
---------
17-AUG-06
```

Listing 1.37 shows how to add an interval to date:

Listing 1.37: Adding the Interval to Date to Produce a New Date

```
select sysdate+a,sysdate+b from ztemp6;
```

The output of Listing 1.37 is as follows:

```
SYSDATE+A SYSDATE+B
--------- ---------
17-AUG-08 19-AUG-06
```

Listing 1.38 shows how to indicate literals of 2 year and 30 days:

Listing 1.38: Indicating Interval Literals of 2 Year and 30 Days

```
insert into ztemp6 values (INTERVAL '2' year,INTERVAL '30' DAY );
```

The output of Listing 1.38 is as follows:

```
1 row created
```

The following code snippet shows how to display data by adding system date in the interval stored in ztemp6:

```
select sysdate+a,sysdate+b from ztemp6;
```

The output of the preceding code snippet is as follows:

```
SYSDATE+A SYSDATE+B
--------- ---------
17-AUG-08 19-AUG-06
17-AUG-08 16-SEP-06
```

Listing 1.39 shows how to indicate interval of 2 years, 2 months, 2 days, 2 hours, 2 min, and 2.2222 seconds:

Listing 1.39: Indicating Interval of 2 Years, 2 Months, 2 Days, 2 Hours, 2 Min, and 2.2222 Seconds

```
insert into ztemp6 values (INTERVAL '2-2' year to month, INTERVAL '2
2:2:2.2222'day to second(4));
```

NOTE

Since 2.2222 exceeds the precision of table datatype, you have to explicitly specify the precision.

The output of Listing 1.39 is as follows:

```
1 row created
```

The following code snippet shows how to display records:

```
select * from ztemp6;
```

The output of the preceding code snippet is as follows:

```
A         B
------    ------
+02-00    +02 00:00:00.000000
+02-00    +30 00:00:00.000000
+02-02    +02 02:02:02.222200
```

NOTE

The interval can be specified as:
(INTERVAL '10:23' HOUR TO MINUTES, INTERVAL '12' HOUR, INTERVAL '34.5677' SECOND(2,4));

To store the date and time data, you can use the datatype date and timestamp. Date stores date as well time in hours, minutes, and seconds. Timestamp is an extension of date and stores precise time in fraction of seconds. You can specify precision in timestamp as TIMESTAMP(5). The default precision is 6, while the maximum precision is 9.

Introducing TIMEZONE and TIMESTAMP

The timestamp with time zone offset stores timestamp and time zone offset. The time zone offset is the difference between the local time zone and UTC (formerly GMT). Its format is as follows:

```
TZH:TZM
```

This specifies the difference in terms of hours and minutes. In local time zone data type, the time is stored as normalized time with reference to UTC. When the time is retrieved, it is converted according to the local time zone of the client machine.

Listing 1.40 shows how to use timestamp with time zone offset:

Listing 1.40: Using Timestamp with Time Zone Offset

```
create table ztemp7(a timestamp,b timestamp with time zone,c timestamp with      local
time zone);
insert into ztemp7 values(to_timestamp('12-MAY-2006 10:23:34.678','DD-MON-YYYY
   HH:MI:SS.FF'),
to_timestamp_tz('12-may-2006 10:23:34.678 -5:00','dd-mon-yyyy hh:mi:ss.ff
   tzh:tzm'),
to_timestamp('12-may-2006 10:23:34.678','dd-mon-yyyy hh:mi:ss.ff'))
/
```

The output of Listing 1.40 is as follows:

```
1 row created
```

The following code snippet shows how to display records:

```
select * from ztemp7;
```

The output of the preceding code snippet is as follows:

```
A
------------------------------------
B
------------------------------------
C
------------------------------------
12-MAY-06 10.23.34.678000 AM
12-MAY-06 10.23.34.678000 AM +05:00
12-MAY-06 10.23.34.678000 AM
```

Listing 1.41: Specifying the TIME_ZONE as Asia/Hong_Kong

```
ALTER SESSION SET TIME_ZONE='Asia/Hong_Kong';
```

The output of Listing 1.41 is as follows:

```
Session altered
```

The following code snippet shows how to display records:

```
select * from ztemp7;
```

The output of the preceding code snippet is as follows:

```
A
---------------------------------------------------------------------------
B
---------------------------------------------------------------------------
C
---------------------------------------------------------------------------
12-MAY-06 10.23.34.678000 AM
12-MAY-06 10.23.34.678000 AM +05:00
12-MAY-06 12.53.34.678000 PM
```

In the preceding example, C will produce value according to the Asia/Hong_Kong time zone.

If the session time zone is same as the database server time zone, then all the time zones (A,B, and C) will produce the same values.

(In the database, the time zone is set as "PST")

```
SQL> alter session set time_zone='PST';
Session altered.
SQL> select * from ztemp7;

A
-----------------------------------------
B
-----------------------------------------
C
-----------------------------------------
12-MAY-06 10.23.34.678000 AM
12-MAY-06 10.23.34.678000 AM +05:00
12-MAY-06 11.23.34.678000 AM
You can set  session time zone (For India )using command as
SQL>  alter session set time_zone='Asia/KOLKATA';

Session altered.

SQL> select sessiontimezone from dual;
SESSIONTIMEZONE
-------------------
Asia/Kolkata
 The database time zone can be obtained as
SQL> SELECT DBTIMEZONE FROM DUAL;

DBTIME
------
+00:00
```

The value '+00.00' indicates that the operating system time zone and the database time zone are set to same value.

Therefore, to store only timestamp information, you can use datatype "TIMESTAMP"; whereas, to store the time stamp and time zone information, when user has specified the time zone, you can use "TIMESTAMP WITH TIME ZONE". To store time stamp with time zone where client is located in multiple countries, you can use "TIMESTAMP WITH LOCAL TIME ZONE".

You can get information about various time zones using view V$TIMEZONE_NAMES as:

```
Select * from V$TIMEZONE_NAMES;
```

The information about client time (with respect to his or her time zone), time stamp, and time with respect to universal time zone is obtained as:

```
SQL> select current_timestamp,localtimestamp,systimestamp from dual;

CURRENT_TIMESTAMP
---------------------------------------------------------------------------
LOCALTIMESTAMP
---------------------------------------------------------------------------
SYSTIMESTAMP
---------------------------------------------------------------------------
```

```
27-DEC-09 11.52.49.609000 AM ASIA/KOLKATA
27-DEC-09 11.52.49.609000 AM
26-DEC-09 10.22.49.609000 PM +5:30
```

In the system, the session time zone is set as "ASIA/KOLKATA", which is 5:30 hours ahead of universal standard time. The database time zone is set as "PST (Pacific Standard Time)" which is eight hours behind universal standard time.

You can extract GMT (Universal coordinated time) using following query

```
SQL>  select c,sys_extract_utc(c) from ztemp7;

C
---------------------------------------------------
SYS_EXTRACT_UTC(C)
---------------------------------------------------
12-MAY-06 10.23.34.678000 AM
12-MAY-06 06.23.34.678000 PM
```

Since PST is eight hours behind GMT, the second value can be obtained by adding eight in the first value.

When the value is stored with time zone, the information about time zone can be extracted using the following command:

```
SQL> select extract(timezone_region from c) from ztemp7;
EXTRACT(TIMEZONE_REGIONFROMC)
----------------------------------------------------------------
Asia/Kolkata
```

The session date can be obtained by using function CURRENT_DATE as

```
Select current_date from dual;
```

To get time_zone offset, the following query is used:

```
SQL> SELECT TZ_OFFSET('Asia/Kolkata') from dual;

TZ_OFFS
-------
+05:30
```

To convert date from one time zone to another, the following NEW_TIME function is used:

```
SELECT TO_CHAR(NEW_TIME(TO_DATE('26-DEC-2009 00:00:00','DD-MON-YYYY
HH24:MI:SS'),'PST','GMT'),'DD-MON-YYYY HH24:MI:SS') FROM DUAL
/
TO_CHAR(NEW_TIME(TO_
--------------------
26-DEC-2009 08:00:00
```

In the preceding example, the time in "PST" is converted into "GMT".

Converting Character Data to Timestamp

The following functions are used to convert character string to time stamp data:

- TO_TIMESTAMP()
- TO_TIMESTAMP_TZ()
- CAST()

Working with The TO_TIMESTAMP() Function

The TO_TIMESTAMP(str,format) function is used to convert string into timestamp. For example:

```
SELECT TO_TIMESTAMP('26-DEC-2009 14:12:12.11111','DD-MON-YYYY HH24:MI:SS.FF') FROM DUAL
 /
TO_TIMESTAMP('26-DEC-200914:12:12.11111','DD-MON-YYYYHH24:MI:SS.FF')
26-DEC-09 02.12.12.111110000 PM
```

SS.FF indicated seconds in fractions.

Working with The TO_TIMESTAMP_TZ() Function

The following TO_TIMESTAMP_TZ(str,format) function converts string to timestamp with time zone:

```
 SELECT TO_TIMESTAMP_TZ('26-DEC-2009 02:12:12.11111 GMT','DD-MON-YYYY HH24:MI:SS.FF TZR')
FROM DUAL
 /

TO_TIMESTAMP_TZ('26-DEC-200902:12:12.11111GMT','DD-MON-YYYYHH24:MI:SS.FFTZR
26-DEC-09 02.12.12.111110000 AM GMT
```

Working with The CAST() Function

You can use the cast () function to convert a string to datatype, as follows:

```
TIMESTAMP WITH LOCAL TIME ZONE.

SELECT CAST(TO_TIMESTAMP_TZ('26-DEC-2009 02:12:12.11111 GMT','DD-MON-YYYY HH24:MI:SS.FF
TZR')
  AS TIMESTAMP WITH LOCAL TIME ZONE)
 FROM DUAL
 /

CAST(TO_TIMESTAMP_TZ('26-DEC-200902:12:12.11111GMT','DD-MON-YYYYHH24:MI:SS.
------------------------------------------------------------------------------------------
--------
26-DEC-09 02.12.12.111110 AM
```

Working with Tables

As already discussed, you need to create a table to store data in a database. However, you need to keep following points in mind before creating a table:

- The maximum number of columns in a table can be 1000
- The maximum value of a number can be (999...38 times) $\times 10^{125}$ and minimum value can be (-999…38 times) $\times 10^{125}$
- The maximum number of tables and maximum number of rows are unlimited and their sizes are controlled only by the space available
- The file name has a maximum size of 255 characters
- The maximum length of the literal, i.e. constant, is 4000 bytes in SQL statement

Let's now learn how to modify a table.

You can add a column in the existing table using the ALTER TABLE command.

Listing 1.42 shows how to add a column using the add clause:

Listing 1.42: Adding a Column Using the Add Clause

Displaying structure of tpcm

```
desc tpcm;
```

Listing 1.42 displays the structure of tpcm.

The output of Listing 1.42 is as follows:

```
Name                                  Null?     Type
------------------------------------- --------  --------------
RN                                              NUMBER
P                                               NUMBER
C                                               NUMBER
M                                               NUMBER
NAME                                            VARCHAR2(10)
```

The following code snippet shows how to use the add clause:

```
alter table tpcm add (total number);
```

The output of the preceding code snippet is as follows:

```
Table altered
```

The following code snippet displays the structure of tpcm again:

```
desc tpcm;
```

The output of the preceding code snippet is as follows:

```
Name                                  Null?     Type
------------------------------------- --------  --------------
RN                                              NUMBER
P                                               NUMBER
C                                               NUMBER
M                                               NUMBER
NAME                                            VARCHAR2(10)
TOTAL                                           NUMBER
```

Listing 1.43 shows how to drop a column:

Listing 1.43: Dropping a Column

```
alter table tpcm drop column total;
desc tpcm;
```

The output of Listing 1.43 is as follows:

```
Name                                  Null?     Type
------------------------------------- --------  --------------
RN                                              NUMBER
P                                               NUMBER
C                                               NUMBER
M                                               NUMBER
NAME                                            VARCHAR2(10)
```

Listing 1.44 shows how to rename a column:

Listing 1.44: Renaming Column

```
alter table tpcm rename column name to sname;
```

The output of Listing 1.44 is as follows:

```
Table altered
```

The following code snippet displays the structure of tpcm:

```
desc tpcm;
```

The output of the preceding code snippet is as follows:

```
Name                                       Null?     Type
----------------------------------------  --------  -------------
 RN                                                  NUMBER
 P                                                   NUMBER
 C                                                   NUMBER
 M                                                   NUMBER
 SNAME                                               VARCHAR2(10)
```

Listing 1.45 shows how to modify a column with new datatype:

Listing 1.45: Modifying the Column with New Datatype

```
alter table tpcm modify(sname varchar2(5));
alter table tpcm modify(sname varchar2(5));
```

The output of Listing 1.45 is as follows:

```
                        *
ERROR at line 1:
ORA-01441: cannot decrease column length because some value is too big
```

In this output, you can see that an error is displayed. This is because when you reduce the precision, the existing data should be according to precision; otherwise, the modifications are not done. For example, if the existing data in some columns is of 15 characters and you are decreasing precision to 10 characters, then an error would be generated.

NOTE

You can only decrease the length if there is no data in the respective column.

However, when you are increasing precision, there is no constraint, as shown in the following code snippet:

```
alter table tpcm modify(sname varchar2(15));
```

The output of the preceding code snippet is as follows:

```
Table altered
```

NOTE

You can also give a new datatype to column, if the existing data satisfies the new definition.

Listing 1.46 shows how to rename a table:

Listing 1.46: Renaming a Table

```
rename tpcm to zpcm;
```

The output of Listing 1.46 is as follows:

```
   Table renamed
```

Dropping column may take more time if there is a large amount of data. In such a case, you can mark some columns as unused and then drop those columns.

Listing 1.47 shows how to mark columns as unused and drop them:

Listing 1.47: Marking Column as Unused and Dropping the Column

```
alter table zpcm set unused column m;
```

The output of Listing 1.47 is as follows:

```
Table altered
```

The following code snippet shows how to drop an unused column:

```
alter table zpcm drop unused columns;
```

The output of the preceding code snippet is as follows:

```
Table altered
```

The following code snippet shows how to display structure of zpcm:

```
desc zpcm;
```

The output of the preceding code snippet is as follows:

```
Name                                     Null?    Type
---------------------------------------- -------- --------------
 RN                                               NUMBER
 P                                                NUMBER
 C                                                NUMBER
 SNAME                                            VARCHAR2(15)
```

Listing 1.48 shows how to specify the default value to column, so that when this value is not mentioned in the insert statement, the default value can be used:

Listing 1.48: Specifying the Default Value to Column

```
alter table zpcm modify (p number default 70);
```

The output of Listing 1.48 is as follows:

```
Table altered
```

The following code snippet shows how to insert values:

```
insert into zpcm(rn,c,sname) values(9,89,'sahil');
```

The output of the preceding code snippet is as follows:

```
1 row created
```

The following code snippet shows how to display records:

```
select * from zpcm;
```

The output of the preceding code snippet is as follows:

```
RN          P          C SNAME
-- ---------- ---------- -------
 9         70         89 sahil
```

Summary

This chapter introduced you to various components of SQL and datatypes used in Oracle. The chapter also discussed the basic operations that can be performed using SQL, such as creating table, inserting data in the table, updating existing data in the table, and modifying structure of the table.

In the next chapter, you learn about the set operations in SQL.

Exercise

Using data given in Appendix A, solve the following queries:

- Give the name of the manager of employee ANIL
- Give salary of employee of ACC
- Give the names of cities in which TATA is located
- Give names of employees having salary greater than 2000 and less than 6000
- Give names of employees having salary greater than 2000 and less than 6000 and having company ACC
- Give names of employee having VIJAY as manager

2

Set Operations

A table can be defined as a relation, i.e. a set of elements. Therefore, in a relational database all data is stored in the form of sets. A query returns a set of rows, so you can do additional set operations on the output of a query. You can combine results of multiple queries using different set operations. The common set operations are union, intersect, minus, testing membership of element in the set, testing whether set is empty or not and Cartesian product.

This chapter introduces above-mentioned operations performed on sets, with some examples. You also learn about other operations, such as those involving the use of clauses and multicolumn subqueries. Toward the end of the chapter, you learn about retrieving data from multiple tables and performing the alias operation on a table.

Let's begin by knowing about the basic operations performed on sets.

Basic Set Operations

The three basic set operations are:

- Union
- Intersect
- Minus

Let's discuss each operation in detail in the following sections.

The Union Operation

Using union you combine output of two or multiple sets.

Suppose there are two sets, S and R

```
S = {a,b,c}
R = {x,y,z}
```

Then the output of R union S is:

```
R U S = {a,b,c,x,y,z}
```

An important condition for performing operations on sets is that the elements of one set must be compatible with the elements of the other set. If the set element of one set has only one part then the set element of the other set must also have only one part, of course, with compatible data type. So following sets cannot be combined.

```
S={ <anil,100>,<sunil,2000>}
R={anil,ajay}
```

The issue of compatibility between set elements can be better understood by taking an example, as shown in Listing 2.1:

Listing 2.1: Getting the Cities having the ACC or TATA Companies

```
select city from company where cname = 'ACC'
union
select city from company where cname = 'TATA';
```

The output of Listing 2.1 is as follows:

```
CITY
------
CHENNAI
DELHI
MUMBAI
NAGPUR
```

You cannot write the following statement:

```
select cname,city from company
where cname = 'ACC'
union
select city from company
where cname = 'TATA';
```

This is because the first set produces two parts, while the second set has an element with a single part. In such a case, you can make the two queries compatible by adding a dummy column, as shown in the following code snippet:

```
select cname, city from company
where cname = 'ACC'
union
select '', city from company
where cname = 'TATA';
```

The output of the preceding code snippet is as follows:

```
CNAME            CITY
---------     ----------
ACC              CHENNAI
ACC              NAGPUR
                 DELHI
                 MUMBAI
```

Let's discuss the intersect operation next.

The Intersect Operation

The intersect operation is used to find the common elements in the given sets. Suppose you have two sets, S and R, as shown in the following code snippet:

```
S = {a,b,c}
R = {a,x,y}
```

Performing the intersect operation in the preceding code snippet produces the following output:

```
S intersect R = {a}
```

Listing 2.2 shows the use of the intersect operation:

Listing 2.2: Retrieving the Name of the City Common to the ACC and TATA Companies

```
select city from company where cname ='ACC'
intersect
select city from company where cname = 'TATA';
```

The output of Listing 2.2 is as follows:

```
No rows selected
```

After learning about the intersect operation, let's discuss the minus operation.

The Minus Operation

The minus operation is used to find elements that are present in one set but not in the other.

Suppose you have two sets, S and R, as shown in the following code snippet:

```
S = {a,b,c}
R = {a,x,y}
```

Perform the minus operation in the preceding code snippet produces the following output:

```
S minus R = {b,c}
```

You can see that the elements {b,c} are present in set S but not in set R. The element a is present in both sets, so does not appear in the output. Similarly, look at the following code snippet:

```
R minus S = {x,y}
```

Listing 2.3 shows the use of the minus operation:

Listing 2.3: Finding the Cities where the ACC Company is Located, but not the TATA Company

```
select city from company where cname = 'ACC'
minus
select city from company where cname = 'TATA';
```

The output of Listing 2.2 is as follows:

```
CITY
-------
CHENNAI
NAGPUR
```

As stated earlier, in all set operations, the sets involved should be compatible; otherwise, the queries return error. For example, the query shown in the following code snippet is incorrect:

```
select city from company where cname = 'ACC'
union select salary from emp_company;
```

The output of the preceding code snippet is as follows:

```
ERROR at line 1:
ORA-01790: expression must have same datatypes as corresponding expression
```

This preceding output returns error because the first set consists of character datatype, while the second set consists of numeric datatype. Now, let's look at the following code snippet:

```
select city from employee
union
select cname, city from company;
```

In the preceding code snippet, the first set consists of an element of a single field, while the second set consists of elements of two fields. Therefore, the sets in the two queries are incompatible with each other.

All the preceding operations produce distinct values and remove duplicates. Here are some more examples of set operations

Listing 2.4: Displaying the Names of the Employees of the ACC Company Living in Nagpur

```
select ename from employee
where city = 'NAGPUR'
intersect
select ename from emp_company
where cname = 'ACC';
```

The output of Listing 2.4 is as follows:

```
ENAME
----------
ANIL
```

Listing 2.5: Displaying the Names of Employees in Nagpur not working in the ACC Company

```
select ename from employee
where city = 'NAGPUR'
minus
select ename from emp_company
where cname = 'ACC';
```

The output of Listing 2.5 is as follows:

```
No rows selected
```

Listing 2.6: Displaying the Names of Employees living in Nagpur, working in ACC, and having Shift A

```
select ename from employee
where city = 'NAGPUR'
intersect
select ename from emp_company
where cname = 'ACC'
intersect
select ename from emp_shift
where shift = 'A';
```

The output of Listing 2.6 is as follows:

```
ENAME
----------
ANIL
```

Listing 2.7: Displaying the names of Employees Living in Nagpur, working in the ACC Company, and not working in Shift A

```
(select ename from employee
where city='NAGPUR'
intersect
select ename from emp_company
where cname='ACC')
minus
select ename from emp_shift
where shift='A';
```

The output of Listing 2.7 is as follows:

```
No rows selected
```

Listing 2.8: Displaying the Names of Employees Living in Nagpur or MUMBAI

```
select ename from employee
where city='NAGPUR'
union
select ename from employee
where city='MUMBAI';
```

The output of Listing 2.8 is as follows:

```
ENAME
----------
ANIL
SHANKAR
SUNIL
```

You can use the `UNION ALL` operation if you do not want to remove duplicates. In general, the `UNION ALL` operation is quicker than the `UNION` operation. You can use brackets to impose the precedence of operations; otherwise, operations are performed in the top to bottom order.

Listing 2.9: Displaying the Employee Names using the UNION and UNION ALL Operators

```
select ename from emp_company
union
select ename from emp_company
union all
select ename from emp_company;
```

The output of Listing 2.9 is as follows:

```
ENAME
----------
AJAY
AMOL
ANIL
JAYA
PRAKASH
SHANKAR
SUNIL
VIJAY
ANIL
SHANKAR
JAYA
SUNIL
VIJAY
PRAKASH
AJAY
AMOL

16 rows selected.
```

The output is 16 rows because the first two select queries are combined by using the `UNION` operator, which gives the results in 8 rows. These 8 rows are then combined by using the `UNION ALL` operator, which selects all the rows, irrespective of the duplicate rows, thereby resulting in 16 rows.

Listing 2.10: Displaying the Employee Name using the UNION ALL and UNION Operators

```
select ename from emp_company union all
select ename from emp_company union
select ename from emp_company;
```

The output of Listing 2.10 is as follows:

```
ENAME
----------
AJAY
AMOL
ANIL
JAYA
PRAKASH
SHANKAR
SUNIL
VIJAY

8 rows selected
```

Listing 2.9 and Listing 2.10 show how the output varies, when the `UNION` and `UNION ALL` operators are used interchangeably. The output of Listing 2.10 is 8 rows because the first two select queries are combined by using `UNION ALL` operator, which results in 16 rows. These 16 rows are then combined by using the UNION operator, which dismisses the duplicate rows, and gives the result as 8 rows.

Therefore, you can see the difference clearly. In the Listing 2.9, first the `union` operation is performed and then the `union all` is executed so the duplicates are not removed. In Listing 2.10, first the `union all` is executed and then, `union` is executed. This way all the duplicates are removed in the result.

Other Set Operations

The other set operations are testing membership of element in the set (IN clause), checking whether set is empty or not (EXISTS clause) and Cartesian product. These set operations are mainly used in retrieving data from multiple tables and retrieving data from one table when condition is given with reference to another table or same table.

*The **In** Clause*

The `In` clause is used where the membership of an element has to be tested against a given set. The following code snippet shows the use of the IN clause:

```
a in {a,b,c} is TRUE.
```

The In clause can be used only in `where` condition and returns either `TRUE` or `FALSE`.

Following query shows use of IN clause.

Listing 2.11: Finding the Names of Employee working in the ACC Company and the Cities they Live in, using the IN Clause

```
select ename, city from employee
where ename in(select ename from
emp_company where cname = 'ACC');
```

the output of Listing 2.11 is as follows:

```
ENAME              CITY
ANIL               NAGPUR
AJAY               CHENNAI
```

In the above query, the subquery:

```
(select ename from emp_company where cname = 'ACC')
```

will produce a set of `employee names` working for company `ACC`. For every row of the table `employee`, it is checked whether `ename` is a member of that set.

Usage of `IN` is described in the following examples.

Listing 2.12: Displaying the employees living in the city MUMBAI and having their company located in the city DELHI

```
select ename from emp_company where ename in (select     ename from employee
   where city = 'MUMBAI') and cname in (select cname from company where city          =
'DELHI');
```

Result:

```
ENAME
---------
SHANKAR
```

The first subquery returns the set of names of employees who are residing in the city `MUMBAI`. Thus, the `ename` of row of table `emp_company` is tested for membership in the above set. Similarly, the second subquery returns a list of companies located at `DELHI`. The only rows of `emp_company` are selected which are members of both sets.

Listing 2.13: Displaying the names of employees living in the same city where SUNIL is residing

```
select ename from employee where city in (select city from employee where
   ename = 'SUNIL');
```

Result:

```
ENAME
------
SUNIL
SHANKAR
```

IN is used when a condition is given with reference to another table.

You can directly mention the INLIST instead of subquery as:

```
select ename, city from employee where city in('NAGPUR','MUMBAI');
```

The query selects employees of cities NAGPUR and MUMBAI.

Listing 2.14: Displaying the names of employees having living city same as Ajay

```
select e.ename, e.city
from employee e
where e.city
in
(select e1.city                              --Delhi
from employee e1
where e1.ename='AJAY');
```

Result:

```
ENAME      CITY
---------- -------
AJAY       CHENNAI
JAYA       CHENNAI
```

If city of AJAY is DELHI, then the subquery produces DELHI and the main query produces all employees in that city.

Listing 2.15: Displaying the names of employees along with their living cities having shift A and company ACC

```
select e.ename, e.city
from employee e where e.ename in
(select c.ename from emp_company c where c.cname='ACC')
                                 -- Suppose query produces anil sunil
 and e.ename in (select s.ename from emp_shift s where s.shift='A');
                                 -- Suppose query produces ajay sunil
                                 -- The output of query will be sunil
```

Result:

```
ENAME      CITY
---------- ----------
ANIL       NAGPUR
```

Listing 2.16: Displaying the names of employees with their living city having company city MUMBAI

```
select e.ename, e.city
from employee e --Main
where e.ename in
(select c.ename  --All employees of ACC,TATA; ajay sunil vijay
from emp_company c       --Q1
where c.cname in
(select m.cname          -- Suppose query produces ACC TATA
from company m           --Q2
where m.city='MUMBAI') );
```

Result:

```
ENAME      CITY
---------- ----------
SHANKAR    MUMBAI
JAYA       CHENNAI
SUNIL      MUMBAI
VIJAY      DELHI
PRAKASH    KOLKATA
```

The query Q2 produces all companies in `MUMBAI`. Query Q1 produces all employees in those companies. The main query produces all employees with their living city having those companies.

Listing 2.17: Displaying the names of employees having living city same as company city

```
select e1.ename                              --ajay
from employee e1                             --Main
where e1.city in                             -- delhi
(select c1.city                              -- delhi
from company c1                              --Q1
where c1.cname in (select m1.cname           --tata
from emp_company m1                          --Q2
where m1.ename=e1.ename));
```

Result:

```
ENAME
----------
ANIL
SHANKAR
JAYA
SUNIL
VIJAY
AJAY

6 rows selected
```

The query is written using principle that for every row of main query table, the subquery is evaluated:

- Suppose the row is having ename `ajay` then in the subquery Q2, `e1.ename` will have the value `ajay` and subquery Q2 produces company of `ajay`.
- The query Q1 produces city of that company, say `delhi`. In the main query, `e1.city`, if the living city of `ajay` equals `delhi` only then will `ajay` be the result, else no.

In this example, the column of main query table is used in subquery Q2. According to the scope rule, you can use the column of the table mentioned in the `FROM` clause anywhere in its `SELECT` or `WHERE` condition, including the subqueries. According to the same rule, you cannot use `Emp_company` table column of Q2 in the main query. The query having reference to table of main query is called a correlated sub query.

Listing 2.18: Displaying the names of employees having same company city as company city of Ajay

```
select e1.ename                              --all employees working in ACC,TATA
from emp_company e1 where e1.cname in
(select c1.cname                             -- ACC,TATA
from company c1 where c1.city in
(select c2.city                              -- MUMBAI
from company c2
where c2.cname in                            --ACC
(select e2.cname
from emp_company e2 where e2.ename='AJAY')));
```

Result:

```
ENAME
----------
ANIL
JAYA
SUNIL
AJAY
AMOL
```

The **Exists** Clause

The exists clause is used for testing whether a given set is empty or not. It is used in where condition. An exists clause on an empty set returns False, while on a nonempty set it returns True. The meaning of exists is as follows:

```
exists {a,b,c} = True
and
exists{  } = False
```

Listing 2.19: Displaying the names of employees, using EXISTS, living in the same city where SUNIL is living

```
select emp1.ename from employee emp1 where exists(select emp2.city from employee
  emp2 where emp2.ename = 'SUNIL' and emp1.city = emp2.city);
```

Result:

```
ENAME
----------
SUNIL
SHANKAR
```

The query is executed as follows:

- For each row of the data source which is given after the from clause, the where condition is evaluated.
- If the first row is of SHANKAR, then emp1.city gives the city of SHANKAR.
- The subquery returns something when city of SHANKAR is same as city of SUNIL.

NOTE

What a query returns is not important. The only important question is whether a query returns something or nothing.

Thus, the subquery is translated as:

```
select emp2.city from employee emp2
where emp2.ename = 'SUNIL'
and emp2.city = 'NAGPUR';
```

Here:

- NAGPUR is the city of SHANKAR for the first row.
- If the query returns no row, then exists on empty set becomes False.

You can write the subquery as:

```
select 'X' from employee emp2, employee emp1
where emp2.ename = 'SUNIL'
and emp2.city = emp1.city;
```

If the where condition is satisfied then the query returns X, i.e. something, and exists returns TRUE.

Here are some more examples.

Listing 2.20: Displaying the salary of employee living in DELHI

```
select salary from emp_company where exists (select 'X' from employee
where employee.city = 'DELHI' and employee.ename = emp_company.ename);
```

Result:

```
SALARY
------
 5000
```

Listing 2.21: Displaying the names of employees other than AMOL using NOT EXISTS

```
SELECT * FROM emp_company WHERE not EXISTS(select ename from employee where
employee .ename =emp_company.ename);
```

Result:

```
ENAME      CNAME           SALARY          JDATE
-------- ----------     ----------   ---------
AMOL       ACC               1000        17-MAR-95
```

This query will output the result when AMOL is in Emp_company table, but not in Employee table.

NOTE

The query can be written by using minus and not exists operations. The not exists clause is just the reverse of exists, i.e. not exists {} returns true.

You can convert any query using IN into EXISTS by following these steps: If the query is:

```
select salary from emp_company where emp_company.ename
in (select employee.ename  from employee
where employee.city = 'DELHI');
```

Then:

- The condition specified using IN (Underlined in the above query) is appended in sub query to the where condition.
- Replace IN with EXISTS
- In the select of sub query, use any single character constant.

Thus, the query is converted as:

```
select salary from emp_company where exists (select 'X'  from employee
where employee.city = 'DELHI' and employee.ename = emp_company.ename);
```

Result:

```
    SALARY
 ---------
      5000
```

Here are some examples of query using exists.

Listing 2.22: Displaying the names of employees having living city same as Ajay

```
select e.ename, e.city
from employee e
where
exists
(select 'X'
from employee e1
where e1.ename='AJAY'
and e.city = e1.city);
```

Result:

```
ENAME      CITY
---------- ----------
AJAY       CHENNAI
JAYA       CHENNAI
```

Listing 2.23: Displaying the names of employees with their living city, having shift B, and company CMC

```
select e.ename,e.city
from employee e
where exists
(select 'X' from emp_company c where c.cname='CMC'and e.ename=c.ename)
   and exists (select 'X' from emp_shift s where s.shift='B'and
   e.ename=s.ename);
```

Result:

```
ENAME      CITY
---------- ----------
SUNIL      MUMBAI
```

Listing 2.24: Displaying the names of employees with their living city and company city MUMBAI

```
select e.ename,e.city
from employee e
where exists
(select'X' from emp_company c
where e.ename=c.ename and exists
(select 'X'
from company m
where c.cname = m.cname and m.city='MUMBAI') );
```

Result:

```
ENAME      CITY
---------- ----------
SHANKAR    MUMBAI
JAYA       CHENNAI
SUNIL      MUMBAI
VIJAY      DELHI
PRAKASH    KOLKATA
```

Listing 2.25: Displaying the names of employees having living city same as company city

```
select e1.ename from employee e1
where exists
(select 'X'
from company c1
where c1.city = e1.city and exists
(select 'X'
from emp_company m1
where m1.ename=e1.ename and c1.cname=m1.cname));
```

Result:

```
ENAME
----------
ANIL
SHANKAR
JAYA
SUNIL
VIJAY
AJAY

6 rows selected
```

Listing 2.26: Displaying the names of employees having same company city as company city of Ajay

```
select e1.ename from emp_company e1
where exists
(select 'X' from company c1
where e1.cname = c1.cname and exists
(select 'X' from company c2
where c1.city = c2.city and exists
(select 'X' from emp_company e2
where e2.cname = c2.cname and e2.ename='AJAY')));
```

Result:

```
ENAME
----------
ANIL
JAYA
SUNIL
AJAY
AMOL
```

The `IN` and `EXIXTS` clauses are useful in `UPDATE` and `DELETE` statements where a condition has to be specified on more than one table.

NOTE

If the subquery refers to a table column of main query, then it is called a correlated subquery. If subquery returns a single value, then it is called a scalar subquery.

Using Multicolumn Subqueries

You can compare elements having multiple values with the set of elements. This is called a multicolumn subquery. This is explained in the following example:

```
create table empdep(empno number,deptno number,salary number)
/
create table empcity(empno number,deptno number,city varchar2(30))
/
insert into empdep values(1,10,1200)
/
insert into empdep values(2,20,2200)
/
insert into empdep values(3,10,3000)
/
insert into empcity values(1,10,'NAGPUR')
/
insert into empcity values(2,20,'DELHI')
/
insert into empcity values(3,10,'NAGPUR')
/
select * from empdep;
```

Result:

```
    EMPNO     DEPTNO      SALARY
---------- ---------- ----------
        1         10        1200
        2         20        2200
        3         10        3000
```

Listing 2.27: Displaying all records

```
select * from empcity;
```

Result:

```
    EMPNO      DEPTNO              CITY
----------   -------              -----
        1         10               NAGPUR
        2         20               DELHI
        3              10          NAGPUR
```

Listing 2.28: Writing a multiple column subquery

```
select e1.empno,e1.deptno,e1.salary
from empdep e1 where (e1.empno,e1.deptno)
in(select e2.empno,e2.deptno from empcity e2 where city='NAGPUR');
```

Result:

```
EMPNO      DEPTNO     SALARY
---------- ------- ----------
   1         10       1200
   3         10       3000
```

Retrieving Data from Multiple Tables

In many cases, the user may require to retrieve data from multiple tables. Suppose you want to retrieve `employee name`, `salary`, and living `city` then you have to get data from tables—`Employee` and `Emp_company`. With SQL, you can retrieve data from multiple tables by using the Cartesian product.

Using Cartesian Product

Let's understand Cartesian product with the help of the following example.

Suppose there are two sets `R` and `S`:

```
R = {a,b}
S = {x,y}
```

Then the Cartesian product `R X S` is as follows:

```
CP = R X S = {(a,x),(a,y),(b,x),(b,y)}
```

Here, `X` denotes the Cartesian product. In the Cartesian product, each element of one set is combined with every element of another set to form the resultant elements of Cartesian product.

In the above example, element `a` of `R` is combined with every element of `S` to form elements (a,x), (a,y) of Cartesian product. Similarly, the element `b` is combined with every element of `S` to form elements (b,x) and (b,y) of Cartesian product. Suppose:

```
V = {m,n}
```

then:

```
R * V = {(a,m),(a,n)(b,m),(b,n)}
R X S X V = {(a,x,m),(a,x,n), (a,y,m),(a,y,n), (b,x,m),(b,x,n) (b,y,m),(b,y,n)}
```

Thus, if `R` consists of `M` elements and `S` consists of `N` elements, then the Cartesian product of `R` and `S` will consists of `M x N` elements. Since the table is the set, you can perform Cartesian product on tables. Each row is treated as an element of the set.

Suppose the query is to give `employee name`, `salary`, and their living `city`. Here you require data from two tables—`Emp_company` and `Employee`—and you have to form a Cartesian product of `Emp_company` and `Employee`.

The Cartesian product forms a data source just like a table in which:

- Columns are `UNION` of all the columns of tables, which are involved in Cartesian product. Each column in a virtual data source is referred to as `tablename.columnname` (The column `ename` of `Employee` is identified as `employee.ename`)
- Each row in the virtual data source is formed by combining each row of one table with every row of another table.

Thus, the Cartesian product or join of two tables gives the virtual data source having columns as:

```
employee.ename,employee.city,emp_company.ename
emp_company.cname,emp_company.salary,emp_company.jdate
```

Suppose the data in the tables `Emp_company` and `Employee` is as follows:

Emp_company

ename	cname	salary	jdate
ANIL	ACC	1500	01-MAY-89
SHANKAR	TATA	2000	10-JUL-90
JAYA	CMC	1800	07-JUN-91
SUNIL	CMC	1700	01-JAN-89

Employee

ename	city
ANIL	NAGPUR
SHANKAR	MUMBAI
JAYA	CHENNAI
SUNIL	MUMBAI

So the Cartesian product will be:

employee ename	employee city	emp_company ename	emp_company cname	emp_company salary	emp_company jdate
ANIL	**NAGPUR**	**ANIL**	**ACC**	**1500**	**1-may-89**
ANIL	NAGPUR	SHANKAR	TATA	2000	10-jul-90
ANIL	NAGPUR	JAYA	CMC	1800	7-jun-91
ANIL	NAGPUR	SUNIL	CMC	1700	1-may-89
SHANKAR	MUMBAI	ANIL	ACC	1500	1-may-89
SHANKAR	**MUMBAI**	**SHANKAR**	**TATA**	**2000**	**10-jun-90**
SHANKAR	MUMBAI	JAYA	CMC	1800	7-July-91
SHANKAR	MUMBAI	SUNIL	CMC	1700	1-jan-89
JAYA	CHENNAI	ANIL	ACC	1500	1-May-89
JAYA	CHENNAI	SHANKAR	TATA	2000	10-july-90
JAYA	**CHENNAI**	**JAYA**	**CMC**	**1800**	**7-Jun-91**
JAYA	CHENNAI	SUNIL	CMC	1700	1-Jan-89
SUNIL	MUMBAI	ANIL	ACC	1500	1-may-89
SUNIL	MUMBAI	SHANKAR	TATA	2000	10-july-90
SUNIL	MUMBAI	JAYA	CMC	1800	7-June-91
SUNIL	**MUMBAI**	**SUNIL**	**CMC**	**1700**	**1-Jan-89**

Out of the 16 rows, not all rows are carrying relevant information. Only those, which are marked bold, carry relevant information. Row no. 1 is relevant because the first part (information from the table `Employee`) of first row gives `city` of `ANIL`, while the second part Information from table `Emp_company` gives company information of `ANIL`.

The second row is not relevant because the first part gives information about `ANIL` while the second part gives company information about `SHANKAR`. The criteria for relevance of information is:

```
employee.ename = emp_company.ename
```

The complete query is written as:

```
select employee.ename,emp_company.salary,employee.city
from employee, emp_company
where emp_company.ename = employee.ename;
```

Listing 2.29: Displaying information of employees in company TATA

```
select employee.ename,emp_company.salary,employee.city
from employee, emp_company where emp_company.ename = employee.ename
and emp_company.cname = 'TATA';
```

Result:

```
ENAME          SALARY    CITY
----------  ----------  ----------
SHANKAR          2000    MUMBAI
VIJAY            5000    DELHI
PRAKASH          3000    KOLKATA
```

The first condition of the query is implicit (not mentioned in query), while the second condition is explicit:

```
emp_company.cname = 'TATA'
```

i.e. specified in the problem. When the Cartesian product is formed, the first condition is important and is used for getting relevant information.

Thus, in Cartesian product you have to add additional implicit conditions because a Cartesian product forms all possible combinations of rows and all rows do not carry relevant information. Implicit conditions are required to filter out such irrelevant combinations. In the above problem, the implicit condition is:

```
employee.ename = emp_company.ename
```

You can represent the condition of Cartesian product by arranging columns of Cartesian product in the following way and then specify the condition on rows, i.e. which rows are acceptable. The above query can be presented as:

```
employee.ename                 employee.city
      X
emp_company.ename                      emp_company.cname
      X                                TATA
emp_company.city               emp_company.jdate
```

The conditions are specified as if `X` is `employee.ename`. `X` is also `emp_company.ename` = `'TATA'`. Thus those rows are retrieved that will satisfy these conditions. Following are the examples of Cartesian product.

Listing 2.30: Displaying the names of employees whose company is located in city DELHI

```
select emp_company.ename
from emp_company, company where emp_company.cname = company.cname
and company.city = 'DELHI';
```

Result:

```
ENAME
----------
SHANKAR
VIJAY
PRAKASH
```

This query requires information from two tables—`Emp_company` and `Company`, Thus a Cartesian product is formed with the following condition on columns:

```
emp_company.ename          emp_company.cname
                                 X
emp_company.sal            emp_company jdate
company.cname              company.city
  X                            'DELHI'
```

The implicit condition is as follows:

```
emp_company.cname = company.cname
```

Since we want only companies that are located in `DELHI`, the following condition has to be written:

```
company.city = 'DELHI'
```

Listing 2.31: Displaying the names of employees living in the same city where their company is located

The condition `employee.city = company.city` gives the rows which satisfy conditions specified in query. The query can be written as:

```
select employee.ename
from employee,emp_company,company
where employee.ename = emp_company.ename
and emp_company.cname = company.cname
and employee.city = company.city;
```

Result:

```
ENAME
----------
ANIL
SHANKAR
JAYA
SUNIL
VIJAY
AJAY

6 rows selected
```

This query requires data from three query tables—`Employee`, `Emp_company`, and `Company`. The conditions on the value of columns are specified as:

```
employee.ename             employee.city
  X                              Z
emp_company.ename          emp_company.cname
  X                              Y
emp_company.sal            emp_company.jdate
company.cname              company.city
  Y                              Z
```

Listing 2.32: Displaying the names of employees living in city MUMBAI and having company located in city DELHI

```
select employee.ename
from employee,emp_company,company
where employee.ename = emp_company.ename
and emp_company.cname = company.cname
and employee.city = 'MUMBAI'
and company.city = 'DELHI';
```

Result:

```
ENAME
----------
SHANKAR
```

This query requires data from three query tables—`Employee`, `Emp_company`, and `Company`:

```
employee.ename              employee.city
   X                        MUMBAI
emp_company.ename           emp_company.cname
   X                            Y
emp_company.sal             emp_company.jdate
emp_company.cname           company.city
   Y                             DELHI
```

Listing 2.33: Displaying the names of managers and salary of employee SUNIL

```
select emp_company.salary,manager.mname
from emp_company,manager
where emp_company.ename = 'SUNIL'
and emp_company.ename = manager.ename;
```

Result:

```
SALARY   MNAME
-------  ----------
1700     JAYA
```

Self Join (Using Alias of Tables)

Suppose the query is to make a list of employees living in the city where `SUNIL` is living. This query requires data from one table—`Employee`. Suppose you write query as

```
select employee.ename
from employee
where employee.ename = 'SUNIL';
```

Result:

```
ENAME
----------
SUNIL
```

The query is obviously wrong because it will give `SUNIL` as output. If you manually solve the query then you will see that the query is referring the table two times—once for finding out `city` of `SUNIL`, and the second time for finding employee having the same city.

To answer such queries, we assume that we have two tables, `employee1` and `employee2` having identical data and identical columns. When we form a Cartesian product of two such tables, we will get four columns. Suppose `X` represents the `city` of `SUNIL`, then we will retrieve those rows in which the city of `employee` is also `X`. In the above condition, we are fetching those rows such that if `X` represents the city of `SUNIL`, then `X` will be the city of `employee`. Therefore, we will select `emp2.ename` as output. When the same table is referred twice or with a different name, you can use renaming/aliasing operation. The aliasing effect will be only for the query; the table is not permanently renamed.

Renaming is done using the following syntax:

```
<tablename>      <newname>
```

Note that renaming has effect only on the current execution of query. The conditions can be stated as:

```
      emp1                                        emp2
ename            city                    ename              city
SUNIL             X                                          X
```

Listing 2.34: Retrieving name of employees having same living city same as SUNIL

```
select emp2.ename
from employee emp1, employee emp2
where emp1.city = emp2.city
and emp1.ename = 'SUNIL'
/
```

Result:

```
ENAME
----------
SHANKAR
SUNIL
```

In the query, we have renamed employee as `emp2` and `emp2`.

Listing 2.35: Displaying the names of employee having same company city as SUNIL

```
select distinct(employee_cmp2.ename)
from emp_company employee_cmp1,company company1,
  emp_company employee_cmp2,company company2
Where employee_cmp1.cname = company1.cname
and employee_cmp1.ename = 'SUNIL'
and employee_cmp2.cname = company2.cname
and company2.city = company1.city
/
```

Result:

```
ENAME
----------
JAYA
AJAY
ANIL
SHANKAR
VIJAY
PRAKASH
AMOL
SUNIL
8 rows selected.
```

This query requires two tables—`emp_company` and `company`—twice. The conditions on columns are given as:

```
  employee_cmp1                          company1
ename  cname  sal   jdate          cname                  city
SUNIL   X                               Z                   X

        employee_cmp2                          company2
ename   cname     sal   jdate     cname          city
          Y                                Y                Z
```

Summary

In this chapter, you have learned about the various set operations such as Union, Intersect, and Minus. You have also learned about the In Clause, join clause and Cartesian Product.

In the next chapter, you will learn about the SQL Operators.

Exercise

Try the following example using only IN and EXISTS

1. List name of employees having living city same as 'Ajay'
2. List name of Employees with their living city having shift B and company 'ACC'
3. List name of employees with their living city having company city 'MUMBAI'
4. List name of employees having living city same as company city
5. List name of employee having same company city as company city of 'Ajay'

Try the following example using Cartesian Product

1. List name of employees having company located in 'Nagpur'
2. List name of employees having company located in 'Nagpur' and shift is B
3. List name of employees having company located in 'Nagpur' and shift is B and those who are living in MUMBAI
4. List name of employees having same working city as there living city and shift B
5. List name of employees having living city nagpur and salary more than 2000

Try the following example using self join

1. List name of employees having same company as company of Vijay
2. List name of employees having same company as company of Vijay and salary more than 1000.
3. List name of employees having same company as company of Vijay and shift B
4. List name of employees having same company as company of Vijay and same living city as Ajay
5. List name of employees having same company city as company city of Vijay
    - Give name of employee living in the same city where their manager also is living.
    - Give the salary of manager of employee living in `city` 'MUMBAI'.

This chapter gave you an insight into set operation. The next chapter will give details about the operators used in SQL.

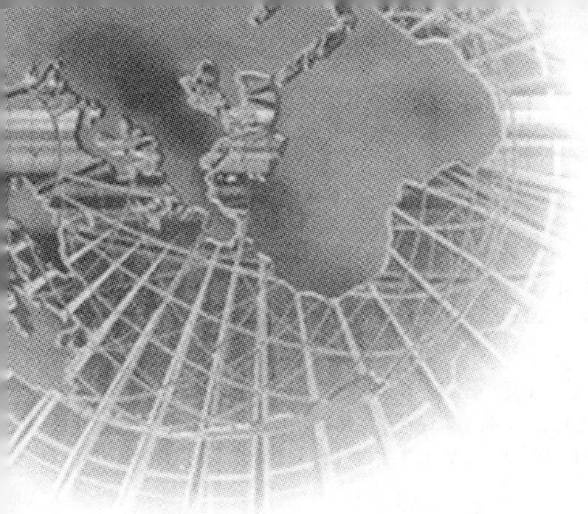

3

SQL Operators

Structured Query Language (SQL) is widely used by Relational Database Management Systems (RDBMSs), such as Microsoft SQL Server and Oracle, to perform common database operations, such as querying, inserting, updating, and deleting data. These operations are performed by using SQL operators. An operator is a symbol that represents an action, which is performed on one or more expressions to produce the desired results. In SQL, there are various types of operators, such as value, logical, and query expression operators. These operators also help you to perform a number of functions, such as numeric functions, date functions, character functions, and row functions.

In this chapter, you learn about different types of operators available in SQL, such as value, logical, and query expression operators. Next, you learn about functions provided by SQL, such as number, character, date, and some other functions. Further, the chapter describes pseudo-columns. In the end, you learn to define substitution variables.

Let's start by learning about value operators.

SQL Arithmetic Operators

Arithmetic operators are used to perform different arithmetic operations, such as addition and subtraction.

Table 3.1 lists different types of arithmetic operators:

Table 3.1: Listing Arithmetic Operators

<table>
<tr><th>Arithmetic Operator</th><th>Description</th></tr>
<tr><td>+, -</td><td>Provide sign for a number expression
Example:<pre>select - (salary) from emp_company;</pre>Output:<pre>-(SALARY)

     -1500
     -2000
     -1800
     -1700
     -5000
     -3000
     -8000
     -1000

8 rows selected</pre></td></tr>
<tr><td>*, /</td><td>Allow you to multiply and divide values
Example:<pre>select (salary * 1.5) from emp_company;</pre>Output:<pre>(SALARY*1.5)

        2250
        3000
        2700
        2550
        7500
        4500</pre></td></tr>
</table>

Table 3.1: Listing Arithmetic Operators

Arithmetic Operator	Description

	` 12000`
	` 1500`
	
	`8 rows selected`

+	Allow you to add and subtract values
	Example:
	`select (salary + 1000) from emp_company;`
	Output:
	`(SALARY+1000)`
	`-------------`
	`2500`
	`3000`
	`2800`
	`2700`
	`6000`
	`4000`
	`9000`
	`2000`
	
	`8 rows selected`

Let's now learn about logical operators.

SQL Logical Operators

Logical operators are used to combine Boolean conditions given in the where clause. In other words, logical operators are used to test a specified condition. On the basis of the test performed, the logical operators return either true or false.

Table 3.2 describes different types of logical operators:

Table 3.2: Describing Logical Operators

Logical Operator	Description

AND	Combines two logical conditions; it returns true if both conditions are `True`.
	Example:
	`select ename from emp_company where salary > 1000 and cname = 'ACC';`
	Output:
	`ENAME`
	`-----`
	`ANIL`
	`AJAY`

Table 3.2: Describing Logical Operators

Logical Operator	Description
OR	Combines two logical conditions; it returns `true` if any one of the logical conditions is `true`. Example: `select ename from emp_company where salary > 2000 or cname = 'ACC';` Output: ENAME ---------- ANIL VIJAY PRAKASH AJAY AMOL
NOT	Reverses the result of a logical expression. Example: `select ename from emp_company where not(cname = 'ACC');` Output: ENAME ---------- SHANKAR JAYA SUNIL VIJAY PRAKASH

Let's now learn to write queries using ALL and ANY

The following code snippet shows the name of employees having highest salary:

```
select ename
  from emp_company
  where salary >= all(select salary from emp_company);
```

The output of the preceding code snippet is as follows:

```
ENAME
----------
Ajay
```

You can write the query shown in the following code snippet to retrieve the name of employees who are not having lowest salary:

```
select ename
  from emp_company
  where salary > any(select salary from emp_company);
```

The output of the preceding code snippet is as follows:

```
ENAME
----------
AJAY
VIJAY
PRAKASH
SHANKAR
```

```
JAYA
SUNIL
ANIL
```

The following code snippet retrieves the name of employees from ACC having highest salary:

```
select e1.ename
   from emp_company e1
   where e1.cname='ACC' and
         e1.salary >=All(select e2.salary
                        from emp_company e2
                        where e2.cname='ACC');
```

The output of the preceding code snippet is as follows:

```
ENAME
----------
AJAY
```

Let's now learn about query expression operators.

SQL Query Expression Operators

Query expression operators are used to combine the results of multiple queries.

Table 3.3 lists different types of query expression operators:

Table 3.3: Describing Query Expression Operators

Query Expression Operator	Description

union	Returns all distinct rows from different queries.
	Example:
	`select cname from company where city = 'NAGPUR'`
	`Union`
	`select cname from company where city = 'MUMBAI';`
	Output:
	`CNAME`
	`----------`
	`ACC`
	`CMC`
	`TATA`

intersect	Returns all distinct rows returned by all queries individually. A row is returned if it appears in the result of each query.
	Example:
	`select cname from company where city = 'NAGPUR' intersect`
	`select cname from company where city = 'MUMBAI';`
	Output:
	`no rows selected`

minus	Returns all distinct rows returned by the first query, but not by second query.
	Example:
	`select cname from company where city = 'NAGPUR'`
	`minus`
	`select cname from company where city = 'MUMBAI';`

Table 3.3: Describing Query Expression Operators	
Query Expression Operator	**Description**

	Output:
	`CNAME`
	`----------`
	`ACC`

SQL Functions

SQL Server provides you a number of built-in functions to help you perform complex operations easily and quickly. For example, you can use the LENGTH() function to retrieve the length of a string. These functions are divided into various categories, such as number functions, character functions, and date functions, depending on the arguments they take. In this section, you learn about the built-in functions provided by SQL, starting with the number functions.

Number Functions

The number functions are used with numeric data. They take a number as an argument. These functions are provided to implement processing that is otherwise not possible with other SQL clauses. Table 3.4 lists the number functions available in SQL:

Table 3.4: Listing Number Functions	
Function	**Description**
ABS (n)	Provides absolute value of n Example: `ABS (-9)=9`
CEIL(n)	Gives smallest integer greater than or equal to n Example: `CEIL (9.5) = 10`
FLOOR (n)	Gives largest integer less than or equal to n Example: `FLOOR (10.5) = 10`
MOD (m,n)	Gives remainder, after dividing m by n Example: `MOD (17, 5) = 2`
POWER (M,N)	Returns the value of specified expression (m) raised to the power n, where n is integer Example: `POWER (3, 3)`

ROUND (N, M)	Rounds n to m decimal places
	Example:
	`ROUND (10.586, 2) = 10.59`
	`ROUND (153.456,-2) = 200`

Table 3.4: Listing Number Functions

Function	Description

TRUNC (n, m)	Truncates n to m decimal places
	Example:
	`TRUNC (10.586, 2) = 10.58`
	`TRUNC (156.56,-2) =100`

SIGN (n)	Returns -1 if n<0; 1 if n>0; 0 if n=0
	Example:
	`SIGN (-5) = -1`
	`SIGN (5) = 1`
	`SIGN (0) = 0`

SQRT (n)	Gives square root of n Example: `SQRT (9) = 3`

The number functions can be used with columns having numeric type, as shown in the following code snippet:

```
select mod(salary, 100) from emp_company;
```

NOTE

Oracle allows rounding and truncating of numbers before decimal points. When you round by –2, you get a number of xxx00. If you round by –3, you get xxx000. For example, ROUND(153.456)will produce x00. Since 153 is >= 150, the middle value x will be 2. So you get 200. ROUND(149.78,-2) will give 100. ROUND and TRUNC are used to produce statistical results, which are discussed in Chapter 9 (Advanced Queries).

Let's now learn about character functions.

Character Functions

The character functions mainly operate on character data. Table 3.5 lists character functions available in SQL:

Table 3.5: Listing Character Functions

Function	Description
ASCII (char)	Gives the *American Standard Code for Information Interchange* (ASCII) value of first character. Example: `ASCII ('ABC') = 65`
CHR (n)	Gives the ASCII value of the n character. Example: `CHR (65) = A`
INTICAP (char)	Capitalizes the first letter of char. Example: `INTICAP ('ANIL') = Anil`
INSTR (char1, char2, n, m)	Gives mth occurrence of char2 in char1. It starts searching from n and returns a numeric value. The first character is having index 1. Example: `INSTR ('abcabdebd','bd',1,1) = 5`

Table 3.5: Listing Character Functions

<table>
<tr><th>Function</th><th>Description</th></tr>
<tr><td></td><td>In the preceding example, the first occurrence of bd starts from position 5, if m = 1 is provided.
<pre>INSTR ('abcabdbd', 'bd',1,2) = 8</pre>The second occurrence of bd starts from 8 so the function returns 8.</td></tr>
<tr><td>LENGTH (char)</td><td>Returns length of a string.
Example:
<pre>length ('abc') = 3</pre></td></tr>
<tr><td>LOWER (char)</td><td>Converts all characters into lower case.
Example:
<pre>LOWER (ABC) = abc</pre></td></tr>
<tr><td>LPAD (char1, n, char2)</td><td>Pads char 1 to the left side of char 2 by length n.
Example:
<pre>LPAD ('Nagpur',8, 'city') gives 'cityNagpur'
SQL> select lpad('aaaabbbb',13,'xyz') from dual;

LPAD('AAAABBBB',13,'XYZ')
----
xyzxyaaaabbbb

SQL> select lpad('aaaabbbb',5,'xyz') from dual;

LPAD('AAAABBBB',5,'XYZ')
----
aaaab</pre></td></tr>
<tr><td>LTRIM (char, set)</td><td>Trims characters upto the first character from left side, not in the set. The set is given as second argument. In the following example, set consists of two characters, N and a. The trimming starts from left side of string and stops when the character, which is not in the set, is encountered.
Example:
<pre>LTRIM ('Nagpura', 'Na') = agpura</pre></td></tr>
<tr><td>RPAD (char1, n, char2)</td><td>Pads char1 to right with sequence of characters in char2
Example:
<pre>RPAD ('Nagpur', 4, 'city')= Nagpurcity</pre></td></tr>
<tr><td>RTRIM (char, set)</td><td>Trims the character from the right side upto the last character, which is not in set
Example:
<pre>RTRIM ('Nagpur', (u, r) = Nagp</pre>In the preceding example, Nagpur is trimmed upto p since it is not in the set</td></tr>
</table>

Table 3.5: Listing Character Functions

Function	Description
SOUNDEX (char)	Matches character string having same pronunciation. Example: `soundex ('son') = soundex ('sun')` In the preceding example, if you compare the strings, `son` and `sun`, it will return `FALSE`; if you compare its sound, then it will return `TRUE`, since both are producing the same sound.
SUBSTR (char, m, n)	Provides a substring of char, beginning with the m character and ending with the n character. Example: `substr ('17-MAY-99', 4 , 3) = MAY`
UPPER (char)	Converts all letters of char into upper case. Example: `UPPER ('abc')= ABC`
TRANSLATE (char, from_c, to_c)	Translates character set in `from_c` to character set in `to_c`. Example: `Translate ('MUMBAI', 'M', 'A') = 'MUMBAI'`

Listing 3.1 shows the use of substr function:

Listing 3.1: Using the SUBSTR **Function**

```
select substr (to_char(jdate),4,3) from emp_company;
```

The output of Listing 3.1 is as follows:

```
SUB
---
MAY
JUL
JUN
JAN
JAN
MAY
APR
MAR

8 rows selected
```

NOTE

The character functions can be used with columns having character data.

For example, consider the following code snippet:

```
select substr (to_char(jdate), 4,3) from emp_company;
```

In the preceding code snippet, to_char is a conversion function that converts date to character to produce the month of joining date.

Let's now learn about date functions.

Date Functions

Date functions are used to process data present in the date format. Table 3.6 lists date functions available in SQL:

Table 3.6: Describing Date Functions

Function	Description
ADD_MONTHS (d,n)	Adds n months to date. Example: `add_months ('17-may-99',2) = 17-jul-99`
LAST_DAY (d)	Specifies the date of the last day of month. Example: `last_day ('17-may-99') = 31-may-99`
MONTHS_BETWEEN (d1,d2)	Specifies the number of months between two dates, d1 and d2. If d2 is more than d1, it returns negative value. Example: `months_between ('17-may-99', '19-jul-99') = -2.0645161`
NEXT_DAY (d, char)	Returns the date of the first day of week named by char that is equal to or later than the date d. Suppose you want to find Wednesday after date 20-DEC-99, then you can call this function as shown in the following example: Example: `next_day ('20-dec-99', 'wed')= 22-dec-99`

TRUNC (value, timeunit)	Truncates date according to unit of time. For example truncating date using month gives first day of month. **Example:**
	`sql> select trunc(to_date('16-dec-2009'),'mon') from dual;`
	`01-DEC-09`
	`sql> select trunc(to_date('16-dec-2009'),'q')from dual;`
	`01-OCT-09`
	`sql> select trunc(to_date('16-dec-2009'),'yy')from dual;`
	`01-JAN-09`

EXTRACT(FMT FROM DATE)	Extracts time component from a date expression. Example: `extract(year from date'2003-08-02')=2003`

Listing 3.2 shows how to display date:

Listing 3.2: Displaying Date

```
select sysdate from dual;
```

The output of Listing 3.2 is as follows:

```
SYSDATE
---------
19-AUG-06
```

Listing 3.3 shows how to extract a day from a date:

Listing 3.3: Extracting a Day from a Date

```
select extract(day  from sysdate) from dual;
```

The output of Listing 3.3 is as follows:

```
EXTRACT(DAYFROMSYSDATE)
-----------------------
                     19
```

Listing 3.4 shows how to extract an year from a date:

Listing 3.4: Extracting an Year from a Date

```
select extract(year from sysdate) from dual;
```

The output of Listing 3.4 is as follows:

```
EXTRACT(YEARFROMSYSDATE)
------------------------
                    2006
```

Listing 3.5 shows how to extract a month from a date:

Listing 3.5: Extracting a Month from a Date

```
select extract(month  from sysdate) from dual;
```

The output of Listing 3.5 is as follows:

```
EXTRACT(MONTH FROM SYSDATE)
-------------------------
                        8
```

Let's now learn about some other functions, which do not fall in any of the preceding categories of functions.

Other Functions

These are common functions which operate on data having character, number, and date data types. Table 3.7 lists some other functions of SQL:

Table 3.7: Describing Other Functions

Function	Description
DECODE (expr, s1,r1, s2, r2, ... , default)	Returns r1, if the `expr` expression is equal to `s1`, and if `expr` is equal to `s2`, it returns `r2`. However, if `expr` does not match to `s1` or `s2`, it returns a default value. Example: `DECODE ( X, 'A', 50, 'B', 10, 80)` In the preceding example, if the value of `X` is `A`, the DECODE function returns `50`; if the value is `B`, it returns `10`; otherwise, `80` is returned. If default is not written, it returns null. The data type of `expr` and `s1`, `s2,s3...sn` should be same.
GREATEST (e1, e2 ...)	Returns the greatest among `e1, e2`.... All expressions are converted to the type of the first expression before comparison is done. Example: `GREATEST  (10, 20, 30) returns 30`
LEAST (e1, e2 ...)	Returns the least of smallest among `e1, e2`..... Example: `LEAST (10, 20, 30) returns 10`
NVL (F, E)	Returns the `E` expression, if `F` is null. `F` can be of any type. The type of `E` should be the same as that of F.

After learning about different functions available in SQL, let's learn about pseudo-columns.

Pseudo-Columns

Pseudo-columns are used to pass additional information to a row. A pseudo-column is not actually part of rows as other columns, but exists due to the row property. You cannot modify or update pseudo-columns, but use them to retrieve data. You can refer to pseudo-columns in the similar manner as you refer to other columns of a table in `select` statements. Let's learn about different types of pseudo-columns in the next section, starting with the LEVEL pseudo-column.

*The **LEVEL** Pseudo-Column*

The LEVEL pseudo-column returns a level of a row in a tree-structured query. It returns level 1 for a root node. The child node has one additional level than the parent. It can be used in a `select` statement where `connect by` is used.

NOTE

The connect by queries are discussed in detail in chapter 9, Advanced Queries.

Listing 3.6 shows how to display a level of a row:

Listing 3.6: Displaying a Level of a Row

```
select level, ename from manager connect by ename = mname start with ename =    'VIJAY';
```

The output of Listing 3.6 is as follows:

```
LEVEL    ENAME
1        VIJAY
```

Let's now learn about the ROWID pseudo-column.

*The **ROWID** Pseudo-Column*

The ROWID pseudo-column gives the location of a row on disk in the database where the row is physically stored.

Listing 3.7 shows how to display the location of a row:

Listing 3.7: Displaying the Location of a Row in a Database

```
select rowid, emp_company.ename from emp_company;
```

The output of Listing 3.7 is as follows:

```
ROWID                  ENAME
------------------     ----------
AAAMCZAAEAAAALIAAA     ANIL
AAAMCZAAEAAAALIAAB     SHANKAR
AAAMCZAAEAAAALIAAC     JAYA
AAAMCZAAEAAAALIAAD     SUNIL
AAAMCZAAEAAAALIAAE     VIJAY
AAAMCZAAEAAAALIAAF     PRAKASH
AAAMCZAAEAAAALIAAG     AJAY
AAAMCZAAEAAAALIAAH     AMOL
8 rows selected
```

Each `ROWID` has four parts. The format of `ROWID` is as follows:

```
filename blocknumber offset
```

Let's understand the first rowid, AAAMczAAEAAAALIAAA:

- AAAMcz—Represents the data object number that identifies the database segment. Schema objects in the same segment, such as a cluster of tables, have the same data object number.
- AAE—Represents the file number that identifies the data file, which contains the row. File numbers are unique within a database.
- AAAALI—Represents the block number that identifies the data block, which contains the row. Block numbers are relative to their data file, not their tablespace. Therefore, two rows in the same tablespace, but in different data files, can have the same block number.
- AAA—Represents the row number that identifies the row in the block.

Let's now learn about the ROWNUM pseudo-column

The *ROWNUM* Pseudo-Column

The ROWNUM pseudo-column gives a sequence in which rows are retrieved from the database. In other words, the ROWNUM pseudo-column is used to add sequence number to the output.

Listing 3.8 shows how to display the sequence of rows:

Listing 3.8: Displaying the Sequence of Retrieved Rows

```
select rownum, ename from employee;
```

The output of Listing 3.8 is as follows:

```
ROWNUM          ENAME
----------      ----------
1               ANIL
2               SHANKAR
3               JAYA
4               SUNIL
5               VIJAY
6               PRAKASH
7               AJAY

7 rows selected
```

The ROWNUM pseudo-column is also used to limit rows in the output.

Listing 3.9 shows how to limit rows in the output:

Listing 3.9: Limiting Rows in the Output

```
select rownum, ename from employee where rownum < 5;
```

The output of Listing 3.9 is as follows:

```
ROWNUM          ENUM
---------       ---------
1               Anil
2               Shankar
3               Jaya
4               Sunil
```

If you want to retrieve rows from the top of the table, you can write TOP-N queries to use ROWNUM, as shown in Listing 3.10:

Listing 3.10: Displaying the Top 3 Employees According to Salary

```
select ename,salary
from(select ename,salary
from emp_company
order by salary desc)
where rownum < 4
/
```

The output of Listing 3.10 is as follows:

```
ENAME           SALARY
----------  ----------
AJAY              8000
VIJAY             5000
PRAKASH           3000
```

Let's now learn about the ROWSCN pseudo-column.

The **ROWSCN** Pseudo-Column

The ROWSCN pseudo-column gives approximate System Change Number (SCN) when the row is last modified. SCN is the number generated by Oracle to record the sequence of transaction. In other words, it is system change number that is generated by Oracle when the transaction is committed.

Listing 3.11 shows the code to display SCN when a row is last modified:

Listing 3.11: Displaying SCN

```
select ora_rowscn, sname from zpcm;
```

The output of Listing 3.11 is as follows:

```
ORA_ROWSCN                 SNAME
----------                 ---------------
    418737                 SAHIL
```

Listing 3.12 displays SCN of a row which is last modified:

Listing 3.12: Displaying SCN for a Row which is Last Modified

```
select scn_to_timestamp(ora_rowscn), sname from zpcm;
```

The output of Listing 3.12 is as follows:

```
SCN_TO_TIMESTAMP(ORA_ROWSCN)            SNAME
---------------------------------       ---------------
29-JUN-06 04.47.15.000000000 PM         SAHIL
```

Let's now learn about the SYSDATE pseudo-column.

The **SYSDATE** Pseudo-Column

The SYSDATE pseudo-column gives the current date and time of the system.

Listing 3.13 shows the code to display the current date and time using the SYSDATE pseudo-column:

Listing 3.13: Displaying the Current Date and Time

```
select sysdate, ename from emp_company;
```

The output of Listing 3.13 is as follows:

```
SYSDATE   ENAME
--------- ----------
19-AUG-06 ANIL
19-AUG-06 SHANKAR
19-AUG-06 JAYA
19-AUG-06 SUNIL
19-AUG-06 VIJAY
19-AUG-06 PRAKASH
19-AUG-06 AJAY
19-AUG-06 AMOL

8 rows selected
```

Let's now learn about the UID pseudo-column.

The **UID** Pseudo-Column

The UID pseudo-column gives a number that identifies the user, since Oracle is used in a multiuser environment. In other words, `UID` is the way to identify a user of Oracle.

Listing 3.14 the use of the **UID** pseudo-column:

Listing 3.14: Identifying the User

```
select UID from DUAL;
```

The output of Listing 3.14 is as follows:

```
       UID
----------
        57
```

Let's now learn about the USER pseudo-column.

The **USER** Pseudo-Column

The USER pseudo-column is used to retrieve the user name. Listing 3.15 shows how to retrieve the user name using the USER pseudo-column:

Listing 3.15 shows the code to retrieve the user name:

Listing 3.15: Retrieving the User Name

```
select user, ename from emp_company;
```

The output of Listing 3.15 is as follows:

```
USER                           ENAME
------------------------------ ----------
SCOTT                          ANIL
SCOTT                          SHANKAR
SCOTT                          JAYA
SCOTT                          SUNIL
SCOTT                          VIJAY
SCOTT                          PRAKASH
SCOTT                          AJAY
SCOTT                          AMOL

8 rows selected
```

NOTE

The select statement cannot be completed without the from clause. At times, you may require information for the from clause, which you can only get by using a pseudo-column. Therefore, if you want to retrieve UID, write a select statement shown in the following code snippet:

```
select UID from DUAL;
```

If you want to display system date, write the following select statement:

```
select sysdate from DUAL;
```

After learning about pseudo-columns, let's learn to define single and double ampersand variables.

Defining Single and Double Ampersand (&) Variables

You can use either single ampersand (`&`) or double ampersand (`&&`). If you use single ampersand before string, SQLPLUS does not define a variable. Therefore, when the same variable is referenced, it will ask for the value of the variable. Listing 3.16 shows how to use single ampersand (&):

Listing 3.16: Using Single Ampersand (&)

```
select Avg(&col), Max (&col) from emp_company;
```

The output of Listing 3.16 is as follows:

```
Enter value of col:
```

Listing 3.17 shows how to use double ampersand (&&):

Listing 3.17: Using Double Ampersand (&&)

```
select Avg(&&col), Max (&&col) from emp_company;
```

On the other hand, `&&` is used to define variables. When a variable is defined by using `&&` and is referenced again, SQLPLUS will use the same value and will not ask for a new value. In other words, a double ampersand is used for queries in which the same variable is used more than once. In Listing 3.17, `col` is used more than once.

Summary

In this chapter, you have learned about different types of operators available in SQL, including value, logical, and query expression operators. You have also learned about functions provided by SQL, such as number, character, date, and some other functions. Moreover, you have learned about pseudo-columns, such as UID, SYSDATE, and ROWSCN. Finally, you have learned to define substitution variables using single (&) and double (&&) ampersands.

Exercise

Write following queries

1. List name of employees who joined in Jan-2000.
2. List name of employees whose name starts with A.
3. List name of employees in lowercase.
4. List name of companies having string length of three characters.
5. List name of employees having salary in multiples of 1000.

4

Aggregate Functions and Group By Clause

Aggregate Functions

Aggregate functions are used for performing group operations. Aggregate functions are used to calculate single values for groups of rows. For example, data in the table Emp_company is given as follows:

```
select * from emp_company;
```

The output of the preceding code snippet is as follows:

```
ENAME      CNAME           SALARY        JDATE
--------- ----------  ----------   ---------
ANIL       ACC               1500        01-MAY-89
SHANKAR    TATA              2000        10-JUL-90
JAYA       CMC               1800        07-JUN-91
SUNIL      CMC               1700        01-JAN-88
VIJAY      TATA              5000        03-JAN-88
PRAKASH    TATA              3000        27-MAY-89
AJAY       ACC               8000        30-APR-95
AMOL       ACC               1000        17-MAR-95

8 rows selected
```

Listing 4.1 shows the code to list the maximum salary in all companies:

Listing 4.1: List Maximum Salary in All Companies

```
select max(salary)
from emp_company;
```

The output of Listing 4.1 is as follows:

```
MAX(SALARY)
-----------
   8000
```

In the preceding output, `max` is the aggregate function.

NOTE

Other aggregate functions are min, sum, avg, count, variance, and stdev (standard deviation).

Listing 4.2 shows the code to display the maximum salary of employees of ACC:

Listing 4.2: Maximum Salary of Employees of ACC

```
select max(salary)
from emp_company
where cname = 'ACC';
```

The output of Listing 4.2 is as follows:

```
MAX(SALARY)
-----------
   8000
```

The query is evaluated as follows:

First, the data source is chosen, it may be a single table or a join, a data source on which the `WHERE` condition is evaluated. In the absence of the `GROUP BY` clause, a single group is formed from the rows, which are selected by the `WHERE` condition. On the selected group, the aggregate function is evaluated. In the absence of the `GROUP BY` clause, the query having the aggregate function returns a single row.

Whenever you are using an aggregate function in `SELECT`, other expressions in the `SELECT` statement should also represent the group property, as shown in the following code snippet:

```
select ename,max(salary) from emp_company;
```

The output of the preceding code snippet is as follows:

```
select ename,max(salary) from emp_company
        *
ERROR at line 1:
ORA-00937: not a single-group group function
```

The preceding output returns an error, `not a single-group group function` because one group can have only one MAX `salary`, but multiple `ename`. So, `ename` cannot be a group property.

The following code snippet will not return an error:

```
select avg(salary),max(salary) from emp_company;
```

The preceding query will not return an error because `AVG` and `MAX` are group properties.

The output of the preceding code snippet is as follows:

```
AVG(SALARY)      MAX(SALARY)
-----------   ------------
   3000     8000
```

You cannot use aggregate functions in the `where` condition directly. Instead, you can use the `in` clause if you want to compare row values with a group value. Listing 4.3 displays the name of employees who are having the maximum salary:

Listing 4.3: Displaying the Name of Employees having Maximum Salary:

```
select ename from emp_company
where salary in (select max(salary) from emp_company);
```

The output of Listing 4.3 is as follows:

```
ENAME
-----
Ajay
```

Listing 4.4 shows the code to count the number of employees working in ACC:

Listing 4.4: Counting the Number of Employees Working in ACC

```
select count(ename) from emp_company where cname = 'ACC';
```

The output of Listing 4.4 is as follows:

```
COUNT(ENAME)
-----------
    3
```

If no employees are working in ACC, then the query in Listing 4.4 will return zero. If `max` is used and no row is selected by the `where` condition, then null is returned, as shown in the following code snippet:

```
select max(salary)
from emp_company where cname = '1';
```

The output of the preceding code snippet is as follows:

```
MAX(SALARY)
------------
Returns null value
```

Listing 4.5 shows the use of the count function:

Listing 4.5: Using the count Function to Return the Number of Rows

```
select count(salary) from emp_company where cname='1'
/
```

The output of Listing 4.5 is as follows:

```
COUNT(SALARY)
--------------------
     0
```

Listing 4.6 shows the use of the NVL function:

Listing 4.6: Using the NVL Function to Return Some Value Instead of Null Value

```
select nvl(max(salary),0) from emp_company where cname = '1'
/
```

The output of Listing 4.6 is as follows:

```
NVL(MAX(SALARY),0)
------------------
      0
```

Listing 4.7 displays the number of employees living in MUMBAI:

Listing 4.7: Displaying the Number of Employees Living in MUMBAI

```
select count(ename) from employee where city ='MUMBAI';
```

The output of Listing 4.7 is as follows:

```
COUNT(ENAME)
------------
          2
```

Listing 4.8 displays the number of employees having shift A:

Listing 4.8: Displaying the Number of Employees having Shift A

```
select count(*) from emp_shift where shift = 'A';
```

The output of Listing 4.8 is as follows:

```
COUNT(*)
---------
  1
```

Listing 4.9 displays the names of employees with their city and maximum salary in TATA:

Listing 4.9: Displaying the Names of Employees with their City and Maximum Salary in TATA

```
select e.ename,e.city from employee e where e.ename in
(select c.ename from emp_company c where  c.cname = 'TATA'
and c.salary in (select max(c1.salary)
from emp_company c1 where c1.cname = 'TATA'))
/
```

The output of Listing 4.9 is as follows:

```
ENAME      CITY
---------- ---------
VIJAY      DELHI
```

Listing 4.10 displays the names of the employee having maximum salary in the Company, where SUNIL is working:

Listing 4.10: Displaying the Names of the Employee having Maximum Salary in Company, where SUNIL is working

```
select e.ename from emp_company e where e.salary in
(select max(e1.salary) from emp_company e1
where e1.cname in (select e2.cname from emp_company e2
where e2.ename = 'SUNIL'))
and e.cname in (select e3.cname from emp_company e3
where e3.ename = 'SUNIL')
/
```

The output of Listing 4.10 is as follows:

```
ENAME
----------
JAYA
```

Listing 4.11 displays the names of employees having maximum salary in their Company:

Listing 4.11: Displaying the Names of Employees having Maximum Salary in their Company

```
select e1.ename
from emp_company e1 where e1.salary in
(select max(e2.salary)
from emp_company e2 where e1.cname=e2.cname)
/
```

The output of Listing 4.11 is as follows:

```
ENAME
----------
JAYA
VIJAY
AJAY
```

Let's learn about the `GROUP BY` clause.

The **GROUP BY** Clause

The `GROUP BY` clause is used to compute aggregate functions of a group.

Listing 4.12 displays the names of companies and the maximum salary in that company:

Listing 4.12: Displaying the Names of Companies and the Maximum Salary in that Company

```
select cname,max(salary)
from emp_company group by cname;
// group by expression
```

The output of Listing 4.12 is as follows:

```
CNAME      MAX(SALARY)
---------- -----------
ACC               8000
TATA              5000
CMC               1800
```

In the preceding output, `cname` is called `group by` expression. When `GROUP BY` is specified, then all the rows having the same value of `group by` expression are combined into one group. If the total number of groups is equal to the total number of distinct values of `group by` expression, then for each group the aggregate function is evaluated. The total number of rows, which are given as output, depend on the total number of groups. In the `select` statement, you can write or use `group by` expression plus any additional group property. Since, cname is a `group by` expression, it can be used in `SELECT`. This is because there is only one `cname` for the group.

Listing 4.13 calculates the number of employees for each company:

Listing 4.13: Calculate the Number of Employees for Each Company

```
select cname,count(ename)
from emp_company group by cname;
```

The output of Listing 4.13 is as follows:

```
CNAME      COUNT(ENAME)
---------- ------------
ACC                   3
TATA                  3
CMC             2
```

The last row in CNAME is blank because one row in cname is having the null value.

Let's learn about the having clause.

The **HAVING** Clause

The HAVING clause is used to provide condition on a group of rows. The where clause is used to provide condition on the row value but the having clause is used to provide condition on the group value.

Listing 4.14 displays the companies having more than one employee:

Listing 4.14: Displaying the Companies having More than One Employee

```
select cname,count(ename)
from emp_company group by cname
having count(ename) > 1;
```

The output of Listing 4.14 is as follows:

```
CNAME      COUNT(ENAME)
---------- ------------
ACC                   3
TATA                  3
CMC                   2
```

In the preceding output, groups are first formed on `cname` and then, for each group, rows with `HAVING` condition are evaluated. The rows that satisfy the `having` condition are given in the result.

Therefore, `ACC` will not be in the result because it does not satisfy the `HAVING` condition. Remember that the `WHERE` condition is used only for comparing row values, while the `HAVING` condition is used for comparing group values, such as `count`, `min`, `max`, etc. The general execution of a query is done in the following ways:

- `The From` clause determines the data source— it can be a join or a simple table.
- For each row in data source, the `where` condition is evaluated and rows are selected
- On the selected rows, groups are formed according to the `GROUP BY` expression.
- For each group, the `HAVING` condition is applied only to rows. Those group rows are given as output that satisfy the `having` condition.

Listing 4.15 shows the code to find the average salary of each company:

Listing 4.15: Finding the Average Salary of Each Company

```
select cname,avg(salary)
from emp_company group by cname;
```

The output of Listing 4.15 is as follows:

```
CNAME      AVG(SALARY)
---------- -----------
ACC               3500
TATA        3333.33333
CMC               1750
```

Listing 4.16 displays the average salary of each company except ACC:

Listing 4.16: Displaying the Average Salary of Each Company Except ACC

```
select cname,avg(salary)
from emp_company
where cname != 'ACC'
group by cname;
```

The output of Listing 4.16 is as follows:

```
CNAME      AVG(SALARY)
---------- -----------
TATA        3333.33333
CMC               1750
```

Listing 4.17 shows the code to find the names of companies having an average salary of more than 1500:

Listing 4.17: Finding the Names of Companies having Average Salary More than 1500

```
select cname,avg(salary)
from emp_company
group by cname
having avg(salary) > 1500;
```

The output of Listing 4.17 is as follows:

```
CNAME      AVG(SALARY)
---------- -----------
ACC               3500
TATA        3333.33333
CMC                    1750
```

Listing 4.18 displays the average salary of a company only for the employees living in DELHI:

Listing 4.18: Displaying the Average Salary of Company Only for the Employees Living in DELHI

```
select cname,avg(e.salary)
from emp_company e where e.ename in
(select l.ename from employee l where l.city='DELHI')
group by e.cname;
```

The output of Listing 4.18 is as follows:

```
CNAME      AVG(E.SALARY)
---------- -------------
TATA                5000
```

Listing 4.19 shows the code to find the name of a company having the highest average salary:

Listing 4.19: Finding the Name of Company having the Highest Average salary

```
select e.cname,avg(e.salary)
from emp_company e
group by cname
having avg(e.salary) >= all(select avg(c.salary)
from emp_company c
group by c.cname);
```

The output of Listing 4.19 is as follows:

```
CNAME      AVG(E.SALARY)
---------- -------------
ACC                 3500
```

Let's learn to use the `WITH` clause.

Using the **WITH** Clause

Using the `WITH` clause, you can reduce the overheads for computing the same queries. Suppose, you want to use the result of a certain query repeatedly, you can mark that query using the `WITH` clause. Internally, Oracle forms temporary tables based on the result of a query and use that table for the rest of the query evaluation. The following code snippet shows the use of the `WITH` clause:

```
select cname, sum(salary) from emp_company group by cname;
```

The output of preceding code snippet is as follows:

```
CNAME      SUM(SALARY)
---------- -----------
ACC              10500
TATA             10000
CMC               3500
```

The following code snippet shows the code to compute the average salary of all companies and names of companies having the total salary more than the average salary.

```
with companysalary as( select cname, sum(salary) totalsal
from emp_company group by cname),
companyavgsalary as(select avg(totalsal) avgsal from companysalary)
select cname,totalsal from companysalary
where totalsal >(select avgsal from companyavgsalary)
/
```

In the preceding code snippet, the first and second query are named as `COMPANYSALARY` and `COMPANYAVGSALARY`, respectively.

The output of the preceding code snippet is as follows:

```
CNAME        TOTALSAL
----------  ----------
ACC              10500
TATA             10000
```

Using the WITH clause, you can compute complex calculations by dividing query into simple queries. For example, you can calculate the ratio of the salary of ANIL and SUNIL as:

```
with
anilsal as (select salary s1 from emp_company where ename='anil'),
sunilsal as (select salary s2 from emp_company where ename='sunil')
select t1.s1,t2.s2,t1.s1/t2.s2
from anilsal t1,sunilsal t2
/
```

Output

```
        S1          S2       T1.S1/T2.S2
----------  ----------  -----------
      1500        1700   .882352941
```

Let's learn to use the `order by` clause.

The **ORDER BY** Clause

You can sort your data using various ways using the `ORDER BY` clause.

Listing 4.20 shows the code to sort the output:

Listing 4.20: Sorting the Output on ename

```
select ename,cname
from emp_company
order by ename;
```

or

```
select ename,cname
from emp_company
Order by 1;
```

In the preceding listing, `1` means first column in the `SELECT` statement.

The output of Listing 4.20 is as follows:

```
ENAME       CNAME
----------  --------
AJAY        ACC
ANIL        ACC
Ashok
JAYA        CMC
```

```
PRAKASH     TATA
SHANKAR     TATA
SUNIL       CMC
VIJAY       TATA

8 rows selected
```

Listing 4.21 displays the output in descending order:

Listing 4.21: Displaying the Output in Descending Order

```
select ename,cname
from emp_company
order by 1 desc;
```

The output of Listing 4.21 is as follows:

```
ENAME       CNAME
---------- --------
VIJAY       TATA
SUNIL       CMC
SHANKAR     TATA
PRAKASH     TATA
JAYA        CMC
ANIL           ACC
AMOL        ACC
AJAY        ACC

8 rows selected
```

You can mention multiple columns in the `ORDER BY` clause.

Listing 4.22 shows the code to sort on cname in ascending order, and if cname is same, then it is sorted on ename in descending order:

Listing 4.22: Sorting on cname in Ascending Order, and if cname is same, then it is sorted on ename in Descending Order

```
select ename,cname
from emp_company
order by 2 asc,1 desc;
```

The output of Listing 4.22 is as follows:

```
ENAME       CNAME
---------- -------
ANIL        ACC
AMOL        ACC
AJAY        ACC
SUNIL       CMC
JAYA        CMC
VIJAY       TATA
SHANKAR     TATA
PRAKASH     TATA

8 rows selected
```

NOTE

ORDER BY is evaluated in the last phase of query execution.

Summary

This chapter threw light on aggregate functions and `GROUP BY` clause. The next chapter stresses on modifying data in the existing table.

Exercise

- List the number of employees living in `MUMBAI`.
- List the number of employees having shift `A`.
- List the names of employees with their living city having maximum salary in `TATA`.
- List the name of the employees having maximum salary in a company where `SUNIL` is working.
- List the names of employees having maximum salary in their `company`.
- Find out the average salary given by each `company`.
- Find out the average salary given by each company except `ACC`.
- Find out the names of companies `HAVING` average salary more than `1500`.
- Find out the average salary given by a company only for the employees living in `DELHI`.
- Find out the name of the company `HAVING` highest average salary.

5

Updating and Deleting Data in Existing Table (DML)

Until now, we have discussed how to insert and retrieve data. You might have to change or update the existing data of the table while insertion or deletion of data is being carried out.

Let's say, an employee has left the company, ACC and joined the company, TATA or there is a raise of 20% in an employee's salary. In such conditions, it is necessary to update the existing rows of the table. This is done using the UPDATE statement (a part of data manipulation language (DML) of SQL) in SQL.

The **UPDATE** Statement

The UPDATE statement is used to update existing rows in a table. Using the UPDATE statement, you can update the rows of maximum one table at a time. The UPDATE statement may update a single row or multiple rows at a time. If the where condition is not written, then all rows will be updated.

The syntax for the UPDATE statement is as follows:

```
update<Table name> set column 1= ,column2 = ........
where <condition>
```

The UPDATE statement first evaluates the condition specified, and if the condition is true, the table is updated.

NOTE

You can use only one table name with the UPDATE statement.

Listing 5.1 shows the code to increase the salary of an employee by 20%:

Listing 5.1: Increasing the Salary of an Employee by 20%

```
update emp_company set salary = salary * 1.2;
```

The output of Listing 5.1 is as follows:

```
8 rows updated
```

Listing 5.2 shows the code to update the salary of an employee of a company, ACC:

Listing 5.2: Updating the Salary of Employee of the ACC Company

```
update emp_company set salary = salary * 1.2
where cname = 'ACC';
```

The output of Listing 5.2 is as follows:

```
3 rows updated
```

In the preceding output, only those rows are updated, which have cname = ACC.

In case the user wants to specify a condition with respect to two or more tables, then it can be done using an IN or EXIXTS clause.

NOTE

The user cannot use join or Cartesian product for specifying such conditions which refers to other tables.

Listing 5.3 shows the code to update the salary of SUNIL, only if both ANIL and SUNIL are working in the ACC company. The condition using the IN or EXISTS clause is used to check whether ANIL is employed with the ACC company; another condition is used to check whether SUNIL is employed with the ACC company.

Listing 5.3: Updating the Salary of SUNIL, only if both ANIL and SUNIL are Working in the Company ACC – the condition using IN, or EXISTS clause is used to check whether ANIL is employed with ACC company; another condition is used to check whether SUNIL is also employed with ACC company

```
update emp_company set salary = salary + 100
where ename = 'SUNIL' and cname ='ACC'
and exists (select e1. ename from emp_company e1 where
e1.ename = 'ANIL' and e1. cname = 'ACC');
```

The query in Listing 5.3 is as follows:

```
select e1.ename from emp_company e1 where
e1.ename = 'ANIL' and e1.cname = 'ACC';
```

Listing 5.3 returns a row, only if ANIL is working in ACC. The row is updated only if SUNIL is working in ACC and ANIL is also working in ACC.

The output of Listing 5.3 is as follows:

```
0 row updated
```

Listing 5.4 shows the code to decrease the salary of VIJAY by 100, if both VIJAY and SUNIL are living in CHENNAI:

Listing 5.4: Decreasing the Salary of VIJAY by 100, if both are Living in CHENNAI

```
update emp_company set salary = salary - 100 where ename = 'VIJAY' and
ename in(select e1.ename from employee e1 where e1.city = 'CHENNAI') and exists
  (select emp1.ename from employee emp1 where emp1.ename = 'SUNIL' and         emp1.city
  = 'CHENNAI');
```

The condition in Listing 5.4 is as follows:

```
ename in
(select e1.ename from employee e1 where e1.city = 'CHENNAI')
```

In Listing 5.4, the IN and EXISTS clauses would return a row, only if SUNIL is living in CHENNAI, while the condition checks whether VIJAY is living in CHENNAI or not. Rows are updated only if both are living in CHENNAI.

The output of Listing 5.4 is as follows:

```
0 row updated
```

The query with the IN and EXISTS clauses would return a row, only if SUNIL lives in CHENNAI, while the condition checks whether or not VIJAY is living in CHENNAI. Rows are updated only if both are living in CHENNAI. Listing 5.5 shows the code to increase the salary of employees by 15% who are living in CHENNAI:

Listing 5.5: Increasing the Salary of Employee by 15% who are Living in City CHENNAI

```
update emp_company
set salary = salary * 1.5
where ename in
(select ename from employee where city = 'CHENNAI');
```

The output of Listing 5.5 is as follows:

```
2 rows updated
```

Listing 5.6 shows the code to update all employees of ACC having a salary greater than 8000 and living in MUMBAI, who are to be shifted to TATA:

Listing 5.6: Updating all Employees of ACC having a Salary Greater than 8000 and Living in MUMBAI, who are to be Shifted to TATA

```
update emp_company
set cname = 'TATA'
where cname = 'ACC' and salary > 8000
and ename in
(select ename from employee where city = 'MUMBAI');
```

The output of Listing 5.6 is as follows:

```
0 row updated
```

Listing 5.7 shows the code to update all employees of ACC, living in MUMBAI, and having a salary greater than 8000, who are to be shifted to TATA (the salary in new company is 20% more than original salary):

Listing 5.7: Updating all Employees of ACC, Living in MUMBAI, and having a Salary Greater than 8000, who are to be Shifted to TATA. The salary in new company is 20% more than original salary.

```
update emp_company
set cname = 'TATA',salary = 1.2 * salary
where cname = 'ACC'
and salary > 8000
and ename
in
(select ename from employee where city = 'MUMBAI');
```

The output of Listing 5.7 is as follows:

```
0 row updated
```

Listing 5.8 shows the code to decrease the salary of employee VIJAY by 100, and increasing the salary of employee SUNIL by 100 (in this case, we require two UPDATE statements as it cannot be stated in a single UPDATE statement, using DECODE you can try using single statement):

Listing 5.8: Decreasing the Salary of Employee VIJAY by 100, and Increasing the Salary of Employee SUNIL by 100 (in this case, we require two UPDATE statements as it cannot be stated in a single UPDATE statement, using DECODE you can try using single statement):

```
update emp_company
set salary = salary - 100
where ename = 'VIJAY';

update emp_company
set salary = salary + 100
where ename = 'SUNIL';
```

The output of Listing 5.8 is as follows:

```
0 row updated
```

Listing 5.9 decreasing the salary of VIJAY by 100 and increasing the salary of SUNIL, if and only if both are working for company, ACC (it requires two UPDATE statements. For each UPDATE statement, you need to check whether VIJAY and SUNIL are working in company, ACC):

Listing 5.9: Decreasing the Salary of VIJAY by 100 and Increasing the Salary of SUNIL, if and Only if Both are Working for Company, ACC

```
update emp_company
set salary = salary - 100
where ename = 'VIJAY'
and cname = 'ACC'
and exists (select e1.ename from emp_company e1 where
e1.ename = 'SUNIL' and e1.cname = 'ACC');

update emp_company
set salary = salary + 100
where ename = 'SUNIL'
and cname = 'ACC'
and exists (select e1.ename from emp_company e1
where e1.ename = 'VIJAY' and e1.cname = 'ACC');
```

The output of Listing 5.9 is as follows:

```
0 row updated
```

There are occasions where the user wants to assign the value of one column to some other column.

Listing 5.10 shows the code to assign salary of VIJAY to salary of SUNIL where salary of SUNIL is unknown (the salary can be retrieved using the SELECT statement and then using it in the UPDATE statement; this facility is given by SQL itself):

Listing 5.10: Assigning a Salary of VIJAY to Salary of SUNIL where Salary of SUNIL is Unknown

```
update emp_company
set salary = (select e1.salary from  emp_company e1 where e1. ename = 'SUNIL')
where ename = 'VIJAY';
```

The output of Listing 5.10 is as follows:

```
1 row updated
```

The SELECT statement is used to calculate the required value to be used in an assignment statement. The condition for using SELECT statement is that it should return only one value.

NOTE

If the SELECT statement returns more than one value, the UPDATE statement would give an error.

Listing 5.11 shows the code to update the salary of VIJAY, by giving him salary that is the sum of his salary and SUNIL's salary:

Listing 5.11: Updating the Salary of VIJAY, by giving him Salary that is the Sum of his Salary and SUNIL's Salary

```
update emp_company
set salary = (select (emp_company.salary + ec1.salary)
from emp_company ec1 where ec1.ename = 'SUNIL')
where ename = 'VIJAY';
```

The output of Listing 5.11 is as follows:

```
1 row updated
```

The select statement returns the sum of VIJAY and SUNIL's salary.

Listing 5.12 shows the code to update the salary and company of VIJAY by giving him the same salary as that of SUNIL's and the same company as that of ANIL's:

Listing 5.12: Updating the Salary and Company of VIJAY by giving him the Same Salary as that of SUNIL's and the Same Company as that of ANIL's

```
update emp_company
set salary = (select ec1.salary
from emp_company ec1 where ec1.ename = 'SUNIL'),
cname = (select ec2.cname from emp_company ec2
where ec2.ename = 'ANIL')
where ename = 'VIJAY';
```

In Listing 5.12, first query returns the salary of SUNIL and the second query returns the company name of ANIL, both the columns (salary and ename) of VIJAY are thus updated.

The output of Listing 5.12 is as follows:

```
1 row updated
```

Listing 5.13 shows the code to update the salary of employee, VIJAY by adding 50% average salary of company, ACC.

Listing 5.13: Updating the Salary of Employee VIJAY by Adding 50% Average Salary of Company, ACC

```
update emp_company EC1
set salary =(select 0.5*avg(EC2.salary)+EC1.SALARY
from emp_company  EC2 where EC2.cname = 'ACC')
where EC1.ename = 'VIJAY';
```

The output of Listing 5.13 is as follows:

```
1 row updated
```

Listing 5.14 shows the code to update the salary of employee, VIJAY and giving him max salary of the company where SUNIL is working.

Listing 5.14: Updating the `salary` of Employee, `VIJAY` and giving him `max salary` of Company of `SUNIL`

```
update emp_company ec1
set salary = (select max(salary)
from emp_company ec1
where ec1.cname
in (select ec2.cname from
emp_company ec2
where ec2.ename = 'SUNIL'))
where ename = 'VIJAY';
```

The output of Listing 5.14 is as follows:

```
1 row updated
```

Let's learn to use delete statement.

The **DELETE** Statement

Deleting Row from a Table (DML)

In this topic, we will discuss the deletion of rows from a table. The insertion, updation, and deletion would complete the data manipulation operation for handling the database. The deletion of rows is done using `DELETE` statement in SQL. The `DELETE` statement only deletes rows and not the table, i.e. the table would exist although rows from the table are deleted. You can again insert the rows in a table by using `INSERT` statement.

Suppose the user wants to restrict deletion of certain rows. In this case, the user can use the `WHERE` clause in `DELETE` statement.

Listing 5.15 shows the code to delete all rows from employee table having city, `CHENNAI`

Listing 5.15: Deleting all Rows from Employee Table having City, `CHENNAI`

```
delete employee where city = 'CHENNAI';
```

In this case, the user cannot use join or Cartesian product for specifying the condition of multiple tables.

The output of Listing 5.15 is as follows:

```
2 rows deleted
```

To specify condition with reference to multiple tables in the `WHERE` statement, it is better to use `IN` or `EXISTS` clause.

Listing 5.16 shows the code to delete rows from the `Emp_company` table, which contain employees living in `MUMBAI`:

Listing 5.16: Deleting Rows from the `Emp_company` Table, which contain Employees Living in `MUMBAI`

```
delete emp_company
where ename in (select ename
from     employee where city = 'MUMBAI');
```

The output of Listing 5.16 is as follows:

```
2 rows deleted
```

The alternate way to write the query in Listing 5.16 using the `exists` clause is as follows:

```
delete emp_company where exists (select 'x'
from employee where employee.ename = emp_company.ename
and city = 'MUMBAI');
```

The output of Listing 5.16 is as follows:

```
2 rows deleted
```

Listing 5.17 shows the code to delete rows of the `Emp_company` table having salary greater than `8000`:

Listing 5.17: Deleting Rows of the `Emp_company` table having Salary Greater than `8000`

```
delete emp_company where salary > 8000;
```

The output of Listing 5.17 is as follows:

```
0 rows deleted
```

Listing 5.18 shows the code to delete rows of the `Emp_company` table with salary greater than `8000`, employee living in `CHENNAI`, and his company is located in `MUMBAI`:

Listing 5.18: Deleting rows of the `Emp_company` table with salary greater than `8000`, employee living in `CHENNAI`, and his company is located in `MUMBAI`

```
delete emp_company where salary > 8000
and ename in (select ename from employee where city = 'CHENNAI') and
cname in (select cname from company where city = 'MUMBAI');
```

The output of Listing 5.18 is as follows:

```
0 rows deleted
```

Using the `EXISTS` clause:

```
delete emp_company where salary > 8000
and exists (select employee.ename from employee
where    employee.city = 'CHENNAI') and exists
(select company.cname from company
where emp_company.cname = company.cname
and company. city = 'MUMBAI');
0 rows deleted
```

Let's learn how to delete the entire table.

Dropping the Table

There is a difference in deleting a table and deleting all rows in a table. Suppose you have executed the following code snippet:

```
delete employee;
```

The preceding code snippet would delete all rows from the table, but will not delete the table. So, you can insert rows later on.

Listing 5.19 shows the code to delete the entire table:

Listing 5.19: Deleting the Entire Table

```
drop table employee;
```

The output of Listing 5.19 is as follows:

```
Table dropped
```

The preceding output shows that that `Employee` table is `dropped`. Inserting rows into a table, which is dropped, would return an error stating that the table does not exist.

Renaming the Table

The user can rename a table using the `RENAME` command.

Listing 5.20 shows the code to rename the table, `Employee` as `emp`:

Listing 5.20: Renaming the Table `Employee` as `emp`

```
rename employee to emp;
```

The output of Listing 5.20 is as follows:

```
Table renamed
```

Once the table is renamed, the table name `Employee` will not be valid.

Inserting Data Using Query (DML)

If the user wants to transfer data from one table to another, the `INSERT` statement is used, irrespective of whether the data is in processed or unprocessed form. While using the `INSERT` statement, the `SELECT` statement is used. The `SELECT` statement decides the rows that need to be transferred to another table.

Listing 5.21 shows the code to transfer employee names from the `Employee` table to the `Emp_shift` table:

Listing 5.21: Transferring Employee Names from the `Employee` Table to the `Emp_shift` Table

```
insert into emp_shift (ename) select ename from employee;
```

The output of Listing 5.21 is as follows:

```
5 rows created
```

Listing 5.22 shows the code to insert employee names along with shift `A`:

Listing 5.22: Inserting Employee Names Along with Shift `A`

```
insert into emp_shift (ename,shift) select ename,'A' from employee;
```

The output of Listing 5.22 is as follows:

```
5 rows created
```

The output of Listing 5.22 is employee's name along with shift `A`, which will be inserted in the `Emp_shift` table.

NOTE

It is important that the type of columns mentioned in the INSERT statement should be compatible with the type produced by the SELECT statement. Suppose in the INSERT statement, the type of first column produced by the SELECT statement is character and the target column is numeric. In that case, an error will be returned. That means the query should produce the data, which should be compatible with the specified columns of the table in which the data is to be inserted.

Listing 5.23 shows the code to insert a row in the `Emp_company` table with employee name as `ANIL`, and `salary` equal to the average salary of company, `ACC`:

Listing 5.23: Inserting a Row in the `Emp_company` Table with Employee Name as `ANIL`, and `salary` Equal to the Average Salary of Company, `ACC`

```
insert into emp_company (ename,salary) select 'ANIL',
avg(salary) from emp_company where cname = 'ACC';
```

The output of Listing 5.23 is as follows:

```
1 row created
```

Listing 5.24 shows the code to insert rows in `Employee` table with employee of the `ACC` company, having the same city as `ACC`:

Listing 5.24: Inserting Rows in `Employee` with Employee of Company `ACC`, having the Same City as `ACC`

```
insert into employee (ename,city)
select e1.ename, c2.city
from emp_company e1, company c2 where
e1.cname = 'ACC'
and e1.cname= c2.cname;
```

The output of Listing 5.24 is as follows:

```
6 rows created
```

Creating Table Using Query

Earlier, we have discussed creating a table by specifying the column and their datatypes. We can also create tables by specifying some additional information or using a query.

Listing 5.25 shows the code, where the user wants that the column `ename` of `Emp_company` should not have null values, while inserting or updating data, i.e. it should not accept `null` value in column `ename` (this can be done by specifying not `null` constraint while creating the table):

Listing 5.25: The user wants that the column `ename` of `Emp_company` should not have null values, while inserting or updating data, i.e. it should not accept `null` value in column `ename`. This can be done by specifying not `null` Constraint while Creating the Table

```
create table emp_company (ename char(10) not null,
cname char(10), salary number(7,2), jdate date);
```

The output of Listing 5.25 is as follows:

```
Table created
```

The `not null` constraint is required for the column without which the row will not have any meaning. Therefore, if the row in `Emp_company` is:

ename	cname	salary	Jdate
	ACC	100	12-MAY-95

then it will not have any meaning.

NOTE

The NOT NULL constraint can be the specification to any number of columns and will take NULL specification by default.

Listing 5.26 Creating table, `emp_company1` with three columns—`ename, cname,` and `salary` having the same datatypes as of the columns from `emp_company`:

Listing 5.26: Creating Table `emp_company1` with Three Columns—`ename, cname,` and `salary`—having the same datatypes as of the columns from `emp_company`

```
create table emp_company1 as
select ename EMP_NAME,cname,salary from emp_company where cname = 'ACC';
```

The output of Listing 5.26 is as follows:

```
Table created
```

After the table has been created, the result of Listing 5.26 is inserted into the table `emp_company1`.

The datatypes of created tables are always enlarged to accommodate any expression. The numeric type is enlarged to NUMBER.

create table ztemp8 as select ename | | 'Employee' empname, salary+100 salary100 from emp_company;

```
Table created
```

The structure of table ztemp8 is:

```
desc ztemp8
 Name                   Null?       Type
 ---------------------- --------   ----------------------------
 EMPNAME                           VARCHAR2(28)
 SALARY100                         NUMBER
```

Listing 5.27 shows the code to give a different column name and modifying specification (giving a different table name for the second query as it will give an error, the table with same name, already exists):

Listing 5.27: Giving a different column name to new table and modifying specification of columns of new table

```
create table emp_company2 (en not null,cn,sal) as
select ename,cname,salary from emp_company where cname = 'ACC';
```

The output of Listing 5.27 is as follows:

```
Table created
```

The table emp_company2 is created.

NOTE

The user can write any SQL SELECT statement in query. If all columns in query are well defined, then one can omit column specifications while creating a table.

Summary

You must now be familiar with modifying data in a table using UPDATE, delete, and insert statements. The next chapter will throw light on views.

Exercise

1. Increase the Salary of employees by 30%.
2. Decrease the salary of Sunil by 200.
3. Create a Table using Query.
4. Insert the data using the DML statements.
5. Delete the emp_company were salary is less than 4000.

6

Views

Usually data is stored in multiple tables to avoid redundancy or repetition in same table. Sometimes, writing a query on different relations or table become more complex than writing a query on a single table. Therefore, views are used to give a simplified representation of data. Views are used just like a table for the queries. The use of the views can be understood using the following example.

Suppose you want to display the names of employees living in the same city where their employer organization is located, you will write the following query.

```
select emp_company.ename
from emp_company, employee, company
where emp_company.ename = employee.ename
and emp_company.cname = company.cname
and employee.city = company.city;
```

In the preceding code snippet, you have to join the three tables with the appropriate where condition. Suppose instead of these three tables, you have a single table, shown in the following code snippet:

```
emp_cmp_emp with column as
emp_cmp_emp
ename    cname    sal    jdate    lcity    ccity
```

In the table shown in preceding code snippet, `lcity` is living city and `ccity` is company city. In this case, you can write the query as shown in the following code snippet:

```
select ename
from emp_cmp_emp
where lcity = ccity;
```

Therefore, for the user the second query is simpler than the first.

Creating Views

A view can be created by using the statement shown in the following code snippet:

```
create view emp_cmp_emp as
select emp_company.ename,
emp_company.cname,
emp_company.salary,
emp_company.jdate,
employee.city lcity,
company.city ccity
from emp_company, employee, company
where emp_company.ename = employee.ename
and emp_company.cname = company.cname;
```

The output of the preceding code snippet is given as follows:

```
View created
```

The columns in views are the same as that of the `SELECT` statement used. For the user, view is used as an ordinary table in the `SELECT` statement, so user can use view in the FROM clause, but view does not have its own storage. When data is retrieved from view, it is actually retrieved from the table that constitutes the view. Therefore, when you retrieve data from the view `emp_cmp_emp`, data is actually retrieved from tables, `Emp_company`, `Employees`, and `Company`.

NOTE

Views are generally used to retrieve data, not to manipulate them.

You can perform DML operation using views, as shown in Listing 6.1:

Listing 6.1: Creating View V1

```
create view V1 as
select ename,cname, salary

from emp_company
where cname = 'ACC';
```

The output of Listing 6.1 is given as follows:

```
View created
```

You can insert data using view as

Listing 6.2: Inserting data

```
insert into V1 values ('Ashok','',1200.00);
```

The output of Listing 6.2 is given as follows:

```
1 row created
```

The following row is inserted into the `Emp_company` table, since view is based on it:

ename	cname	salary	jdate
Ashok	–	1200.00	

For `cname` and `jdate` null values are inserted.

Listing 6.3 shows a row created by using View V1:

Listing 6.3: Displaying a Row by using View V1

```
select * from V1
where cname = 'ACC';
```

The output of Listing 6.3 is given as follows:

```
no rows selected
```

The row selected in Listing 6.3 would not appear in the result since the company name (cname) of row is not ACC as no value is inserted for cname as shown in the preceding table. If you want to avoid this inconsistency, you can create view with CHECK OPTION.

Listing 6.4: Creating a View V2 using CHECK OPTION

```
create view V2
as select ename, salary
from emp_company
where cname = 'ACC'
with CHECK OPTION;
```

The output of Listing 6.4 is given as follows:

```
View created
```

If views are created with CHECK OPTION, insertion and deletion will not be permitted on the rows, as they would not be selected by using the view query. Therefore, the insertion in V1 is not permitted, because cname in the row is having company ACC.

You can name the constraint to specify condition of the CHECK OPTION, as shown in the following code snippet:

```
create view V2
as select ename, salary
from emp_company
where cname = 'ACC'
with check option constraint ck_v1;
```

NOTE

If a query contains GROUP BY, Group function, DISTINCT clauses or ROWNUM, DML operations using views are not permitted. If a column is added in the table, the view may not work properly. This problem can be eliminated by dropping and recreating the view.

You can create a view to retrieve company name and its average, maximum, and minimum salary, as shown in Listing 6.5:

Listing 6.5: Creating a view for retrieving company name, its average salary, its maximum salary, and minimum salary

```
create view V3 as
select emp_company.cname,
max(salary)Maximum, min(salary)Minimum,
avg (salary)Average from emp_company group by emp_company.cname;
```

The output of Listing 6.5 is given as follows:

```
View created
```

Creating view v4 for providing employee name, salary, and living city

Listing 6.6: Creating a view that gives information about employee name, salary, and living city

```
create view v4 as
select emp_company.ename, emp_company.salary, employee.city
from emp_company, employee where emp_company.ename= employee.ename;
```

The output of Listing 6.6 is given as follows:

```
View created
```

If you create a view with one base table and some columns with column expression, then you cannot update that column using view. However, such columns can be used in the `WHERE` condition. Suppose you create a view as shown in the following code snippet:

```
create view emp_sal as Select ename,salary+100 sal100
from emp_company;
```

The output of the preceding code snippet is given as follows:

```
View created
```

You can update column `ename` using view. In addition, you can check which columns can be updated by using view `USER_UPDATABLE_COLUMNS`. Suppose you want to check updatable columns in view EMP_SAL.

```
select * from user_updatable_columns where table_name='emp_sal';
```

The output of the preceding code snippet is given as follows:

```
OWNER          TABLE_NAME                 COLUMN_NAME                 UPD   INS   DEL
------------------------------ ------------------------------ ------------------
SCOTT          EMP_SAL                    ENAME                       YES   YES   YES
SCOTT          EMP_SAL                    SAL100                      NO    NO    NO
```

The column `sal100` can be used in the `WHERE` condition.

If you write following statement

```
delete emp_sal where sal100=1000;
```

then it will delete all the rows with salary `900`, i.e. if salary is `900` then `sal100` is `1000(900+100)`.

Using FORCE VIEW clause

You can create view even if base tables are not in existence by using CREATE FORCE VIEW option as:

```
create force view v1 as select ename, salary from emp_company;
```

using READ ONLY option using views

You can create view using READ ONLY option. When view is created using READ ONLY option then any DML operation on the view results in error.

Listing 6.7: Creating a view with emp_sal_read using READ ONLY

```
create view emp_sal_read_only as
select * from emp_company
with read only constraint emp_company_read_only;
/
```

The output of Listing 6.7 is given as follows:

Though view is created, you cannot do DMP operation using view.

```
insert into emp_sal_read_only values('ashok','acc',4500,'12-dec-2009');
insert into emp_sal_read_only values('ashok','acc',4500,'12-dec-2009');
*
ERROR at line 1:
ORA-42399: cannot perform a DML operation on read-only view
```

Getting Information about views.

You can get the view query using USER_VIEWS.

Listing 6.8: Listing View Query from USER_VIEWS

```
select text from  user_views where view_name='emp_sal';
```

The output of Listing 6.8 is given as follows:

```
TEXT
------------------------------------------------
select ename, salary+100 sal100
from emp_company
```

Dropping Views

You can drop view using the DROP VIEW command, as shown in Listing 6.9:

Listing 6.9: Dropping view

```
drop view emp_sal;
```

Changing view query

You can change view query using command CREATE OR REPLACE

```
create or replace view emp_sal_read_only as
select * from emp_company where salary>3000
with read only constraint emp_company_read_only
/
```

NOTE

The concept of key preserving joins is given in Chapter 10, Integrity Constraints.

Now, let's explore the concept of synonyms in detail.

Synonyms

Synonyms are used for giving another name to a table so that the user can refer the table very conveniently. Suppose table is having very long name like Emp_company, using synonym it can be referred as ec.

Listing 6.10: Referring Table Emp_company

```
create synonym ec
for emp_company;
```

The output of Listing 6.10 is given as follows:

```
Synonym created
```

Now you can refer table `Emp_company` with `ec`

You can retrieve data from table ec as shown in Listing 6.11:

Listing 6.11: Retrieving Data from Table Emp_company

```
select * from ec;
```

The output of Listing 6.11 is given as follows:

```
ENAME       CNAME          SALARY    JDATE
---------- -------      ------ ---------
ANIL         ACC          1500.00   1-MAY-89
SHANKAR     TATA          2000.00    10-JUN-90
JAYA        CMC           1800.00    07-JUN-91
SUNIL       CMC           1700.00    01-JAN-98
VIJAY       TATA          5000.00    03-JAN-88
PRAKASH     TATA          3000.00    27-MAY-89
AJAY         ACC          8000.00    30-APR-95
AMOL         ACC          1000.00    17-MAR-95
ASHOK                      1200.00

7 rows selected
```

You can drop synonyms given to tables if required, as shown in Listing 6.12:

Listing 6.12: Dropping synonyms

```
drop synonym ec;
```

The output of Listing 6.12 is given as follows:

```
Synonym dropped
```

Now you can no longer refer the name `ec` for the `Emp_company` table. A user can create a public synonym as shown in the following code snippet:

```
create public synonym ec for emp_company;
```

A public synonym is available for all users. If same synonym is public and private, then private synonym is having more precedence.

Miscellaneous Facilities of **Sqlplus**

You can create simple reports using sqlplus. You can set titles, footers using reporting facility of sqlplus.

*Creating Reports with **Sqlplus***

You can create or format output data in a simple way by using sqlplus. This facility includes title, header, footer, data grouping, and computation of grouped data.

Giving Title Output

You can give a title to output by using the `TTITLE` command. The syntax of the command is as follows:

```
ttitle text
```

The title can be provided to output by using the TTITLE command, as shown in Listing 6.13:

Listing 6.13: Giving Title to Output using the TTITLE Command

```
ttitle 'This is my title'
select * from employee;
```

The output of Listing 6.13 is given as follows:

```
 Thu 19 May                                          Page          1
                                 This is my title

ENAME      CITY
---------- ----------
ANIL       NAGPUR
SHANKAR    MUMBAI
JAYA       CHENNAI
SUNIL      MUMBAI
VIJAY      DELHI
PRAKASH    KOLKATA
AJAY       CHENNAI

7 rows selected
```

You also can add print specification to title by using either of the following syntax:

```
ttitle <prsp>
```

Or

```
tti[tle] [printspec [text|variable] ...]|[off|on]
```

In the preceding syntax `<prsp>` defines the print specifications, which are as follows:

- `COL n`—Skips column `n` of current line
- `SKIP n`—Skips `n` lines, if `n` is specified. Otherwise one line is skipped
- `TAB n`—Skips `n` columns forward
- `LEFT, CENTER` **or** `RIGHT`—Aligns data to left, center, and right on the current line
- `FORMAT` **Character expression**—Specifies the display format of the column. The format specification must be a text constant, such as `A10` or `$9,999`, and not a variable.

Listing 6.14: Displaying TTITLE as employee for the following query

```
ttitle employees
select * from employee;
```

The output of Listing 6.14 is given as follows:

```
Mon Aug 14                                                  page     1
                                 emplyees

ENAME      CITY
---------- ----------
ANIL       NAGPUR
SHANKAR    MUMBAI
JAYA       CHENNAI
SUNIL      MUMBAI
VIJAY      DELHI
PRAKASH    KOLKATA
AJAY       CHENNAI

7 rows selected
```

You can also indent TTITLE, as shown in Listing 6.15:

Listing 6.15: Indenting TTITLE

```
ttitle col 4 "Employee 1" col 60 "Employee 2"
select * from employee;
```

The output of Listing 6.15 is given as follows:

```
Employee 1                                                       Employee 2
ENAME      CITY
---------- ----------
ANIL       NAGPUR
SHANKAR    MUMBAI
JAYA       CHENNAI
SUNIL      MUMBAI
VIJAY      DELHI
PRAKASH    KOLKATA
AJAY       CHENNAI

7 rows selected
```

In addition, you can show title with date, as given in Listing 6.16:

Listing 6.16: Displaying TITLE with Date

```
ttitle left "General Report" right "28 DEC 95"skip center "EMPLOYEE LIST"
select * from employee;
```

The output of Listing 6.16 is given as follows:

```
General Report                                                          28 DEC 95
                                   EMPLOYEE LIST
ENAME      CITY
---------- ----------
ANIL       NAGPUR
SHANKAR    MUMBAI
JAYA       CHENNAI
SUNIL      MUMBAI
VIJAY      DELHI
PRAKASH    KOLKATA
AJAY       CHENNAI

7 rows selected
```

You can switch off TTITLE by using the code snippet shown in Listing 6.17:

Listing 6.17: Switching Off TTITLE

```
ttitle off;
select * from employee;
```

The output of Listing 6.17 is given as follows:

```
ENAME      CITY
---------- ----------
ANIL       NAGPUR
SHANKAR    MUMBAI
JAYA       CHENNAI
SUNIL      MUMBAI
VIJAY      DELHI
PRAKASH    KOLKATA
AJAY       CHENNAI

7 rows selected
```

This will not display title in any output; therefore, the next time a `SELECT` statement is given, the title would not be displayed.

Showing Timing in Output

You can create your own timing area and can see its current as well as accumulated time. The command can be given in one of the following ways:

```
timing start my_area;
```

or

```
timi start my_area:
```

NOTE

The syntax for showing timing is TIMI[NG] [START text|SHOW|STOP]. Therefore, we can give TIMI instead of TIMING, as both works in the same manner.

The preceding command will create a timing area defined by the name `my_area, which` becomes the current timing area. Therefore, whenever SQL executes a command, it adds the execution time of that command to the time stored in the current timing area.

NOTE

You can give a name of your own choice to the timing area. In addition, several timing areas can coexist.

You can show the timing area as

Listing 6.18: Issuing the Command

```
timing show:
```

The output of Listing 6.18 is given as follows:

```
timing for: my_area
Elapsed: 00:00:22.20
```

The execution of command given in 6.18 displays the current timing area's title and accumulated time.

You can remove the timing area by using the code shown in Listing 6.19:

Listing 6.19: Removing the Timing Area

```
TIMING STOP:
```

The output of Listing 6.19 is given as follows:

```
timing for: my_area
Elapsed: 00:00:47.64
```

This command displays the current timing area's title and accumulated time and then removes the timing area.

Outputting Data to File or Printer

The `SPOOL` command is used for outputting data to the printer or file. The user can copy or spool the displayed output with the help of `spool` either in the system printer or file.

Listing 6.20: Spooling output of SQL statement to a File

```
spool myfile:
```

The `SPOOL` command does two tasks at the same time—it makes spooling `ON` and directs the forthcoming matter to the `myfile` file with the extension `lst` by default. If the user has typed the spool command, then the output of the command will go into the `myfile` file, as shown in Listing 6.21:

Listing 6.21: Outputting to myfile

```
select * from employee;
```

The output of Listing 6.21 is given as follows:

```
ENAME      CITY
--------   --------
ANIL       NAGPUR
SHANKAR    MUMBAI
```

```
JAYA        CHENNAI
SUNIL       MUMBAI
VIJAY       DELHI
PRAKASH     KOLKATA
AJAY        CHENNAI

7 rows selected
```

NOTE

The output is displayed on screen, and the command is saved in the spool file. If the user has not mentioned any file name, then the spool adds a default file type depending upon the operating system in use.

You can stop the spooling by using the code provided in Listing 6.22:

Listing 6.22: Stopping the spooling using Command

```
spool off
```

This command makes SQL stop spooling.

You can also stop the spooling and print to file by using the code/command shown in Listing 6.23:

Listing 6.23: Stop spooling and Printing to File

```
spool out
```

The command will make SQL to stop spooling as well as printing to the file.

NOTE

You can use SET TERMOUT OFF to spool output without displaying it on the screen.

The user can write the output in file or printer by giving the `NEWPAGE` command. The syntax of `NEWPAGE` is as follows:

```
NEWP[AGE] {1|n|NONE}
```

The command given in preceding syntax sets the number of blank lines to be printed from the top of each page to the top of the table title. This is shown in Listing 6.24:

Listing 6.24: Setting the number of blank lines to be printed from the top of each page to the top of the table title

```
newpage 4:
select * from employee;
```

The output of Listing 6.24 is given as follows:

```
ENAME       CITY
----------  ----------
ANIL        NAGPUR
SHANKAR     MUMBAI
JAYA        CHENNAI
SUNIL       MUMBAI
VIJAY       DELHI
PRAKASH     KOLKATA
AJAY        CHENNAI

7 rows selected
```

The NEWPAGE command can be used in conjunction with the `SPOOL` command. It facilitates the user if he wants to advance the spooled output `n` lines beyond the beginning of the next page. The NEWPAGE command is used to advance `four` lines past the beginning of next page in the spooled file.

Computing Data at the Time of Output

One can perform computation on a group of selected rows by using some commands. Let's consider table `Emp_company` with fields `ename`, `cname`, `salary`, **and** `jdate`. The following code snippet computes the sum of salary on cname:

```
break on cname;
compute sum of salary on cname;
select * from emp_company order by cname;
```

The explanation of commands present in the preceding code snippet is as follows:

- In the very first command, the BREAK `ON` option specifies that the table element `cname` is used as a break. This implies that computation would be done on `cname` and as the computation gets over, SQL prints the `sum` of salary at each break.
- The second command computes the `sum` of salary by considering `cname` as the break.
- The third command displays the output.

The output of the preceding code snippet is given as follows:

```
ENAME      CNAME          SALARY JDATE
---------- ---------- ---------- ---------
ANIL       ACC              2160 01-MAY-89
VIJAY                       2484 03-JAN-88
AMOL                        1440 17-MAR-95
           ********** ----------
           sum              6084

JAYA       CMC              2484 07-JUN-91
           ********** ----------
           sum              2484

PRAKASH    TATA             3600 27-MAY-89
           ********** ----------
           sum              3600

ENAME      CNAME          SALARY JDATE
---------- ---------- ---------- ---------
ANIL                        2028
ASHOK                       1200
           ********** ----------
           sum              3228

7 rows selected
```

NOTE

You can use other clauses with compute commands, such as AVG, COUNT, MAXIMUM, MINIMUM, NUMBER, and VARIABLE.

Next section defines specification for printing columns in detail.

Defining Specification for Printing Columns

This command specifies how a column and column heading should be formatted in the report. Any number of `COLUMN` commands may be entered for different columns as well as for the same column. If several `COLUMN` commands apply to the same clause and column, the last one entered will control the printing. The syntax of the command is provided as follows:

```
COL[UMN] [{column | expr} [option...] ]
```

In the command given in preceding syntax, `on/off` is one of the possible options, as it controls the status of display attributes for a column. `OFF` disables the attributes for a column without affecting the attributes' definition, whereas `ON` reinstates the attributes. You can use on/off option by using either of the commands shown in Listing 6.25:

Listing 6.25: Turning the output format specification for a column ON or OFF

```
COLUMN cname ON/OFF
```

or

```
COL cname ON/OFF
```

This command turns the output format specification for a column `ON` or `OFF` without affecting its content. The current column definitions are shown by using the COLUMN command given in Listing 6.26:

Listing 6.26: Displaying the Current Column Definitions

```
COLUMN
```

The output of Listing 6.26 is given as follows:

```
"column cname ON"
```

A `COLUMN` with no argument displays the current column definition.

Removing column definition

Listing 6.27: Removing the Column Definition Completely

```
column cname clear
```

The above command resets the display attributes for the column to default values.

NOTE

You can also use the CLEAR COLUMNS command to reset the attributes for all columns. This command clears the ATTRIBUTEs for that column.

You can reset the column definition by using the command shown in Listing 6.27:

Listing 6.28: Resetting the column definition to its default conditions, leaving the column defined and ON

```
COLUMN cname DEFAULT
```

You can define a column heading by using the command shown in Listing 6.29:

Listing 6.29: Defining a Column Heading

```
COLUMN cname HEADING "Company"
select * from company;
```

The output of Listing 6.29 is given as follows:

```
Company    CITY
---------- ----------
CMC        MUMBAI
CMC        CHENNAI
TATA       MUMBAI
ACC        NAGPUR
ACC        CHENNAI
TATA       DELHI

6 rows selected
```

You can align the heading of a column as per the given option. The syntax to set the alignment of a column to justify is as follows:

```
COLUMN <column name> JUSTIFY (LEFT/RIGHT/CENTER)
```

The following command is used to justify the alignment of a column:

```
column cname justify (CENTER)
select * from company;
```

The output of the preceding syntax and command is given as follows:

```
Company                    CITY
----------             ----------
ACC                    CHENNAI
TATA                   MUMBAI
ACC                    NAGPUR
CMC                    MUMBAI
                       CHENNAI
TATA                   DELHI

6 rows selected
```

The number column is aligned to the RIGHT and other columns are aligned to the left by default.

Formatting Data

Formatting is used provide different display for data of different datatypes.

Formats

The Char, Numeric, and Date formats are used in BITITLE, TTITLE, and COLUMN commands, respectively. The FORMAT clause is used to control the appearance of displayed data. Date format models are used in the TO_DATE function.

Let's learn about all the formats in detail.

Char Format

A char format consists of letter A followed by the width of the column in characters. If a value does not fit within the width, it will be wrapped or truncated depending on whether SET WRAP or SET TRUNC is ON. The char format is shown in the following code snippet:

```
col cname format A5 heading "company"
select * from company;
```

The output of the preceding code snippet is given as follows:

```
COMPA CITY
----- ----------
ACC   CHENNAI
TATA  MUMBAI
ACC   NAGPUR
CMC   MUMBAI
      CHENNAI
TATA  DELHI

6 rows selected.
```

If the above command is executed and a query is written which will display the data of column cname, then the data in column is printed in width 5.

Numeric Format

A numeric format decides how the numeric data will be printed in the output. There are a number of numeric formats, as shown in Table 6.1:

Table 6.1: Describing the Numeric Data Formats

Format	Description
99999	Determines the width of the data. In the example given the Char Format, the width of data is 5.
099	Displays the leading zeroes in the specified width.
$9999	Displays dollar sign as prefix.
B9999	Displays blank instead of zero.
999MI	Displays – for negative values.
9,999,999	Displays, in the value. Therefore, the value 12345 is printed as 12,345.
99.99	Prints the decimal point in the specified position.
9.999EEEE	Displays the data in scientific position.

The numeric formats can be used in the `COLUMN` statement, as shown in Listing 6.30:

Listing 6.30: Displaying the salary Column in a Format

```
column salary format $9,999,999;
```

The output of Listing 6.30 is given as follows:

```
      SALARY
-----------
      $2,160
      $2,484
      $2,484
      $3,600
      $1,440
      $2,028
      $1,200

7 rows selected
```

Date Format

A date format decides how the dates will be printed on output. The date formats are constructed using the format elements. Suppose the syntax of date format is as follows:

```
'DDth of Month YY'
```

If the date is Aug 17, 2006, then it will be printed as:

```
17th of August 06
```

The description of the elements of the date formats is given in Table 6.2:

Table 6.2: Explaining the Date Formats

Date Format	Description
YYYY,YYY,YY	For printing year
BC or AD	For indicating BC or AD
MM,Month,Mon	For printing month
DDD,DD	For printing day of year or month or week
Dy	For printing name of day

The date formats are specified by using the elements given in Table 6. For example, specify the date format as dd-mon-yy and it will print the date August 17, 2006 as shown in the following syntax:

```
17-August-06
```

The date formats are used in the To_Date function.

Footer of the Report

You can add footer to the output by using the BTITLE command. You can display a title at the bottom of each page of a report by using the BTITLE command, which is shown as follows:

```
BTITLE ON/OFF
```

You can turn the bottom title ON and OFF depending on the command. Listing 6.31 shows an example of selecting a bottom title for the output:

Listing 6.31: Setting Employee as the Bottom Title

```
btitle "EMPLOYEE"
select * from employee;
```

The output of Listing 6.31 is given as follows:

```
ENAME      CITY
---------- ----------
ANIL       NAGPUR
SHANKAR    MUMBAI
JAYA       CHENNAI
SUNIL      MUMBAI
VIJAY      DELHI
PRAKASH    KOLKATA
AJAY       CHENNAI
                                        EMPLOYEE
7 rows selected
```

This above command can be used only after we have used the command BTITLE ON. It will set Employee as the bottom title.

Listing 6.32: Indenting BTITLE

```
BTITLE LEFT "END" RIGHT "GOOD"
select * from employee;
```

The output of Listing 6.32 is given as follows:

```
ENAME      CITY
---------- ----------
ANIL       NAGPUR
SHANKAR    MUMBAI
JAYA       CHENNAI
SUNIL      MUMBAI
VIJAY      DELHI
PRAKASH    KOLKATA
AJAY       CHENNAI

END                                                   GOOD

7 rows selected
```

Performing Action During Printing

The following command causes SQL to display records by `cname`:

```
select * from emp_company order by cname;
```

You can use the `BREAK` command to cause a break and indicate the action to be performed at a `break` next to that as well.

NOTE

Only the BREAK command will be used at a time. When you will issue a new BREAK command, it replaces the preceding one completely.

You can specify a break on cname, as shown in Listing 6.33:

Listing 6.33: Specifying BREAK

```
break on cname;
select * from emp_company order by cname;
```

The output of Listing 6.33 is given as follows:

```
ENAME      COMPA      SALARY JDATE
---------- ----- ----------- ---------
ANIL       ACC        $2,160 01-MAY-89
VIJAY                 $2,484 03-JAN-88
AMOL                  $1,440 17-MAR-95
           ***** -----------
           sum        $6,084

JAYA       CMC        $2,484 07-JUN-91
           ***** -----------
           sum        $2,484

PRAKASH    TATA       $3,600 27-MAY-89
           ***** -----------
END                                                   GOOD

ENAME      COMPA      SALARY JDATE
---------- ----- ----------- ---------
           sum        $3,600

ANIL                  $2,028
ASHOK                 $1,200
```

```
            ***** -----------
            sum         $3,228
END                                                         GOOD

7 rows selected
```

In Listing 6.33, the first command groups all rows having the same `cname` and will cause a `BREAK` when `cname` changes. This effect has been shown in the result of the second command.

Effect of BREAK clause

Listing 6.34: Performing condition on BREAK

```
break on cname skip 3;
select * from emp_company;
```

The output of Listing 6.34 is given as follows:

```
ENAME      COMPA      SALARY JDATE
---------- ----- ----------- ---------
ANIL       ACC        $2,160 01-MAY-89
           ***** -----------
           sum        $2,160

JAYA       CMC        $2,484 07-JUN-91
           ***** -----------
           sum        $2,484
END                                                         GOOD

ENAME      COMPA      SALARY JDATE
---------- ----- ----------- ---------
VIJAY      ACC        $2,484 03-JAN-88
           ***** -----------
           sum        $2,484

PRAKASH    TATA       $3,600 27-MAY-89
           ***** -----------
END                                                         GOOD

ENAME      COMPA      SALARY JDATE
---------- ----- ----------- ---------
           sum        $3,600

AMOL       ACC        $1,440 17-MAR-95
           ***** -----------
           sum        $1,440
END                                                         GOOD

ENAME      COMPA      SALARY JDATE
---------- ----- ----------- ---------
ANIL                  $2,028
ASHOK                 $1,200
           ***** -----------
           sum        $3,228
END                                                         GOOD

7 rows selected
```

Summary

After getting familiar with the concepts of views and reports, it is time to exercise the mind with assignments.

Exercise

1. Create view to compute average salary of each company.
2. Create view to find all information (name, company name, salary, shift) of an employee.
3. Design report to show employee name and their company.

7

Assignment-I

Assignment No. 1

Listing 7.1: Create Tables According to the Following Definition

```
CREATE TABLE DEPOSIT (ACTNO VARCHAR2(5), CNAME VARCHAR2 (18),                    BNAME
VARCHAR2(18), AMOUNT NUMBER(8,2), ADATE DATE);
CREATE TABLE BRANCH(BNAME VARCHAR2(18), CITY VARCHAR2(18));
CREATE TABLE CUSTOMER(CNAME VARCHAR2(19), CITY VARCHAR2 (18));
CREATE TABLE BORROW (LOANNO VARCHAR2(5), CNAME VARCHAR2(18), BNAME VARCHAR2(18),
  AMOUNT NUMBER(8,2));
```

Listing 7.2: Describe Tables, which are Already Created

```
DESC DEPOSIT;
DESC BRANCH;
DESC CUSTOMER;
DESC BORROW;
```

Listing 7.3: Insert the Following Data as Shown

```
INSERT INTO DEPOSIT VALUES ('100','ANIL','VRCE',1000.00,'1-MAR-95');
INSERT INTO DEPOSIT VALUES ('101','SUNIL','AJNI',5000.00, '4-JAN-96');
INSERT INTO DEPOSIT VALUES ('102','MEHUL','KAROLBAGH',3500.00,'17-NOV-95');
INSERT INTO DEPOSIT VALUES ('104','MADHURI','CHANDNI',1200.00,'17-DEC-95');
INSERT INTO DEPOSIT VALUES ('105','PRAMOD','M.G.ROAD',3000.00,'27-MAR-96');
INSERT INTO DEPOSIT VALUES ('106','SANDIP','ANDHERI',2000.00,'31-MAR-96');
INSERT INTO DEPOSIT VALUES ('107','SHIVANI','VIRAR',1000.00,'5-SEP-95');
INSERT INTO DEPOSIT VALUES ('108','KRANTI','NEHRU PLACE',5000.00,'2-JUL-95');
INSERT INTO DEPOSIT VALUES('109','NAREN','POWAI',7000.00,'10-AUG-95');
INSERT INTO BRANCH VALUES ('VRCE','NAGPUR');
INSERT INTO BRANCH VALUES ('AJNI','NAGPUR');
INSERT INTO BRANCH VALUES ('KAROLBAGH','DELHI');
INSERT INTO BRANCH VALUES ('CHANDNI','DELHI');
INSERT INTO BRANCH VALUES ('DHARAMPETH','NAGPUR');
INSERT INTO BRANCH VALUES ('M.G.ROAD','BANGLORE');
INSERT INTO BRANCH VALUES ('ANDHERI','MUMBAI');
INSERT INTO BRANCH VALUES ('VIRAR','MUMBAI');
INSERT INTO BRANCH VALUES ('NEHRU PLACE','DELHI');
INSERT INTO BRANCH VALUES ('POWAI','MUMBAI');
INSERT INTO CUSTOMER VALUES ('ANIL','KOLKATA');
INSERT INTO CUSTOMER VALUES ('SUNIL','DELHI');
INSERT INTO CUSTOMER VALUES ('MEHUL','BARODA');
INSERT INTO CUSTOMER VALUES ('MANDAR','PATNA');
INSERT INTO CUSTOMER VALUES ('MADHURI','NAGPUR');
INSERT INTO CUSTOMER VALUES ('PRAMOD','NAGPUR');
INSERT INTO CUSTOMER VALUES ('SANDIP','SURAT');
INSERT INTO CUSTOMER VALUES ('SHIVANI','MUMBAI');
INSERT INTO CUSTOMER VALUES ('KRANTI','MUMBAI');
INSERT INTO CUSTOMER VALUES ('NAREN','MUMBAI');
INSERT INTO BORROW VALUES ('201','ANIL','VRCE',1000.00);
INSERT INTO BORROW VALUES ('206','MEHUL','AJNI',5000.00);
INSERT INTO BORROW VALUES ('311','SUNIL','DHARAMPETH',3000.00);
INSERT INTO BORROW VALUES ('321','MADHURI','ANDHERI',2000.00);
INSERT INTO BORROW VALUES ('375','PRAMOD','VIRAR',8000.00);
INSERT INTO BORROW VALUES ('481','KRANTI','NEHRU PLACE',3000.00);
```

Assignment No. 2

Selecting Data from Single Table

Listing 7.4: List All Data from the DEPOSIT Table

```
SELECT * FROM DEPOSIT;
```

Listing 7.5: List All Data from the BORROW Table

```
SELECT * FROM BORROW;
```

Listing 7.6: List All Data from the CUSTOMER Table

```
SELECT * FROM CUSTOMER;
```

Listing 7.7: List All Data from the BRANCH Table

```
SELECT * FROM BRANCH;
```

Listing 7.8: List Account Number and Amount of Depositors

```
SELECT ACTNO,AMOUNT FROM DEPOSIT;
```

Listing 7.9: List cname and Account Number of Depositors

```
SELECT CNAME,ACTNO FROM DEPOSIT;
```

Listing 7.10: List Names of Customers

```
SELECT CNAME FROM CUSTOMER;
```

Listing 7.11: List Names of Branches

```
SELECT BNAME FROM BRANCH;
```

Listing 7.12: List Names of Borrowers

```
SELECT CNAME FROM BORROW;
```

Listing 7.13: List Names of Customers Living in the NAGPUR City

```
SELECT CNAME FROM CUSTOMER WHERE CITY = 'NAGPUR';
```

Listing 7.14: List Names of Depositors Having AMOUNT Greater Than 4000

```
SELECT CNAME FROM DEPOSIT WHERE AMOUNT > 4000.00;
```

Listing 7.15: List Account Date of Customer ANIL

```
SELECT ADATE FROM DEPOSIT WHERE CNAME = 'ANIL';
```

Listing 7.16: List Names of All Branches Located in the MUMBAI City

```
SELECT BNAME FROM BRANCH WHERE CITY = 'MUMBAI';
```

Listing 7.17: List Name of Borrower Having Loan No. 206

```
SELECT CNAME FROM BORROW WHERE LOANNO = '206';
```

Listing 7.18: List Names of Depositors Having Account at VRCE

```
SELECT CNAME FROM DEPOSIT WHERE BNAME = 'VRCE';
```

Listing 7.19: List Names of All Branches Located in the DELHI City

```
SELECT BNAME FROM BRANCH WHERE CITY = 'DELHI';
```

Listing 7.20: List Names of Customers who Opened Account after Date '1-12-95'

```
SELECT CNAME FROM DEPOSIT WHERE ADATE > '1-DEC-95';
```

Listing 7.21: List Account Number and Deposit Amount of Customer Having Account Opened between Dates 1-12-95 and 1-6-95

```
SELECT ACTNO, AMOUNT FROM DEPOSIT WHERE ADATE >= '1-JUN-95' AND ADATE <= '1-DEC-
   95';
```

Listing 7.22: List Name of the City where the KAROLBAGH Branch is Located

```
SELECT CITY FROM BRANCH WHERE BNAME = 'KAROLBAGH';
```

Listing 7.23: List Details of Customer ANIL

```
SELECT D1.ACTNO, D1.BNAME, D1.AMOUNT, D1.ADATE, C1. CITY, B1.CITY FROM DEPOSIT
   D1, CUSTOMER C1, BRANCH B1 WHERE D1.CNAME = C1.CNAME AND D1.BNAME = B1.BNAME AND
   D1.CNAME = 'ANIL';
```

Assignment No. 3

Join or Cartesian Product

Listing 7.24: List Name of Customer Having Living City MUMBAI and Branch City DELHI

```
SELECT C1.CNAME FROM DEPOSIT D1,CUSTOMER C1,BRANCH B1 WHERE C1.CITY = 'MUMBAI'
   AND B1.CITY = 'DELHI' AND D1.CNAME = C1.CNAME AND D1.BNAME = B1.BNAME;
```

Listing 7.25: List Names of Customers Having Same Living City as their Branch City

```
SELECT C1.CNAME FROM DEPOSIT D1,CUSTOMER C1,BRANCH B1 WHERE C1.CITY = B1.CITY
   AND D1.CNAME = C1.CNAME AND D1.BNAME = B1.BNAME;
```

Listing 7.26: List Names of Customers who are Borrowers as well as Depositors and Having Living City NAGPUR

```
SELECT C1.CNAME FROM CUSTOMER C1, DEPOSIT D1,BORROW BR1 WHERE C1.CITY = 'NAGPUR'
   AND C1.CNAME = D1.CNAME AND D1.CNAME = BR1.CNAME;
```

Listing 7.27: List Names of Customers who are Depositors and Have Same Branch City as that of Sunil

```
SELECT D1.CNAME FROM DEPOSIT D1,BRANCH B2 WHERE D1.BNAME=B2.BNAME AND B2.CITY IN
   (SELECT B1.CITY FROM DEPOSIT D2,BRANCH B1 WHERE D2.CNAME = 'SUNIL' AND D2.BNAME
   = B1.BNAME);
```

Listing 7.28: List Names of Depositors Having Same Living City as that of SHIVANI and Having Deposit Amount Greater than 2000

```
SELECT D1.CNAME FROM DEPOSIT D1, CUSTOMER C1 WHERE D1.AMOUNT > 2000 AND D1.CNAME =
   C1.CNAME AND C1.CITY IN (SELECT C2.CITY FROM CUSTOMER C2 WHERE C2.CNAME =
   'SHIVANI');
```

Listing 7.29: List Names of Borrowers Having Deposit Amount Greater than 1000 and Loan Amount Greater than 2000

```
SELECT BR1.CNAME FROM BORROW BR1,DEPOSIT D1 WHERE D1.CNAME = BR1.CNAME AND
   D1.AMOUNT > 1000 AND BR1.AMOUNT > 2000;
```

Listing 7.30: List Names of Depositors Having the Same Branch as the Branch of SUNIL

```
SELECT D1.CNAME FROM DEPOSIT D1 WHERE D1.BNAME IN (SELECT D2.BNAME FROM DEPOSIT
   D2 WHERE D2.CNAME = 'SUNIL');
```

Listing 7.31: List Names of Borrowers Having Loan Amount Greater than the Loan Amount of Anil

```
SELECT BR1.CNAME FROM BORROW BR1 WHERE BR1.AMOUNT > ALL (SELECT BR2.AMOUNT FROM
   BORROW BR2 WHERE BR2.CNAME = 'ANIL');
```

Listing 7.32: List Names of Customers Living in the City where Branch of Depositor Sunil is Located

```
SELECT C1.CNAME FROM CUSTOMER C1 WHERE C1.CITY IN (SELECT B1.CITY FROM BRANCH
   B1, DEPOSIT D1 WHERE D1.CNAME = 'SUNIL' AND D1.BNAME = B1.BNAME);
```

Listing 7.33: List LOANNO and LOAN AMOUNT of Borrowers Having the Same Branch as that of Depositor Sunil

```
SELECT LOANNO,AMOUNT FROM BORROW WHERE BNAME IN(SELECT D1.BNAME FROM DEPOSIT D1
   WHERE D1.CNAME = 'SUNIL');
```

Listing 7.34: List LOANNO, LOAN AMOUNT, ACCOUNT NO and DEPOSIT AMOUNT of Customers Living in NAGPUR

```
SELECT BR1.LOANNO, BR1.AMOUNT, D1.ACTNO, D1. AMOUNT FROM DEPOSIT D1,BORROW
   BR1,CUSTOMER C1 WHERE C1.CNAME = D1.CNAME AND D1.CNAME = BR1.CNAME AND C1.CITY
   ='NAGPUR';
```

Listing 7.35: List LOANNO, LOAN AMOUNT, ACCOUNT NO and DEPOSIT AMOUNT of Customers Having Deposit Branch Located in DELHI

```
SELECT BR1.LOANNO, BR1.AMOUNT, D1.ACTNO, D1.AMOUNT FROM DEPOSIT D1,BORROW
   BR1,BRANCH B1 WHERE D1.CNAME = BR1.CNAME AND B1.CITY = 'DELHI' AND D1.BNAME =
   B1.BNAME;
```

Listing 7.36: List LOANNO, LOAN AMOUNT, ACCOUNT NO, DEPOSIT AMOUNT, BRANCH NAME, BRANCH CITY and LIVING CITY of PRAMOD

```
SELECT BR1.LOANNO, BR1.AMOUNT, D1.ACTNO, D1. AMOUNT, D1.BNAME, 1.CITY, C1.CITY
   FROM BORROW BR1, DEPOSIT D1, BRANCH B1, CUSTOMER C1 WHERE C1.CNAME = 'PRAMOD'
   AND D1.CNAME = C1.CNAME AND D1.CNAME = BR1. CNAME AND D1.BNAME = B1.BNAME;
```

Listing 7.37: List Deposit Details and Loan Details of Customer in the City where PRAMOD is Living

```
SELECT D1.ACTNO, D1.BNAME, D1.AMOUNT, D1. ADATE, BR1.LOANNO, BR1.BNAME,
   BR1.AMOUNT FROM DEPOSIT D1, BORROW BR1, CUSTOMER C1 WHERE C1.CNAME = D1.CNAME
   AND D1.CNAME = BR1.CNAME AND C1.CITY IN (SELECT C2.CITY FROM CUSTOMER C2 WHERE
   C2.CNAME = 'PRAMOD');
```

Listing 7.38: List Names of Depositors Having the Same Branch City as that of SUNIL and Having the Same Living City as that of ANIL

```
SELECT D1.CNAME  FROM DEPOSIT D1,  CUSTOMER C1,  BRANCH B1
WHERE D1.CNAME = C1.CNAME  AND D1.BNAME = B1.BNAME AND B1.CITY
IN (SELECT B2.CITY FROM BRANCH B2,  DEPOSIT D2  WHERE D2.CNAME = 'SUNIL' AND
   D2.BNAME = B2.BNAME  AND C1.CITY IN(SELECT C2.CITY FROM CUSTOMER C2 WHERE
   C2.CNAME = 'ANIL'));
```

Listing 7.39: List Names of Depositors Having Amount Greater than 1000 and Having the Same Living City as PRAMOD

```
SELECT D1.CNAME FROM DEPOSIT D1, CUSTOMER C1, CUSTOMER C2 WHERE C1.CITY =
   C2.CITY AND C2.CNAME = 'PRAMOD' AND C1.CNAME = D1.CNAME AND D1.AMOUNT > 1000;
```

Listing 7.40: List City of Customer Having the Same Branch City as that of PRAMOD

```
SELECT C1.CITY FROM CUSTOMER C1, DEPOSIT D1, DEPOSIT D2, BRANCH B1, BRANCH B2
   WHERE D1.BNAME = B1.BNAME AND D2.BNAME = B2.BNAME AND D2.CNAME = 'PRAMOD' AND
   B1.CITY = B2.CITY AND C1.CNAME = D1.CNAME;
```

Listing 7.41: List the Branch City and Living City of PRAMOD

```
SELECT B1.CITY, C1.CITY FROM BRANCH B1, CUSTOMER C1, DEPOSIT D1 WHERE C1.CNAME
   ='PRAMOD' AND C1.CNAME = D1.CNAME AND D1.BNAME = B1.BNAME;
```

Listing 7.42: List the Branch City of SUNIL or the Branch City of ANIL

```
select city from branch, deposit where deposit.bname = branch.Bname and
   (deposit.cname='ANIL'OR DEPOSIT.CNAME ='SUNIL');
```

Listing 7.43: List the Living City of ANIL and the Living City of SUNIL

```
SELECT CNAME,CITY FROM CUSTOMER WHERE CUSTOMER.CNAME = 'SUNIL' OR CUSTOMER.CNAME   =
   'ANIL';
```

Assignment No. 4

Set Operations

Listing 7.44: List All the Customers who are Depositors but Not Borrowers

```
SELECT CNAME FROM DEPOSIT
MINUS
(SELECT CNAME FROM BORROW);
```

Listing 7.45: List All the Customers who are Both Depositors and Borrowers

```
SELECT CNAME FROM DEPOSIT INTERSECT
(SELECT CNAME FROM BORROW);
```

Listing 7.46: List All the Customers, Along with their Amount, who are Either Borrowers or Depositors and Living in NAGPUR

```
SELECT D1.CNAME,D1.AMOUNT FROM DEPOSIT D1, CUSTOMER C1 WHERE C1.CITY = 'NAGPUR'
   AND D1.CNAME = C1.CNAME
UNION ALL
SELECT BR1.CNAME, BR1.AMOUNT FROM BORROW BR1, CUSTOMER C2 WHERE C2.CITY =
   'NAGPUR' AND BR1.CNAME = C2.CNAME;
```

Listing 7.47: List All the Depositors Having Deposit in All the Branches where SUNIL is Having Account

```
SELECT D1.CNAME FROM DEPOSIT D1 WHERE D1.BNAME IN (SELECT D2.BNAME FROM DEPOSIT
   D2 WHERE D2.CNAME = 'SUNIL');
```

Listing 7.48: List all the Customers Living in NAGPUR and Having the Branch City as MUMBAI or DELHI

```
SELECT C1.CNAME FROM CUSTOMER C1, DEPOSIT D1, BRANCH B1 WHERE C1.CITY = 'NAGPUR'
   AND C1.CNAME = D1.CNAME AND D1.BNAME = B1.BNAME AND B1.CITY IN
   ('MUMBAI','DELHI');
```

Listing 7.49: List All the Depositors Living in NAGPUR

```
SELECT D1.CNAME FROM DEPOSIT D1 WHERE D1.CNAME IN (SELECT C1.CNAME FROM CUSTOMER
   C1 WHERE C1.CITY = 'NAGPUR');
```

Listing 7.50: List All the Depositors Living in NAGPUR and Having Branch in DELHI

```
SELECT D1.CNAME FROM DEPOSIT D1 WHERE D1.CNAME IN
((SELECT D2.CNAME FROM DEPOSIT D2 ,
CUSTOMER C1 WHERE C1.CITY = 'NAGPUR' AND D2.CNAME = C1.CNAME)
INTERSECT (SELECT D3.CNAME FROM DEPOSIT D3,  BRANCH B1
WHERE B1.CITY = 'DELHI' AND D3.BNAME = B1.BNAME));
```

Listing 7.51: List the Branch Cities of ANIL and SUNIL

```
SELECT B1.CITY FROM DEPOSIT D1, BRANCH B1 WHERE D1.CNAME IN ('SUNIL','ANIL') AND
   B1.BNAME = D1.BNAME;
```

Listing 7.52: List the Customer Having Deposit Greater than 1000 and Loan Less than 10000

```
SELECT D1.CNAME  FROM DEPOSIT D1 WHERE D1.AMOUNT > 1000
AND D1.CNAME IN (SELECT BR1.CNAME FROM BORROW BR1 WHERE  BR1.AMOUNT < 10000);
```

Listing 7.53: List the Borrowers Having Branch City Same as that of SUNIL

```
SELECT BR1.CNAME FROM BORROW BR1, BRANCH B1 WHERE BR1.BNAME = B1.BNAME AND
   B1.CITY IN (SELECT B2.CITY FROM BORROW BR2, BRANCH B2  WHERE BR2.CNAME =
   'SUNIL' AND BR2.BNAME = B2.BNAME);
```

Listing 7.54: List the Cities of Depositors Having Branch VRCE

```
SELECT C1.CITY FROM CUSTOMER C1 WHERE C1.CNAME IN (SELECT D1.CNAME FROM DEPOSIT
   D1 WHERE D1.BNAME = 'VRCE');
```

Listing 7.55: List the Depositors Having the Same Living City as that of SUNIL and the Same Branch City as that of ANIL

```
SELECT D1.CNAME FROM DEPOSIT D1, CUSTOMER C1, BRANCH B1 WHERE D1.CNAME =
   C1.CNAME AND D1.BNAME = B1.BNAME AND C1.CITY IN (SELECT C2.CITY FROM CUSTOMER C2
   WHERE C2.CNAME = 'SUNIL')
AND
B1.CITY IN (SELECT B2.CITY FROM DEPOSIT D2, BRANCH B2 WHERE D2.CNAME = 'ANIL'
   AND D2.BNAME = B2. BNAME);
```

Listing 7.56: List the Depositors Having Amount Less than 8000 and Living in the Same City as SHIVANI

```
   SELECT D1.CNAME FROM DEPOSIT D1, CUSTOMER C1 WHERE D1.AMOUNT < 8000 AND D1.CNAME =
C1.CNAME AND C1.CITY IN (SELECT C2.CITY FROM CUSTOMER C2 WHERE C2.CNAME =
   'SHIVANI');
```

Listing 7.57: List All the Customers who are Both Depositors and Borrowers and Living in the Same City as ANIL

```
SELECT C1.CNAME FROM CUSTOMER C1 WHERE C1.CNAME IN
((SELECT D1.CNAME FROM DEPOSIT D1)
INTERSECT
```

```
(SELECT BR1.CNAME FROM BORROW BR1))
AND
C1.CITY IN
(SELECT C2.CITY FROM CUSTOMER C2 WHERE C2.CNAME = 'ANIL');
```

Listing 7.58: List All the Cities where Branches of ANIL and SUNIL are Located

```
SELECT B1.CITY FROM BRANCH B1 WHERE B1.BNAME IN
(SELECT D1.BNAME FROM DEPOSIT D1 WHERE D1.CNAME IN ('ANIL','SUNIL'));
```

Listing 7.59: List all the Customer Names and the AMOUNT for Depositors Living in the City where Either ANIL Or SUNIL is Living

```
SELECT D1.CNAME, D1.AMOUNT FROM DEPOSIT D1, CUSTOMER C1
WHERE C1.CNAME = D1.CNAME AND C1.CITY IN
(SELECT C2.CITY FROM CUSTOMER C2 WHERE C2.CNAME IN ('SUNIL','ANIL'));
```

Listing 7.60: List the AMOUNT for the Depositors Living in the City where ANIL is Living

```
SELECT D1.AMOUNT FROM DEPOSIT D1, CUSTOMER C1 WHERE D1.CNAME = C1.CNAME AND
  C1.CITY IN (SELECT C2.CITY FROM CUSTOMER C2 WHERE C2.CNAME = 'ANIL');
```

Listing 7.61: List the Cities which are Either Branch City of ANIL or Living City of SUNIL

```
SELECT B1.CITY FROM BRANCH B1,DEPOSIT D1 WHERE D1.CNAME IN ('SUNIL') AND
  D1.BNAME = B1.BNAME
UNION
(SELECT C1.CITY FROM CUSTOMER C1 WHERE C1.CNAME IN ('ANIL'));
```

Listing 7.62: List the Customers who are Borrowers or Depositors and Having Living City MUMBAI and the Branch City is Same as that of SANDIP

```
SELECT C1.CNAME FROM CUSTOMER C1,BRANCH B1,DEPOSIT D3
WHERE C1.CITY = 'MUMBAI' AND
C1.CNAME IN ((SELECT D1.CNAME FROM DEPOSIT D1)
UNION
(SELECT BR1.CNAME FROM BORROW BR1))
AND
B1.CITY IN
(SELECT B2.CITY FROM DEPOSIT D2, BRANCH B2 WHERE D2.CNAME = 'SANDIP'
AND D2.BNAME = B2.BNAME
AND
C1.CNAME = D3.CNAME AND D3.BNAME = B1.BNAME);
```

Listing 7.63: List the Customers who are Both Borrowers and Depositors and Having the Same Branch City as that of Anil

```
SELECT C1.CNAME FROM CUSTOMER C1,DEPOSIT D1,
BRANCH B1 WHERE  C1.CNAME IN((SELECT BR1.CNAME FROM BORROW BR1) INTERSECT
  (SELECT D2.CNAME FROM DEPOSIT D2))
AND  D1.CNAME = C1.CNAME  AND  D1.BNAME = B1.BNAME
AND  B1.CITY IN(SELECT B2.CITY FROM DEPOSIT D3, BRANCH B2 WHERE D3.CNAME =
  'ANIL' AND D3.BNAME = B2.BNAME);
```

Assignment No. 5

Aggregate Functions

Listing 7.64: List Total Loan

```
SELECT SUM (AMOUNT) FROM BORROW;
```

Listing 7.65: List Total Deposit

```
SELECT SUM(AMOUNT) FROM DEPOSIT;
```

Listing 7.66: List Total Loan Taken from ANDHERI Branch

```
SELECT SUM(AMOUNT) FROM BORROW WHERE BNAME = 'ANDHERI';
```

Listing 7.67: List Total Deposit of Customer Having Account Date Later than 1-JAN-96

```
SELECT SUM(AMOUNT) FROM DEPOSIT WHERE ADATE >'1-JAN-96';
```

Listing 7.68: List Total Deposit of Customers Living in NAGPUR

```
SELECT SUM(D1.AMOUNT) FROM DEPOSIT D1, CUSTOMER C1 WHERE C1.CITY = 'NAGPUR' AND
  C1.CNAME = D1.CNAME;
```

Listing 7.69: List Maximum Deposit of Customers Living in MUMBAI

```
SELECT MAX(D1.AMOUNT) FROM DEPOSIT D1, CUSTOMER C1 WHERE C1.CITY = 'MUMBAI' AND
  C1.CNAME = D1.CNAME;
```

Listing 7.70: List Total Deposit of Customers Having Branch City as DELHI

```
SELECT SUM(D1.AMOUNT) FROM DEPOSIT D1, BRANCH B1 WHERE B1.CITY = 'DELHI' AND
  D1.BNAME = B1.BNAME;
```

Listing 7.71: List Total Deposit of Customers Living in the City where SUNIL is Living

```
SELECT SUM(D1.AMOUNT) FROM DEPOSIT D1,CUSTOMER C1 WHERE D1.CNAME=C1.CNAME AND
  C1.CITY IN  (SELECT C2.CITY FROM CUSTOMER C2 WHERE C2.CNAME = 'SUNIL');
```

Listing 7.72: Count Total Number of Branch Cities

```
SELECT COUNT(DISTINCT CITY) FROM BRANCH;
```

Listing 7.73: Count Total Number of Customer Cities

```
SELECT COUNT(DISTINCT CITY) FROM CUSTOMER;
```

Listing 7.74: List Branch Name and Branch wise Deposit

```
SELECT BNAME, SUM(AMOUNT) FROM DEPOSIT GROUP BY BNAME;
```

Listing 7.75: List City Name and City wise Deposit

```
SELECT B1.CITY, SUM(D1.AMOUNT) FROM BRANCH B1, DEPOSIT D1 WHERE D1.BNAME =
  B1.BNAME GROUP BY B1.CITY;
```

Listing 7.76: List City wise Name and Branch wise Deposit

```
SELECT B1.CITY, SUM(D1.AMOUNT) FROM DEPOSIT D1, BRANCH B1 WHERE D1.BNAME =
  B1.BNAME GROUP BY D1.BNAME,B1.CITY;
```

Listing 7.77: List the Branch wise Deposit of Customer after Account Date 1-JAN-96

```
SELECT SUM(AMOUNT) FROM DEPOSIT WHERE ADATE > '1-JAN-96' GROUP BY BNAME;
```

Listing 7.78: List Branch wise Loan of Customer Living in NAGPUR

```
SELECT SUM(BR1.AMOUNT) FROM BORROW BR1, CUSTOMER C1 WHERE C1.CNAME = BR1.CNAME
  AND C1.CITY = 'NAGPUR' GROUP BY BR1.BNAME;
```

Listing 7.79: Count Total Number of Customers

```
SELECT COUNT(DISTINCT (CNAME)) FROM CUSTOMER;
```

Listing 7.80: Count Total Number of Depositors Branch wise

```
SELECT COUNT(DISTINCT CNAME) FROM DEPOSIT GROUP BY BNAME;
```

Listing 7.81: List Maximum Loan from the VRCE Branch

```
SELECT MAX(AMOUNT) FROM BORROW WHERE BNAME = 'VRCE';
```

Listing 7.82: List Living City wise Loan of Borrowers

```
SELECT SUM(BR1.AMOUNT) FROM BORROW BR1, CUSTOMER C1 WHERE C1.CNAME = BR1.CNAME
  GROUP BY C1.CITY;
```

Listing 7.83: List the Number of Customers who are Depositors as well as Borrowers

```
SELECT COUNT(DISTINCT CNAME) FROM CUSTOMER WHERE CNAME IN
((SELECT CNAME FROM DEPOSIT)
INTERSECT
(SELECT CNAME FROM BORROW));
```

Assignment No. 6

GROUP BY and HAVING Clause

Listing 7.84: List the Branches Having Sum of Deposit More than 4000

```
SELECT BNAME FROM DEPOSIT GROUP BY BNAME HAVING SUM(AMOUNT) > 4000;
```

Listing 7.85: List the Branches Having a Sum of Deposit More than 1000 and Located in MUMBAI

```
SELECT D1.BNAME FROM DEPOSIT D1, BRANCH B1 WHERE D1.BNAME = B1.BNAME
AND B1.CITY = 'MUMBAI' GROUP BY D1.BNAME HAVING SUM(D1.AMOUNT) > 1000;
```

Listing 7.86: List the Names of Customers Having Deposit in the Branches Where the Average Deposit is More than 1000

```
SELECT C1.CNAME FROM CUSTOMER C1 WHERE
C1.CNAME IN (SELECT D1.CNAME FROM DEPOSIT D1 GROUP BY D1.CNAME HAVING
  AVG(D1.AMOUNT) > 1000);
```

Listing 7.87: List the Names of Customers Having Maximum Deposit

```
SELECT D1.CNAME FROM DEPOSIT D1 WHERE D1.AMOUNT IN (SELECT MAX(D2.AMOUNT) FROM
  DEPOSIT D2);
```

Listing 7.88: List the Name of Customers Having Maximum Deposit in the Customers Living in NAGPUR

```
SELECT D.CNAME FROM DEPOSIT D WHERE AMOUNT IN
(SELECT MAX(D1.AMOUNT) FROM DEPOSIT D1, CUSTOMER C1 WHERE
D1.CNAME = C1.CNAME AND C1.CITY = 'NAGPUR');
```

Listing 7.89: List the Name of Branch Having Highest Number of Depositors

```
SELECT D1.BNAME FROM DEPOSIT D1 GROUP BY D1.BNAME
HAVING COUNT(D1.CNAME) >= ALL (SELECT COUNT (D2.CNAME) FROM DEPOSIT D2 GROUP BY
  D2.BNAME);
```

Listing 7.90: Count the Number of Depositors Living in NAGPUR

```
SELECT COUNT (D2.CNAME) FROM DEPOSIT D2, CUSTOMER C1 WHERE
C1.CITY = 'NAGPUR' AND C1.CNAME = D2.CNAME;
```

Listing 7.91: List Names of Customers in POWAI Branch Having More Deposit than All Customer from VRCE Branch

```
SELECT D1.CNAME FROM DEPOSIT D1 WHERE D1.BNAME = 'POWAI'
GROUP BY D1.AMOUNT,D1.CNAME  HAVING D1.AMOUNT > ALL
(SELECT D2.AMOUNT FROM DEPOSIT D2 WHERE D2.BNAME = 'VRCE');
```

Listing 7.92: List Names of Customers in KAROLBAGH Branch Having More Deposit than Any Other Customer in VIRAR Branch

```
SELECT D1.CNAME FROM DEPOSIT D1 WHERE D1.BNAME = 'KAROLBAGH'
GROUP BY D1.CNAME,D1.AMOUNT HAVING D1.AMOUNT > ANY
(SELECT D2.AMOUNT FROM DEPOSIT D2 WHERE D2.BNAME = 'VIRAR');
```

Listing 7.93: List Names of Customers Having Highest Deposit in the Branch where SUNIL is Having Deposit

```
SELECT D1.CNAME FROM DEPOSIT D1 WHERE D1.AMOUNT >= ALL (SELECT D2.AMOUNT FROM
  DEPOSIT D2 WHERE D2.CNAME = 'SUNIL') AND D1.BNAME IN (SELECT BNAME FROM DEPOSIT
  WHERE CNAME='SUNIL');
```

Listing 7.94: List the Highest Deposit of the City where Branch of SUNIL is Located

```
SELECT MAX (AMOUNT) FROM DEPOSIT WHERE BNAME IN (SELECT BNAME FROM BRANCH WHERE
  CITY IN(SELECT CITY  FROM BRANCH WHERE BNAME IN (SELECT BNAME FROM DEPOSIT WHERE
  CNAME ='SUNIL')));
```

Listing 7.95: List Names of Customers Having More Deposit than the Average Deposit in their Respective Branches

```
SELECT D1.CNAME FROM DEPOSIT D1 WHERE AMOUNT >= ANY (SELECT AVG(D2.AMOUNT) FROM
  DEPOSIT D1 , DEPOSIT D2 WHERE D1.BNAME = D2.BNAME GROUP BY D2.BNAME);
```

Listing 7.96: List Names of Customers Having Maximum Deposit Among Deposits of NAGPUR for the VRCE Branch

```
SELECT CNAME FROM DEPOSIT,BRANCH  WHERE DEPOSIT.AMOUNT IN (SELECT MAX(D1.AMOUNT)
  FROM DEPOSIT D1, BRANCH B1
WHERE D1.BNAME='VRCE' AND B1.CITY ='NAGPUR'
AND B1.BNAME= D1.BNAME)AND  BRANCH.BNAME = 'VRCE'
AND BRANCH.CITY ='NAGPUR' AND BRANCH.BNAME= DEPOSIT.BNAME;
```

Listing 7.97: List the Name of the Branch where Number of Depositors is Less than 2

```
SELECT D1.BNAME FROM DEPOSIT D1 GROUP BY D1.BNAME
HAVING COUNT(D1.CNAME) < 2;
```

Listing 7.98: List the Name of the City Having More Customers Living than in NAGPUR

```
SELECT C1.CITY FROM CUSTOMER C1 GROUP BY C1.CITY
HAVING COUNT (C1.CNAME) > ALL (SELECT COUNT (C2.CNAME) FROM CUSTOMER C2 WHERE
  C2.CITY = 'NAGPUR');
```

Listing 7.99: List Names of Branches Having the Number of Depositors More than the Number of Borrowers

```
SELECT D1.BNAME FROM DEPOSIT D1 GROUP BY D1.BNAME
HAVING COUNT(D1.CNAME) > ALL (SELECT COUNT (BR1.CNAME) FROM BORROW BR1
WHERE BR1.BNAME = D1.BNAME GROUP BY BR1. BNAME);
```

Listing 7.100: List the Names of Cities in which the Maximum Number of Branches are Located

```
SELECT B1.CITY FROM BRANCH B1 GROUP BY  B1.CITY
HAVING COUNT(B1.CITY) =(SELECT MAX(COUNT(*)) FROM
BRANCH GROUP BY CITY);
```

Listing 7.101: List the Names of Customers Living in the City where the Maximum Number of Depositors are Located

```
SELECT D1.CNAME FROM DEPOSIT D1, CUSTOMER C1 WHERE D1.CNAME=C1.CNAME AND C1.CITY
  IN (SELECT C2.CITY FROM CUSTOMER C2 GROUP BY C2.CITY HAVING COUNT(C2.CITY)=(
  SELECT MAX(COUNT(*)) FROM CUSTOMER GROUP BY CITY));
```

Listing 7.102: List the Names of Borrowers Having the Same Branch City and Highest Borrower

```
SELECT BR1.CNAME FROM BORROW BR1 WHERE BR1.BNAME IN
((SELECT BR2.BNAME FROM BORROW BR2 GROUP BY BR2.BNAME
HAVING COUNT(BR2.CNAME) >= ALL(SELECT COUNT (BR2.CNAME) FROM
BORROW BR2 GROUP BY BR2.BNAME)));
```

Listing 7.103: Count the Number of Customers Living in the City where Branch is Located

```
SELECT COUNT(C1.CNAME) FROM CUSTOMER C1, DEPOSIT D1, BRANCH B1
WHERE C1.CNAME = D1.CNAME AND B1.BNAME = D1.BNAME AND B1.CITY = C1.CITY;
```

Assignment No. 7

*The **UPDATE** Statement*

Listing 7.104: List 10% Interest to All Depositors

```
UPDATE DEPOSIT
SET AMOUNT = AMOUNT * 0.1;
```

Listing 7.105: List 10% Interest to All Depositors Having the VRCE Branch

```
UPDATE DEPOSIT
SET AMOUNT = AMOUNT * 0.1 WHERE BNAME = 'VRCE';
```

Listing 7.106: List 10% Interest to All Depositors Living in NAGPUR

```
UPDATE DEPOSIT
SET AMOUNT = AMOUNT * 0.1 WHERE CNAME IN
(SELECT CNAME FROM CUSTOMER WHERE CITY = 'NAGPUR');
```

Listing 7.107: List 10% Interest to All Depositors Living in NAGPUR and Having a Branch in MUMBAI

```
UPDATE DEPOSIT
SET AMOUNT = AMOUNT * 0.1 WHERE CNAME IN
(SELECT CNAME FROM CUSTOMER WHERE CITY = 'NAGPUR')
AND
BNAME IN
(SELECT BNAME FROM BRANCH WHERE CITY = 'MUMBAI');
```

Listing 7.108: Add Hundred Rupees to the Deposit of ANIL and Assign it to SUNIL

```
UPDATE DEPOSIT
SET AMOUNT = AMOUNT + 100 WHERE CNAME = 'ANIL';
UPDATE DEPOSIT
SET AMOUNT = (SELECT AMOUNT FROM DEPOSIT WHERE CNAME = 'ANIL')
WHERE CNAME = 'SUNIL';
```

Listing 7.109: Change the Deposit of the VRCE Branch to 1000 and Change the Branch as VRCE_AMBAZARI

```
UPDATE DEPOSIT
SET AMOUNT = 1000,
BNAME = 'VRCE_AMBAZARI' WHERE BNAME = 'VRCE';
```

Listing 7.110: Assign to the Deposit of Anil the Maximum Deposit from the VRCE Branch

```
UPDATE DEPOSIT
SET AMOUNT = (SELECT MAX(AMOUNT) FROM DEPOSIT WHERE BNAME = 'VRCE') WHERE CNAME =
   'ANIL';
```

Listing 7.111: Change the Living City of the VRCE Branch Borrowers to NAGPUR

```
UPDATE CUSTOMER
SET CITY = 'NAGPUR' WHERE CNAME IN
(SELECT CNAME FROM BORROW WHERE BNAME = 'VRCE');
```

Listing 7.112: Update Deposit of Anil. Give Him Maximum Deposit from Depositors in Living City NAGPUR

```
UPDATE DEPOSIT
SET AMOUNT = (SELECT MAX(AMOUNT) FROM DEPOSIT, CUSTOMER WHERE DEPOSIT.CNAME =
   CUSTOMER.CNAME AND CUSTOMER.CITY = 'NAGPUR')
WHERE CNAME = 'ANIL';
```

Listing 7.113: Deposit the Sum of the Deposits of SUNIL and VIJAY in the Account of ANIL

```
UPDATE DEPOSIT
SET AMOUNT = (SELECT SUM(AMOUNT) FROM DEPOSIT WHERE CNAME IN ('SUNIL','VIJAY'))
   WHERE CNAME = 'ANIL';
```

Listing 7.114: Transfer Rs 10 from the Account of ANIL to the Account of SUNIL

```
UPDATE DEPOSIT
SET AMOUNT = AMOUNT - 10 WHERE CNAME = 'ANIL';
UPDATE DEPOSIT
SET AMOUNT = AMOUNT + 10 WHERE CNAME = 'SUNIL';
```

Listing 7.115: Transfer Rs 10 from the Account of Anil to the Account of Sunil if Both are Having the Same Branch

```
UPDATE DEPOSIT
SET AMOUNT = AMOUNT - 10 WHERE CNAME = 'ANIL' AND BNAME IN
(SELECT D1.BNAME FROM DEPOSIT D1 WHERE D1. CNAME = 'SUNIL');
UPDATE DEPOSIT
SET
AMOUNT = AMOUNT + 10 WHERE CNAME = 'SUNIL' AND BNAME IN
(SELECT D2.BNAME FROM DEPOSIT D2 WHERE D2. CNAME = 'ANIL');
```

Listing 7.116: Transfer 10 from the Account of MADHURI to the Account of PRAMOD if Both are Living in NAGPUR

```
UPDATE DEPOSIT
SET AMOUNT = AMOUNT - 10 WHERE CNAME = 'MADHURI' AND CNAME IN
(SELECT C1.CNAME FROM CUSTOMER C1, CUSTOMER C2 WHERE
C2.CNAME = 'PRAMOD' AND C1.CITY = 'NAGPUR' AND C1.CITY = C2.CITY);
UPDATE DEPOSIT
SET
AMOUNT = AMOUNT + 10 WHERE CNAME = 'PRAMOD' AND CNAME IN
(SELECT C2.CNAME FROM CUSTOMER C2, CUSTOMER C4 WHERE
C4.CNAME = 'MADHURI' AND C2.CITY = C4.CITY);
```

Listing 7.117: Transfer 10 from the Account of MADHURI to the Account of PRAMOD if Both are Living in the Same City

```
UPDATE DEPOSIT
SET AMOUNT = AMOUNT - 10 WHERE CNAME = 'MADHURI' AND CNAME IN
(SELECT C1.CNAME FROM CUSTOMER C1, CUSTOMER C2 WHERE
C2.CNAME = 'PRAMOD'  AND C1.CITY = C2.CITY);
UPDATE DEPOSIT
SET
AMOUNT = AMOUNT + 10 WHERE CNAME = 'PRAMOD' AND CNAME IN
(SELECT C2.CNAME FROM CUSTOMER C2, CUSTOMER C4 WHERE
C4.CNAME = 'MADHURI' AND C2.CITY = C4.CITY);
```

Listing 7.118: Transfer 10 from the Account of ANIL to the Account of SUNIL if Both are Having the Same Branches

```
UPDATE DEPOSIT
SET AMOUNT = AMOUNT - 10 WHERE CNAME = 'ANIL' AND BNAME IN
(SELECT D1.BNAME FROM DEPOSIT D1 WHERE D1.CNAME = 'SUNIL');
UPDATE DEPOSIT
SET
AMOUNT = AMOUNT + 10 WHERE CNAME = 'SUNIL' AND BNAME IN
(SELECT D1.BNAME FROM DEPOSIT D1 WHERE D1.CNAME = 'ANIL');
```

Listing 7.119: Add 100 to the Account of all Those Depositors who are Having the Highest Deposit Amount in their Respective Branches

```
UPDATE DEPOSIT
SET AMOUNT = AMOUNT + 100
WHERE CNAME IN
(SELECT D1.CNAME FROM DEPOSIT D1
GROUP BY D1.CNAME HAVING AVG(D1.AMOUNT) >= ALL
(SELECT MAX(D2.AMOUNT) FROM DEPOSIT D2,DEPOSIT D1  WHERE
D1.BNAME = D2.BNAME GROUP BY D2.BNAME));
```

Listing 7.120: Add Rs 10 to the Amount of all Depositors Having Deposit Higher than the Average Deposit

```
UPDATE DEPOSIT SET AMOUNT = AMOUNT + 10
WHERE CNAME IN(SELECT D1.CNAME FROM DEPOSIT D1 GROUP BY D1.CNAME
HAVING AVG(D1.AMOUNT) > ALL (SELECT AVG(D2. AMOUNT) FROM DEPOSIT D2));
```

Listing 7.121: Add 10 to the Amount of all Depositors Having Deposit Higher than the Average Deposit of their Branch

```
UPDATE DEPOSIT SET AMOUNT = AMOUNT + 10 WHERE CNAME IN
(SELECT D1.CNAME FROM DEPOSIT D1 GROUP BY D1.CNAME
HAVING AVG(D1.AMOUNT)  > ALL (SELECT AVG(D2. AMOUNT)
FROM DEPOSIT D2, DEPOSIT D1 WHERE D2.BNAME = D1.BNAME
GROUP BY D2. BNAME));
```

Listing 7.122: Add 10 to the Amount of all Customers Living in the City where their Branch is Located

```
UPDATE DEPOSIT
SET AMOUNT = AMOUNT + 10
WHERE CNAME IN
(SELECT D1.CNAME FROM DEPOSIT D1, BRANCH B1, CUSTOMER C1
WHERE B1.BNAME = D1.BNAME AND B1.CITY = C1.CITY AND
C1.CNAME = D1.CNAME);
```

Listing 7.123: Add 10 to the Amount of all Depositors Having Deposit Higher than the Average Deposit of their Branch

```
UPDATE DEPOSIT SET AMOUNT = AMOUNT + 10 WHERE CNAME IN
(SELECT D1.CNAME FROM DEPOSIT D1,CUSTOMER C1 WHERE
C1.CNAME = D1.CNAME GROUP BY D1.CNAME HAVING
AVG(D1.AMOUNT) >= ALL (SELECT D2.AMOUNT
FROM DEPOSIT D2, CUSTOMER C2,CUSTOMER C1
WHERE D2.CNAME = C2.CNAME AND C2.CITY = C1.CITY));
```

Assignment No. 8

*The **DELETE** Statement*

Listing 7.124: Delete from Customer

```
DELETE FROM CUSTOMER;
```

Listing 7.125: Delete Depositors of Branches Having Number of Customer between 1 and 3

```
DELETE FROM DEPOSIT WHERE CNAME IN
(SELECT D1.CNAME FROM DEPOSIT D1 GROUP BY D1.CNAME HAVING COUNT(D1.CNAME)
  BETWEEN 1 AND 3);
```

Listing 7.126: Delete Branches Having Average Deposit Less than 5000

```
DELETE FROM BRANCH WHERE BNAME IN
(SELECT BNAME FROM DEPOSIT GROUP BY BNAME HAVING AVG(AMOUNT) < 5000);
```

Listing 7.127: Delete Branches Having Maximum Loan More than 5000

```
DELETE FROM BRANCH WHERE BNAME IN
(SELECT BNAME FROM BORROW GROUP BY BNAME HAVING MAX(AMOUNT) > 5000);
```

Listing 7.128: Delete Branches Having Deposit from NAGPUR

```
DELETE FROM BRANCH WHERE
BNAME IN
(SELECT D1.BNAME FROM DEPOSIT D1, CUSTOMER C1
WHERE  D1.CNAME = C1.CNAME AND C1.CITY = 'NAGPUR');
```

Listing 7.129: Delete Deposit of ANIL and SUNIL if Both are Having Branch VIRAR

```
DELETE FROM DEPOSIT WHERE CNAME IN ('ANIL', 'SUNIL') AND
EXISTS
(SELECT * FROM DEPOSIT D1, DEPOSIT D2 WHERE D1.CNAME = 'ANIL' AND D2.CNAME =
  'SUNIL' AND D1.BNAME = D2.BNAME AND D1.BNAME = 'VIRAR');
```

Listing 7.130: Delete Deposit of ANIL and SUNIL if Both are having Living City NAGPUR

```
DELETE FROM DEPOSIT WHERE CNAME IN ('ANIL', 'SUNIL') AND EXISTS
(SELECT * FROM CUSTOMER C1, CUSTOMER C2 WHERE C1.CNAME = 'ANIL' AND C2.CNAME =
  'SUNIL' AND C1.CITY = C2.CITY AND C1.CITY = 'NAGPUR');
```

Listing 7.131: Delete Deposit of ANIL and SUNIL if Both are Having the Same Living City

```
DELETE FROM DEPOSIT WHERE CNAME IN ('ANIL', 'SUNIL') AND EXISTS
(SELECT * FROM CUSTOMER C1, CUSTOMER C2 WHERE C1.CNAME = 'ANIL' AND C2.CNAME =
  'SUNIL' AND C1.CITY = C2.CITY);
```

Listing 7.132: Delete Deposit of ANIL and SUNIL if they are Having Less Deposit than VIJAY

```
DELETE FROM DEPOSIT WHERE CNAME IN ('ANIL', 'SUNIL') AND EXISTS
(SELECT * FROM DEPOSIT D1, DEPOSIT D2 WHERE D1. CNAME IN ('ANIL','SUNIL') AND
  D2.CNAME = 'VIJAY' AND D1.AMOUNT < D2.AMOUNT);
```

Listing 7.133: Delete Deposit of VIJAY

```
DELETE FROM DEPOSIT WHERE CNAME = 'VIJAY';
```

Listing 7.134: Delete Deposit of AJAY if VIJAY is Not a Depositor

```
DELETE FROM DEPOSIT WHERE CNAME = 'AJAY' AND
NOT EXISTS
(SELECT * FROM DEPOSIT WHERE CNAME = 'VIJAY');
```

Listing 7.135: Delete Customers from MUMBAI City

```
DELETE FROM CUSTOMER WHERE CITY = 'MUMBAI';
```

Listing 7.136: Delete Depositors if the Branch is VIRAR and Depositor Name is AJAY

```
DELETE FROM DEPOSIT WHERE CNAME = 'AJAY' AND BNAME = 'VIRAR';
```

Listing 7.137: Delete Depositors Having Deposit Less than 500

```
DELETE FROM DEPOSIT WHERE AMOUNT < 500;
```

Listing 7.138: Delete Borrower Having Loan More than 10000

```
DELETE FROM BORROW WHERE AMOUNT > 10000;
```

Listing 7.139: Delete Borrower Having Loan More than 1000 and the KAROLBAGH Branch

```
DELETE FROM BORROW WHERE AMOUNT > 1000 AND BNAME = 'KAROLBAGH';
```

Listing 7.140: Delete the Names of Those Depositors of the VRCE Branch who Lives in MUMBAI

```
DELETE FROM DEPOSIT WHERE BNAME = 'VRCE' AND CNAME IN
(SELECT CNAME FROM CUSTOMER WHERE CITY = 'MUMBAI');
```

Listing 7.141: Delete Borrower Having Branch Name CHANDNI

```
DELETE FROM BORROW WHERE BNAME = 'CHANDNI';
```

Listing 7.142: Delete Borrower of Branches Having Average Loan Less than 1000

```
DELETE FROM BORROW WHERE CNAME IN
(SELECT BR1.CNAME FROM BORROW BR1 GROUP BY BR1.CNAME HAVING AVG(BR1.AMOUNT) <
  1000);
```

Listing 7.143: Delete Borrower of Branches Having the Minimum Number of Customers

```
DELETE FROM BORROW WHERE
CNAME IN
(SELECT BR1.CNAME FROM BORROW BR1 GROUP BY BR1.CNAME
HAVING COUNT(BR1.CNAME) <= ALL (SELECT COUNT(BR2.CNAME) FROM BORROW BR2
GROUP BY BR2.BNAME));
```

8

Assignment-II

The following schema is required by a Computer training institute to store information:

Schema	Description	Creating table
Course	Information about available courses	create table course (coursecode number(2)not null, coursename varchar2(30), syllabus varchar2(60), lastno number(1));
Batch	Information about batches—one course can have multiple batches	create table batch (batchcode number(5) not null, coursecode number(2) not null, startingdate date not null, duration number(3) not null, coursefees number(10,2) not null, netincome number(10,2), expectedincome number(10,2), lastno number(3));
Advertisement	Information about advertisements in newspaper—the institute Lists advertisement regarding courses	create table advertisement (refcode number(5) not null ,medianame varchar2(30) ,pages number(2) ,advdate date not null ,amount number(10,2));
Enquiry	In response to the advertisement, the institute gets response in the form of enquiries. Each enquiry can be tagged using source of enquiry, i.e. which advertisement	create table enquiry (enquiryno number(8) not null ,fname varchar2(30) ,sname varchar2(30) ,coursecode number(2) ,plotno varchar2(30) ,street varchar2(30) ,city varchar2(30) ,pincode number(6) ,phone number(6) ,enquirydate date not null ,refcode number(5) ,en_st char(1));
Enrollment	Information about enrollments in the batch. Only some enquiries are converted into enrollments	create table enrollment (rollno number(8) not null ,enquiryno number(8) ,batchcode number(5) ,enrollmentdate date not null);
Installment	Information of the student who has enrolled for a particular batch. Students can pay fees in numbers of installments	create table installment (rollno number(8) ,installmentdate date not null ,amount number(10,2) not null ,installmentstatus char(1));

Schema	Description	Creating table
Feespaid	The information about feespaid	create table feespaid (rollno number(8) not null, feespaiddate date not null, chequeno varchar2(10), bankname varchar2(30), remarks varchar2(30), amount number(10,2));
Expenditure	Expenditure details of the institute	create table EXPENDITURE (expcode number(5) ,amount number(10,2) ,expdate date ,chequeno varchar2(30) ,bankname varchar2(30) ,remark varchar2(100) ,batchcode number(5));
Master expenditure	Master file for expenditure	create table expmaster (expcode number(5) not null ,expname varchar2(30) ,exptype varchar2(10) ,netexp number(10,2));

Listing 8.1: Displaying the Structure of the Course Table

```
desc COURSE
```

Result:

```
NAME                     NULL?           TYPE
----------               ------          ------------
COURSECODE               NOT NULL        NUMBER(2)
COURSENAME                               VARCHAR2(30)
SYLLABUS                                 VARCHAR2(60)
LASTNO                                   NUMBER(1)
```

Listing 8.2: Displaying the Structure of the Batch Table

```
desc BATCH
```

Result:

```
NAME                     NULL?           TYPE
----------               ------          ------------
BATCHCODE                NOT NULL        NUMBER(5)
COURSECODE               NOT NULL        NUMBER(2)
STARTINGDATE             NOT NULL        DATE
DURATION                 NOT NULL        NUMBER(3)
COURSEFEES               NOT NULL        NUMBER(10,2)
NETINCOME                                NUMBER(10,2)
EXPECTEDINCOME                           NUMBER(10,2)
LASTNO                                   NUMBER(3)
```

Listing 8.3: Displaying the Structure of the Advertisement Table

```
desc ADVERTISEMENT
```

Result:

```
NAME                 NULL?          TYPE
----------           ------         ------------
REFCODE              NOT NULL       NUMBER(5)
MEDIANAME                           VARCHAR2(30)
PAGES                               NUMBER(2)
ADVDATE              NOT NULL       DATE
AMOUNT                              NUMBER(10,2)
```

Listing 8.4: Displaying the Structure of the ENQUIRY Table

```
desc ENQUIRY
```

Result:

```
NAME                 NULL?          TYPE
----------           ------         ------------
ENQUIRYNO            NOT NULL       NUMBER(8)
FNAME                               VARCHAR2(30)
SNAME                               VARCHAR2(30)
COURSECODE                          NUMBER(2)
PLOTNO                              VARCHAR2(30)
STREET                              VARCHAR2(30)
CITY                                VARCHAR2(30)
PINCODE                             NUMBER(6)
PHONE                               NUMBER(6)
ENQUIRYDATE          NOT NULL       DATE
REFCODE                             NUMBER(5)
EN_ST                               CHAR(1)
```

Listing 8.5: Displaying the Structure of the ENROLLMENT Table

```
desc ENROLLMENT
```

Result:

```
NAME                 NULL?          TYPE
----------           ------         ------------
ROLLNO               NOT NULL       NUMBER(8)
ENQUIRYNO                           NUMBER(8)
BATCHCODE                           NUMBER(5)
ENROLLMENTDATE       NOT NULL       DATE
```

Listing 8.6: Displaying the Structure of the INSTALLMENT Table

```
desc INSTALLMENT
```

Result:

```
NAME                 NULL?          TYPE
----------           ------         ------------
ROLLNO                              NUMBER(8)
INSTALLMENTDATE      NOT NULL       DATE
AMOUNT               NOT NULL       NUMBER(10,2)
INSTALLMENTSTATUS                   CHAR(1)
```

Listing 8.7: Displaying the Structure of the FEESPAID Table

```
desc FEESPAID
```

Result:

```
NAME                NULL?       TYPE
----------          ------      ------------
ROLLNO              NOT NULL    NUMBER(8)
FEESPAIDDATE        NOT NULL    DATE
CHEQUENO                        VARCHAR2(10)
BANKNAME                        VARCHAR2(30)
REMARKS                         VARCHAR2(30)
AMOUNT                          NUMBER(10,2)
```

Listing 8.8: Displaying the Structure of the EXPENDITURE Table

```
desc EXPENDITURE
```

Result:

```
NAME                NULL?       TYPE
----------          ------      ------------
EXPCODE                         NUMBER(5)
AMOUNT                          NUMBER(10,2)
EXPDATE                         DATE
CHEQUENO                        VARCHAR2(30)
BANKNAME                        VARCHAR2(30)
REMARK                          VARCHAR2(100)
BATCHCODE                       NUMBER(5)
```

Listing 8.9: Displaying the Structure of the EXPMASTER Table

```
desc EXPMASTER
```

Result:

```
NAME                NULL?       TYPE
----------          ------      ------------
EXPCODE             NOT NULL    NUMBER(5)
EXPNAME                         VARCHAR2(30)
EXPTYPE                         VARCHAR2(10)
NETEXP                          NUMBER(10,2)
```

Inserting Data into the Tables

COURSE Table

```
INSERT INTO COURSE
VALUES (10,'ORACLE','SQL,PLSQL,JDBC,JSP',2);
```

```
INSERT INTO COURSE
VALUES (20,'JAVA','JAVA CORE JAVA,SERVLETS, JSP,EJB',2);
```

BATCH Table

```
INSERT INTO BATCH
VALUES (20002,20,'01-JUL-01',180,24000,0,0,1);
```

```
INSERT INTO BATCH
VALUES (10002,10,'23-JAN-99',3,4000,2000,0,2);
```

```
INSERT INTO BATCH
VALUES (10001,10,'11-JAN-99',2,3000,0,6000,5);
```

```
INSERT INTO BATCH
VALUES (10003,10,'25-JAN-99',4,3000,0,7000,7);
```

ADVERTISEMENT Table

```
INSERT INTO ADVERTISEMENT
(REFCODE,MEDIANAME,ADVDATE)
VALUES (1001,'Times Of India','12-MAR-00');
```

```
INSERT INTO ADVERTISEMENT
(REFCODE,MEDIANAME,ADVDATE)
VALUES (1002,'Hindustan Times','15-APR-00');
```

ENQUIRY Table

```
INSERT INTO ENQUIRY
(ENQUIRYNO,FNAME,SNAME,COURSECODE,PLOTNO,STREET,CITY,ENQUIRYDATE,REFCODE,EN_ST) VALUES
   (110001,'ANIL','SHARMA',10,'23D','RAMNAGAR','NAGPUR','01-JUL-          00',1001,'Y');
```

```
INSERT INTO ENQUIRY
(ENQUIRYNO,FNAME,SNAME,COURSECODE,PLOTNO,STREET,CITY,ENQUIRYDATE,REF
CODE,EN_ST) VALUES (110002,'SACHIN','NIMJE',20,'20','GANDHI NAGAR','NAGPUR','01-
   SEP-00',1002,'Y');
```

ENROLLMENT Table

```
INSERT INTO ENROLLMENT VALUES (20002001,100826,20002,'01-JUL-00');
```

```
INSERT INTO ENROLLMENT VALUES (20002003, 100827, 20002, '11-JUL-00 ');
```

```
INSERT INTO ENROLLMENT VALUES (20002009, 100844, 20002, '01-JUL-00 ');
```

```
INSERT INTO ENROLLMENT VALUES (20002005, 100830, 20002, '01-JUL-00 ');
```

```
INSERT INTO ENROLLMENT VALUES (20002010, 100845, 20002, '01-JUL-00' );
```

```
INSERT INTO ENROLLMENT VALUES (10001100 ,110001,10001,'01-JUL-00');
```

INSTALLMENT Table

```
INSERT INTO INSTALLMENT VALUES (20002001,'12-AUG-00',5000,'N');
```

```
INSERT INTO INSTALLMENT VALUES (20002001,'12-SEP-00',5000,'N');
```

```
INSERT INTO INSTALLMENT VALUES (20002003,'12-JUL-00',5000,'N');
```

```
INSERT INTO INSTALLMENT VALUES (20002003,'15-SEP-00',5000,'N');
```

```
INSERT INTO INSTALLMENT VALUES (10001100,'15-OCT-00',10000,'Y');
```

FEESPAID Table

```
INSERT INTO FEESPAID VALUES(20002001,'25-JUL-01','','','',5000);
```

```
INSERT INTO FEESPAID VALUES(20002001,'25-AUG-01','','','',5000);
```

```
INSERT INTO FEESPAID VALUES(20002003,'25-JUL-01','','','',5000);
```

```
INSERT INTO FEESPAID VALUES(10001100,'10-JUL-99','','','',3000);
```

```
INSERT INTO FEESPAID VALUES(20002154,'05-JUL-00','','','',24000);
```

EXPENDITURE Table

```
INSERT INTO EXPENDITURE VALUES(100,20000,'12-SEP-00',20002,101,200,20002);
```

EXPMASTER Table

```
INSERT INTO EXPMASTER VALUES (101,'ADVT','CASH',4000);
```

Simple Exercises

Listing 8.10: Displaying the Contents of Course

```
SELECT * FROM COURSE;
```

Result:

```
COURSE   COURSE            SYLLABUS                              LASTNO
CODE     NAME
10       ORACLE            SQL,PLSQL,JDBC,JSP                    2
20       JAVA              JAVA CORE JAVA, SERVLETS, JSP,EJB     2
```

Listing 8.11: Displaying the Contents of BATCH

```
SELECT * FROM BATCH;
```

Result:

```
BATCHCODE COURSECODE STARTINGD DURATION COURSEFEES NETINCOME EXPECTEDINCOME LASTNO
20002            20      01-JUL-01      180       24000         0          0          1
10002            10      23-JAN-99      3         4000          2000       0          2
10001            10      11-JAN-99      2         3000          0          6000       5
10003            10      25-JAN-99      4         3000          0          7000       7
```

Listing 8.12: Displaying the Contents of BATCH for Particular Course Having COURSECODE=10

```
SELECT * FROM BATCH
WHERE COURSECODE = 10;
```

Result:

```
BATCHCODE COURSECODE STARTINGD DURATION COURSEFEES  NETINCOME EXPECTEDINCOME LASTNO
10002            10        23-JAN-99    3         4000          2000       0          2
10001            10        11-JAN-99    2         3000          0          6000       5
10003            10        25-JAN-99    4         3000          0          7000       7
```

Listing 8.13: Displaying the Contents of the BATCH that Starts from a Particular Date, say, STARTINGDATE = 23-JAN-99

```
SELECT * FROM BATCH
WHERE STARTINGDATE = '23-JAN-99';
```

Result:

```
BATCHCODE COURSECODE STARTINGD  DURATION COURSEFEES  NETINCOME EXPECTEDINCOME  LASTNO
10002         10        23-JAN-99     3         4000          2000              0       2
```

Listing 8.14: Displaying the BATCHCODE of BATCH Having a NETINCOME of More than 50000

```
SELECT BATCHCODE FROM BATCH
WHERE NETINCOME > 50000;
```

Result:

```
No rows selected
```

Listing 8.15: Displaying the BATCHCODE of BATCH Having EXPECTEDINCOME More than NETINCOME by 2000

```
SELECT BATCHCODE
FROM BATCH
WHERE EXPECTEDINCOME - NETINCOME > 2000;
```

Result:

```
BATCHCODE
---------
10001
10003
```

Or

```
SELECT BATCHCODE
FROM BATCH
WHERE EXPECTEDINCOME > NETINCOME + 2000;
```

Result:

```
BATCHCODE
---------
   10001
   10003
```

Listing 8.16: Displaying the Enquiries for COURSECODE 10

```
SELECT * FROM ENQUIRY
WHERE COURSECODE = 10;
```

Result:

```
ENQUIRYNO        FNAME          SNAME          COURSECODE     PLOTNO       STREET
---------        -------        ------         ----------     -------      -------
CITY             PINCODE        PHONE          ENQUIRYDA      REFCODE      E
--------         --------       -----          ---------      -------      ---------
110001             ANIL         SHARMA         10             23D          RAMNAGAR
NAGPUR                          01-JUL-00      1001           Y
```

Listing 8.17: Displaying the Names of Persons Having City as NAGPUR

```
SELECT  FNAME,SNAME
FROM  ENQUIRY
WHERE  CITY = 'NAGPUR';
```

Result:

```
FNAME            SNAME
----------       -----------
ANIL             SHARMA
SACHIN           NIMJE
```

Listing 8.18: Displaying the Advertisement Date

```
SELECT ADVDATE FROM ADVERTISEMENT;
```

Result:

```
ADVDATE
--------
12-MAR-00
15-APR-00
```

Listing 8.19: Displaying the ROLLNO for a Particular Batch

```
SELECT ROLLNO
FROM ENROLLMENT
WHERE BATCHCODE = 10001;
```

Result:

```
ROLLNO
--------
10001100
```

Listing 8.20: Displaying all Expenditure Types from EXPMASTER

```
SELECT EXPTYPE
FROM EXPMASTER;
```

Result:

```
EXPTYPE
-------
CASH
```

Listing 8.21: Displaying the Details of Person who Enquired about a Particular Course

```
SELECT * FROM ENQUIRY
WHERE COURSECODE = 10;
```

Result:

```
ENQUIRYNO     FNAME       SNAME      COURSECODE   PLOTNO    STREET
--------      --------    -----      ---------    -------   ---------
CITY          PINCODE     PHONE      ENQUIRYDA    REFCODE   E
--------      --------    -----      ---------    -------   ---------
110001        ANIL        SHARMA     10           23D       RAMNAGAR
NAGPUR        01-JUL-00   1001       Y
```

Listing 8.22: Displaying the Details about ENROLLMENT

```
SELECT * FROM ENROLLMENT;
```

Result:

```
ROLLNO       ENQUIRYNO     BATCHCODE    ENROLLDAT
-------      ----------    ---------    -----------
20002001     100826        20002        01-JUL-00
20002003     100827        20002        11-JUL-00
20002009     100844        20002        01-JUL-00
20002005     100830        20002        01-JUL-00
20002010     100845        20002        01-JUL-00
10001100     110001        10001        01-JUL-00

6 rows selected.
```

Listing 8.23: Displaying the Contents of EXPENDITURE

```
SELECT * FROM EXPENDITURE;
```

Result:

```
EXPCODE AMOUNT   EXPDATE     CHEQUENO BANKNAME REMARK BATCHCODE
------- ------   -------     -------- -------- ------ --------
100     20000    12-SEP-00       20002     101        200      20002
```

Listing 8.24: Displaying the Installments Having Status N

```
SELECT * FROM INSTALLMENT
WHERE INSTALLMENTSTATUS = 'N';
```

Result:

```
ROLLNO       INDATE       AMOUNT     I
------       ---------    ------     ---
20002001     12-AUG-00    5000       N
20002001     12-SEP-00    5000       N
20002003     12-JUL-00    5000       N
20002003     15-SEP-00    5000       N
```

Listing 8.25: Displaying the Syllabus of a Particular Course

```
SELECT SYLLABUS
FROM COURSE
WHERE COURSECODE = 10;
```

Result:

```
SYLLABUS
----------------------
SQL,PLSQL,JDBC,JSP
```

Listing 8.26: Displaying the Contents of Expenditure Master

```
SELECT * FROM EXPMASTER;
```

Result:

```
EXPCODE      EXPNAME      EXPT      NETEXP
101          ADVT         CASH      4000
```

Listing 8.27: Displaying the Contents of FEESPAID

```
SELECT * FROM  FEESPAID;
```

Result:

```
ROLLNO          PAYDATE          AMOUNT     CHEQUENO        BANKNAME         REMARKS
20002001        25-JUL-01        5000
20002001        25-AUG-01        5000
20002003        25-JUL-01        5000
11001100        10-JUL-99        3000
20002154        05-JUL-00        24000
```

Cartesian Product Exercises

Listing 8.28: Displaying the COURSENAME, STARTINGDATE of all Batches

```
SELECT COURSENAME, BATCHCODE, STARTINGDATE
FROM BATCH, COURSE
WHERE BATCH.COURSECODE=COURSE.COURSECODE;
```

Result:

```
COURSENAME       BATCHCODE        STARTINGD
-----------      ----------       ---------
JAVA             20002            01-JUL-01
ORACLE           10002            23-JAN-99
ORACLE           10001            11-JAN-99
ORACLE           10003            25-JAN-99
```

Listing 8.29: Displaying the COURSENAME, BATCHCODE, STARTINGDATE for a Particular BATCH

```
SELECT COURSENAME,BATCHCODE,STARTINGDATE
FROM BATCH,COURSE
WHERE BATCH.COURSECODE = COURSE.COURSECODE
AND BATCH.BATCHCODE = 10001;
```

Result:

```
COURSENAME       BATCHCODE        STARTINGD
----------       ---------        ---------
ORACLE           10001            11-JAN-99
```

Listing 8.30: Displaying media name, date of advertisement for a Specified Course

```
SELECT MEDIANAME,ADVDATE
FROM ENQUIRY,ADVERTISEMENT
WHERE ENQUIRY.REFCODE = ADVERTISEMENT.REFCODE
AND ENQUIRY.COURSECODE = 10;
```

Result:

```
MEDIANAME                ADVDATE
-------------            --------
TIMES OF INDIA           12-MAR-00
```

Listing 8.31: Displaying RollNo and Name of Students for a Particular Batch

```
SELECT ROLLNO,FNAME,SNAME
FROM ENQUIRY,ENROLLMENT
WHERE ENQUIRY.ENQUIRYNO = ENROLLMENT.ENQUIRYNO
AND ENROLLMENT.BATCHCODE = 10001;
```

Result:

```
ROLLNO   FNAME       SNAME
-------- -----       -----
10001100 ANIL        SHARMA
```

Listing 8.32: Displaying the ROLLNO, ADDRESS of Students in Specified BATCH

```
SELECT ROLLNO,PLOTNO,STREET,CITY,PINCODE,PHONE
FROM ENQUIRY,ENROLLMENT
WHERE ENQUIRY.ENQUIRYNO = ENROLLMENT.ENQUIRYNO
AND ENROLLMENT.BATCHCODE = 10001;
```

Or

```
SELECT ROLLNO,(PLOTNO||'
 '||STREET||'
 '||CITY||'
 '||PINCODE||'
 '||PHONE) ADDRESS
FROM ENQUIRY,ENROLLMENT
WHERE ENQUIRY.ENQUIRYNO=ENROLLMENT.ENQUIRYNO
AND ENROLLMENT.BATCHCODE=10001;
```

Result:

```
ROLLNO          PLOTNO          STREET          CITY          PINCODE          PHONE
-------         ------          -------         -----         -------          ------
10001100        23D             RAMNAGAR        NAGPUR
```

Listing 8.33: Displaying the ROLLNO, NAME, and FEESPAID for a Particular BATCH

```
SELECT ENROLLMENT.ROLLNO,FNAME, SNAME, ENROLLMENT. BATCHCODE,          FEESPAID.AMOUNT
FROM ENQUIRY,ENROLLMENT,FEESPAID
WHERE ENQUIRY.ENQUIRYNO = ENROLLMENT.ENQUIRYNO
AND ENROLLMENT.ROLLNO = FEESPAID.ROLLNO
AND ENROLLMENT.BATCHCODE = 10001;
```

Result:

```
ROLLNO          FNAME           SNAME           BATCHCODE          AMOUNT
----------      ----------      ------          ---------          -------
10001100        ANIL            SHARMA           10001             3000
```

Listing 8.34: Displaying the ROLLNO, NAME, INSTALLMENT DATE, AMOUNT for a Particular BATCH

```
SELECT ENROLLMENT.ROLLNO, ENQUIRY.FNAME, ENQUIRY. SNAME,
  INSTALLMENT.INSTALLMENTDATE, INSTALLMENT.AMOUNT
FROM ENQUIRY, ENROLLMENT, INSTALLMENT
WHERE ENQUIRY.ENQUIRYNO = ENROLLMENT.ENQUIRYNO
AND ENROLLMENT.ROLLNO = INSTALLMENT.ROLLNO
AND ENROLLMENT.BATCHCODE = 10001;
```

Result:

```
ROLLNO          FNAME           SNAME           INSTALLME          AMOUNT
---------       ----------      ---------       ----------         ---------
10001100        ANIL            SHARMA          15-OCT-00         10000
```

Listing 8.35: Displaying the COURSENAME and Details of all Batches

```
SELECT COURSE.COURSENAME, BATCH.BATCHCODE, BATCH. STARTINGDATE,          BATCH.DURATION,
  BATCH.COURSEFEES, BATCH. NETINCOME, BATCH.EXPECTEDINCOME,              BATCH.LASTNO FROM
  COURSE, BATCH WHERE COURSE.COURSECODE = BATCH.COURSECODE;
```

Result:

```
COURSENAME      BATCHCODE        STARTINGD       DURATION          COURSEFEES
----------      -------------- ----------        ---------         -----------
NETINCOME       EXPECTEDINCOME  LASTNO
----------      -------------- ----------
JAVA            20002           01-JUL-01        180               24000
0               0               1
```

```
ORACLE            10002           23-JAN-99        3              4000
2000              0               2

ORACLE            10001           11-JAN-99        2              3000
0                 6000            5

ORACLE            10003           25-JAN-99        4              3000
0                 7000            7
```

Listing 8.36: Displaying the ROLLNO, NAME of Students who Paid Fees More than 5000 at a Time

```
SELECT ENROLLMENT.ROLLNO, ENQUIRY.FNAME ||''|| ENQUIRY.SNAME
FROM ENQUIRY,ENROLLMENT,FEESPAID
WHERE ENQUIRY.ENQUIRYNO = ENROLLMENT.ENQUIRYNO
AND ENROLLMENT.ROLLNO = FEESPAID.ROLLNO
AND FEESPAID.AMOUNT > 2000;
```

Result:

```
ROLLNO        ENQUIRY.FNAME||''||ENQUIRY.SNAME
--------      ----------------------------------
10001100      ANILSHARMA
```

Renaming Exercises

Listing 8.37: Displaying the BATCHCODE of Batches Having NETINCOME More than Specified Batch

```
SELECT B.BATCHCODE
FROM BATCH B
WHERE B.NETINCOME > (SELECT B1.NETINCOME
FROM BATCH B1
WHERE B1.BATCHCODE = 10001);
```

Result:

```
BATCHCODE
-----------
   10002
```

Or

```
SELECT B.BATCHCODE
FROM BATCH B, BATCH B1
WHERE B.NETINCOME > B1.NETINCOME
AND B1.BATCHCODE = 10001;
```

Result:

```
BATCHCODE
------------
   10002
```

Listing 8.38: Displaying Names of Persons Having ADDRESS in All Those Cities where a Specified Person is Living

```
SELECT E1.FNAME||' '||E1.SNAME NAME
FROM ENQUIRY E1, ENQUIRY E2
WHERE E1.CITY = E2.CITY
AND E2.FNAME = 'ANIL'
AND E2.SNAME = 'SHARMA';
```

Result:

```
NAME
---------------
ANIL SHARMA
SACHIN NIMJE
```

Listing 8.39: Displaying the BATCHCODE of Batches Having EXPECTEDINCOME More than any Specified Batch. All the Batches Should be of the Same Course

```
SELECT B1.BATCHCODE
FROM BATCH B1, BATCH B2
WHERE B1.EXPECTEDINCOME > B2.EXPECTEDINCOME
AND B1.COURSECODE = B2.COURSECODE
AND B2.BATCHCODE = 10001;
```

Result:

```
BATCHCODE
-----------
10003
```

Listing 8.40: Displaying the Names of Students who are in the Same Batch in which Person ANIL is Enrolled

```
SELECT E1.FNAME||' '||E1.SNAME NAME
FROM ENQUIRY E1, ENQUIRY E2, ENROLLMENT EN1, ENROLLMENT EN2 WHERE E2.FNAME =
   'ANIL'
AND EN1.ENQUIRYNO = E2.ENQUIRYNO
AND EN1.BATCHCODE = EN2.BATCHCODE
AND EN2.ENQUIRYNO = E1.ENQUIRYNO;
```

Result:

```
NAME
--------------
ANIL SHARMA
```

Listing 8.41: Displaying the Names of Students who are Enrolled in the Same Course where ANIL is Enrolled

```
SELECT E1.FNAME||' '||E1.SNAME FROM ENQUIRY E1, ENQUIRY E2, ENROLLMENT
   EN1,ENROLLMENT EN2,BATCH B1,BATCH B2
WHERE E2.FNAME = 'ANIL'
AND   E2.ENQUIRYNO = EN1.ENQUIRYNO
AND   EN1.BATCHCODE = B1.BATCHCODE
AND   B1.COURSECODE = B2.COURSECODE
AND   B2.BATCHCODE = EN2.BATCHCODE
AND   EN2.ENQUIRYNO = E1.ENQUIRYNO;
```

Result:

```
E1.FNAME||''||E1.SNAME
------------------------
ANIL SHARMA
```

IN/EXIST Exercises

Listing 8.42: Displaying the Details of BATCH Having a Specified COURSENAME

```
SELECT * FROM BATCH
WHERE COURSECODE IN
(SELECT COURSECODE
FROM COURSE
WHERE COURSENAME = 'ORACLE');
```

Result:

```
BATCHCODE          COURSECODE       STARTINGD          DURATION          COURSEFEES
----------         ----------       ---------          ----------        ----------
NETINCOME          EXPECTEDINCOME LASTNO
----------         -------------  -------
  10003            10        25-JAN-99            4              3000
   0               7000         7

  10001            10        11-JAN-99            2              3000
   0               6000         5

 10002             10        23-JAN-99            3              4000
  2000             0            2
```

Listing 8.43: Displaying the Names of Persons Enrolled in a Specified BATCH by Using IN

```
SELECT FNAME
FROM ENQUIRY E1
WHERE E1.ENQUIRYNO IN (SELECT ENQUIRYNO FROM ENROLLMENT
WHERE BATCHCODE = 10001);
```

Result:

```
FNAME
----------
ANIL
```

Listing 8.44: Displaying the Names of Persons Enrolled in a Specified BATCH by Using EXISTS

```
SELECT FNAME
FROM ENQUIRY E1
WHERE EXISTS (SELECT * FROM ENROLLMENT
WHERE ENQUIRYNO = E1.ENQUIRYNO
AND BATCHCODE = 10001);
```

Result:

```
FNAME
-------
ANIL
```

Listing 8.45: Displaying Names of Persons Enrolled in a Specified Course

```
SELECT FNAME
FROM ENQUIRY E1,ENROLLMENT EN1
WHERE E1.ENQUIRYNO = EN1.ENQUIRYNO
AND EN1.BATCHCODE
IN (SELECT BATCHCODE
FROM BATCH
WHERE COURSECODE = 10);
```

Result:

```
FNAME
------
ANIL
```

Listing 8.46: Assuming that One Person is Enrolled in Multiple Batches, Listing All Persons Enrolled in All Those Batches where ANIL has Enrolled

```
SELECT FNAME
FROM ENQUIRY E1
WHERE
NOT EXISTS((SELECT EN2.BATCHCODE
```

```
FROM ENQUIRY E2,ENROLLMENT EN2
WHERE E2.FNAME = 'ANIL'
AND E2.ENQUIRYNO = EN2.ENQUIRYNO)
MINUS
(SELECT EN3.BATCHCODE
FROM ENQUIRY E3,ENROLLMENT EN3
WHERE E3.ENQUIRYNO = EN3.ENQUIRYNO
AND E3.FNAME = E1.FNAME));
```

Result:

```
FNAME
-------
ANIL
```

Listing 8.47: Assuming that One Person is Enrolled in Multiple Courses, Listing Names of Persons Enrolled in All Those Courses

```
SELECT FNAME
FROM ENQUIRY E1
WHERE
NOT EXISTS((SELECT EN2.BATCHCODE
FROM ENQUIRY E2,ENROLLMENT EN2
WHERE E2.FNAME = 'ANIL'
AND E2.ENQUIRYNO = EN2.ENQUIRYNO)
MINUS
(SELECT EN3.BATCHCODE
FROM ENQUIRY E3,ENROLLMENT EN3
WHERE E3.ENQUIRYNO = EN3.ENQUIRYNO
AND E3.FNAME = E1.FNAME));
```

Result:

```
FNAME
--------
ANIL
```

Listing 8.48: Assuming One Person is Enrolled in Multiple Batches, Listing Persons Enrolled in All Those Batches where ANIL has Enrolled

```
SELECT E1.FNAME
FROM ENQUIRY E1
WHERE NOT EXISTS
((SELECT B1.COURSECODE
FROM BATCH B1,ENROLLMENT EN1,ENQUIRY E2
WHERE B1.BATCHCODE = EN1.BATCHCODE
AND EN1.ENQUIRYNO = E2.ENQUIRYNO
AND E2.FNAME = 'ANIL')
MINUS
(SELECT B2.COURSECODE
FROM BATCH B2,ENROLLMENT EN2
WHERE B2.BATCHCODE = EN2.BATCHCODE
AND EN2.ENQUIRYNO = E1.ENQUIRYNO));
```

Result:

```
FNAME
-----------
ANIL
```

Listing 8.49: Assuming that One Person is Enrolled in Multiple Courses, Listing Names of Persons Enrolled in All Those Courses in which Anil has Enrolled

```
SELECT E1.FNAME
FROM ENQUIRY E1
WHERE NOT EXISTS
((SELECT B1.COURSECODE
FROM BATCH B1,ENROLLMENT EN1,ENQUIRY E2
WHERE B1.BATCHCODE = EN1.BATCHCODE
AND EN1.ENQUIRYNO = E2.ENQUIRYNO
AND E2.FNAME = 'ANIL')
MINUS
(SELECT B2.COURSECODE
FROM BATCH B2,ENROLLMENT EN2
WHERE B2.BATCHCODE = EN2.BATCHCODE
AND EN2.ENQUIRYNO = E1.ENQUIRYNO));
```

Result:

```
FNAME
--------
ANIL
```

Listing 8.50: Displaying the Names of Students who have Not Paid Any Fees

```
SELECT FNAME
FROM ENQUIRY E1
WHERE EN_ST = 'Y'
AND
NOT EXISTS
(SELECT * FROM ENROLLMENT EN1,FEESPAID F1
WHERE EN1.ENQUIRYNO = E1.ENQUIRYNO
AND EN1.ROLLNO = F1.ROLLNO);
```

Result:

```
FNAME
----------
SACHIN
```

Listing 8.51: Displaying the Names of Persons Enrolled in BATCH Having Starting Date before the Specified Date

```
SELECT FNAME
FROM ENQUIRY E1,ENROLLMENT EN1,BATCH B1
WHERE E1.ENQUIRYNO = EN1.ENQUIRYNO
AND EN1.BATCHCODE = B1.BATCHCODE
AND EXISTS(SELECT * FROM BATCH B2
WHERE STARTINGDATE < '23-JAN-99'
AND B2.BATCHCODE = B1.BATCHCODE);
```

Result:

```
FNAME
----------
ANIL
```

Listing 8.52: Displaying the Names of Students Living in Nagpur and Enrolled in Course 10

```
SELECT FNAME
FROM  ENQUIRY E1
WHERE E1.CITY = 'NAGPUR'
AND EXISTS(SELECT * FROM ENROLLMENT EN1,BATCH B1
WHERE EN1.BATCHCODE = B1.BATCHCODE
```

```
AND EN1.ENQUIRYNO = E1.ENQUIRYNO
AND B1.COURSECODE = 10);
```

Result:

```
FNAME
--------
ANIL
```

Aggregate Function Exercises

Listing 8.53: Displaying the Average Income from Each BATCH

```
SELECT BATCHCODE, AVG(NETINCOME) FROM BATCH
GROUP BY BATCH.BATCHCODE;
```

Result:

```
BATCHCODE AVG(NETINCOME)
--------- --------------
    20002              0
    10002           2000
    10001              0
    10003              0
```

Listing 8.54: Displaying the Names of BATCH Having Average income> 1000

```
SELECT BATCHCODE
FROM BATCH
GROUP BY BATCH.BATCHCODE
HAVING AVG(BATCH.NETINCOME) > 1000;
```

Result:

```
 BATCHCODE
 ----------
     10002
```

Listing 8.55: Finding out the Name of the Course Having Maximum NETINCOME

```
SELECT C.COURSENAME
FROM COURSE C
WHERE C.COURSECODE
IN(SELECT B.COURSECODE
FROM BATCH B
GROUP BY B.COURSECODE
HAVING SUM(B.NETINCOME) >= ALL
(SELECT SUM(B1.NETINCOME)FROM BATCH B1
GROUP BY (B1.COURSECODE)));
```

Result:

```
COURSENAME
---------
ORACLE
```

Listing 8.56: Finding Out the Name of the Course Having the Maximum Difference between NETINCOME and EXPECTEDINCOME

```
SELECT C.COURSENAME
FROM COURSE C
WHERE C.COURSECODE
IN(SELECT B.COURSECODE
FROM BATCH B
GROUP BY B.COURSECODE
HAVING (SUM(B.EXPECTEDINCOME) - SUM(B.NETINCOME)) >= ALL
```

```
(SELECT (SUM(B1.EXPECTEDINCOME) - SUM(B1.NETINCOME)) FROM BATCH  B1
GROUP BY (B1.COURSECODE)));
```

Result:

```
COURSENAME
---------
ORACLE
```

Listing 8.57: Finding Out the Total Fees Paid by a Particular Student

```
SELECT SUM(AMOUNT) FROM FEESPAID
WHERE ROLLNO = 10001100;
```

Result:

```
SUM(AMOUNT)
-----------
   3000
```

Listing 8.58: Finding Out the Difference between Expected Fees and Total Fees for a Particular Roll Number

```
SELECT (BATCH.COURSEFEES - F1.TOTAL)
FROM (SELECT ROLLNO ROLLNO1, SUM(AMOUNT) TOTAL
FROM FEESPAID
GROUP BY (ROLLNO)) F1, BATCH, ENROLLMENT
WHERE F1.ROLLNO1 = ENROLLMENT.ROLLNO
AND ENROLLMENT.BATCHCODE = BATCH.BATCHCODE
AND F1.ROLLNO1 = 10001100;
```

Result:

```
(BATCH.COURSEFEES - F1.TOTAL)
-----------------------------
                0
```

Listing 8.59: Finding Out the Income Course Wise

```
SELECT A.COURSECODE, SUM(B.NETINCOME)
FROM COURSE A, BATCH B
WHERE A.COURSECODE = B.COURSECODE
GROUP BY A.COURSECODE;
```

Result:

```
COURSECODE      SUM(B.NETINCOME)
----------      ----------------
        20                     0
        10                  2000
```

Listing 8.60: Finding Out Sum of Fees and ROLLNO for a Specified Course

```
SELECT D.ROLLNO, SUM(A.AMOUNT)
FROM FEESPAID A, COURSE B, BATCH C, ENROLLMENT D
WHERE B.COURSENAME = 'JAVA'
AND A.ROLLNO = D.ROLLNO
AND D.BATCHCODE = C.BATCHCODE
AND C.COURSECODE = B.COURSECODE
GROUP BY (D.ROLLNO)
/
```

Result:

```
ROLLNO   SUM(A.AMOUNT)
---------        ------------
20002001 10000
20002003 5000
```

Listing 8.61: Finding Out the Total Amount Collected

```
SELECT COUNT(ENQUIRYNO) FROM ENQUIRY
WHERE COURSECODE = 10
/
```

Result:

```
COUNT(ENQUIRYNO)
----------------
   1
```

Listing 8.62: Finding Out the Number of Enquiries for a Specified Advertisement Code

```
SELECT COUNT(ENQUIRYNO) FROM ENQUIRY
WHERE REFCODE = 1001
/
```

Result:

```
COUNT(ENQUIRYNO)
----------------
          1
```

Listing 8.63: Finding Out the Number of Enquires for a Specified Course

```
SELECT COUNT(ENQUIRYNO) FROM ENQUIRY WHERE COURSECODE = 10;
```

Result:

```
COUNT(ENQUIRYNO)
---------------
   1
```

Date Function Exercises

Listing 8.64: Finding Out the Sum of Amount Collected Month Wise

```
SELECT TO_CHAR(A.FEESPAIDDATE,'MM'), TO_CHAR (A. FEESPAIDDATE, 'MON'),
  SUM(A.AMOUNT) FROM FEESPAID A
GROUP BY TO_CHAR(A. FEESPAIDDATE,'MM'), TO_CHAR (A. FEESPAIDDATE, 'MON')
ORDER BY 1;
```

Result:

```
TO       TO_  SUM(A.AMOUNT)
--       ---  -------------
07       JUL          37000
08       AUG           5000
```

Listing 8.65: Finding Out the Sum of Amount Collected Weekly (yearly week)

```
SELECT TO_CHAR(FEESPAIDDATE,'IW'),SUM(AMOUNT)
FROM FEESPAID
GROUP BY TO_CHAR(FEESPAIDDATE,'IW');
```

Result:

```
TO  SUM(AMOUNT)
--  -----------
27        27000
30        10000
34         5000
```

Listing 8.66: Finding Out the Monthly and Weekly Income

```
SELECT TO_CHAR(FEESPAIDDATE,'MON'), TO_CHAR(FEESPAIDDATE, 'WW'), SUM(AMOUNT)
FROM FEESPAID
GROUP BY TO_CHAR(FEESPAIDDATE,'MON'),TO_CHAR(FEESPAIDDATE, 'WW')
/
```

Result:

```
TO_ TO SUM(AMOUNT)
--- -- -----------
JUL 30       10000
AUG 34        5000
JUL 28        3000
JUL 27       24000
```

Listing 8.67: Finding Out the ROLLNO and Name of the Students who have Not Paid the Amount According to their Installment Dates

```
SELECT EN1.ROLLNO,E1.FNAME, E1.SNAME
FROM ENROLLMENT EN1,ENQUIRY E1,INSTALLMENT I1
WHERE EN1.ENQUIRYNO = E1.ENQUIRYNO
AND EN1.ROLLNO = I1.ROLLNO
AND NOT EXISTS (SELECT * FROM FEESPAID F1
WHERE I1.ROLLNO = F1.ROLLNO
AND I1.AMOUNT = F1.AMOUNT
AND I1.INSTALLMENTDATE = F1. FEESPAIDDATE)
/
```

Result:

```
ROLLNO          FNAME           SNAME
----------      -----------     --------------
10001100        ANIL            SHARMA
```

Listing 8.68: Finding Out Expenditure Month Wise

```
SELECT TO_CHAR(EXPDATE,'MM'), TO_CHAR(EXPDATE,'MON'), SUM(AMOUNT)
FROM EXPENDITURE
GROUP BY TO_CHAR(EXPDATE,'MM'), TO_CHAR(EXPDATE,'MON')
ORDER BY 1;
```

Result:

```
TO      TO_     SUM(AMOUNT)
--      ---     -----------
09      SEP     20000
```

Listing 8.69: Finding Out the Date Wise Enrollment for the Previous 15 Days

```
SELECT A.ENROLLMENTDATE, TO_DATE(SYSDATE) - A.ENROLLMENTDATE,          COUNT(A.ROLLNO)
FROM ENROLLMENT A
WHERE TO_DATE(SYSDATE) - A.ENROLLMENTDATE
BETWEEN 1 AND 15
AND BATCHCODE = 1001
GROUP BY A.ENROLLMENTDATE, TO_DATE(SYSDATE) - A.ENROLLMENTDATE
ORDER BY 1;
```

Result:

```
no rows selected
```

Listing 8.70: Finding Out the Quarterly Income for a Specified Course

```
SELECT TO_CHAR(STARTINGDATE,'Q'),SUM(NETINCOME)
FROM BATCH WHERE COURSECODE = 10
GROUP BY TO_CHAR(STARTINGDATE,'Q');
```

Result:

```
T SUM(NETINCOME)
- --------------
1           2000
```

Listing 8.71: Finding Out Monthly AVG Fees Paid

```
SELECT TO_CHAR(FEESPAIDDATE,'MM'), TO_CHAR(FEESPAIDDATE, 'MON'), AVG(AMOUNT)
FROM FEESPAID
GROUP BY TO_CHAR(FEESPAIDDATE,'MM'), TO_CHAR(FEESPAIDDATE,'MON')
ORDER BY 1;
```

Result:

```
TO        TO_       AVG(AMOUNT)
--        ---       -----------
07        JUL          9250
08        AUG          5000
```

Listing 8.72: Finding Out Monthly Expenditure

```
SELECT TO_CHAR(EXPDATE,'MM'),
TO_CHAR (EXPDATE,'MON'), AVG(AMOUNT)
FROM EXPENDITURE
GROUP BY TO_CHAR(EXPDATE,'MM'),
TO_CHAR (EXPDATE, 'MON')
ORDER BY 1;
```

Result:

```
TO        TO_       AVG(AMOUNT)
--        ---       -----------
09        SEP         20000
```

Listing 8.73: Calculating Date Wise Response for an Advertisement

```
SELECT TO_CHAR(ENQuiryDATE),COUNT(ENQUIRYNO)
FROM ADVERTISEMENT,ENQUIRY
WHERE ADVERTISEMENT.REFCODE = ENQUIRY.REFCODE
GROUP BY TO_CHAR(ENQuiryDATE);
```

Result:

```
TO_CHAR(E         COUNT(ENQUIRYNO)
---------         ----------------
01-JUL-00                 1
01-SEP-00                 1
```

SQL Function Exercises

Listing 8.74: Finding Out Details of Persons Having Spelling like ANIL

```
SELECT * FROM ENQUIRY
WHERE FNAME LIKE 'ANIL'
/
```

Result:

```
ENQUIRYNO     FNAME        SNAME        COURSECODE     PLOTNO      STREET
---------     -----        -----        -----------    -------     --------
CITY          PINCODE      PHONE        ENQUIRYDA      REFCODE     E
------        --------     --------     -----------    --------    ------
110001        ANIL         SHARMA        10              23D        RAMNAGAR
NAGPUR        01-JUL-00    1001         Y
```

Listing 8.75: Finding Out the Number of Persons whose Name Starts with S

```
SELECT COUNT(FNAME) FROM ENQUIRY
WHERE FNAME LIKE 'S%';
```

Result:

```
COUNT(FNAME)
-----------
   1
```

Listing 8.76: Replacing All Names with the First Character Capital and Others in Lower Case

```
UPDATE ENQUIRY
SET FNAME = INITCAP(FNAME);
SELECT INITCAP(FNAME) FROM ENQUIRY;
```

Result:

```
INITCAP(FNAME)
------------------
ANIL
SACHIN
```

Listing 8.77: Displaying Amount in the Format Rs. 99,999,99

```
SELECT TO_CHAR(EXPECTEDINCOME,'99,999,99')
FROM BATCH
/
```

Result:

```
TO_CHAR(EX
----------
         0
         0
     60,00
     70,00
```

Listing 8.78: Assume that the Statistics of Fees Collected is as Follows:

LOW	HIGH	NO OF STUDENTS
1	1000	3
1001	2000	5

```
SELECT TRUNC(A.AMOUNT, -3) + 1, ROUND((TRUNC(A. AMOUNT, -3) + 500), -3),
  COUNT(*)
FROM FEESPAID A
GROUP BY TRUNC(A.AMOUNT, -3), ROUND((TRUNC(A. AMOUNT, -3) +500), -3);
```

Result:

```
TRUNC(A.AMOUNT, -3) +1  ROUND((TRUNC(A.AMOUNT, -3) +500), -3)   COUNT(*)
----------------------- -------------------------------------   --------
3001                              4000                          1
5001                              6000                          3
24001                             25000                         1
```

Listing 8.79: Finding the Statistics for a Particular Course

```
SELECT TRUNC(A.AMOUNT,-3), ROUND((TRUNC(A.AMOUNT, -3) +500), -3), COUNT(*)
FROM FEESPAID A,ENROLLMENT B,BATCH C
WHERE A.ROLLNO = B.ROLLNO
AND B.BATCHCODE = C.BATCHCODE
AND C.COURSECODE = 10
GROUP BY TRUNC(A.AMOUNT, -3), ROUND((TRUNC(A.AMOUNT, -3) +500), -3);
```

Result:

```
TRUNC(A.AMOUNT, -3)      ROUND((TRUNC(A.AMOUNT, -3) +500), -3)   COUNT(*)
-------------------      --------------------------------------- --------
  3000                   4000                                       1
```

Listing 8.80: Finding Out the Closing Amount for Each Batch

```
select b.batchcode, sum(f.amount) from feespaid f, enrollment e, batch b
  where f.rollno =e.rollno and b.batchcode=e.batchcode group by b.batchcode
/
```

Result:

```
BATCHCODE        SUM(F.AMOUNT)
----------       -------------
   20002          15000
   10001           3000
```

Delete/Update Exercises

Listing 8.81: Deleting All Rows from COURSE

```
delete course;
```

Result:

```
2 rows deleted
```

Listing 8.82: Deleting All Rows from BATCH Having Specified BATCHCODE

```
DELETE BATCH
WHERE BATCHCODE = 10001;
```

Result:

```
1 row deleted
```

Listing 8.83: Deleting All Rows from BATCH which is Not Having Any Specified EXPECTEDINCOME

```
DELETE BATCH
WHERE EXPECTEDINCOME = 0;
```

Result:

```
2 rows deleted
```

Listing 8.84: Deleting All Rows from ENQUIRY for a Specified COURSENAME

```
DELETE ENQUIRY
WHERE COURSECODE IN
(SELECT COURSECODE FROM COURSE WHERE COURSENAME = 'ORACLE');
```

Result:

```
1 rows deleted
```

Listing 8.85: Deleting All Rows from enquiry, which are Six Months before SYSDATE and are Not Having enrollment

```
DELETE ENQUIRY
WHERE MONTHS_BETWEEN(SYSDATE,ENQUIRYDATE) > 6
AND EN_ST = 'N';
```

Result:

```
0 rows deleted
```

Listing 8.86: Updating BATCH set NETINCOME According to FEESPAID

```
UPDATE BATCH B
SET B.NETINCOME = (SELECT SUM(AMOUNT)
FROM  FEESPAID F1, ENROLLMENT EN1, BATCH B1
WHERE F1.ROLLNO = EN1.ROLLNO
AND EN1.BATCHCODE = B1.BATCHCODE
```

```
AND B1.BATCHCODE = B.BATCHCODE)
WHERE EXISTS (SELECT * FROM FEESPAID F2, ENROLLMENT
EN2, BATCH B2
WHERE F2.ROLLNO = EN2.ROLLNO
AND EN2.BATCHCODE = B2.BATCHCODE
AND B2.BATCHCODE = B.BATCHCODE);
```

Result:

```
2 rows updated
```

Listing 8.87: Updating SET EXPECTEDINCOME from INSTALLMENT

```
update BATCH d
set EXPECTEDINCOME = (select sum(a.AMOUNT)
from INSTALLMENT a,ENROLLMENT b,BATCH c
where a.ROLLNO = b.ROLLNO
and b.BATCHCODE = c.BATCHCODE
and b.BATCHCODE = d.BATCHCODE)
where d.BATCHCODE in
(SELECT BATCHCODE from ENROLLMENT,INSTALLMENT
WHERE ENROLLMENT.ROLLNO = INSTALLMENT.ROLLNO
AND ENROLLMENT.BATCHCODE = d.BATCHCODE);
```

Result:

```
2 rows updated
```

Listing 8.88: Updating LASTNO of COURSE Having Data from BATCH

```
UPDATE COURSE C1
SET C1.LASTNO = (SELECT COUNT(*)
FROM BATCH B1
WHERE B1.COURSECODE = C1.COURSECODE)
WHERE C1.COURSECODE IN
(SELECT B2.COURSECODE FROM BATCH B2
WHERE B2.COURSECODE = C1.COURSECODE);
```

Result:

```
2 rows updated
```

Listing 8.89: Deleting duplicate Rows from ENQUIRY

```
DELETE ENQUIRY A
WHERE A.ROWID NOT IN
(SELECT MAX(A1.ROWID) FROM ENQUIRY A1 WHERE A1.ENQUIRYNO = A.ENQUIRYNO);
```

Result:

```
0 rows deleted
```

9

Advanced Queries

This chapter explains the facilities provided in Structured Query Language (SQL) to retrieve information from the tree structured data and a few other advanced techniques to get information, which are used to fulfill practical needs of software applications used in banks, shops, insurance etc.

Hierarchical Queries

The hierarchical structure (Tree structure) represents the relationship between the various entities in ascending (top–down) or descending order like a tree. For example, the relationship between an employee and his/her manager is hierarchical or Tree structured, as shown in Figure 9.1:

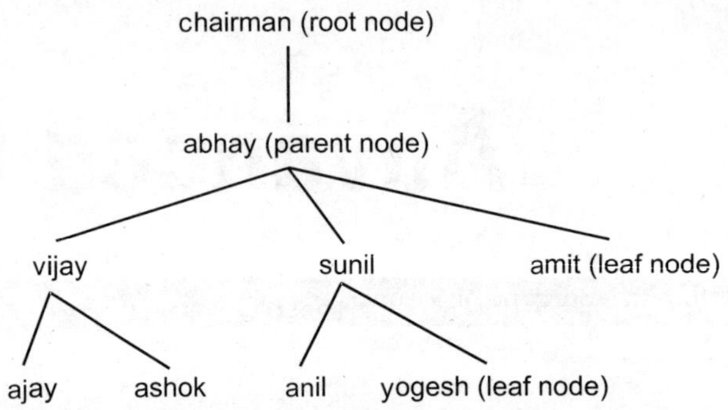

Figure 9.1: Displaying the Relationship in Hierarchical Structure

In Figure 9.1, the information of the entity is represented as node and relationship between entities is represented as links.

Table 9.1 shows the structure of the Emp2 table:

Table 9.1: Showing the Structure of the Emp2 Table

ENAME	MNAME	SALARY	RATING
ajay	vijay	1000	2
ashok	vijay	1000	1
anil	sunil	1500	2
yogesh	sunil	1500	1
vijay	abhay	3000	3
sunil	abhay	3000	1
amit	abhay	3000	2
abhay	chairman	5000	1
chairman		8000	1

Listing 9.1 shows how to create the preceding table and insert data in it:

Listing 9.1: Creating the Table and Inserting Data

```
create table emp2(ename varchar2(10), mname varchar2(10), salary number,
  rating number);
insert into emp2 values('&ename', '&mname', &salary, &rating);
```

In the `Emp2` table, the data is arranged in tree or hierarchical structure. Oracle provides direct support to extract information from the hierarchical structure.

If the table contains hierarchical data, you can select rows in the hierarchical order by using the hierarchical query clause. Listing 9.2 shows how to use the hierarchical query clause:

Listing 9.2: Using the Hierarchical Query Clause

```
select ename,mname,salary,level from emp2 start with mname='abhay' connect
  by prior ename=mname;
```

The output of Listing 9.2 is as follows:

```
ENAME     MNAME          SALARY     LEVEL
-------- ----------     ---------- ---------
amit      abhay          3000       1
sunil     abhay          3000       1
anil      sunil          1500       2
yogesh    sunil          1500       2
vijay     abhay          3000       1
ajay      vijay          1000       2
ashok       vijay          1000       2
```

In Listing 9.2:

- `start with` specifies the root rows of the query
- `connect by` specifies the relationship between the parent and child rows
- You must use `prior` operator to refer to a parent row

The query in Listing 9.2 is evaluated as follows:

start with ⟶ condition ⟶ connect by condition

- First, the root row(s) that satisfies the `start with` condition is selected.
- Oracle selects the child rows of each root row. Each child row must satisfy the condition of the `connect by` clause with respect to one of the root rows. Suppose the first row where `ename is vijay` is selected as root row. Then, the next row is selected in which `mname` is `ename` of parent row, that is, `vijay. Prior ename=mname` means the next row is selected such that ename of parent row is mname of current row. Oracle also selects the children of the parent rows by using the `connect by` clause for each parent row. The level is pseudo column, which indicates distance of any row from first root row.
- If the query contains the `where` clause, then it will be applied to each row before applying the start with clause.
- To find the children of the parent row, Oracle evaluates the `prior` expression of the `connect by` clause for the parent row and other expressions for each row in the table.
- The `connect by` condition can contain other conditions to further filter the rows selected by the query.
- The `connect by` condition cannot contain a subquery.
- If the `connect by` condition results in a loop in the hierarchy, Oracle returns an error. A loop occurs if one row is both the parent and a child of another row directly or indirectly.

Following figure shows how to evaluate an expression for the parent row of the child row in the hierarchical query using PRIOR.

The effect of prior `ename = mname`

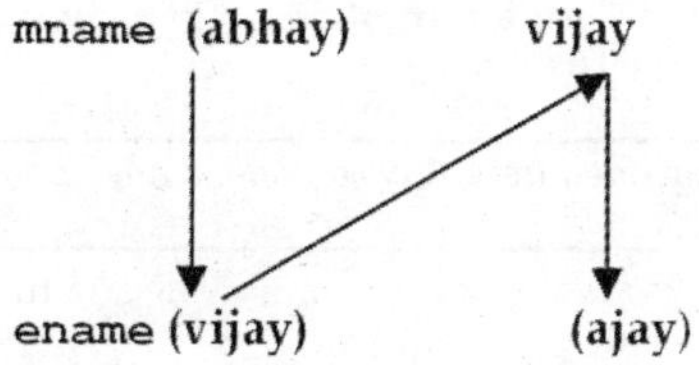

Listing 9.3: Displaying Rows without using the Start By Clause

```
Select ename, mname, level from emp2 connect by prior ename = mname;
```

If you do not use the start with clause in the query, every row acts as a root row. The output of Listing 9.3 is as follows:

```
ENAME      MNAME           LEVEL
---------- ---------- ----------
vijay      abhay               1
ajay       vijay               2
ashok      vijay               2
amit       abhay               1
sunil      abhay               1
anil       sunil               2
yogesh     sunil               2
abhay      chairman            1
vijay      abhay               2
ajay       vijay               3
ashok      vijay               3

ENAME      MNAME           LEVEL
---------- ---------- ----------
amit       abhay               2
sunil      abhay               2
anil       sunil               3
yogesh     sunil               3
anil       sunil               1
yogesh     sunil               1
ajay       vijay               1
ashok      vijay               1
chairman                       1
abhay      chairman            2
vijay      abhay               3

ENAME      MNAME           LEVEL
---------- ---------- ----------
ajay       vijay               4
ashok      vijay               4
amit       abhay               3
sunil      abhay               3
anil       sunil               4
yogesh     sunil               4

28 rows selected
```

The preceding output shows the `ename`, `mname`, and their `level` values. For each row returned by a hierarchical query, the `level` pseudocolumn returns `1` for a root node, `2` for a child of a root, and so on.

NOTE

A root node is the highest node within an inverted tree. A child node is any non-root node. A parent node is any node that has children. A leaf node is any node without children.

Listing 9.4 shows the effect of reversing the connect by condition:

Listing 9.4: Effect of Reversing CONNECT BY condition

```
select ename,mname,level from emp2 connect by prior mname = ename;
```

In Listing 9.4, the effect of prior `mname = ename` is as follows:

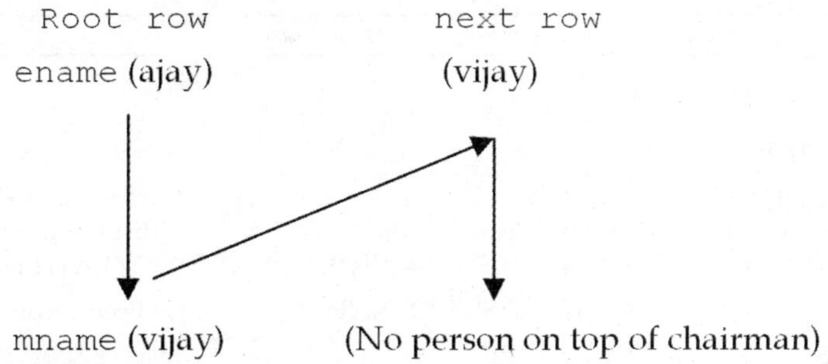

Suppose first row having mname as vijay is selected, then the next row having ename as vijay is selected.

The output of Listing 9.4 is as follows:

```
ENAME      MNAME           LEVEL
---------- ---------- ----------
abhay      chairman            1
chairman                       2
ajay       vijay               1
vijay      abhay               2
abhay      chairman            3
chairman                       4
amit       abhay               1
abhay      chairman            2
chairman                       3
anil       sunil               1
sunil      abhay               2

ENAME      MNAME           LEVEL
---------- ---------- ----------
abhay      chairman            3
chairman                       4
ashok      vijay               1
vijay      abhay               2
abhay      chairman            3
chairman                       4
chairman                       1
sunil      abhay               1
abhay      chairman            2
chairman                       3
vijay      abhay               1

ENAME      MNAME           LEVEL
---------- ---------- ----------
abhay      chairman            2
chairman                       3
yogesh     sunil               1
sunil      abhay               2
```

```
abhay       chairman              3
chairman                          4

28 rows selected.
```

NOTE

If you wish to print this part of the tree, you can use the `START WITH` clause.

Let's now learn to use pseudocolumns.

Using Pseudocolumns

You can use pseudocolumns, such as LEVEL to display hierarchy of tree, CONNECT_BY_ISLEAF to test whether the node has a child or not, and SYS_CONNECT_BY_PATH to display the path from the root node. Listing 9.5 shows the use of CONNECT_BY_ISLEAF and SYS_CONNECT_BY_PATH pseudocolumns:

Listing 9.5: Using CONNECT_BY_ISLEAF and SYS_CONNECT_BY_PATH Pseudocolumns

```
select ename,connect_by_isleaf isleaf,
sys_connect_by_path(ename,'/') abspath,
level
from emp2
start with ename='chairman'
connect by prior ename=mname
/
```

The output of Listing 9.5 is as follows:

```
ENAME            ISLEAF          ABSPATH                          LEVEL
----------     ----------      --------------------             ----------
chairman              0        /chairman                          1

abhay                 0         /chairman/abhay                   2
ENAME              ISLEAF       ABSPATH                           LEVEL
---------- ----------           ----------------------            -------
amit                  1         /chairman/abhay/amit               3

sunil                 0         /chairman/abhay/sunil              3

ENAME              ISLEAF       ABSPATH                            LEVEL
---------- ----------           ----------------------            -------
anil                  1         /chairman/abhay/sunil/anil        4

yogesh                1         /chairman/abhay/sunil/yogesh       4

ENAME              ISLEAF       ABSPATH                            LEVEL
---------- ----------           ----------------------            -------

vijay                 0         /chairman/abhay/vijay             3


ENAME              ISLEAF       ABSPATH                            LEVEL
---------- ----------           ----------------------            -------
ajay                  1         /chairman/abhay/vijay/ajay        4

ashok                 1         /chairman/abhay/vijay/ashok       4

9 rows selected
```

NOTE

If there is a cycle in a query, then the query is terminated by the following error:

ERROR:

ORA-01436: CONNECT BY loop in user data

When same node is ancestor or successor of another node directly or indirectly, then it is known as cycle. For example, if data is as follows:

ENAME	MNAME
abhay	vijay
vijay	saurav
saurav	abhay

In the preceding data, abhay is ancestor as well as successor of saurav so there is cycle.

If you want to display the data containing a cycle, you can use the CONNECT BY `NOCYCLE` clause, if CONNECT BY LOOP exists in query.

CONNECT _BY_ISCYCLE indicates 1 when cycle is detected. Listing 9.6 shows the code to display the data containing a cycle using the `ISCYCLE` pseudocolumn:

Listing 9.6: Using the ISCYCLE Pseudocolumn

```
select ename,connect_by_isleaf isleaf,
sys_connect_by_path(ename,'/') abspath,
level ,
connect_by_iscycle cycle
from emp2
start with ename='vijay'
connect by nocycle prior ename=mname
/
```

The output of Listing 9.6 is as follows:

```
ENAME          ISLEAF          ABSPATH              LEVEL        CYCLE
----------     ----------      ----------           -------      --------
vijay          0               /vijay               1            0
ajay           1               /vijay/ajay          2            0
ashok          1               /vijay/ashok         2            0
```

If you want to preserve the relationship but sort in order by siblings then you can use ORDER BY SIBLING clause. Listing 9.7 shows the use of the ORDER BY SIBLING clause:

Listing 9.7: Using the ORDER BY SIBLING Clause

```
select ename,connect_by_isleaf isleaf,
sys_connect_by_path(ename,'/') abspath,
level
from emp2
start with ename='chairman'
connect by  prior ename=mname
order  siblings by ename
/
```

The output of Listing 9.7 is as follows:

```
ENAME          ISLEAF     ABSPATH                              LEVEL
----------   ----------   ------------------------------    ----------
chairman        0                /chairman                            1
abhay           0                /chairman/abhay                      2
amit            1                /chairman/abhay/amit                 3
sunil           0                /chairman/abhay/sunil                3
anil            1                /chairman/abhay/sunil/anil           4
```

```
yogesh          1           /chairman/abhay/sunil/yogesh          4
vijay           0           /chairman/abhay/vijay                 3
ajay            1           /chairman/abhay/vijay/ajay            4
ashok           1           /chairman/abhay/vijay/ashok           4

9 rows selected.
```

Following are some examples of CONNECT BY clause

Example 1: Listing 9.8 shows the code to display the name of employees working under SUNIL:

Listing 9.8: Displaying the Name of Employees

```
select ename from emp2 connect by prior ename = mname  start with mname =
  'sunil';
```

The output of Listing 9.8 is as follows:

```
ENAME
------
ANIL
YOGESH
```

Example 2: Suppose one additional table DEPT which is used to store information of departments as follows.

```
create table dept(ename varchar2(10), dname varchar2 (10));
```

The data in the table is as follows:

```
ENAME           DNAME
--------        ----------
AJAY            SECURITY
ASHOK           SECURITY
ANIL            ACCOUNTS
YOGESH          ACCOUNTS
VIJAY           PERSONNEL
SUNIL           PERSONNEL
AMIT            PRODUCTION
ABHAY           MANAGEMENT
CHAIRMAN        MANAGEMENT
```

Listing 9.9 shows the code to display the number of employees department wise, who are working under ABHAY:

Listing 9.9: Displaying the Number of Employees Department Wise

```
select count(*), d.dname from(select ename e1 from emp2 connect by prior
  ename = mname
start with mname = 'abhay')z, dept d
where z.e1 = d.ename group by d.dname;
```

The output of Listing 9.9 is as follows:

```
  COUNT(*)      DNAME
----------      ----------
         2      SECURITY
         2      ACCOUNTS
         1      PRODUCTION
         2      PERSONNEL
```

Let's understand the query given in Listing 9.9 by dividing it into the following steps:

- **Step 1**—In step 1, the connect by clause is used, as shown in the following code snippet:

```
select ename e1 from emp2
connect by prior ename = mname
start with mname = 'abhay';
```

The output of the preceding code snippet is as follows:

```
E1
----------
AMIT
SUNIL
ANIL
YOGESH
VIJAY
AJAY
ASHOK

7 rows selected
```

Since the employees of ABHAY are not given directly, the query will act as a data source for the outer query. Such queries are called inline views. They are executed only once for the outer query.

- **Step 2**—The ename from step 1 is then used for determining the department of each employee of vijay, as shown in the following code snippet:

```
select count(*),d.dname from(data from step 1)z,dept d
where z.e1 = d.ename group by  d.dname;
```

Example 3: Suppose you want to display name of employees who are not managers.

Listing 9.10 shows the code to display the name of employees who are not managers:

Listing 9.10: Displaying the Name of Employees Other than Managers

```
select e1.ename from emp2 e1
where    not exists
(select distinct e2.mname from emp2 e2 where e2.mname = e1.ename);
```

The output of Listing 9.10 is as follows:

```
ENAME
------
YOGESH
AMIT
AJAY
ANIL
ASHOK
```

Example 4: You can display the employee's level wise by grouping by level as shown in Listing 9.11:

Listing 9.11: Displaying the Employees Level Wise

```
select count('no_of_emp'),level from emp2
connect by prior ename = mname
start with ename = 'chairman'
group by level;
```

The output of Listing 9.11 is as follows:

```
COUNT('NO_OF_EMP')        LEVEL
   1                        1
   1                        2
   4                        4
   3                        3
```

Let's understand the query given in Listing 9.11 by dividing it into the following steps:

- **Step 1**—In the query, the first step is to evaluate the name and level of each employee, as shown in the following code snippet:

```
select ename, mname, level from emp2 connect by prior ename = mname start
  with ename = 'chairman';
```

The output of the preceding code snippet is as follows:

```
ENAME                    MNAME                    LEVEL
chairman                                   1
abhay                    chairman                   2
amit                     abhay                      3
sunil                    abhay                      3
anil                     sunil                      4
yogesh                   sunil                      4
vijay                    abhay                      3
ajay                     vijay                      4
ashok                    vijay                      4

9 rows selected.
```

- **Step 2**—After evaluating the name and level of each employee, the CONNECT BY condition (CONNECT BY LEVEL) is applied to the result, as shown in Listing 9.12:

Listing 9.12: Displaying the Name of the Employees at Level 3

```
select z1.ename from
(select ename e1, level l1 from emp2
connect by prior ename = mname
start with ename = 'chairman')z, emp2 z1
where z.l1 = 3 and
z.e1 = z1.ename;
```

The output of Listing 9.12 is as follows:

```
ENAME
----------
VIJAY
SUNIL
AMIT
```

Listing 9.13 shows the code to display the total salary of the employees at level 3:

Listing 9.13: Displaying the Total Salary of the Employees at Level 3

```
select sum(salary)
from emp2 z3 where
z3.ename in(select distinct z1.ename from
(select ename e1,level l1 from emp2
connect by prior ename = mname
start with ename = 'chairman')z,emp2 z1
where z.l1 = 3 and
z.e1 = z1.ename);
```

The output of Listing 9.13 is as follows:

```
SUM(SALARY)
-----------
   9000
```

Let's understand the query given in Listing 9.13 by dividing it into the following steps:

- Step 1:

```
select distinct z1.ename from
(select ename e1,level l1 from emp2
connect by prior ename = mname
start with ename = 'chairman')z, emp2 z1;
```

The output of preceding code snippet is as follows:

```
ENAME
------
AMIT
ANIL
VIJAY
YOGESH
ABHAY
CHAIRMAN
ASHOK
SUNIL
AJAY

9 rows selected.
```

- **Step 2**—The data of step 1 acts as a data source for the outer query, as shown in the following code snippet:

```
select sum(salary)
from emp2 z3 where
z3.ename in(data from step 1)
where z.l1 = 3 and
z.e1 = z1.ename);
```

Listing 9.14 shows the code to retrieve the manager having the highest rating at level 3:

Listing 9.14: Finding the Manager Having the Highest Rating at Level 3

```
select z3.ename
from emp2 z3 where
z3.ename in(select z1.ename from
(select ename e1,level l1 from emp2
connect by prior ename = mname
start with ename = 'chairman')z, emp2 z1
where z.l1 = 3 and z.e1 = z1.ename) and
z3.rating in(select max(rating)
from emp2 z3 where
z3.ename in(select z1.ename from
(select ename e1,level l1 from emp2
connect by prior ename = mname
start with ename = 'chairman')z, emp2 z1
where z.l1 = 2 and
z.e1 = z1.ename));
```

The output of Listing 9.15 is as follows:

```
ENAME
-----
SUNIL
```

Let's understand the query given in Listing 9.15 by dividing it into the following steps:

- **Step 1**—In step 1, we have calculated the level of each employee starting from the highest level, as shown in the following code snippet:

```
select ename e1,level l1 from emp2
connect by prior ename = mname
start with ename = 'chairman';
```

The output of preceding code snippet is as follows:

```
E1              L1
------    ------------
CHAIRMAN         1
ABHAY            2
AMIT             3
SUNIL            3
ANIL             4
YOGESH           4
VIJAY            3
AJAY             4
ASHOK            4

9 rows selected.
```

- **Step 2**—In step 2, we have selected the name of the employees at level 3, as shown in the following code snippet:

```
select z3.ename
from emp2 z3 where
z3.ename in(select z1.ename from
(data from step 1)z, emp2 z1
where z.l1 = 3 and
z.e1 = z1.ename);
```

The output of preceding code snippet is as follows:

```
ENAME
-----
VIJAY
SUNIL
AMIT
```

- **Step 3**—In step 3, we have selected the name of the employees having maximum rating at level 3, as shown in the following code snippet:

```
select max(rating)
from emp2 z3 where
z3.ename in(select z1.ename from
(data from step 1)z, emp2 z1
where    z.l1 = 2 and
z.e1 = z1.ename);
```

The output of preceding code snippet is as follows:

```
MAX(RATING)
-----------
     1
```

- **Step 4**—The data from step2 acts as a table and where condition is applied using that data.

```
(data from step 2)
  and
z3.rating in
(data from step 3);
```

Listing 9.15 shows the code to retrieve the number of employees at the third highest level:

Listing 9.15: Retrieving the Number of Employees at the Third Highest Level

```
select count(z3.e1) from
(select ename e1,level l1 from emp2 connect by prior ename = mname
start with ename = 'chairman')z3,(select z2.l1 l1 from
(select distinct level l1 from emp2
```

```
connect by prior ename = mname
start with ename = 'chairman')z1,
(select distinct level l1 from emp2
connect by prior ename = mname
start with ename = 'chairman')z2
where z2.l1 >= z1.l1
group by z2.l1
having count(*) = 3)z4
where z3.l1 = z4.l1;
```

The output of Listing 9.15 is as follows:

```
Count(z3.E1)
------------
3
```

Let's understand the query given in Listing 9.15 by dividing it into the following steps:

- **Step 1**—The level of each employee starting from the highest level is determined, as shown in the following code snippet:

```
select distinct level l1 from emp2
connect by prior ename = mname start with ename = 'chairman';
```

The output of preceding code snippet is as follows:

```
L1
---
1
2
3
4
```

- **Step 2**—The third highest level is determined, as shown in the following code snippet:

```
select z2.l1 l1 from
(data from step 1)z1, (data from step 1)z2 where
z2.l1 >= z1.l1 group by z2.l1 having count(*) = 3;
```

The output of preceding code snippet is as follows:

```
L1
--
3
```

- **Step 3**—The name and level of each employee is retrieved, as shown in the following code snippet:

```
select ename e1, level l1 from emp2 connect by prior ename = mname
start with ename = 'chairman';
```

The output of preceding code snippet is as follows:

```
E1              L1
--------        ------
CHAIRMAN           1
ABHAY              2
AMIT               3
SUNIL              3
ANIL               4
YOGESH             4
VIJAY              3
AJAY               4
ASHOK              4

9 rows selected.
```

- **Step 4**—Performing count on the basis of data retrieved in step 3 and 4

```
select count(*) from
(data from step 3)z3, (data from step 2)z4 where
z3.l1 = z4.l1;
```

Similar to retrieving number of employees at level 3, you can retrieve the number of employees along with the sum of their salaries at level 2, as shown in Listing 9.16:

Listing 9.16: Retrieving the Number of Employees and the Sum of their Salaries at Level 2

```
select count('no_of_emp'), sum(z3.s1) from
(select ename e1,salary s1, level l1 from emp2 connect by prior
ename = mname
start with ename = 'chairman')z3,
(select z2.l1 l1 from
(select distinct level l1 from emp2
connect by prior ename = mname
start with ename = 'chairman')z1,
(select distinct level l1 from emp2
connect by prior ename = mname
start with ename = 'chairman')z2
where z2.l1 >= z1.l1 group by z2.l1
having count(*) = 2)z4 where z3.l1 = z4.l1;
```

The output of Listing 9.16 is as follows:

```
COUNT('NO_OF_EMP')          SUM(Z3.S1)
------------------          ---------
   1                        5000
```

Let's understand the query given in Listing 9.16 by dividing it into the following steps:

- Step 1:

```
select ename e1,salary s1, level l1 from emp2 connect by prior ename = mname
start with ename = 'chairman';
```

The output of preceding code snippet is as follows:

```
E1              S1              L1
-------         -------
CHAIRMAN        8000            1
ABHAY           5000            2
AMIT            3000            3
SUNIL           3000            3
ANIL            1500            4
YOGESH          1500            4
VIJAY           3000            3
AJAY            1000            4
ASHOK           1000            4

9 rows selected.
```

- Step 2:

```
select distinct level l1 from emp2
connect by prior ename = mname start with ename = 'chairman';
```

The output of preceding code snippet is as follows:

```
L1
-------
1
2
3
4
```

- Step 3:

```
select count('no_of_emp'), sum(z3.s1) from
(select ename e1,salary s1, level l1 from emp2 connect by prior
ename = mname start with ename = 'chairman')z3, (select z2.l1 l1 from
(select distinct level l1 from emp2 connect by prior ename = mname
start with ename = 'chairman' )z1,
(select distinct level l1 from emp2 connect by prior ename = mname
start with ename = 'chairman')z2
where z2.l1 >= z1.l1
group by z2.l1 having count(*) = 2)z4
where z3.l1 = z4.l1;
```

The output of preceding code snippet is as follows:

```
COUNT('NO_OF_EMP') SUM(Z3.S1)
------------------ ----------
                 1       5000
```

Consider the tree structure:

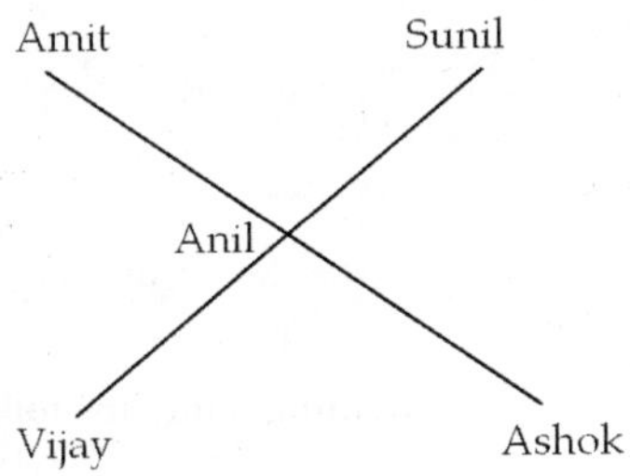

The following code snippet creates the Emp4 table:

```
create table emp4(ename varchar2(10),mname varchar2(10));
```

The output of preceding code snippet is as follows:

```
Table created
```

Now, enter the data given in Table 9.2 into the Emp4 table:

Table 9.2: Data to be Entered in the Emp4 Table

ENAME	MNAME
vijay	anil
ashok	anil
anil	amit
anil	sunil
amit	sunil

Submit the query written in the following code snippet for the preceding tree structure:

```
select ename, mname,level from emp4 connect by prior ename = mname;
```

The output of preceding code snippet is as follows:

```
ENAME      MNAME           LEVEL
---------- ---------- ----------
VIJAY      ANIL                1
ASHOK      ANIL                1
AMIT       ANIL                1
```

```
ANIL        SUNIL              1
VIJAY       ANIL               2
ASHOK       ANIL               2
AMIT        ANIL               2
AMIT        SUNIL              1

8 rows selected.
```

Listing 9.17 shows the code to submit a query to generate a tree structure:

Listing 9.17: Submitting a Query for Generating a Tree Structure

```
select ename, mname, level from emp4 connect by prior mname = ename;
```

The output of Listing 9.17 is as follows:

```
ENAME      MNAME           LEVEL
---------- ---------- ----------
AMIT       ANIL                1
ANIL       SUNIL               2
AMIT       SUNIL               1
ANIL       SUNIL               1
ASHOK      ANIL                1
ANIL       SUNIL               2
VIJAY      ANIL                1
ANIL       SUNIL               2

8 rows selected.
```

Let's now learn about advanced queries.

Advanced Queries

*Running **sum***

Create a table with the data given in Table 9.3:

Table 9.3: Data Given for Creating a Table

sr	amt
1	5
2	4
3	8

Listing 9.18 shows how to create a table and perform a query for sum:

Listing 9.18: Creating a Table and Performing a Query for sum

```
create table z(sr number, amt number);
select z2.sr,z2.amt, sum(z1.amt) from z z1,z z2 where
z1.sr <= z2.sr group by z2.sr,z2.amt;
```

The output of Listing 9.18 is as follows:

```
        SR        AMT   SUM(Z1.AMT)
---------- ----------   -----------
         3          8    17
         2          4    9
         1          5    5
```

Let's understand the query given in Listing 9.18 by dividing it into the following steps:

- Step 1:

  (Running sum is nothing but the cumulative sum of `amt` of each row in table `z`.)

  - Taking the self join of table `z`.

NOTE

A self join is a join of a table to itself. This table appears twice in the FROM clause along with table aliases. To perform a self join, Oracle combines and returns rows of the table that satisfy the join condition.

```
select * from z z1,z z2;
```

The output of preceding code snippet is as follows:

```
SR AMT    SR      AMT
---- ----  -----   -----
1 5       1        5
1 5       2        4
1 5       3        8
2 4       1        5
2 4       2        4
2 4       3        8
3 8       1        5
3 8       2        4
3 8       3        8

9 rows selected.
```

- **Step 2**—The `join` condition is applied, as shown in the following code snippet:

```
select * from z z1,z z2 where z1.sr <= z2.sr
/
```

The output of preceding code snippet is as follows:

```
SR AMT    SR      AMT
--- -----   ----   ------
1 5       1        5
1 5       2        4
1 5       3        8
2 4       2        4
2 4       3        8
3 8       3        8

6 rows selected.
```

- **Step 3**—The group by z2.sr is applied to form groups based on same value of z2.sr `(GROUP BY z2.sr)`.
- **Step 4**—The `sum (z1.amt)` is calculated for each group. By applying `group by z2.sr, z2.amt`, three groups will be formed—`sum(z1.amt)` is calculated for each group. For the first group, the sum is 5, for the second group it is 9, and for the third group it is 17.

This concept can also be used to determine any `max` value from a certain table, as shown in Listing 9.19:

Listing 9.19: Displaying the 2nd max Amount from z

```
select z2.amt from z z1,z z2 where
z2.amt <= z1.amt
group by z2.amt
having count(z2.amt) = 2;
```

The output of Listing 9.19 is as follows:

```
AMT
---------
   5
```

In Listing 9.19:

- The having clause is used when the condition is specified to a group, not to an individual row.
- After selecting the number of rows for each group, `amt` of the group having the number of rows equal to 2 is selected. To calculate the third highest, replace 2 by 3.

Listing 9.20 shows the code to retrieve sr at which sum is maximum:

Listing 9.20: Retrieving sr at which sum is Maximum

```
select z5.sr from(select z2.sr, sum(z1.amt)amt from z z1, z z2 where
z1.sr <= z2.sr group by z2.sr)z5 where
z5.amt in(select max(z4.amt) from (select z2.sr, sum(z1. amt)amt from z
  z1, z z2 where
z1.sr <= z2.sr group by z2.sr)z4);
```

The output of Listing 9.20 is as follows:

```
SR
------
  3
```

Let's understand the query given in Listing 9.20 by dividing it into the following steps:

- **Step 1**—The running sum is calculated, which acts as data source, as shown in the following code snippet:

```
(select z2.sr, sum(z1.amt)amt from z z1, z z2
Where z1.sr <= z2.sr group by z2.sr);
```

The output of preceding code snippet is as follows:

```
SR        AMT
------- ----------
  1          5
  2          9
  3          17
```

- **Step 2**—The maximum running sum, that is, `max(z4.amt)` is retrieved, as shown in the following code snippet:

```
(select max(z4.amt) from (select z2.sr, sum(z1. amt)amt from z z1, z z2
Where z1.sr <= z2.sr group by z2.sr)z4)
```

The output of preceding code snippet is as follows:

```
MAX(Z4.AMT)
-----------
   17
```

- **Step 3**—The amount, determined by Step 1, is compared with `max(z4.amt), as shown in the following code snippet:`

```
select z2.sr,sum(z1.amt)amt from z z1, z z2 where
z1.sr <= z2.sr group by z2.sr;
```

The output of preceding code snippet is as follows:

```
   SR        AMT
--------- ----------
   1          5
   2          9
   3          17
```

You can retrieve serial wise running sum for z if there are multiple rows for each sr, as shown in Listing 9.21:

Listing 9.21: Retrieving the serial wise (sr) running sum for the table z if table is having multiple rows for each sr

```
select z2.z2sr, sum(z1.z1amt) from (select sr z1sr, sum(amt) z1amt from z
group by sr)z1,
(select sr z2sr, sum(amt)z2amt from z group by sr)z2 where
z1.z1sr <= z2.z2sr group by z2.z2sr,z2.z2amt;
```

The output of Listing 9.21 is as follows:

```
Z2SR              SUM(Z1.Z1AMT)
-----    -------------
  1                   5
  2                   9
  3                   17
```

Let's understand the query given in Listing 9.21 by dividing it into the following steps:

- **Step 1**—The sum of amount for each `sr` is calculated, as shown in the following code snippet:

```
(select sr z2sr, sum(amt)z2amt from z group by sr);
```

The output of preceding code snippet is as follows:

```
Z2SR       Z2AMT
------- ----------
  1          5
  2          4
  3          8
```

- **Step 2**—Then the self join of data from Step 1 is taken, as shown in the following code snippet:

```
select sr z2sr, sum(amt)z2amt from z group by s
select z2.z2sr, sum(z1.z1amt) from
(select sr z1sr, sum(amt) z1amt
from z group by sr)z1,
(select sr z2sr, sum(amt)z2amt from z group by sr)z2 where
z1.z1sr <= z2.z2sr
group by z2.z2sr,z2.z2amt;
```

The output of preceding code snippet is as follows:

```
Z2SR              SUM(Z1.Z1AMT)
------    -------------
 1                  5
 2                  9
 3                  17
```

*Additional Queries Based on Running **Sum***

In this section, we learn some additional queries based on running sum:

Listing 9.22: Displaying the Name of Branches having 5th Highest Total Deposit (The data is described in Chapter 7)

```
select z1.bname, z1.tamt from(select d1.bname,sum (d1.amount)tamt from
deposit d1 group by d1.bname)z1,
(select distinct sum(d2.amount)tamt from deposit d2 group by d2.bname) z2
where z2.tamt >= z1.tamt group by z1.bname, z1.tamt
having count(z1.bname) = 5;
```

The output of Listing 9.22 is as follows:

```
BNAME                   TAMT
-------------     ----------
ANDHERI                 2000
```

Let's understand the query given in Listing 9.22 by dividing it into the following steps:

- **Step 1**—The sum of each branch is calculated, which acts as a data source, as shown in the following code snippet:

```
select d1.bname,sum (d1.amount)tamt from deposit d1 group by d1.bname;
```

The output of preceding code snippet is as follows:

```
BNAME                    TAMT
------------------    ----------
VRCE                     1000
AJNI                     5000
KAROLBAGH                3500
CHANDNI                  1200
M.G.ROAD                 3000
VIRAR                    1000
POWAI                    7000
ANDHERI                  2000
NEHRU PLACE              5000

9 rows selected.
```

- **Step 2**—The distinct sum of each branch is retrieved, as shown in the following code snippet:

```
select distinct sum(d2.amount)tamt from deposit d2 group by d2.bname;
```

The output of preceding code snippet is as follows:

```
TAMT
-----
 1000
 5000
 1200
 3500
 2000
 3000
 7000
7 rows selected
```

- **Step 3**—The Cartesian product of Step 1 and Step 2 is calculated, as shown in the following code snippet:

```
select z1.bname, z1.tamt from(select d1.bname,sum (d1.amount)tamt from deposit
d1 group by d1.b
(select distinct sum(d2.amount)tamt from deposit d2 group by d2.bname) z2
group by z1.bname, z1.tamt;
```

The output of preceding code snippet is as follows:

```
BNAME                    TAMT
------------------ ----------
AJNI                     5000
VRCE                     1000
POWAI                    7000
VIRAR                    1000
ANDHERI                  2000
CHANDNI                  1200
M.G.ROAD                 3000
KAROLBAGH                3500
NEHRU PLACE              5000

9 rows selected
```

- **Step 4**—The `WHERE` condition that determines the number of rows selected for each Branch `(GROUP BY bname)` is applied, as shown in the following code snippet:

```
select z1.bname, z1.tamt from(select d1.bname,sum (d1.amount)tamt from deposit
d1 group by d1.bname)z1,
(select distinct sum(d2.amount)tamt
from deposit d2 group by d2.bname) z2
where z2.tamt >= z1.tamt
group by z1.bname, z1.tamt;
```

The output of preceding code snippet is as follows:

```
BNAME                    TAMT
------------------ ----------
CHANDNI                  1200
NEHRU PLACE              5000
M.G.ROAD                 3000
VIRAR                    1000
ANDHERI                  2000
KAROLBAGH                3500
POWAI                    7000
AJNI                     5000
VRCE                     1000
9 rows selected.
```

- **Step 5**—`count(z1.bname)` will select the name of the branch of which 9 rows are selected.

```
select z1.bname, z1.tamt from(select d1.bname,sum (d1.amount)tamt from deposit
d1 group by d1.bname)z1,
(select distinct sum(d2.amount)tamt from deposit d2 group by d2.bname) z2
where z2.tamt >= z1.tamt
group by z1.bname, z1.tamt
having count(z1.bname) = 5;
```

The output of preceding code snippet is as follows:

```
BNAME                    TAMT
------------------ ----------
ANDHERI                  2000
```

Listing 9.23: Displaying those Customers having Addresses in all those cities where ANIL is Living

```
select d3.cname from deposit d3
where not exists (select c2.city from customer c2 where c2.cname =
d3.cname)minus(select c1.city from customer c1 where c1.cname = 'ANIL');
```

The output of Listing 9.23 is as follows:

```
CNAME
----------
ANIL
```

Let's understand the query given in Listing 9.23 by dividing it into steps.

- **Step 1**—Since `Anil` is living in multiple cities, we first retrieve Anil's cities, as shown in the following code snippet:

```
select c1.city from customer c1 where c1.cname = 'ANIL';
```

The output of preceding code snippet is as follows:

```
CITY
---------------
KOLKATA
```

- **Step 2**—We have retrieved the cities in which customers are living, as shown in the following code snippet:

```
select c2.city from customer c2,deposit d3 where c2.cname = d3.cname;
```

The output of preceding code snippet is as follows:

```
CITY
-------------
KOLKATA
DELHI
BARODA
NAGPUR
NAGPUR
SURAT
MUMBAI
MUMBAI
MUMBAI

9 rows selected.
```

- **Step 3**—We have then minus the multiple cities of customers from ANIL's cities, as shown in the following code snippet:

```
(select c2.city from customer c2,
deposit d3  where c2.cname = d3.cname)minus
(select c1.city from customer c1 where c1.cname = 'ANIL');
```

The output of preceding code snippet is as follows:

```
CITY
-------------
BARODA
DELHI
MUMBAI
NAGPUR
SURAT
```

- **Step 4**—We have used the exists operator. If `exists` returns true, then customers do not have address in all those cities where `ANIL` is living, else it satisfies the condition, as shown in the following code snippet:

```
select d3.cname from deposit d3
where not exists (select c2.city
from customer c2 where c2.cname =
d3.cname)minus(select c1.city
from customer c1 where c1.cname = 'ANIL');
```

The output of preceding code snippet is as follows:

```
CNAME
----------
ANIL
```

Deleting Duplicate Rows

If you want, you can delete duplicate rows from a table by using the delete statement.

Listing 9.24 shows how to delete duplicate rows from a table:

Listing 9.24: Deleting Duplicate Rows

```
delete z z1
where(z1.sr,z1.amt)in
(select z2.sr,z2.amt from z z2
group by z2.sr,z2.amt having count(*) > 1);
```

The output of Listing 9.24 is as follows:

```
0 rows deleted
```

You can also use the `rowid` pseudocolumn to delete duplicate rows from a table.

NOTE

The rowid pseudocolumn specifies the location of the row on the disc.

Let's delete repeated rows from the z table. The structure of z table is given in Table 9.4:

Table 9.4: Displaying the Structure of the z Table

SR	AMT
1	5
2	4
3	8
1	5
3	8
1	5
2	4
2	4

Listing 9.25 shows how to delete rows from z using rowid:

Listing 9.25: Using the rowid Pseudocolumn

```
delete z z1 where
z1.rowid < any
(select z2.rowid from z z2
where z1.sr = z2.sr
and z1.amt = z2.amt);
```

The output of Listing 9.25 is as follows:

```
5 rows deleted
```

The following code snippet displays remaining records from the z table:

```
select * from z;
```

The output of preceding code snippet is as follows:

```
SR AMT
----     ----
3  8
1  5
2  4
```

The other way of deleting records is shown in the following code snippet:

```
delete z z1
where(z1.sr,z1.amt)in
(select z2.sr,z2.amt from z z2
where 1 < (select count(*)
from z z3 where
z2.sr = z3.sr and
z2.amt = z3.amt) and
z1.rowid < z2.rowid);
```

The output of preceding code snippet is as follows:

```
5 rows deleted
```

Implementing Contain All Functionality

Table 9.5 shows the structure of the company table:

Table 9.5: The Structure of the Company Table

Cname	City
ACC	NAGPUR
ACC	KOLKATA
HLL	NAGPUR
HLL	MUMBAI
TATA	NAGPUR
TATA	KOLKATA
TATA	DELHI

Listing 9.26 shows how to implement the contain all functionality:

Listing 9.26: Retrieving the Names of Companies Located in Those Cities Where ACC is Located

```
select distinct c1.cname
from company c1
where not exists
((select c2.city
 from company c2
 where c2.cname='acc')
minus
(select c3.city
 from company c3
 where c3.cname=c1.cname));
```

The output of Listing 9.26 is as follows:

```
CNAME
--------------------
ACC
TATA
```

Data Transformation using ***DECODE***

Table 9.6 shows the data of the marks table:

Table 9.6: The marks Table

RN	PHY	CHE	MATHS
1	79	89	90
2	70	80	91
3	65	75	85
4	60	68	98
5	55	57	93

Listing 9.27 shows the code to display the data of the marks table:

Listing 9.27: Displaying the Data of marks

```
select * from marks;
```

The output of Listing 9.27 is as follows:

```
        RN        PHY        CHE      MATHS
---------- ---------- ---------- ----------
         1         79         89         90
         2         70         80         91
         3         65         75         85
         4         60         68         98
         5         55         57         93
```

Listing 9.28: Using Decode to Give Grade

```
select rn,phy,decode((trunc(phy/25)),0,'A',1,'B',2,'C','D') from marks;
```

The output of Listing 9.28 is as follows:

```
        RN        PHY D
---------- ---------- -
         1         79 D
         2         70 C
         3         65 C
         4         60 C
         5         55 C
```

Transforming Row Data Column Wise

Listing 9.29 shows the code to display the data from the Emp_company table (see Appendix A) according to a specified condition:

Listing 9.29: Displaying the Data from the emp_company Table

```
select cname,sum(salary) from emp_company group by cname;
```

The output of Listing 9.30 is as follows:

```
CNAME      SUM(SALARY)
---------- -----------
ACC              10500
TATA             10000
CMC               3500
```

The following code snippet shows how to display data using Decode:

```
select decode(cname,'acc',salary,0) acc,
decode(cname,'tata',salary,0) tata,
decode(cname,'cmc',salary,0) cmc,
decode(cname,null,salary,0) other
from emp_company
/
```

The output of preceding code snippet is as follows:

```
       ACC       TATA        CMC      OTHER
---------- ---------- ---------- ----------
      1500          0          0          0
         0       2000          0          0
         0          0       1800          0
         0          0       1700          0
         0       5000          0          0
         0       3000          0          0
      8000          0          0          0
```

```
    1000          0          0          0

8 rows selected.
```

The following code snippet shows the query editing for calculating the sum of decode value in each company

```
edit decode2
select sum(decode(cname,'acc',salary,0)) acc,
sum(decode(cname,'tata',salary,0)) tata,
sum(decode(cname,'cmc',salary,0)) cmc,
sum(decode(cname,null,salary,0))other
from emp_company
/
@decode2
```

The output of preceding code snippet is as follows:

```
       ACC       TATA        CMC      OTHER
---------- ---------- ---------- ----------
      9500      10000       3500       1200
```

TOP-N Queries

You can use inline views to make top-n queries. Top-n queries are used to retrieve top-n rows from a table. Listing 9.30 shows how to retrieve top three employees salary wise from a table:

Listing 9.30: Retrieving Top Three Employees Salary Wise

```
select ename,salary
from (select ename,nvl(salary,0) salary
from emp_company
order by salary desc)
where rownum < 4
/
```

The output of Listing 9.30 is as follows:

```
ENAME          SALARY
---------- ----------
AJAY             8000
VIJAY            5000
PRAKASH          3000
```

Summary

Now that you have understood the hierarchical and advanced queries, it's time to explore integrity constraints.

Exercise

1. Implement contain all functionality.
2. Retrieving the Number of Employees and the Sum of their Salaries.
3. Retrieving the Names of Companies Located in Those Cities Where HLL is Located.
4. Retrieve the top three employees on the basis of salaries.

10

Integrity Constraints

Integrity constraints are the rules in real life, which are to be imposed on the data. If the computer data is not satisfying the constraint then it is considered as inconsistent. For example if marks in percentage are 105 then is not valid because marks cannot exceed 100 if they are expressed in percentage. This is explained using following example. Table 10.1 lists the data of a student:

Table 10.1: Student Table

Student			
	RN	**Name**	**City**
R1	1	AMIT	NAGPUR
R2	2	AJAY	MUMBAI
R3	2	ASHOK	DELHI
R4	3	ABHAY	

In the preceding table, rows, R2 and R3 are not valid because two students should not have the same roll number. Row, R4 is not valid because every student should have a living city.

Table 10.2 lists the marks obtained by a student:

Table 10.2: Student Marks Table

Student marks			
	RN	**YEAR**	**MARKS**
R5	1	1	85.2
R6	5	1	76
R7	3	1	109
R8	3	2	A

In the Student marks table, `R6` is not a valid row because student with roll number 5 does not exist (i.e. does not exist in the table `student`). Rows, `R7` and `R8` are not valid because the percentage value is not correct. These rules are to be enforced on data because of the presence of these rules in real life. These rules are called integrity constraints. The data, which is not obeying integrity constraints, is called inconsistent data. Every software must enforce integrity constraints, otherwise inconsistent data is generated. Following are the five integrity constraints:

- Domain constraints
- Key constraints
- Functional dependency
- Multivalued dependency
- Miscellaneous constraints

(The discussion on constraints Functional dependency, Multivalued dependency are out of scope of the book).

Let's learn about domain and key constraints in detail.

Domain Constraints

It means every data should have proper data type, proper range, and proper format. It also deals with the question of whether null values are acceptable for data. A domain means a set of permitted values. Domain constraints are handled by defining proper data type, specifying `NOT NULL` constraint, if necessary, and by specifying `CHECK` constraint.

Listing 10.1 shows the code to specify constraints in a table:

Listing 10.1: Specifying Constraints in a Table

```
create table student_marks
(rn number(3) not null,
year number(1) not null,
marks number(5,2) not null,
remarks varchar2(20),
constraint ck_student_marks_rn
check (rn between 1 and 250),
constraint ck_student_marks_year
check (year between 1 and 3),
constraint ck_student_marks_marks
check (marks between 0 and 100));
```

In the preceding listing, data written inside bracket after `CHECK` is a boolean condition and should be simple (It should contain column names or constants). A constraint name (i.e. any name such as `abc` and `xyz`) should be unique for the user (the common practice is `<ck><table name><column name>`).

The output of Listing 10.1 is as follows:

```
Table created
```

The table is created with the specified constraints

NOTE

We cannot use SQL statement in `CHECK` constraints.

Following is the example of CHECK constraint

For the table Student check constraints should implement the following points:

- RN should have a range from `1` to `250` and null values are not acceptable
- First character of a name should be between `A` and `Z`
- City should have length 3 and all the characters should be in uppercase

Listing 10.2 shows the code to apply CHECK constraints:

Listing 10.2: Using CHECK Constraints

```
create table student'
(rn number(3) not null,
city varchar2(20) not null,
name varchar2(30) not null,
constraint ck1_student_rn
check (rn between 1 and 250),
constraint ck2_student_name
check(name between 'a' and 'z'),
constraint ck3_student_city
check(length(city) between 1 and 3 and city between 'a' and 'z'),
check (substr(name,1,1) between 'a' and 'z'),
constraint ck4_student_city
check (length (city) = 3 and city = upper (city)));
```

The output of Listing 10.2 is as follows:

```
Table created
```

The constraints are enforced for any DML operation under any condition. The DML operation is rejected, if for any row which is affected by DML statement, violates the constraints. Such a DML operation will have null effect on the data, as shown in the following code snippet:

```
Update student_marks set marks = marks + 20;
```

Its effect is either full or null. Effect of any DML statement is either full or null. That is, if the `update` statement is supposed to update 10 rows but, due to the constraint violation, is unable to update three rows then the rest of the seven rows are also not updated. So, the effect of `update` statement is either updation of 10 rows or updation of no rows. This is called *statement level atomicity*.

Key Constraints

Key constraints can be explained using the following terms:

- **Superkey**—Refer to the set of attributes or columns, which uniquely identify the entity. Entity means a thing, which is having physical or conceptual meaning, e.g. student, department, vehicle, or subject. Superkey can be `Voterid`, `Reg. no.` of vehicle, `Phone No.`, `Account no.` in Bank, or `Enrollment No.` in university.
- **Candidate key**—Refer to the superkey without any extraneous or minimal attributes, or for which any proper subset is not the superkey. If a superkey is having any proper subset that is also a superkey, then it is not called a candidate key, as shown in Table 10.3:

Table 10.3: Following table lists information of students of a particular class

Class	RN	Name	Marks	Superkeys
				RN(This is also a candidate key) RN,NAME RN,NAME, MARKS

Table 10.4 shows `Student_college table`, representing the marks of all students in the college:

Table 10.4: Student_college Table

Year	Branch	RN	Name	Marks	EN
1	CS	1	Anil	79.8	5585

The preceding table contains the following superkeys:

- Superkey = `(Year, branch, RN)`, which is also a candidate key
- Superkey = `EN`, which is also a candidate key

NOTE

The set of attributes (EN, RN) is a superkey but not a candidate key because `RN` is extraneous.

- **Primary key**—Refers to the superkey, which is chosen by the designer for recognizing an entity. It is the choice among multiple superkeys. Table 10.5 represents sports information in table `sports` in two different ways:

Table 10.5: sports Table

EN	Name of sports—suitable for university
5585	T
5585	C

Or

RN	Year	Branch	Name of sports—suitable for college
1	1	CS	T
1	1	CS	C

NOTE

In the first representation EN is the primary key, while in the second representation (RN, Year, Branch) the primary key. EN is not suitable for college because it is not decided by college administration.

Let's learn to create a primary key.

Primary Key

A primary key is the candidate key that is used by the database designer for identifying an entity. It depends merely on the choice of the designer among various candidate keys under a given condition. There is no fixed rule for choosing the primary key, but generally it is the key that can be controlled by the user. This key is specified while creating table.

Characteristics of a Primary Key are as follows:

- There should be at the most one Primary Key for a table.
- Primary Key columns do not accept null values.
- Primary Key columns do not accept duplicate values. If Primary Key is composite, then uniqueness is determined by the combination of columns.
- It is recommended that Primary Key columns should be short and numeric.
- Primary Key is implemented by `UNIQUE INDEX`.

Listing 10.3 shows the code to create a table with primary key:

Listing 10.3: Creating a Table with Primary Key

```
create table student
(rn number(3), name varchar2(30), year date, univ  varchar2(10),
branch varchar2(20), en number(4), constraint uk1_student_en unique(en),
constraint pk1_student primary key (rn, year, branch));
```

The output of Listing 10.3 is as follows:

```
Table created
```

Table 10.6 shows the table created with primary key:

Table 10.6: Table with Primary Key

year	branch	RN	name	univ	EN
1	cs	1	Amit	Abc univ	
1	mm	2	Ashok	Xyz univ	
1	cs	3	Ajay		

Let's learn to create unique key.

Unique Key

Since one table can have at the most one primary key, to avoid duplicates in other database columns, a unique key can be defined. Unique key can be defined according to the table definition given earlier. The following are the characteristics of unique key:

- ❒ Unique key columns do not accept duplicate values
- ❒ One table can have a number of unique keys
- ❒ The same combination of columns should not make both unique and primary keys
- ❒ By default, unique key columns accept null values, unless `not null` constraint is specified
- ❒ UK is implemented by `UNIQUE INDEX`

Suppose you wish to create a table, ABC, with the following specifications:

- ❒ A & B—PK
- ❒ C & D—UK
- ❒ E—UK

Listing 10.4 shows the code to create a table ABC with the preceding specifications:

Listing 10.4: Creating Table ABC

```
create table abc
(a number(2), b number(2), c number(2), d number(2),
e number(2), constraint pk1_abc primary key (a,b),
constraint uk1_abc unique (e), constraint uk2_abc unique (c,d));
```

The output of Listing 10.4 is as follows:

```
Table created
```

Listing 10.5: Inserting Rows in Table ABC

```
insert into ABC values (1, 1, 1, 1, 1);
```

The output of Listing 10.5 is as follows:

```
1 row created
```

Insert values in table ABC using the following code snippet:

```
insert into ABC values (1, 1, 2, 3, 5);
```

The output of preceding code snippet is as follows:

```
*
ERROR at line 1:
ORA-00001: unique constraint (SYS.PK1_ABC) violated
Error at line 1 i.e., insert into ABC …
unique constraint (student1.pk_ABC) violated (i.e., Duplicate values 1,1)
```

The following code snippet provides the code to insert values in table ABC with null value in column B:

```
insert into ABC values (1, null, 5, 4, 2);
```

The output of preceding code snippet is as follows:

```
*
ERROR at line 1:
ORA-01400: cannot insert NULL into ("SYS"."ABC"."B")
Cannot create null into ('student.pk_ABC',"B")
```

The following code snippet provides the code to insert values in table ABC with null value in columns, A and B:

```
insert into ABC values (null, null, 7, 8, 9);
```

The output of preceding code snippet is as follows:

```
ERROR at line 1:
ORA-01400: cannot insert NULL into ("SYS"."ABC"."A") Cannot insert null
```

The following code snippet provides the code to insert values in table ABC with null value in column D:

```
insert into ABC values (1, 2, 1, null, 7);
```

The output of preceding code snippet is as follows:

```
1 row created
```

The following code snippet provides the code to insert values in table ABC with null value in column D:

```
insert into ABC values (1, 3, 1, null, 8);
```

The output of preceding code snippet is as follows:

```
ERROR at line 1:
ORA-00001: unique constraint (SYS.UK2_ABC) violated
Unique constraint (student1.UK_ABC) violated-check
```

The following code snippet provides the code to insert values in table ABC with null value in columns, C and D:

```
insert into ABC values (1, 4, null, null, 9);
```

The output of preceding code snippet is as follows:

```
1 row created
```

The following code snippet provides the code to insert values in table ABC with null value in columns C and D:

```
insert into ABC values (1, 5, null, null, 10);
```

The output of preceding code snippet is as follows:

```
1 row created
```

The following code snippet provides the code to insert values in table ABC with null value in columns, C,D, and E:

```
insert into ABC values (1, 7, null, null, null);
```

The output of preceding code snippet is as follows:

```
1 row created
```

Listing 10.6 displays all data in table ABC:

Listing 10.6: Displaying all Data in Table ABC

```
select * from ABC;
```

The output of Listing 10.6 is as follows:

```
A       B       C       D       E
---     ----    ---     ---     ---
1       1       1       1       1
1       3       1               8
1       4                       9
1       5                       10
1       7
```

Let's learn to create the foreign key.

Foreign Key

Foreign key is the constraint on the data of one table due to the data of another table. Suppose we have tables, `student` and `Student_marks`. Table 10.7 represents the master table:

Table 10.7: Master TableParent or master table

student		
RN	**Name**	**City**
1	Amit	NAGPUR
2	Sunil	MUMBAI
3	Vijay	DELHI

The preceding table, student is called parent table or master table. Table 10.8 represents the details table:

Table 10.8: Details Table		
Child or details table		
	Student_marks	
RN	**Year**	**perc**
1	1	78
1	2	59
5	1	65

Here `student` is called parent table or master table, Table 10.8, while `Student_marks` is the child or details table. If all the students who have enrolled are having entries in `Student table`, then the following rows are either accepted or rejected:

- Row `R6` is not accepted, because RN5 is not present in table `Student table`.
- Rows `R2` and `R3` are accepted, because these are the students whose examination data is not available

`RN` in `Student_marks` table is the foreign key referencing `RN` of `student` table. It is also called *referential integrity,* i.e. `Student_marks` (RN) is a subset of `student(RN)` for all DML operations.

Foreign key relationship imposes the following restrictions:

- INSERTION
  - **Parent**—No restriction
  - **Child**—Restriction
- UPDATION
  - **Parent**—Restriction
  - **Child**—Restriction
- DELETION
  - **Parent**—Restriction
  - **Child**—No Restriction

The deletion operation is handled theoretically in the following four ways:

- **No deletion**—Specifies that if corresponding rows are present in the child table, then the parent row is not allowed to be deleted.
- **Cascade deletion**—Specifies that if the parent row is deleted, then the corresponding child rows are also deleted.
- **Set to null**—Specifies that if the parent row is deleted, then the foreign key column in the corresponding child table gets `null` value, if nulls are accepted.
- **Set to default**—Specifies that if a row in the parent table is deleted, the corresponding row and corresponding column in the child table gets the predefined value that would not violate the foreign key constraints.

NOTE

Oracle handles deletion in two ways:

1. *No deletion*
2. *Cascade deletion*
3. *Set to Null*

There are different ways of handling nulls in the foreign key. So, the foreign key can be implemented in the following three ways:

- **Match full**—Refers to those rows that are accepted in the child table and have corresponding data in parent table, or all the foreign key columns having `null` values. It will accept rows `R1`, `R2`, and `R3`.
- **Match partial**—Refers to those rows that are accepted in child table and have corresponding data in the parent table. If any of the foreign key columns has null value then the `not null` value should be present in the parent table. It will accept the rows, `R1`, `R2`, `R3`, and `R4`.
- **Match none**—Refers to only those values that are accepted in child table and have corresponding data in the parent table or any of the foreign key columns having `null` value. It will accept `R1`, `R2`, `R3`, `R4`, and `R5`.

Suppose you have data where, in the parent table, (B, C) is the primary key, and in the child table, (B, C) is the foreign key. Table 10.9 represents the parent table:

Table 10.9: Parent Table

Parent		
A	**B**	**C**
1	2	3
2	5	9

Table 10.10 represents the parent table:

Table 10.10: Child Table

Child			
	A	**B**	**C**
R1	7	2	3
R2	9	5	9
R3	7	NULL	NULL
R4	1	2	NULL
R5	8	NULL	10

NOTE

Oracle uses the match none implementation.

Let's learn to implement the foreign key.

Implementation of Foreign Key

Following command indicates how the foreign key is specified in CREATE TABLE

```
create table student_marks
(RN1                                          --child column
year                                          --child column
marks                                         --child column
constraints FK_student_marks
Foreign key (RN1)                             --child column
References student (RN) on delete cascade     --parent table for set null
                                              --use 'References student
                                              --(RN) on delete set null'
```

Foreign key constraints are always defined on child columns. The columns of child table having constraint foreign key (i.e. RN1) must have a constraint as primary key or unique key in the corresponding columns of parent table, i.e. RN. Parent table column and child table column need not have the same name, only the data type should be the same. The parent table columns which are referred should be the primary key or unique key of the parent table, as shown in Table 10.11:

Following example specifies composite foreign key

Table 10.11: Parent Table Containing Primary Key (B, C)

Parent		
A	**B**	**C**
1	2	3
2	5	9

Table 10.12 shows the child table that contains the constraint foreign key:

Table 10.12: Child Table Containing Foreign Key (E, F) Referencing Parent (B, C)

Child		
D	**E**	**F**
7	2	3
9	5	9

NOTE

In the absence of the clause on delete cascade, no deletion is assumed.

Listing 10.7 shows the code to create parent table:

Listing 10.7: Creating Parent Table

```
create table parent
 (a number(2), b number(2), c number(2),
 constraints pk_parent primary key(b,c));
```

The output of Listing 10.7 is as follows:

```
Table created
```

Listing 10.8 shows the code to implement table, if (E, F) of child table are defined as foreign key, referencing (B, C):

Listing 10.8: Implementing Table, if (E, F) of Child Table is Defined as Foreign Key, Referencing (B, C)

```
create table child
(d number(2), e number(2), f number(2),
constraints fk_child foreign key (e,f)
references parent (b,c));
```

The output of Listing 10.8 is as follows:

```
Table created
```

NOTE

In some cases parent table or child table may be the same table.

Following table show the example having foreign key referencing same table

Table 10.13 shows Employee table containing columns ename, mname, and salary:

Table 10.13: employee Table

Employee		
ename	**mname**	**salary**
Anil		1000
Sunil	Anil	500
(parent column)	(child column)	

Listing 10.9 shows the code to define constraint in the preceding table, when the data in mname should be the subset of data from ename

Listing 10.9: Defining Constraint on Employee Table

```
create Table employee_mgr
 (mname varchar2(20), ename varchar2(20) primary key,
 salary number(8,2), constraints FK1_employee_mgr foreign key (ename)
 references employee (ename));
```

The output of Listing 10.9 is as follows:

```
Table created
```

Employee table does not have a primary key. So, let's first make `ename column` in `employee` table as primary key. Listing 10.10 shows the code to make ename of employee as the primary key:

Listing 10.10: Making ename of employee as the Primary Key

```
alter table employee add constraint pk_employee primary key(ename);
```

The output of Listing 10.10 is as follows:

```
Table altered
```

NOTE

If multiple tables are involved in a foreign key relationship, then it is better to define it using diagrams. Figure 10.1 shows the diagram containing multiple tables that are involved in a foreign key relationship:

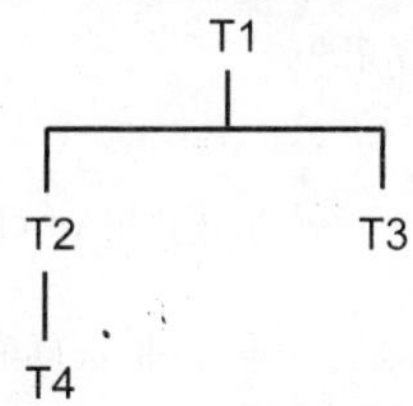

Figure 10.1: Graph indicating in which sequence tables are created

Figure 10.1 gives the order in which tables should be created, i.e. top to bottom. If parent–child relationship is in existence for multiple tables forming a chain and a delete cascade clause is to be used in the top link of the chain, it should be used in the remaining part of the chain to have its effect on the entire chain.

Let's learn how to enable or disable a constraint.

Enabling/Disabling a Constraint

If the constraints are present, then for each DML operation, constraints are checked by executing certain codes internally. It may slow down the DML operation marginally. For massive DML operations, such as transferring data from one table to another because of the presence of constraint, the speed will be considerably slower. To improve the speed in such cases, the following methods are adopted:

The following code snippet shows the code to disable constraint:

```
alter table employee
disable constraint pk_employee;                          --constraint name
```

The following code snippet shows the code to enable constraint:

```
alter table employee
enable constraint pk_employee;
```

While enabling the constraint, if the existing data is violating the constraint, then constraints are not enabled and an error message, giving the name of the constraint, is displayed. Suppose you have tables `T1` and `S`. If you want to transfer rows from table `S` to table `T1`, table `T1` must be empty or having data different from that in `S` `(There should not be primary key violation)`. Listing 10.11shows the code to create table T1:

Listing 10.11: Creating Table T1

```
create Table T1
(A number(2), B number(2),
constraint PK_T1 primary key (A,B));
```

The Output of Listing 10.11 is as follows:

```
Table created
```

Alter table T1 using the following code snippet:

```
Alter table T1
disable constraint PK_T1;
```

The output of preceding code snippet is as follows:

```
Table altered
```

Listing 10.12 shows the code to create table S:

Listing 10.12: Creating Table S

```
CREATE TABLE S
 (C NUMBER(2), D NUMBER(2));
```

The output of Listing 10.12 is as follows:

```
Table created
```

The following code snippet shows how to insert data in table `S`:

```
insert into S values (30, 50);
```

The output of preceding code snippet is as follows:

```
1 row created
```

Listing 10.13 displays the records of table S:

Listing 10.13: Displaying Records of Table S

```
Select * from s;
```

The output of Listing 10.13 is as follows:

```
C D
---        ---
30 50
```

Listing 10.14 shows the code to transfer all the rows from table S to table T1 by disabling the constraint and then enabling the constraint:

Listing 10.14: Transferring all the Rows from Table S to Table T1 by Disabling the Constraint and then Enabling the Constraint

```
insert into T1 (A,B)
 select C,D from S;
```

The output of Listing 10.14 is as follows:

```
1 row created
```

Let's learn to enable a constraint.

Enabling a constraint

The constraints are enabled using `enable constraint` clause.

Listing 10.15 shows the code to enable constraint of table, T1:

Listing 10.15: Enabling Constraint of Table T1

```
alter table T1
enable constraint PK_T1;
```

The output of Listing 10.15 is as follows:

```
Table altered
```

If the existing rows do not satisfy the constraints, then the constraints are not enabled. In such a case, such rows are found using exception. The script is given in file `UTLEXCPT.SQL` in `rdbms/admin` directory of Oracle installation.

Listing 10.16 shows the code to create table, EXCP_TABLE, with the given columns:

Listing 10.16: Creating Table EXCP_TABLE

```
create table excp_table
(row_id rowid, owner varchar2(30),
table_name varchar2(30), constraint varchar2(30));
```

The output of Listing 10.16 is as follows:

```
Table created
```

Listing 10.17 displays columns of table EXCP_TABLE:

Listing 10.17: Displaying Columns of Table EXCP_TABLE

```
desc EXCP_TABLE;
```

The output of Listing 10.17 is as follows:

```
NAME              NULL?              TYPE
----------        --------           -----------------
ROW_ID            ROWID
OWNER                                VARCHAR2(30)
TABLE_NAME                           VARCHAR2(30)
CONSTRAINT                           VARCHAR2(30)
```

Listing 10.18 shows the code to use EXCEPTION INTO clause:

Listing 10.18: Using EXCEPTION INTO Clause

```
alter table t1
enable constraint pk_t1
exceptions into excp_table;
```

In Listing 10.18 `EXCEPTION INTO` clause adds rows in the table without deleting the existing rows.

The output of Listing 10.18 is as follows:

```
Table altered
```

Suppose you want to delete rows in table `T1` that are violating the constraint, then you can do it in following steps:

- **Step 1** — Deleting existing rows in the EXCP_TABLE

The command shown in the following code snippet:

```
delete excp_table;
```

- **Step 2** — Adding row ids of T1 which are violating constraint in the EXCP_TABLE

Listing 10.19: Adding rows in Table EXCP_TABLE which are Violating the Constraint

```
alter table t1
enable constraint pk_t1
exceptions into excp_table;
```

The output of Listing 10.19 is as follows:

```
Table altered
```

- **Step 3**—Deleting rowid from T1 which are violating constraint

The following code snippet provides the code to delete rows:

```
delete t1
where rowid
in (select row_id from excp_table);
```

The output of the preceding code snippet is as follows:

```
0 rows deleted
```

After deleting rows from T1 which are violating constraint, the constraint can be enabled.

The following code snippet provides the code to altering table T1 by enabling constraint PK_T1:

```
alter table T1
enable constraint PK_T1;
```

The output of the preceding code snippet is as follows:

```
Table altered
```

Let's learn to use NOVALIDATE clause.

NOVALIDATE Clause

If `NOVALIDATE clause` is specified when the constraint is enabled then it does not `validate` the existing data according to constraint. Constraint is enforced only on future DML operations. This clause is not valid for primary key or unique key constraint. When a constraint is enabled, Oracle locks all the rows in the table. Therefore, other users cannot perform any DML operation on the table.

However, with the `NOVALIDATE` clause, no lock is applied on the table, so the other user can perform DML operation on the table. When the system is not busy, data is validated using the `VALIDATE` clause. NOVALIDATE clause is specified in the following code snippet:

```
alter table t
enable novalidate constraint pk1_t ;
if you want to validate data then use
alter table t
enable validate constraint pk1_t ;
```

Let's learn about initially immediate deferrable.

Initially Immediate Deferrable

Suppose the constraint uses the `DEFERRABLE clause` then the enforcement of constraint is deferred, until `commit` is issued by the user. Let's learn it using table `T2`.

Listing 10.20 shows the code to create table T2 and inserting data in it:

Listing 10.20: Creating Table T2 and Inserting Data

```
create table t2
(a number(2), b number(2),        c number(2),
constraint ck_a check (a>1), constraint ck_b check (b>1),
constraint ck_c check (c>1)
initially deferred deferrable);
```

The output of the Listing 10.20 is as follows:

```
Table created
```

Table 10.14 shows the data of table T2:

Table 10.14: Table T2

```
A     B     C
---   ---   ---
2     3     4
2     2     5
2     6     0
```

The following code snippet provides the command to commit a transaction:

```
commit;
```

The output of the preceding code snippet is as follows:

```
Commit complete
```

The clause `DEFERRABLE` causes postponing of the enforcement of constraint checking. Therefore, no error is issued even though second and third row violates the constraint. If you issue `COMMIT`, the whole transaction is rolled back and you will not get all the rows that were inserted prior to it. If `INITIALLY DEFERRED` is specified then that constraint is checked at the end of the transaction.

If the rows that are manipulated by the transaction do not satisfy the constraint, then the whole transaction is rolled back. When `INITIALLY IMMEDIATE` is specified, which is also the default setting, then the constraints are enforced at the end of every DML statement.

When the clause `DEFERRABLE` is used, the behavior of constraint can be changed in the transaction by using the `SET CONSTRAINT` command, as shown in Listing 10.21:

Listing 10.21: Enforcing the Constraint IMMEDIATE

```
set constraint ck_c immediate;
```

The output of Listing 10.21 is as follows:

```
Constraint set
```

The following code snippet shows the command to defer the constraint CK_C:

```
set constraint ck_c deferred;
```

The output of the preceding code snippet is as follows:

```
Constraint set
```

Listing 10.22 shows the code to change all constraints to IMMEDIATE:

Listing 10.22: Changing all Constraints to IMMEDIATE

```
set constraint all immediate;
```

The output of Listing 10.22 is as follows:

```
Constraint set
```

NOTE

If the constraint is NOT DEFERRABLE, then it cannot be manipulated using the SET CONSTRAINT command. These facilities are provided to tackle various situations in the practical application where data is made according to the constraint at the end of the transaction.

Updatable Join Views

You can perform DML operations on join views, if the join in the view query is key preserving join. The DML operations are permitted only on key preserved table. A table is key preserved if every key of the table can also be a key of the result of the join. In short, any row in the key preserved table should be mapped to, at the most, one row of the join. The property of key preservation is due to schema definition and not due to data. The following code snippet shows the two tables when joined will give updatable join view:

```
create table newparent(a number(2), b number(2),
constraint pk1_parent primary key(a));
create table newchild(a number(2), c number(2),
constraint fk1_child foreign key(a) references newparent(a));
select * from newparent;
```

The output of the preceding code snippet is as follows:

```
      A          B
------- ----------
      1          2
      2          4
      8          3
```

The following code snippet provides the command to display records from newchild table:

```
select * from newchild;
```

The output of the preceding code snippet is as follows:

```
         A          C
---------- ----------
         1          2
         2          2
         8          2
         8          5
```

Listing 10.23 shows the code to create join views:

Listing 10.23: Creating Join Views

```
select p.a pa,p.b pb,c.a ca,c.c cc
from newparent p,newchild c where p.a=c.a;
```

The output of Listing 10.23 is as follows:

```
     PA         PB         CA         CC
------- ---------- ---------- ----------
      1          2          1          2
      2          4          2          2
      8          3          8          2
      8          3          8          5
```

In the preceding output, the child is key preserving table, while the parent is not a key preserving table because one row of parent (1, 2) is mapped to three rows of view. If you use primary key in the join condition, then the other table become key preserving table. Listing 10.24 shows the code to create view to make the child table a key preserving table:

Listing 10.24: Creating View having key preserving join (Child table a Key Preserving Table

```
create view parent_child as
select p.a pa,p.b pb,c.a ca,c.c cc
from newparent p,newchild c
where p.a=c.a;
select * from parent_child;
```

The output of Listing 10.24 is as follows:

```
   PA         PB         CA         CC
----- ---------- ---------- ----------
    1          2          1          2
    2          4          2          2
    8          3          8          2
    8          3          8          5
```

If you use columns of non key preserving table in DML operation then error is generated as follows

The following code snippet provides code to insert values using view:

```
insert into parent_child(pa,pb) values (4,7);
```

The output of the preceding code snippet is as follows:

```
                                 *
ERROR at line 1:
ORA-01779: cannot modify a column which maps to a non key-preserved table
```

For the column of key preserving table no error is generated.

The following code snippet provides code to insert values using view:

```
insert into parent_child(ca,cc) values(8,2);
```

The output of the preceding code snippet is as follows:

```
1 row created
```

Listing 10.25 displaying rows from Parent_child view:

Listing 10.25: Displaying Rows

```
select * from parent_child;
```

The output of Listing 10.25 is as follows:

```
    PA         PB         CA         CC
------ ---------- ---------- ----------
     1          2          1          2
     2          4          2          2
     8          3          8          2
     8          3          8          5
     8          3          8          2
```

Listing 10.26 shows the code to update table Parent_child:

Listing 10.26: Updating Table

```
update parent_child set cc=1 where cc= 2;
```

The output of Listing 10.26 is as follows:

```
4 rows updated
```

Listing 10.27 shows the command to commit transaction:

Listing 10.27: Committing the Transaction

```
commit;
```

The output of Listing 10.27 is as follows:

```
Commit complete
```

Summary

This chapter has given idea about various types of integrity constraints and how they are specified in Oracle. In the next chapter, you will learn about Analytical Queries.

Exercise

1. Add primary key constraint for table Employee on column ename.
2. Add check constraint on Emp_company such that minimum salary of ACC is 3000.
3. Add foreign key constraint on ename for table Emp_company

11

Analytical Queries

If you need an Information on:	See page:

Analytical Functions

Analytical functions are used mainly for the analysis of data as required by decision-making managers. A manager may want to know the answers to queries, such as the top ten products sold in the rainy season, the region where a product has fewer sales, or the effect of advertisement cost on profit.

Such queries are called as analytical queries and they are computation-intensive and process a large number of rows. These queries are statistical in nature and do not require much data detail, such as name or address of customers. For such queries, data is generally stored in separate database servers called data warehouse servers. Servers that manage data on a daily basis are called OLTP (Online Transaction Processing) servers (for example, the server used to reserve railway tickets). This is If analytical queries are fired to the OLTP server, it will hamper the work of the OLTP server because they are quite computation intensive and require large memory resources, like memory and CPU.

Architecture of a Warehouse Server

A warehouse server contains slightly outdated data because the OLTP server populates it after a certain period. This is not a problem for warehouse queries as they are statistical in nature and results based on 1,00,000 rows or 90,000 rows do not differ much. The technique of extracting data from the warehouse is called data mining. Figure 11.1 shows the architecture of a warehouse server:

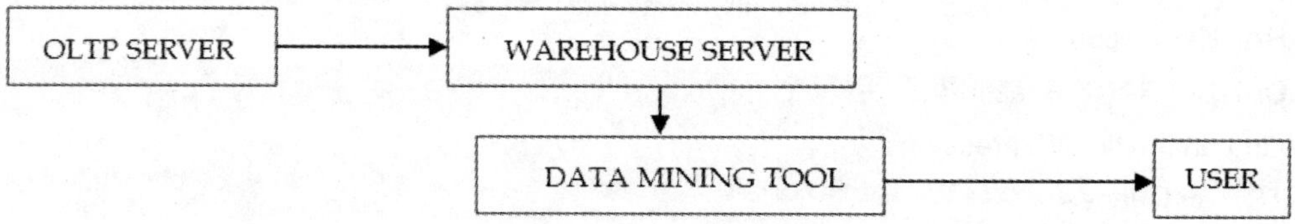

Figure 11.1: Displaying the Architecture of a Warehouse Server

Oracle has embedded analytical functions in SQL statements to cater to most of the requirements of data mining. These functions are categorized as follows:

- **Ranking**—For calculates ranks, percentiles, and *n*-tiles of the values in a result set. For example, finding the top 10 products sold in the northern region in a particular month.
- **Windowing**—For calculating the cumulative and moving aggregates such as 7-day moving average of shares of the ACC company.
- **Reporting**—For calculating shares; for example, the market share of a product among products of the same category.
- **Lag/Lead**—For comparing values of two rows; for example, finding the increase value of the current row compared to the previous row.
- **First/Last**—For calculating the first or last value in an ordered group, such as the value of sales on the last date of a month.
- **Linear regression**—For calculating linear regression and other statistics (such as slope and intercept) which are used in planning.
- **Inverse percentile**—Calculates the value in a data set that corresponds to a specified percentile.
- **Hypothetical rank and distribution**—Calculates the rank or percentile that a row would have if inserted into a specified data set. For example, the rank of a student if he has 87 marks.

TIP

The table structure and data used in queries are given in Appendix A.

Table 11.1 shows sample sales data to create a table:

Table 11.1: Sales Data to Create a Table

PRODID	NOT NULL NUMBER(6)
CUSTID	NOT NULL NUMBER
TIMEID	NOT NULL DATE
CHANNELID	NOT NULL CHAR(1)
PROMOID	NOT NULL NUMBER(6)
QUANTITY	NOT NULL NUMBER(3)
AMOUNT	NOT NULL NUMBER(10,2)

Listing 11.1: Shows sample data of sales table

```
select * from sales_data where rownum < 11;
```

The output of Listing 11.1 is as follows:

```
    PRODID     CUSTID TIMEID    C    PROMOID   QUANTITY     AMOUNT
---------- ---------- --------- - ---------- ---------- ----------
     94653       7290 01-JAN-98 S       9999         18       1422
     46360      22340 01-JAN-98 S       9999          6        114
      4105      37280 01-JAN-98 C       9999          7        553
        85     180430 01-JAN-98 T       9999          2        236
      7145     136490 01-JAN-98 P       9999          3        195
     10880       2630 01-JAN-98 I       9999         14        280
      2595      16480 01-JAN-98 I       9999          4        196
      6315       6910 01-JAN-98 S       9999          2         78
     37195      49900 01-JAN-98 T       9999          9         90
      4885       6900 01-JAN-98 C       9999          4        752

10 rows selected
```

Let's now discuss some basic functions used to use analytical queries, starting with the RANK function.

The **RANK** Function

The `RANK` function is used to grade data depending on certain criteria. Let's understand the use of the RANK function by using the PCM table.

Listing 11.2: Shows sample data of PCM table:

```
select * from PCM;
```

The output of Listing 11.2 is as follows:

```
ROLLNO           NAME   PHYSICS        CHEMISTRY     MATHS
---------        -----  ---------      ------- --    ------
1                ANIL   67             89            76
2                SUNIL  89             65            99
3                AJAY   77             95            94
4                SUSHIL 75             92            91
```

You can now use the RANK function to display the total marks of the students according to their rank, as shown in Listing 11.3:

Listing 11.3: Displaying Rank Based on Total Marks

```
select name, total, rank() over (order by total desc)
from
(select name,(physics+chemistry+maths) total from pcm);
```

The output of Listing 11.3 is as follows:

```
NAME                  TOTAL  RANK()OVER(ORDERBYTOTALDESC)
-----------------  ----------  ----------------------------
AJAY                    266                            1
SUSHIL                  258                            2
SUNIL                   253                            3
ANIL                    232                            4
```

You can also rank the marks the students obtained in a particular subject, as shown in Listing 11.4:

Listing 11.4: Displaying Rank Based on Marks Obtained in Physics

```
select name, physics, rank() over (order by physics desc) rnk
from pcm;
```

The output of Listing 11.4 is as follows:

```
NAME     PHYSICS       RNK
-------  -----         ----
SUNIL         89       1
AJAY          77       2
SUSHIL        75       3
ANIL          67       4
```

From the preceding example, it is clear that the RANK function is used to rank the items in a group; for example, finding the top three salaried employees of a company or the top five items sales-wise. To understand the ranking process better, let's learn the steps used in the evaluation of a query containing the analytic function `RANK()`:

1. Evaluation of the `JOINS`, `WHERE`, `GROUP BY`, and `HAVING` clauses in the specified order.
2. Use of the preceding operation to decide the resultsets of the rows.
3. Formation of partitions according to the partition expression. Rows that have the same value as that of the partition expression are grouped under the same partition.
4. Evaluation of the analytical function.
5. Processing of the `ORDER BY` clause of the main query to generate the output.

Syntax of the ***RANK*** Function

The syntax to use the RANK function is as follows:

```
RANK() OVER
([PARTITION BY <value expression1> [, …]]
ORDER BY <value expression2> [collate clause] [ASC|DESC] [NULLS FIRST|NULLS      LAST] [,
…])
```

The following is a brief description of the various elements in the preceding syntax:

- `RANK()` – Refers to the ranking function.
- `PARTITION BY <value expression1>`–Specifies how the rows in the resultset are partitioned. In its absence, all rows are partitioned into one group. The partition expression can be either a column expression or an aggregate expression.

- ORDER BY <value expression2>—Specifies how the rows are sorted. This expression can be either a column expression or an aggregate expression. You can also explicitly specify how nulls are to be treated.

By default, nulls have the highest values. For example, consider the following code snippet:

```
... ORDER BY amount desc nulls first'...
```

The preceding code snippet shows that when the ORDER BY clause is used with the DESC (descending) option, null values are considered as the highest. Therefore, the fields with null values appear first and the other fields appear after them. For example, consider the query in the following code snippet:

```
select amount from abc order by amount desc;
```

The output of this query selects the amount field of the abc table, with the null amount appearing first, followed by the other amounts in the table, in descending order.

Suppose you have sales data that is arranged year-wise and channel-wise, and you want to rank the sales per year and per channel. For this, you can use the RANK() function. Let's first look at the data without using the RANK() function, as shown in the following code snippet:

Listing 11.5: Displaying Data of Sales Year-Wise and Channel-Wise without using the RANK() Function

```
select to_char(timeid,'yyyy'),
channelid,to_char (sum(amount),'999,999,999,999.99')
from sales_data group by to_char(timeid,'yyyy'),channelid;
```

The output of Listing 11.5 is as follows:

```
TO_C          C       TO_CHAR(SUM(AMOUNT))
----          -       -------------------
1998          C             1,305.00
1998          P               195.00
1998          S             1,614.00
1998          T               326.00
1998          I               476.00
```

The ranking operation is performed such that least sale gets rank one, and for the highest sale, the rank is the highest. To find out ranks, the data is first arranged in ascending order of according to the sum(amount) column and then the ranks are determined according to their order.

Listing 11.6 shows you how to use the RANK() function to arrange data year and channel:

Listing 11.6: Displaying Data Ranked According to the Year and Channel by using the RANK() Function

```
select rank() over (order by sum(amount)) default_rank,
   to_char(timeid,'yyyy'),channelid,to_char(sum(amount),'999,999,999,999.99')
from sales_data group by to_char(timeid,'yyyy'), channelid;
```

The output of Listing 11.6 is as follows:

```
DEFAULT_RANK    TO_C    C        TO_CHAR(SUM(AMOUNT))
------------    ----    -        -------------------
           1    1998    P                195.00
           2    1998    T                326.00
           3    1998    I                476.00
           4    1998    C              1,305.00
           5    1998    S              1,614.00
```

You can see that both queries perform the same task. In the first query, data is displayed year-wise and channel-wise, and in the second query this data is ranked according to the year and channel by using the RANK() function.

Next, let's discuss the use of partitions in the ranking operation.

Using Partitions

Suppose you want to calculate channel sales for each year according to their rank. For this, you can use a partition clause. The rows in the resultset are partitioned according to the partition expression and the rows that have the same value of the partition expression are grouped in one partition. The ranks are determined for each partition.

Listing 11.7 shows the use of partitions:

Listing 11.7: Partitioning the Rows of the Year 1999 and Determining the Ranks in each Partition

```
select rank() over (PARTITION BY to_char(timeid,'yyyy') order by sum(amount))
  default_rank, to_char(timeid,'yyyy'), channelid,
  to_char(sum(amount),'999,999,999,999.99')
from sales_data group by to_char(timeid,'yyyy'), channelid;
```

The output of Listing 11.7 is as follows:

```
DEFAULT_RANK     TO_C             C        TO_CHAR(SUM(AMOUNT)
------------     ----             -        -------------------
   1             1998             P                 195.00
   2             1998             T                 326.00
   3             1998             I                 476.00
   4             1998             C               1,305.00
   5             1998             S               1,614.00
```

Let's now discuss the DENSE_RANK function.

The **DENSE_RANK** Function

The main difference between the `RANK()` function and the `DENSE_RANK()` function is that in the `DENSE_RANK()` function, there is no gap between the ranks. Let's understand this better with an example. Listing 11.8 shows the use of the RANK function:

Listing 11.8: Using the RANK() Function

```
select rank() over (order by trunc(sum(amount),-3)) default_rank,
  to_char(timeid,'yyyy'), channelid,to_char (trunc(sum(amount),-
  3),'999,999,999,999.99')
from sales_data group by to_char(timeid,'yyyy'), channelid;

DEFAULT_RANK     TO_C             C       TO_CHAR(TRUNC(SUM(A
-----------      ----             -      --------------------

   1             1998             I                      .00
   1             1998             P                      .00
   1             1998             T                      .00
   4             1998             C                 1,000.00
   4             1998             S                 1,000.00
```

Listing 11.9: Using the DENSE_RANK() Function

```
select dense_rank() over (order by trunc(sum(amount),-3)) default_rank,
  to_char(timeid,'yyyy'), channelid, to_char(trunc(sum(amount),-
  3),'999,999,999,999.99')
from sales_data group by to_char(timeid,'yyyy'), channelid;
```

The output of Listing 11.9 is as follows:

```
DEFAULT_RANK     TO_C             C         TO_CHAR(TRUNC(SUM(A
------------     ----             -         -------------------
   1             1998             I                      .00
   1             1998             P                      .00
   1             1998             T                      .00
```

```
2          1998          C          1,000.00
2          1998          S          1,000.00
```

The output of Listing 11.8 shows three rows ranked 1, and the next rank starts at four, while in the output of Listing 11.9, rank 2 comes after the first three rows marked 1Thus there is no gap between ranks.

Ordering on Multiple Expressions

You can specify the order in which you want multiple expressions to appear. If the value of the first expression is the same as the value of the second expression, the value of second expression is considered.

Listing 11.10 shows the principle of ordering being used to order rows

Listing 11.10: Ordering Rows According to Amount and Quantity Criteria

```
select rank() over (order by trunc(sum(amount),-2),
  to_char(sum(quantity),'999,999,99')desc) default_rank, to_char(timeid,'yyyy'),
  channelid, to_char(trunc(sum(amount),-2), '999,999,999,999.99'),
  to_char(sum(quantity),'999,999,99') from sales_data                    group by
to_char(timeid,'yyyy'), channelid;
```

The output of Listing 11.10 is as follows:

```
DEFAULT_RANK    TO_C    C    TO_CHAR(TRUNC(SUM(A    TO_CHAR(SUM
------------    ----    -    -------------------    -----------
1          1998    P               100.00           3
2          1998    T               300.00           11
3          1998    I               400.00           18
4          1998    C             1,300.00           11
5          1998    S             1,600.00           26
```

In the preceding output, the rows have been ordered by using `amount` and `quantity`, and in the rows where the `quantity` is the same (shown highlighted), the `amount` is used for the ordering.

Let's discuss the TOP_N function next.

The **TOP_N** Queries

Using inline views (using query as data source in the `FROM` clause), you can list the first N rows to show the top three sales.

Listing 11.11: Using inline views to list the first N rows

```
select * from (select rank() over (order by trunc(sum(amount),-2),
  to_char(sum(quantity),'999,999,99') desc) default_rank,
  to_char(timeid,'yyyy'),channelid,to_char(trunc(sum(amount),-
  2),'999,999,999,999.99'),to_char(sum(quantity),'999,999,99')
from sales_data group by to_char(timeid,'yyyy'),channelid)
where default_rank < 4;
```

The output of Listing 11.11 is as follows:

```
DEFAULT_RANK    TO_C          C        TO_CHAR(TRUNC(SUM(A      TO_CHAR(SUM
------------    ----          -        -------------------      -----------
1               1998          P                100.00              3
2               1998          T                300.00             11
3               1998          I                400.00             18
```

In Listing 11.11, the inner query returns rows with their ranks and the main query returns rows that have ranks lower than 4.

After learning about the TOP_N function, let's discuss the CUME_DIST function.

The **CUME_DIST** Function

The CUME_DIST function is used to calculate the fraction of the number of rows below the current row, including the current row, according to the rank and total number of rows.

Listing 11.12 shows the use of the CUME_DIST function:

Listing 11.12: Using the CUME_DIST Function to Calculate the Fraction

```
select rank() over (order by sum(amount)) default_rank,cume_dist() over (order
  by sum(amount)) default_dist,to_char(timeid,'yyyy'), channelid, to_char
  (sum(amount), '999,999,999,999.99') from sales_data
  group by to_char(timeid,'yyyy'), channelid;
```

The output of Listing 11.12 is as follows:

```
DEFAULT_RANK     DEFAULT_DIST     TO_C          C        TO_CHAR(SUM(AMOUNT)
------------     ------------     ----          -        -------------------
   1                .2            1998          P                195.00
   2                .4            1998          T                326.00
   3                .6            1998          I                476.00
   4                .8            1998          C              1,305.00
   5                 1            1998          S              1,614.00
```

You can see from the preceding output that there are two rows below the second rank row, and there are 5 rows in all. Therefore, the fraction is 2/5, i.e. 0.4. The formula used in this case is rank/total rows.

We discuss the PERCENT_RANK function next.

The **PERCENT_RANK** Function

You can calculate the PERCENT RANK (percentile) as shown in the following code snippet:

```
(Rank of the rows in partition - 1)/(Total number of rows in partition - 1]
```

Listing 11.13 shows the use of the PERCENT_RANK function:

Listing 11.13: Using the PERCENT_RANK Function

```
select rank() over (order by sum(amount)) default_rank,percent_rank() over
  (order by sum(amount)) per_rank,to_char(timeid,'yyyy'),
  channelid,to_char(sum(amount), '999,999,999,999.99')
from sales_data
group by to_char(timeid,'yyyy'), channelid;
@an10
```

The output of Listing 11.13 is as follows:

```
DEFAULT_RANK     PER_RANK         TO_C          C        TO_CHAR(SUM(AMOUNT)
------------     ----------       ----          -        -------------------
   1                0             1998          P                195.00
   2                .25           1998          T                326.00
   3                .5            1998          I                476.00
   4                .75           1998          C              1,305.00
   5                1             1998          S              1,614.00
```

PERCENT_RANK gives percentile value of that row. Let's now discuss the NTILE(N) function.

The **NTILE(N)** Function

The `NTILE(N)` function is used to calculate tertiles, quartiles, and other common statistics. This function divides the rows into N buckets and distributes the rows in the buckets according to rank. The number of rows in each bucket is equal to or more than that in the other bucket. For example, let's suppose there are 50 rows and 5 buckets. In this case, 10 rows are added for each bucket. If there are 55 rows and 10 buckets, then there will be 6 rows for the first 5 buckets, and 5 rows for the next 5 buckets.

Listing 11.14 shows the use of the NTILE(N) function:

Listing 11.14: Using the NTILE(N) Function

```
select rank() over (order by trunc(sum(amount),-2)) default_rank, ntile(4) over
   (order by trunc(sum(amount),-3))
   rw_num,to_char(timeid,'yyyy'),channelid,to_char(trunc(sum(amount),-
   2),'999,999,999,999.99')
from sales_data
group by to_char(timeid,'yyyy'), channelid;
```

The output of Listing 11.14 is as follows:

```
DEFAULT_RANK     RW_NUM        TO_C        C      TO_CHAR(TRUNC(SUM(A
-------------    ---------     ----        -      -------------------
   1             1             1998        P                   100.00
   2             1             1998        T                   300.00
   3             2             1998        I                   400.00
   4             3             1998        C                 1,300.00
   5             4             1998        S                 1,600.00

@an11
```

Next, we discuss the ROW_NUMBER function.

The **ROW_NUMBER** Function

The ROW_NUMBER function assigns a unique rank to each row, even if it has the same value of order by expression. If rank is used, then the rows get the same rank if their order, by expression, has the same value.

Listing 11.15 shows the use of the ROW_NUMBER function:

Listing 11.15: Assigning a Unique Rank to Rows by using the ROW_NUMBER Function

```
select rank() over (order by trunc(sum(amount),-6)) default_rank,row_number()
   over (order by trunc(sum(amount),-2))
   rw_num,to_char(timeid,'yyyy'),channelid,to_char(trunc(sum(amount),-
   2),'999,999,999,999.99') from sales_data
   group by to_char(timeid,'yyyy'), channelid;
```

The output of Listing 11.15 is as follows:

```
DEFAULT_RANK     RW_NUM        TO_C        C      TO_CHAR(TRUNC(SUM(A
------------     ----------    ----        -      -------------------
   1             1             1998        P                   100.00
   1             2             1998        T                   300.00
   1             3             1998        I                   400.00
   1             4             1998        C                 1,300.00
   1             5             1998        S                 1,600.00
```

After learning about the ROW_NUMBER function, let's move on and discuss windowing functions.

Windowing Functions

Windowing functions are used to calculate moving averages, centered averages, cumulative sums, and first and last values in time frame. They return values for each row and these values depend on the values of other rows.

Syntax of Windowing Functions

```
{SUM|AVG|MAX|MIN|COUNT|STDDEV|VARIANCE|FIRST_VALUE|LAST_VALUE}
  ({<value expression1> | *}) OVER
    ([PARTITION BY <value expression2>[,…]]
      ORDER BY <value expression3> [collate clause>]
              [ASC| DESC] [NULLS FIRST | NULLS LAST] [,…]
```

```
        ROWS | RANGE
          {{UNBOUNDED PRECEDING | <value expression4> PRECEDING}
          | BETWEEN
      {UNBOUNDED PRECEDING | <value expression4> PRECEDING}
         AND{CURRENT ROW | <value expression4> FOLLOWING}}
```

The following is a brief description of the various elements used in the preceding

- FIRST_VALUE—Returns the value of the first row in the window.
- LAST_VALUE—Returns the value of last row in the window.
- PARTITION BY—Determines how the rows in the resultset are to be partitioned; similar to the RANK () function.
- ORDER BY—Determines the sorting of rows within each partition.
- ROWS | RANGE—Determines the rows in the window for the current row. When ROWS is specified, then <value expression4> should be evaluated as an integer. Suppose the rows are 1, 2, 3, 4, 5, 6, 7, 8, 9, and you have specified the following:

```
...ROWS between 3 preceding AND 2...following
```

Then:

- For 3, rows 1, 2, 3, 4, 5 are considered.
- For 5, rows 2, 3, 4, 5, 6, 7 are considered.

NOTE

If you want to consider the rows of one side, then BETWEEN is not specified; for example, ROWS 3 preceding....

- RANGE—Specifies the time interval:

```
range between interval '1' day preceding and interval '1' day following.
```

For example, If the given dates are 1, 2, 5, 6, 7, 8, 10, then:

- For date 2, the window is 1, 2 (there is no data of date 3)
- For 6, window is 5, 6, 7
- The INTERVAL can be specified in terms of DAY, MONTH, and YEAR

The following are some examples illustrating the use of windowing functions:

Listing 11.16: Using the Windowing Function to Calculate the Running or Cumulative Sum According to Time

```
create table shares
(cname varchar2(10),
sdate date,
price number(4));
select * from shares;
```

The output of Listing 11.16 is as follows:

```
CNAME      SDATE          PRICE
---------- --------- ----------
ACC        12-JUN-06        700
ACC        13-JUN-06        704
ACC        14-JUN-06        712
ACC        15-JUN-06        723
TATA       12-JUN-06        500
TATA       13-JUN-06        512
TATA       14-JUN-06        520
TATA       15-JUN-06        523

8 rows selected
```

You can display records according to a condition, as shown in the following code snippet:

```
select cname,sdate,price,
avg(price)
over(partition by cname order by sdate rows unbounded preceding) csum
from shares;
```

The output of the preceding code snippet is as follows:

```
CNAME      SDATE          PRICE       CSUM
---------- --------- ---------- ----------
ACC        12-JUN-06        700        700
ACC        13-JUN-06        704        702
ACC        14-JUN-06        712 705.333333
ACC        15-JUN-06        723        723
TATA       12-JUN-06        500        500
TATA       13-JUN-06        512        506
TATA       14-JUN-06        520 510.666667
TATA       15-JUN-06        523     513.75

8 rows selected
```

Listing 11.17: Evaluating a Windowing Function

```
select * from sales_data where custid = 37280 and rownum<11;
```

The output of Listing 11.17 is as follows:

```
 PRODID  CUSTID    TIMEID        C     PROMOID    QUANTITY      AMOUNT
---------- --------- -------------------- --------- -------------------
 4105      37280   01-JAN-98    C          9999          7         553
```

Listing 11.18: Writing a Query with the ROWS UNBOUNDED PRECEDING Expression

```
select timeid,amount,sum(amount) over(order by timeid rows unbounded preceding)
  cum_amt  from sales_data where rownum < 11 order by 1;
```

The output of Listing 11.18 is as follows:

```
TIMEID        AMOUNT    CUM_AMT
--------- ---------- ----------
01-JAN-98       1422       1422
01-JAN-98        114       1536
01-JAN-98        553       2089
01-JAN-98        236       2325
01-JAN-98        752       3077
01-JAN-98        280       3357
01-JAN-98        196       3553
01-JAN-98         78       3631
01-JAN-98         90       3721
01-JAN-98        195       3916

10 rows selected.
```

The evaluation of a windowing function is similar to the analytical function. In Listing 11.18, the window for each row is calculated based on the window expression `ROWS UNBOUNDED PRECEDING`. The aggregation operation is performed for all the rows in that window. The first row does not have a preceding row. Therefore, `SUM(AMOUNT)` is evaluated to 1422. The third row has three preceding rows (including the third row), so `SUM(AMOUNT)` is calculated as the sum of 1422, 114 and 553, i.e. 2089.

Finding the Cumulative Sum of Amount Channel Wise

In this case, rows are partitioned according to `channelid`. For each channel, the rows are ordered and the cumulative sum is calculated by defining windows of the previous rows.

Listing 11.19 shows the use of PARTITION BY function

Listing 11.19: Calculating the Cumulative Sum

```
select timeid,amount,channelid, sum(amount) over(partition by channelid order by
   timeid rows unbounded preceding) cum_amt
from sales_data where  rownum < 11 order by 3,1;
```

The output of Listing 11.19 is as follows:

```
TIMEID          AMOUNT C     CUM_AMT
--------- ----------       -----------
01-JAN-98          553 C         553
01-JAN-98          752 C        1305
01-JAN-98          196 I         196
01-JAN-98          280 I         476
01-JAN-98          195 P         195
01-JAN-98          114 S         114
01-JAN-98         1422 S        1536
01-JAN-98           78 S        1614
01-JAN-98           90 T          90
01-JAN-98          236 T         326

10 rows selected.
```

Finding the Sales of the Last Date Channel Wise

Here it is similar to the previous example, except that instead of `SUM`, the `LAST_VALUE` function is used.

Listing 11.20 shows the use of the LAST_VALUE function:

Listing 11.20: Using the LAST_VALUE Function

```
select timeid,amount, channelid , last_value(amount) over(partition by
channelid order by timeid rows between unbounded preceding and unbounded
following) last_amt from sales_data where rownum < 11 order by 3,1;
```

The output of Listing 11.20 is as follows:

```
TIMEID          AMOUNT          C    LAST_AMT
---------   ----------          - ----------
01-JAN-98          553          C          752
01-JAN-98          752          C          752
01-JAN-98          196          I          280
01-JAN-98          280          I          280
01-JAN-98          195          P          195
01-JAN-98          114          S           78
01-JAN-98         1422          S           78
01-JAN-98           78          S           78
01-JAN-98           90          T          236
01-JAN-98          236          T          236

10 rows selected
```

Finding the Moving Average

Here it is similar to the previous except that the `AVG` function is used for aggregation.

Listing 11.21 shows the use of the WINDOWING function to calculate the moving average:

Listing 11.21: Using the AVG Function

```
SELECT TIMEID,AMOUNT,CHANNELID,AVG(AMOUNT) OVER(ORDER BY TIMEID ROWS UNBOUNDED
   PRECEDING) LAST_AMT
FROM SALES_DATA WHERE ROWNUM < 11 ORDER BY 1;
```

The output of Listing 11.21 is as follows:

```
TIMEID          AMOUNT  C  LAST_AMT
--------- ---------- - ----------
01-JAN-98       1422  S       1422
01-JAN-98        114  S        768
01-JAN-98        553  C 696.333333
01-JAN-98        236  T     581.25
01-JAN-98        752  C      615.4
01-JAN-98        280  I      559.5
01-JAN-98        196  I 507.571429
01-JAN-98         78  S    453.875
01-JAN-98         90  T 413.444444
01-JAN-98        195  P      391.6

10 rows selected
```

Calculating the 7 Days' Moving Average

The 7-day moving average is the average of the values of the last 7 days in a given data according to the date. If the data is available for the last 5 days, then only 5 days are considered.

Listing 11.22 shows you how to calculate the average of values of the last 7 days, based on the date:

Listing 11.22: Calculating the Average of Values of the Last 7 Days According to the Date

```
SELECT TIMEID,AMOUNT, CHANNELID,
AVG(AMOUNT) OVER(ORDER BY TIMEID RANGE INTERVAL
'7' DAY PRECEDING) LAST_AMT
FROM SALES_DATA WHERE ROWNUM < 11 ORDER BY 1;
```

The output of Listing 11.22 is as follows:

```
TIMEID          AMOUNT  C  LAST_AMT
--------- ---------- - ----------
01-JAN-98       1422  S      391.6
01-JAN-98        114  S      391.6
01-JAN-98        553  C      391.6
01-JAN-98        236  T      391.6
01-JAN-98        752  C      391.6
01-JAN-98        280  I      391.6
01-JAN-98        196  I      391.6
01-JAN-98         78  S      391.6
01-JAN-98         90  T      391.6
01-JAN-98        195  P      391.6

10 rows selected.
```

Apart from calculating the average of values for a number of days, you can also calculate the average of a range of rows, as discussed in the following section.

Calculating the Average of the Previous Rows and the Current Row

You can specify the WINDOW using time interval by using the `RANGE` clause. For example, consider the data provided in Table 11.2:

Table 11.2: Table with Sample Data

Date	Amt
1-JAN-2010	100
5-JAN-2010	50
6-JAN-2010	40
9-JAN-2010	10
10-JAN2010	60

According to above data, window if window with preceding 1 row is given in terms of date then for date 5-JAN-2010 will have only one row (of amount 50), for the date 6-JAN-2010 the window will have two rows (of date 5-JAN-2010 and 6-JAN-2010).

Listing 11.23 shows the use of the RANGE clause to specify the absolute range of rows:

Listing 11.23: Specifying the absolute range of rows by using the RANGE clause

```
SELECT TIMEID,AMOUNT,CHANNELID, AVG(AMOUNT) OVER(ORDER BY TIMEID RANGE BETWEEN
   '1' PRECEDING AND CURRENT ROW) CALC_AMT FROM SALES_DATA
WHERE ROWNUM < 11 ORDER BY 1;
```

The output of Listing 11.23 is as follows:

```
TIMEID           AMOUNT      C       CALC_AMT
-------- -------             --      -------
01-JAN-98          1422      S      391.6
01-JAN-98           114      S      391.6
01-JAN-98           553      C      391.6
01-JAN-98           236      T      391.6
01-JAN-98           195      P      391.6
01-JAN-98           280      I      391.6
01-JAN-98           196      I      391.6
01-JAN-98            78      S      391.6
01-JAN-98            90      T      391.6
01-JAN-98           752      C      391.6

10 rows selected.
```

Defining a Variable-Size Window

Variable size window means number of rows in the window are not fixed but can vary according to value of current row.

You can define a function based on the column of the current row to define user-defined window boundaries.

Listing 11.24: Calculating the Moving Average of the Last 2 Working Days (i.e., rows of Saturday and Sunday are excluded)

```
create or replace function calc_days(fdate date) return number as
begin
   if (to_char(fdate,'dy') = 'mon') or (to_char(fdate,'dy')='tue') then
          return(4);
   else
          return(2);
   end if;
end;
```

The output of Listing 11.24 is as follows:

```
Function created
```

After creating the function, it needs to be tested, as shown in Listing 11.25:

Listing 11.25: Executing the Function

```
declare
    a number;
    begin
    a:= calc_days('23-JUN-06');
    dbms_output.put_line(a);
    end;
    /
```

The output of Listing 11.25 is as follows:

```
PL/SQL procedure successfully completed.
```

The function returns 4 for Monday and Tuesday, and for other days it returns 2. You can use the function to specify a window.

NOTE

CALC_DAYS(TIMEID) returns 4 for Monday and Tuesday, and 2 otherwise.

```
select timeid,amount,channelid, avg(amount) over(order by timeid range between
   calc_days(timeid) preceding   and current row) calc_amt
from sales_data
where custid = 37280 and rownum < 11
order by 1;
```

The sample output is

```
TIMEID          AMOUNT          C       CALC_AMT
---------       ----------      -       ----------
01-JAN-98       553             C        553
```

Reporting Functions

Reporting functions are used to provide aggregate values of partitions to every row in the partition. These functions are useful to calculate market share and comparing row value with aggregated value.

Syntax of a Reporting Function

You can specify the function using following syntax

```
{SUM | AVG | MAX | MIN | COUNT | STDDEV | VARIANCE}
   ([ALL | DISTINCT] {<value expression1> | *})
       OVER ([PARTITION BY <value expression2>[,…]])
```

You can use any column name or column expression, or aggregation in place of the value `expression1`. Partition expressions can be similar to the previous functions. For each row, the aggregate functions such as `MAX` and `SUM` are evaluated for that partition.

Listing 11.26 shows you the use of reporting functions:

Listing 11.26: Using Reporting Functions to Calculate the Ratio of Sales to the Total Sales for each Channel

```
select timeid,amount,channelid, sum(amount) over(partition by channelid)        calc_amt,
amount/sum(amount) over(partition by channelid) perc from sales_data
where rownum < 11 order by 3,1;
```

The output of Listing 11.26 is as follows:

```
TIMEID          AMOUNT    C         CALC_AMT        PERC
--------- ----------    -         ---------- ----------
01-JAN-98          553    C         1305      .423754789
01-JAN-98          752    C         1305      .576245211
01-JAN-98          196    I          476      .411764706
01-JAN-98          280    I          476      .588235294
01-JAN-98          195    P          195               1
01-JAN-98          114    S         1614      .07063197
01-JAN-98         1422    S         1614      .881040892
01-JAN-98           78    S         1614      .048327138
01-JAN-98           90    T          326       .27607362
01-JAN-98          236    T          326      .72392638

10 rows selected
```

Finding the Ratio of Channel Sales to Maximum Sales

Here you have to use the MAX function as an aggregate function. The following query calculates the maximum value in a given set of values which can be compared with the current row value.

Listing 11.27: Using the MAX Function to compare current value with maximum value

```
select channelid,sum(amount) sum_amt,max(sum(amount)) over()
calc_amt,sum(amount) / max(sum(amount)) over() ratio
from sales_data where rownum < 11
group by channelid order by 1;
```

The output of Listing 11.27 is as follows:

```
C    SUM_AMT   CALC_AMT           RATIO
- ---------- ----------      ----------
C       1305       1614      .808550186
I        476       1614      .294919455
P        195       1614      .120817844
S       1614       1614               1
T        326       1614      .201982652
```

Let's now discuss the RATIO_TO_REPORT function.

The RATIO_TO_REPORT Function

The RATIO_TO_REPORT function is used to calculate the market share with reference to some column. It finds the ratio of the values of the rows to the sum of those values in a partition. For example, you can use the RATIO_TO_REPORT function to find out the ratio of sale of date in a channel to the total sales in that channel.

Syntax of the RATIO_TO_REPORT Function

The syntax to use the RATIO_TO_REPORT function is as follows:

```
RATIO_TO_REPORT
(<value expression1>) OVER
([PARTITION BY <value expression2>[,…]])
```

The following is a brief description of the various elements in the preceding syntax:

- PARTITION BY—Specifies the set for which the sum is calculated
- value expression2—Refers to the sum that is calculated over the partition. This sum is used in the denominator, while the numerator is the value of value expression1.

Listing 11.28 shows the use of the RATIO_TO_REPORT function:

Listing 11.28: Using the RATIO_TO_REPORT Function to Calculate the Ratio of Sale of Date to Total Sale in a Channel

```
select timeid, amount,channelid, sum(amount) over(partition by channelid)
   calc_amt,ratio_to_report(amount) over(partition by channelid) rat
from sales_data
where rownum < 11
order by 3,1;
```

The output of Listing 11.28 is as follows:

```
TIMEID        AMOUNT     C   CALC_AMT        RAT
--------- ----------     - ----------    ----------
01-JAN-98        553     C       1305    .423754789
01-JAN-98        752     C       1305    .576245211
01-JAN-98        196     I        476    .411764706
01-JAN-98        280     I        476    .588235294
01-JAN-98        195     P        195             1
01-JAN-98        114     S       1614    .07063197
01-JAN-98       1422     S       1614    .881040892
01-JAN-98         78     S       1614    .048327138
01-JAN-98         90     T        326     .27607362
01-JAN-98        236     T        326    .72392638
10 rows selected
```

After learning about the RATIO_TO_REPORT function, let's discuss the LAG/LEAD functions.

The LAG/LEAD Functions

The LAG/LEAD functions are used to compare the value of the current row with the values of the previous or next rows without taking a Cartesian product. The LAG function is used for previous rows, and the LEAD function is used for the next rows. The target row is specified in terms of an offset value with respect to the value of the current row.

Syntax of the ***LAG/LEAD*** *Functions*

The syntax to use the LAG/LEAD functions is as follows:

```
{LAG | LEAD}
   (<value expression1>, [<offset>[, <default>]]) OVER
      ([PARTITION BY <value expression2>[,…]]
       ORDER BY <value expression3> [collate clause>]
      [ASC | DESC][NULLS FIRST | NULLS LAST][,…])
```

The following is a brief description of the elements in the preceding syntax:

- PARTITION BY and ORDER BY are having the same meaning as specified in RANKING or WINDIWING functions.
- value expression1—Specifies a column expression or an aggregation

Let's now learn more about the LAG/LEAD functions through some examples. Consider the query in the following code snippet:

```
select timeid,channelid,amount
from sales_data
where custid = 37280
and timeid = '01-jan-98';
```

The output of the preceding code snippet is as follows:

```
TIMEID           C      AMOUNT
---------        - ----------
01-JAN-98        C         553
```

Listing 11.29 shows the use of the LAG function:

Listing 11.29: Using the LAG function to Calculate the Ratio of Sale for the Current Date to sale of previous date

```
select timeid,channelid,amount,
lag(amount,1)over(order
by timeid)lg1, amount/lag(amount,1)over(order by timeid) ratio_lag,
   lead(amount,1)over(order by timeid) ld1, amount/lead(amount,1)over(order by
   timeid) ratio_lead
from sales_data
where custid = 16480
and timeid = '01-jan-98'
order by 1;
```

The output of Listing 11.29 is as follows:

```
TIMEID           C      AMOUNT        LG1  RATIO_LAG           LD1 RATIO_LEAD
---------        -   --------- ---------- ---------- ---------- ----------
01-JAN-98        I         196
```

You can see that `LAG(AMOUNT,1)` gives the value of the amount of the previous row, while `LEAD(amount,2)` gives the value of the amount of the next second row. The rows being compared should be from a single partition.

If offset value is out of bound, then the default value is used. If default value is not specified, then the null value is returned as shown in the following code snippet:

```
select timeid,channelid,amount,
lag(amount,5,2)over(order by timeid)lg1, amount/lag(amount,1)over( order by
   timeid) ratio_lag,
lead(amount,1)over(order by timeid) ld1, amount/lead(amount,1)over(order by
   timeid) ratio_lead
from sales_data where timeid = '01-jan-98'
order by 1;
```

The output of the preceding code snippet is as follows:

```
TIMEID           C     AMOUNT        LG1       RATIO_LAG        LD1      RATIO_LEAD
---------        - ---------- ----------      ---------- ----------      ----------
01-JAN-98        S       1422          2                        114      12.4736842
01-JAN-98        S        114          2      .080168776        553      .206148282
01-JAN-98        C        553          2      4.85087719        236      2.34322034
01-JAN-98        T        236          2       .42676311        195      1.21025641
01-JAN-98        P        195          2      .826271186        280       .696428571
01-JAN-98        I        280       1422      1.43589744        196      1.42857143
01-JAN-98        I        196        114              .7        78        2.51282051
01-JAN-98        S         78        553      .397959184        90         .866666667
01-JAN-98        T         90        236      1.15384615        752        .119680851
01-JAN-98        C        752        195      8.35555556

10 rows selected.
```

Let's now discuss the FIRST/LAST functions.

The **FIRST/LAST** Functions

The FIRST/LAST functions are used to return the aggregate value for a set of rows, which ranks first or last, respectively, in a set of rows defined by partition. Ranks are determined by using the ORDER BY clause. The set of rows within a partition that has the first or last rank is taken and its aggregate value is calculated.

*Syntax of the **FIRST/LAST Functions***

The syntax for using the FIRST/LAST function is as follows:

```
[MIN | MAX | COUNT | SUM | AVG | STDDEV | VARIANCE ] (<expression>)
KEEP ( DENSE_RANK [FIRST | LAST] ORDER BY <order by expression> [,…]
[ASC|DESC] [NULLS FIRST| NULLS LAST] )
```

The following is a brief description of the elements in the preceding syntax:

- ORDER BY—Indicates how the rows in the set are arranged
- FIRST/ LAST—Determines the row set to be taken for aggregation. The aggregation function is one of the above aggregation functions as mentioned in syntax..

Let's now explore some examples to understand the use of the FIRST/LAST function:

Listing 11.30: Comparing the Current Date Values with the Values present in the Last Date of a Year

```
select timeid, amount, min(amount)  KEEP (DENSE_RANK Last ORDER BY (timeid))
  over() minvalue
from sales_data where to_char(timeid,'yyyy')='1998';
```

The output of Listing 11.30 is as follows:

```
TIMEID          AMOUNT   MINVALUE
--------- ---------- ----------
01-JAN-98         1422         78
01-JAN-98          114         78
01-JAN-98          553         78
01-JAN-98          236         78
01-JAN-98          195         78
01-JAN-98          280         78
01-JAN-98          196         78
01-JAN-98           78         78
01-JAN-98           90         78
01-JAN-98          752         78

10 rows selected.
```

Note the following in the preceding example:

- The condition selects the rows from the year
- LAST ORDER BY selects the last date of the year
- MIN(amount) selects the amount of sales for the date

Listing 11.31: Finding the Sale on the Last Day of Each Month

```
select to_char(timeid,'mon'), amount
from sales_data s
where to_char(timeid,'yyyy') = '1998'
and
timeid in
(select max(s1.timeid)
from sales_data s1
where  to_char(s1.timeid,'yyyy') = '1998'
and to_char(s.timeid,'mon')=to_char(s1.timeid,'mon'))
order by to_char(timeid,'mm');
```

The output of Listing 11.31 is as follows:

```
TO_     AMOUNT
---  ----------
JAN       1422
JAN        114
JAN        553
JAN        236
JAN        752
JAN        280
JAN        196
JAN         78
JAN         90
JAN        195
10 rows selected
```

In the preceding example, the inner subquery returns the last date of each month and the main query returns the sale for that date.

Listing 11.32: Using the FIRST/LAST Function Instead of a Subquery

```
select to_char(timeid,'mon'), min(amount)  KEEP
(DENSE_RANK last ORDER BY (timeid)) lastvalue
from sales_data where to_char(timeid,'yyyy') = '1998'
group by to_char(timeid,'mon'), to_char(timeid,'mm')
order by to_char(timeid,'mm');
```

Listing 11.33:

```
TO_  LASTVALUE
--- ----------
jan         78
```

In the preceding example, for each month, the rows are sorted according to timeid, and the last row is selected because the LAST function is used. The aggregation function MIN is evaluated for the rows having the last rank.

Regression

Regression is used to find the relation between two properties and estimate the other property values when the value of the first property is given. For example, when you decrease the price of an item, then the quantity of sales for that item will increase. Likewise, when spend more money in advertisements, the sales will increase.

In linear regression, we find the linear relationship between two properties from specified data. This is done by using the line fitting method. In this method, points are plotted on the X-Y axis and a line is drawn between these points so that the distance between the points and the line is the minimum. Suppose you have a data table with two columns, `QUANTITY` and `AVG_PRICE and having data as follows:`

```
select * from sales_price;
```

The output of the preceding code snippet is as follows:

```
  QUANTITY  AVG_PRICE
---------- ----------
       100        100
       120         90
       150         80
       140         84
```

You can plot the points on the X-Y axis and fit the line as shown in Figure 11.2:

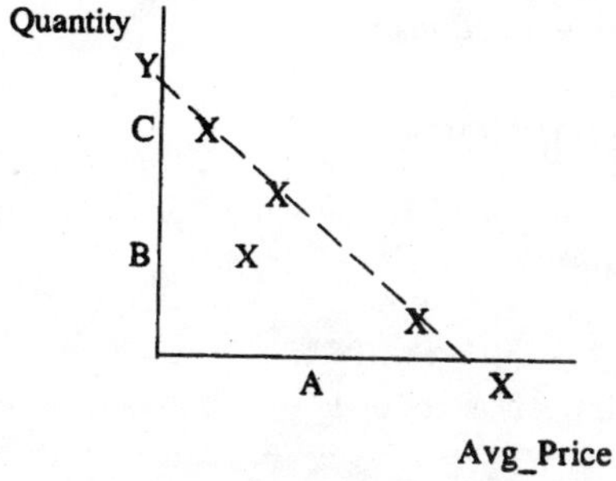

Figure 11.2: Plotting Points on the X-Y Axis

In Figure 11.2, the points are marked as X. After the line is approximated, you can find the Y-value (Quantity), if the X-value is known (if A is given then you can get B). The equation of line is as follows:

```
Y = mX + C
```

In the preceding equation:

- `m` is the slope of the line
- `C` is the Y intercept (point at which line intercepts the Y-axis)

Oracle provides the facility for calculating the slope, intercept, and number of `NOT NULL` rows, which are used in regression analysis (if the first or second value is `NULL`, then the row is not considered). Consider the following code snippet:

```
select
regr_slope(s.quantity, s.avg_price) slope,
regr_intercept(s.quantity, s.avg_price) intcpt,
regr_r2(s.quantity, s.avg_price) rsqr,
regr_count(s.quantity, s.avg_price) count,
regr_avgx(s.quantity, s.avg_price) avg_avg_price,
regr_avgy(s.quantity, s.avg_price) avg_quantity from sales_price s;
```

The output of the preceding code snippet is as follows:

```
SLOPE          INTCPT          RSQR          COUNT        AVG_AVG_PRICE    AVG_QUANTITY
----------   ----------     ----------     ---------    -------------    ------------
-2.5330396     351.674009     .987456134     4                     88.5           127.5
```

For each regression function, the input is `(Y-axis value, X-axis value)`. `REGR_R2 (s.quantity, s.avg_price)`. `RSQR` gives the quality of regression and its value is between 0 and 1.

NOTE

If the value is close to 1, the regression is considered good.

`REGR_AVGX(s.quantity, s.avg_price)` gives the average of the X-value, i.e. `avg_price`, and `REGR_AVGY(s.quantity, s.avg_price)` gives the average of the Y-value, i.e. quantity sold.

Listing 11.33 shows how to calculate Y value if X value is given.

Listing 11.33: Calculating the Value of the Quantity Sold for Price X = 95

```
select 95 x,(-2.5330396*95 + 351.674009) y
from dual;
```

The output of Listing 11.33 is as follows:

```
     X              Y
----------     ----------
    95         111.035247
```

In the preceding example, the expression of `Y` is `mX + C`.

Let's now learn about inverse percentile functions.

The Inverse Percentile Functions

Inverse percentile functions are used to calculate the value for certain cumulative distributions. Consider the query shown in the following code snippet:

```
select timeid,quantity
from sales_data where timeid = '01-jan-98';
```

The output of the preceding code snippet is as follows:

```
TIMEID      QUANTITY
--------- ----------
01-JAN-98         18
01-JAN-98          6
01-JAN-98          7
01-JAN-98          2
01-JAN-98          3
01-JAN-98         14
01-JAN-98          4
01-JAN-98          2
01-JAN-98          9
01-JAN-98          4

10 rows selected.
```

Listing 11.34 shows you how to find the cumulative distribution of data in the preceding output:

Listing 11.34: Finding Cumulative Distribution

```
select timeid,quantity,cume_dist()over(order by quantity)
from sales_data
where timeid ='01-jan-98';
```

The output of Listing 11.34 is as follows:

```
TIMEID      QUANTITY   CUME_DIST()OVER(ORDERBYQUANTITY)
--------- ----------   --------------------------------
01-JAN-98          2                                 .2
01-JAN-98          2                                 .2
01-JAN-98          3                                 .3
01-JAN-98          4                                 .5
01-JAN-98          4                                 .5
01-JAN-98          6                                 .6
01-JAN-98          7                                 .7
01-JAN-98          9                                 .8
01-JAN-98         14                                 .9
01-JAN-98         18                                  1

10 rows selected.
```

*Syntax of the INVERSE **PERCENTILE** Functions*

The syntax to use PERCENTILE functions is as follows:

```
[PERCENTILE_CONT | PERCENTILE_DISC](<constant expression>)
WITHIN GROUP (ORDER BY <single order by expression>
[ASC|DESC][NULLS FIRST| NULLS LAST])
OVER ([PARTITION BY <value expression> [,…]])
```

In the preceding syntax:

- `WITHIN GROUP` gives the value for each row in the query
- The `ORDER BY` clause should be numeric or of the datetime type because interpolation is used in the calculation for `PERCENTILE_CONT`.
- `NULLS` are ignored for calculations

Listing 11.35 shows the use of PERCENTILE functions

Listing 11.35: Finding the Value of the Quantity Sold for which the Cumulative Distribution is 0.5

```
select percentile_disc(0.5) within group
(order by quantity) as perc_disc,
percentile_cont(0.5) within group
(order by quantity) as perc_cont
from sales_data where timeid ='01-jan-98';
```

The output of Listing 11.35 is as follows

```
PERC_DISC  PERC_CONT
---------- ----------
   4        5
```

In the preceding example, `PERCENTILE_DISC(x)` finds the first cumulative value, which is equal to or greater than x (`x = 0.5`). Therefore, it finds the value of quantity for which cumulative sale is `50%`, i.e. `0.5`. The value is 4 as given by the highlighted row in the output of Listing 11.34.

The steps to calculate `PERCENTILE_CONT(x) (USING INTERPOLATION)` is as follows:

1. Determine the row number `RN` by the formula `RN= (1 + x* (N - 1))`, where N (the number of rows) `=10, x = 0.5; therefore, RN = 1 + 0.5(9) = 5.5`
2. Determine CRN by using ceil(RN) = ceil(5.5)=6
3. Determine FRN by using floor(RN) = floor(5.5)=5

The formula is:

```
(CRN - RN) * (VALUE OF ROW AT FRN)+(RN - FRN)* VALUE OF ROW AT CRN
PERCENTILE_CONT(0.5) = (6 - 5.5)*(value of row 5) + (5.5 - 5)*(value of row 6]
= 0.5 * 4 + 0.5 * 6
= 5
```

Listing 11.36 shows how to use inverse percentile function

Listing 11.36: Displaying the Output for Each Row

```
select timeid,quantity,
percentile_disc(0.2) within group
(order by quantity) over()as perc_disc,
percentile_cont(0.2) within group
(order by quantity)over() as perc_cont
from sales_data where  timeid = '01-jan-98';
```

The output of Listing 11.36 is as follows:

```
TIMEID       QUANTITY     PERC_DISC      PERC_CONT
--------- ----------    ----------     ----------
01-JAN-98           2            2      2.8
01-JAN-98           2            2      2.8
01-JAN-98           3            2      2.8
01-JAN-98           4            2      2.8
01-JAN-98           4            2      2.8
01-JAN-98           6            2      2.8
01-JAN-98           7            2      2.8
01-JAN-98           9            2      2.8
```

```
01-JAN-98          14          2          2.8
01-JAN-98          18          2          2.8

10 rows selected
```

Hypothetical Rank

It is used to calculate the rank of a row, if it is inserted with some value. For example suppose you are interested in finding rank of student if student gets 85 marks then you can use hypothetical function.

Syntax of the Hypothetical Rank

The syntax of hypothetical rank is

```
[RANK|DENSE_RANK|PERCENT_RANK|CUME_DIST](<constant expression>[,...] )
WITHIN GROUP (ORDER BY <order by expression> [ASC|DESC][NULLS FIRST|NULLS
LAST][,...])
```

In the preceding syntax:

- `ORDER BY` gives the sorting order on which the ranks are to be based
- The expression `constant expression` is evaluated as constant

If we take the data from the previous listing (Listing 11.36), what will be the rank of row if a row with quantity 10 is inserted. The row will have rank 2 because 10 will come after 7 (value of the 1st row).

Following listing shows how to use hypothetical rank

Listing 11.37: Finding the percent_rank, dense_rank and cume_dist of the Given Row

```
select rank(10) within group
(order by quantity) as hrank,
percent_rank(10) within group
(order by quantity) as perc_rank,
cume_dist(10) within group
(order by quantity) as cume_rank
from sales_data where custid = 37280 and timeid = '01-jan-98';
```

The output of Listing 11.37 is as follows:

```
   HRANK           PERC_RANK         CUME_RANK
--------           ----------        ----------
       2           1                 1
```

Summary

In this chapter, you have learned about the concept of analytical queries. In the next chapter, you will learn about ROLLUP and CUBE.

Exercise

(Use Sales_data)

1. Name of top 5 products in terms of sales in JAN-2010.
2. Find out growth of sale of product having code 85 in FEB-2003 as compared to sale in JAN-2003.
3. Find out market share of product having code 85 for each channel with reference to channel.

12

Understanding ROLLUP and CUBE

Rollup and Cube are used to calculate aggregate functions on multiple groups in the single query. Using Rollup and Cube, performance will be improved because instead of executing multiple queries single query is executed.

Understanding **ROLLUP**

Cube and Rollup grouping is used in data warehousing, which generates business intelligence information that is required for decision-making by medium and high-level managers.

Suppose you have data on departmental sale and you want the information regarding the `time` and `region of the sale` and `departments in which the sale has occurred` and the `profit` from the sale. In other words, you are interested in finding out department wise, region wise, and total sale of the year. This can be done by using the rollup feature in the group by clause. If you want to use the `rollup` command, you need to use the additional clause `Group by Rollup (time, region, dept)`. The output will display the department wise sale and then it will `rollup` to the region. Rollup means it will find out the total sale of the region.

Suppose the first three rows in a table gives the total sale for the Central region. After finding out the total sale for each region by writing a query, if we wish to find the total sale for the year 1996, we can write another query. The same thing can be repeated for the year 1997, and this becomes tiring. However, you can have the aggregation in N dimensions without using additional queries with the help of the `rollup` facility.

Let's first create and insert data into the table, sales.

Listing 12.1, 12.2, and 12.3 shows the syntax to create the sample sales table, insert data in it, and display the inserted data:

Listing 12.1: Creating the sales Table

```
create table sales (time number, region varchar2(15), dept varchar2(15), profit
  number);
```

Output of Listing 12.1 is given as follows:

```
Table created
```

Listing 12.2: Inserting Data into the sales Table

```
insert into sales values(1996, 'Central', 'pen_sales', 34000);
insert into sales values(1996, 'Central', 'pen_sales', 41000);
insert into sales values(1996, 'Central', 'book_sales', 74000);

insert into sales values(1996, 'east','pen_sales', 89000);
insert into sales values(1996, 'east','book_sales',100000);
insert into sales values(1996, 'east', 'book_sales', 15000);

insert into sales values(1996, 'west', 'pen_sales', 87000);
insert into sales values(1996, 'west', 'book_sales', 86000);
insert into sales values(1997, 'Central', 'pen_sales', 82000);

insert into sales values(1997, 'Central', 'book_sales', 85000);
insert into sales values(1997, 'east', 'pen_sales', 101000);
insert into sales values(1997, 'east', 'book_sales', 137000);

insert into sales values(1997, 'west', 'pen_sales', 96000);
insert into sales values(1997, 'west', 'book_sales', 97000);
```

Listing 12.3: Displaying the Data of the sales Table

```
select * from sales;
```

Output of Listing 12.3 is given as follows:

```
TIME        REGION       DEPT          PROFIT
------      ---------    ----------    ----------
1996        CENTRAL      PEN_SALES      34000
1996        CENTRAL      PEN_SALES      41000
1996        CENTRAL      BOOK_SALES     74000
1996        EAST         PEN_SALES      89000
1996        EAST         BOOK_SALES    100000
1996        EAST         BOOK_SALES     15000
1996        WEST         PEN_SALES      87000
1996        WEST         BOOK_SALES     86000
1997        CENTRAL      PEN_SALES      82000
1997        CENTRAL      BOOK_SALES     85000
1997        EAST         PEN_SALES     101000
1997        EAST         BOOK_SALES    137000
1997        WEST         PEN_SALES      96000
1997        WEST         BOOK_SALES     97000

14 rows selected.
```

The data in the table using GROUP BY clause is listed as follows

Listing 12.4: Using GROUP BY

```
select time, region, dept, sum(profit) as profit from sales
group by time, region, dept;
```

Output of Listing 12.4 is given as follows:

```
 TIME        REGION       DEPT              PROFIT
 -----       -----        ---------         ---------
 1997        WEST         PEN_SALES          96000
 1997        EAST         BOOK_SALES        137000
 1997        WEST         BOOK_SALES         97000
 1996        CENTRAL      BOOK_SALES         74000
 1996        EAST         PEN_SALES          89000
 1997        CENTRAL      BOOK_SALES         85000
 1996        CENTRAL      PEN_SALES          75000
 1996        EAST         BOOK_SALES        115000
 1996        WEST         BOOK_SALES         86000
 1996        WEST         PEN_SALES          87000
 1997        CENTRAL      PEN_SALES          82000

 1997        EAST         PEN_SALES         101000

12 rows selected
```

Here, the rows are produced by using group by, but without using rollup. The output contains regular aggregation rows that would be produced by `GROUP BY` without using `ROLLUP`. Therefore, you are having rows, which are having the same values of year, region, and department.

In the following query the data is first aggregated on (Time, region, dept), then aggregation is done on (Time, region) and finally aggregation is done on (Time).

Listing 12.5: Using ROLLUP

```
select time, region, dept,
sum(profit) as profit from sales
group by rollup(time,region,dept);
```

Output of Listing 12.5 is given as follows:

```
TIME        REGION       DEPT          PROFIT
----------  ------------ ------------  -------
1996        EAST         PEN_SALES     89000
1996        EAST         BOOK_SALES    115000
1996        EAST                       204000
1996        WEST         PEN_SALES      87000
1996        WEST         BOOK_SALES     86000
1996        WEST                       173000
1996        CENTRAL      PEN_SALES      75000
1996        CENTRAL      BOOK_SALES     74000
1996        CENTRAL                    149000
1996                                   526000
1997        EAST         PEN_SALES     101000
1997        EAST         BOOK_SALES    137000
1997        EAST                       238000
1997        WEST         PEN_SALES      96000
1997        WEST         BOOK_SALES     97000
1997        WEST                       193000
1997        CENTRAL      PEN_SALES      82000
1997        CENTRAL      BOOK_SALES     85000
1997        CENTRAL                    167000
1997                                   598000
                                      1124000
21 rows selected.
```

Rollup produces rows that give subtotals for each combination of time and region across departments. So you will have rows, like 1996, central region and 1996, eastern region. After producing the second-level subtotals of aggregation across region, department for each combination with time, you will have rows for 1996 and 1997. After the aggregation of the second-level subtotals, it will produce the grand total row. Therefore, the output contains the following:

- First-level aggregation using group (Time, region, dept)
- Second-level aggregation using group (Time, region)
- Third level aggregation using group (Time)
- A grand total row

Using Partial Rollup

Partial ROLLUP can be specified by using the following syntax:

```
group by time, rollup (region, department)
```

It indicates that the rollup is specified as region and department. It will produce aggregation of region and department sales for each value of time. So it will produce rows as 1996, central region. Since no rollup is specified for the time, you will not have the total aggregation of rows as a grand total row, which was present earlier.

Listing 12.6 provides the code to use the partial ROLLUP:

Listing 12.6: Using Partial ROLLUP

```
select time, region, dept, sum(profit) as profit from sales
group by time, rollup(region, dept);
```

Output of Listing 12.6 is given as follows:

```
      TIME          REGION          DEPT                 PROFIT
  ----------    ------------    ---------------     ----------
      1996          EAST            PEN_SALES             89000
      1996          EAST            BOOK_SALES           115000
      1996          EAST                                 204000
      1996          WEST            PEN_SALES             87000
      1996          WEST            BOOK_SALES            86000
      1996          WEST                                 173000
      1996          CENTRAL         PEN_SALES             75000
      1996          CENTRAL         BOOK_SALES            74000
      1996          CENTRAL                              149000
      1996                                               526000
      1997          EAST            PEN_SALES            101000
      1997          EAST            BOOK_SALES           137000
      1997          EAST                                 238000
      1997          WEST            PEN_SALES             96000
      1997          WEST            BOOK_SALES            97000
      1997          WEST                                 193000
      1997          CENTRAL         PEN_SALES             82000
      1997          CENTRAL         BOOK_SALES            85000
      1997          CENTRAL                              167000
      1997                                               598000

  20 rows selected
```

You can observe the following points from the output:

- There are regular aggregation rows that would be produced by `GROUP BY` without using `ROLLUP`
- There are first-level subtotals aggregating across `Department` for each combination of `Time` and `Region`
- There are second-level subtotals aggregating across `Region` and `Department` for each `Time` value
- No grand total row is produced

Create a Group within a Group

You know that grouping is always done on certain combinations. For example, grouping is always done on `TIME` and `REGION`, as shown in Listing 12.7:

Listing 12.7: Grouping on TIME and REGION

```
select time, region, dept, sum(profit) as profit from sales
group by rollup((time,region),dept);
```

Output of Listing 12.7 is given as follows:

```
TIME            REGION          DEPT                     PROFIT
----------      ------------    ---------------     ----------
1996            EAST            PEN_SALES                89000
1996            EAST            BOOK_SALES              115000
1996            EAST                                    204000
1996            WEST            PEN_SALES                87000
1996            WEST            BOOK_SALES               86000
1996            WEST                                    173000
1996            CENTRAL         PEN_SALES                75000
1996            CENTRAL         BOOK_SALES               74000
1996            CENTRAL                                 149000
1997            EAST            PEN_SALES               101000
1997            EAST            BOOK_SALES              137000
1997            EAST                                    238000
```

```
1997          WEST          PEN_SALES         96000
1997          WEST          BOOK_SALES        97000
1997          WEST                           193000
1997          CENTRAL       PEN_SALES         82000
1997          CENTRAL       BOOK_SALES        85000
1997          CENTRAL                        167000
                                            1124000

19 rows selected.
```

Understanding **CUBE**

A cube is used when you are interested in finding out aggregation of multiple dimensions or multiple combinations of multiple dimensions. Suppose you have a table containing `time`, `region`, and `department`; and you want to find out the total sale for the year 1996, or the total pen sales, or the total pen sales in the central region for all time. That means you are interested in combinations of multiple dimensions. In such cases, cubes are very useful as they help in producing aggregations without writing multiple queries.

NOTE

A cube is specified in GROUP BY clause similar to ROLLUP.

Listing 12.8 shows the code to use a cube to ascertain product aggregations:

Listing 12.8: Using a CUBE to Product Aggregations

```
select time,nvl(region,0) region, dept, sum(profit) as profit from sales
group by cube(time, region, dept);
```

Output of Listing 12.8 is given as follows:

```
TIME          REGION        DEPT              PROFIT
----------    ------------- --------------- ----------
              0                              1124000
              0             PEN_SALES         530000
              0             BOOK_SALES        594000
              EAST                            442000
              EAST          PEN_SALES         190000
              EAST          BOOK_SALES        252000
              WEST                            366000
              WEST          PEN_SALES         183000
              WEST          BOOK_SALES        183000
              CENTRAL                         316000
              CENTRAL       PEN_SALES         157000
              CENTRAL       BOOK_SALES        159000
1996          0                               526000
1996          0             PEN_SALES         251000
1996          0             BOOK_SALES        275000
1996          EAST                            204000
1996          EAST          PEN_SALES          89000
1996          EAST          BOOK_SALES        115000
1996          WEST                            173000
1996          WEST          PEN_SALES          87000
1996          WEST          BOOK_SALES         86000
1996          CENTRAL                         149000
1996          CENTRAL       PEN_SALES          75000
1996          CENTRAL       BOOK_SALES         74000
```

```
1997          0                                598000
1997          0               PEN_SALES        279000
1997          0               BOOK_SALES       319000
1997          EAST                             238000
1997          EAST            PEN_SALES        101000
1997          EAST            BOOK_SALES       137000
1997          WEST                             193000
1997          WEST            PEN_SALES         96000
1997          WEST            BOOK_SALES        97000
1997          CENTRAL                          167000
1997          CENTRAL         PEN_SALES         82000
1997          CENTRAL         BOOK_SALES        85000

36 rows selected
```

Using the Partial Cube

When you specify less number of dimensions in the `cube` clause, the combinations are generated only for the dimensions that you have specified. Suppose, you specify a `group by time, cube(region, dept)`, then combinations are generated only for `region` and `dept` along with `time`. Therefore, in the output you will have rows, such as `1996; central; pen_sales 1996; and central except central, pen_sales row.` Listing 12.9 shows the code that is used to make partial cube.

Listing 12.9: Using Group by time, cube (region, dept)

```
select time, region, dept, sum(profit) as profit from sales
group by time, cube(region, dept);
```

Output of Listing 12.9 is given as follows:

```
TIME          REGION          DEPT            PROFIT
----------    -------------   -------------   ----------
1996                                          526000
1996                          PEN_SALES       251000
1996                          BOOK_SALES      275000
1996          EAST                            204000
1996          EAST            PEN_SALES       89000
1996          EAST            BOOK_SALES      115000
1996          WEST                            173000
1996          WEST            PEN_SALES       87000
1996          WEST            BOOK_SALES      86000
1996          CENTRAL                         149000
1996          CENTRAL         PEN_SALES       75000
1996          CENTRAL         BOOK_SALES      74000
1997                                          598000
1997                          PEN_SALES       279000
1997                          BOOK_SALES      319000
1997          EAST                            238000
1997          EAST            PEN_SALES       101000
1997          EAST            BOOK_SALES      137000
1997          WEST                            193000
1997          WEST            PEN_SALES       96000
1997          WEST            BOOK_SALES      97000
1997          CENTRAL                         167000
1997          CENTRAL         PEN_SALES       82000
1997          CENTRAL         BOOK_SALES      85000

24 rows selected
```

Grouping Set

A CUBE can specify all combinations; however, if you are interested in certain combinations, you can specify them by using GROUPING SET. The usage of GROUPING SET is shown in the following listings:

Listing 12.10: Using the GROUPING SET

```
select region, dept, sum(profit) as profit from sales
group by grouping sets(region,dept);
```

Output of Listing 12.10 is given as follows:

```
REGION      DEPT                    PROFIT
----------  ------------        ----------
west                                366000
Central                             316000
east                                442000
            pen_sales               530000
            book_sales              594000
```

Listing 12.11: Grouping Two Combinations (time, region) and dept

```
select time, region, dept, sum(profit) as profit from sales
group by grouping sets((time,region),dept);
```

Output of Listing 12.11 is given as follows:

```
TIME        REGION          DEPT            PROFIT
----------  -------------   ------------    ----------
  1996      WEST                                173000
  1997      CENTRAL                             167000
  1997      WEST                                193000
  1997      EAST                                238000
  1996      CENTRAL                             149000
  1996      EAST                                204000
                            PEN_SALES           530000
                            BOOK_SALES          594000
8 rows selected.
```

Listing 12.12: Performing grouping on (region, time) and (dept, time)

```
select time, region, dept, sum(profit) as profit from sales
group by grouping sets(region,dept), grouping sets(time);
```

Output of Listing 12.12 is given as follows:

```
TIME        REGION          DEPT            PROFIT
----------  -------------   ------------    ----------
 1996       CENTRAL                             149000
 1997       WEST                                193000
 1996       EAST                                204000
 1997       CENTRAL                             167000
 1996       WEST                                173000
 1997       EAST                                238000
 1997                       PEN_SALES           279000
 1997                        BOOK_SALES         319000
 1996                       BOOK_SALES          275000
 1996                        PEN_SALES          251000

10 rows selected.
```

Grouping Clause

The grouping clause is specified in the `SELECT` clause and used to find out the dimension that is rolled up in the aggregated row. This is shown in Listing 12.13:

Listing 12.13: Using GROUPING

```
select time, region, dept, sum(profit) as profit,
grouping (time) as t, grouping (region) as r,
grouping (dept) as d from sales
group by rollup (time, region, dept);
```

Output of Listing 12.13 is given as follows:

```
TIME    REGION     DEPT          PROFIT    T    R    D
------  --------   --------      -------   --   --   --
1996    EAST       PEN_SALES     89000     0    0    0
1996    EAST       BOOK_SALES    115000    0    0    0
1996    EAST                     204000    0    0    1
1996    WEST       PEN_SALES     87000     0    0    0
1996    WEST       BOOK_SALES    86000     0    0    0
1996    WEST                     173000    0    0    1
1996    CENTRAL    PEN_SALES     75000     0    0    0
1996    CENTRAL    BOOK_SALES    74000     0    0    0
1996    CENTRAL                  149000    0    0    1
1996                             526000    0    1    1
1997    EAST       PEN_SALES     101000    0    0    0
1997    EAST       BOOK_SALES    137000    0    0    0
1997    EAST                     238000    0    0    1
1997    WEST       PEN_SALES     96000     0    0    0
1997    WEST       BOOK_SALES    97000     0    0    0
1997    WEST                     193000    0    0    1
1997    CENTRAL    PEN_SALES     82000     0    0    0
1997    CENTRAL    BOOK_SALES    85000     0    0    0
1997    CENTRAL                  167000    0    0    1
1997                             598000    0    1    1
                                 1124000   1    1    1

21 rows selected.
```

The output highlights the following points:

- In the third row, 1996, central grouping for department indicates 1 and for time and region, it is 0. It implies that in third row the dimension department is rolled up.
- If you see the row in which 1996 is specified, then grouping bit (generated by grouping function) for region and department is 1 and for time it is 0. In other words, the 1 in grouping indicates that the specified expression in not involved in aggregation and null in group expression is the result of cube or rollup.
- If grouping indicates 0 and group by column is null, then it implies that the column is involved in aggregation; however, the group by column is null because of the null value stored in the base table.
- For the grand total row, the grouping bit for time, region, and department is 1.
- In the fifth row, the null in the group column indicates null in the base table, while 0 in the grouping indicates that the column is involved in aggregation.
- In the sixth row, null in group column indicates that column is not involved in aggregation.

Listing 12.14: Using the Grouping on Emp_company Table

```
select cname,sum(salary),grouping(cname)
from emp_company
group by rollup(cname);
```

Output of Listing 12.14 is given as follows:

```
CNAME       SUM(SALARY)   GROUPING(CNAME)
----------  -----------   ---------------
                   2400                 0
                   2400                 1
```

GROUP_ID Clause

The GROUP_ID clause is used to find out the duplicate rows in the query, which may be generated by rollup or cube clause. The first occurrence of the row, groupid value 1, for second occurrence generates 2 etc.

Listing 12.15: Using GROUP_ID

```
select time, region, dept, sum(profit) as profit,
group_id() grid from sales
group by rollup (time, region),rollup(time, dept)
order by 5
```

Output of Listing 12.15 is given as follows:

```
  TIME            REGION            DEPT                PROFIT         GRID
---------  ---------------  ---------------  ----------  ----------
  1997                                              598000            0
  1997          WEST                                193000            0
  1997          CENTRAL           PEN_SALES          82000            0
  1997          WEST              PEN_SALES          96000            0
  1997          EAST              PEN_SALES         101000            0
  1996          CENTRAL           BOOK_SALES         74000            0
  1996          WEST              BOOK_SALES         86000            0
  1996          EAST              BOOK_SALES        115000            0
  1997          CENTRAL                             167000            0
  1997          EAST              BOOK_SALES        137000            0
  1997          WEST              BOOK_SALES         97000            0

  TIME            REGION            DEPT                PROFIT         GRID
------     ---------------  ---------------     ----------  ----------
  1997          CENTRAL           BOOK_SALES         85000            0
  1996                            PEN_SALES         251000            0
  1996                            BOOK_SALES        275000            0
  1997                            PEN_SALES         279000            0
  1997                            BOOK_SALES        319000            0
  1996          EAST              PEN_SALES          89000            0
  1996          WEST              PEN_SALES          87000            0
  1996          CENTRAL           PEN_SALES          75000            0
                                                   1124000            0
  1996          EAST                                204000            0
  1996          WEST                                173000            0

  TIME            REGION            DEPT                PROFIT         GRID
------     ---------------  ---------------     ----------  ----------
  1996          CENTRAL                             149000            0
  1997          EAST                                238000            0
```

```
  1996                                               526000          0
  1997          CENTRAL                              167000          1
  1997          WEST                                 193000          1
  1997          EAST                                 238000          1
  1996          CENTRAL                              149000          1
  1996          WEST                                 173000          1
  1996          EAST                                 204000          1
  1997                          PEN_SALES            279000          1
  1996                          BOOK_SALES           275000          1

  TIME          REGION          DEPT                 PROFIT       GRID
------   ---------------   ---------------       ---------- ----------
  1996                          PEN_SALES            251000          1
  1997                          BOOK_SALES           319000          1
  1997                                               598000          1
  1996                                               526000          1
  1997                                               598000          2
  1996                                               526000          2

39 rows selected.
```

Summary

The chapter has provided utility of ROLLUP and CUBE operations. Using ROLLUP and CUBE, you can improve your performance in multiple aggregations. In the next chapter joins are introduced.

Exercise

Using Sales table

1. Write a query to provide aggregate profit on groups (Time, Region) and (Region).
2. Write a query to provide aggregate profit on all combinations of groups formed by Region and Time.

13

Understanding Joins

The joins provide an alternative syntax according to the SQL-1999 standard. They do not add any additional functionality. Oracle provides all types of join operations like natural join, cross join and outer join.

Natural Join

When you have a Cartesian product with equality condition using columns having the same name in the `where` condition, it is called a natural join. Suppose two table T and S are having column with same name A then in the natural join the where condition T.A=S.A is implicit.

Suppose you want to retrieve name, living city and salary of the employee then you will write query as

Listing 13.1: Retrieving Name, Living City, and Salary of an Employee

```
select e.ename,e.city,c.salary
from employee e , emp_company c
where e.ename=c.ename
/
```

The output of Listing 13.1 is given as follows:

```
ENAME               CITY                SALARY
ANIL                NAGPUR              1500
SHANKAR             MUMBAI              2000
JAYA                CHENNAI             1800
SUNIL               MUMBAI              1700
VIJAY               DELHI               5000
PRAKASH             KOLKATA             3000
AJAY                CHENNAI             8000

7 rows selected.
```

The above query can also be written as follows.

Listing 13.2: Using the JOIN Clause

```
select ename,city,salary
from employee natural join emp_company
/
```

The output of Listing 13.2 is given as follows:

```
ENAME               CITY                SALARY
-----               -----               ------
ANIL                NAGPUR              1500
SHANKAR             MUMBAI              2000
JAYA                CHENNAI             1800
SUNIL               MUMBAI              1700
VIJAY               DELHI               5000
PRAKASH             KOLKATA             3000
AJAY                CHENNAI             8000

7 rows selected.
```

When you specify a natural join, a Cartesian product is computed and the `where` condition is constructed by using columns of the same name from the tables involved in join operation. If we use the qualifier name in natural join an error can occur as follows.

```
select e.ename,city,salary from employee e natural join emp_company c
/
```

The output of the preceding syntax, which shows the error, is as follows:

```
select e.ename,city,salary
       *
ERROR at line 1:
ORA-25155: column used in NATURAL join cannot have qualifier
```

Cross Join

Cross join is another way of specifying Cartesian product. In the Listing 13.3 query is specified using Cartesian product and using CROSS JOIN.

Listing 13.3: Using a Cartesian Product

```
select e.ename,e.city,c.salary
from employee e, emp_company c
/
```

Alternatively, you can write the same query by using a new syntax of CROSS JOIN, which is as follows:

```
select e.ename,city,salary
from employee e cross join emp_company c
/
```

The output of the preceding query is given as follows:

```
ENAME      CITY           SALARY
---------- ---------- ----------
ANIL       NAGPUR           1500
ANIL       NAGPUR           2000
ANIL       NAGPUR           1800
ANIL       NAGPUR           1700
ANIL       NAGPUR           5000
ANIL       NAGPUR           3000
ANIL       NAGPUR           8000
ANIL       NAGPUR           1000
SHANKAR    MUMBAI           1500
SHANKAR    MUMBAI           2000
SHANKAR    MUMBAI           1800
SHANKAR    MUMBAI           1700
SHANKAR    MUMBAI           5000
SHANKAR    MUMBAI           3000
...
56 rows selected.
```

Using the Column Clause

If you want to perform a natural join on a specified column name, you can use the following syntax:

```
join <table name> using <column name>
```

If you specify `JOIN using`, you cannot specify natural join. The equality condition in the `WHERE` clause is constructed by using the column name specified in the `WHERE` condition. The following listings provide the examples where the 'WHERE clause' and 'USING clause' are used:

Listing 13.4: JOIN using where condition

```
select c.ename, m.mname, c.salary
from manager m, emp_company c
where c.ename = m.ename
and salary < 3000
/
```

The output of Listing 13.4 is given as follows:

```
ENAME             MNAME            SALARY
------   -------            -------
ANIL              AJAY             1500
SHANKAR           VIJAY            2000
JAYA                               1800
SUNIL             JAYA             1700
```

Listing 13.5: JOIN using column

```
manager.ename = emp_company.ename
select ename,mname,salary
from manager join emp_company using(ename)
where salary < 3000
/
```

The output of Listing 13.5 is given as follows:

```
ENAME          MNAME          SALARY
------         -------        -------
ANIL           AJAY           1500
SHANKAR        VIJAY          2000
JAYA                          1800
SUNIL          JAYA           1700
```

The clause `JOIN using (ename)` in the above query, constructs the `where` condition as shown as follows

```
manager.ename=emp_company.ename
```

Using ON Clause

The ON clause is similar to the `WHERE` clause as you can put multiple conditions in the `ON` clause. The syntax to use the ON clause is as follows:

```
ON(Con1 and/or Con2 and/or...)
```

In the preceding syntax, `Con1` and `Con2` are conditions that are connected by using relational operators, such as `AND/OR`. Following two queries are equivalent and the first query is written using 'WHERE' condition while second query is written using 'ON clause'.

```
select c.ename, m.mname,c.salary
from manager m , emp_company c
where c.ename = m.ename and salary > 3000
/
```

The output of the preceding syntax is given as follows:

```
ENAME          MNAME          SALARY
-------        -------        --------
VIJAY                         5000
AJAY                          8000
```

The second query is as follows:

```
select c.ename, m.mname,c.salary
from manager m join emp_company c
on (c.ename = m.ename and salary > 3000)
/
```

The output of the preceding syntax is given as follows:

```
ENAME          MNAME          SALARY
------         ------         ------
VIJAY                         5000
AJAY                          8000
```

OUTER JOIN

OUTER JOIN is used when you want to get all rows from one table as output. In natural join, the row is in the output only if it is joined with the corresponding row in another table. In OUTER JOIN, the row is in the output even if it does not have a corresponding row in another table. In this case, the row is joined with an imaginary row of another table. Suppose you have the data of the Emp_shift table and the manager table. You need to perform natural join and outer join operations with the help of these tables.

Listing 13.6: Showing the data in Emp_shift table

```
select * from emp_shift;
```

The output of the Listing 13.6 is given as follows:

```
ename           shift
--------        -------
ANIL            A
SUNIL           B
VIJAY           B
PRAKASH         C
4 rows selected.
```

Listing 13.7: Displaying the data of the manager table

```
select * from manager;
```

The output of the Listing 13.7 is given as follows:

```
ENAME           MNAME
------          ------
ANIL            AJAY
SHANKAR         VIJAY
JAYA
SUNIL           JAYA
VIJAY
PRAKASH         SHANKAR
AJAY
7 rows          selected.
```

The procedure to perform the natural join by using the Emp_shift table and the manager table is shown in Listing 13.8:

Listing 13.8: Performing the Natural Join

```
select ename,mname,shift
from manager natural join emp_shift
/
```

The output of Listing 13.8 is given as follows:

```
ENAME           MNAME           S
------          ------          ---
ANIL            AJAY            A
SUNIL           JAYA            B
VIJAY                           B
PRAKASH         SHANKAR         C
```

In case of natural JOIN, only four rows having ename in both the tables are obtained as output The row of one table that does not has an entry in another table; would not appear in the output of Listing 13.8. For example, SUNIL has an entry in the manager table, but do not have the corresponding entry in the `Emp_shift` table; therefore, it will not appear in the output of Listing 13.8. If you want to display all data in Manager table then outer join is used. The procedure to perform `the OUTER JOIN` by using the Emp_shift table and the Manager table is shown in Listing 13.9:

Listing 13.9: Using outer join to produce employee name, manager name and shift of all employees. (if the employee does not have the shift, then only the employee name and manager name is displayed)

```
select m.ename,mname,shift
from manager m left outer join emp_shift s
on (m.ename = s.ename)
/
```

The output of Listing 13.9 is given as follows:

```
ENAME      MNAME      S
---------- ---------- -
ANIL       AJAY       A
SUNIL      JAYA       B
VIJAY                 B
PRAKASH    SHANKAR    C
SHANKAR    VIJAY
AJAY
JAYA

7 rows selected.
```

In case of OUTER JOIN, all rows from `Manager` are produced and the row that cannot be joined with row from `Emp_shift` is joined with an imaginary row of `Emp_shift`. For example, the row of `SUNIL`. This is shown in the following code snippet:

```
select m.ename,mname,shift
from manager m , emp_shift s
where (m.ename = s.ename(+));
```

You can produce all rows by using the code shown in Listing 13.10:

Listing 13.10: Producing all Rows of the EMP_SHIFT Table

```
select m.ename,mname,shift
from manager m right outer join emp_shift s
on (m.ename = s.ename)
/
```

The output of Listing 13.10 is given as follows:

```
ENAME      MNAME      S
ANIL       AJAY       A
SUNIL      JAYA       B
VIJAY                 B
PRAKASH    SHANKAR    C
```

NOTE

Right outer join means all rows from right table (Emp_shift) are produced.

FULL OUTER JOIN

In case of FULL OUTER JOIN, rows from both the table are produced. In the case of natural join rows are produced only if where condition is true. The code to use the full outer join is shown in Listing 13.11:

Listing 13.11: Using the Full Outer Join

```
select m.ename, mname, shift
from manager m full  outer join emp_shift s
on (m.ename = s.ename)
/
```

The output of Listing 13.11 is given as follows:

```
ENAME      MNAME       S
-----      -----      ----
ANIL       AJAY       A
SHANKAR    VIJAY
JAYA
SUNIL      JAYA       B
```

```
VIJAY                B
PRAKASH     SHANKAR  C
AJAY

7 rows selected.
```

The output of Listing 13.11 displays:

- All rows from the manager table, which are having corresponding rows in the `Emp_shift table`
- All rows from the manager table, which are not having corresponding rows in the `Emp_shift table`
- All rows from the `Emp_shift table`, which are not having corresponding rows in the manager table

Alternatively, you can perform the full outer join operation on the `Emp_shift table` and the manager table, as shown in the following code snippet:

```
select m.ename,mname,shift
from manager m,emp_shift s
where (m.ename = s.ename(+))
union
select m.ename,mname,shift
from manager m,emp_shift s
where (m.ename(+) = s.ename)
```

Generating Histogram Using Decode

You can generate histogram using `DECODE function` and outer join. Let's understand this with the help of an example. Suppose, a table contains marks and grades of students. Marks are given within the range of `25` and there are four types of grades. If no student falls in a certain grade then the row corresponding to that grade would not appear. If you store all grades in the `GRADEMASTER` table, and the data in it as follows.

```
select * from grademaster;
```

Output if the preceding code syntax:

```
G
-
A
B
C
D
```

The following listings serve as examples of the cases when no student falls in certain grade:

Listing 13.12: Displaying a case where there are no students in a certain grade using DECODE

```
select decode(trunc(phy/25),4,'a',3,'a',2,'b',1,'c','d') grade
from marks
/
```

The output of Listing 13.12 is given as follows:

```
G
-
A
B
B
B
B
```

Listing 13.13: Following query produces number of students in each grade. For grade 'C' and 'D' no row is produced.

```
select decode(trunc(phy/25),4,'a',3,'a',2,'b',1,'c','d') grade,
count(1) cnt
```

```
from marks
group by decode(trunc(phy/25),4,'a',3,'a',2,'b',1,'c','d')
/
```

The output of Listing 13.13 is given as follows:

```
G        CNT
- --------
A          1
B          4
```

You can produce all rows with the help of outer join and DECODE:

Listing 13.14: Producing all rows (for grade 'C' and 'D') using outer join and using DECODE

```
select g.g,nvl(m.cnt,0)
from
(select decode(trunc(phy/25),4,'a',3,'a',2,'b',1,'c','d') grade,
count(1) cnt
from marks
group by decode(trunc(phy/25),4,'a',3,'a',2,'b',1,'c','d'))m,
grademaster g
where g.g=m.grade(+)
/
```

The output of Listing 13.14 is given as follows:

```
G NVL(M.CNT,0)
- ------------
A            1
B            4
D            0
C            0
```

Summary

This chapter familiarized you to joins. The next chapter focuses on Scalar sub queries.

Exercise

Write following queries using JOIN operation.

1. List name of employees having company located in 'NAGPUR'.
2. List name of employees having company located in 'NAGPUR' and shift is B.
3. List name of employees having company located in 'NAGPUR' and shift is B and those who are living in MUMBAI.
4. List name of employees having same working city as there living city.
5. List name of employees having living city NAGPUR and the salary more than 2000.

14

Scalar Subqueries

The scalar subquery is the query that returns single row and single column values. You can use such queries as an expression in SELECT, WHERE and ORDER BY clauses. When such a query returns no row, it returns the NULL value. On the other hand, if it returns more than one row, then Oracle returns error. Although scalar subqueries represent queries more naturally, they are resource intensive and may not be more efficient. So using them is not advisable.

In this chapter, you learn about scalar subqueries and how to use them in Oracle.

Use of Scalar Subquery in the **SELECT** Clause

Listing 14.1 shows how to use the scalar subquery in the SELECT clause:

Listing 14.1: Comparing the salary of employee with the maximum salary of employee in that company

```
spool on
edit scale1

select ename,salary,cname,
(select max(salary) from emp_company r where r.cname = s.cname) max_salary from
  emp_company s
/
@scale1
```

The output of Listing 14.1 is as follows:

```
ENAME          SALARY        CNAME               MAX_SALARY
-----          ------        -----               ----------
ANIL          1500           ACC                    8000
SHANKAR        2000          TATA                   5000
JAYA           1800          CMC                    1800
SUNIL          1700          CMC                    1800
VIJAY          5000          TATA                   5000
PRAKASH        3000          TATA                   5000
AJAY           8000          ACC                    8000
AMOL           1000          ACC                    8000

8 rows selected.
```

NOTE

The SCALE1 file is required to run the preceding query.

The subquery specified in brackets should return only one value; otherwise, Oracle returns an error. The WHERE condition is applied and rows are selected for each row in the datasource. In addition, the subquery is evaluated for each selected row. For example, if you take row of ANIL, then company of ANIL is ACC and the subquery returns maximum salary of employees in ACC.

Use of Scalar Subquery in the **WHERE** Clause

Listing 14.2 shows how to use the scalar subquery in the WHERE clause:

Listing 14.2: Displaying names of employees having maximum salary in a company

```
select ename,salary,cname,(select max(salary) from emp_company r where r.cname =
  s.cname) max_salary
from emp_company s
where salary = (select max(salary) from emp_company r where r.cname = s.cname)
/
```

The output of Listing 14.2 is as follows:

```
ENAME          SALARY         CNAME          MAX_SALARY
JAYA           1800           CMC            1800
VIJAY          5000           TATA           5000
AJAY           8000           ACC            8000
```

In this case, the subquery is evaluated for each row in the data source and the return value of query is compared with the row value. For example, the following condition is satisfied for the VIJAY row and the row is returned in the result:

```
salary = max(salary)
```

Use of Scalar Subquery in the **ORDER BY** Clause

You can use a scalar subquery in the `ORDER BY` clause. Here, you will get a list of employees ordered by maximum salary in their company. Listing 14.3 shows how to use the scalar subquery in the ORDER BY clause:

Listing 14.3: Displaying employees ordered by maximum salary in their company

```
  select ename,salary,cname,(select max(salary) from emp_company r where r.cname =
  s.cname) max_salary
from emp_company s
order by (select max(salary) from emp_company r where r.cname = s.cname)
/
@SCALE3
```

The output of Listing 14.3 is as follows:

```
ENAME          SALARY         CNAME          MAX_SALARY
--------       -------        --------       -----------
SUNIL          1700           CMC            1800
JAYA           1800           CMC            1800
VIJAY          5000           TATA           5000
PRAKASH        3000           TATA           5000
SHANKAR        2000           TATA           5000
AJAY           8000           ACC            8000
AMOL           1000           ACC            8000
ANIL           1500           ACC            8000

8 rows selected.
```

Summary

In this chapter, you have learned to use the SELECT, WHERE, and ORDER BY clauses is the scalar subqueries. After understanding scalar subqueries, let's explore Case expressions in the next chapter.

Exercise

1. Compare the salary of employee with the maximum salary of employee.
2. Displaying names of employees having maximum salary in a company.

15

Case Expressions

A case expression is just like a `DECODE` statement. Oracle 11g supports two types of case expressions. `Case` is used for outputting one value from an input value by using simple mapping or complex mapping.

In this chapter, you learn to use various case expressions, such as simple as well as searched case statements. The chapter also discusses the usage of various functions, such as `NULLIF`, NVL2, and `COALESCE in detail.`

Simple **CASE** Statement

Simple case statement is used to provide one to one mapping of data. You can use it for providing alternate names to data.

Table 15.1 shows the data of the `Emp_shift` table:

Table 15.1: Data of the Emp_shift Table

ENAME	S
ANIL	A
SHANKAR	B
	C
	D

Suppose, Listing 15.1 contains data of the Emp_shift table:

Listing 15.1: Displaying Data of the Emp_shift Table

```
select ename, s from emp_shift;
```

The output of Listing 15.1 is as follows:

```
ENAME        S
----------   -
ANIL         A
SHANKAR      B
             C
             D
```

In cases, where you want to produce some other values, such as `A_SHIFT, B_SHIFT` instead of just producing characters, the `CASE` statement is used. The value of shift in each row is matched with the value specified in `WHEN` using the equality operator and in the order specified. When a certain value is matched, the expression specified in `THEN` is returned as output. If nothing is matched, then the `ELSE` expression is returned.

The following query describes the usage of the CASE statement:

Listing 15.2: Using the CASE…WHEN…ELSE Statement

```
select ename,(case s
when 'a' then 'a_shift' when 'b' then 'b_shift'
when 'c' then 'c_shift'
else 'any_shift'
end) as shift_name from emp_shift;
```

The output of Listing 15.2 is as follows:

```
ENAME      SHIFT_NAM
---------- ---------
ANIL       A_SHIFT
SHANKAR    B_SHIFT
           C_SHIFT
           ANY_SHIFT
```

Searched **CASE** Statement

The searched CASE statement is similar to the simple CASE statement, but the match expression can be specified in a more generalized way. Instead of equality matching, the conditions in WHEN are evaluated in the order and the THEN expression is produced for the condition which is true. If no condition is true, then the ELSE expression is returned. Therefore, for the shifts A and B, the first expression is true. So the result, MORNING_SHIFT, is returned.

Listing 15.3 displays the query for using the searched CASE statement:

Listing 15.3: Using the searched CASE statement

```
SELECT ENAME,(CASE
WHEN SHIFT < 'C' THEN 'MORNING_SHIFT'
WHEN SHIFT < 'D' THEN 'EVENING_SHIFT'
ELSE 'NIGHT_SHIFT' END) AS SHIFT_NAME FROM EMP_SHIFT;
```

The output of Listing 15.3 is as follows:

```
ENAME      SHIFT_NAME
---------- -------------
Anil       MORNING_SHIFT
Shankar    MORNING_SHIFT
           EVENING_SHIFT
           NIGHT_SHIFT
```

The **NULLIF** Function

The NULLIF function produces the NULL value, if the expression has a specified value. In the following example, if shift has the value D, then NULL is produced. If shift does not have the value D, then the value of shift is returned as the result. Therefore, the NULLIF function acts as a complement of the NVL function. Listing 15.4 shows the syntax of using the NULLIF function:

Listing 15.4: Using the NULLIF Function

```
select ename,nullif(shift,'d') from emp_shift;
```

The output of Listing 15.4 is as follows:

```
ENAME      N
---------- -
ANIL       A
SHANKAR    B
           C
```

The NVL2 Function

The NVL2(X, VALUE1, VALUE2) function returns VALUE1, if X is not null; otherwise, it returns VALUE2

```
select mname,nvl2(mname,'specified','not specified') from manager;
```

Output of preceding code syntax:

```
MNAME                          NVL2(MNAME,'SPECIFIED','NOTSPECIFIED')
------------------------------ --------------------------------
AJAY                           SPECIFIED
VIJAY                          SPECIFIED
                               NOT SPECIFIED
JAYA                           SPECIFIED
                               NOT SPECIFIED
SHANKAR                        SPECIFIED
                               NOT SPECIFIED

7 rows selected.
```

The **COALESCE** Function

The `COALESCE` function takes `n` arguments and produces the first argument, which has the first `not null` value. Table 15.2 contains the data of the `TEST1` table:

Table 15.2: Data of the TEST1 Table

A	B	C
10		30
	21	31
12	22	32

Listing 15.5 shows the syntax to create the TEST1 table:

Listing 15.5: Creating the TEST1 Table

```
create table test1
(a number(3),
b number(3),
c number(3));
```

The output of Listing 15.5 is as follows:

```
Table created
```

Listing 15.6 shows the syntax to insert records in a table:

Listing 15.6: Inserting Records in Table

```
insert into TEST1 values(10,'' , 30);
insert into TEST1 values('' ,21, 31);
insert into TEST1 values(12, 22, 32);
```

Listing 15.7 shows the syntax to display records in a table:

Listing 15.7: Displaying Records of the TEST1 Table

```
select * from test1;
```

The output of Listing 15.7 is as follows:

```
     A          B          C
------   ----------   ----------
    10                    30
               21         31
    12         22         32
3 rows displayed.
```

Listing 15.8 shows how to insert another record in the table:

Listing 15.8: Inserting another Record

```
insert into test1 values(null,null,33);
```

The output of Listing 15.8 is as follows:

```
1 row created
```

Listing 15.9 shows the syntax of using the COALESCE command:

Listing 15.9: Using the COALESCE command

```
select c,coalesce(a,b,0) result
from test1;
```

The output of Listing 15.9 is as follows:

```
  C        RESULT
 ---     ----------
 30         10
 31         21
 32         12
 33          0
```

When you use the `COALESCE` command, the order is specified as `A`, `B`. In other words, the `COALESCE` command first produces the value of `A`. If the value of `A` is `not null`, the `RESULT` will be `10` that is the value of `A`. If `A` has the null value, then `B` is produced. In this case, `c = 31`, value of `A` is `null`, and B is `not null`. Therefore, it produces the `RESULT 21` that is value of `B`. If both `A` and `B` have `null` values, then `0` is produced as a result. In this case, where `c = 33`, the value of `A`, `B` is `null`. The result produced is `0`.

Summary

In this chapter, you learned about different case expressions, such as simple as well as searched case statements. You also learned to use various functions, such as `NULLIF`, NVL2, and `COALESCE`. The next chapter will throw light on multiple insert and merge.

Exercise

1. Write the statement using the case expressions.
2. Make use of NULLIF function
3. Make use of NVL2 function
4. Make use of COALESCE statement

16

Multitable Insert and Merge

From Oracle 10g there is an enhanced facility of loading data in the table using the `SELECT` statement. Using this facility you can:

- Load data in multiple tables in single `INSERT` statement
- Load multiple rows in the same table in single `INSERT` statement
- Load data conditionally in the table

If the preceding facilities are not available, you have to write multiple `INSERT` statements, which involve parsing overheads and tend to be slower. The `MERGE` facility implements the much-required functionality of updating data in the table.

Multitable **INSERT** Statement

There are four types of multitable `INSERT` statements:

- Unconditional `INSERT` statement
- Pivoting `INSERT` statement
- Conditional `INSERT` statement
- `INSERT FIRST` statement

*Unconditional **INSERT** Statement*

Using the unconditional **INSERT** statement, you can `insert` data into multiple tables using a single `INSERT` statement. Let's create a table to understand the meaning of this statement, as shown in Listing 16.1:

Listing 16.1: Creating the emp_cmp_shift Table

```
create table emp_cmp_shift (ename varchar2(30),cname varchar2(30),shift          char(3));
```

The output of Listing 16.1 is as follows:

```
Table created
```

Listing 16.2 shows the code to create the emp_cmp_mgr table:

Listing 16.2: Creating the emp_cmp_mgr Table

```
create table emp_cmp_mgr(ename varchar2(30),cname varchar2(30),mname
  varchar2(30));
```

The output of Listing 16.2 is as follows:

```
Table created
```

Listing 16.3 shows the code to display the structure of the emp_cmp_shift table:

Listing 16.3: Displaying Structure of the emp_cmp_shift Table

```
desc emp_cmp_shift;
```

The output of Listing 16.3 is as follows:

```
Name              Null?            Type
--------          ---------        ------
ENAME                              VARCHAR2(30)
CNAME                              VARCHAR2(30)
SHIFT                              CHAR (3)
```

Listing 16.4 shows the code to display the structure of the emp_cmp_mgr table:

Listing 16.4: Displaying Structure of the emp_cmp_mgr Table

```
desc emp_cmp_mgr;
```

The output of Listing 16.4 is as follows:

```
Name          Null?         Type
-------     --------      ---------
ENAME                       VARCHAR2(30)
CNAME                       VARCHAR2(30)
MNAME                       VARCHAR2(30)
```

Listing 16.5 shows the code to insert data into two tables using a query:

Listing 16.5: Inserting Data into Two Tables using a Query

```
insert all
into emp_cmp_shift values(ename,cname,shift)
into emp_cmp_mgr values(ename,cname,mname)
select e.ename,cname,mname,shift
from emp_company e ,manager,emp_shift
where e.ename = manager.ename
and e.ename = emp_shift.ename
/
```

Listing 16.5 executes the query and processes the output rows of the query one by one. For each row, there are four column values, which are given as follows:

```
ANIL              ACC               AJAY              A
```

The output of Listing 16.5 is as follows:

```
8 rows created
```

In the preceding output, values are inserted according to the columns of the query mentioned in the `INTO` clause of the respective tables. Therefore, the single row of query is inserted in multiple tables.

Listing 16.6 displays the records of the emp_cmp_shift table:

Listing 16.6: Displaying Records of the emp_cmp_shift Table

```
select * from emp_cmp_shift;
```

The output of Listing 16.6 is as follows:

```
ENAME              CNAME            SHI
--------    ------------     -----
ANIL              ACC               A
SUNIL             CMC               B
VIJAY             TATA              B
PRAKASH           TATA              C
```

Listing 16.7 displays the records of the emp_cmp_mgr table:

Listing 16.7: Displaying Records of the emp_cmp_mgr Table

```
select * from emp_cmp_mgr;
```

The output of Listing 16.7 is as follows:

```
ENAME       CNAME          MNAME
-------   ----------      -------
ANIL          ACC          AJAY
SUNIL         CMC          JAYA
VIJAY         TATA
PRAKASH       TATA         SHANKAR
```

In the `INTO` clause, you cannot use the full qualifier name, because it gives an error, which is shown in the following code snippet:

```
into emp_cmp_mgr values(e.ename,cname,mname)
                         *
ERROR at line 3:ORA-00904: "E"."ENAME": invalid identifier
```

Let's learn about pivoting insert statement.

*Pivoting **INSERT** Statement*

You can use pivot `INSERT` statement for inserting data in the same table multiple times. The number of rows inserted will depend on how many times you have used the `INTO` clause. Listing 16.8 shows an example of pivot `INSERT` statement, which inserts data into table `emp_cmp_mgr` from `emp_cmp_shift`:

Listing 16.8: Displaying All Records of emp_cmp_shift

```
select * from emp_cmp_shift;
```

The output of Listing 16.8 is as follows:

```
ENAME       CNAME               SHI
--------  ----------            ------
ANIL        ACC                 A
SUNIL       CMC                 B
VIJAY       TATA                B
PRAKASH     TATA                C
```

Listing 16.9 shows the code to insert data into the emp_cmp_mgr table:

Listing 16.9: Inserting Data into the emp_cmp_mgr Table

```
insert all
into emp_cmp_mgr values (ename,cname,'ASHOK')
into emp_cmp_mgr values (ename,cname,'ASHWIN')
select ename,cname from emp_cmp_shift
/
```

The output of Listing 16.9 is as follows:

```
8 rows created.
```

In Listing 16.9, one row of query output is inserted twice in the `emp_cmp_mgr` table. The name of the manager of the second group is `ASHOK`, while the manager of the third group is `ASHWIN`.

Listing 16.10 displays all data of the emp_cmp_mgr table after insertion:

Listing 16.10: Displaying the Data of the emp_cmp_mgr Table after Insertion

```
select * from emp_cmp_mgr;
```

The output of Listing 16.10 is as follows:

```
ENAME                           CNAME             MNAME
------------------------------------------------------------
ANIL                            ACC               AJAY
SUNIL                           CMC               JAYA
VIJAY                           TATA
PRAKASH                         TATA              SHANKAR
ANIL                            ACC               ASHOK
SUNIL                           CMC               ASHOK
VIJAY                           TATA              ASHOK
PRAKASH                         TATA              ASHOK
ANIL                            ACC               ASHWIN
SUNIL                           CMC               ASHWIN
VIJAY                           TATA              ASHWIN
PRAKASH                         TATA              ASHWIN
```

Let's learn about the conditional insert statement.

*Conditional **INSERT** Statement*

The conditional `INSERT` statement inserts data into the table only if the `when` condition is satisfied. Suppose you have three tables.

Table 16.1 lists the data of table emp_acc:

Table 16.1: Displaying Data of the emp_acc Table

Name	Null?	Type
ENAME		VARCHAR2(30)
SALARY		NUMBER(7,2)
JDATE		DATE

Table 16.2 lists the data of the emp_tata table:

Table 16.2: Displaying Data of the emp_tata Table

Name	Null?	Type
ENAME		VARCHAR2(30)
SALARY		NUMBER(7,2)
JDATE		DATE

Table 16.3 lists the data of the emp_cmc table:

Table 16.3: Displaying Data of the emp_cmc Table

Name	Null?	Type
ENAME		VARCHAR2(30)
SALARY		NUMBER(7,2)
JDATE		DATE

Listing 16.11 shows the code to load data of a table, conditionally into three tables:

Listing 16.11: Loading Data of a Table, Conditionally into Three Tables

```
insert all
when cname = 'ACC' then
into emp_acc values(ename,salary,jdate)
when cname = 'TATA' then
into emp_tata values (ename,salary,jdate)
when cname = 'CMC'  and ename in (select ename from emp_shift where shift = 'A')
  then
into emp_cmc values (ename,salary,jdate)
select ename,cname,salary,jdate
from emp_company
/
```

Listing 16.11 is executed as follows:

- The WHEN condition is evaluated for each row obtained as an output by the query.
- The row value is inserted depending on the INTO clause in the table for which the WHEN condition is true.
- If, for the same row, two WHEN conditions are true, then the row values are inserted into two tables.
- If the row has company ACC, the first when condition is satisfied and row values are inserted into the emp_acc table. In this listing, each when condition is evaluated. In the when clause, you can give any relational condition or subqueries.

Listing 16.12: Displaying the data in the emp_acc table, which is used in the previous insert statement

```
select * from emp_acc;
```

The output of the Listing 16.12 is as follows:

```
ENAME          SALARY         JDATE
-----          ------         -------
ANIL           1500           01-MAY-89
AJAY           8000           30-APR-95
AMOL           1000           17-MAR-95
```

Listing 16.13: Displaying the data in the emp_tata table, which is used in the previous insert statement

```
select * from emp_tata;
```

The output of the Listing 16.13 is as follows:

```
ENAME          SALARY         JDATE
-------        -------        ---------
SHANKAR        2000           10-JUL-90
VIJAY          5000           03-JAN-88
PRAKASH        3000           27-MAY-89
```

Let's learn about the insert first statement.

The ***INSERT FIRST*** Statement

In case of the `INSERT FIRST` statement, `when` conditions are evaluated one by one and the row is inserted into that table for which the first `when` condition is true. If no condition is satisfied then the table mentioned in the `ELSE` part is used for insertion.

Listing 16.14 shows how to use the INSERT FIRST statement:

Listing 16.14: Using the INSERT FIRST Statement

```
insert first
when cname = 'ACC' then
into emp_cmc values(ename,salary,jdate)
when ename = 'TATA' then
into emp_tata values(ename,salary,jdate)
else
into emp_all  values(ename,salary,jdate)
select ename,cname,salary,jdate from emp_company;
select * from emp_all;
```

The output of Listing 16.14 is as follows:

```
ENAME          SALARY         JDATE
-------        -------        ---------
SHANKAR        2000           10-JUL-90
JAYA           1800           07-JUN-91
SUNIL          1700           01-JAN-88
VIJAY          5000           03-JAN-88
PRAKASH        3000           27-MAY-89
```

For each output row, `when` condition is evaluated in an order from top to bottom. If the row is of TATA company, the row is inserted into `emp_tata`. If the row is not of the `ACC` or `TATA` company, then `when` the condition returns false, the `ELSE` part is executed, and the row is inserted into the `emp_all` table. The difference between `INSERT FIRST` and `INSERT ALL` is that in the `INSERT FIRST` at the most one row is inserted into the table, while in `INSERT ALL,` rows may be inserted into multiple tables.

The MERGE Statement

The MERGE statement merges data of one table with that of another table. It uses the MATCH condition to determine the existence of the rows. If the given row exists, then it updates the row. Otherwise, it inserts the row.

Listing 16.15: Command to select the data of emp_company table

```
select * from emp_company;
```

The output of Listing 16.15 is as follows:

```
ENAME          CNAME          SALARY         JDATE
------         ------         -------        ---------
ANIL           ACC            1500           01-MAY-89
SHANKAR        TATA           2000           10-JUL-90
JAYA           CMC            1800           07-JUN-91
SUNIL          CMC            1700           01-JAN-88
VIJAY          TATA           5000           03-JAN-88
PRAKASH        TATA           3000           27-MAY-89
AJAY           ACC            8000           30-APR-95
AMOL           ACC           1000            17-MAR-95

8 rows selected.
```

Listing 16.16: Displaying the records of the emp_all table:

```
select * from emp_all;
```

The output of the Listing 16.16 is as follows:

```
ENAME          SALARY         JDATE
------         -----          ---------
SHANKAR        2000           10-JUL-90
JAYA           1800           07-JUN-91
SUNIL          1700           01-JAN-88
VIJAY          5000           03-JAN-88
PRAKASH        3000           27-MAY-89

5 rows selected.
```

Listing 16.17 shows the code to merge data:

Listing 16.17: Merging Data

```
merge into emp_all a
using emp_company b
on (a.ename = b.ename)
when matched then
      update set a.salary = b.salary + 100
when not matched then
     insert (a.ename,a.salary,a.jdate)
     values(b.ename,b.salary,b.jdate);
select * from emp_all;
```

The output of Listing 16.17 is as follows:

```
ENAME          SALARY         JDATE
-------        ------         ----------
Shankar        2100           10-JUN-90
Jaya           1900           07-JUN-91
Sunil          1800           01-JAN-98
Vijay          5100           03-JAN-88
```

```
Prakash          3100          27-MAY-89
Ajay             8000          30-APR-95
Anil             1500          01-MAY-89
Amol             1000          17-MAR-95

8 rows selected.
```

In the preceding output, data from the Emp_company table is merged with data of the emp_all table. The emp_all table changes as a result. The processing is done for each row in the Emp_company table in the following ways:

- If the row is similar to the row of ANIL, i.e. it is not present in the emp_all table according to the match condition, then the row is inserted into emp_all using the INSERT statement.
- If the row is similar to the row of SHANKAR, i.e. it is present in the emp_all table, then the condition is matched and the UPDATE statement is executed.

The MERGE statement reduces the number of statements that otherwise you would want to write for the same functionality. It also serves to avoid the number of table scans required for the same functionality.

Summary

This chapter discussed about multiple insert and merge. The next chapter will give idea about regular expressions.

Exercise

The following table lists the marks. Suppose data about marks is given as follows:

ROLLNO	NAME	PHYSICS	CHEMISTRY	MATHS
1	ANIL	78	74	82
2	SUNIL	72	82	88
3	AJAY	81	92	99

1. Write a multi table insert statement to insert data above data in the following table:

ROLLNO	NAME	SUBJECT	MARKS
1	ANIL	PHYSICS	78
1	ANIL	CHEMISTRY	74
1	ANIL	MATHS	82

2. Write a merge statement to insert/update data in the following table:

ROLLNO	NAME	SUBJECT	MARKS
1	ANIL	PHYSICS	78

17

Regular Expression

Sometimes strings are searched using patterns. In such cases, instead of searching exact string, pattern searching is required. You can use the `LIKE` operator for pattern searching. Suppose you want to search the email string having `yahoo.com` or `rediff.com` at the end of some text. In such case, you can search the specified pattern using the `LIKE` operator. The only limitation of using the LIKE operator is that you have to write some complex condition for a successful pattern searching. Instead of writing a complex condition for pattern searching, you can use regular expression. Regular expression is the language for specifying complex patterns in the strings. For example, pattern `a(b+|c)d` indicates the pattern which starts with `a` followed by one or more `b` or single `c` and `d` at the end.

In this chapter, you learn how to specify patterns using regular expressions, in which you learn about metacharacters, such as +, *, and \. Next, you learn about the REGEXP_SUBSTR, REGEXP_REPLACE, REGEXP_LIKE functions.

Specifying Patterns using Regular Expressions

You can use some metacharacters such as |, \ and character classes for specifying regular expressions. Oracle provides SQL functions, such as `REGEXP_INSTR`, `REGEXP_LIKE`, `REGEXP_REPLACE`, and `REGEXP_SUBSTR` for handling regular expressions. The `REGEXP_INSTR` function searches regular expression in the string similar to `INSTR`.

Metacharacters

The metacharacters used in specifying regular expressions are as follows:

- +
- .
- *
- {m}
- {m,}
- {m,n}
- [xyz..]
- [^xyz..]
- |
- \
- ^
- $
- [:class:]

Let's discuss these in detail.

The + Metacharacter

The + metacharacter matches one or more occurrences of a preceding character or subexpression. The subexpression is specified using brackets. Oracle begins searching with the first character in the string. Listing 17.1 shows how to use the + metacharacter to examine the specified string and search the words with one or more occurrences of B followed by C:

Listing 17.1: Examining the string and looking for occurrences of words with one or more occurrences of B followed by C (Using the + Metacharacter)

```
SELECT REGEXP_INSTR('ABBCDFFGR','B+C') FROM DUAL;
```

The output of Listing 17.1 is as follows:

```
REGEXP_INSTR('ABBCDFFGR','B+C')
-------------------------------
                              2
```

This query returns the starting position of a pattern. In this case, we are searching the pattern where one or more than one B is followed by C and, in this case, this pattern is 2.

The . Metacharacter

The . metacharacter matches with any one character. The a.b regular expression matches with expressions, such as acb and adb.

The * Metacharacter

The * metacharacter is similar to +, but matches with zero or more occurrences. The regular expression a*b matches with the expressions, such as b, ab, aaab, and aaaaaab.

The {m} Metacharater

The {m} metacharacter matches with exact m occurrences of a preceding character or subexpression. For example, ab{2}c matches with abbc.

The {m,} Metacharacter

The {m,} metacharacter matches with minimum m occurrences of a preceding character or subexpression. For example, ab{2,}c matches with abbc, abbbc, and abbbbc.

The {m,n} Metacharacter

The {m,n} metacharacter matches with minimum m and maximum n occurrences of preceding character or subexpression. For example, ab{2,4}c matches with expressions, such as abbc, abbbc, and abbbbc.

The [xyz..] Metacharacter

The [xyz..] metacharacter matches with any character specified in the list. For example, a[cdf]b matches with acb, adb, and afb.

The [^xyz..] Metacharacter

The [^xyz] character matches with any character not in list. For example, a[^cdf]b matches with expressions, such as agb, ahb, and abb.

The | Metacharacter

The | metacharacter is also known as the OR operator. For example, a(b|c)d matches with abd or adb.

The \ Metacharacter

The \ metacharacter is the escape character. It shuts the special meaning of a character. For example, ab/++c matches with strings, ab+c and ab++c.

The ^ Metacharacter

The ^ metacharacter is called beginning of line anchor and matches with any matching pattern only if it occurs at the beginning of line.

The $ Metacharacter

The $ metacharacter is called end of line anchor. It matches with any matching pattern, only if it occurs at the end of line. The following code snippet shows the use of the $ metacharacter:

```
select regexp_instr('abbccdf bbc','(b+c)$') from dual;
```

The output of the preceding code snippet is as follows:

```
REGEXP_INSTR('ABBCCDFBBC','(B+C)$')
-----------------------------------
                                  9
```

Another matching pattern is shown in the following code snippet:

```
select regexp_instr('abbccdf bbc','b+c') from dual;
```

The output of the preceding code snippet is as follows:

```
REGEXP_INSTR('ABBCCDFBBC','B+C')
--------------------------------
                               2
```

In the preceding code snippet, this string has 2 matching patterns but the first one appears at the second position. Therefore, the output is 2. The second time this pattern appears is not considered.

The [:class:] Metacharacter

The [:class:] metacharacter matches with any character in the specified character class. The classes are as follows:

- alnum(alphanumeric)
- alpha
- cntrl(all control characters)
- lower
- upper
- print(all printable characters)
- punct(all punctuation characters)
- space(all space characters)

Some examples of using the [:class:] metacharacter are as follows:

Listing 17.2: Returning the Position in the ABBCDFFBBCFFGBBCFFGGR String, in which Pattern with One or More Occurrences of B Followed by C and Four Occurrences of G or F

```
SELECT REGEXP_INSTR('ABBCDFFBBCFFGBBCFFGGR','B+C[(G|F)]{4}') FROM DUAL;
```

The output of Listing 17.2 is as follows:

```
REGEXP_INSTR('ABBCDFFBBCFFGBBCFFGGR','B+C[(G|F)]{4}')
-----------------------------------------------------
                                                   14
```

Listing 17.3: Returning the Position of the Character Other than D in the ABBCDFFBBCFFGBBCFFGGR String (Search Starts from Position 1)

```
SELECT REGEXP_INSTR('ABBCDFFBBCFFGBBCFFGGR','[^D]') FROM DUAL;
```

The output of Listing 17.3 is as follows:

```
REGEXP_INSTR('ABBCDFFBBCFFGBBCFFGGR','[^D]')
--------------------------------------------
                                           1
```

Listing 17.4: Returning the Position of the F Character in ABBCD HJHF SDFFB BCFF GBBCFFGGR, Only if it is the End of Line

```
SELECT REGEXP_INSTR('ABBCD HJHF SDFFB BCFF GBBCFFGGR','[$F]') POS FROM DUAL;
```

The output of Listing 17.4 is as follows:

```
       POS
----------
        10
```

In Listing 17.4, lines are separated by spaces and searching starts from position 1.

Listing 17.5: Returning the Starting Position of Four Contiguous Digits in ABBCD H123 1234B BCFF GBBCFFGGR

```
SELECT REGEXP_INSTR('ABBCD H123 1234B BCFF GBBCFFGGR','[[:digit:]]{4}') POS FROM
   DUAL;
```

The output of Listing 17.5 is as follows:

```
       POS
----------
        12
```

Listing 17.6: Returning the Position of Second Occurrence of Nonblank Character (Search Starts from Position 1)

```
SELECT
REGEXP_INSTR('ABBCD HJHF SDFFB, BCFF GBBCFFGR, AA', '[^ ]+', 1, 2)
   "REGEXP_INSTR"
FROM DUAL;
```

The output of Listing 17.6 is as follows:

```
REGEXP_INSTR
------------
           7
```

Listing 17.7: Returning the Position of the Character Other than B in BBBBBBCC (Search Starts from Position 1)

```
SELECT REGEXP_INSTR('BBBBBBCC','[^B]') FROM DUAL;
```

The output of Listing 17.7 is as follows:

```
REGEXP_INSTR('BBBBBBCC','[^B]')
-------------------------------
                              7
```

Listing 17.8: Examining the String and Searching for Occurrences of Words Beginning with r or o, Regardless of Case, Followed by Any Four Alphabetic Characters

```
SELECT
REGEXP_INSTR('ABBRD HJHF ODFFB, BCFF RBBCFFGR, AA',
'[r|o][[:alpha:]]{4}',2,2,1,'i') "REGEXP_INSTR"
FROM DUAL;
```

The output of Listing 17.8 is as follows:

```
REGEXP_INSTR
------------
          29
```

Oracle begins searching from the second character in the string and returns the position of the character following the second occurrence of a five-letter word beginning with o or r, regardless of case. In Listing 17.8, i stands for ignore case.

Listing 17.9: Examining the String and Searching for Occurrences of Words Beginning with R or O, Considering the Case, Followed by Any Four Alphabetic Characters

```
SELECT
REGEXP_INSTR('ABBRD HJHF ODFFB, BCFF RBBCFFGR, AA',
   '[R|O][[:alpha:]]{4}',3,2,1,'c')
"REGEXP_INSTR" FROM DUAL;
```

The output of Listing 17.9 is as follows:

```
REGEXP_INSTR
------------
          29
```

Oracle begins searching from the third character and returns the position of the character following the second occurrence of a five letter word beginning with R or O, considering case. In Listing 17.9, c at the end of the function indicates case is considered.

Listing 17.10: Searching for Occurrences of Words Beginning with R or O, in Lowercase, Followed by Any Four Lowercase Alphabetic Characters

```
SELECT
REGEXP_INSTR('Abbrd Hjhf Odffb, Bcff Rbbcffgr, Aa',
'[R|O][[:lower:]]{4}',2,1,1,'i') "REGEXP_INSTR"
FROM DUAL;
```

The output of Listing 17.10 is as follows:

```
REGEXP_INSTR
------------
          17
```

Oracle begins searching from the second character and returns the position of the character following the first occurrence of a five-letter word beginning with R or O in lowercase.

Listing 17.11: Examining the String and Searching for Occurrences of Words Beginning with R or O, in Uppercase, Followed by Four Uppercase Alphabetic Characters

```
SELECT REGEXP_INSTR('ABBRD HJHF ODFFB, BCFF RBBCFFGR, AA',
'[R|O][[:upper:]]{4}', 2, 2, 0, 'i') "REGEXP_INSTR"
FROM DUAL;
```

The output of Listing 17.11 is as follows:

```
REGEXP_INSTR
------------
  24
```

Oracle begins searching from the second character in the string.

Listing 17.12: Examining the String and Searching for Occurrences of Words Beginning with R or O, in Uppercase, Followed by Any Four Uppercase Alphabetic Characters

```
SELECT REGEXP_INSTR('ABBRD HJHF ODFFB, BCFF RBBCFFGR, AA',
'[R|O][[:upper:]]{4}', 2, 1, 1, 'i') "REGEXP_INSTR"
FROM DUAL;
```

The output of Listing 17.12 is as follows:

```
REGEXP_INSTR
------------
          17
```

Oracle begins searching from the second character and returns the position of the character following the first occurrence of a five letter uppercase word beginning with R or O in uppercase.

Listing 17.13: Examining the String and Searching for Occurrences of Words Beginning with R or O, in Lowercase, Followed by Any Four Lowercase Alphabetic Characters

```
SELECT REGEXP_INSTR('Abbcd Hjhf Sdffb, Bcff Gbbcffgr, aa',
'[R|O][[:lower:]]{4}', 2, 2, 1, 'i') "REGEXP_INSTR"
FROM DUAL;
```

The output of Listing 17.13 is as follows:

```
REGEXP_INSTR
------------
     0
```

Oracle begins searching from the second character and returns the position of the character following the second occurrence of a five-letter lowercase word beginning with R or O in lowercase.

Listing 17.14: Examining the String and Searching for the Position of http:// Followed by One or More Alphanumeric Characters and Optionally, a Period (.)

```
SELECT
REGEXP_INSTR('ABBCCD GFDAAA,http://www.oracle.com/products',
'http://([[:alnum:]]+\.?){3,4}/?',1,1) "REGEXP_INSTR" FROM DUAL;
```

The output of Listing 17.14 is as follows:

```
REGEXP_INSTR
------------
          15
```

Oracle searches for a minimum of three and a maximum of four occurrences of this substring between `http://`, and either a slash (/) or end of string.

Listing 17.15: Examining the String and Searching for the Position of http:// Followed by One or More Lowercase Characters and Optionally, a Period (.)

```
SELECT
REGEXP_INSTR('ABBCCD     GFDAAA,http://www.rediff.mail.com.com/products',
'http://([[:lower:]]+\.?){3,4}/?',1,1,1) "REGEXP_INSTR" FROM DUAL;
```

The output of Listing 17.15 is as follows:

```
REGEXP_INSTR
------------
          46
```

Oracle searches for a minimum of three and a maximum of four occurrences of this substring between `http://`, and either a slash (/) or end of string.

Using the **REGEXP_SUBSTR** FUNCTION

You can extract the substring, which matches the pattern defined by a regular expression, by using the REGEXP_SUBSTR function. Some examples of extracting substrings using the REGEXP_SUBSTR function are given as follows:

Listing 17.16: Examining the String and Searching the First Substring Bounded by Commas

```
SELECT
REGEXP_SUBSTR('ABBCD HJHF SDFFB, BCFF GBBCFFGR, AA',
',[^,]+,') "REGEXPR_SUBSTR" FROM DUAL;
```

The output of Listing 17.16 is as follows:

```
REGEXPR_SUBSTR
----------------
, BCFF GBBCFFGR,
```

In Listing 17.16, Oracle searches for a comma followed by one or more occurrences of non-comma characters followed by a comma, and returns the substrings, including the leading and trailing commas.

Listing 17.17: Examining the String and Searching for the First Substring Starting with http://, Followed by One or More Occurrences of Lowercase Letters Followed by Zero or One Dot Followed by Zero or a Slash

```
SELECT REGEXP_SUBSTR('ABBCCD GFDAAA,http://www.rediff.mail.com/products',
'http://([[:lower:]]+\.?){1,3}/?',1,1) "REGEXP_SUBSTR" FROM DUAL;
```

The output of Listing 17.17 is as follows:

```
REGEXP_SUBSTR
-----------------------
http://www.rediff.mail.
```

In Listing 17.18, search starts from position one for the 1st occurrence.

Listing 17.18: Examining the String and Searching for the First Occurrence of Substring Starting with d, Followed by One or More Occurrences of Lowercase Letters; Followed by Zero or One Comma

```
SELECT REGEXP_SUBSTR('AbbccdGfdaaa,ccaa,bbag gg',
'd([[:lower:]]+,?){1,3}',1,1) "REGEXP_SUBSTR" FROM DUAL;
```

The output of Listing 17.18 is as follows:

```
REGEXP_SUBSTR
--------------
daaa,ccaa,bbag
```

In Listing 17.18, Oracle searches for minimum of one and maximum of three occurrences of this substring. Search starts from position one.

Listing 17.19: Examining the String and Searching for the First Occurrence of Substring Starting with d, Followed by One or More Occurrences of Lowercase Letters

```
SELECT REGEXP_SUBSTR('AbbccdGfdaaa,ccaa,bbag gg',
'd([[:lower:]]+){1,3},?',1,1) "REGEXP_subSTR" FROM DUAL;
```

The output of Listing 17.19 is as follows:

```
REGEX
-----
daaa,
```

In Listing 17.19, Oracle searches for minimum of one and maximum of three occurrences of this substring. Search starts from position one.

Listing 17.20: Examining the String and Searching for the First Occurrence of Substring Starting with d, Followed by One or More Occurrences of Uppercase Letters and Optionally by a Comma

```
SELECT REGEXP_SUBSTR('AbbccdGfdaaa,ccaa,bbag gg',
'd([[:upper:]]+,?){1,3}',1,1) "REGEXP_subSTR" FROM DUAL;
```

The output of Listing 17.20 is as follows:

```
RE
--
dG
```

In Listing 17.20, Oracle searches for minimum of one and maximum of three occurrences of this substring. Search starts from position one.

Listing 17.21: Examining the String and Searching for the First Occurrence of Substring Starting with D, Followed by One or More Occurrences of Uppercase Letters and Optionally by a Comma

```
SELECT  REGEXP_SUBSTR('ABBCCDGFDAAA,CCAA,BBAG GG',
'D([[:upper:]]+,?){1,3}',1,1) "REGEXP_SUBSTR" FROM DUAL;
```

The output of Listing 17.21 is as follows:

```
REGEXP_SUBSTR
-----------------
DGFDAAA,CCAA,BBAG
```

In Listing 17.21, Oracle searches for minimum of one and maximum of three occurrences of this substring. Search starts from position one.

Listing 17.22: Examining the String and Searching for the First Occurrence of Substring Starting with D, Followed by One or More Occurrences of Alphanumeric Characters and Optionally by a Comma

```
SELECT REGEXP_SUBSTR('ABBCCDGFDAAA,CCAA,BBAG GG',
'D([[:alnum:]]+,?){1,2}',1,1) "REGEXP_SUBSTR" FROM DUAL;
```

The output of Listing 17.22 is as follows:

```
REGEXP_SUBSTR
-------------
DGFDAAA,CCAA,
```

In Listing 17.22, Oracle searches for minimum of one and maximum of two occurrences of this substring. Search starts from position one.

Listing 17.23: Examining the String and Searching for the First Occurrence of Substring Starting with D, Followed by One or More Occurrences of Alphanumeric Characters

```
SELECT REGEXP_SUBSTR('ABBCCDGFDAAA,CCAA,BBAG GG',
'D([[:alnum:]]+)',1,1) "REGEXP_SUBSTR" FROM DUAL;
```

The output of Listing 17.23 is as follows:

```
REGEXP_
-------
DGFDAAA
```

Listing 17.24: Examining the String and Searching for the First Occurrence of Substring Starting with D, Followed by One or More Occurrences of Alphanumeric Characters

```
SELECT REGEXP_SUBSTR('ABBCCDGFDAAA  L,CCAA,BBAG GG',
'D([[:alnum:]]+)',1,1) "REGEXP_SUBSTR" FROM DUAL;
```

The output of Listing 17.24 is as follows:

```
REGEXP_
-------
DGFDAAA
```

Listing 17.25: Examining the String and Searching for the First Occurrence of Substring Starting with C, Followed by One or More Occurrences of Uppercase Characters

```
SELECT REGEXP_SUBSTR('ABBCCDGfdaac  L,CCAA,BBAG GG','C([[:upper:]]+)',1,1,'c')
"REGEXP_subSTR" FROM DUAL;
```

The output of Listing 17.25 is as follows:

```
REGE
----
CCDG
```

In Listing 17.25, search starts from position one considering case of characters.

Listing 17.26: Examining the String and Searching for the First Occurrence of Substring Starting with C Followed by One or More Occurrences of Characters Other than G

```
SELECT REGEXP_SUBSTR('ABBCCDGfdaac','C[^G]+',1,1)
"REGEXP_subSTR" FROM DUAL;
```

The output of Listing 17.26 is as follows:

```
REG
---
CCD
```

Listing 17.27: Examining the String and Looking for the First Occurrence of Substring Starting Optionally with comma, Followed by One or More Occurrences of Character f and then by d

```
SELECT REGEXP_SUBSTR('ABB,CCDGfdaac',',?[$f]+d',1,1)
"REGEXP_subSTR" FROM DUAL;
```

The output of Listing 17.27 is as follows:

```
RE
--
fd
```

Listing 17.28: Examining the String and Searching for the First Occurrence of Substring Starting Optionally with comma, Followed by Character Other than A

```
SELECT REGEXP_SUBSTR('ABB,CCDGfdaac',',?[^A]',1,1)
"REGEXP_SUBSTR" FROM DUAL;
```

The output of Listing 17.28 is as follows:

```
R
-
B
```

Let's now learn about the REGEXP_REPLACE function.

Using the **REGEXP_REPLACE** Function

The REGEXP_REPLACE function allows you to replace the pattern of a string by another pattern. Some examples of replacing patterns using the REGEXP_REPLACE function are explained as follows:

Listing 17.29: Replacing the Pattern Starting with B and Ending with C, with One Character in between them

```
SELECT REGEXP_REPLACE('(ABBCD)(HJHF)(SDFFB BCFF FBBCFFGGR)',
'(B).(C)','\2-\1') POS FROM DUAL;
```

The output of Listing 17.29 is as follows:

```
POS
-----------------------------------
(AC-BD)(HJHF)(SDFFB BCFF FC-BFFGGR)
```

In Listing 17.29, the pattern has two components:

- \2 indicates second component (C)
- \1 indicates first component (B)

Listing 17.30: Replacing the Pattern, Dot (.), with the Specified String

```
SELECT REGEXP_replace('www.yahoo.com   ',
'(.)','\1 ') "REGEXP_replace" FROM DUAL;
```

The output of Listing 17.30 is as follows:

```
REGEXP_replace
------------------------------
w w w . y a h o o . c o m
```

In Listing 17.30, the dot is replaced by dot followed by one space (.).

Listing 17.31: Replacing the Pattern, Comma (,), with the Specified String

```
SELECT  REGEXP_replace('class,project,workspace',
'(,)','\1s ') "REGEXP_replace" FROM DUAL;
```

The output of Listing 17.31 is as follows:

```
REGEXP_replace
---------------------------
class,s project,s workspace
```

In Listing 17.31, the comma is replaced by ,s and \1 indicates pattern number 1.

Listing 17.32: Replacing the Pattern, Comma (,), with the Specified String

```
SELECT REGEXP_replace('class,project,workspace,',
'(,)','R\1 ') "REGEXP_replace" FROM DUAL;
```

The output of Listing 17.32 is as follows:

```
REGEXP_replace
------------------------------
classR, projectR, workspaceR,
```

In Listing 17.32, comma is replaced by R, followed by a comma and a space.

Listing 17.33: Examining the String and Searching for Two or More Spaces

```
SELECT REGEXP_replace('class,  project,  workspace' ,
'( ){2,}',' ') "REGEXP_replace" FROM DUAL;
```

The output of Listing 17.33 is as follows:

```
REGEXP_replace
--------------------------
class, project, workspace
```

In Listing 17.33, Oracle replaces each occurrence of two or more spaces with a single space.

Listing 17.34: Examining the String and Searching for Two or More Consecutive Occurrences of B

```
SELECT REGEXP_replace('ABB,CCDGfdaac','(B){2,}','V')
"REGEXP_replace" FROM DUAL;
```

The output of Listing 17.34 is as follows:

```
REGEXP_repla
------------
AV,CCDGfdaac
```

In Listing 17.34, Oracle replaces each occurrence of two or more `B` with `V`.

Listing 17.35: Examining the String and Searching for Occurrences of B Followed by C

```
SELECT REGEXP_REPLACE('ABB,CCDGfdaac', '(B).(C)','T,W') POS FROM DUAL;
```

The output of Listing 17.35 is as follows:

```
POS
-------------
ABT,WCDGfdaac
```

In Listing 17.35, Oracle replaces each occurrence of this with `T, W`.

Listing 17.36: Examining the String and Searching for Occurrences of B Followed by a Comma

```
SELECT REGEXP_replace('BB,BBBB,BBB,BBB','B,',' ') "REGEXP_replace" FROM DUAL;
```

The output of Listing 17.36 is as follows:

```
REGEXP_repla
------------
B BBB BB BBB
```

In Listing 17.36, Oracle replaces each occurrence of this with one space.

Listing 17.37: Examining the Code without Treating the String as Multiple Lines

```
SELECT REGEXP_REPLACE('FGHBG
HGGB
FFFB','B$','T',1,1) REPLACE FROM DUAL;
```

The output of Listing 17.37 is as follows:

```
REPLACE
---------------
FGHBG
HGGB
FFFT
```

In Listing 17.37:

- `FGHBG HGGB FFFB` is the source string.
- `B$` is a regular expression.
- `T` is a replacement string.
- `1` indicates position from where search begins.
- The next parameter `1` indicates the number of occurrence.
- `m` indicates the matching parameter. The value `m` indicates that the string should be treated as multiple lines.

Listing 17.38: Examining the String by Treating it as Multiple Lines

```
SELECT REGEXP_REPLACE('FGHBG
HGGB
FFFB','B$','T',1,1,'m') REPLACE FROM DUAL;
```

The output of Listing 17.38 is as follows:

```
REPLACE
---------------
FGHBG
HGGT
FFFB
```

Listing 17.39: Replacing the First Occurrence of B with m Option

```
SELECT REGEXP_REPLACE('FGHCG
HGGB
FFFB','B.','T',1,1,'m') REPLACE FROM DUAL;
```

The output of Listing 17.39 is as follows:

```
REPLACE
--------------
FGHCG
HGGB
FFFB
```

In the output, the first occurrence of `B` is not replaced by `T`. This is because, the pattern is `B.` and we have the `m` option for parameter. The `m` option does not match the newline character. Moreover, it considers the string as multiline.

Listing 17.40: Replacing the First Occurrence of B. Using the n Option

```
SELECT REGEXP_REPLACE('FGHCG
HGGB
FFFB','B.','T',1,1,'n') REPLACE FROM DUAL
/
```

The output of Listing 17.40 is as follows:

```
REPLACE
--------------
FGHCG
HGGTFFFB
```

In the output, the first occurrence of `B` is replaced by `T`. This is because, the pattern is `B.` and we have the `n` option for parameter. The `n` option allows the period (`.`), which is the match-any-character character, to match the newline character. If you omit this parameter, the period does not match the newline character.

Using the **REGEXP_LIKE Function**

The REGEXP_LIKE function is similar to the `LIKE operator`. It searches and returns the rows having the specified pattern. It can be used only in the `WHERE` condition.

Listing 17.41 shows the use of the REGEXP_LIKE function:

Listing 17.41: Searching Rows with the Specified Pattern

```
SELECT 1 FROM DUAL
WHERE REGEXP_LIKE('FGHCG
HGGB
FFFB','B.','n') ;
```

The output of Listing 17.40 is as follows:

```
         1
---------
         1
```

In case you omit n, the condition will return false.

Now that you are familiar with regular expression, let us understand statistical functions.

Summary

In this chapter, we have learned about the regular expression and its functions. You have also learned about specifying patterns with regular expression. In this chapter, you have also come across various examples showing the usage of regular expressions.

Exercise

1. Examining the string and looking for occurrences of words with one or more occurrences of B followed by F.
2. Returning the Position of the L Character in SQL PL/SQL, Only if it is the End of Line.
3. Replacing the Pattern, Dot (.), with the Specified String.
4. Replacing the First Occurrence of A. Using the n Option.

18

Statistical Functions

Oracle has introduced many statistical functions for data analysis and data mining. These features are very useful in determining statistical relationship in the data. You can use various statistics to test such hypothesis. For example, you can use statistical functions to determine similarity of marks of the two classes.

Variance

Variance is calculated as deviation of value from mean. It is calculated as the sum of square of distances from the mean divided by the total number of values of the data of minus one.

Listing 18.1 shows the code to calculate variance (standard deviation):

Listing 18.1: Calculating Variance (Standard Deviation)

```
select avg(phy), variance(phy), stddev(phy) from marks;
```

The output of Listing 18.1 is as follows:

```
  AVG(PHY) VARIANCE(PHY) STDDEV(PHY)
---------- ------------- -----------
      65.8          85.7  9.25742945
```

Listing 18.2 shows the code to calculate variance (average):

Listing 18.2: Calculating Variance (Average)

```
select power((phy-65.8),2),phy,65.8 avg from marks;
```

The output of Listing 18.2 is as follows:

```
POWER((PHY-65.8),2)        PHY        AVG
------------------- ---------- ----------
             174.24         79       65.8
              17.64         70       65.8
                .64         65       65.8
              33.64         60       65.8
             116.64         55       65.8
```

Listing 18.3 shows the code to calculate variance (sum):

Listing 18.3: Calculating Variance (sum)

```
select sum(power((phy-65.8),2)) sm from marks;
```

The output of Listing 18.3 is as follows:

```
        SM
----------
     342.8
```

Listing 18.4 shows the code to calculate the variance of data:

Listing 18.4: Calculating Variance using 'sum' and 'count' Function

```
select sum(power((phy-65.8),2)) sm,sum(power((phy-65.8),2))/(count(1)-1)
  var from marks;
```

The output of Listing 18.4 is as follows:

```
        SM        VAR
---------- ----------
     342.8       85.7
```

Listing 18.5 shows the code to calculate the square root of variance:

Listing 18.5: Calculating Square Root of Variance

```
select var_pop(phy),sum(power((phy-65.8),2)) sm,sum(power((phy-
  65.8),2))/(count(1)) var from marks;
```

The output of Listing 18.5 is as follows:

```
VAR_POP(PHY)          SM        VAR
------------ ---------- ----------
       68.56      342.8      68.56
```

The standard deviation is calculated as the square root of variance. The `VAR_POP` is similar to variance, but the denominator is taken as the number of values, instead of (number of values -1).

Listing 18.6 shows the code to calculate the sample of variance similar to variance:

Listing 18.6: Calculating the Sample of Variance Similar to Variance

```
select var_samp(phy),sum(power((phy-65.8),2))/(count(1)-1) var from marks;
```

The output of Listing 18.6 is as follows:

```
VAR_SAMP(PHY)        VAR
------------- ----------
         85.7       85.7
```

Let's learn how to calculate covariance.

Covariance

The covariance is calculated to determine whether a change in two variables is similar. If it is similar, then you will get positive covariance, as shown in the following expression:

```
(Sum(expr1*expr2)- sum(expr1)*sum(expr2)/n)/n
```

In the preceding expression, `n` is the total number of values.

Listing 18.7 shows the code to calculate covariance using the COVER_POP command:

Listing 18.7: Calculating Covariance Using the COVER_POP Command

```
select covar_pop(phy,che),covar_pop(phy,maths) from marks;
```

The output of Listing 18.7 is as follows:

```
COVAR_POP(PHY,CHE) COVAR_POP(PHY,MATHS)
------------------ --------------------
             88.16               -14.12
```

Listing 18.8 shows the code to calculate covariance using the 'SUM' function:

Listing 18.8: Calculating Covariance Using the SUM Function

```
select (sum(phy*che)-sum(phy)*sum(che)/5)/5 from marks;
```

The output of Listing 18.8 is as follows:

```
(SUM(PHY*CHE)-SUM(PHY)*SUM(CHE)/5)/5
------------------------------------
                               88.16
```

Listing 18.9 shows the code to use the COVER_SAMP function

Listing 18.9: Using the COVER_SAMP Function

```
select (sum(phy*che)-sum(phy)*sum(che)/5)/(5-1), covar_samp(phy,che) from
  marks;
```

The output of Listing 18.9 is as follows:

```
(SUM(PHY*CHE)-SUM(PHY)*SUM(CHE)/5)/(5-1) COVAR_SAMP(PHY,CHE)
---------------------------------------- -------------------
                                   110.2               110.2
```

The `COVAR_SAMP` is similar to `COVAR_POP`, except that the denominator is `(N-1)`.

Correlation

Correlation is used to check whether there is any relationship between two variables.

Spearman Rank-Correlation Coefficient

Coefficient of correlation is a measure of the closeness of association between two variables. It computes a correlation coefficient from a very large set of data of two variables. Spearman Rank-correlation coefficient is a method of performing correlation analysis when the information is sufficient to rank the values.

NOTE

Spearman's rank correlation coefficient, which is named after Charles Spearman, is often denoted by the Greek letter ρ (rho). The principle, ρ, is simply a special case of the Pearson product-moment coefficient in which the data is converted to ranks before calculating the coefficient. However, the following formula is normally used to calculate ρ:

$$\rho = 1 - \frac{6\sum D^2}{N(N^2 - 1)}$$

The preceding formula is defined as follows:

- *The raw scores are converted to ranks*
- *D refers to the difference between the ranks of corresponding given values of X and Y*
- *N refers to the number of pairs of values*

- If the two rankings are the same, the coefficient has value 1
- If one ranking is the reverse of the other, the coefficient has value -1
- For all other arrangements, the value lies between -1 and 1
- Increasing values imply increasing agreement between the rankings
- If the rankings are independent, the coefficient has value 0

Let's learn about correlation having perfect inverse correlation.

Correlation Having Perfect Inverse Correlation

Inverse correlation between variables means that if one variable is increasing, other is decreasing.

Table 18.1 shows the following data of the product table:

Table 18.1: Displaying Product Table

Product	DEMAND_RANK	SUPPLY_RANK
A	1	5
B	2	4
C	3	3
D	4	2
E	5	1

- **The data input for the query**—Specifies `DEMAND_RANK` and `SUPPLY_RANK` columns of `product` table
- **The data output from the query**—Refers to the rank correlation coefficient

The following code snippet shows the command to select the product table:

```
select * from product;
```

The output of the preceding code snippet is as follows:

```
PRODUCT                    DEMAND_RANK SUPPLY_RANK
-------------------- ----------- -----------
A                                1           5
B                                2           4
C                                3           3
D                                4           2
E                                5           1

5 rows selected
```

Listing 18.10 shows the code for correlation having perfect inverse correlation:

Listing 18.10: Showing Perfect Inverse Correlation

```
select corr_s (demand_rank, supply_rank, 'coefficient')
   coefficient,corr_s(demand_rank,supply_rank, 'two_sided_sig')
   two_sided_p_value,corr_s(demand_rank,supply_rank, 'one_sided_sig')
   one_sided_p_value  from product
/
```

The output of Listing 18.10 is as follows:

```
COEFFICIENT TWO_SIDED_P_VALUE ONE_SIDED_P_VALUE
----------- ----------------- -----------------
         -1                 0                 0
```

The preceding output measures the degree of association between DEMAND_RANK and SUPPLY_RANK using Spearman rank-correlation coefficient. The method for computing Spearman rank correlation is described in following calculations:

PRODUCT	DEMAND RANK	SUPPLY RANK	DIFF BET TWO RANKS(D)	DIFF SQUARED (D*D)
A	1	5	-4	16
B	2	4	-2	4
C	3	3	0	0
D	4	2	2	4
E	5	1	4	16
				40

In the preceding data:

- Number of paired observations = N = 5
- Difference between two ranks = D
- Square of difference = D*D

The formula can be given as follows:

$$rs = 1 - \frac{6\sum D^2}{N(N^2-1)}$$

```
= 1- [6*(sum of D*D)]/N((N*N)-1)]
= 1-[6(40)/120]
= -1
```

In the preceding formula, -1 indicates perfect inverse correlation between demand rank and supply rank.

Let's learn about the data having perfect correlation.

Data Having Perfect Correlation

Suppose you have the following table, where two variables are increasing with the same amount, then there is a perfect correlation.

Table 18.2: Displaying the product1 Table

Product	DEMAND_RANK	SUPPLY_RANK
A	1	1
B	2	2
C	3	3
D	4	4
E	5	5

In Table 18.2, the following are the fields of data input and output:

- **The data input for the query**—Specifies DEMAND_RANK and SUPPLY_RANK columns of product1 table
- **The data output from the query**—Represents rank correlation coefficient

The following code snippet shows the command to select the product1 table:

```
select * from product1;
```

The output of preceding code snippet is as follows:

```
PRODUCT              DEMAND_RANK SUPPLY_RANK
-------------------- ----------- -----------
A                              1           1
B                              2           2
C                              3           3
D                              4           4
E                              5           5

5 rows selected
```

Listing 18.11 shows the code for calculating correlation:

Listing 18.11: Showing Perfect Correlation

```
select corr_s(demand_rank,supply_rank, 'coefficient') coefficient,
corr_s(demand_rank,supply_rank, 'two_sided_sig') two_sided_p_value,
corr_s(demand_rank,supply_rank, 'one_sided_sig')   one_sided_p_value
from product1
/
```

The output of Listing 18.11 is as follows:

```
COEFFICIENT TWO_SIDED_P_VALUE ONE_SIDED_P_VALUE
----------- ----------------- -----------------
          1                 0                 0
```

The preceding output measures the degree of association between DEMAND_RANK and SUPPLY_RANK using Spearman rank-correlation coefficient. Therefore, generating information to compute the Spearman rank-correlation coefficient is as follows:

```
PRODUCT  DEMAND RANK  SUPPLY  DIFF BET TWO   DIFF SQUARED
                       RANK    RANKS(D)        (D*D)
-------  -----------  ------- ------------  ------------
   A          1         1       0                0
   B          2         2       0                0
```

```
C        3        3        0        0
D        4        4        0        0
E        5        5        0        0
                                 -----
                                    0
```

In the preceding data:

- Number of paired observations = `N = 5`
- Difference between two ranks = `D`
- Square of difference = `D*D`

The formula can be given as follows:

$$rs = 1 - \frac{6\sum D^2}{N(N^2-1)}$$

```
= 1- [6*(sum of D*D)]/N((N*N)-1)]
= 1-[6(0)/120]
= 1
```

In the preceding formula, `1` indicates perfect co-relation between demand rank and supply rank.

Let's learn about other correlating coefficients.

Other Correlation Coefficients

Apart from the above correlation coefficient, some coefficients are used to describe the relationship between two data sets.

Pearson Coefficient

The Pearson coefficient is used to calculate whether or not there is a relationship between two variables, i.e. both are decreasing or increasing in general. Suppose you have the following data in Table 18.3:

Table 18.3: Displaying Marks Table

Rn	Phy	Che	Maths
1	79	89	90
2	70	80	91
3	65	75	85
4	60	68	98
5	55	57	93

In Table 18.3, there is a correlation between physics marks and chemistry marks. If a student is getting good marks in physics, he is likely to get good marks in chemistry. In such a case, the coefficient tends towards 1.

You will also notice that there is negative correlation between physics marks and mathematics marks. If a student is getting good marks in physics, he is likely to get less marks in mathematics. In such a case, the coefficient tends towards -1. On the other hand, if there is no relation between the variables, then the coefficient tends towards 0. The following code snippet shows the command to select the marks table:

```
select * from marks;
```

The output of the preceding table is as follows:

```
        RN        PHY        CHE      MATHS
---------- ---------- ---------- ----------
         1         79         89         90
         2         70         80         91
```

```
        3          65          75          85
        4          60          68          98
        5          55          57          93

  5 rows selected
```

Listing 18.12 shows the code to find coefficient:

Listing 18.12: Finding Coefficient

```
select corr(phy,che) p_c, corr(phy,maths) p_m from marks;
```

The output of Listing 18.12 is as follows:

```
       P_C          P_M
----------   ----------
.982824845   -.40374008
```

The coefficient is calculated, as shown in the following expression:

```
COVAR_POP(expr1, expr2) / (STDDEV_POP(expr1) * STDDEV_POP(expr2))
```

Let's learn about CORR_K.

CORR_K

The correlation function, also called CORR_K, calculates the Kendall's correlation coefficient. It calculates the number of concordant and discordant pairs of two variables. If the pair is having increasing values of both variables, then it is concordant; otherwise, it is discordant.

Let's learn about the analysis of variance.

Analysis of Variance (ANOVA)

The one-way analysis of variance function helps us to test the significance of the differences among more than two sample means. Depending on the variance within the group and variances among the mean of group, estimate mean squares within group and mean squares between are computed.

Suppose you have the following data in the `sales_new` table (Table 18.4):

Table 18.4: Displaying the sales_new Table

Area	ZoneA	ZoneB
s	45	59
n	40	43
n	50	47
s	39	51
s	53	39
n	44	49

The following code snippet shows the contents of the sales_new table.

```
select * from sales_new;
```

The output of the preceding code snippet is as follows:

```
AREA                      ZONEA      ZONEB
------------------- ---------- ----------
s                            45         59
n                            40         43
n                            50         47
s                            39         51
```

```
s                              53          39
n                              44          49

6 rows selected
```

Listing 18.13 shows the code to use the ANOVA function:

Listing 18.13: Showing the Analysis of Variance Function

```
select
  stats_one_way_anova(area,zoneb, 'f_ratio') f_ratio,
  stats_one_way_anova(area,zoneb, 'sig') significance,
        stats_one_way_anova(area,zoneb, 'mean_squares_between') msq_bet,
        stats_one_way_anova(area,zoneb, 'mean_squares_within') msq_with,
        stats_one_way_anova(area,zoneb, 'df_between') df_bet,
        stats_one_way_anova(area,zoneb, 'df_within') df_with,
        stats_one_way_anova(area,zoneb, 'sum_squares_between') sq_bet,
        stats_one_way_anova(area,zoneb, 'sum_squares_within') sq_with
        from sales_new
/
```

The output of Listing 18.13 is as follows:

```
F_RATIO          SIGNIFICANCE    MSQ_BET          MSQ_WITH          DF_BET          DF_WITH
----------       ------------    ----------       ----------        ----------      -------
SQ_BET           SQ_WITH
----------       ----------
.301204819    .612323595  16.6666667      55.3333333          1           4
16.6666667       221.333333
```

Calculation 18.1: Computing the Sample Mean (sm) of ZONE_A and ZONE_B of the sales_new Table

```
S ZONEB          N ZONEB
---------        ----------
  59               43
+ 51           +   47
+ 39           +   49
---------        ---------
  149/3            139/3
```

The result of the preceding calculation is as follows:

```
S ZONEB   N ZONEB
---------   ---------
= 49.67   = 46.34
```

Calculation 18.2: Computing the Grand Mean (G.M.) as a Weighted Average of Sample Means using the Relative Sample Sizes as Weights

```
G.M. = (3/6)49.67+(3/6)46.34
```

The result of preceding calculation is as follows:

```
G.M. = 48
```

Calculation 18.3: Computing Variances within the Samples and within Column Variance

Suppose:

- Sample mean = `sm`
- Grand mean = `gm`
- Size of jth sample = `nj`

and the values of nj, sm, and gm are as follows:

```
nj sm    G.M.
3  49.67  48
3  46.34  48
```

The result of the preceding calculation is as follows:

```
sm-gm               (sm-gm)*(sm-gm) nj*(sm-gm)*(sm-gm)
------      ------------------    ----------------------
1.67                     2.7889                    8.3667
-1.66                    2.7556                    8.2668
                                        -----------------

                                               Σ 16.6335

σ^2b = Between column variance
     = 16.6335
```

To calculate within column variance, the following steps should be taken:

1. Calculate variance of ZONE_A and ZONE_B:

```
          S ZONE B                          N ZONE B
     (x-sm)       (x-sm)2            (x-sm)         (x-sm)2
     (59-49.67)    87.04           (43-46.34)     11.15
     (51-49.67)    1.768           (47-46.34)     0.435
     (39-49.67)    113.84          (49-46.34)     7.075
                   ------                         -------

                 Σ 202.64                       Σ 18.66
S12 = 202.64/ 2
    = 101.32

S22 = 18.66 / 2
    = 9.33

σ^2 = (nj-1/nT-k)*(x-sm)2

nT = total sample size

k = number of samples

σ^2 = [(2/4) * (101.32)]+ [(2/4)*(9.33)]
        = 50.66 +4.665
        = 55.325
    = WITHIN-COLUMN VARIANCE

F-RATIO = Between column variance / WITHIN-COLUMN VARIANCE
          = 16.6335 / 55.325
          = 0.3006
```

If the value of the F-RATIO is nearer to 1, then two datasets are similar. If the value of the F-RATIO is larger than one, then two datasets are dissimilar.

Let's learn about chi-square test.

Chi-Square

The Chi-square test calculates whether or not more than two population proportions can be considered equal. This test can also be used to determine if the two attributes are independent of each other.

Suppose you have the following data in the `rainfall` table (Table 18.5):

Table 18.5: Displaying the Rainfall Table

Rainfall	Expected	Observed
Y_1990	50	45
Y_1991	35	32
Y_1992	45	40
Y_1993	40	45
Y_1994	33	40

Table 18.5 is used to explain Chi-square test.

- **The data input for the query**—Represents `EXPECTED` and `OBSERVED` columns of the `Rainfall` table
- **The data output from the query**—Represents the observed value of Chi-square

The following code snippet shows the command to select the rainfall table:

```
select * from rainfall;
```

The output of the preceding code snippet is as follows:

```
RAINFALL               EXPECTED   OBSERVED
-------------------- ---------- ----------
Y_1990                       50         45
Y_1991                       35         32
Y_1992                       45         40
Y_1993                       40         45
Y_1994                       33         40

5 rows selected
```

Listing 18.14 shows the code to find Chi-square:

Listing 18.14: Finding Chi-square

```
select stats_crosstab
  ( expected,observed, 'chisq_obs') chi_squared,
        stats_crosstab
        (expected,observed, 'chisq_sig') p_value,
        stats_crosstab
        (expected,observed,'phi_coefficient') phi_coefficient,
        stats_crosstab
        (expected,observed, 'chisq_df') degree_freedom,
        stats_crosstab
        (expected,observed,'cont_coefficient') cont_coefficient,
        stats_crosstab
        (expected,observed,'cramers_v') cramers_v
        from rainfall
     /
```

The output of Listing 18.14 is as follows:

```
CHI_SQUARED      P_VALUE     PHI_COEFFICIENT       DEGREE_FREEDOM    CONT_COEFFICIENT
-----------  --------   --------------- ---------------   ---------------
CRAMERS_V
----------
10 .265025915      1.41421356             8       .816496581
 1.
```

Calculation 18.5: Computing chi-square statistic from the rainfall table

f_o = Observed

f_e = Expected

a. Subtract f_e from f_o for each of the five values of table rainfall.

b. Square each of the differences.

c. Divide each squared differences by f_e.

d. Add all the five values

The formula for calculating Chi-square (χ^2) is as follows:

```
x²: = (fo- fe)²/fe
```

The values of f_o and f_e to be inserted into the formula are as follows:

```
fo          fe          fo - fe         (fo - fe)*( fo - fe)
---      ---------    ------------     --------------------
45          50             -5                  25
32          35             -3                   9
40          45             -5                  25
45          40              5                  25
40          33              7                  49
```

The result of the preceding calculation is as follows:

```
(fo - fe)*( fo - fe)/ fe
--------------------------------------------
                0.5
                0.25
                0.55
                0.62
                1.48
----------------------------
Chi-squared value = 3.4
```

If the value of Chi-square is close to 0, it indicates similarity in two data sets.

Let's learn about F_Test.

F_Test

F_Test calculates f_statistic, which is a ratio of variance of one group to another. If the value of f varies from 1, it indicates significant differences in variances.

To explain F_TEST Sales_new table as given ANOVA test is used.

Listing 18.15 shows the code to find f_statistic:

Listing 18.15: Finding f_statistic

```
select
   stats_f_test(area,zoneb, 'statistic') f_stat,
          stats_f_test(area,zoneb, 'df_num') df_num,
          stats_f_test(area,zoneb, 'df_den') df_den,
          stats_f_test(area,zoneb, 'one_sided_sig') one_sig,
          stats_f_test(area,zoneb, 'two_sided_sig') two_sig
          from sales_new
          /
```

The output of Listing 18.15 is as follows:

```
      F_STAT     DF_NUM     DF_DEN      ONE_SIG      TWO_SIG
---------- ---------- ----------   ----------   ----------
.092105263          2          2  .084337349   .168674699
```

Calculation 18.6: Computing Sample Mean (sm) of Both Areas of ZONEB of the Sales_new Table

```
S ZONEB    N ZONEB
---------    ----------
  59             43
+ 51       +     47
+ 39       +     49

---------        ---------
  149/3         139/3
```

The result of the preceding calculation is as follows:

```
S ZONEB  N ZONEB
-------  -------
= 49.67  = 46.34
```

Calculation 18.7: Steps to Compute Within Column Variance of the Sales_new Table

Step1: Calculate variance for each area i.e. s and n

```
         S ZONE B                          N ZONE B

    (x-sm)        (x-sm)2           (x-sm)      (x-sm)2

    (59-49.67)     87.04          (43-46.34)    11.15
    (51-49.67)     1.768          (47-46.34)    0.435
    (39-49.67)     113.84         (49-46.34)    7.075
                   ------                      -------
                 Σ 202.64                     Σ 18.66

Variance of S ZONEB = σ2 =  (x-sm)2 / N
Total no. of items in the population = N
Each item in population == X

σ2 = 202.64 / 3
  = 67.54

Variance of N ZONEB       = σ2
                  = (x-sm)2 / N

σ2 = 8.66 / 3
  = 6.22
Step2: Calculate F_statistics.
F_STAT = variance of one group /variance of another group
     = 6.22 / 67.54
     = 0.092
```

If the value of F_STAT differs significantly from 1, then it indicates dissimilarity of two data sets.

Let's learn about KS_TEST.

K-S TEST (Kolmogorov-Smirnov Test)

Kolmogorov-Smirnov test (K-S_Test) is a nonparametric goodness-of-fit test of a theoretical frequency distribution. It finds the relative cumulative distributions for both observed frequencies and expected frequencies, and then tests their differences. K-S_Test is always a one-tailed test.

Suppose you have the following data in the `kol_s` table (Table 18.6):

Table 18.6: Displaying the kol_s Table

Grade	Score
A	30
B	100
A	440
B	500
A	130

Table 18.6 is used to explain the K-S_TEST.

- **The data input for the query**—Represents `GRADE` and `SCORE` columns of the `kol_s` table
- **The data output from the query**—Represents the value of `K-S_statistic`

The following code snippet shows the command to select the data of the kol_s table:

```
select * from kol_s;
```

The output of the preceding code snippet is as follows:

```
GRADE            SCORE
---------------- ----------
  A              30
  B              100
  A              440
  B              500
  A              130

5 rows selected
```

Listing 18.16 shows the code to evaluate the data of kol_s table with K-S_Test

Listing 18.16: Evaluating Data of the kol_s Table with **K-S_TEST**

```
select stats_k-s_test(grade,score, 'statistic') ks_statistic,
stats_k-s_test(grade,score, 'sig') significance
from kol_s
/
```

The output of Listing 18.16 is as follows:

```
KS_STATISTIC     SIGNIFICANCE
------------     ------------
          .5     .779627873
```

If KS_statistics is less than significant value, then two data sets are considered as equal.

Let's learn about the STATS_MODE test.

MODE

The function `STATS_MODE` test is useful in finding out the observation, which occur the maximum number of times in a sample. Suppose you have the data in `the mode1` table (Table 18.7):

Table 18.7: Displaying mode1 Table

ID	Val
1	10
2	23
3	39
3	32

The above data is used to explain MODE function.

- **The data input for the query**—Represents `ID` column of `mode1` table
- **The data output from the query**—Represents the value, which occurs the maximum number of times in sample

The following code snippet shows the command to select the mode1 table:

```
select * from mode1;
```

The output of preceding code snippet is as follows:

```
ID          VAL
-------     -------
1           10
2           23
3           39
3           32

4 rows selected
```

Listing 18.17 shows the code to find the mode of id with stats_mode test

Listing 18.17: Finding Mode of Id with stats_mode Test

```
select stats_mode(id) from mode1
/
```

The output of Listing 18.17 is as follows

```
STATS_MODE(ID)
--------------
  3
```

In table, `mode1`, the mode is displayed as 3, as it occurs twice while the other observations occur only once.

Let's learn about Mann-Whitney test.

Mann-Whitney Test (**MW_TEST**)

The MW_Test is a non-parametric test which takes into account rank of the data of the sample observations. We use this test when two populations are involved. Using this test, we can determine whether independent samples are from the same population or from different populations having the same distribution.

Suppose you have the in the `M_WHITNEY1` table describing section strengths at various sections (Table 18.8):

Table 18.8: Displaying the M_WHITNEY1 Table

Section	Strength
A	35
B	40
A	45
A	50
B	55
A	60
B	65
A	70
A	75
B	80
B	85
A	90
A	95
A	100
B	30
B	105
A	110
B	115
B	120
A	125
B	130
A	135
B	140

Above table is used to explain the concept of Mann Whitney test.

- **The data input for the query**—Represents `SECTION` and `STRENGTH` columns of `M_WHITNEY1` table
- **The data output from the query**—Represents the sample value of U statistic and critical value `z` for test

The following code snippet shows the command to select the M_WHITNEY1 table:

```
select * from M_WHITNEY1;
```

The output of preceding code snippet is as follows:

```
SECTION              STRENGTH
----------------     ----------
A                       35
B                       40
A                       45
```

```
A                   50
B                   55
A                   60
B                   65
A                   70
A                   75
B                   80
B                   85
A                   90
A                   95
A                  100
B                   30
B                  105
A                  110
B                  115
B                  120
A                  125
B                  130
A                  135
B                  140

23 rows selected
```

Listing 18.18 shows the code to find the sample value of U statistic and critical value z:

Listing 18.18: Finding the Sample Value of U Statistic and Critical Value z

```
select stats_mw_test(section,strength, 'u_statistic') u_statistic,
   stats_mw_test(section,strength) p_value,
stats_mw_test(section,strength, 'statistic') statistic
from m_whitney1
/
```

The output of Listing 18.18 is as follows:

```
U_STATISTIC                P_VALUE         STATISTIC
-----------                ----------      ----------
60                         .711923151      -.36927447
```

Consider the above table M_WHITNEY1 with section and strength of different classes. Let's now perform the ranking of strength.

The query does the calculation according to the following steps.

Step1: Calculating ranks in each data set.

```
SECTION A     RANK          SECTION B        RANK
--------      ----          ----------       -------
35            2             40               3
45            4             55               6
50            5             65               8
60            7             80               11
70            9             85               12
75            10            30               1
90            13            105              16
95            14            115              18
100           15            120              19
110           17            130              21
125           20            140              23
135           22
```

```
        -----                                   -----
        Σ 138                                   Σ 138
```

In the preceding calculation:

- n1 = number of observations in SECTION A = 12
- n2 = number of observations in SECTION B = 11
- R1 = sum of the ranks of strength of SECTION A = 138
- R2 = sum of the ranks of strength of SECTION B = 138

Step2: Calculate U statistic using the following formula:

```
U = n1(n2)+[n1(n1+1)/2]-R1
```

The result of preceding formula is as follows:

```
U_STATISTIC       = 12(11)+[12(12+1)/2]-138
U_STATISTIC       = 72
```

To get the critical value of z, we calculate mean μ_u and standard error σu, as shown in the following expression:

```
μu = n1n2/2
    = 12(11)/2
    = 66

σu =  [[n1*n2(n1+n2+1)]/12]1/2
    =  [[132(24)]/12]1/2
    = 16.24
```

The output of the preceding expression is given as follows:

```
z = U-μu /σu
  = 72-66/16.24
z = 0.369
```

If U_statistics is less than critical value z, then data sets are similar.

Let's learn about Wilcoxon Signed-Rank tests.

Wilcoxon Signed-Rank Test (**WSR_TEST**)

Wilcoxon Signed-Rank tests are based on plus minus signs of the difference between the sample observations and the hypothesized mean μ. The magnitude of this difference is used to test the null hypothesis's test statistic and it can be calculated by finding mean and variance of the sample.

Table 18.9 lists the data of the MACHINE table:

Table 18.9: Displaying the MACHINE Table

NEW_MAC	OLD_MAC
10	12
11	14
12	10
9	11
15	16
8	11
20	22

Table 18.9: Displaying the MACHINE Table

NEW_MAC	OLD_MAC
14	16
10	8
13	11
14	15
10	8
7	10
17	16
18	20

In Table 18.9, following are the fields of data input and output:

- **The data input for the query**—Represents `NEW_MAC` and `OLD_MAC` columns of `MACHINE` table
- **The data output from the query**—Represents the value of `Z` test statistic

The following code snippet shows the command to select the MACHINE table:

```
select * from machine;
```

The output of the preceding code snippet is as follows:

```
NEW_MAC      OLD_MAC
----------  ----------
10              12
11              14
12              10
9               11
15              16
8               11
20              22
14              16
10              8
13              11
14              15
10              8
7               10
17              16
18              20

15 rows selected
```

Listing 18.19 shows the code to perform WSR_TEST:

Listing 18.19: Performing WSR_TEST

```
select stats_wsr_test(new_mac,old_mac, 'statistic') z_statistic,
stats_wsr_test(new_mac,old_mac, 'one_sided_sig') onesignificance,
stats_wsr_test(new_mac,old_mac, 'two_sided_sig') tosignificance
from machine
/
```

The output of Listing 18.19 is as follows:

```
Z_STATISTIC ONESIGNIFICANCE TOSIGNIFICANCE
----------- --------------- --------------
-1.5163508       .935284663 .129430674
```

Calculation 18.9: Computing Z test statistic

The result of the preceding calculation is as follows:

```
  NEW_MAC(x)    OLD_MAC      Difference          Rank
     (x)          (y)          (x-y)
  ----------    -------      ----------    ------
      10          12            -2            8
      11          14            -3            14
      12          10             2            8
       9          11            -2            8
      15          16            -1            2
       8          11            -3            14
      20          22            -2            8
      14          16            -2            8
      10           8             2            8
      13          11             2            8
      14          15            -1            2
      10           8             2            8
       7          10            -3            14
      17          16             1            2
      18          20            -2            8
```

Therefore,

$S_+ = 34$ and $S_- = 86$

In the preceding data

- S_+ =sum of values of ranks with positive difference
- S_- =sum of values of ranks with negative difference
- N = size of sample. In this case it is 15

So:

$$\mu_{S+} = \mu_{S-} = n(n+1)/4$$
$$= 15(16)/4$$
$$= 60$$

$$\sigma^2_{S+} = \sigma^2_{S-} = n(n+1)(2n-1)/24$$
$$= 15(16)(29)/24$$
$$= 290$$

$$Z = S_+ - \mu_{S+} / \sigma_{S+} \quad \text{or} \quad Z = S_- - \mu_{S-} / \sigma_{S-}$$

$$= 34-60/17.02$$
$$= -1.52$$

If value of WSR_statistics is less than the significant value, then the two data sets are equal.

Now, let's learn about binomial test.

BINOMIAL_TEST

It is used for variables having two possible values such as Y or N. In the following data, the number of rows having value, Y are 50%, while the number of rows having value, N are also 50%. The binomial test is used to test the probability of getting 68% Y value or the probability of getting more than 68% of Y value.

Table 18.10 lists the data of the ANSWER table:

Table 18.10: Displaying the ANSWER Table

Y_OR_N	Score
Y	50
N	176
Y	100
Y	80
N	95
N	60

In Table 18.10, following are the fields of data input and output:

- **The data input for the query**—Represents Y_OR_N column of ANSWER table
- **The data output from the query**—Represents real proportion

The following code snippet shows the command to select the ANSWER table:

```
select * from answer;
```

The output of the preceding code snippet is as follows:

```
Y_OR_N                    SCORE
-------------------- ----------
Y                            50
N                           176
Y                           100
Y                            80
N                            95
N                            60

6 rows selected
```

Listing 18.20 shows the code to use BINOMIAL_TEST:

Listing 18.20: Using BINOMIAL_TEST

```
select avg(decode(y_or_n, 'y', 1, 0)) real_proportion,
stats_binomial_test
(y_or_n, 'y', 0.68, 'exact_prob') exact, stats_binomial_test
(y_or_n, 'y', 0.68, 'one_sided_prob_or_less') prob_or_less
from answer
/
```

The output of Listing 18.20 is as follows:

```
REAL_PROPORTION      EXACT                 PROB_OR_LESS
--------------- ----------          ------------
             .5  .206066156          .293559337
```

Summary

With this chapter, you must have had in depth knowledge of statistical functions. These functions are used for data analysis in various conditions. The chapter also introduces how to use these functions and in which form, these functions expects their data. The next chapter will focus on some model queries.

Exercise

Suppose the following data is given in the PCM (Physics, Chemistry, Maths) table

RN	P	C	M
1	67	54	87
2	65	73	62
3	66	61	82
4	82	74	90
5	45	56	65
6	86	92	92

1. Test whether data in Physics and Chemistry is similar using different correlation coefficients.
2. Test whether data in Physics and Maths is similar using F_statistics.
3. Test whether data in Maths and Chemistry is similar using the Mann-Whitney Test.

19

Model Queries

Model queries are introduced in Oracle to support spreadsheet like calculations. These are also called inter row queries. These queries use a relational table as an array of values.

This chapter discusses concept of model queries and various functionalities associated with model queries.

Dimensions and Cells in model query

For model query, user has to select some columns as dimensions then the values in the rows are referred using dimensions and these values are stored in cells. This is explained as follows.

Consider a table with data shown in Table 19.1:

Table 19.1: Data for a Sample Table

RN	P	C	M	CLASS
1	78	67	98	A
2	90	70	87	B
3	80	60	85	A
4	93	75	93	B

In Table 19.1, each value is stored in a cell. For example, if you consider `RN` as one dimension and `CLASS` as another dimension, then the value of `P(1,A)` can be calculated as follows:

```
P(1,A) = 78,
P(2,B) = 90
```

You can also construct expressions by using these values, as follows:

```
P(1,A)+P(3,A) = 78+80
              = 158
```

Let's now learn to construct a model query.

Construction of a Model Query

Models queries are constructed using dimensions and cells.

Suppose a table, `ABCD`, contains the data shown in Table 19.2:

Table 19.2: Data for the ABCD Table

A	B	C	D
1	1	1	10
1	2	1	20
1	3	1	30
1	1	2	15
1	2	2	25
1	3	2	35

Now, suppose you send a query shown in the following code snippet:

```
select * from abcd;
```

The output of the preceding code snippet is as follows:

```
         A          B          C          D
    ------ ---------- --------- ---------
         1          1          1         10
         1          2          1         20
         1          3          1         30
         1          1          2         15
         1          2          2         25
         1          3          2         35

6 rows selected
```

Let's now use the data in the preceding output to write a spreadsheet query, as shown in Listing 19.1:

Listing 19.1: Writing a Spreadsheet Query

```
select a,b,c,d from abcd
  model
    partition by (c)
    dimension by (a, b)
    measures (d)
    ignore nav
    unique dimension
    rules upsert sequential order
    (d[a=1, b=3] = d[1, 1] + d[1, 2]+12);
```

The output of Listing 19.1 is as follows:

```
         A          B          C          D
---------- ---------- ---------- ----------
         1          1          1         10
         1          2          1         20
         1          3          1         42
         1          1          2         15
         1          2          2         25
         1          3          2         52

6 rows selected
```

The following is a brief description of the various elements that appear in Listing 19.1:

- `PARTITION BY (C)` —Indicates the number of groups of rows. Therefore, all the rows that have the same value of `C` will be in one partition or group.
- `DIMENSION BY (A, B)` —Indicates how the cells in the spreadsheet are selected.
- `MEASURES`—Indicate the value of a cell.
- `NAV`—Indicates not available values or null values.
- `UNIQUE DIMENSION`—Indicates that the cell should be unique. Otherwise, an error is generated.
- `UPSERT`—Indicates that a value should be updated if a target cell is available; otherwise, it will make a new row using expression specified in query.

NOTE

Updation is done at the query level and not at the table level.

Additional Clauses in Model Query

Users can use multiple expressions, iterations in model queries.

The following are some examples that make use of additional clauses in a model query:

Listing 19.2: Generating the value for D[1,4] and D[1,6] for Each Partition

```
select a, b, c, d from abcd
  model
    partition by (c)
    dimension by (a, b)
    measures (d)
    ignore nav
    unique dimension
    rules upsert sequential order
    (d[1, for b in (4, 6)] = d[cv( ), 2] + d[cv( ), 2]);
```

The output of Listing 19.2 is as follows:

```
         A          B          C          D
---------- ---------- ---------- ----------
         1          1          1         10
         1          2          1         20
         1          3          1         30
         1          4          1         40
         1          6          1         40
         1          1          2         15
         1          2          2         25
         1          3          2         35
         1          4          2         50
         1          6          2         50

10 rows selected
```

In Listing 19.2, `CV` indicates the current value, and is written in place of the dimension `(a)`. In this way, it uses the current value of `a`.

Listing 19.3: Generating the value for d[1,4] and d[1,6] for Each Partition using PRESENTNNV function

```
select a, b, c, d from abcd
  model
    partition by (c)
    dimension by (a, b)
    measures (d)
    ignore nav
    unique dimension
    rules upsert sequential order
    (d[1, for b in (4, 6)] = presentnnv(d[1, 4], d[1,3], 17));
```

The output of Listing 19.3 is as follows:

```
         A          B          C          D
---------- ---------- ---------- ----------
         1          1          1         10
         1          2          1         20
         1          3          1         30
         1          4          1         17
         1          6          1         17
         1          1          2         15
         1          2          2         25
```

```
        1          3          2         35
        1          4          2         17
        1          6          2         17

10 rows selected
```

In Listing 19.3, `PRESENTNNV` checks whether the specified value is null or not available. If `cell [1,2]` exists and is not null, the value of `cell [1,3]` is assigned to `cell [1,4]`; otherwise, the default value `17` is assigned.

Listing 19.4: Generating the value for D[1,4] and D[1,6] for Each Partition when D[1,2] is Present

```
select a, b, c, d from abcd
  model
    partition by (c)
    dimension by (a, b)
    measures (d)
    ignore nav
    unique dimension
    rules upsert sequential order
    (d[1, for b in (4, 6)] = presentnnv(d[1, 2], d[1,1], 17));
```

Since D[1,2] is present value D[1,1] is assigned to D[1,4] and D[1,6]

The output of Listing 19.4 is as follows:

```
        A          B          C          D
--------- ---------- ---------- ----------
        1          1          1         10
        1          2          1         20
        1          3          1         30
        1          4          1         10
        1          6          1         10
        1          1          2         15
        1          2          2         25
        1          3          2         10
        1          4          2         15
        1          6          2         15
```

Listing 19.5: Using the PRESENTV Function to Generate the Value for D[1,4] and D[1,6] for Each Partition

```
select a, b, c, d from abcd
  model
    partition by (c)
    dimension by (a, b)
    measures (d)
    ignore nav
    unique dimension
    rules upsert sequential order
    (d[1, for b in (4, 6)] = presentv(d[1, 4], d[1,3], 10));
```

The output of Listing 19.5 is as follows:

```
         A          B          C          D
---------- ---------- ---------- ----------
         1          1          1         10
         1          2          1         20
         1          3          1         30
         1          4          1         10
         1          6          1         10
```

```
         1          1          2         15
         1          2          2         25
         1          3          2         35
         1          4          2         10
         1          6          2         10

10 rows selected
```

In Listing 19.5, PRESENTV indicates the current value. As D[1,4] is absent, the default value 10 is assigned to D[1,6].

Listing 19.6: Assigning a Value to d[1,6] by Using the ITERATE Clause for Each Partition

```
select a, b, c, d from abcd
model
partition by (c)
    dimension by (a, b)
    measures (d,0 cnt)
    ignore nav
    unique dimension
    rules iterate(10) until(d[1,3]-previous(d[1,3])  >3)
    (
d[1,3]=d[1,3]*1.1,
cnt[1,3]=cnt[1,3]+1,
d[1, 6] = cnt[1,3]
);
```

The output of Listing 19.6 is as follows:

```
         A          B          C          D
---------- ---------- ---------- ----------
         1          1          1         10
         1          2          1         20
         1          3          1       36.3
         1          6          1          2
         1          1          2         15
         1          2          2         25
         1          3          2       38.5
         1          6          2          1
```

The query in Listing 19.6 is explained as follows:

- The value of CNT which is also called as measure is additionally defined and initialized to 0
- The initial value of D[1,3] is 20
- After the first iteration, D[1,3] has the value 33, i.e. 30*1.1 and CNT gets the value 1
- After the second iteration, D[1,3] has the value 36.3 and CNT gets the value 2.
- After the second iteration, the iteration condition is TRUE and the iteration is terminated
- The last value of D[1,3] is 36.3 and that of CNT is 2, which is assigned to D[1,6]

Listing 19.7: Generating a Value for d[1,3] for Each Partition and Displaying the Data in Sorted Order

```
select a,b,c,d from abcd
  model
    partition by (c)
    dimension by (a, b)
    measures (d)
    ignore nav
    unique dimension
```

```
        rules upsert sequential order
        (d[a=1, b=3] = d[1, 1] + d[1, 2]+12) order by a,b,c;
```

The output of Listing 19.7 is as follows:

```
         A          B          C          D
---------- ---------- ---------- ----------
         1          1          1         10
         1          1          2         15
         1          2          1         20
         1          2          2         25
         1          3          1         42
         1          3          2         52

6 rows selected
```

In Listing 19.7, the `ORDER BY` clause is used to order the rows selected by the query.

Listing 19.8: Generating the Value for d[3] for Each Partition by Using Other Cell Values

```
select b,c,d from abcd
    model
      partition by (c)
      dimension by (b)
      measures (d)
      ignore nav
      unique dimension
        rules upsert sequential order
       (d[3] = d[1]*d[1]);
```

The output of Listing 19.8 is as follows:

```
         B          C          D
---------- ---------- ----------
         1          1         10
         2          1         20
         3          1        100
         1          2         15
         2          2         25
         3          2        225

6 rows selected
```

NOTE

If a row with cell[3] is not present, then new row is inserted.

Listing 19.9: Generating the Value for d[1,1,1] for Each Partition

```
  select a,b,d from abcd
      model
         partition by (c)
         dimension by (a,b,c)
         measures (d)
         ignore nav
     unique dimension
         rules upsert sequential order
         (d[1,1,1] = d[1,2,1]+d[1,3,1]-10);
```

The output of Listing 19.9 is as follows:

```
         A          B          D
---------- ---------- ----------
         1          1         40
         1          2         20
         1          3         30
         1          1         15
         1          2         25
         1          3         35
         1          1        -10

7 rows selected
```

In Listing 19.9, if the row with `cell[1,1]` is not present, then the new row is inserted.

Listing 19.10: Generating the Value for a Cell with the Dimensions a=1, a=2, b=1, and b=2 and the value of c as 1 for Each Partition

```
select a,b,d from abcd
  model
    partition by (c)
    dimension by (a,b,c)
    measures (d)
    ignore nav
    unique dimension
    rules upsert sequential order
    (d[for a in(1,2),for b in(1,2),1] = presentv
       (d[1,3,12],d[1,3,2],100));
```

The output of Listing 19.10 is as follows:

```
         A          B          D
---------- ---------- ----------
         1          1        100
         1          2        100
         1          3         30
         2          1        100
         2          2        100
         1          1         15
         1          2         25
         1          3         35
         1          1        100
         1          2        100
         2          1        100
         2          2        100

12 rows selected
```

In Listing 19.10, `PRESENTV` indicates the current value. If `cell[1,3,12]` exists, then the value of `cell[1,3,2]` is assigned. Otherwise, the default value `100` is assigned.

Listing 19.11: Generating the Value for a Cell with the Dimensions a=1 and a=2, and the Value of c as 1 for Each Partition

```
select a,b,c,d from abcd
  model
    partition by (c)
    dimension by (a,b)
    measures (d)
```

```
      ignore nav
    unique dimension
      rules upsert sequential order
      (d[for a in(1,2),1] =presentv (d[1,4],d[1,3],120));
```

The output of Listing 19.11 is as follows:

```
         A          B          C          D
---------- ---------- ---------- ----------
         1          1          1        120
         1          2          1         20
         1          3          1         30
         2          1          1        120
         1          1          2        120
         1          2          2         25
         1          3          2         35
         2          1          2        120

8 rows selected
```

In Listing 19.11, `PRESENTV` indicates the current value. If `cell[1,4]` exists, then the value of `cell[1,3]` is assigned. Otherwise, the default value `120` is assigned.

Listing 19.12: Generating the Value for a Cell with the Dimensions a=1, b=4, b=6, and the value of c as 1 for Each Partition

```
select a,b,d from abcd
  model
    partition by (c)
    dimension by (a,b,c)
    measures (d)
    ignore nav
  unique dimension
    rules upsert sequential order
    (d[1,for b in(4,6),1] =d[cv(),1,1]+d[cv(),2,1]);
```

The output of Listing 19.12 is as follows:

```
         A          B          D
---------- ---------- ----------
         1          1         10
         1          2         20
         1          3         30
         1          4         30
         1          6         30
         1          1         15
         1          2         25
         1          3         35
         1          4          0
         1          6          0

10 rows selected
```

In Listing 19.12, `CV` indicates the current value and is written in place of the dimension `(a)`. In this way, it uses the current value of `a`.

Let's now discuss PIVOT queries.

The PIVOT Query

PIVOT queries are introduced in Oracle 11g to change the display of output of queries by rotating rows into columns and vice versa.

Suppose you have the data shown in the following table:

```
      TIME REGION          DEPT                PROFIT
  -------- --------------- --------------- ----------
      1996 Central         pen_sales            34000
      1996 Central         pen_sales            41000
      1996 Central         book_sales           74000
      1996 east            pen_sales            89000
      1996 east            book_sales          100000
      1996 east            book_sales           15000
      1996 west            pen_sales            87000
      1996 west            book_sales           86000
      1997 Central         pen_sales            82000
      1997 Central         book_sales           85000
      1997 east            pen_sales           101000

      TIME REGION          DEPT                PROFIT
  -------- --------------- --------------- ----------
      1997 east            book_sales          137000
      1997 west            pen_sales            96000
      1997 west            book_sales           97000
```

Suppose you want to show the year on the horizontal axis and department on the vertical axis, you can write the query as shown in the following code snippet:

```
@pivot1
select * from
(
select dept,time,profit
from sales)
pivot
(
sum(profit) for time in (1996 as y1996,1997 as y1997)
)
order by 2;
```

Result:

```
DEPT                 Y1996      Y1997
--------------- ---------- ----------
pen_sales           251000     279000
book_sales          275000     319000
```

The steps to execute a pivot query are as follows:

1. The (SELECT DEPT,TIME,PROFIT FROM SALES) query provides data for the PIVOT query
2. Two additional columns for 1996 and 1997 are created, by using the following clause:

   ```
   time in (1996 as y1996,1997 as y1997)
   ```
3. SUM(PROFIT) is displayed as a cell value.
4. Other columns, such as Dept, form the rows of the display.
5. The output is sorted on the second column.

After learning about pivot queries, let's discuss how to display data for multiple columns.

Displaying Data for Multiple Columns

You can use multiple columns in PIVOT clause. The query in the following code snippet shows how to form pivot columns by combining year and region:

```
select * from
(
select dept,time,region,profit
from sales)
pivot
(
sum(profit) for (time,region) in (
(1996,'east') as east_1996,
(1996,'west') as west_1996,
(1996,'central') as central_1996
)
)
order by 2
/
```

The output of the preceding code snippet is as follows:

```
DEPT            EAST_1996  WEST_1996 CENTRAL_1996
--------------- ---------- ---------- ------------
pen_sales            89000      87000
book_sales          115000      86000
```

Next, we discuss the use of multiple aggregate functions to display data.

Displaying Data by using Multiple Aggregate Functions

You can also mention multiple aggregate functions in PIVOT clause.

The query in the following code snippet shows the creation of two aggregate functions and four columns:

```
select * from
(
select dept,time,region,profit
from sales)
pivot
(
avg(profit) as avg_amt,
sum(profit) as sum_amt
for (time,region) in (
(1996,'east') as east_1996,
(1996,'west') as west_1996
)
)
order by 2
/
```

The output of the preceding code snippet is as follows:

```
DEPT     EAST_1996_AVG_AMT  EAST_1996_SUM_AMT  WEST_1996_AVG_AMT  WEST_1996_SUM_AMT
-------------- ---------------- ---------------- ----------------- -----------------
book_sales              57500            115000              86000             86000
pen_sales               89000             89000              87000             87000
```

Let's now learn the use of multiple aggregate functions and rows to display data.

Displaying Data by using Multiple Aggregate Functions and Multiple Rows

You can use multiple functions and multiple aggregate functions with multiple rows in the output. The query in the following code snippets shows you how to create columns by using time, and create aggregate functions and rows by using the remaining columns of the query, i.e. DEPT, REGION:

```
select * from
(
select dept,time,region,profit
from sales)
pivot
(
avg(profit) as avg_amt,
sum(profit) as sum_amt
for (time) in (
(1996) as y1996,
(1997) as y1997
)
)
order by 2
/
```

The output of the preceding code snippet is shown as follows:

```
DEPT            REGION          Y1996_AVG_AMT Y1996_SUM_AMT Y1997_AVG_AMT Y1997_SUM_AMT
--------------- --------------- ------------- ------------- ------------- -------------
book_sales      Central                 74000         74000         85000         85000
pen_sales       Central                 37500         75000         82000         82000
book_sales      east                    57500        115000        137000        137000
pen_sales       east                    89000         89000        101000        101000
book_sales      west                    86000         86000         97000         97000
pen_sales       west                    87000         87000         96000         96000
6 rows selected.
```

Let's now discuss the UNPIVOT clause.

The UNPIVOT Clause

The UNPIVOT clause is used to convert columns into rows. This clause is particularly used with columns having similar values. The clause creates additional columns mentioned in the query.

Consider the query in the following code snippet:

```
SELECT * FROM PCM;
```

The output of the preceding code snippet is as follows:

```
ROLLNO        NAME                 PHYSICS      CHEMISTRY      MATHS
------------------------------ ---------- ----------      ----------
1             anil                  67        98              87
2             sunil                 47        88              80

3             vijay                 87        91              47
4             ashok                 97        92              67
```

Now consider the query in the following code snippet:

```
select *
from pcm
unpivot
(
```

```
marks for subject in (physics,chemistry,maths)
);
```

The output of the preceding code snippet is as follows:

```
ROLLNO          NAME                          SUBJECT          MARKS
------------------------------               -----           ----------
  1          anil                          PHYSICS              67
  1          anil                          CHEMISTRY            98
  1          anil                          MATHS              87
  2          sunil                         PHYSICS              47
  2          sunil                         CHEMISTRY            88
  2          sunil                         MATHS                80
  3          vijay                         PHYSICS              87
  3          vijay                         CHEMISTRY            91
  3          vijay                         MATHS                47
  4          ashok                         PHYSICS              97
  4          ashok                         CHEMISTRY            92

                NAME                       SUBJECT          MARKS
 ------------------------------           -----           ----------
  4          ashok                         MATHS                67
 /
```

The query in the preceding code snippet creates a new column, SUBJECT, in the output. Each row displays NAME, subject which displays columns names of the unpivoted columns. In this case PHYSICS,CHEMISTRY and MATHS are unpivoted). For each unpivoted column, an additional row is created, which includes NAME, the name of the unpivoted column and Marks.

Summary

In this chapter, you have learned about Model queries and pivot queries, which are very useful in data analysis and presentation of data in various formats. The next chapter will quiz you on the concepts of SQL.

Exercise

Consider as table storing car sales

CAR	REGION	SALES
ZEN	SOUTH	123
ZEN	NORTH	34
ALTO	SOUTH	432
ALTO	NORTH	321
SANTRO	SOUTH	421
SANTRO	NORTH	521

1. Write a query to provide addition of 1st and 3rd row.
2. Write a query to provide average of 1st, 3rd and 5th row,
3. Write a query to provide REGION on X –axis and CAR on Y-axis and SALES as cell value.

20

SQL Quiz

DATATYPES

1. What is the maximum number of columns in a table?
2. Write the maximum and minimum values for `number(5,2)`
3. What are the limits on `CHAR` and `VARCHAR2` columns? What is the main difference between `CHAR` and `VARCHAR2`?
4. What will happen if you declare `CHAR` and `VARCHAR2` without size?
5. What is the suitable datatype for storing images, pictures, and files?
6. What is the utility of `BFILE`?
7. How will you store date with exact time in the `DATE` format?
8. Does Oracle has `BOOLEAN` type for columns?
9. What is the difference between `LONG` and `CLOB`?
10. How will you specify values that are mandatory for a column?

JOINS

1. When do you use a join?
2. How many tables can you have in an operation?
3. When do you use the `ALIAS` table?
4. What are implicit and explicit conditions in join? Why is explicit condition required? How many tables can you use for joins?

SET Operation

1. What is the difference between `UNION` and `UNION ALL`?
2. When are the two queries said to be compatible?
3. Suppose the queries are not set compatible, then how will you set them compatible?
4. When should you use `IN`?
5. What steps are to be followed for converting `IN` query to `EXISTS`?
6. What will happen if `EXISTS` query returns constant set of rows?
7. What is the scope of the object name?

Miscellaneous

1. How will you suppress special meaning of characters, such as `%` in the `LIKE` operator?
2. What is the output of the `MONTHS_BETWEEN(DATE1,DATE2)` function?
3. Can you set the default format for `NUMBER` and `DATE`?
4. What is the meaning of `TRUNCATE` and `ROUND` for date?
5. How will you put `DATE` in words?
6. What is the utility of `TRUNCATE` and `ROUND` functions?

7. Explain the following functions along with an example:
   - RTRIM
   - RPAD
   - INSTR
8. How you will display the date of last Sunday in a month?

UPDATE, DELETE, INSERT

1. Can you use `SELECT` statement for updating value (in the `SET` clause)?
2. What will you do if you are updating one table and the condition gives reference to another table?
3. What is the difference between `TRUNCATE` and `DELETE`?
4. What steps will you follow in order to drop the `NOT NULL` column?
5. Can you decrease the width of a column, if it is having data?
6. What steps will you follow in order to add the `NOT NULL` column?
7. If you want to create a column with a name having spaces, how will you create it?

CONSTRAINTS

1. What is use of the `CHECK` constraint?
2. Can you use `SYSDATE` or `USERNAME` in `CHECK` constraint?
3. What are the different methods of implementing uniqueness to column values?
4. What is the difference between `UNIQUE` key and `PRIMARY` key?
5. How is the `PRIMARY` key or `UNIQUE` key implemented?
6. Why should a primary key be `SHORT` and `NUMERIC`?
7. What is the behavior of null values in case of composite `UNIQUE` key?
8. What is the meaning of foreign key?
9. Can you refer to the same table in the declaration of foreign key?
10. How are null values handled in a foreign key?
11. How is the deletion of `PARENT` handled?
12. Why is updating a parent not allowed, if the child row is inserted from another transaction?
13. Why should you disable and enable constraints?
14. What is the use of `ENABLE NOVALIDATE`?
15. Can you apply `ENABLE NOVALIDATE` for primary key or unique key?
16. How will you find rows that are violating the constraints?
17. What is the meaning of immediate and deferred constraints?
18. Can you make primary or unique key as deferred constraint?
19. What will happen if, at the time of `COMMIT`, there is a violation of deferred constraint? Justify its behavior.
20. How will you get information about constraints?
21. What are the default settings of constraints?
22. How will you get information about the column involved in constrain definition?

Analysis Queries

1. Define analysis queries.
2. What is architecture of data warehouse?
3. What types of analysis queries are provided by Oracle?
4. Describe each feature of analysis queries with an example.
5. What is the meaning of regression? How will you use regression?

VIEWS

1. What is the use of views?
2. On which of the views is DML option permitted?
3. How will you determine which of the columns of a table are updatable?
4. What is the effect of `WITH CHECK OPTION`?
5. What is the meaning of key preserving join and key preserving table?
6. What is the use of the `INSTEAD OF` trigger?
7. Can you write the `INSTEAD OF` trigger as statement trigger?
8. What is the meaning of virtual columns? Can virtual columns participate in the `SET` clause of `UPDATE` or `INSERT`?
9. What is the effect of virtual column in the `WHERE` condition?

JOINS, SCALER Subqueries, and **MERGE** Statement

1. What are the different types of joins provided by Oracle?
2. What is the meaning of full outer join?
3. When will you use the `USING` clause?
4. Can you use the `SELECT` statement in the `SELECT` clause of SQL? Why it is not recommended?
5. How will you insert the same row in multiple tables?
6. What are the different types of `INSERT` statements?
7. What is the meaning of the `INSERT FIRST` statement?
8. What is the utility of the `MERGE` statement?

Unit II

PL/SQL

21

PL/SQL Program Features

PL/SQL is a language used in all Oracle products. It is a language which has procedural features known as SQL statements. The procedural features are variables, control statements, such as `IF...THEN`, `FOR` loop, and `WHILE` loop, subprograms, and exceptions.

In this chapter, you learn about PL/SQL programs, block structured language, and work area cursor. Next, you learn about control structures, modularity, and packages. Further, you learn about the concept of data abstraction and information hiding. You also learn how to handle errors in a program. The chapter also explains the architecture of PL/SQL. In the end, you learn about database triggers and advantages of PL/SQL.

Nature of PL/SQL Programs

PL/SQL is used in stored procedures, programs, packages, forms, and reports; and does not have conventional input and output statement (read and write) as other languages. The input is taken mainly from the table, while the output is stored in the table. The features of PL/SQL programs are described using the following sample programs:

Listing 21.1: Creating the month_collection Table

```
Create table month_collection
(Mon number, total number);
```

Listing 21.2: Finding the Total Fees Collected for One Month and Storing it in month_collection

```
declare
  mn number;
  cursor c1 is
  select amount, feespaiddate from feespaid;
  amount number;
  spaydate char(10);
  procedure sum_n_sub(a in number, b in number, c out number, d out number)
  is e number:= 0;
begin
  c := a+b;
  d := a-b;
  return;
end;                                            -- end of proc sum_n

begin
  for z in c1 loop
        spaydate := to_char( z. feespaiddate, 'dd-mm-yyyy');
               mn := to_number (substr(spaydate,4,2));
               update month_collection
               set total = total + z.amount
               where mon = mn;
               if sql%notfound then
                      insert into month_collection values (mn, z.amount);
               end if;
  end loop;
sum_n_sub(3,1,x,y);
sum_n_sub(m,n,x,y);
end;
/
```

The PL/SQL program has multiple sections, which are described as follows:

1. **Declaration section**—Consists of variable declaration as well as procedure and function declarations; however, all these components are optional. The declaration section is shown in the following code snippet:

```
declare
   mn number;
   cursor c1 is
   select amount, feespaiddate from feespaid;
   amount number;
   spaydate char(10);
   procedure sum_n_sub(a in number, b in number, c out number, d out number)
   is e number:= 0;
      begin
   c := a+b;
   d := a-b;
   return;
      end;
/
```

2. **Body section**—Consists of the body of a program, which is defined within the BEGIN and END keywords. The body section is defined in the following code snippet:

```
begin
   for z in c1 loop
         spaydate := to_char( z. feespaiddate, 'DD-MM-YYYY');
                 mn := to_number (substr(spaydate,4,2));
                 update month_collection
                 set total = total + z.amount
                 where mon = mn;
                 if SQL%NOTFOUND then
                         insert into month_collection values (mn, z.amount);
                 end if;
   end loop;
sum_n_sub(3,1,x,y);
sum_n_sub(m,n,x,y);
end;
```

The body section consists of the following components:

- Assignment statement
- Control statement
- Iteration statement
- Call to subprogram
- SQL statements

Let's discuss these components in detail.

Assignment Statement

The assignment statement is used to assign value to a variable. The syntax of assignment statement is as follows:

```
variable:= expr;
mn := to_number (substr(spaydate,4,2));
```

Control Statement

The control statement is used to define conditions in a program. It consists of the if and IF...ELSE statements, as shown in the following code snippet:

```
if sql%notfound then
                        insert into month_collection values (mn, z.amount);
end if;
```

Iteration Statement

The iteration statement is used to iterate the values of a variable. It consists of statements, such as for loops and while loops, as shown in the following code snippet:

```
for z in c1 loop
 ….
 End loop;
```

Call to subprogram

You can call subprograms which are declared in the declaration section, as shown in the following code snippet:

```
sum_n_sub(3,1,x,y);
```

SQL Statements

You can use SELECT, INTO, DML statement, as shown in the following code snippet:

```
update month_collection
             set total = total + z.amount
```

All these components and concepts are discussed using following programs.

Some Sample programs

1. Write a program to add two numbers.

   You can execute a program by performing the following steps:

   a. Login to Oracle using SQLPLUS

   b. Type edit add0

The editor opens for the add0.sql file. In the editor, you can write the following program to add two numbers:

```
declare
x number:=90;
y number:=34;
z number;
begin
 z:= x+y;
 dbms_output.put_line(z);
end;
/
```

After writing the program, you can exit the editor and give the following command that displays output of DBMS_OUTPUT.PUT_LINE(), which is similar to PRINTF in the C language. The file is executed using @ADD0:

```
set serveroutput on

@add0
124

PL/SQL procedure successfully completed.
```

2. Write a program to find out the biggest of three numbers.

   The program to find the biggest of three numbers is as follows:

```
declare
x number := 45;
y number := 60;
z number := 23;
big number;
begin
big := x;
```

```
if(y > big) then
big := y;
end if;
if(z > big) then
big := z;
end if;
dbms_output.put_line('the big number is '||to_char(big));
end;
/
```

The preceding program declares the IF statement. When the condition in the IF statement is satisfied, code between if and END IF is executed.

3. Write a program to find out sum of first 5 numbers, that is, 1+2+3+4+5.

   The program to find the sum of first 5 numbers is as follows:

```
declare
x number := 0;
begin
x := 0;
for i in 1..5 loop
 x := x + i;   --A
end loop;
dbms_output.put_line('sum is '||to_char(x));
end;
/
```

In the preceding program, the FOR loop is executed 5 times. The i variable is called as counter and is implicitly declared as integer. The counter is initialized with 1 and incremented by 1 in each iteration. The loop is terminated when i exceed 5. The A statement is executed five times. The symbol before A is known as single line comment.

4. Write a program to retrieve values from a table.

   The program to retrieve values from a table is as follows:

```
declare
x number := 0;
y number:=0;
z number;
begin
select salary  into x from emp_company where ename='anil';
select salary into y from emp_company where ename='sunil';
z := x / y;
dbms_output.put_line('+ value is '||to_char(z));
end;
/
```

The preceding program fetches values from a database using the SELECT … INTO statement. You can write any query in the SELECT … INTO statement, ensuring it returns single row. The statement generates an error if more than one row or zero row is returned. The x variable is called target variable and should have datatype s compatible with the value it will store.

5. Write a program to handle errors using exceptions.

   The program to handle errors using exceptions is as follows:

```
declare
 x number :=34;
 y number:=0;
 z number(2);
```

```
    begin
      z:=x/y;   --a
      z:=z+10 --g
      dbms_output.put_line('z value '||to_char(z)); --b
      exception
      when zero_divide then
      z:=0; --c
      dbms_output.put_line('z value  excp '||to_char(z)); --d
      when others then
      z:=0; --e
      dbms_output.put_line('z value  excp value '||to_char(z)); --f
    end;
   /
```

The preceding program generates an error at statement A. The code for handling the error is written at the end of body of program. Since the error is divide by zero, the program control is transferred to statement c after execution of statement a. If the ratio calculated goes above value 99, then the value cannot be stored in z and the error is generated. Exception OTHERS is called generalized exception handler and it can catch any exception. In this case, control is transferred to statement e.

6. Using subprograms.

   You can use subprograms like procedures and functions to modularize your application. The subprograms are written in declaration section and can be invoked in the body of program. The subprograms are written using formal parameters and called using actual parameters. Following program is using procedure to print salary of specified employee.

```
declare
zename varchar2(20);
procedure printsalary(pename in varchar2) is
x number;
begin
 select salary
 into x
 from emp_company
 where ename=pename;
 dbms_output.put_line(x);
end;
begin
 printsalary('ANIL'); -- call to procedure
 zename:='SUNIL';
 printsalary(zename);
end;
/
```

The formal parameter PENAME is used to pass the value of employee name. The specification

PENAME in VARCHAR2 indicates that PENAME is IN parameter and its value cannot be changed inside subprogram The procedure is called using procedure name. The actual parameter can be constant literal like 'ANIL' or a variable.

7. Using stored procedure

Oracle is having very good facility of storing application logic using stored subprograms. In the stored subprograms the code is stored in compiled form so the execution efficiency is greater. The stored subprogram can be called from any software like VB, Java which can connect with Oracle. Following procedure makes addition of three numbers.

```
create or replace procedure add3(x1 in number,x2 in number,x3 in number,y out number) as
 begin
```

```
 y:=x1+x2+x3;
 end;
the procedure can be called using following program.

declare
  x number :=12;
  y number:=3;
  z number:=56;
  w number;
 begin
   add3(x,y,z,w); --call to procedure
    dbms_output.put_line(w);
end;
/
```

8. Using stored functions

   When you want to use output of subprogram in the expressions then it is better to use functions. The function is having return value.

```
create or replace function fadd2(x number,y number)return number as
z number;
begin
z:=x+y;
return(z);
end;
/
program for using function
declare
a number;
begin
a:=fadd2(12,56)+fadd2(4,6); --use of function
dbms_output.put_line(a);
end;
/
```

The function call FADD2(12,56) returns 78.

Following sections discuss components of PLSQL in detail.

Block-Structured Language

PL/SQL is a block-structured language. Each block is supposed to perform one logical unit of job. The block can be a named block (procedure, function) or an anonymous block and it can have any number of nested blocks.

Each block has the following three parts:

- A declarative part
- An executable part
- An exception handling part (For handling abnormal conditions during the program execution)

The declarative and exception handling parts are optional.

Each block may look as shown in the following code snippet:

```
                                        --Declarative part
Declare
  i number;
begin
                                        --Executable part
```

```
    i := 5;
    - - - -
                                      --Exception handling part
    Exception
    When value_error then
    - - - -
  end;
```

When execution of statement generates some error, control can be diverted to the exception control section depending on the nature of error. The executable and exception parts may have subblocks or nested blocks. Some examples of programs with nested blocks are as follows:

Listing 21.3: Using Nested Blocks in a Program

```
  <<A>>
  Declare                              --start of Block A
    i number ;
  begin
    i := 5 ;
    Declare                            --start of Block B
          j number;
          begin
          j := 10;
                exception
                when value_error then
          j :=15;
          end;                                --end of Block B
    i := i+1;
    Exception
    when value_error then
    i := 20;
  end;                                 --end of Block A
  /
```

In Listing 21.3, block B is a subblock or nested block of block A

Listing 21.4: Show the Usefulness of Nested Blocks

```
  declare                                     --start of block A
    i number;
  begin
    i := 5;
    i := i+1;
    exception
    when value_error then
    declare                            --start of block B
            j number ;
    begin
          j := 10;
          j := j +1;
          exception
          when value_error then
          j := 20;
    end;  --  end of block b
  end;                                        --end of block A
  /
```

In Listing 21.4, the nested block B, is defined in the exception handler of block A. The advantages of nested blocks are as follows:

- Allowing you to declare variables close to where they are used.
- Allowing you to solve any complex problem by dividing it into small problems and making a block for each small problem. This strategy is known as the divide and conquer strategy.

Declarative Part

PL/SQL enforces the declaration of a variable before its use in the executable area. Therefore, PL/SQL does not allow any forward reference. The syntax to declare a variable is as follows:

```
varname vartype;
```

In the preceding syntax, `vartype` is any SQL datatype, such as `CHAR`, `DATE`, and `NUMBER` or PL/SQL datatype, such as `BOOLEAN`.

The following code snippet declares the `mn` variable as `NUMBER`, which holds two digits:

```
mn number(2);
```

You can also initialize variables during its declaration, as shown in the following code snippet:

```
mn number(2):= 15;
```

You can also use composite datatypes, such as nested tables and variable always and records using `TABLE`, `VARRAY` and `RECORD` datatype. The name of a variable also follows a standard conversion:

- Variable names should begin with alphabets
- Variable names should not have more than 30 characters

The constants are declared similar to variables, except that a keyword `CONSTANT` should be added while declaring a constant. For example, the following code snippet shows how to declare the `pi constant`:

```
pi constant real := 3.14;
```

Work Area **Cursor**

Oracle uses temporary work area cursor for storing the output of SQL statements. There are two types of cursors, implicit and explicit. Oracle maintains an implicit cursor for all DML statements and queries, which returns one row. The name of the cursor is SQL. On the other hand, you need to define an explicit cursor to use it. The following code snippet shows how to define an explicit cursor programmatically:

```
cursor c1 is
select amount, feespaiddate
from feespaid;
```

NOTE

The set of rows returned by the SELECT statement is known as a resultset. You learn more about cursors in chapter-24.

Similar to the rows of a file, the rows in the cursor are accessed sequentially. The PL/SQL program opens the cursor, processes the rows, and closes the cursor. The cursor pointer marks the current position of the row. The cursor is controlled by `OPEN`, `FETCH`, and `CLOSE` statements. The `FETCH` statement retrieves the row from the cursor and advances the pointer to the next row. The `OPEN` statement executes the query associated with the cursor, identifies the resultset, and positions the pointer on the first row. The close statement disables the cursor.

In this section, you learn about:

- For loop
- Cursor variables

Let's discuss these in detail.

FOR Loop in a Cursor

The cursor `FOR` loop is an easy way to handle a cursor. The `FOR` loop opens the cursor, fetches the rows, and closes the cursor after all rows have been processed. The following code snippet shows the FOR loop in a cursor:

```
for Z in c1 loop
      - - - -
end loop;
```

In the preceding code snippet, the cursor for loop implicitly declares `Z` as a record, which can hold rows, returned for the cursor.

Cursor Variables

Cursor variables are used when you do not want to tie any specific query to a cursor. You can tie a cursor variable to any compatible query, pass it to subprograms, and assign new values to it. Listing 21.5 shows how to open a cursor variable:

Listing 21.5: Opening a Cursor Variable using a procedure

```
create Procedure open_cursor
(generic_cursor in OUT
generic_cursor_type, status number) is

begin
    if status = 1 then
         open generic_cursor
         for select total
         from month_collection;
     end if;
    if status =2 then
         open generic_cursor
         for select total
         from year_collection;
     end if;
end open_cursor;
/
```

Attributes

Attributes are properties, which are used to refer to the datatype and structure without repeating its definition. In this section, you learn about the following attributes:

- %TYPE
- %ROWTYPE

Let's discuss these attributes one by one.

%TYPE

The %TYPE attribute provides datatype information of a database table column or variable. For example, suppose you want to declare a variable having the same type as amount of table `feespaid`. In this case, you can declare the variable, as shown in the following code snippet:

```
x    feespaid.amount%type;
```

So it is not necessary that you should know the datatype of `amount` of table `feespaid`. If the column definition of `amount` is changed, the datatype of x changes accordingly.

%ROWTYPE

The PL/SQL record stores information, which is related and consists of different datatypes. Suppose you want to declare variable Z that holds the value of one row of table feespaid. In this case, you can declare the variable, as shown in the following code snippet:

```
x  feespaid%rowtype;
```

In the preceding code snippet, we have declared x as a record. The fields of x have the same name as columns of feespaid and the same datatype. The amount field in the record is referred as x.amount. You can also give the cursor name for referencing a row in a cursor, as shown in the following code snippet:

```
Z  c1%rowtype;
```

Suppose that the cursor has two field's namely feespaiddate and amount. Then Z may have values shown in Table 21.1:

Table 21.1: Showing the values of Z

Feespaiddate	Amount
12-Mar-1999	2000
14-Jun-1999	4000

About Control Structures

The data is processed using control statements. The different types of control structure are as follows:

- Conditional (IF ... THEN ... ELSE)
- Iterative (FOR LOOP, WHILE ... LOOP, LOOP ... EXIT, WHEN)
- Changing flow (GOTO statements)

Let's discuss these control structures in detail.

Conditional Control

You may need to change the flow of program depending upon certain conditions. To modify the flow of program, you can use the IF... THEN and IF ... THEN ... ELSE statements. The clauses and parts used in these statements are as follows:

- IF—Defines a condition
- THEN—Defines the set of actions, which are done, if the condition is true
- ELSE—Performs actions only if the condition is false

Listing 21.6 shows the use of the conditional control structure:

Listing 21.6: Using Conditional Control

```
declare
    cnt number;
     batch_code enrollment.batchcode % type;
     cursor c1 is
     select * from
     enrollment;

                 --  The program finds number of students in batch 10001
begin
     cnt := 0;
     batch_code := 10001;
     for Z in c1 loop
         if  Z.batchcode = 10001 then
```

```
                cnt := cnt +1;
                end if;
        end loop;
    end;
    /
```

In Listing 21.6, the flow of program changes according to the row fetched by the cursor.

Iterative Control

You can use the iterative control structures when you want to repeat some instructions many times. PL/SQL provides the following types of iterative controls.

- FOR....LOOP.....END LOOP
- WHILE....LOOP.....END LOOP
- LOOP...EXIT WHEN

Let's discuss these in detail.

FOR.....LOOP.....END LOOP

The FOR....LOOP.....END LOOP iterative control structure specifies a range of integers. The statements under this control are executed once for each integer. Listing 21.7 shows the use of the FOR....LOOP.....END LOOP iterative control structure:

Listing 21.7: Using FOR....LOOP.....END LOOP

```
declare
    amt number(10,2);
    i number;
begin
    amt := 2000;
    for i in 1..10 loop
         amt := (amt *15/100) +amt;
    end loop;
end;
/
```

In Listing 21.7, we have added 15% interest for 10 years.

WHILE.....LOOP.....END LOOP

In `WHILE.....LOOP.....END LOOP`, the condition is associated with a sequence of statements. Before iteration of loop, the condition is evaluated. If the condition evaluates to `TRUE`, then the sequence of statements are executed. However, if the condition evaluates to false, the loop is terminated. Listing 21.8 shows the use of the `WHILE.....LOOP.....END LOOP` iterative control structure:

Listing 21.8: Using WHILE.....LOOP....END LOOP

```
declare
   amt number(10,2);
   i number;
begin
   amt := 2000;
   i := 1;
   while (i<=10)  loop
         amt := (amt * 15/100) + amt;
         i := i +1;
   end loop;
end;
/
```

LOOP ... EXIT WHEN

In `LOOP.....EXIT.....WHEN`, the loop is terminated when the condition after `WHEN` is evaluated to `TRUE`. Listing 21.9 shows the use of the `LOOP.....EXIT.....WHEN` iterative control structure:

Listing 21.9: Using LOOP ... EXIT ... WHEN

```
declare
   amt number(10,2);
   i  number;
begin
   amt :=2000;
   i := 1;
   LOOP
        amt := amt * 15/100 + amt;
        i := i + 1;
   EXIT WHEN (i >14);
   END LOOP;
end;
/
```

Changing the Flow of Program

You can use the `GOTO` statement to change the flow of a program. Listing 21.10 shows How to change the flow of a program:

Listing 21.10: Using the GOTO Statement

```
If amout > 500 then
   GO TO high_amt;
End If;
...............
<<high_amt>>
amount := amout -1000;
```

Modularity

Modularity implies dividing an application into manageable well-defined modules. In the divide and conquer approach, a complex problem is divided into small problems that can be easily solved. Each small problem is implemented as one program unit. PL/SQL provides three ways of implementing modularity. These ways are as follows:

- PL/SQL blocks
- Procedures and functions
- External procedures

You are already familiar with nested blocks. The procedures and functions are called subprograms. They are similar to a block having a definition part, declarative part, an executable part, and exception handling part. In the definition part, parameters are defined for calling subprograms. The procedure or function is intended to one unit of job—the procedure can take input and pass output using parameters; the function can take input and its name is used for returning output. Listing 21.11 shows the use of procedures:

Listing 21.11: Updating the Net Income of a Batch Using a Procedure

```
create or replace Procedure updatebatch (rlno in number, amt in number) as
bcode number;
begin
   select batchcode
   into bcode
   from enrollment
```

```
    where rollno = rlno;
    update batch
    set netincome = netincome+amt
    where batchcode = bcode;
end updatebatch;
/
```

In Listing 21.11, the procedure updates net income of a batch.

Listing 21.12 shows the use of functions:

Listing 21.12: Calculating the Net Income from a Particular Course

```
create or replace Function calcourseamt (code number) return number as
netincomeamt number;
begin
   select sum(netincome)
   into netincomeamt from batch
   where coursecode = code;
   return (netincomeamt);
end calcourseamt;
/
```

External Procedures

Some tasks, which involve complex calculations or interface with machine hardware, cannot be done efficiently in PL/SQL. Such tasks can be done very easily in other languages, such as C. PL/SQL provides an interface with these languages.

The interface is given in terms of Dynamic Link Library (DLL). The object code of the module, written in third generation language, is stored as DLL and is registered with PL/SQL. At the execution time, PL/SQL calls the library and runtime, similar to PL/SQL subprograms. Listing 21.13 registers `C.ROUTINE C_SIN` as an external function:

Listing 21.13: Registering c.routine c_sin as an External Function

```
create function pl_sin1 (x float)
return float as external
library mathlib
name "c_sin"
language c;
/
```

You need to create MATHLIB library before running the preceding listing.

Package

Packages are used to group related procedure functions, variables, and cursors. The interface between the packages is simple and clear, and it gives more clarity to the application. Package consists of two parts, specification and body. The specification part is available externally, while the body is not accessible from outside. Listing 21.14 shows the code for creation of package.

Listing 21.14: Providing the Function CALCOURSEAMT and Procedure UPDATEBATCH under one package to be Used by Other Modules

```
create or replace package sample as x number;
procedure updatebatch (rlno in number, amt in number);
function calcourseamt (code number) return number ;
end sample;
/
```

Listing 21.16: Creating an Object Type

```
create type enrollment as object
(rollno number (8),
enquiryno number (8),
batchcode number (5),
member procedure enroll(enqno number),
member procedure cancel(rollno in number)) ;
```

The variables, which form data structures, are called attributes. The functions and procedures, which operate on data, are called methods.

Objects are used to break the large system into small logical entities. Software, which is developed using objects, is more modular and maintainable. Once the objects are properly created, they can be used in other programs.

Information Hiding

The process of hiding the unnecessary details and providing the necessary information, which is required for algorithm design and data structure design, is known as information hiding. The information hiding is supported by data abstraction and data encapsulation.

Information Hiding for an Algorithm

The information hiding for an algorithm is implemented through a top-down design. For example, if some application is using the updatebatch procedure, it should only know what is input to the procedure and what the procedure does. The implementation details should be hidden from the application. Any changes made in implementation should not affect the calling application.

Information Hiding for Data structures

Information hiding for data structures is implemented by data encapsulation. A set of utility programs is implemented, which operates on the data. You can manipulate the data only through utility programs. You need not to know the representation of data. The implementation of subprograms can be hidden, if the package is used. In a package, only the specification is visible, and not implementation.

Error Handling

PL/SQL provides the facility of exception for handling errors or abnormal conditions. The abnormal conditions can be predefined, such as `ZERO_DIVIDE`, or user defined, such as `HIGH_AMT`. If the exception occurs during program execution, it can be handled by an exception handler. The exception handler is written at the end of the block. The user-defined exceptions are declared in the declaration section. Listing 21.17 shows the code to handle exceptions:

Listing 21.17: Calculating Installment Amount for a Particular Rollno

```
create or replace procedure calcinstallment (prollno in number, insamt out
  Number) is high_amt exception;
begin
  select sum(amount)
  into insamt from installment
  where rollno=prollno;
  if insamt > 100000 then
        raise high_amt;
  end if;
  exception
  when high_amt then
        dbms_output.put_line('exception raised');
end calcinstallment;
/
```

In Listing 21.17, `high_amt` is a user-defined exception and it is raised explicitly. When an exception is raised, the control goes to the exception handler without executing further statements. The statements in exception handler are executed and the block is terminated.

If an error, such as `ZERO_DIVIDE` occurs, then a predefined exception is raised. It is not explicitly raised. Oracle errors can also be handled using exceptions.

Architecture of PL/SQL

The module, which is responsible for compiling and executing PL/SQL programs, is called PL/SQL engine. PL/SQL engine can reside in the:

- Oracle server
- Oracle tools, such as forms and reports

The two locations can be independent. When the tool is lacking PL/SQL engine then it has to rely on the server for executing PL/SQL code.

PL/SQL Engine in the Oracle Sever

PL/SQL engine processes PL/SQL blocks as well as single SQL statements. It is used for processing the following types of blocks:

- **Anonymous Blocks**—Represents the blocks, which can be send by Oracle precompilers to the server at the time of execution, in the interactive tool, such as SQL plus. On the server, they are compiled and executed.
- **Stored Subprograms**—Refers to procedures, functions or packages, which are created using SQL plus. They are stored in a compiled form in the database. They can be accessed by all the users, who are connected to the system. When a call is made to the subprograms, they are executed by the PL/SQL on the server.

Though several users call the same stored subprogram many times, only one copy of it is maintained in the memory. Therefore, the user can take advantage of shared memory by reducing the disk I/O. Some of the advantages of stored subprograms are higher productivity, better performance, memory utilization, security, and integrity of application. Since several users are using the same subprogram for same computations, each user need not have to write the code.

PL/SQL Engine in Oracle Tools

When the PL/SQL engine is provided on the client side, it executes the non-SQL part on client, while SQL statements are sent to the server. Therefore, work is divided between the client and server. It is advantageous if the client and server reside on two machines. If PL/SQL block does not have an SQL statement, then there is no call on server-side. This helps in reducing the network traffic.

Database Triggers

Triggers are the stored subprograms associated with the tables. They are stored in compiled form and are automatically executed when some DML operations are performed on the table. They are used for providing complex validation, security, auditing, and replication of data. The code of database triggers is executed by PL/SQL engine on the server side.

Advantages of PL/SQL

PL/SQL is a language, which is used in almost all Oracle products. It offers various advantages.

Support for SQL

PL/SQL does have procedural features as well as non-procedural features, through SQL. Since SQL is a non-procedural language, it is very easy to perform database operations using SQL. PL/SQL features, such as variables, iteration statements, and conditional statements, make it more flexible for programming.

Support for Object Oriented Programs

Object oriented programming is used to reduce the cost and time for developing applications. The code developed using objects have more reusability, modularity, and maintainability. It provides features, such as information hiding and data encapsulation. The object oriented features are supported by packages and object types.

Better Performance

When PL/SQL block is processed, not the individual statements but the entire block is sent to the server. Therefore, if the PL/SQL block contains a large number of SQL statements, it results in one call i.e. call to execute block to the server. Without PL/SQL, each SQL statement will be a result in one call. This implies that PL/SQL helps in reducing network traffic.

Portability

Applications developed in PL/SQL are portable across any platform and on all operating systems.

Higher Productivity

PL/SQL adds processing power in Oracle tools, such as forms and reports. You can do procedural programming in these tools.

Integration with Oracle

PL/SQL supports all SQL datatypes using `%TYPE`. `%ROWTYPE` attributes help in integration with Oracle data dictionary.

Summary

The chapter introduced you various features of PL/SQL. Most of the application development in Oracle is done using PL/SQL. All the features which are outlined in this chapter are discussed in detail in next chapters.

Exercise

1. What is PL/SQL block?
2. What is syntax of declaration of variable and constant?
3. How many ways you can declare subprograms in PL/SQL?
4. What is advantage of package over procedure?
5. What is the use of exception handling?

Better Performance

Higher Productivity

Integration with Oracle

Summary

Exercise

22

PL/SQL Datatypes

PL/SQL is made up of various elements such as character sets, lexical units, datatypes, and expressions. The basic conceptual elements that make up PL/SQL are as follows:

- Lexical units
- Datatypes
- User-defined subtypes
- Datatype conversion
- Declarations
- Naming conversion
- Scope and visibility
- Assignments
- Expressions and comparisons
- Functions

Let's begin by discussing lexical units.

Lexical Units

A PL/SQL program can be written by using the following set of characters:

- A ... Z, a.... z, 0 ... 9
- Tabs, spaces, carriage returns
- symbols such as (), +, - ,* , /,< >, =, !, ~ , ; , : , ., ' , @ , % , " , #, $, & , - , ! , {}, ? , and [ ]

Meaningful groups of characters are called lexical units. The following are some of the common lexical units used in PL/SQL:

- Delimiters
- Identifiers, reserved words
- Literals
- Comments

For example, consider the following code snippet:

```
xx : = y +10;                    --sum
```

The lexical units in the preceding code snippet are as follows:

- Identifiers—`xx, y`
- Compound symbol— :=
- Simple symbol—+ , ;
- Numeric literal—`10`
- Comment—`--sum`

A space or punctuation must separate identifiers., the lexical units must be separated by spaces to improve readability of code. Spaces should not be allowed in compound symbols. For example, the code in the following code snippet is illegal because there is no space between `END` and `IF`:

```
If x > y THEN
    x : = 10;
ENDIF;
```

Similarly, the assignment symbol := is illegal when it is written as : = (blank between two characters).

Always indent lines by using space and tabs, as shown in the following code snippet:

```
IF x > 100 THEN
    y := 50;
```

```
ELSE
     y := 100;
END IF;
```

Let's now learn about the common lexical units of PL/SQL, starting with delimiters.

Delimiters

A delimiter is a symbol, which carries a special meaning in PL/SQL. The symbol may be single or compound.

Let's briefly describe the various single and compound delimiters in the following sections.

Single Symbols

Table 22.1 describes the various single symbols used in PL/SQL:

Table 22.1: Single Symbols of PL/SQL

Single Symbol	Description
+	Addition operator
-	Subtraction/negation operator
*	Multiplication operator
/	Division operator
=	Relational operator
<	Relational operator
>	Relational operator
(	Expression or list delimiter
)	Expression or list delimiter
;	Statement terminator
%	Attribute indicator
,	Item separator
.	Component selector
@	Remote access indicator
'	Refers to the character string delimiter
"	Refers to the quoted identifier delimiter
:	Refers to the post variable indicator

Compound Symbols

Table 22.2 describes the various compound symbols used in PL/SQL:

Table 22.2: Compound Symbols of PL/SQL

Compound Symbols	Description
**	Refers to the exponentiation operator
< >	Relational operator
!=	Relational operator

Table 22.2: Compound Symbols of PL/SQL	
Compound Symbols	**Description**
~	Relational operator
>=	Relational operator
<=	Relational operator
:=	Assignment operator
=>	Association operator
..	Range operator
||	Concatenation operator
<<	Beginning label delimiter
>>	Ending label delimiter
--	Single line comment indicator
/*	Multiline comment delimiter
*/	Multiline comment delimiter

After learning about delimiters, let's discuss identifiers.

Identifiers

Identifiers are used for naming constants, variables, exceptions, the cursor, cursor variables, subprograms, and packages. Some examples of identifiers are as follows:

- a
- abc#
- salecode
- sale$amount

Identifiers can have letters, numerals, dollar signs, underscores, and number signs. The beginning identifier should always be a letter. Table 22.3 shows some examples of illegal identifiers:

Table 22.3: Illegal Identifiers	
Illegal Identifier	**Reason**
1abc	Beginning with a numeral
abc&cd	Ampersand sign
ab/cd	Slash sign
ab cd	Blank space

PL/SQL is not case-sensitive. So all the following identifiers have the same meaning:

- abc
- Abc
- aBc
- ABC

The length of an identifier should not exceed 30 characters. It is recommended that reusable and meaningful names should be used in place of identifiers.

Let's now discuss another important lexical unit known as reserved word.

Reserved Words

Some words convey a special meaning in PL/SQL and so should not be used as identifiers. Such words are called reserved words. Table 22.4 provides a list of reserved words in PL/SQL:

Table 22.4: Reserved Words in PL/SQL

ARRAY	AT	AUTHID	AVG
BEGIN	BINARY	BODY	BOOLEAN
BULK	CASE	CHAR_BASE	CLOSE
COALESCE	COLLECT	COMMIT	CONSTANT
CURRVAL	CURSOR	DAY	DECLARE
DO	ELSIF	END	EXCEPTION
EXECUTE	EXIT	EXTENDS	EXTRACT
FALSE	FETCH	FORALL	FUNCTION
GOTO	HEAP	HOUR	IF
INDICATOR	INTERFACE	INTERVAL	ISOLATION
JAVA	LIMITED	LOOP	MAX
MIN	MINUTE	MOD	MONTH
NATURAL	NATURALN	NEW	NEXTVAL
NOCOPY	NULLIF	NUMBER_BASE	OCIROWID
OPAQUE	OPEN	OPERATOR	ORGANIZATION
OTHERS	OUT	PACKAGE	PARTITION
PLS_INTEGER	POSITIVE	POSITIVEN	PRAGMA
PRIVATE	PROCEDURE	RAISE	RANGE
REAL	REF	RELEASE	RETURN
REVERSE	ROLLBACK	ROWTYPE	SAVEPOINT
SECOND	SEPARATE	SPACE	SQL
SQLCODE	SQLERRM	STDDEV	SUBTYPE
SUM	TIME	TIMESTAMP	TIMEZONE_REGION
TIMEZONE_ABBR	TIMEZONE_MINUTE	TIMEZONE_HOUR	TRUE
TYPE	USE	VARIANCE	WHEN
WHILE	WORK	WRITE	YEAR
ZONE			

From Table 22.4, we can see that reserved words such as DECLARE, BEGIN, END, and LOOP should never be used as identifiers. Therefore, the following declaration generates compilation error:

```
DECLARE
    BEGIN BOOLEAN;
```

Reserved words can be embedded in an identifier. Therefore, the identifier BEGIN_TIME is legal.

Predefined Identifiers

The identifiers declared in the package STANDARD, such as VALUE_ERROR, are globally declared. You should not declare identifiers with the same name because that way the original meaning of the identifier will be lost.

Quoted Identifiers

Quoted identifiers can have any printable character, including blank spaces, but excluding double quotes. Therefore, the following identifiers are legal:

- " ab/bc"
- "a+b"
- "items (10)"
- "first name"
- "** High Amount **"

The maximum length of an identifier can be 30 characters, ignoring double quotes. You can use PL/SQL reserved words in quotes, but that is not allowed. Some words are reserved words in PL/SQL, but not in SQL. For such words, double quotes are used and the word is written in upper case. For example, the use of word 'type' in PL/SQL, in the following code snippet, returns an error:

```
select salary, type                     --compilation error.
```

However, the following statement doesn't return any error:

```
select salary, "TYPE"
```

The column type should always appear in uppercase and it is better to use views for such columns.

After learning about different types of identifiers, let's move on and discuss literals.

Literals

A literal is an explicitly defined character, string, numeric, or Boolean value not represented by an identifier. Let's discuss the different types of literals in the following sections.

Numeric Literals

A numeric literal is used in arithmetic expressions. The integer literal is optionally signed without a decimal point.

For example:

```
050    + 7    -18    0    + 15281
```

A real literal is optionally signed without a decimal point, as shown in the following example:

```
8.889    0.5    -15.3    8.0    8
```

In the preceding example, the numbers 8.0 and 8 are taken as real literals. Numeric literals can be written in scientific notation, but should not have a dollar sign or commas. For example, the following are valid real literals:

```
2E8 (2 x10^8), 2.3 E3 (2.3 x 10^3), - 4E5, -8.8 E10, -1.7 E-5
```

The following are illegal real literals:

```
$300, (1,2,9,300)
```

Character Literal

Character literals are single characters enclosed in single quotes. The character can be any printable character. For example, `'Z'`, `'a'`, `'*'`, `'%'`

The `'Z'` and `'a'` in the preceding example are different. The character literals `0 to 9` can be used in numeric expressions, and converted to corresponding integers.

String Literals

A string literal is a sequence of zero or more characters enclosed in single quotes. Some examples of string literals are as follows:

- `'High Amount'`
- `'ABC corporation'`
- `'01-JAN -1998'`
- `'$5,000.00'`

PL/SQL is case-sensitive within string literals. Therefore, the following different literals are different:

```
'abc'
'Abc'
```

Boolean Literals

Booleans literals are predefined values `TRUE` and `FALSE`. They are values, not strings.

Let's now learn about comments.

Comments

A comment is used for documentation and to improve the readability of code. Comments are used to describe the purpose of a module or statement. A comment can be single line or multiline.

Single Line Comment

A single line comment starts with a -- symbol. The length of this comment can be till the end of a line. The following is an example of a single line comment:

```
select batchcode
from batch;                          --selecting batchcode from batch
```

If the comment sign (two hyphens) is placed at the beginning of a line, then the whole line becomes a comment, as shown in the following example:

```
                    --SELECT batchcode from batch;
```

In the preceding example, the `SELECT` statement is entirely commented.

Multiline Comment

Multiline comments are enclosed by `/* ... */` (as in C language) and can span multiple lines. A section of code can be commented by using multiline comments. For example, in the following code snippet, the entire `IF` statement is commented:

```
x := x +1;
/* IF x =10 THEN
        y := 20 ;
   ELSE
        y := 40;
*/
z := z + 5 ;
```

Comments cannot be nested. For example, the following statement is illegal:

```
/* IF… /* THEN
.
.
.
*/
*/
```

You cannot use single line comment in precompilers. In precompilers, the end of the line is ignored and therefore the entire code beginning from the single line comment becomes part of the comment. It is better to use multiline comments in precompilers, such as pro*C.

After learning about the common lexical units used in PL/SQL, let's discuss datatypes, which is an important element in PL/SQL.

Datatypes

Datatypes are used to specify the type of values a variable can have. A datatype specifies a storage format, constraint, or a valid range of values, and is attached to variables and constants. Consider the following statement:

```
i   integer;
```

In the preceding statement, `i` can hold only integer value.

Figure 22.1 shows the various types of datatypes used in PL/SQL:

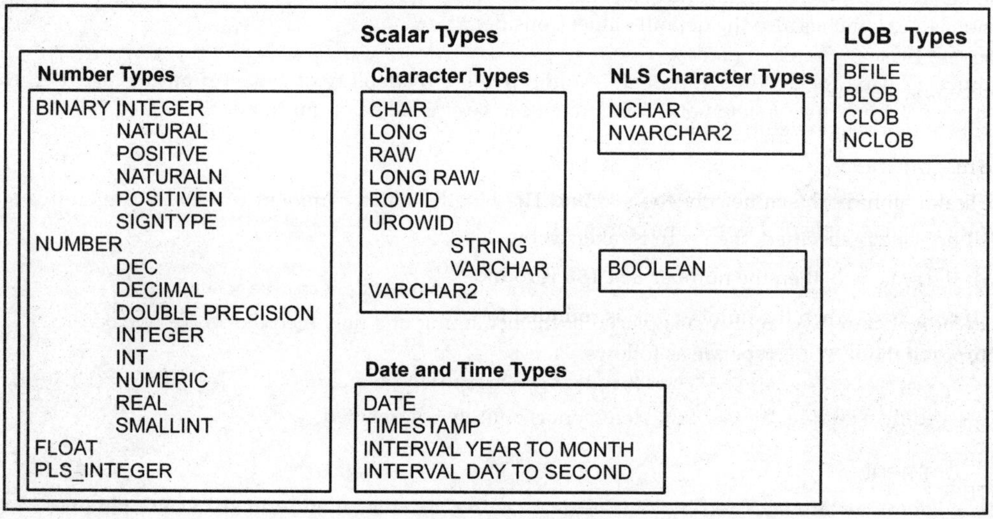

Figure 22.1: Datatypes in PL/SQL

The following is a brief description of the various types of datatypes:

- **Scalar datatype**—Refers to datatypes that do not have any internal component
- **Composite datatype**—Refers to datatypes that have internal components, which can be manipulated individually
- **Reference datatype**—Refers to datatypes which in turn refer to the value of other data items. These datatypes are also called pointers.
- **LOB datatype**—Specifies the location of large objects. These datatypes are also called locators.

Scalar Datatypes

Scalar datatypes are divided into four categories: NUMBER, CHARACTER, BOOLEAN, and DATE/TIME.

Number Types

A number type allows you to store numeric data, such as integers, real numbers, and floating-point numbers. Number types are further divided into several categories, as discussed in the following sections.

The BINARY_INTEGER Type

The BINARY_INTEGER type is used to store signed integers (both positive and negative). The range of these integer values is from -2**31 to 2**31. The BINARY_INTEGER type requires less storage space compared to a number datatype. However, the operations performed by the BINARY_INTEGER type are slower than those performed by the PLS_INTEGER type. The BINARY_INTEGER type has the following subtypes:

- `NATURAL` — Allows `INTEGER` numbers
- `POSITIVE` — Allows only positive numbers
- `NATURALN` — Allows `NATURAL`, but no null values can be assigned
- `POSITIVEN` — Allows `POSITIVE`, but no null values can be assigned
- `SIGNTYPE` — The valid values in the datatype are `-1, 0, +1` (useful for tri-state logic).

*The **NUMBER** Type*

The NUMBER type is used for storing fixed and floating point numbers of any size. For number datatype, precision i.e. total number of digits and scale, i.e. where rounding occurs, can be specified. The maximum value of precision is `38`, which is also the default value. Consider the following statement:

```
x number;
```

In the preceding statement:

- `x` will have precision value of `38`
- The magnitude range is `1.0 x 10^-130` to `9.99 x 10^125`
- The scale can have the value between `-84` and `127`
  - If no scale is specified, then zero is taken as the default value
  - If the scale is `2`, then the number `3.1458` is rounded to `3.15`
  - If scale is `-2`, then the number `746` is rounded to `700`

The subtypes of the `NUMBER` type are as follows:

- `DEC`
- `DECIMAL`
- `DOUBLE PRECISION`
- `INTEGER`
- `INT`
- `NUMERIC`
- `REAL`
- `SMALLINT`

Subtypes are mainly provided to ensure compatibility with ANSI or IBM datatypes.

The *FLOAT Type*

The FLOAT type is subtype of the NUMBER type. In the `FLOAT type`, scale is not specified, and the precision is specified in `BINARY` format. The maximum precision value of a FLOAT type is `126` binary digits, which is approximately equal to `38` decimal digits. You can convert a precision value from binary format to decimal format by multiplying the binary precision value by 0.30103. Similarly, you can convert a precision value from decimal format to binary format by multiply the value by 3.32193.

You can specify a FLOAT type variable as shown in the following statement:

```
x FLOAT(10);
```

The PLS_INTEGER Type

The PLS_INTEGER type is preferred over the BINARY_INTEGER type because of its better performance. Both PLS_INTEGER and BINARY_INTEGER have almost the same characteristics. Both have a magnitude range from -2**31 to 2**31. The PLS_INTEGER type requires less storage space and performs operations faster. This is because PLS_INTEGER uses machine arithmetic, while BINARY_INTEGER uses library arithmetic.

A calculation overflow in PLS_INTEGER gives rise to an exception. However, in the case of BINARY_INTEGER calculation, no exception is raised if the result of the calculation is stored in the NUMBER variable. Oracle recommends the use of the PLS_INTEGER type instead of the BINARY_INTEGER type.

SIMPLE_INTEGER

Oracle 11g introduced new datatype SIMPLE_INTEGER to increase efficiency of computation. It has the following characteristics:

- Stores values ranging from -2 ^31 to 2^31
- Cannot store NULL value.
- In case of overflow the value is wrapped from positive to negative and negative to positive. After adding 1 in maximum value most negative number is obtained.

Character Types

A character type is used to process character data, such as alphanumeric text and words. Let's discuss the various categories of character types in the following sections.

The CHAR Datatype

The CHAR datatype is used for storing character data of fixed length. The data is internally stored according to the database character set (ASCII, EBCDIC ...). The following statement shows you how to declare a CHAR datatype variable:

```
x CHAR(5);
```

In the preceding statement, x can hold 5 bytes of data. Therefore, if the data consists of characters that require more than 1 byte but less than 5 bytes, lesser characters are stored and rest of the remaining space will be taken by null bytes. The maximum number of bytes is 32767. If no size is specified, then the default size 1. The maximum length of a CHAR datatype column is 2000 bytes. You cannot put data in a CHAR variable from a LONG column, if the length exceeds 32767. The CHAR datatype has CHARACTER as its subtype, which has similar characteristics, and it is given for compatibility with previous versions.

The LONG Datatype

The LONG datatype is used for storing large text. It is similar to the VARCHAR2 datatype with a maximum length 32760 bytes. The maximum length of a long database column is 2**31 bytes. So the value from long columns cannot be retrieved in LONG variables, if it exceeds 32760 bytes. LONG columns can store text documents, large texts. They can take part in UPDATE, INSERT or SELECT operations, but not in comparison operations (WHERE, CONNECT, GROUP BY).

The RAW Datatype

The RAW datatype is used to store images, digitized picture, or sound. In the RAW datatype, the internal conversion is not done according to the character set (ASCII). PL/SQL does not interpret raw data, like varchar2. The maximum length of a RAW datatype is 32767 bytes. The syntax to declare a RAW datatype variable is as follows:

```
x RAW (10) ;              --10 bytes
```

The maximum length of a RAW datatype column is 2000 bytes. You can insert a RAW datatype value to a LONG RAW datatype column and vice versa, provided the sizes of both the datatypes match.

The LONG RAW Datatype

The LONG RAW datatype is used for storing large binary images. It is not interpreted by PL/SQL as long data. The maximum length of the LONG RAW datatype is 32760 bytes, and the maximum length of a LONG RAW datatype column is 2**31 bytes (2GB). Therefore, a LONG RAW datatype column can be put in a LONG RAW variable, if the size of the datatype column is less than or equal to 32760 bytes.

The ROWID Datatype

ROWID is a pseudocolumn, which is associated with every table. It gives information about the location of row.

The ROWID provides the following information:

- Data object number
- Data file number
- Data block number
- Offset within a block

ROWID provides fastest way of retrieving data from a table. If it is a clustered table, then two rows may have the same ROWID. The ROWID information can be put in the ROWID variable. The ROWID variable can be declared as:

```
x   ROWID;
x := 'AAAH62AAIAAABgyAAA';
```

The ROWID variable can be compared with WHERE clause with ROWID column. Oracle provides the DBMS_ROWID package to manipulate ROWID.

Oracle has two types of rowid's—physical rowid and logical rowid. A physical rowid identifies a row in an ordinary table, while a logical rowid identifies a row in an index-organized table. The physical rowid has the following components as given in following example:

```
select rowid, batchcode from batch;
```

The output of the preceding example:

```
ROWID                        BATCHCODE
-----------------            ---------
AAAH62AAIAAABgyAAA          20002
AAAH62AAIAAABgyAAB          10002
AAAH62AAIAAABgyAAC          10001
```

In the preceding output, the string AAAH62AAIAAABgyAAA has the format OOOOOOFFFBBBBBBRRR where:

- AAAH62 (OOOOOO) —Identifies the database segment
- AAI (FFF) —Identifies the file number
- AAABgy (BBBBBB) —Identifies the block number within a file
- AAA (RRR) —Identifies the offset within the block.

The UROWID Datatype

Oracle provides a new type called UROWID to store both logical and physical rowid's. It is recommended that you use UROWID rather than ROWID.

The rowid to character conversion or vice versa is done by using functions, such as ROWIDTOCHAR, or CHARTOROWID, if the ROWID datatype is used. Such functions are not required for the UROWID datatype. Instead, normal assignment expressions are used with the UROWID.

The VARCHAR2 Datatype

The VARCHAR2 datatype is used for storing variable length character data. The character data is stored internally according to the database character set. The maximum length of the VARCHAR2 datatype is 32767 bytes. If the data consists of multibyte characters, then it stores fewer numbers of characters. The maximum width of a VARCHAR2 datatype column is 4000 bytes. You can declare a VARCHAR2 datatype variable as shown in the following statement:

```
x    varchar2(10);
```

As you know, the maximum width of a LONG database column is 2GB. Therefore, to put a LONG datatype column into a VARCHAR2 variable, the column data should be less than 32767 bytes. The VARCHAR2 datatype has the following subtypes:

- STRING
- VARCHAR

Both are similar to the VARCHAR2 datatype and are given for backward compatibility.

The NLS Character Type

Short for National Language Support, NLS character types are used to provide an environment for different languages, such as Japanese, which contains thousands of characters and each character may require single or multiple bytes. NLS is used to process single as well as multibyte data and convert between character set. PL/SQL V8 supports two data character sets, the database character set, used for identifiers, source code, and the national character set for national language data with NLS. Number and data formats adapt automatically to the language conversion which can be specified when a session is created. NLS provides two datatypes, NCHAR and NVARCHAR2, to store character strings created from the national character set. Let's discuss these two datatypes next.

***The NCHAR** Datatype*

The NCHAR datatype is used to store character data of a fixed length. The data is internally stored according to the national character set (US7ASII or variable width encoding JA16SJIS). The maximum length of the NCHAR datatype is 32767 bytes and the default value is 1. You can declare a NCHAR datatype variable as shown in the following statement:

```
x    NCHAR (10);
```

If the character set is of a fixed width, then the size is in characters; otherwise, it is in bytes. The maximum width of the NCHAR database column is 2000 bytes. You cannot insert a CHAR value in a NCHAR column or vice versa.

The NVARCHAR2 Datatype

The NVARCHAR2 datatype is used for storing variable length NLS character data. The data is represented internally in the format which depends on the national character set. The NVARCHAR2 datatype may be of fixed width encoding (WE8EBCDIC 37C) or variable width encoding, such as JA16DBLS. The maximum width of the NVARCHAR2 datatype is 32767 bytes. You can declare an NVARCHAR2 datatype variable as shown in the following statement:

```
x varchar2 (50);
```

For a fixed width character set, size is in number of characters and for a variable width character set, the size is in terms of bytes. The maximum width of an NVARCHAR2 datatype column is 4000 bytes. Therefore, the conversion from an NVARCHAR2 variable and an NVARCHAR2 column depends on the size of data. You cannot convert the VARCHAR2 datatype to the NVARCHAR2 datatype or vice versa.

Let's now continue our discussion on the remaining datatypes of the scalar type, which is the BOOLEAN datatype, the DATE datatype, the TIMESTAMP datatype, the INTERVAL YEAR TO MONTH datatype, and the INTERVAL DAY TO SECOND datatype.

The BOOLEAN Datatype

The BOOLEAN datatype can store the TRUE, FALSE or NULL value. NULL represents an inapplicable or unknown value. These three values are used to return the result of conditions in functions. They are the corresponding column in database, so there is no transfer of data between a BOOLEAN variable and database column.

The DATE Datatype

The DATE datatype stores date and time information. It gives the time in the seconds format, which is calculated from midnight. The default value of the date is the first day of the current month. The range of valid date values is from January 1, 4712 BC to December 31, 4712 AD. The Julian date is the number of days since January 1, 4712 BC. The TO_DATE and TO_CHAR functions are used to convert a date value to the Julian date, which is given in the format 'J'. PL/SQL automatically converts date values in character format, to the DATE values. The NLS_DATE_FORMAT parameters are used to specify the default format of the date. The default format may be 'DD-MON-YY'. The date values can be added or subtracted. For example subtraction of two date values return the number of days between dates. The system date can be obtained from the pseudocolumn SYSDATE.

The TIMESTAMP Datatype

The TIMESTAMP datatype is used for storing seconds and fraction of seconds. Oracle provides the TIMESTAMP datatype, which stores the year, month, day, hour, minute, and second. The syntax is for using the TIMESTAMP datatype is as follows:

```
TIMESTAMP[(precision)]
```

In the preceding syntax, the optional parameter precision specifies the number of digits in the fractional part of the seconds field. It can have a length between 0 and 9, but the default is 6.

```
declare
   x timestamp(3);
begin
   x := '22-jun-2003 06:48:53.275';

end;
/
```

Here the default timestamp format is set by the Oracle initialization parameter NLS_TIMESTAMP_FORMAT.

The INTERVAL YEAR TO MONTH Datatype

The INTERVAL YEAR TO MONTH datatype is used to store and manipulate the intervals of years and months. The syntax to use the INTERVAL YEAR TO MONTH datatype is as follows:

```
INTERVAL YEAR[(precision)] TO MONTH
```

In the preceding syntax, precision specifies the number of digits in the YEAR field. The valid precision values are between 0 and 4, and the default value is 2. The following code snippet shows the use of the INTERVAL YEAR TO MONTH datatype :

```
DECLARE
   X INTERVAL YEAR(3) TO MONTH;
BEGIN
   X := INTERVAL '104-3' YEAR TO MONTH;         --interval literal 105 years
                                                --and 3 months
   X := '105-3';                                --implicit conversion from
                                                --character type
   X := INTERVAL '105' YEAR;                    --Can specify just the years
   X := INTERVAL '3' MONTH;                     --Can specify just the months
END;
/
```

The INTERVAL DAY TO SECOND Datatype

The INTERVAL DAY TO SECOND datatype is used to store and manipulate time intervals measured in days, hours, minutes, and seconds. The syntax to use the INTERVAL DAY TO SECOND datatype is as follows:

```
INTERVAL DAY[(leading_precision)] TO
SECOND[(fractional_seconds_precision)]
```

In the preceding syntax, INTERVAL DAY[(leading_precision)] TO and SECOND[(fractional_seconds_precision)] refers to the values to include in days and seconds fields respectively. These values can range from 0 to 9. The default values of the two fields are 2 and 6, respectively. The following code snippet shows you how to declare the variable of type `INTERVAL DAY TO SECOND`:

```
declare
   x interval day(3) to second(3);
begin
   x:= interval '5' day;
end;
```

The operation between two date variables can be stored in the interval datatypes, while the operation between date variable and interval can be stored in date.

LOB Types

Short for Large Object Binary, LOB types are used for storing large unstructured data, such as graphics images, and sound files. The maximum size of data that a LOB type can store is 4 GB. LOB allows random, piece wise access to the data. The LOB type differs from the `LONG` or `LONG RAW` type in the following ways:

- The LOB type can be an attribute to another object type
- The maximum size of LOB data is 4 GB, while maximum size of `LONG` data is 2 GB
- The LOB type supports random access, while the `LONG` type supports only sequential access
- LOB stores locators, which specify the position of LOB data. LOB data can be inline (inside the row) or in an external operating system file. `LONG` data is always inline.
- Database columns such as `BLOB`, `CLOB` or `BFILE` store locators. `BLOB`, `CLOB` or `NCLOB` data is stored in a database inline or out of line. `BFILE` data is stored in external operating system file.
- LOB types are manipulated by using the `DBMS_LOB` package through LOB locators. The LOB location cannot span DML transactions or sessions. Therefore, you cannot retrieve the locator in one transaction and use it in another transaction.

Let's now discuss the various LOB types in the following sections.

BFILE

In the `BFILE`, the data is stored in external operating system file whose size is maximum 4 GB. The `BFILE` variable stores the locator of the file, i.e. the full path name of the operating system file. The number of `BFILE`s opened at one time depends on the initialization parameter `SESSION_MAX_OPEN_FILES`, which is system-dependent.

`BFILE`s are read only files. Users cannot modify them. `BFILE` does not take part in the transactions. To use `BFILE`, DBA has to ensure that the file exists and the user has permission to read the file.

BLOB (Binary large object)

It is used for storing large raw data, such as graphics or sound files. The size of `BLOB` cannot exceed 4 GB. BLOB stores the locator, which provides information about the location of data. The data may be stored in the row (inline) or outside the raw (out of line). BLOB can take part in transactions and is manipulated by package `DBMS_LOB`. The `BLOB` locators cannot span DML transactions or sessions.

CLOB (Character large object)

These are similar to BLOB, but store single byte character data. CLOB can be stored inline or out of line. CLOB stores a locator, which provides the location of data. The size of CLOB cannot exceed 4 GB. They can participate in transactions. They are manipulated by package DBMS_LOB. The locator cannot span DML transactions and session.

NCLOB

They are similar to CLOB, but contain single byte or fixed width multibyte NCHAR data.

Let's now discuss the various user-defined subtypes available in PL/SQL.

User-Defined Subtypes

In PL/SQL, base types, such as number, char, and define a set of acceptable values and types to perform operations on data. Subtypes, which are used to improve the readability of a program, define the same set of operations, but on subset of the values of the data. A subtype does not introduce a new type, but places a constraint on its base type. PL/SQL has many predefined subtypes in the STANDARD package. For example, the subtype string is VARCHAR2. Subtypes can also provide compatibility with ANSI and IBM types.

Defining Subtypes

You can declare a subtype in the declare section of PL/SQL block by using the following syntax:

```
SUBTYPE subtypename IS
        Base-type-name;
```

In the preceding syntax, Base-type-name is any scalar or user-defined PL/SQL type or %Type or %ROWTYPE. The following are some examples of subtypes:

```
DECLARE
SUBTYPE LASTDATE IS DATE;
TYPE STUDENTLIST IS
     TABLE OF VARCHAR2(10);
SUBTYPE STUDENTENROLL IS STUDENTLIST;
TYPE TIME_RECORD IS
RECORD (MIN INTEGER,
               HOUR INTEGER);
STARTINGTIME TIME_RECORD;
SUBTYPE SROLLNO IS ENROLLMENT.ROLLNO%TYPE;
SUBTYPE STUDENT_REC IS ENROLLMENT%ROWTYPE;
```

When you declare a subtype, you should not mention the constraint on its base type.

Listing 22.1: Displaying illegal Subtype Declarations

```
declare
    subtype salaryamount is
                      number(10,2);
    subtype ename is
                      varchar2(30),
```

Listing 22.2: Defining Constrained Subtypes by Using the Indirect Way

```
declare
    ename varchar2(30);
    subtype empname is
                      ename%type;
```

Subtypes adopt the size and datatype of database columns, but no constraints, such as NOT NULL.

Using Subtypes

Subtypes improve the readability of a program by detecting out of range values. Consider the following code snippet:

```
declare
    subtype numvalue is
                number;
    x  numvalue(1,0);
```

In the preceding code snippet, `x` is a variable that can store values ranging from `-9` to `9`. If you assign a value that is out of this range, then PL/SQL raises the `VALUE_ERROR` exception.

Type Compatibility

The variables of different subtypes are interchangeable, according to the following rules:

- An unconstrained subtype is interchangeable with its base type.

Listings 22.23 shows an example of the preceding rule:

Listing 22.3: Assigning the Value of x to y

```
declare
   subtype numvalue is number;
   x    number(10,2);
   y    numvalue;
begin
   y := x;
```

- Subtypes are interchangeable if they have the same base type.

Listings 22.4 shows an example of the preceding rule:

Listing 22.4: Assigning the Value of x to y

```
declare
    subtype numvalue1 is number (10);
    subtype numvalue2 is number (10);
    x  numvalue1;
    y  numvalue2;
begin
    y := x;
```

- Subtypes are interchangeable if they are from same datatype family.

Listing 22.5: Assigning the Value of x to y

```
declare
     subtype charvalue is char;
     subtype varchar value is varchar2;
     x  charvalue;
     y  varcharvalue;
begin
     y := x;
```

Datatype Conversion

Sometimes, you may need to convert a value from one datatype to another. For example, if you want extract the value of a particular month, you have to extract the value from the date value. You can covert one data type to another either implicitly or explicitly.

Explicit Conversion

Explicit conversion of a datatype is performed by using built-in functions such as `TO_DATE`, `TO_NUMBER`, and `TO_CHAR`, For example

```
X NUMBER:= TO_NUMBER('45');
```

Implicit Conversion

When the variable of one datatype is assigned to the variable of another datatype then PL/SQL converts the first datatype variable to the second datatype variable. In-general, right-hand value of expression is controlled by the datatype of left-hand variable. This type of conversion is called implicit conversion. When such a conversion is not possible, PL/SQL generates an error.

Explicit conversion can take place when there is compatibility between the target datatype and the source value. For example, if `x` is a character string with the value `56` and `y` is a number variable, implicit computation can take place, as shown in the following expression:

```
y := x;
```

Listing 22.6: Performing Implicit Conversion where tm1 and tm2 are Character Values Representing Time in Seconds

```
declare
    tm1 char(5);
    tm2 char(5);
   diff number(5);
begin
    select to_char(sysdate,'sssss')
    into tm1
    from dual;
    tm2 := '10000';
   diff := tm1 - tm2;
/* implicit conversion is taking place in above expression  */
end;
```

Listing 22.6, the `SELECT ... INTO` statement, before assigning a value of a column to a variable, the implicit conversion could be done. It is possibly done when `DATE` column is assigned to `VARCHAR2` variable. Implicit conversion in PL/SQL is performed according to the following figure. ('x' in second row, third column indicates that implicit conversion is possible for 'CHAR' to 'DATE' datatype).

Source Datatype (Y-axis) Dataype (X-axis)									
	1	2	3	4	5	6	7	8	9
	BIN-INT	CHAR	DATE	LONG	NUMBER	PLS-INT	RAW	ROWID	VARCHAR2
1	x	x			x	x		x	x
2	x	x	x		x	-	-	-	x
3	-	x	x		x	-	-	-	x
4	-	x		x		-	-	x	x
5	x	x			x	-	x	-	x
6	x	x			x	x	-	-	x
7	-	x				-	-	-	x
8	-	x				-	-	-	x
9	x	x	x	x	x	x	x	x	-

For a conversion to be successful, the source datatype values should be convertible to the target datatype values. For example, the character value `15-OCT-1992` can be converted to the `DATE` variable, but the value `15-OCT-1992` cannot be converted to the `DATE` variable.

Implicit vs. Explicit Conversion

You should generally avoid implicit conversion because it is unpredictable and may change from one version to another. When explicit conversion is used the application is more reliable and easier to maintain.

Let's now learn about different datatype conversions.

Conversion of **DATE** Values

When you convert a value from the `DATE` column to a `CHAR` or `VARCHAR2` variable, PL/SQL calls the `TO_CHAR` function implicitly. The `CHAR` value is according to the default `DATE` format. To obtain `CHAR` value in other formats, such as Julian date, `TO_CHAR` has to be called with other format.

A `CHAR` or `VARCHAR2` value is converted to the `DATE` value by implicit conversion, only if the `CHAR` or `VARCHAR2` value is in the default `DATE` format. For example, if the default `DATE` format is `DD-MON-YY`, then the character string should be in a similar format, for example `19-JUL-06`. If the `CHAR` value is not in a different format, implicit conversion cannot take place. If the character string is in another format, then the TO_DATE function is used, and the required format has to be mentioned as a parameter.

Conversion of **RAW** and **LONG RAW** Values

When a `RAW` or `LONG RAW` value is converted to a character value (`CHAR` or `VARCHAR2`), the binary value is converted to the character value. Each binary byte is converted to a pair of characters, and each half part of the byte (nibble) is converted to a hexadecimal equivalent character. For example, if the byte is `1010 1110`, then it is converted as `AD`. The `RAWTOHEX` function performs the same conversion.

When a character value is converted to a `RAW` or `LONG RAW` value, each pair of characters is converted to a hexadecimal equivalent binary byte. For example, if the characters are `AA`, the binary byte obtained is `1001 1001`. If the character does not have any hexadecimal equivalent, PL/SQL raises an exception.

Conversion of the **NLS Value**

When an upper case character set name is passed as an argument, the `NLS_CHARSET_ID` function returns the `ID` number of the corresponding character set. Similarly, when an `ID` is passed, the `NLS_CHARSET_NAME` function returns the corresponding character set name.

Declarations

Variables and constants are declared in the declaration part of the PL/SQL block, subprogram, or package. You can change the values of variables during program execution, but not the values of constants. When a variable is declared, a storage space is allocated to it according to the datatype of the variable.

Listing 22.7: Declaring Variables

```
jdate date;    -- 1
item_count  pls_integer := 0 ;                     --2
pi constant real := 3.14159 ;                      --3
radius real := 1;                                  --4
perimeter real := 2 * pi * radius;                 --5
```

By default, variables are initialized to `NULL`. The assignment operator is used to initialize a variable. In the second statement (Listing 22.7), the `item_count` is initialized to `0` and `pi` is declared as a constant. The word `CONSTANT` should be used before the specified type. In addition, `CONSTANT` and has to be initialized with some value; otherwise, a compilation error is returned.

The DEFAULT Value

You can use the DEFAULT value instead of the assignment operator. Therefore, you can also declare item_count as shown in the following example:

```
item_count  pls_integer   default 0;
```

In the preceding code DEFAULT is used when variables have typical values. For non-typical values, the assignment operator can be used.

Listing 22.8: Using DEFAULT Declaration when working days in the week are 5

```
working_days integer default 5 ;
```

DEFAULT is also used to initialize subprograms, cursor parameters and user-defined records.

The NOT NULL Type

If a variable is specified as the NOT NULL type, then it cannot have a null value. The following are some examples of using the NOT NULL type:

Listing 22.9: Declaring variables by using the NOT NULL Constraint

```
empcode NUMBER(6) NOT NULL := 100000;
```

If you try to assign a null value to a variable, then PL/SQL raises an unhandled exception VALUE_ERROR. When NOT NULL is used, the variable should be initialized to some value. If a variable is not initialized to some value, then an error is returned.

Listing 22.10: Not Initializing Value to a Variable

```
empcode NUMBER(6) NOT NULL;                --Not valid
```

The subtypes POSITIVEN are predefined as NOT NULL and have to be initialized, as shown in the following code snippet:

```
empcode positiven := 100000;               --valid
empcode positiven ;                        --Not valid
```

Forward Reference

PL/SQL does not allow forward reference, that is, the variable has to be declared before using it. In other words, if perimeter is using a constant pi and radius, then the declarations of pi and radius need to be preceded before the declaration of perimeter.

Listing 22.11: Showing invalid declaration of perimeter

```
perimeter number(10) := 2 *  pi * radius;
pi constant REAL := 3.14;
radius number(7,2) := 1;
```

In Listing 22.11, the variable and constant referred in perimeter are forward reference, and therefore above code is invalid.

Using %TYPE

%TYPE is used to give the datatype of a predefined variable and database column. The following examples show the use of %TYPE:

Listing 22.12: Declaring the Datatype of the itemcode Variable

```
declare
      itemcode  number(10);
      icode     itemcode%type;
```

In Listing 22.12, the datatype of icode is NUMBER(10), which is the same as that of itemcode.

Listing 22.13: Initializing the icode Variable

```
icode itemcode%type := 1000;
```

Listing 22.14: Initializing the Datatype of itemmaster.itemcode to the icode Variable

```
icode  itemmaster.itemcode%Type;
```

Listing 22.15: Declaring icode when another User manager Owns the itemmaster table

```
icode  manager.itemmaster.itemcode%Type;
```

The declaration shown in Listing 22.15 offers two advantages, it is not necessary to know the datatype of `itemcode`, and when the definition of `itemmaster` is changed, the variable sets automatically change the datatype.

The `NOT NULL` constraint of a database column is not automatically available to the variable defined by using the `%Type` declaration. Therefore, if the itemcode column in `itemmaster` has the `NOT NULL` constraint, then the statements, shown in the following code snippet, do not generate any error:

```
declare
      icode  itemmaster.itemcode%type;
begin
      icode := null;
```

Using %ROWTYPE

`%ROWTYPE` is used to provide record datatype to a variable. The variable declared using %ROWTYPE can store rows of the table or row fetched from the cursor.

Listing 22.16: Storing a Row of the course Table into a Variable using %ROWTYPE

```
course%rowtype;
```

Suppose a cursor is declared as shown in the following code snippet:

```
cursor c1 is
select coursecode, coursename
from course;
```

In the following code snippet, the variable `Y` is used for holding a row from the cursor. This variable is declared as shown in the following:

```
y c1%rowtype;
```

The fields of the record declared by using `%ROWTYPE` inherits the datatype from columns. The datatype of `y.coursecode` is the same as the datatype of `coursecode` in the `course` table. The fields of the records are referenced by using the dot notation and they behave the same as ordinary variables. You can assign a value for `coursecode`, as shown in the following:

```
x.coursecode := 50;
```

Listing 22.17: Using the cursor row type to Define a Packaged Cursor

```
create package enqanalysis as
    cursor E1 return enquiry%rowtype;
end enqanalysis;
/
Create package body enqanalysis as
     cursor E1 return enquiry%rowtype is
               select * from enquiry;
               end enqanalysis;
/
```

Aggregate Assignment

You can assign a variable of `%ROWTYPE` to a variable of `%ROWTYPE`, if both are defined in the same way. For example variable b can be assigned to a in the following code.

Listing 22.18: Assigning a `%`ROWTYPE Variable to another

```
declare
    a enquiry%rowtype;
```

```
b enquiry%rowtype;
cursor c1 is
select * from enquiry;
c  c1%rowtype;
```

The following assignment in the body of the program is legal:

```
a := b:
```

However, the following assignment is illegal because `c` is defined with the base as `cursor`:

```
a := c;
```

Another way of doing aggregate assignment is by putting data in a variable by using the `SELECT .... INTO` clause or the `cursor FETCH` statement.

Listing 22.19: Performing aggregate assignment in another way

```
Select *
into a
from enquiry
or
Fetch c1 into c;
```

Records, however, cannot be inserted in the same way. Therefore, the following statement is illegal:

```
Insert into enquiry values (a);
```

Similarly, records cannot be used in the `UPDATE` statement. You can use individual fields in the record in both the `INSERT` and `UPDATE` statements. Therefore, the following statements are legal:

```
INSERT INTO enquiry values (a. enqno, .....);
UPDATE Enquiry
Set enqno = c1.enqno
................
```

The variables of the `%ROWTYPE` type cannot be initialized in the `DECLARE` section.

Using Aliases

Aliases are used when the cursor is defined with an expression, as shown in the following code snippet:

```
declare
    cursor c1 is
    select amount * 0.1
    from feespaid;
    x  c1%rowtype;
```

In the preceding code snippet, the declaration of `x` is illegal because the expression is used in `cursor` and the alias is not defined for the expression.

The declaration in the following code snippet is legal:

```
declare
    cursor c1 is
    select (amount * 0.1) interest from feespaid;
    x  c1%rowtype;
```

In the preceding code snippet, the expression is defined. The field `X` is accessed as `x.interest`.

Restrictions on Forward References

PL/SQL does not allow forward references. If a variable is referred before a declaration, it is termed as an illegal declaration. The declarations shown in the following code snippet are illegal:

```
x    integer := 20 * y;
y    integer := 10;
```

Similarly, PL/SQL does not allow declaration of multiple variables on the same line. Therefore, declarations in the following code snippet are illegal:

```
x, y, z   integer;
```

Naming Conventions

A PL/SQL program can access objects when:

- They are of the same user
- They are of other users
- They are of a remote database

Listing 22.20: Accessing the find_amount Procedure

```
find_amount ( );                    --Accessing own object
u1. find_amount ( );                --Accessing object of user u1
find_amount@remote network
                                    --Accessing object or remote mode named as
                                    --Remote network.
                                    --The data link name is remote_network.
u1.find_object@remote_network
                                    --Qualified name of remote node object.
```

You can use synonyms to refer to object names, which are long, particularly for remote objects.

Scoping

A declared identifier name should be unique. Variables and parameters cannot have the same name in the same scope. Therefore, the declarations shown in the following code snippet are illegal:

```
declare
   x   integer;
   x   real;                        --illegal because of  duplicate declaration.
function f( x in char )             --illegal because of triplicate declaration
```

Case Sensitivity

The names of constants, variables, and parameters are not case-sensitive. However, data that is held by a variable is always case-sensitive. Therefore, the declarations shown in the following code snippet will have the same effect:

```
declare
      item_code number (8);                  --A
      item_code number (8);                  --B
```

In the preceding code snippet, both A and B have the same effect.

Listing 22.21: Allocating values to some character variable

```
x :=   'ABC';                                --C
x :=  'abc' ;                                --D
```

As you can see in Listing 22.21, in the case of C, the value ABC is assigned whereas, in case of D, a different value, abc (lowercase), is assigned.

Name Resolution

Sometimes, the names of local variables and parameters are the same as that of database tables. In such cases, the names of the local variables and parameters take precedence over the database tables. Suppose you have CNT as a counter and a table name, as shown in the following statement:

```
FOR  CNT IN 1...10 LOOP
     ..........
```

```
        UPDATE CNT                                        ---Error
         SET ..........
         ................
    END LOOP;
```

The preceding statement returns an error. Similarly, the following statement fails because `CNT` refers to the name of the formal parameter:

```
    Create Procedure calc_cnt (cnt NUMBER) IS
         x number;
    Begin
         SELECT rate
         INTO x
         FROM cnt
        WHERE ITEMCODE = 'A001';
    End;
```

You can use `username.tablename` in PL/SQL for referring such tablenames. Therefore, the preceding statement can be written as follows:

```
    create procedure calc_cnt (cnt number) is
        x   number;
    begin
        select  rate
        into x
        from username.cnt
        where itemcode = ' a001';
    end;
```

It is always recommended to change the names of parameters and variables in PL/SQL code. When a name of a parameter or variable clashes with the name of a column, the name of the column takes precedence over the name of the parameter or variable. This is exactly the reverse compared to the table.

Listing 22.22: Deleting all the Rows from the bill Table

```
    declare
        rate number(5) := 1000;
    begin
        delete from bill
        where  rate = rate;
```

In Listing 22.22, all the rows from the table are deleted irrespective of whether the `rate` is `1000` or not. You can avoid such ambiguity by renaming the variable as follows:

```
    my_rate number(5) := 1000;
```

You can also avoid ambiguity by using either a block qualifier or subprogram qualifier.

Using the Block Qualifier

The following code snippet shows the use of the block qualifier:

```
    << nblock>>                                       -- give a name to block
    declare
           rate number (5) := 1000;
    begin
           delete from  bill
           where rate = nblock.rate;
```

Using the Subprogram Qualifier

The following code snippet shows the use of the subprogram qualifier:

```
    function calc_cnt (rate number)
                            return real is
```

```
begin
      select  ........
      into  ----
      from bill
      where rate    =    calc_cnt.rate;
        column name      parameter reference
```

Scope and Visibility

Scope is the part of a program unit in which the identifier can be referenced. For example, in the following code snippet, x is declared in a program as number:

```
DECLARE
      x    number;
BEGIN
      ................
         ............
END
```

In the preceding code snippet, the scope of x is from DECLARE to END.

The identifier is visible only in the region in which you can reference the identifier by using an unqualified name. In the preceding code snippet, x is visible from DECLARE to END. In general, identifiers are visible in their scope, until they are declared again in a subblock.

Identifiers are called local in the block in which they are declared. If the identifiers are referenced in a subblock, then they are called global variables in the subblock. The time identifier cannot be declared twice in the same block. Identifiers can be declared in two different blocks. In that case, they would be considered two distinct entities. However, when identifiers are declared in nested blocks, their referencing is resolved according to their scope and visibility.

Listing 22.23: Declaring an Identifier in a Block

```
DECLARE
  Y   REAL;                --Outer Y                      --A
BEGIN
  .................
                                                          --Block1
  DECLARE
        Y INTEGER;         -- Inner Y                     --B
  BEGIN
                                                          --Block2
        Y : = 5 ;          --Referencing Inner Y          --E
  END;                                                    --C
  Y : = 5.34;              --Referencing outer Y          --D
END ;
```

In Listing 22.23, the identifier Y is declared in two blocks. The scope of Outer Y is to the end of the block, i.e. statement D. The scope of the inner block is from B to C. When Y is referenced in statement E, then it is referring inner Y. This is according to the rule that the reference of an identifier is always decided on its nearness of declaration. The nearest declaration of Y at statement E is in Block 2. Therefore, it is referencing that declaration, i.e. Y as integer. Since Y in statement E is referring to Inner Y, the Outer Y is not visible in Block 2. Therefore, the scope of Outer Y is the entire Block 1, and is visible from A to B, and from C to D. Outer Y is not visible from B to C. In the absence of a re-declaration of Y inside Block 2, the scope of Outer Y is the entire Block 1, and is visible from block A to D. The scope of Inner Y is in the entire Block 2, i.e. from B to C, and is visible from B to C. In a block, the identifier can be referenced if it is declared in the block or in the parent block.

Listing 22.24: Referencing an Identifier if it is Declared in the Parent Block or in the Block itself

```
<<block1>>
declare
      x integer;
      y integer;
begin    -- block 1
                                   --identifiers available are x,y
       declare                             --start of block 2
             x char,
             z integer;
       begin
                                   --identifiers available are
                                   --x,y,z (x as char)
       end;                        --end of block 2

       declare                     --start of block 3
             w real;
       begin
                                   --identifiers available are x, y, w
               z : = 5
                                   --this reference is illegal because z is
                                   --not declared in the block neither it is
                                   --declared in parent block
       end;                        --end of block 3
                                   --identifiers available are x,y
end;                               --end of block 1
```

In Listing 22.24:

- Block 1 is the parent block of block 2 and block 3
- In block 3, the identifiers x, y, w can be referenced
- In block 2, the identifiers x, y, z can be referenced
- The x in block 2 references x, which is declared in block 2. If you want to reference x in block 2 with x declared in block 1, then you can explicitly mention it in block 2. It can be referred as block 1.x. block 1 is called a qualifier and can also be the name of a subprogram.

The following code snippet...

```
Procedure pro1
      x  char;
      Function f1 ......
            x  integer;
      begin
            If pro1.x = 'A' then
               ...........
```

In the preceding code snippet, pro1. x refers to its declaration of x in the procedure.

Assignment

Variables are initialized to NULL every time a block or subprogram is entered, unless they are explicitly initialized. Variables are initialized in the DECLARE section as shown in the following code snippet:

```
DECLARE
    x  integer := 5;
    ..................
```

If any variable is used in an expression having a NULL value, then the expression is evaluated to NULL. Consider the following example:

```
x := x + 1;
```

In the preceding example, if x has a NULL value, then the expression is evaluated to NULL.

Only TRUE, FALSE or NULL values can be assigned for Boolean variables. You can apply the condition in an expression that returns either TRUE or FALSE. Consider the example in the following code snippet:

```
DECLARE
   x  Boolean;
BEGIN
      ...............
      x :=  (rate < 100);
```

In the preceding code snippet, if the value of rate is less than 100, x gets the TRUE value; otherwise it gets the FALSE value.

Database Value

You can use the SELECT statement to put database values to variables. The SELECT statement should return only one row. The variables, which are mentioned in SELECT statement, should be type compatible with the columns mentioned in the SELECT statement.

Listing 22.25: Putting rate and qty in a Variable

```
select rate, qty
into x,y from  bill
where  billno = 0;
```

In Listing 22.25, x should be type compatible with rate and y should be type compatible with qty. So, now you can declare the variables as shown in the following syntax:

```
x bill.rate%type:
y bill.qty%type;
```

Expressions and Comparisons

The simplest expression consists of a single variable or constant. Expressions are constructed by using operands and operators. The (-) negation operator operates on single operand, while * and / (multiplication and division) operators operate on two personals. The expressions are evaluated by using operator precedence to have unique values. The order of precedence is shown in Table 22.5 (from highest to lowest):

Table 22.5: Operator Precedence

Operator	Operation
* *, NOT	Exponentiation, logical negation
+, -	Identify, negation
+, -, ||	Addition, subtraction, concatenation
=, !=, <, >, <=, >=	Comparison
IS NULL, LIKE	Comparing nulls, string pattern matching
Between, In	Checking range and membership in the set
AND	Conjunction
OR	Inclusion

Each expression is evaluated according to precedence—from left to right.

Consider the following expression:

```
A * B + C + D
```

In the preceding expression, first A * B is evaluated and the result is added to C, and, finally, the result is added to D. Parentheses can be used to improve the readability, even if they are not required. Parentheses are provided to override the default precedence. Consider the following expression:

```
A * (B+C) + D
```

In the preceding expression, B + C is first evaluated and then the result is multiplied by A.

Logical Operators

Logical operators are used to connect two Boolean expressions. The operators used in PL/SQL are AND, OR, and NOT.

- a AND b returns true, only if a and b both are true
- a OR b returns true, only if any one of them returns true
- NOT a returns compliment of a

Table 22.6 displays summarize results of the operators (here T represents true, while F represents false):

a	b	a AND b	a OR b
T	T	T	T
T	F	F	T
F	T	F	T
F	F	F	F
NULL	T	NULL	T
NULL	F	F	NULL
NULL	NULL	NULL	NULL

a	NOT a
T	F
F	T
NULL	NULL

The involvement of NULL returns NULL in the expression.

Order of Evaluation in **AND**

When AND is used in a Boolean expression, the evaluation stops as soon as a condition is evaluated to FALSE.

Consider the following condition:

```
C1 AND C2 AND C3 ......
```

In the preceding condition, if C3 and C2 are evaluated to FALSE, then C3 is not evaluated and FALSE is returned.

Order of Evaluation in **OR**

When OR is used, the evaluation stops when the first TRUE is evaluated. Consider the following condition:

```
C1 OR C2 OR C3
```

In the preceding condition, if C1 is evaluated to FALSE, then C2 is evaluated. If C2 is evaluated to TRUE, then further evaluation stops and TRUE is returned:

```
If (X= 0) OR (Y/X < 1), Then
....
```

In the preceding condition, the condition `X = 0` is evaluated first. If `X` is `zero`, then the second condition is not evaluated, and the exception `DIVIDE_BY_ZERO` is not raised.

NOTE

It is always better to use parentheses in case of multiple operators. Consider the following expression:

```
NOT C1 AND C2
```

The preceding expression is interpreted as follows:

```
(NOT C1) AND C2.
```

The expression is interpreted in this way because `NOT` has precedence over `AND`. Suppose you want the complement of `C1` and `C2`, then it is better to write it as shown in the following expression:

```
NOT( C1 and C2).
```

Comparison Operator

Comparison operators are used to compare values or expressions. They return results as `TRUE`, `FALSE` or `NULL`. They are used in the `WHERE` clause, the DML statement, and the conditional control statement.

Let's now learn about the various comparison operators.

Relational Operator

Table 22.7 gives a list of the various relational operators

Table 22.7: Relational Operators

Relational Operator	Description
=	Is equal
< >, ! =, ~ =	Not equal
<	Less than
>	Greater than
<=	Less than equal
> =	Greater than equal

IS NULL Operator

The IS NULL operator returns TRUE if the operand has a NULL value. Consider the statements in the following code snippet:

```
X := null;
if X IS NULL then ....
...........
```

In the preceding code snippet, `X IS NULL` returns `TRUE`. Consider the expression in the following code snippet:

```
if X := NULL then
.............
```

In the preceding code snippet, X returns `FALSE` because comparison using `NULL` always returns `FALSE`.

LIKE Operator

`The LIKE` operator is used to compute character values with a pattern. It returns `TRUE` if the pattern matches the value; otherwise, it returns `FALSE`.

Listing 22.26: Displaying all Items Starting with A from the item Table using LIKE operator

```
Select itemname
from item
where itemname LIKE 'A%';
```

NOTE

You can use _ (Underscore) to match one character exactly, and % to match zero or more characters.

BETWEEN Operator

The Between operator is used to check whether a value lies in a range or not. Consider the following condition:

```
X BETWEEN 10 and 100
```

The preceding condition checks whether X is greater than or equal to 10, and less than or equal to 100.

IN Operator

The IN operator tests whether a value is a member of a given set or not. Consider the following statement:

```
x in ( 10,20,30)
```

The preceding statement checks if x has a value of 10, 20, or 30. The complement of IN is NOT IN, which is written as follows:

```
not in (10,20,30)
```

Concatenation Operator

The concatenation operator is used to connect two character strings. Consider the following statement:

```
X : = ' blue' || 'color';
```

In the preceding statement, the value bluecolor is assigned to the variable X. If both the operands have the CHAR datatype, then the operator returns a CHAR value; otherwise, it returns a VARCHAR2 value.

Boolean Expression

Boolean expressions return TRUE, FALSE or NULL. Complex boolean expressions are connected by using AND, OR and NOT. They can be used in the WHERE condition or in the if .. then statement. There are three kinds of boolean expressions sets:

- Arithmetic expressions
- Character expression
- Date expressions

Arithmetic Expression

Arithmetic expressions are used to compare numbers.

Listing 22.27: Comparing Two Numbers using the Less Than Operator (<)

```
if (X < Y ) then ......
```

Character Expressions

Character strings are also compared similar to numbers. The comparison is passed on internal ordering of character set. It is called as collating sequence. Internally, characters are stored as numbers according to a standard, such as ASCII and EBCDIC. In ASCII, A is represented as 65, while B is represented as 66. In other words, B > A is true for the ASCII character set.

Date Expression

Dates are also compared similar to numbers. The more recent date is said to have a larger value than the earlier dates. Consider the following code snippet:

```
date1 := ' 01-FEB-96';
date2 := '01-MAR-98'
then
date2 > date1 is TRUE
```

Real numbers should not be compared for equality or inequality because they are stored as approximate values. For example, the following condition may return `TRUE` or `FALSE`:

```
X := 5;
if ( X = 5.0)
then
....................
```

In the preceding condition, one value is compared for two values. In such a case, it is better to use parentheses.

Listing 22.28: Finding whether X is in the Range of 5 and 10:

```
( X > 5 ) and ( X < 10)
```

The following statement, however, is illegal:

```
5 < X < 10                    --illegal statement
```

A Boolean variable is itself either `TRUE` or `FALSE`. Therefore, it is not necessary to use `TRUE` or `FALSE` in comparisons. If you want to check whether the Boolean variable `Y` has the value `TRUE`, you can write it as:

```
if  X
then
```

Instead of:

```
if (X = TRUE)
then
.........
```

NULL Behavior

`NULL` is handled according to the following rules:

- A comparison involving NULL always returns NULL.
- When `NULL` is connected with the `AND` operator, the rest of the conditions are not evaluated unless `NULL` occurs initially.
- When `NULL` is connected with the `OR` operator, the other conditions are evaluated even though `NULL` does not occur initially.
- The complement of `NULL` and `NOT (NULL)` also yield `NULL`.
- In an expression, the value of expression becomes `NULL`, if `NULL` is used in evaluation.

Consider the following expression:

```
X : = Y+7;
```

The preceding expression gives a `NULL` value if `Y` is `NULL`. A comparison of two variables having `NULL` values returns `NULL`. Consider the following code snippet:

```
a := null;
b := null;
if ( a = b)
then
........
```

In the preceding code snippet, the condition `a = b` returns `NULL`, not `TRUE`.

If the value of a condition is `NULL` in the `IF` statement, then the associated sequence of statements is not executed. Consider the following code snippet:

```
a : = null;
b : = null;
if ( a = b)
```

```
    then
    .................                              -- A
    else
    .................                              -- B
    end if;
```

In the preceding code snippet, statement A is not executed when the value of the condition is TRUE, because it is an indeterminate statement. Instead, statement B is executed. Two statements having conditions written in a similar manner may give different results if NULLs are involved. Consider the following statement where a code written in two ways:

Listing (i):

```
    if ( a > b)
    then
       c := a;
    else
       c := b;
    end if ;
```

Listing (ii):

```
    if NOT ( a > b)
    then
       c := b;
    else
       c := a;
    end if;
```

In listing (i) and (ii), if both a and b are NOT NULL, then the effect of the statements remains the same. If either a or b is null, then, in the case of Listing (i), b is assigned to c, while in the case of Listing (ii), a is assigned to c.

A zero length string is treated as NULL. Consider the following statement:

```
    insert into course (coursecode, syllabus)
    values (a001, '  ');
```

In the preceding statement, the NULL value is assigned in the column syllabus. Now, consider the following statement:

```
    X := '     ';
```

The preceding statement assigns a NULL value to X. You can assign a NULL value, as shown in the following:

```
    X := SUBSTR ( `abc', 4,0);
```

The NULL string is tested by using the IS NULL operator. During concatenation, the null values are ignored. Suppose you write:

```
    X := 'big' || null || 'apple'
```

then the value of X is bigapple.

Functions

Any function, with some exceptions, that takes the NULL argument, returns NULL. Consider the following statement:

```
    X := null;
    Y := substr ( x,1,0);
```

In the preceding statement, null is assigned to Y.

Null can be compared in the DECODE function as:

```
    Y := DECODE( X, NULL, 100, 'L', 250, ` N', 300);
```

If X has the value NULL, then 100 is assigned to Y.

The NVL functions return the value of the second argument, if its first argument is NULL. Therefore, if you write:

```
Y := NVL ( X,100);
```

the function returns 100, since X is NULL.

If NULL is passed as a second argument, to the REPLACE function, then the first argument is returned. Consider the following code snippet:

```
X := ' abbc';
Y : = REPLACE (X, NULL, 'd' );
```

In the preceding code snippet, Y gets the value abbc.

If NULL is passed as a third argument, then every occurrence of the second argument is removed.

```
Y : = REPLACE (X, 'b', NULL );
```

Therefore, Y gets the value ac.

Built-in Functions in PL/SQL

Table 22.8 lists the various built-in functions used in PL/SQL:

Table 22.8: Lists the various built-in functions used in PL/SQL

Type	Function
Number	ABS, ACOS, ASIN, ATAN, ATAN2,CEIL, COS,COSH, EXP,FLOOR, LN, LOG, MOD, POWER, ROUND, SIGN, SIN, SINH, SQRT, TAN, TANH, TRUNC
Error Reporting	SOLCODE, SQLERRM
Character	ASCII, CHR, CONCAT, INITACAP, INSTR, INSTRB, LENGTH, LENGTHB, LOWER, LPAD, LTRIM, NLS_INITCAP, NLS_LOWER, NLS_UPPER, NLSSORT, REPLACE, RPAD, RTRIM, SOUNDEX, SUBSTR, SUBSTRB, TRANSLATE, UPPER
Conversion	CHARTOROWID, CONVERT, HEXTORAW, NLS_CHARSET_ID, NLS_CHARSET_NAME, RAWTOHEX, ROWIDTOCHAR, TO_CHAR, TO_DATE, TO_LABEL, TO-MULTIBYTE, TO_NUMBER, TO_SINGLE_BYTE
Date	ADD_MONTHS, LAST_DAY, MONTHS_BETWEEN, NEW_TIME, NEXT_DAY, ROUND, SYSDATE, TRUNC
MISC	DECODE, DUMP, CREATES, LEAST, NVL,UID, USER, USERENV, VSIZE

Summary

The chapter introduced various concepts of PL/SQL such as lexical units, datatypes, user-defined subtypes, datatype conversion and scope rules. The next chapter discusses various control structures.

Exercise

1. Name different datatypes in PL/SQL.
2. What are different numeric datatypes provided in PL/SQL?
3. What is the difference between CHAR and VARCHAR2?
4. What are different scope rules for referencing variables?
5. What is the use of subtypes?

23

Understanding Control Structure

Control structures are used to modify the flow of programs. These structures give processing capability to a program. The processing capabilities include branching of the program flow, providing iterations, and changing values of variables.

Table 23.1 lists various control statements:

Table 23.1: Control Statements

Control statement	Control structure

Conditional control statement	`IF.....THEN`
	`IF.....THEN.....ELSE`
	`IF.....THEN.....ELSIF`

Iterative statement/Iterative control	`WHILE.....LOOP.....END LOOP`
	`FOR.....LOOP.....END LOOP`
	`LOOP.....END LOOP`

Unconditional branching statement	`GOTO`
Sequential control statement	`NULL` statement

Figure 23.1 indicates the structure of the control statements, mentioned in Table 23.1:

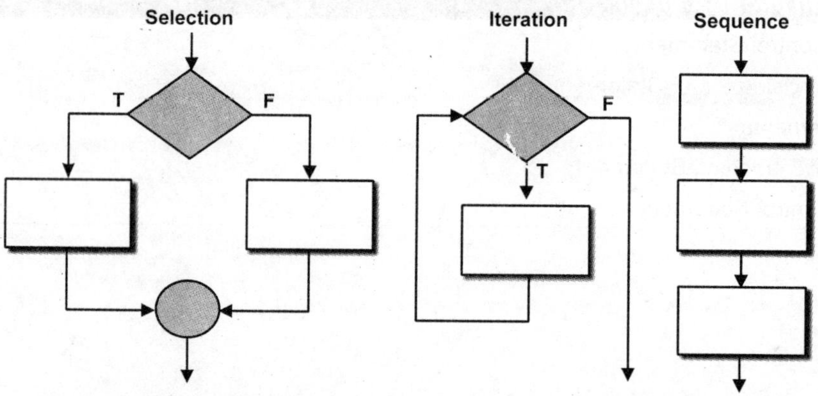

Figure 23.1: Showing the Structure of the Control Statements

Conditional Control Statements

The basic control structure is used in writing any computer program. The `IF` statement is used to change the flow of program conditionally. Whether or not the statement is executed depends on the value of the condition. The three types of IF statements are:

- IF.....THEN
- IF.....THEN.....ELSE
- IF.....THEN.....ELSIF

Let's now discuss each of these three types of `IF` statements.

The IF.....THEN Statement

The following code snippet shows the syntax of the IF.....THEN statement:

```
IF condition THEN
   Statements
END IF;
```

In this case, if the condition is satisfied, then the statements are executed. The following are some examples of using the IF.....THEN statement:

Listing 23.1: Calculating the Biggest among the Three Given Numbers

```
                                             --A, B, C are three numbers
big := A;
if B > big
then
   big := B;
end if;
if C > big
then
   big := C;
end if;
```

You can also write the `IF` statement in a single line as follows:

```
if c > big then big := c; end if;
```

Listing 23.2: Writing a Complete Program to Find the Biggest Number using the IF.....THEN Statement

```
declare
   x number;
   y number;
   z number;
   big number;
begin
   z := 10;
   x := 100;
   y := 50;
   big := x;
   if(y > big)
   then

                    big := y;
   end if;
   if(z > big)
   then
           big := z;
   end if;
   dbms_output.put_line(' The highest is  '|| to_char(big));
end;
/
```

The output of Listing 23.2 is as follows:

```
The highest is 100

PL/SQL procedure successfully completed
```

The IF.....THEN.....ELSE Statement

The IF.....THEN statement adds the ELSE keyword. ELSE is used to provide an alternate sequence of statements, if the condition is not TRUE.

The following code snippet shows the syntax of the IF.....THEN.....ELSE statement:

```
IF condition THEN
   Statements A;
ELSE
   Statements B;
END IF;
```

If the condition is satisfied, then statements A are executed, else statements B are executed. The preceding code snippet can also be written as:

```
if ( A > B ) then
   big := A;
else
   big := B ;
end if ;
if (C > big ) then
   big : = C;
end if;
```

You can nest IF statements as shown in the following code snippet:

```
if A > B then
   if A > C then
           big : = A;
   else
           big : = C;
   end if;
else
   if B > C
   then
           big : = B;
   else
           big : = C;
   end if
end if;
```

The IF.....THEN.....ELSIF Statement

When several mutually exclusive conditions are combined, the IF.....THEN.....ELSIF statement can be used. The following code snippet shows the use of the IF.....THEN.....ELSIF statement:

```
IF condition 1
THEN
   Statement A;
ELSIF condition 2
THEN
   Statement B;
ELSE
   Statement C;
END IF;
```

If condition 1 is satisfied, then Statement A is executed. If condition 1 is false, but condition 2 is satisfied, then Statement B is executed. If both the conditions 1 and 2 are false, then Statement C is executed. The following examples show the use of the IF.....THEN.....ELSIF statement:

Listing 23.3: Finding the Biggest among the Three Numbers using the IF.....THEN.....ELSIF Statement

```
IF (A>B) and (A>C) then
  big := A;
ELSIF (B>C) then
  big := B;
ELSE
  big := C;
END IF;
```

Listing 23.4: Finding the Biggest Number by Directly Assigning Values to Variables

```
Declare
  x number := 45;
  y number := 60;
  z number := 23;
  big number;
begin
  big := x;
  if(y > big) then
              big := y;
  else
              if(z > big) then
                     big := z;
              end if;
  end if;
  dbms_output.put_line('the biggest number is '||to_char(big));
end;
/
```

The output of Listing 23.4 is as follows:

```
The biggest number is 60

PL/SQL procedure successfully completed
```

Listing 23.5: Writing a Condition for Assigning Discount According to the Value of the Amount

```
if amount > 50000 then
  discount := 50;
elsif amount > 40000 then
  discount := 40;
elsif amount > 30000 then
  discount := 30;
else
  discount := 5 ;
end if;
```

The `ELSIF` statement can be used to provide an equivalent construct of `CASE` or `SWITCH`.

Listing 23.6: Giving Grades According to the Marks using the IF....THEN.....ELSIF Statement

```
declare
  X number := 45;
  begin
        if (X<40) then
                      dbms_output.put_line('F');
        ELSIF (X<=60) then
                      dbms_output.put_line('S');
        ELSIF (X<75) then
                      dbms_output.put_line('I');
```

```
        else
                         dbms_output.put_line('D');
        end if;
    end;
    /
```

The output of Listing 23.6 is as follows:

```
S

PL/SQL procedure successfully completed
```

Guidelines for Using the **IF** Statement

Although you can use any type of IF statement in your program, it is recommended that you use the `ELSIF` statement, instead of `IF....THEN......ELSE` statement. Let's take an example to understand this better.

Listing 23.7: Writing the Program Syntax using the IF.....THEN.....ELSE Statement

```
if condition1 then
   statement a;
else
   if condition2 then
          statement b;
   else
          if condition3 then
                    statement c;
          end if;
   end if;
end if;
```

The preceding program can be written more easily by using the IF.....THEN.....ELSIF statement, as shown in Listing 23.8:

Listing 23.8: Writing the Program Syntax using the IF.....THEN.....ELSIF Statement

```
if condition1 then
   statement a;
elsif condition2 then
   statement b;
elsif condition 3 then
   statement c;
end if;
```

You can also connect multiple conditions using operators, such as and, or in the `IF` statement.

Listing 23.9: Writing Multiple Conditions using (and) and (or) Operators

```
Declare
   marks number :=45;
begin
   if (marks<40) and (marks>0) then
          dbms_output.put_line('fail');
   end if;
   if (marks<60) and (marks>=40) then
          dbms_output.put_line('pass');
   end if;
end;
/
```

The output of Listing 23.9 is as follows:

```
pass

PL/SQL procedure successfully completed
```

Iterative Statements

Iterative statements are used to execute some statements repeatedly. There are three forms of iterative statements:

- FOR.....LOOP..... END LOOP
- WHILE..... LOOP.....END LOOP
- LOOP..... END LOOP

Let's discuss each of these in detail.

The FOR.....LOOP.....END LOOP Statement

FOR LOOP iterates over a specified range of integers. Then number of iterations is known prior to loop execution in FOR LOOP.

The following code snippet shows the syntax of the FOR.....LOOP.....END LOOP statement:

```
FOR counter IN lower bound  .. upper bound LOOP
  Statements;
END LOOP;
```

Now, let's see some examples of using the FOR.....LOOP.....END LOOP statement:

Listing 23.10: Calculating sum s: = 1 + 2 + 3+..... + 100

```
s:= 0;
for i in 1..... 100 loop
  s:= s + i;
end loop;
```

In this case, the loop iterates for 100 times. i is called as counter. The lower bound is 1 and upper bound is 100. The values of the lower bound and the upper bound are evaluated one prior to the execution of the loop. They are never evaluated again. Inside the loop, the value of the counter is initially equal to the lower bound, and it is incremented each time for each iteration. The final value of counter is upper bound.

Listing 23.11: Condition where the Lower Bound is Same as the Upper Bound

```
for i in 10..10 loop
  k: = i;
end loop;
```

In this case, the loop is executed once and k is assigned a value of 10.

Listing 23.12: Condition where the Lower Bound is More than the Upper Bound

```
k:= 5;
for i in 11 .. 10 loop
  k:= 10;
end loop;
```

In this case, the loop is not executed and the value of k remains 5.

Inside the loop, the counter acts as a constant and any attempt to modify its value results in an error. Consider the following code snippet:

```
for i in 1..10 loop
  k:= 5;                    --a
  x:= i + 1;                --b
  i := k + 1;               --c
end loop;
```

In the preceding code snippet, statement b is legal because it is referring the value of counter i. However, statement c is not legal because it is modifying the counter variable i.

The loop ranges—the values of upper bound and lower bound—can be variables, expressions, or literals, but they should be evaluated as integer. The lower bound needs not be one, but counter is always incremented by 1. Therefore, the following statements are legal:

```
For K IN -10 ..10 LOOP
FOR K In 0 .. ROUND ( X/Y)
FOR K IN ASCII ('A') .. ASCII('Z')
```

PL/SQL does not have the facility of incrementing the counter by some other value. For example, the BASIC language provides the following facility:

```
for k = 5 to 20 step 5
                                    --statement a;
next k;
```

In this case, the values of k are 5, 10, 15, 20. You can build the BASIC structure in PL/SQL using the MOD function.

Listing 23.13: Building a Condition Using the MOD Function

```
for k in 5..20 loop
  if (mod (k,5) = 0) then
        statement a;
  end if;
end loop;
```

In this case, the statement is evaluated four times. Inside the IF statement, the value of k would be 5, 10, 15, 20. A more efficient statement can be written as follows:

```
for i in 1..4 loop
  k :=  i * 5;
  statement a ;
end loop;
```

Listing 23.14: Dynamically Determining the Values of Upper or Lower Bound at Runtime

```
select count (enrollno) into x from student;
for i in 1 .. x  loop
  statement a;
end loop;
```

In this case, the value of X can be determined at runtime.

Listing 23.15: Displaying Even Numbers between 1 to 10

```
begin
  for i in 1..10 loop
        IF(mod(i,2)=0) THEN
               dbms_output.put_line('i is '||to_char(i));
        end if;
  end loop;
end;
/
```

The output of Listing 23.15 is as follows:

```
i is 2
i is 4
i is 6
i is 8
i is 10

PL/SQL procedure successfully completed
```

Listing 23.16: Displaying the Sum of Numbers from 1 to 10

```
declare
  x number := 0;
begin
  x := 0;
  for i in 1..10 loop
        x := x + i;
  end loop;
  dbms_output.put_line('sum is '||to_char(x));
end;
/
```

The output of Listing 23.16 is as follows:

```
sum is 55

PL/SQL procedure successfully completed
```

Listing 23.17: Displaying each Character in the String on Each Line

```
declare
  x varchar2(20) := 'abcdf';
begin
  for j in 1..length(x) loop
        for i in j..length(x) loop
                        dbms_output.put(substr(x,i,1));
                dbms_output.new_line;
        end loop;
        exit;
  end loop;
end;
/
```

The output of Listing 23.17 is as follows:

```
a
b
c
d
f

PL/SQL procedure successfully completed
```

Scope of Counter Variable

You need not declare the counter variable because it is implicitly declared in the `FOR.....LOOP.....END LOOP`.

If the counter is not explicitly declared, then its reference outside the loop is illegal.

```
declare
  x number;
begin
  for i in 1 .. 10 loop
        x := x + 1;
  end loop;
  x := i;                          --illegal reference of i
end;
/
```

If the counter variable is explicitly declared, then inside the loop the reference of counter variable is always for the counter in `FOR.....LOOP.....END LOOP`.

Consider the following code snippet:

```
declare
   i integer;
   x integer;
begin
   i := 10;
   for i in 1..100 loop
          x := i;
   end loop;
end;
/
```

The output of the preceding code snippet is as follows:

```
PL/SQL procedure successfully completed
```

In this case, you will notice that in the inside loop, `i` is the counter, and not a variable. This is explicitly declared in the main program.

If you want to refer the variable in the main program, then you can use a label for referencing a variable. Consider the following code snippet:

```
<< mainprg>>
declare
   x  integer;
   i integer;
begin
   x := 10;
   i := 5;
   For i in 1..100 LOOP
          x := mainprg.i;
   end loop;
dbms_output.put_line(x);
end;
/
```

In this case, `x` always assigns a value of `5`, because `mainprg.i` refers to a variable declared in `mainprg`.

Listing 23.18 shows how to use labels in nested FOR statements:

Listing 23.18: Using Labels in Nested FOR Statements

```
<< outer >>
   for i in 1.....25 loop
<< inner >>
   for i in 1.....10 loop
          statement a ;
          x := outer.i;
   end loop;
end loop outer;
```

In this case, the `outer.i` refers to the value of counter `i` defined in the outer loop.

The EXIT Statement

You can use the `EXIT` statement to terminate a loop prematurely (before the counter reaches the upper bound). The following examples show the use of the EXIT statement:

Listing 23.19: Terminating x when Value of x goes above 25

```
for x in 1...100 loop
   x := k * ... ;
   exit when (x > 25);
end loop;
```

The EXIT statement terminates the current loop.

Listing 23.20: Terminating the Outer Loop using Labels

```
<< outer>>
for i in 1..30 loop
   for k in 1...100 loop
         x := k * ...;
         exit outer when (x > 30);
   end loop;
end loop outer;
```

Listing 23.21: Showing the Use of the EXIT Statement

```
declare
   k number := 1;
begin
   <<A>>
   for j in 1..5 loop
         <<B>>
         for i in 1..10 loop
                     if(j=i) then
                           exit A;
                     end if;
                     dbms_output.put_line(' '||to_char(k));
                     k := k + 1;
         end loop;
   end loop;
end;
/
```

The output of Listing 23.21 is as follows:

```
PL/SQL procedure successfully completed
```

The WHILE.....LOOP.....END LOOP Statement

Unlike FOR.....LOOP.....END LOOP, the number of iterations in the WHILE loop is not fixed.

The following code snippet shows the syntax of the WHILE..... LOOP..... END LOOP statement:

```
WHILE condition LOOP
   statement A ;
END LOOP;
```

When a condition is TRUE, the loop is executed, else the loop gets terminated. The following examples show the use of the WHILE..... LOOP..... END LOOP statement:

Listing 23.22: Calculating Sum (s:= 1+2+3+.....100)

```
s := 0;
i :=  0:
while (i < = 100) loop
   s:= s + i;
   i := i +1;
end loop;
```

In this case, the loop is executed until it reaches 100. It is the responsibility of the programmer to ensure that the condition becomes FALSE after some iteration; otherwise, the loop executes infinitely. The loop would execute infinitely in the absence of the following statement:

```
i := i + 1;
```

When the WHILE loop is encountered, the condition is evaluated first. If it is TRUE, the loop statements are executed and the control goes to the top of the loop. On the other hand, if the condition is FALSE or NULL, the loop gets terminated.

Listing 23.23: Displaying Odd Numbers in the Range from 1 to 21

```
declare
  i number :=1;
begin
  while(i <=21) loop
        dbms_output.put_line(to_char(i));
        i:= i+2;
  end loop;
end;
/
```

The output of Listing 23.23 is as follows:

```
1
3
5
7
9
11
13
15
17
19
21
PL/SQL procedure successfully completed
```

Listing 23.24: Substituting the Character b with #

```
declare
  s1 varchar2(20) := 'abbdgbfbghb';
  c char := 'b';
  i number:=1;
  s2 varchar2(1);
  d char := '#';
  s4 varchar2(24):='';
  len number:=0;
begin
  len:= length(s1);
  while(i<= len) loop
        s2 := substr(s1,i,1);
        if(s2=c) then
                       s2:= d;
        end if;
               s4 := s4||s2;
               i:= i+1;
  end loop;
        dbms_output.put_line(s4);
end;
/
```

The output of Listing 23.24 is as follows:

```
a##dg#f#gh#

PL/SQL procedure successfully completed
```

The LOOP ..... END LOOP Statement

The `LOOP.....END LOOP` statement provides infinite loops. Consider the following code snippet:

```
s := 0;
i := 0;
loop
   s:= s + 1;
   i := i+1;
end loop;
```

In this case, you notice that the statements execute infinitely.

You need to use the EXIT statement to terminate the infinite loop, as shown in the following code snippet:

```
DECLARE
   x number;
   i number;
BEGIN
   ...........
   ...........
   EXIT WHEN (i >100);
END;
```

Listing 23.25: Terminating an Infinite Loop using the EXIT statement

```
s:= 0;
i := 0;
loop
   s := s + i;
   i := i + 1;
   exit when (i >100);
end loop;
```

Alternatively, you can use the EXIT statement as:

```
s := 0;
i := 0;
loop
   s:= s + i;
   i := i +1;
   if (i >100)
   then
           exit;
   end if;
end loop;
```

NOTE

Listing 23.25 is just a sample code explaining the use of EXIT in loops, so that the loops are not executed infinitely.

The `EXIT` statement should be placed inside the loop; however, it cannot be used to terminate the local block.

NOTE

To terminate the PL/SQL block prematurely, the RETURN statement can be used.

You can use labels to specify which loop has to be terminated. This is used for terminating the outer loop in case of nested loops. By default, `EXIT` always terminates the current loop.

Now, consider the following code snippet:

```
<< outer >>
LOOP
        ............
        ............
<< Inner>>
        LOOP
              ............          -- a
   EXIT outer when (X > 20);
              ............          -- b
   EXIT when (X >10);
         END LOOP;
END LOOP outer;
```

In this case, statement A terminates the outer loop, while statement B terminates the inner loop.

The `WHILE` and `FOR` loops are recommended over the `LOOP.....END LOOP` statement.

Listing 23.26: Printing Even Numbers in the 1.....10 Range

```
declare
   x number;
begin
   x := 2;
   loop
          dbms_output.put_line(x);
          x:= x + 2;
          exit when (x >10);
   end loop;
end;
/
```

The output of Listing 23.26 is as follows:

```
2
4
6
8
10
PL/SQL procedure successfully completed
```

Unconditional Branching Statement

The `GOTO` statement is used for unconditional branching. It is better to avoid the use of `GOTO`, because it results in complex and unstructured code, which is difficult to understand. It is recommended that you use exception, rather than `GOTO`, to branch from deep nested structure. The following are some examples of the unconditional branching statement.

Listing 23.27: Calculating the Sum of 100 Numbers using the GOTO Statement

```
s:= 0;
i := 0;
<< abc>>
s:= s + i;
i :=  i + 1;
if i <=100 then
   goto abc;
end if;
```

If the value of `i` is below 100, the control transfers to the statement having the `abc` label. The label should be unique in the scope and must precede an executable statement in the block.

Listing 23.28: Using GOTO to Branch to the Enclosing Block

```
Declare
   X integer:= 0;
Begin
   << abc>> X := X +1;
   Begin
           ............
           ............
           GOTO abc;
   End;
End;
/
```

`The GOTO` statement cannot branch either to `IF` statement or `LOOP` statement, or sub blocks. The following are some of the examples of using the GOTO statement:

Listing 23.29: Showing How GOTO is Illegal when it Branches into the IF Statement

```
declare
   x number;
   y number;
begin
   x:= 5;
   goto abc;
   <<abc>>
   begin
           if (x>500) then
                   y:= 10;
           end if;
   end;
end;
/
```

The output of Listing 23.29 is as follows:

```
PL/SQL procedure successfully completed
```

Listing 23.30: Showing How GOTO is Illegal when it Branches into Sub Block

```
declare
   x number;
   y number;
begin
   x := 5;
   goto abc;
   begin
           <<abc>>
           y:=10;
   end;
end;
/
```

The output of Listing 23.30 is as follows:

```
PL/SQL procedure successfully completed
```

The following code snippet shows how the `GOTO` statement cannot branch out of a subprogram:

```
DECLARE
   .........
   procedure calc_rate Is
BEGIN
   ..................
   GOTO abc;
END;
BEGIN
   <<abc>>
   Y:=10;
```

Similarly, the following code snippet shows how the `GOTO` statement cannot branch from the exception handler into the current block:

```
DECLARE
   Y NUMBER;
BEGIN
   ...............
   <<abc>>
   Y := 10;
              ...............
   EXCEPTION
   WHEN_OTHERS
        GOTO abc;
END;
```

In this case, the label should not precede non-executable statements, like `END LOOP`, `END IF` or `END` statement. Therefore, the following statements are not legal:

```
DECLARE
   X NUMBER;
BEGIN
   ...............
   GOTO abc;
   IF (x < 200) THEN
   ...............
   <<abc>>
   END IF;
END;
```

The best way to avoid writing such illegal statements is by adding `NULL` before the non-executable statement as shown in the following code snippet:

```
GOTO abc:
IF (X > 100)  THEN
   <<abc>>
   NULL;
END IF;
```

Sequential Control Statement

The `NULL` statement is used to improve the readability of a program. It makes the meaning and action of conditional statements clear. Consider the following code snippet:

```
if a > 190 then
   bonus(emp_id);
else
   null;
end if;
```

In this case, the `NULL` statement specifies that only the employee with `a>190` shall get bonus. It passes the control to the next statement. The NULL statement can also be used as shown in the following code snippet:

```
exception
when zero_divide then
  handle_zero_divide;
when no_data_found then
  handle_no_data_found;
when too_many_rows then
  null;
end;
```

The NULL statement, in this case, makes sure that the exception condition `TOO_MANY_ROWS` is not overlooked, even though no action is necessary for it.

Listing 23.31: Using the NULL Statement to Make a Program More Readable

```
if (rate > 500) then
  discount:= 10;
else
  null;
end if;
```

In this case, `IF` indicates that only for a purchase above `Rs.500`, a discount of `10%` is given.

NOTE

In case, you want to refer a procedure named calc_amt in the main program, but are not much sure of its definition, you can create a procedure by using NULL.

You can create stubs for designing applications. Stubs are the dummy subprograms, which allow you to put off their definition until the main program is tested. Consider the following code snippet:

```
DECLARE
  ...
BEGIN
  NULL;
END;
...
...
```

Whatever statement may be in the executable part of the subprogram, we can test the structure of the subprogram by using the `NULL` statement in place of the actual executable part, i.e. the `NULL` statement would meet the requirement of having at least one statement in the executable part of a subprogram.

Summary

In this chapter, you learned about three types of IF statements, namely IF.....THEN.....END IF, IF.....THEN.....ELSE, and IF.....THEN.....ELSIF. Next you learned about various loop statements, such as FOR.....LOOP..... END LOOP, WHILE..... LOOP.....END LOOP, and LOOP..... END LOOP. The chapter also discusses about unconditional branching and sequential control statements. After understanding control structures, let's now learn to interact with Oracle.

Exercise

1. Write a program to find out addition of number from 100 to 1000.
2. Write a program to print every combination of characters abcde.
3. Write a program to locations of x,y,z in string xxsczxysxz.

24

Interaction with Oracle

PL/SQL is mainly used to process data stored in Oracle. Using PL/SQL, you can fetch data from Oracle database, process it, and store the result of the processing back into the Oracle database. PL/SQL interacts with Oracle in the following ways:

- SELECT.....INTO statement
- Cursor
- DDL and dynamic SQL
- Transaction control statements

The SELECT.....INTO Statement

When a single value or row has to be fetched from a database, then the `SELECT.....INTO` statement can be used. Listing 24.1 shows the code to fetch the salary of employee, ANIL and calculate the grade according to its value:

Listing 24.1: Fetching the Salary of Employee ANIL and Calculating the Grade According to its Value

```
declare
   x number;
begin
   select salary
   into x
   from emp_company
   where ename='anil';
       if x < 1000 then
           dbms_output.put_line('a');
   elsif x < 2000 then
           dbms_output.put_line('b');
   elsif x < 3000 then
           dbms_output.put_line('c');
   else
           dbms_output.put_line('d');
   end if;
end;
/
```

The output of Listing 24.1 is as follows:

```
B
PL/SQL procedure successfully completed.
```

The value of salary is put into `x` using the `SELECT.....INTO` statement. This statement should return single rows; otherwise, an exception is raised.

Listing 24.2 displays coursename corresponding to coursecode:

Listing 24.2: Displaying coursename Corresponding to coursecode

```
create or replace procedure displaycoursename ( ccode in number ) is
   cname course.coursename%type;
begin
   Select coursename
   into  cname from  course
   where coursecode = ccode;
   dbms_output.put_line ( ' The name of course is ' || cname);
end;
/
```

The output of Listing 24.2 is as follows:

```
Procedure created
```

Listing 24.3 shows the code to execute the procedure, displaycoursename:

Listing 24.3: Executing the displaycoursename Procedure

```
exec displaycoursename(10);
```

The output of Listing 24.3 is as follows:

```
The name of course is ORACLE

PL/SQL procedure successfully completed
```

In Listing 24.3, the procedure is executed as:

```
execute displaycoursename(10);
```

The `SELECT.....INTO` statement should use proper number of variables of proper datatype after the `INTO` clause. Suppose, you select `coursecode` and `coursename`. In that case, it is represented, as shown in the following code snippet:

```
declare
   x course.coursecode%type;
   y course.coursename%type;
begin
   select coursecode, coursename
   into x ,y
   from course
   where coursecode  = 10;
      ...................
```

If the list of variables after the `INTO` clause does not have variables of proper datatypes, then an error is generated, as shown in the following code snippet:

```
declare
   X course.coursecode%type;
   Y course.coursename%type;
begin
   SELECT coursecode, coursename
   INTO X
      ...................
```

In the preceding code snippet, two values are selected, but `INTO` is having only one variable. Thus, the statement returns error.

If the variables are not of proper datatypes, an error is generated, as shown in the following code snippet:

```
declare
   x course.coursecode%type ;
   y course.coursename%type;
begin
   select coursename
   into x from course;
      ..................
```

In the preceding code snippet, datatypes of `coursename` and variable `x` are not compatible.

User can use the variable of `%ROWTYPE` to store a single row, as shown in the following code snippet:

```
declare
   x course% rowtype;
begin
   select *
   into x from course
```

```
    where coursecode = 10;
      ........................
    if x.coursecode = 10 then
    ......................
```

In the preceding code snippet, variable x is of the %ROWTYPE datatype, and can store the entire row. Each element of the row can be referred as x.coursecode, x.coursename, and x.syllabus.

User has to ensure that the SELECT.....INTO statement should return one row. If no row is selected, then an exception NO_DATA_FOUND is raised. If more than one row is selected, then an exception TOO_MANY_ROWS is raised.

Listing 24.4 displays the coursename by considering exceptions:

Listing 24.4: Displaying coursename by Considering Exceptions

```
set serveroutput on
create or replace Procedure displaycoursename (ccode IN number ) as
cname course.coursename%type;
begin
  select coursename
  into cname from course
  where coursecode = 10;
  dbms_output.put_line( ' The course name is ' || cname);
exception
when no_data_found then
  dbms_output.put_line('The required course is not present');
when too_many_rows then
  dbms_output.put_line('The required coursecode has many names');
end;
/
```

The output of Listing 24.4 is as follows:

```
Procedure created
```

Listing 24.5 shows the code to execute a procedure:

Listing 24.5: Executing the Procedure

```
exec displaycoursename(10);
```

The output of Listing 24.5 is as follows:

```
The course name is ORACLE

PL/SQL procedure successfully completed
```

NOTE

It is always recommended to write exception handlers for NO_DATA_FOUND and TOO_MANY_ROWS, when SELECT.....INTO is used.

Let's learn about cursors.

Cursor

Cursors are used when you want to manipulate data of many rows. When SELECT.....INTO or any DML statement is issued, Oracle internally opens the cursor. This is called the implicit cursor. It is named as SQL. When queries return more than one row, then the cursor has to be defined explicitly. This is called as explicit cursor.

The cursor can be declared in the declaration part of the PL/SQL block, subprogram, and package. The cursor is the temporary work area in which you can store the results of SQL statements. The cursors are used as sequential files. To manipulate a cursor, you have to open it using the OPEN statement. You can fetch the rows from the cursor using the FETCH statement. After fetching the rows, the cursor is closed using the CLOSE statement. All these operations are implicitly performed using cursor FOR loop, which is used for processing the data of cursor. Several queries are processed by opening multiple cursors at a time.

The following are some simple Cursor Programs:

1. The following program prints employee name and salary using the FOR...LOOP cursor:

```
declare
cursor c1 is
select ename en,salary
from emp_company;    ---A
begin
 for z in c1 loop                              --B
    dbms_output.put_line('data is '||z.en||' '||z.salary); --C
  end loop;

end;
/
```

In the preceding program, statement A declares a cursor. In the cursor declaration, you have to specify cursor name (c1) and select the query, which is attached to the cursor.

The statement B indicates cursor FOR...LOOP. The variable z indicates loop variable. The variable z is capable of storing one row of query and its type is RECORD. The fields or column values can be accessed using . extension as z.en or z.salary.

2. The following program calculates average salary of an employee in the Emp_Company table:

```
declare
cursor c1 is
select salary
from emp_company;
x number:=0;
y number:=0;
countx number:=0;
avgx number := 0;
begin
 for z in c1 loop
       x := x + nvl(z.salary,0);
    countx := countx + 1;
 end loop;
 avgx := x/countx;
 dbms_output.put_line(avgx);

end;
/
```

In the preceding program, the NVL function is used to handle null values in salary.

Cursor Declaration

Cursors are declared in the DECLARE section of the PL/SQL block. The CURSOR has to be declared before referencing it, since PL/SQL does not allow forward declarations.

The following is the syntax for cursor declaration:

```
declare
  cursor <cursor name> Is
  <Select statement>
```

Listing 24.6 shows the code to declare a CURSOR that takes data from batch:

Listing 24.6: Declaring a CURSOR that Takes Data from Batch

```
declare
   cursor c1 is
   Select * from batch;
```

In Listing 24.6, `c1` is the cursor name.

Listing 24.7 shows the code to specify a return datatype in cursor definition:

Listing 24.7: Specifying a Return Datatype in Cursor Definition

```
cursor c1
return batch%ROWTYPE is
select * from batch;
```

The cursor name should not be a PL/SQL declared variable name. It should be an undeclared identifier. Scope rules for the variables are also applicable to the cursor.

NOTE

You can name the cursor same as the table name, but it is not recommended.

Listing 24.8 shows the code to pass parameters to cursors:

Listing 24.8: Passing Parameters to Cursors

```
cursor c1 ( ccode number default 10) is
select * from batch
where coursecode = ccode;
```

In Listing 24.8, `CCODE` is the parameter whose value is provided during execution.

Listing 24.9 shows the code to open the cursor with parameter:

Listing 24.9: Opening the Cursor with Paramefer

```
open c1(20);
```

In Listing 24.9, the cursor has the row corresponding to `coursecode 20`. If no parameter is passed, it has the default value `10`. The formal parameter is the `IN` parameter, so that you cannot return values in actual parameters. The parameter can only be referred in the specified query. Therefore, the scope of the parameter is local to cursor.

NOTE

You cannot impose NOT NULL constraint on the parameters.

Let's learn how to open a cursor.

Opening a Cursor

You need to open a cursor before fetching rows from it. The opening cursor executes the query and selects the rows, which satisfy the query criteria. If a cursor is opened for updation using the `FOR UPDATE` statement, the rows get locked. The following code snippet shows the command to use the `CURSOR`:

```
Open c1;
```

Listing 24.10 shows the code to use the CURSOR through various cursor related statements:

Listing 24.10: Using the Cursor through Various Cursor Related Statements

```
declare
   cursor c1 is
   select * from batch;
   z c1%rowtype;
```

```
begin
  Open c1;
  fetch c1 into Z;
  while (c1%found) loop
  dbms_output.put_line ( 'Batchcode is '  || z.batchcode);
  fetch c1 into Z;
  end  loop;
  close c1;
end;
/
```

The following points explain the code in Listing 24.10:

- Opening `c1` does not fetch any rows. It only selects the rows, which satisfies the search criteria. The `FETCH` statement actually returns rows.
- The while loop is iterated for a number of rows returned by query. Each iteration fetches a new row from the cursor. The row values are accessed using the target variable z. When all rows are finished, then the cursor attribute c1%found returns true.
- After all rows are fetched, cursor is closed.

The output of Listing 24.10 is as follows:

```
Batchcode is 20002
Batchcode is 10002
Batchcode is 10001
Batchcode is 10003

PL/SQL procedure successfully completed
```

Cursor using parameter

If some computation has to repeat for similar rows, then the parametric cursor is used, as shown in the following code snippet:

```
declare
  cursor c1(ccode varchar2) is
  Select * from batch where coursecode=ccode;
  z c1%rowtype;
begin
  Open c1('10');
  fetch c1 into Z;
  while (c1%found) loop
  dbms_output.put_line ( 'Batchcode is '  || z.batchcode);
  fetch c1 into z;
  end  loop;
  close c1;
end;
/
```

If the cursor is declared using parameters, then the value of parameter can be passed in the `open` statement. Suppose you have declared the cursor, as shown in the following code snippet:

```
declare
  cursor c1 (ccode number) is
  select * from batch
  Where coursecode = ccode;
  z c1%rowtype;
```

```
begin
   Open c1 ('10');
   fetch c1 into Z;
          .............
```

In the preceding code snippet, `Open c1('10')` opens the cursor. The value of parameter is `10`. It fetches the rows corresponding to `CCODE` equals to `10`.

It is better to use a unique identifier for formal parameter of cursor. When the formal parameter is declared with default value, and the `cursor` is opened without parameter, then the default value of parameter is taken, as shown in the following code snippet:

```
declare
   cursor c1 ( ccode number default 10) is
   select *
   from batch
   where coursecode = ccode;
   Z c1%rowtype;
begin
   open c1;
   .............
```

In the preceding code snippet, the cursor is opened without parameter. Therefore, the value of parameter, `CCODE`, is taken as `10`.

You can also use the named notation for passing a parameter. For example, to open a `CURSOR` with value `20`, you can use the `OPEN` statement, as shown in the following code snippet:

```
open c1 ( ccode => 20);
```

Suppose `x` and `y` are two parameters to the `c2` cursor. In that case, they can be passed to the c2 cursor, as shown in the following code snippet:

```
open c2 (X =>5, Y =>10);
```

Fetching Rows from Cursor

Rows are fetched from the cursor using the `fetch` statement. Fetching of rows gets the current row of cursor, and advances the cursor pointer to the next row. For example, the cursor `c1` has rows A, B, C, D, E.

->A	A	A
B	->B	B
C	C	->C
D	D	D
E	E	E

The following code snippet shows the effect of the `FETCH` statement on pointer:

```
Fetch c1 into x          Fetch c1 into x          Fetch c1 into x
       X = A                    X = B                    X = C
```

In the preceding code snippet, the first fetch statement returns value `A` to `x` and moves the pointer to `B` and the next fetch statement returns value `B` to `x` and moves the pointer to `C`.

Thus, the fetching operation is similar to accessing data in a sequential file. The `fetch` statement should put data in variables having compatible datatypes, as shown in the following code snippet:

```
declare
   cursor c1 is
   Select batchcode, startingdate from batch;
   bcode batch.batchcode%type;
   sdate batch.startingdate%type;
   z c1%rowtype;
```

```
begin
   open c1;
   fetch c1 into bcode, sdate;             --A
   fetch c1 into z;                        --B
   fetch c1 into bcode;                    --C
   close c1;
end;
/
```

In the preceding code snippet, statement A and B are valid statements, while C is not a valid statement. In C, only one variable is used, while fetch is producing two values at a time.

You can mention any two variables having datatypes `CHAR` and `DATE` for the above `FETCH` statement. You can use the record type variable, such as `z`, having two components, char and date.

NOTE

It is recommended to use %type and %rowtype declaration for variables. It gives compatible datatypes for the variables.

The rows, which are fetched in the cursor, are decided by the existing conditions of the `SELECT` statement when the cursor is open. Listing 24.11 shows the code to define a cursor:

Listing 24.11: Defining a Cursor

```
declare
   X number;
   cursor C1 is
   Select * from batch
   where coursecode = X;
begin
   X := 10;
   open c1;                                --A
   fetch c1 into z;                        --B
   X := 20;                                --C
         fetch c1 into z;                        --D
End;
/
```

The output of Listing 24.11 is as follows:

```
PL/SQL procedure successfully completed
```

In the preceding output, the cursor is opened at `A`, and the time value of `coursecode` is `10`. So, all the rows, having `coursecode` equal to `10`, are selected. Even if you change the value of `X` later on at statement `C`, the rows fetched from the cursor correspond to the value of `coursecode` equal to `10`. This is because rows are defined at the time of opening the cursor. If you want to fetch the rows for `coursecode` that equals to `20` then you have to close and reopen the cursor again.

When all rows are fetched from the cursor, the next `fetch` statement does not generate any error. Only the result of such fetch statement is indeterminate, i.e. target variables are having indeterminate values. Such conditions are determined using cursor attributes `%found` and `%NOTFOUND`. For the 'end of cursor' condition of cursor `c1`, the attribute `c1%found` returns `FALSE`; otherwise, it returns `true`.

Closing a ***Cursor***

When the cursor work is over, the cursor has to be closed. The cursor is closed using the `CLOSE` statement, as shown in the following code snippet:

```
CLOSE C1;
```

When the cursor is closed, any other resources such as the memory associated with cursor, is released. Oracle has a limit on the maximum number of cursors, which are opened at a time. The limit is set by the parameter `MAX_OPEN_CURSOR`. Any operation, such as fetch on closed cursor raises the exception, `INVALID_CURSOR`.

Sometimes, program may do an abnormal exit due to an error in statement. So, the cursor may remain open. In such cases, you have to ensure that the cursor is closed by writing an exception handler for the `OTHERS` exception, as shown in the following code snippet:

```
declare
   cursor cl is
           ...............
begin
   Open cl;
   fetch ........
   Close cl;
Exception
When others then
   close cl;
end;
```

In case of error conditions, exception handler for `OTHERS` is executed, this closes the cursor.

NOTE

Closing the cursor in normal termination and abnormal termination is the duty of a programmer.

Listing 24.12 displays the name and salary of employees working in ACC:

Listing 24.12: Displaying the Name and Salary of Employees Working in ACC

```
declare
   cursor c1(pcname varchar2) is
   select ename,salary
   from emp_company
   where cname=pcname;
   z c1%rowtype;
begin
   open c1('acc');
   fetch c1 into z;
   while(c1%found) loop
          dbms_output.put_line
          (' name '||z.ename||' sal '||to_char(z.salary));
          fetch c1 into z;
   end loop;
   close c1;
end;
/
```

The output of Listing 24.12 is as follows:

```
NAME ANIL SAL 1500
NAME AJAY SAL 8000
NAME AMOL SAL 1000
PL/SQL procedure successfully completed
```

Let's learn about cursor FOR loop.

*Using Cursor **FOR** Loops*

Cursor `FOR` loop is used for opening the cursor, fetching a row from the cursor, and closing the cursor. It is used generally when all the rows in a cursor are to be processed.

Listing 24.13 shows the code to calculate the number of rows in a batch:

Listing 24.13: Calculating the Number of Rows in a Batch

```
declare
   cnt number;
   cursor c1 is
   select batchcode
   from batch;
begin
   cnt := 0;
   for z in c1 loop
           cnt := cnt +1;
                dbms_output.put_line(z.batchcode);
   end loop;
   dbms_output.put_line ( TO_CHAR(cnt));
end;
/
```

Listing 24.13 can be defined as follows:

- z is called as a loop index, which is implicitly declared with the c1%ROWTYPE datatype. The records are fetched one by one. The fields of the implicitly declared record store the value of the row, which is fetched from the cursor.
- Inside the cursor FOR loop, you cannot refer another cursor with the same name. You can implicitly refer to a record only in the FOR loop. It is not referred outside the loop.

The output of Listing 24.13 is as follows:

```
20002
10002
10001
10003
4

PL/SQL procedure successfully completed
```

Listing 24.14 shows the sequence of statements that are illegal because of implicitly defined cursor loop variable, which is referred outside the loop:

Listing 24.14: Showing Illegal Statements

```
declare
   cnt number;
   cursor c1 is
   select batchcode
   from batch;
begin
   cnt := 0;
   for z in  c1 loop
           cnt := cnt + 1;
   end loop;
   dbms_output.put_line (z.batchcode);          -- illegal
end;
/
```

The output of Listing 24.14 is as follows:

```
ERROR at line 11:
ORA-06550: line 11, column 24:
PLS-00201: identifier 'Z.BATCHCODE' must be declared
ORA-06550: line 11, column 2:
PL/SQL: Statement ignored
```

The output of Listing 24.14 shows the error that occurred in line 11. The cursor is closed irrespective of the loop being terminated normally or abnormally (premature termination). Even if the exception is raised and the control goes outside the FOR loop, the cursor is closed.

NOTE

The compilation of the program in Listing 24.14 results in an error stating:
PLS-00302: component BATCHCODE must be declared.

Listing 24.15 displays the total salary of all employees of ACC using cursor:

Listing 24.15: Displaying the Total Salary of all Employees of ACC using Cursor

```
declare
   cursor c1 is
   select ename,salary from emp_company
   where cname='acc';
   total number := 0;
begin
   for z in c1 loop
           total := total+z.salary;
           dbms_output.put_line(z.ename||'     '||to_char(z.salary));
   end loop;
   dbms_output.put_line(total);
end;
/
```

The output of Listing 24.15 is as follows:

```
ANIL   1500
AJAY   8000
AMOL      1000
10500

PL/SQL procedure successfully completed
```

Using the For loop for Parametric Cursor

You can use the FOR LOOP for parametric cursor. The program given in Listing 24.15 can be written using the FOR loop cursor, as shown in the following code snippet:

```
declare
   cursor c1(ccode varchar2) is
   Select * from batch where coursecode=ccode;
   z c1%rowtype;
begin
   for z in c1('10')  loop
   dbms_output.put_line ( 'Batchcode is '  || z.batchcode);
   end  loop;
   end;
/
```

Listing 24.16 displays the average value of shares of ACC and TATA:

Listing 24.16: Displaying the Average Value of Shares of ACC and TATA

```
declare
   cursor c1 is
   select cname cn,sdate,price from shares;
   x number:=0;
   y number:=0;
   countx number:=0;
```

```
      avgx number := 0;
      county number:=0;
      avgy number := 0;
   begin
      for z in c1 loop
            if(z.cn='acc') then
                              x := x + z.price;
                              countx := countx + 1;
                      end if;
            if(z.cn='tata') then
                              y := y + z.price;
                              county := county + 1;
                      end if;
      end loop;
      avgx := x/countx;
      avgy := y/county;
      dbms_output.put_line(avgx);
      dbms_output.put_line(avgy);
   end;
   /
```

The output of Listing 24.16 is as follows:

```
705.33333333333333333333333333333333333
513.75

PL/SQL procedure successfully completed
```

You can use parameters as given in following example, while using the cursor.

Listing 24.17 shows an example where the outer loop selects the subject and inner loop prints student names having marks between 50 and 90:

Listing 24.17: Showing an Example of Outer Loop and Inner Loop with Parameter

```
declare
   cursor c1(psubject varchar2,plmarks number,phmarks number) is
   select rn,subject,marks from student
   where subject=psubject and marks between plmarks and phmarks ;
   cursor c2 is select subject from student;
begin
   for w in c2 loop
         for z in c1(w.subject,50,90) loop
                        dbms_output.put_line('subject is '||w.subject||' rn is
                 '||to_char(z.rn));
         end loop;
   end loop;
end;
/
```

The output of Listing 24.17 is as follows:

```
SUBJECT IS Physics RN IS 1
SUBJECT IS Chemistry RN IS 2
SUBJECT IS Maths RN IS 3
SUBJECT IS Biology RN IS 4

PL/SQL procedure successfully completed
```

Let's learn how to substitute subqueries in place of cursor.

Substituting Subqueries in Place of Cursor

You can substitute a query in place of cursor in the FOR loop cursor.

Listing 24.18 displays all the batchcode from batch table:

Listing 24.18: Displaying all the batchcode from the Batch Table

```
declare
   cnt number;
begin
   cnt := 0;
   for z in (select batchcode from batch)loop
          cnt := cnt + 1;
          dbms_output.put_line (z.batchcode);
   end loop;
end;
/
```

The output of Listing 24.18 is as follows:

```
20002
10002
10001
10003
20001

PL/SQL procedure successfully completed
```

Let's learn to use aliases for field.

Using Aliases for Fields

You can refer the expression in the SELECT clause in the query using aliases.

Listing 24.19 shows the code to sum 10% of netincome:

Listing 24.19: Summing 10% of netincome

```
declare
   sumamt number;
   cursor c1 is
   select batchcode, 0.1 * netincome nincome
   from batch;
begin
   sumamt := 0;
   For Z in c1 loop
          sumamt := sumamt + Z.nincome;
   end loop;
   dbms_output.put_line (TO_CHAR(sumamt));
end;
/
```

In Listing 24.19, `nincome` is the alias for the expression `0.1 * netincome`.

The output of Listing 24.19 is as follows:

```
200

PL/SQL procedure successfully completed
```

Let's learn how to pass parameters to cursor.

Passing Parameters to Cursor

The parameters are passed to cursor after the name of cursor in the cursor `FOR` loop.

Listing 24.20 shows the code to calculate netincome for a specific batch:

Listing 24.20: Calculating netincome for a Specific Batch

```
declare
   sumamt number := 0;
   btcode number;
   cursor c1 (pbtcode number) is
   select netincome from batch
   where batchcode = pbtcode;
begin
   sumamt := 0;
   btcode := 20001;
   for z in c1 (btcode) loop
         sumamt := sumamt + z.netincome;
   end loop;
   dbms_output.put_line ('the income for batch is ' ||  to_char (sumamt));
end;
/
```

In Listing 24.20, only those rows are fetched from `CURSOR` that have `batchcode` equals to `20001`, i.e. the value of `btcode` at that time.

The output of Listing 24.20 is as follows:

```
The income for batch is 0

PL/SQL procedure successfully completed
```

Listing 24.21 shows the code to explain nested loop

Listing 24.21: Nested Loops in Cursor For Loop

```
declare
   cursor c1(psubject varchar2,plmarks number,phmarks number) is
   select rn,name,marks
   from student
   where subject=psubject
   and marks between plmarks and phmarks ;
   cursor c2 is
   select subject from student;
begin
   for w in c2 loop
         for z in c1(w.subject,50,90) loop
                        dbms_output.put_line('subject is '||w.subject||' rn is
                  '||to_char(z.rn) || ' name is ' || z.name);
         end loop;
   end loop;
end;
/
```

The output of Listing 24.21 is as follows:

```
SUBJECT IS PHYSICS RN IS 1 NAME IS AMIT
SUBJECT IS CHEMISTRY RN IS 2 NAME IS ANIL
SUBJECT IS MATHS RN IS 3 NAME IS AJAY
SUBJECT IS BIOLOGY RN IS 4 NAME IS SACHIN

PL/SQL PROCEDURE SUCCESSFULLY COMPLETED
```

Listing 24.22 shows the code to display car sales in south and north region assuming that you have car sales for each region:

Listing 24.22: Displaying Car Sales in South and North Region using the Parametric Cursor

```
declare
   cursor c1(pregion varchar2) is
   select car,region,qty
   from carsales
   where region=pregion;
   sumx number :=0;
begin
   for z in c1('n') loop
                  sumx := sumx+z.qty;
   end loop;
   dbms_output.put_line(sumx);
   sumx := 0;
   for z in c1('s') loop
          sumx := sumx+z.qty;
   end loop;
   dbms_output.put_line(sumx);
end;
/
```

The output of Listing 24.22 is as follows:

```
10
20

PL/SQL procedure successfully completed
```

Listing 24.23 Shows the use of cursor for aggregate query.

Listing 24.23: Printing Total Car Sales Using Aggregate Query

```
declare
   cursor c1 is
   select car,sum(qty) sum_qty
   from carsales
   group by car
   order by car;
begin
   for z in c1 loop
          dbms_output.put_line(z.car ||' '||z.sum_qty);
   end loop;
end;
/
```

The output of Listing 24.23 is as follows:

```
BMW 15
HONDA CITY 10
MERCEDES 20
WAGON R 25

PL/SQL procedure successfully completed
```

Let's learn about cursor attributes.

Cursor Attributes

Cursor attributes provide the current information of cursor. Each cursor has four attributes, `%FOUND`, `%ISOPEN`, `%NOTFOUND`, and `%ROWCOUNT`. The syntax of cursor attributes is as follows:

```
cursorname%attribute
```

If the cursor name is `c1`, and the attribute is `%FOUND`, then it can be written, as shown in the following code snippet:

```
c1%FOUND
```

NOTE

The attributes are referred only in PL/SQL. They cannot be referred in the SQL statement.

Let's learn about the %FOUND attribute.

*The **%FOUND** Attribute*

The %FOUND attribute provides information about the recent fetch operation. If a recent `FETCH` statement results in successful fetching of rows, it returns `TRUE`; otherwise, it returns `FALSE`. If it is referred before the first `FETCH` operation, it returns `NULL`. If referred before the opening cursor or after the closing cursor, it raises the exception, `INVALID_CURSOR`.

Listing 24.24 shows the code to test whether the specified batchcode is present or not:

Listing 24.24: Testing whether the Specified batchcode is Present or Not

```
create or replace function testbatchcode (bcode number) return boolean as
   cursor c1 is
   select 'x'
   from batch
   where batchcode = bcode;
   flag boolean;
   z c1%rowtype;
begin
   open c1;
   fetch c1 into z;
   if c1%found then
         flag  := true;
   else
         flag := false;
   end if;
   close c1;
   return (flag);
end;
/
```

The output of Listing 24.24 is as follows:

```
Function created
```

If the specified `batchcode` is present, then the cursor successfully fetches a row and `c1%FOUND` returns `TRUE`. Using this attribute, you can construct a condition for `WHILE.....LOOP.....END LOOP` for fetching rows from cursor.

Listing 24.25 shows the code to calculate batchcode having fifth maximum netincome:

Listing 24.25: Calculating batchcode having Fifth Maximum netincome

```
declare
   amt number := 0;
   cnt number := 0;
```

```
   cursor c1 is
   select netincome
   from batch
   order by netincome desc;
   Z c1%rowtype;
begin
   open c1;
   fetch c1 into Z;
   while (c1%found) and (cnt <= 5) loop
         cnt := cnt +1;
         fetch c1 into Z;
        end loop;
   if cnt = 5 then
         dbms_output.put_line ('The amount is' || TO_CHAR ( Z.netincome));
   else
         dbms_output.put_line ('The required rows are not present');
   end if;
        close c1;
end;
/
```

In Listing 24.25, the `WHILE` loop is terminated when the cursor has less than five rows (using `c1%FOUND`) or when rows are fetched from cursor.

The output of Listing 24.25 is as follows:

```
The amount is 0

PL/SQL procedure successfully completed
```

Listing 24.26 shows the code to calculate the total number of rows in a batch, where you can write equivalent WHILE loop in place of FOR loop

Listing 24.26: Calculating the Total Number of Rows in a Batch using the Equivalent WHILE Loop in Place of the FOR loop

```
declare
   totalrows number := 0;
   cursor c1 is
   select batchcode
   from batch;
   Z c1%rowtype;
begin
   open c1;
   fetch c1 into Z;
   WHILE c1%FOUND LOOP
         totalrows := totalrows +1;
         fetch c1 into Z;
   END LOOP;
        close c1;
   dbms_output.put_line('The no of rows are ' ||  TO_CHAR(totalrows));
end;
/
```

In Listing 24.26, you can see that one `fetch` statement is executed before using `c1%FOUND and` one `fetch` statement is provided before the `WHILE` loop. Inside the `WHILE` loop, the fetch is required so that the rows are fetched one by one. The `WHILE` loop is terminated when the last fetch operation is unable to fetch a new row.

The output of Listing 24.26 is as follows:

```
The no of rows are 4
PL/SQL procedure successfully completed
```

Let's learn about %NOTFOUND attribute.

The %NOTFOUND Attribute

The %NOTFOUND attribute is the complement of %FOUND. %NOTFOUND returns FALSE when %FOUND returns TRUE and vice versa. Similar to FETCH, %NOTFOUND returns NULL before the first FETCH statement.

Listing 24.27 shows the code to calculate the number of rows in a batch using LOOP.....END LOOP and %NOTFOUND:

Listing 24.27: Calculating the Number of Rows in a Batch using LOOP.....END LOOP and %NOTFOUND

```
declare
   cnt number := 0;
   cursor c1 is
   select batchcode
   from batch;
   z c1%rowtype;
begin
   cnt := 0;
   open c1;
   loop
          fetch c1 into z;
          exit when c1%notfound;
          cnt := cnt +1;
   end loop;
   close c1;
   dbms_output.put_line( ' the number of rows are ' ||  to_char(cnt));
end;
/
```

The output of Listing 24.27 is as follows:

```
The number of rows are 4

PL/SQL procedure successfully completed
```

When the fetch operation is unsuccessful, c1%NOTFOUND returns TRUE and loop gets terminated.

The %ISOPEN Attribute

The %ISOPEN attribute returns TRUE if the cursor is open; otherwise, it returns FALSE. It is used for the global cursor, when the programmer is not sure whether the cursor is opened or not.

Listing 24.28 shows the code to open the cursor if the cursor is not opened:

Listing 24.28: Opening the Cursor if the Cursor is Not Opened

```
if c1%isopen then
   dbms_output.put_line ( ' cursor already opened ' );
else
   open c1;
end if;
```

Let's learn about the %ROWCOUNT attribute.

The %ROWCOUNT Attribute

The %ROWCOUNT attribute provides the number of rows, which are currently fetched from the cursor. When the cursor is opened, %ROWCOUNT is equal to zero. The %ROWCOUNT attribute, if referred before opening a cursor or after closing a cursor, raises the exception, INVALID_CURSOR.

Listing 24.29 displays the value of %ROWCOUNT after a successful fetch operation:

Listing 24.29: Displaying the Value of %ROWCOUNT after a Successful Fetch Operation

```
declare
   cursor c1 is
   select batchcode
   from batch;
   Z c1%ROWTYPE;
begin
   open c1;
   dbms_output.put_line (TO_CHAR(C1%ROWCOUNT));     -- Prints 0
   fetch c1 into Z;
   dbms_output.put_line (TO_CHAR(C1%ROWCOUNT));     -- Prints 1
   Fetch c1 into Z;
   dbms_output.put_line (TO_CHAR( C1%ROWCOUNT));      -- Prints2
   close c1;
   dbms_output.put_line(TO_CHAR(C1%ROWCOUNT));
                                    -- raises exception INVALID_CURSOR
end;
/
```

The output of Listing 24.29 is as follows:

```
0
1
2
declare
*
ERROR at line 1:
ORA-01001: invalid cursor
ORA-06512: at line 14
```

Table 24.1 summarizes the values of attributes, in different conditions:

Table 24.1: Values of Attributes

	%FOUND	%NOTFOUND	%ISOPEN	%ROWCOUNT
Before Open	E	E	F	E
After Open	N	N	T	O
Before first fetch	N	N	T	O
After first fetch	T	F	T	1
Before middle fetch	T	F	T	1
After middle fetch	T	F	T	D
Before last fetch	T	F	T	D
After last fetch	F	T	T	D
Before close	F	T	T	D
After close	E	E	F	E

In Table 24.1, n : NULL, T : TRUE, F : FALSE, E : Exception INVALID CURSOR, and D : Data Dependant 1, 2, 3 (Depends on number of rows fetched).

Implicit **Cursor** Attributes

Implicit cursor attributes are used to test the outcome of DML statement and SELECT.....INTO statement. The attributes always refer to the recent SQL statement. Before any SQL statement, the attributes have NULL values. The name of cursor is SQL and the attributes are referred as SQL%FOUND.

*The **%FOUND** Attribute*

The SQL%FOUND attribute returns TRUE, if INSERT, DELETE, UPDATE, or SELECT statement affects at least one row. Otherwise, SQL%FOUND returns FALSE. Before this statement, it returns NULL.

Listing 24.30 shows the code to add the given amount in a given batchcode (if the specified batchcode is not present then it inserts a row in batch with netincome 0)

Listing 24.30: Adding the Given Amount in a Given Batchcode

```
declare
  bcode batch.batchcode%type;
  amt number(10,2) := 0;
begin
  bcode := 20001;
  amt :=10000;
  Update batch
  Set netincome = amt
  where batchcode = bcode;
  IF SQL%NOTFOUND THEN
insert into batch (coursecode,batchcode,
  netincome,startingdate,duration,lastno,coursefees)
  values (1,bcode,0,'1-jan-2003',30,0,1000);
  END IF;
end;
/
```

The output of Listing 24.30 is as follows:

```
PL/SQL procedure successfully completed
```

The output of Listing 24.30 shows the successfully completed message.

NOTE

The attributes always refer to the recent SQL statement.

Listing 24.31 shows the code to refer an attribute to SQL statement in a procedure:

Listing 24.31: Referring Attribute to SQL Statement in a Procedure

```
update batch
set netincome = amt
where batchcode = bcode;
calcamt ;                                  --procedure call
if SQL%NOTFOUND THEN
                                         --Refers to sql statement referred in
                               --procedure not FOR UPDATE statement.
```

Listing 24.32 shows the code to store the value of SQL%NOTFOUND in a variable (to refer update statement it is better to store value of SQL%NOTFOUND in a variable)

Listing 24.32: Storing the Value of SQL%NOTFOUND in a Variable

```
update batch
netincome = amt
where batchcode=bcode;
x := sql%notfound;
calcamt;
if x then
   ...............
```

In the normal `SELECT.....INTO` statement, it is useless to use `SQL%NOTFOUND` because the statement raises the exception, `NO_DATA_FOUND`.

Listing 24.33 shows the code to raise NO_DATA_FOUND exception:

Listing 24.33: Raising NO_DATA_FOUND Exception

```
declare
   ...............
begin
   select netincome
   into amt
   from batch
   where batchcode=bcode;
   IF SQL%NOTFOUND then
           A;
   END IF;
   Exception
   When no_data_ found then
           B;
end;
```

In Listing 24.33, when `SELECT.....INTO` fails to return any row, exception `NO_DATA_FOUND` is raised, and the IF statement is never executed. Therefore, it is useless to write code that tests the outcome of statements and performs some action. However, if you are using only one exception handler `OTHERS`, then you can use the attribute, as shown in Listing 24.34:

Listing 24.34: Using Exception Handler OTHERS

```
select netincome
into amt
from batch
where batchcode = bcode;
exception
when OTHERS then
   if SQL%NOTFOUND then
        ..............
   end if;
   if ...........
        ..............
   end if;
end;
```

When a group function is used in the `SELECT.....INTO` statement, the exception, `NO_DATA_FOUND` is never raised and `SQL%NOTFOUND` also returns `FALSE`. The group function always returns a value or a null.

The following code snippet shows how a group function works in the `SELECT.....INTO` statement:

```
.........
select avg(netincome)
into avg_amt
```

```
from batch
where coursecode = code;
                                        --It never raises exception NO_DATA_FOUND
IF SQL%NOTFOUND THEN
                                        --It is tested but never returns true
   A;                                   --This code is never executed
END IF;
Exception
WHEN NO_DATA_FOUND THEN
   B;                                   --never executed
```

Let's learn about the SQL%ISOPEN attribute.

The SQL%ISOPEN Attribute

The SQL cursor is closed by Oracle when execution of a query is completed. So, `SQL%ISOPEN` always returns `FALSE`.

The SQL%NOTFOUND Attribute

The SQL%NOTFOUND attribute is a complement to SQL%FOUND. So, if SQL%FOUND returns TRUE, SQL%NOTFOUND returns FALSE.

The SQL%ROWCOUNT Attribute

The `SQL%ROWCOUNT` attribute returns the number of rows affected by `INSERT`, `UPDATE`, or `DELETE` statement. If no rows are affected or the `SELECT.....INTO` statement returns no rows, then the value of `SQL%ROWCOUNT` is zero. When the `select.....into` statement returns more than one row, the `TOO_MANY_ROWS` exception is raised; `%ROWCOUNT` returns a value and not the number of rows, which satisfies the condition. Suppose you want to perform an action in which more than 20 rows are updated, use the following code snippet:

```
update .........
IF SQL%ROWCOUNT > 20 THEN
   A;
END IF;
```

Let's learn about the cursor variables.

Cursor Variables

Cursor variables are used when you want to use the cursor facility but do not want to bind the cursor to a specific query. The cursor variable points to the current row in the resultset of the query similar to the cursor. The difference between the cursor and cursor variable is similar to the difference between constant and variable. While the cursor is tied to only one specific query, the cursor variable can be tied to many such types of compatible queries.

Listing 24.35 shows the code to calculate the number of rows in total course and batch:

Listing 24.35: Calculating the Number of Rows in Total Course and Batch

```
declare
   type rec_type is record
      (code number);
      Type cur_num_type is
   ref cursor return rec_type;                         --A
   cur_num cur_num_type;                               --B
   x   rec_type;                                       --x number;
   pcnt  number;
   ccnt  number;
```

```
begin
Open cur_num
   FOR select batchcode
        from batch order by startingdate;                   -- C
   Fetch cur_num into x;                                    -- D
   pcnt := 0;
   WHILE cur_num%found Loop                                 -- D
        pcnt := pcnt + 1;
        FETCH cur_num into x;
   END LOOP;
   DBMS_OUTPUT.PUT_LINE ( 'Number of rows in batch are ' || TO_CHAR(pcnt));
        close cur_num;
   OPEN cur_num  --E
   FOR Select coursecode
        from course;
Fetch cur_num into X;
   ccnt := 0;
   WHILE cur_num%found Loop
        ccnt := ccnt +1;
        Fetch cur_num into X;
   END LOOP;
   DBMS_OUTPUT.PUT_LINE ('Number of rows in course are ' || TO_CHAR(ccnt));
   CLOSE cur_num; --F
end;
/
```

The output of Listing 24.35 is as follows:

```
Number of rows in batch are 5
Number of rows in course are 2

PL/SQL procedure successfully completed
```

In the preceding output, a cursor variable is created that requires two steps. The first step is to declare type of cursor type rows and second step is to declare variable of that type. The syntax for the type declaration is as follows:

```
Type cursortypename is REF cursor
   RETURN return_type;
```

In the preceding syntax, `cursortypename` is any valid object name. `RETURN_TYPE` defines the type of row a cursor can store. It must be a record or a `rowtype` of a database table. The following code snippet shows the valid declaration of cursor type rows:

```
Declare
   type batchcurtype is Ref cursor
        return batch%rowtype;
```

The following code snippet shows the cursor, which holds the data of one row in the batch table:

```
batch_rec batch%rowtype;                                   --1
Type batchcurtype is REF Cursor
   RETURN batch_rec;
```

In the preceding code snippet, the first statement defines the record of the type row of the batch table and then the record is used to define the data type cursor, as shown in the following code snippet:

```
                                                  --cursor data type
   Type batch_rec is Record
   (Batchcode number(5),
```

```
    startingdate date);                          --2
    Type batchcurtype IS REF cursor
         RETURN batch_rec;
```

The following points define the preceding code snippet:

- Statement 2 defines the record explicitly having fields `batchcode` and `startingdate`
- The record is used to define cursor variable type
- After declaring the proper datatypes of cursor, the cursor variable is declared, as shown in the following code snippet:

```
batchcur batchcurtype;
```

- The cursor variable types can be declared in any PL/SQL block, subprogram, or package.

NOTE

The cursor variables cannot be declared in the package. They do not have persistent similar to package variables.

- The cursor variables are similar to pointers of C or Pascal. Pointers hold the address of object, instead of the value of object. When a cursor variable is declared, it is the pointer that is created, and not the object.
- In PL/SQL, a pointer is declared as `REF X`, which is interpreted as a pointer with reference to the object X. Therefore, a cursor variable has the datatype `REF CURSOR`. When multirow query has to be processed, Oracle opens an unnamed area for processing the information. To access information in that unnamed area, either explicit cursor is used, which names such an area or cursor variable is used that has address to such an area. A cursor variable can point to any such area, which stores the result of queries.
- Cursor variables allow sharing of resultset generated by the query. Since, the work area in which the resultset is stored is not owned by the client or server, they can share a pointer to process the information in that work area. Therefore, you can process certain rows from the server-side and certain rows from the client-side. The work area remains accessible as long as the cursor variable points to it.

NOTE

Resultset is a set of rows selected by query.

- Cursor variables follow general scoping rules. When the block in which the cursor variable is terminated, life of a variable also ends.

Weakly Typed ***Cursor***

When a return type is not mentioned, the cursor is called as a weakly typed cursor. The following code snippet shows an example of the weakly typed cursor:

```
DECLARE
   Type batch_cur IS REF CURSOR RETURN batch%rowtype;
   Type wk_cur IS REF CURSOR;
```

In the preceding code snippet, the `batch_cur` is a strongly typed cursor, because the return type is associated with the cursor. On the other hand, `wk_cur` is a weakly typed cursor, because no datatype is associated with the cursor. Any query can be associated with the weakly typed cursor. In case of a strongly typed cursor, only type compatible queries are associated. The weakly type cursor is more flexible but more error prone.

Listing 24.36 shows the code to use cursor variables:

Listing 24.36: Using cursor Variables

```
declare
        type rec_type is record
         (code number);

   Type cur_num_type is
   ref cursor ;                                    --A
```

```
    cur_num cur_num_type;                                        --B
    x   rec_type;
    pcnt  number;
    ccnt  number;
begin
    Open cur_num
    FOR select batchcode
          from batch;                                            -- C
    Fetch cur_num into x;                                        -- D
    pcnt := 0;
    WHILE cur_num%found Loop                                     -- D
          pcnt := pcnt + 1;
          FETCH cur_num into x;
    END LOOP;
    DBMS_OUTPUT.PUT_LINE ( 'Number of rows in batch are ' || TO_CHAR(pcnt));
         close cur_num;
    OPEN cur_num                                                 --E
    FOR Select coursecode
          from course;
Fetch cur_num into X;
    ccnt := 0;
    WHILE cur_num%found Loop
          ccnt := ccnt +1;
          Fetch cur_num into X;
    END LOOP;
    DBMS_OUTPUT.PUT_LINE ('Number of rows in course are ' || TO_CHAR(ccnt));
    CLOSE cur_num;                                               --F
end;
/
```

Listing 24.36 can be explained as follows:

- The statement `OPEN.....FOR` associates a query with the cursor variable and its syntax is as follows:

```
OPEN cursorvariablename
FOR Select statement;
```

- You cannot pass the parameters in the `OPEN.....FOR` statement. Similarly, the select statement should not use the `FOR UPDATE` clause. The query can refer PL/SQL variables, parameters, and functions.
- The `OPEN.....FOR` statement opens the same cursor variable for a different query. When the same cursor variable opens the new query, the previous query is lost. When normal cursor is opened or is already opened, the exception, `CURSOR_ALREADY_OPEN` is raised. Such is not the case with cursor variable.

The output of Listing 24.36 is as follows:

```
Number of rows in batch are 5
Number of rows in course are 2

PL/SQL procedure successfully completed
```

- The following code snippet shows an example to explain how the cursor variable is used to reduce the code:

```
declare
type rectype is record -c defines record type
(
 rn number,
 name varchar2(30),
 p number,
 c number,
```

```
    m number
    );
   z rectype; --d  defines variable of record type
   type curtype  is  ref cursor return rectype; --a define cursor data type
   c1 curtype; --b define variable of cursor type

   status number:=2;

   begin
    if(status=1) then
      open c1 for  --4
      select rn,name,p,c,m
      from pcm
      order by p;
    end if;
    if(status=2) then
      open c1 for  --4
      select rn,name,p,c,m
      from pcm
      order by c;
    end if;
    if(status=3) then
      open c1 for  --4
      select rn,name,p,c,m
      from pcm
      order by m;
    end if;
    fetch c1 into z; --2
    while(c1%found) loop  --3
      dbms_output.put_line(rpad(z.rn,2) ||' '||rpad(z.name,30)||' '||z.p||' '||z.c||'
     '||z.m); --4
      fetch c1 into z; --5
     end loop;--6
    close c1; --7
   end;
   /
```

In the preceding code snippet, statements marked by 2,3,4,5,6,7 defines processing on cursor data. Value of status defines which query is binded to the cursor. Thus, by changing status you can change data for processing. This is very useful when you are having similar processing but data is different.

Opening a *Cursor* Variable in Stored Procedure

You can write a stored procedure for opening a cursor variable that is passed as a formal parameter. The parameter type must be of the `IN OUT` type.

Listing 24.37 shows the code to open a cursor variable in a package:

Listing 24.37: Opening a Cursor Variable in a Package

```
   create or replace package batch_data as
         type batch_curtype is
         ref cursor return batch%rowtype;
         procedure open_batch( batchcur in out batch_curtype);
   end batch_data;
   /
   create or replace package body batch_data as
```

```
.        procedure open_batch (batchcur in out batch_curtype) is
         begin
      open batchcur
      for select *
               from batch;
         end open_batch;
   end batch_data;
   /
```

The output of Listing 24.37 is as follows:

```
Package created
Package body created
```

Listing 24.38 shows the code to open a cursor variable in a package to display batch codes:

Listing 24.38: Opening a Cursor Variable in a Package to Display Batch Codes

```
declare
   x batch_data.batch_curtype ;
   z batch%rowtype;
begin
   batch_data.open_batch(x);
   loop
         fetch x into z;
         exit when x%notfound;
         dbms_output.put_line('value of batchcode '||z.batchcode);
   end loop;
   close x;
end;
/
```

The output of Listing 24.38 is as follows:

```
value of batchcode 20002
value of batchcode 10002
value of batchcode 10001
value of batchcode 10003
value of batchcode 20001

PL/SQL procedure successfully completed
```

You can write a standalone procedure to open a cursor. The cursor data type must be declared in some package. For example, the type declaration is in package `batchdata`, and it is used in the procedure `OPEN_BATCH_CUR`, as shown in the following code snippet:

```
CREATE PACKAGE batchdata AS
      TYPE batch_curtype is
      REF CURSOR RETURN batch%rowtype;
      .............
END batchdata;

CREATE PROCEDURE open_batch_cur ( X IN OUT batch_data.batch_curtype) AS
begin
   OPEN X FOR select * from batch;
end;
/
```

Listing 24.39 shows the code to take some parameter that can change the type of query:

Listing 24.39: Taking Some Parameter that can Change the Type of Query

```
create or replace procedure open_batch_cur (x in out batch_data.batch_curtype,
  ch in number) as
begin
  if ch = 1 then
        open x for select *
                    from batch
                    where coursecode =10;
  elsif ch = 2 then
        open x for select *
        from batch
        where startingdate > '01-nov-1998';
  end if;
end;
/
```

In Listing 24.39, both the queries are having different where conditions but the same return type. The code in Listing 24.39 has two queries, which are as follows:

```
1) open x for select *
   from batch
   where coursecode =10;
```

```
2) OPEN X for Select *
   FROM batch
   WHERE startingdate > '01-NOV-1998';
```

The `WHERE` conditions of these queries is different, but their return types are same.

The output of Listing 24.39 is as follows:

```
Procedure created
```

Listing 24.40 shows the code to use weak type declaration to bind queries having different datatypes:

Listing 24.40: Using Weak Type Declaration to Bind Queries having Different Datatypes

```
create or replace package gen_batch_data as
  type generic_cur is ref cursor;
end gen_batch_data;
/
create or replace procedure open_batch_cur( x in out gen_batch_data.generic_cur,
                                            ch in number ) as
begin
  if ch = 1 then
        open x for select batchcode,coursecode
                    from batch;
  elsif  ch = 2 then
        open x for select batchcode,netincome
                    from batch;
  end if;
end;
/
```

The output of Listing 24.40 is as follows:

```
Procedure created
```

The weak type declaration gives more flexibility, but the fields should be referred correctly after opening the cursor; otherwise, an error is returned.

Listing 24.41 shows the code to use procedure:

Listing 24.41: Using Procedure

```
declare
   bcode batch.batchcode%type;
   netincome batch.netincome%type;
   code batch.coursecode%type;
   X gen_batch_data.generic_cur;
   ch number;
begin
   ch := 2;
   open_batch_cur( X, ch);
                                 --fetch X into bcode, ccode;     Error
         loop
         fetch x into bcode,netincome;
         exit when x%notfound;
         dbms_output.put_line('batch is '||bcode);
         end loop;
         close x;
end;
/
```

In Listing 24.41, statements for `ch = 2` the query, which is binded, is as follows:

```
select batchcode,netincome
from batch;
```

In the `fetch` statement, data is fetched into the variables having compatible data types.

The output of Listing 24.41 is as follows:

```
batch is 20002
batch is 10002
batch is 10001
batch is 10003
batch is 20001

PL/SQL procedure successfully completed
```

The preceding output shows the result of statements executed in Listing 24.41.

NOTE

A programmer has to ensure that operations are done correctly; otherwise, runtime errors are generated.

Let's learn how to fetch data from cursor.

Fetching Data from **Cursor**

Similar to a cursor, data is fetched using the cursor variable by the `FETCH` statement. The syntax of the `FETCH` statement is as follows:

```
FETCH <CURSOR varname>
INTO <variable List>
```

In the syntax of the fetch statement, variable list should have compatible variables as opened cursor.

Similar to a cursor, rows in the resultset are determined only at the time the cursor is opened. In case, the set of rows is to be changed, the cursor must be reopened.

In the case of weak type declaration, the fetch statement should be used properly. If the choice is `1`, then the statement should be written, as shown in the following code snippet:

```
Fetch X into bcode, ccode;
```

If the choice is 2, the fetch statement should be written, as shown in the following code snippet:

```
Fetch X into bcode, netincome;
```

If a variable is having non-compatible datatype, then an error occurs. In case of strong type, the error occurs at compile time, while for the weak type the error occurs at runtime. In case of weak type, the exception, ROWTYPE_MISMATCH is generated.

If the exception is properly trapped and the fetch statement is executed with proper datatypes, then no rows are lost. If the procedure is used for fetching the cursor, then the variable should have IN declaration. If the procedure is opening and fetching rows, then it should have IN OUT declaration.

When the fetch operation is done on a not opened cursor or closed cursor, the exception, INVALID_CURSOR is raised.

*Closing the **Cursor***

When the cursor work is finished, the cursor is closed using the statement, as shown in the following code snippet:

```
close <cursor varname>
```

In case, the number of cursors opened goes above the limit MAX_CURSOR_OPEN, Oracle may generate an error. When a cursor is reopened, the previous query is automatically lost.

When an attempt is made to close an already closed cursor or not opened cursor then an exception, INVALID_CURSOR, is raised.

*Reducing Network Traffic by using **Cursor** Variables*

You can reduce the network traffic by grouping multiple OPEN.....FOR statements.

Listing 24.42 shows the code to open three cursors:

Listing 24.42: Opening Three Cursors

```
declare
type curtype is ref cursor;
batch_cur curtype;
course_cur curtype;
enquiry_cur curtype;
begin
   open  batch_cur for
          select * from batch;
   open  course_cur for
                 select * from course;
   open  enquiry_cur for
                 select * from enquiry;
end;
/
```

The output of Listing 24.42 is as follows:

```
PL/SQL procedure successfully completed
```

If issued from the client side, the PL/SQL block opens the preceding cursor in a single round trip. On the client side, the cursor variables can be used to open a cursor. After the cursor operations are over, the cursor is closed.

Listing 24.43 shows the code to close a cursor

Listing 24.43: Closing a Cursor

```
declare
type curtype is ref cursor;
batch_cur curtype;
course_cur curtype;
```

```
enquiry_cur curtype;
begin
   open  batch_cur for
         select * from batch;
   open  course_cur for
              select * from course;
   open  enquiry_cur for
              select * from enquiry;
   close batch_cur;
   close  course_cur;
   close enquiry_cur;
end;
```

The output of Listing 24.43 is as follows:

```
PL/SQL procedure successfully completed
```

Listing 24.44 shows the code to use cursor variable:

Listing 24.44: Using the Cursor Variable

```
declare
   type curtype is ref cursor;
   c1 curtype;
   z emp_company%rowtype;
   status number:=1;
begin
   if (status=1) then
         open c1 for
         select *
         from emp_company
         where cname='acc'
         order by salary;
   else
         open c1 for
         select *
         from emp_company
         where cname='acc'
         order by ename;
   end if;
   fetch c1 into z;                                             --A
   while(c1%found) loop
         dbms_output.put_line
         (' name '||z.ename||' sal '||to_char(z.salary));
         fetch c1 into z;
   end loop;
   close c1;                                                    --B
end;
```

In Listing 24.44, the code from A to B is constant. Depending on the type of query, the cursor is opened and data is processed. Thus, a lot of coding is reduced. The output row of cursor can be taken in a variable, and the type declared using the table%ROWTYPE or record type.

The output of Listing 24.44 is as follows:

```
NAME Amol SAL 1000
NAME Anil SAL 1500
NAME Ajay SAL 8000

PL/SQL procedure successfully completed
```

Listing 24.45 shows the code to use variables to fetch value from cursor:

Listing 24.45: Using Variables to Fetch Value from Cursor

```
declare
   type curtype is ref cursor;
   c1 curtype;
   status number:=1;
   x varchar2(20);                                          --emp_company.ename%type;
   y number;
begin
   if (status=1) then
         open c1 for
         select ename,salary
         from emp_company
         where cname='acc'
         order by salary;
   else
         open c1 for
         select ename,salary
         from emp_company
         where cname='acc'
         order by ename;
   end if;
   fetch c1 into x,y;
   while(c1%found) loop
         dbms_output.put_line
         (' name '||x||' sal '||to_char(y));
         fetch c1 into x,y;
   end loop;
   close c1;
end;
```

The output of Listing 24.45 is as follows:

```
NAME Amol SAL 1000
NAME Anil SAL 1500
NAME Ajay SAL 8000

PL/SQL procedure successfully completed
```

Listing 24.46 shows the code to use record type to fetch values from cursor:

Listing 24.46: Using Record Type to Fetch Values from Cursor

```
declare
   type emprec is record
   (ename varchar2(20),
   salary number);
   type curtype is ref cursor;
   c1 curtype;
   z emprec;                        --cursor row variable using record type
   status number:=1;
begin
   if (status=1) then
         open c1 for
         select ename,salary
         from emp_company
```

```
        where cname='acc'
        order by salary;
    else
        open c1 for
        select ename,salary
        from emp_company
        where cname='acc'
        order by ename;
    end if;
    fetch c1 into z;
    while(c1%found) loop
        dbms_output.put_line
        (' name '||z.ename||' sal '||to_char(z.salary));
        fetch c1 into z;
    end loop;
    close c1;
end;
```

The output of Listing 24.46 is as follows:

```
Name Amol SAL 1000
NAME Anil SAL 1500
NAME Ajay SAL 8000

PL/SQL procedure successfully completed
```

Let's learn about the exception in cursor.

Exception in **Cursor**

The cursor variable can be assigned to another variable having the same data type, if both the variables are strongly typed.

Listing 24.47 shows the code to assign cursor variable to another variable:

Listing 24.47: Assigning Cursor Variable to Another Variable

```
declare
   type batch1 is ref cursor
   return batch%rowtype;
   type batch2 is ref cursor
   return batch%rowtype;
   x batch1;
   y batch1;
   z batch2;
begin
   x := y ;                                        --A
   z := x ;                                        --B; will throw error
end;
```

In Listing 24.47, statement A is a legal statement and statement B is not legal because both x and z have different data types, even though they are having the same return types. So, statement B raises the exception.

The output of Listing 24.47 is as follows:

```
ERROR at line 11:
ORA-06550: line 11, column 7:
PLS-00382: expression is of wrong type
ORA-06550: line 11, column 2:
PL/SQL: Statement ignored
```

If you want both the variables to point to the same work area, the assignment operation should be done after the query is bound.

Listing 24.48 shows the code to use the assignment operator:

Listing 24.48: Using the Assignment Operator

```
declare
   type batch1 is ref cursor return batch%row type;
   x  batch1;
   r  batch%rowtype;
   y  batch1;
begin
   y := x;
                                          --the above statement is useless because x
                                          --is not pointing to any work area.
   open x for select *
                    from batch;
   fetch x into r;
                                          -- fetch first row from cursor
   fetch y into r;
                                          -- raise exception invalid cursor
exception
when invalid_cursor then
   y := x;
   fetch y into r;
                                          -- fetches record from cursor
   open y for select *
   from batch;
                                          --it reuses work area for another query
   fetch x into r;
end;
```

Since both x and y point to the same query area, the code in Listing 24.48 fetches the first row from the old batch.

The output of Listing 24.48 is as follows:

```
PL/SQL procedure successfully completed
```

When a parameter having a different datatypes is passed to a procedure, an exception, ROWTYPE_MISMATCH is raised.

Listing 24.49: Passing a parameter with different datatypes to a procedure:

Listing 24.49: Passing a Parameter with Different Datatypes to a Procedure

```
declare
   type batchcur is ref cursor
   return  batch%rowtype;
   type coursecur is ref cursor
   return course%rowtype;
   x batchcur;
   y coursecur;
   procedure open_batch (batchcursor in out batchcur) is
   begin
         open batchcursor for select * from batch;
   end;
begin
   open_batch (y);                                 -- it raises exception
end;
/
```

The output of Listing 24.49 is as follows:

```
ERROR at line 13:
ORA-06550: line 13, column 2:
PLS-00306: wrong number or types of arguments in call to 'OPEN_BATCH'
ORA-06550: line 13, column 2:
PL/SQL: Statement ignored
```

In the preceding output, a row type mismatch occurs, because `Y` does not have a datatype as formal parameter.

Exceptions due to Aliasing

Exceptions may arise during aliasing. Aliasing occurs when some work area is referred by more than one variable.

Listing 24.50 shows the code to performing aliasing:

Listing 24.50: Performing Aliasing

```
declare
   type batchcur is ref cursor
   return batch%rowtype;
   x batchcur;
   r batch%rowtype;
   y batchcur;
begin
   open x for select * from batch;
   fetch x into r;                          -- first row is fetched
   y := x;
   fetch y into r;                          -- second row is fetched
   close y;                                 -- cursor area is closed
            fetch x into r;                 -- raises exception
                                            -- invalid_cursor


end;
```

The output of Listing 24.50 is as follows:

```
declare
*
ERROR at line 1:
ORA-01001: invalid cursor
ORA-06512: at line 13
```

Aliasing also occurs when the same actual parameters are passed to a procedure twice, and both formal parameters are passed into `IN` parameters.

Listing 24.51 shows the code to understand the cursor in procedure:

Listing 24.51: Understanding the Procedure

```
create or replace procedure opencur(c1 in out batch_data.batch_curtype, c2 in
   out batch_data.batch_curtype) is
begin
   open c1 for select *
                      from batch
                      where coursecode = 10;
   open c2 for select *
                    from batch
                    where coursecode = 20;
end;
```

The output of Listing 24.51 is as follows:

```
Procedure created
```

Listing 24.52 shows the code to call the procedure:

Listing 24.52: Calling the Procedure

```
declare
   x batch_data.batch_curtype ;
   z batch%rowtype;
begin
   opencur(x,x);
   loop
          fetch x into z;
          exit when x%notfound;
          dbms_output.put_line('value of batchcode '||z.batchcode);
   end loop;
   close x;
end;
/
```

Listing 24.52 gives an indeterminate result.

The output of Listing 24.52 is as follows:

```
value of batchcode 20002

PL/SQL procedure successfully completed
```

Let's lean about the restrictions on cursor variables.

Restrictions on **Cursor** Variables

The following are the restrictions on cursor variables:

- The cursor `FOR.....LOOP.....END LOOP` cannot be used for cursor variable.
- Cursor variables cannot be used in dynamic SQL.
- Cursor variable cannot be used in package, because it does not have a persistent state.
- The column in the table cannot have the `REF CURSOR` datatype.
- The nested table, array, and index by table cannot store the value of cursor variable.
- Nulls cannot be assigned to cursor variables.
- The query associated with cursor variable cannot have `FOR UPDATE` clause.
- Cursor variable cannot be compared for equality, inequality, or nullity.
- Remote procedures cannot accept cursor variables. So, passing the value of cursor variable from one server to another is not possible.
- If the cursor host variable is passed to PL/SQL fetching, then using it from server side is not possible unless both, open and fetch, are in server call.

The following code snippet shows an invalid way of using cursor:

```
Declare
   Type curtype is Ref cursor
   return batch%row type;
   curvar curtype;
   currec batch%rowtype;
Begin
   ..........
   For currec In curvar loop
        .................                        -- Invalid loop
```

Let's learn about the use of the cursor in package.

Use of **Cursor** in Package

The cursor specification is declared in the package specification, while its implementation can be defined in the body of the package.

Listing 24.53 shows the code to create the packaged specifications for the batchcur cursor:

Listing 24.53: Creating the Packaged Specifications for the batchcur Cursor

```
create or replace package batch_data as
      type batch_curtype is
      ref cursor return batch%rowtype;
      procedure open_batch( batchcur in out batch_curtype);
      cursor x is select * from batch;   --allowed
                                                   --y batch_curtype; not allowed
      function give_one_row return batch%rowtype;

end batch_data;
/
```

The following points define the code in Listing 24.53:

- The cursor is referred as `packagename.cursorname`
- The program also defines cursor `Y` that is not visible outside, i.e. user cannot use it.
- The function `GIVE_ONE_ROW` returns only one row at a time

The output of Listing 24.53 is as follows:

```
Package created
```

Listing 24.54 shows the code to create or replace the package body of batch_data

Listing 24.54: Creating or Replacing Package Body batch_data

```
cursor y is select * from batch;
procedure open_batch (batchcur in out batch_curtype) is
begin
   open batchcur
   for select *
            from batch;
      end open_batch;
      function give_one_row return batch%rowtype is
      z batch%rowtype;
      begin
         fetch x into z;
         if x%notfound then
                  close x;
                  open x;
         else
                  return z;
         end if;
      end;
   begin     --initialization
         open x;
end batch_data;
```

The output of Listing 24.54 is as follows:

```
PL/SQL procedure successfully completed
```

Listing 24.55 shows the code to use cursors in packages to display batchcodes:

Listing 24.55: Using Cursors in Packages to Display Batchcodes

```
declare
  z batch%rowtype;
begin
   z := batch_data.give_one_row;
   dbms_output.put_line('batchcode '||z.batchcode);
   z := batch_data.give_one_row;
   dbms_output.put_line('batchcode '||z.batchcode);
end;
/
```

The output of Listing 24.55 is as follows:

```
batchcode 20002
batchcode 10002

PL/SQL procedure successfully completed
```

The packaged cursor is used, as shown in the following code snippet:

```
Open batch_data.X;
  .............
Close batch_data.X;
```

Let's learn about cursor expressions.

Cursor Expressions

The cursor expression returns the cursor specified by the cursor query. The syntax of cursor query is as follows:

```
CURSOR(subquery).
```

This processes related rows of multiple tables. The cursor expression returns the cursor as a column that can be processed using loop.

Listing 24.56 shows the code to fetch the cursor column in target refcursor variable:

Listing 24.56: Fetching the Cursor Column in Target refcursor Variable

```
declare
   type refcursor is ref cursor;
   cursor c1 is
   select c.coursename,
   cursor(select b.batchcode
   from batch b where b.coursecode=c.coursecode) bcode
   from course c;
   b_cur refcursor;
   coursename course.coursename%type;
   batchcode batch.batchcode%type;

begin
   open c1;
   loop                                                  --for c1
        fetch c1 into coursename, b_cur;
        exit when c1%notfound;
        dbms_output.put_line('coursename '||coursename);
        loop                                             -- for b_cur
               fetch b_cur into batchcode; -- no need to open
               exit when b_cur%notfound;
```

```
                dbms_output.put_line('batchcode '||batchcode);
        end loop;                                       --of b_cur

    end loop;                                           -- end of c1
    close c1;
  end;
```

In Listing 24.56, cursor `c1` is called as parent cursor. The inner cursor `bcode` automatically opens, when the parent row is fetched. You have to close only the parent cursor.

The output of Listing 24.56 is as follows:

```
coursename ORACLE
batchcode 10002
batchcode 10001
batchcode 10003
coursename JAVA
batchcode 20002

PL/SQL procedure successfully completed
```

Let's learn about DDL and dynamic SQL.

DDL and Dynamic SQL

PL/SQL does not support DDL or dynamic SQL directly, but the user can issue such statements using the `DBMS_SQL` package.

When a PL/SQL program is submitted, first it is compiled and then executed. The variable types and reference to database objects are resolved at compile time, by checking the definitions stored in the data dictionary. The program variables are assigned strong addresses by the compiler so that Oracle can look for the address at runtime. This process is called as binding. If the binding is done at the compile time, it is called as static or early binding. It has more execution efficiency because all look up processes are done at compile time. The compiler produces machine-readable code, which is just executed.

If binding is done at runtime, then it is called as dynamic or late binding. Late binding has more flexibility, because the name of the object is decided at runtime. However, it is not efficient because the look up process is done at runtime or execution time.

The early binding of PL/SQL makes it efficient, but imposes certain restrictions on PL/SQL code. For example, you write a procedure, which creates a table as shown in the following code snippet:

```
create procedure crtable (tname in varchar2) as
  create table tname(batchcode ...);
end;
```

The procedure in the preceding code snippet cannot be complied because the name of the table is unknown when the procedure is complied. To overcome the limitation of preceding code snippet, the package `DBMS_SQL` is used.

Listing 24.57 shows the code to use the package DBMS_SQL:

Listing 24.57: Using the Package DBMS_SQL

```
                                --Procedure for dropping table
                                --Procedure for dropping table
create or replace procedure drtable (tname in varchar2) as
  cursorid integer;
begin
  /* open new cursor and retun it's cursor id*/
  cursorid := dbms_sql.open_cursor;
  /* parse and execute dynamic sql statment */
```

```
    dbms_sql.parse (cursorid, 'drop table' || tname, dbms_sql.native);
    /* close cursor */
    dbms_sql.close_cursor(cursorid);
       exception
       when others then
                 dbms_sql.close_cursor (cursorid);
end drtable;
/
```

The output of Listing 24.57 is as follows:

```
Procedure created
```

After learning about DDL and dynamic SQL, let's learn about transaction control statements.

Transaction Control Statements

The transaction processing in Oracle is centered around two concepts, session and transaction. A session is created when a user connects to Oracle, and is discontinued when a user disconnects from Oracle. Oracle allows many sessions to work simultaneously and store computer rescues. To have multiple sessions, Oracle has to control concurrency, i.e. maintain data integrity when multiple sessions access the same data at the same time.

For example, consider a railway reservation system where a table is maintained to show the availability of reservations, as shown in Table 24.2:

Table 24.2: Railway Reservation Table

Train Resv		
Txcno	**Date**	**AvRes**
GT	1-DEC-98	5
TN	1-DEC-98	3

Suppose multiple terminals are doing reservations for any train, and two customers Cl and C2 (from different terminals) want reservations 4 and 3, respectively, for GT on 1-DEC-98. The operators from both these terminals see that the adequate reservations are available and perform the reservation. This makes the data inconsistent, because the available reservations were 5 but reservations done are 7.

Oracle controls the concurrency using the concept of locking. Lock gives temporary ownership of the resource to the user. For example, if a user updates a row in a table, then, before updating, Oracle places lock on that row. If another user tries to update the same row `R1`, then Oracle also attempts to put lock on that row `R1`. Since `R1` is already locked, the second attempt fails. Locking is done implicitly; however, the user can also make explicit locking.

Locking could result in a dead lock also, i.e. locking is done in such a way that users cannot proceed. For example, user `u1` has locked free row `R1` and proceeds to lock the row `R2`. Meanwhile, user `u2` has already locked the row `R2` and proceeds to lock row `R1`. In this case, both the users wait for each other and this condition is called a deadlock. Deadlock can be avoided by proper ordering of requests.

Oracle also ensures the read consistent view of data for the query. Thus, the query will see the data, which is present at that time. When the query begins execution and the data gets updated by another user then the query will always fetch data which is present when query begun its execution. The following code snippet shows the query issued by a user:

```
Update enquiry
Set enrollstatus = 'Y'
Where Enrollstatus = 'P';
```

Suppose, the table enquiry has 10 blocks and the update statement requires reading and updating rows of 10 blocks. The SQL statement is submitted and by the time it completely executes, another user changes the data of block 9. The first user's query still refers to the old data of block, i.e. the data, which was present when the query was submitted. Oracle uses the `Rollback` segment to record the old data of the `update` statement. This data is used to provide read consistent view of the data.

Oracle uses transaction to group multiple SQL statements into single logical unit of work.

Listing 24.58 shows the code to transfer Rs.100 from Sunil's account to Anil's account:

Listing 24.58: Transferring Rs.100 from Sunil's Account to Anil's Account

```
                                    --A
update deposit
set amount = amount +100
where cname = 'Anil';
                                    --B
update deposit
set amount = amount -100
where cname= 'Sunil';
                                    --C
```

Suppose both Anil and Sunil have deposited the amount of Rs.1000. Table 24.3 lists the data at point A, B, and C:

Table 24.3: Deposited Amount

	Anil	Sunil
A	1000	1000
B	1100	1000
C	1100	900

The data at A and C represents consistent data. To have consistent data, the effect of the statements should be full or null. When it is null, the database state is A, and when it is full, the database state is C. Both are at consistent states. To have this effect, we will place the `COMMIT` statement before and after the update statement.

Listing 24.59 shows the code to place the COMMIT statement before and after update statements:

Listing 24.59: Placing the COMMIT Statement before and after Update Statements

```
commit;
Update deposit set amount= amount +100
where customername  = 'ANIL';
Update deposit Set amount = amount - 100
where customername  = 'SUNIL';
commit;
```

The output of Listing 24.59 is as follows:

```
Commit complete
1 row updated
1 row updated
Commit complete
```

The statements between two successive commits constitute a transaction. A transaction is the single logical unit of work. The effect of transaction is full or null. This property of transaction is called as atomicity of transaction.

A transaction starts when you submit the first SQL statement after connecting to Oracle and ends when you issue a `COMMIT` statement. `COMMIT` is also issued implicitly when you submit the DDL statement, such as `CREATE TABLE`, `DROP TABLE` OR `ALTER TABLE`. The `COMMIT` statement makes changes permanent (done after the last commit). When a user commits data, only the other users see the changed data.

The `COMMIT` statement releases all locks, which comprises rowlocks and table blocks. You can use comment with commit. It is specially used in distributed transactions.

You can also use comment as commit in doubt transaction. The transaction id and comment text is stored in the data dictionary. The text can be retrieved in case of failure in distributed database.

Rollback *Statement*

Rollbacks are used to undo changes, which are made during a transaction. Rollbacks also end the current transaction. You can issue a statement, as shown in the following code snippet:

```
delete batch;
```

In the preceding code snippet, the given statement deletes all the rows. You require data of the `batch` table as an afterthought. In this case, you can undo the changes by using rollback, as shown in the following code snippet:

```
rollback;
```

`ROLLBACK` undoes all changes made up to the last commit. `ROLLBACK` is also used to make corrective action in case of failure in processing the current transaction.

Suppose a user tries to insert a row in the table `course` and later realizes that such course was already present. In that case, he can issue rollback to undo the insertion.

Listing 24.60 shows the code to use ROLLBACK:

Listing 24.60: Using ROLLBACK

```
begin
   insert into course
   values ( ....);
   if check_duplicate then
         rollback;
   end if;
end;
```

In Listing24.60, `CHECK_DUPLICATE` is a user defined function to check for similar courses.

Statement ***ROLLBACK***

Statement `ROLLBACK` is used to impose atomicity on statement. Atomicity at the statement level means that the affect of statement is either full or null. When any DML statement is issued, Oracle issues implicit save point. Save point is used for storing the inter-immediate state of the database, which can be restored at a later point of time (detail explanation is in next section). In case of failure of a DML statement, the state prior to DML statement is restored.

The following code snippet shows the statement in a transaction issued by a user:

```
Insert into  ......                        --A
.............                              --C
update enrollment
Set .......
where batchcode = '10001';                 --B
```

The preceding code snippet can be defined as follows:

- Statement A is successfully executed and statement B is taken for execution.
- Statement B intends to modify some of the rows in the enrollment table. During execution, 5 rows are modified but the 6th row shows some constraint violation. In such a case, Oracle makes save point prior to the start of DML statement B.
- At point C, 5 rows are updated and the database state is restored. The work done up to C is retained; only the partial affect of statement B is undone.

Therefore, statement level atomicity ensures definiteness for execution of the SQL statement, i.e. effect of statement is full or null. It is not ambiguous.

Savepoint

Savepoint is used to store intermediate state in a transaction. It allows the user to undo a part of transaction. Suppose a user has to issue some statements, as shown in the following code snippet:

```
Insert into .........          --A
Delete from ..........         --B
Update ..........              --C
Update ..........              --D
```

The user has issued statements A, B, and C, and he is sure about the effect of those statements. He is unsure about the outcome of statement D. To save data, the user restores it, as shown in Listing 24.61:

Listing 24.61: Restoring Data

```
Insert into ............       -- A
Delete from ..........         -- B
Update ............            -- C
Savepoint  SA;
Update ...........             -- D
if not_proper_update then
  rollback to SA;
end if;
```

In the preceding code snippet, if the updation is not proper, the state after C is restored and a suitable update is given. The part of transaction, i.e. statement D, is undone.

NOTE

User can issue limited number of savepoints in a session.

Savepoint is an undeclared identifier. All the savepoints, which are issued after the savepoint, are erased when the user rollbacks to the specified savepoint. The following code snippet shows an example of savepoint and rollback:

```
Insert .........               --A
Savepoint A;
Insert .........               --N
Savepoint B;
Insert .........               --L
Savepoint C;
............
Rollback to B;                 --X
...........
Rollback to A;                 --Y
...........
Rollback to C;                 --Z
```

When a user `ROLLBACKS` to savepoint `B`, the affect of statement `L` is undone and the savepoint `C` is erased. In that case, it is legal to rollback to provision save point, i.e. `A` but not to savepoint `C`. Therefore, the statement `Y` is valid, but statement `Z` is invalid.

NOTE

In the case of simple ROLLBACK and COMMIT ALL, the savepoints are erased.

When you use the same identifier, which is used earlier again in a savepoint, the savepoint moves from its old position to the current position. Consider the code provided in the following code snippet:

```
Savepoint SA;                  --A
Insert into .......            --B
Savepoint  SA;                 --C
```

```
Insert into ........                  --D
Rollback to SA;                       --E
```

In case of the preceding code snippet, at the time `ROLLBACKS` is executed, the state at statement `C` is restored, unlike state `A`.

In the case of a recursive program, the savepoint can also be issued when the program is called again. Then the new savepoint is made and when rollback is done, savepoint state is restored to recent the savepoint.

Implicit Savepoint

Oracle issues implicit save point before executing any DML statement. When a statement fails to execute, the database state is restored to savepoint. Therefore, any partial effect made by DML statement is undone. If the stored subprogram raises an unhandled exception, then values of out variables are not updated, and the database work is undone.

Ending of Transactions

It is better to end transactions explicitly using `COMMIT` or `ROLLBACK`. Outcome of the program depends on the environment, if transaction is not explicitly committed or rolled back. For example, in SQL plus, if you do not make `COMMIT` or `ROLLBACK` in the program, the final state depends on the statements used after the program. If you issue any DDL or DCL statement, the changes are committed. Oracle also commits changes, if the user exits normally from the program.

Read Only Transactions

Read only transaction is used to provide the same data for the queries in a transaction. Suppose you have a transaction, as shown in the following code snippet:

```
Select sum (amount) into X
from feepaid;                                 --A
 ...............
Select sum (amount ) into Y
from feepaid;                                 --B
```

In the preceding code snippet, both statements, A and B, refer the same data but at different times. Suppose a user has executed statement A and before he submits the second statement, another user updates the table and commits the data. When the feepaid field is referred second time at statement B, the result is not same since the data has changed. Read only transactions are used to provide the same view of data in a transaction, which is implemented as shown in the following code snippet:

```
Commit;
SET TRANSACTION READ ONLY;                    --C
Select sum (amount)
into X
from feepaid;                                 --A
                ...........
  select sum (amount)
  into Y
  from feepaid;                               --B
  ..........
  Commit;                                     --D
```

In the preceding code snippet, statement C marks the transaction as read only. It should be the first statement in the transaction. The statement A and B returns the same data, irrespective of the updation of table from other sessions. The statement D marks the end of transaction. All the queries return information, which is present at the beginning of the transaction.

Restrictions

There are some restrictions on read only transactions, which are as follows:

- DML statement
- Queries with the FOR UPDATE clause

But you can use SELECT INTO, OPEN, FETCH, CLOSE, LOCK TABLE, COMMIT, and ROLLBACK statement in the read only transaction.

FOR UPDATE Clause

The FOR UPDATE clause is used to lock specific rows of a table before updating rows. By default, the rows are locked when a user attempts to update the row. Consider the statement shown in the following code snippet:

```
update batch
set expectedincome = 1.1 * expectedincome;
```

In the preceding code snippet, when the statement is submitted, the first attempt is made to lock rows, which are being updated.

Listing 24.62 shows the code to lock rows before updation:

Listing 24.62: Locking the Rows before Updation

```
declare
   cursor cl is
   select batchcode, expectedincome from batch
   for update;
   z  cl%rowtype;
begin
   open cl;
   loop
          fetch cl into z;
          exit when cl%notfound;
          update batch
          set expectedincome = 1.1 * expectedincome
          where current of cl;
   end loop;
   close cl;
end;
```

The rows are locked when the cursor is opened and not locked when the rows are fetched. Therefore, if you issue commit while the rows are fetched, then an error is returned. The rows, which are going to be updated, are not available to others, because any of the rows in the set is locked. If another user does not perform the locking, Oracle waits until the rows are available.

The output of Listing 24.62 is as follows:

```
PL/SQL procedure successfully completed
```

If you don't want to wait, then you can use the NOWAIT clause in the FOR UPDATE statement, as shown in Listing 24.63: shows the NOWAIT Clause in the FOR UPDATE Statement

Listing 24.63: Using the NOWAIT Clause in the FOR UPDATE Statement

```
cursor cl is
select batchcode, expectedincome
from batch
for update nowait;
```

If NOWAIT is not specified, then waiting may be indefinite. If a table is remote in the distributed database, then the waiting limit is imposed by the DISTRIBUTED_LOCK_TIMEOUT parameter.

If the error refers to multiple tables using join or Cartesian product, then locking is confined to the table whose column is mentioned in the `FOR UPDATE` clause, as shown in Listing 24.64:

Listing 24.64: Locking batch Table

```
cursor c1 is
select batch.batchcode,batch.expectedincome,
course.coursename From batch, course
where batch.coursecode = course.coursecode
for update of batchcode;
```

The code in Listing 24.64 locks the `batch` table when the cursor is opened.

NOTE

Rows from both the tables get locked if you write the following code:
FOR UPDATE OF batchcode, coursename

Let's learn to explicitly lock a table using the LOCK TABLE statement.

Explicit Locking using ***LOCK TABLE***

You can explicitly lock a table using the `LOCK TABLE` statement. Oracle provides different types of locks with different restrictions. The table locks are released when a user commits the data.

Listing 24.65 shows the code to lock table in ROW SHARE mode:

Listing 24.65: Locking Table in ROW SHARE Mode

```
lock table batch
in row share mode nowait;
```

The output of Listing 24.65 is as follows:

```
Table(s) Locked
```

It allows many users to lock the table, but only one user can place exclusive lock.

NOTE

Any type of lock never stops other users from querying the table and no query places any lock on the table. Different types of locks are discussed in the chapters ahead.

Let's learn about fetching across commit.

Fetching Across ***COMMIT***

If you open a cursor, which is `FOR UPDATE`, then locks are placed on those rows, which are selected by the cursor query. The locks are released when you issue the `COMMIT` statement. When the user executes the next `fetch` statement, he gets an error.

Listing 24.66 shows the code to observe how the code generates an error when the next fetch statement is executed:

Listing 24.66: Observing how the Code Generates an Error when the Next Fetch Statement is Executed

```
declare
   cursor c1 is
   select batchcode,expectedincome
   from batch
   for update;
   z  c1% rowtype;
begin
   open c1;                                          -- A
   fetch c1 into z;                                  -- B
   commit;                                           -- C
```

```
    fetch c1 into z ;
  end;
```

In Listing 24.66, statement A opens the cursor and locks are placed on rows. `COMMIT` at statement C releases locks on the rows. The next fetch statement at D generates the error, fetching across commit.

The output of Listing 24.66 is as follows:

```
Declare
*
ERROR at line 1:
ORA-01002: fetch out of sequence
ORA-06512: at line 11
```

Here:

- Statement A opens the cursor and locks are placed on rows.
- `COMMIT` at statement C releases locks on the rows.
- The next fetch statement at D generates the error 'fetching across commit'.

If you want fetch across commit, then you can use `ROWID` in the update statement instead of `CURRENT OF` clause, as shown in Listing 24.67:

Listing 24.67: Using ROWID, Instead of CURRENT OF in Update Statement

```
Declare
  Cursor c1 is
  select batchcode, expectedincome, rowid
  from batch;
  z c1%rowtype;
begin
  open c1;
  fetch c1 into z;
  update batch
  set netincome=1.1*netincome
  where rowid = z.rowid;
  commit;
  fetch c1 into z;
  close c1;
end;
/
```

In Listing 24.67, rows are not locked when the user opens the cursor. So, another user might update the rows.

The output of Listing 24.67 is as follows:

```
PL/SQL procedure successfully completed
```

To have a consistent view of data of the cursor, the rollback segment is used. This rollback segment is not released, until the cursor is closed. If the rows are very large, then very large rollback tablespace is required. During runtime, there will be allocation of space. This will decrease the speed when many rows are updated. If you commit data after a certain interval, then rollback requirement will be reduced. Listing 24.68 shows the program that requires less rollback segment space:

Listing 24.68: Frequently Committing Data

```
declare
  cursor c1 is
  select batchcode, expectedincome, rowid
  from batch;
  z c1%rowtype;
    cnt number:=0;
begin
```

```
    open c1;
    fetch c1 into z;
       while(c1%found) loop
    update batch
    set netincome=1.1*netincome
    where rowid = z.rowid;
       if(mod(cnt,100)=0) then
    commit;
       end;
       cnt:=cnt+1;
    fetch c1 into z;
       end loop;
    close c1;
 end;
```

Let's learn about size limitation in PL/SQL.

Size Limitation in PL/SQL

PL/SQL compiler limits the number of identifiers, keywords, and operators (these are commonly called as tokens) of one unit, i.e. block, subprogram, and package. When the limit is crossed, Oracle returns an error, program to large.

For a package, the strategy is to divide the package into smaller packages. For the blocks, it is better to divide large blocks into smaller ones. A table or packaged variables can be used to pass the data between the blocks.

Listing 24.69 shows the code to divide a block into two blocks:

Listing 24.69: Dividing a Block into Two Blocks

```
declare
   x  batch.batchcode % type;
   y batch.expectedincome % type;
begin
   x :=  .........
   y :=  .........
   insert into temp
   values ( x,y);
end;

declare
   x batch.batchcode % type;
   y batch.expectedincome% type;
begin
   select batchcode, expectedincome
   into x,y
   from temp
   where ......;
   ............
   update  .........
   set col := x;
end;
```

In Listing 24.69, block is divided into two blocks. In the temporary table temp values of variables are kept. Second block uses values of these variables.

Returning Clause and Single Set Aggregate

You can take output in terms of values and aggregates, using the returning expression of DML statements. The structure of PCM table is given as follows:

```
desc pcm
```

Result:

```
 Name                                      Null?    Type
 ----------------------------------------- -------- ----------------
 RN                                        NOT NULL NUMBER
 P                                         NOT NULL NUMBER
 C                                                  NUMBER
 M                                                  NUMBER
 NAME                                               VARCHAR2(30)
 TOTAL                                              NUMBER
declare
  x number;
  y number;
begin
  insert into pcm values(5, 'suhas',87,96,94)
  returning physics, maths into x,y;
  dbms_output.put_line(x);
  dbms_output.put_line(y);
end;
```

Result:

```
87
94

PL/SQL procedure successfully completed
```

Listing 24.70: Observing how the DML Statement Affects More than One Row and Returns an Error

```
declare
  x number;
  y number;
begin
  update pcm set maths=maths+1 returning physics, maths into x,y;
  dbms_output.put_line(x);
  dbms_output.put_line(y);
end;
/
```

The output of Listing 24.70 is as follows:

```
declare
*
ERROR at line 1:
ORA-01422: exact fetch returns more than requested number of rows
ORA-06512: at line 5
```

In case of update it returns new value:

Suppose data in table PCM is

```
select * from pcm;
```

The output of preceding code snippet is as follows:

```
ROLLNO          NAME           PHYSICS      CHEMISTRY       MATHS
---------       ----------     ----------   ----------      ----------
    1           anil            67           89              76
    2           sunil           89           65              99
    3           ajay            77           95              94
    4           sushil          75           92              91
    5           suhas           87           96              94
```

Listing 24.71 shows the code to return the value of updated row:

Listing 24.71: Returning Value of Updated Row

```
declare
  x number;
  y number;
begin
  update pcm set maths=maths+1 where rollno=1
  returning physics, maths into x,y;
  dbms_output.put_line(x);
  dbms_output.put_line(y);
end;
/
```

The output of Listing 24.71 is as follows:

```
67
79
```

Listing 24.72 shows the code to return the value of deleted row:

Listing 24.72: Returning the Value of Deleted Row

```
declare
  x number;
  y number;
begin
  delete pcm  where rollno=1
  returning physics, maths into x,y;
  dbms_output.put_line(x);
  dbms_output.put_line(y);
end;
```

The output of Listing 24.72 is as follows:

```
67
79
```

When the DML statement affects more than one row, then you can use aggregate function in returning clause, as shown in Listing 24.73:

Listing 24.73: Using Aggregate Function in Returning Clause

```
declare
  x number;
  y number;
begin
  update pcm set maths=maths+1
  returning sum(physics),sum(maths) into x,y;
  dbms_output.put_line(x);
  dbms_output.put_line(y);
end;
/
```

The output of Listing 24.73 is as follows:

```
395
382
```

Using **WITH CHECK OPTION**

You can use `WITH CHECK OPTION` in DML statement to enforce additional constraint on DML operation.

Listing 24.74 shows the code to use WITH CHECK OPTION:

Listing 24.74: Using WITH CHECK OPTION

```
insert into
(select rollno,physics,chemistry,maths,name
from pcm where physics between 1 and 100
with check option)
values(7,120,78,87,'anand');
from pcm where physics between 1 and 100
```

The output of Listing 24.74 is as follows:

```
      *
ERROR at line 3:
ORA-01402: view WITH CHECK OPTION where-clause violation
```

Let's learn about the SQL facilities provided in PL/SQL.

SQL Facility in PL/SQL

Table 24.4 shows the usage of SQL features in PL/SQL:

Table 24.4: Features of PL/SQL

SQL feature in PL/SQL	Description
DML Statements	To manipu'ate data, a user can use `INSERT`, `UPDATE`, `DELETE`, `SELECT`, and `LOCK TABLE` command. The `SELECT` statement without `INTO` cannot be used in PL/SQL body.
Transaction Control Statements	You can use transaction control statements, such as `COMMIT`, `ROLLBACK`, and `SAVEPOINT`. To make a read only transaction, the user can use `SET TRANSACTION` statement. You can explicitly allocate the rollback segment using the `SET ROLLBACK` statement.
SQL Functions	You can use SQL functions, such as `SUBSTR`, `ADD_MONTHS`, etc. in SQL as well as in procedural statements. You can use group functions, such as AVG, MIN, MAX, SUM, COUNT, STDDEV, and VARIANCE in SQL statement, but not in procedural statement.
SQL Pseudocolumns	Pseudocolumns are used to provide certain information. They can be used in SQL statement, but not in procedural statements. Pseudocolumns are not columns, which store any data. PL/SQL uses the following pseudocolumns: • CURVAL • NEXTVAL • LEVEL • ROWID • ROWNUM

Table 24.4: Features of PL/SQL

SQL feature in PL/SQL	Description
Comparison Operators	PL/SQL uses comparison operators, such as `ALL`, `ANY`, `SOME`, `BETWEEN`, `EXISTS`, `IN`, `IS NULL`, and `LIKE`.
SET Operators	The set operators, which are used to combine results of two queries, can be used in SQL statement. Set operators are given as follows: • INTERSECT • MINUS • UNION • UNION ALL

Summary

The chapter introduced you how PLSQL program can interact with ORACLE. Using PLSQL program you can fetch data using cursor, making changes using DML statements and control execution of transaction. After this, the next chapter will introduce you to collections and records.

Exercise

- Evaluate the number of enquiries, which result in enrollment, and which do not result in enrollment.
- Print the `batchcode` for which the `netincome` does not exceed `90%` of expected income.
- Print `rollno` and name of students who have not cleared their installments.
- Calculate the number of advertisements having more than `5` enrollments.
- Calculate the number of advertisements having more than `10` enquires.
- Calculate the statistics of advertisement day wise given in the following table:

DAY	No of Enq.	No of Enroll
MONDAY	15	5
TUESDAY	17	10

- Calculate the statistics of advertisement `amount` wise given in the following table :

Day	Expense	Collection
MONDAY	5000	30,000
TUSDAY	6000	70,000
....	....	....

- Calculate computer `Expenditure` month wise
- Calculate `Expenses` and `collection` month wise
- Calculate day wise statistics of the batch given in the following table:

Day	No. of Enrollment
-15	1
-14	2
-13	8
0	:
1	5
2	2
15	0

- Write a program, which displays the number of batches for a course, and the number of enrollments for a course.
- Write a program, which displays the names of batches as well as their starting date (name of students and enrollment date).

25

Collections and Records

PL/SQL provides new data types, like records, VARRAY, and nested tables to manipulate a set of data as a whole object. The object is considered as a collection. A collection is an ordered group of elements having the same data type, for example marks of the students of a particular class. Collections are used just like ordinary data type and they can be passed as parameter. They can be attribute of object type or instances of an object type.

PL/SQL provides two types of collections—VARRAY and nested table. VARRAY is like an array in programming languages, like C, Pascal, having only single dimension. Nested table is also like a one-dimensional array but it does not have limit on upper bound.

VARRAY and Nested Table Structure

Suppose you declare two variables as shown in the following syntax:

```
declare
   Type vtype is VARRAY (10) of INTEGER;
   Type vtab IS TABLE of NUMBER;
   X vtype;
   Y vtab;
```

In the preceding syntax, X and Y are two variables and you have stored 10 values in both `X` and `Y`. The values in `X` can be stored as:

23	18	17	5	2	53	88	8	3	7
1	2	3	4	5	6	7	8	9	10

The elements of VARRAY are referred as `X(1)` and `X(2)` .....

The values in `Y`, with no upper bound are:

23	18	17	5	2	53	88	8		3		7	81	
1	2	3	4	5	6	7	8	9	10	11	12	13	14

The elements of nested table are referred as `Y(1),Y(2)` .....

The difference between VARRAY and nested table is that there is fixed upper bound in case of VARRAY, whereas in nested table there is no upper bound. Therefore, you can store unlimited values in nested tables.

The second difference between VARRAY and nested table is that varrays are not sparse. Therefore, you cannot delete an individual element from VARRAY. On the other hand, the nested table is initially dense; however, when you delete any element using a built-in procedure, it can be sparse. If VARRAY is a column of the database table, then the data of VARRAY is stored along with the row of table. Such type of storage is called as data in line.

When a nested table is stored as a column of database table, the data in the nested table is stored separately in a store table. Such a type of storage is called as data out of line storage. When VARRAY is stored in a database, the ordering and subscripts are retained, which is not the case of nested table. You can write a program using VARRAY, as shown in Listing 25.1:

Listing 25.1: Writing a Program using VARRAY

```
declare
   type vmarktype is
   varray(10) of  integer;                          --A
   total integer;
   x vmarktype;                                     --B
begin
   x := vmarktype ( 15, 36, 25, 18, 17);            --C
   total := x.count;                                --D
   for i in 1 .. total  loop
```

```
            dbms_output.put_line(x(i));                    --E
      end loop;
   end;
   /
```

Output of Listing 25.1 is given as follows:

```
   15
   36
   25
   18
   17

   PL/SQL procedure successfully completed
```

- The following points explain the output of Listing 25.1:
- The statement A declares `vmarktype` as datatype, representing a VARRAY of integer. The upper bound of VARRAY is 10.
- The statement B declares the variable `x` of datatype `vmarktype`.
- The statement C is the initialization of an array in which `vmarktype` is called as a constructor method that is used to assign an element to the array. The constructor method has the same name as a data type.
- The statement D assigns the number of elements in the collection to total variable.
- The statement E prints the values of element of an array. The ith element in the array is referred as `x(i)`.

You can write a program using the nested table, as shown in Listing 25.2:

Listing 25.2: Writing a Program using the Nested Table

```
   declare
      type vmarktype is
      table of integer;                                    --A
      y vmarktype;                                         --B
            total number;
   begin
      y :=  vmarktype(15, 30, 25, 18, 10);                 --C
      total := y.count;                                    --D
      for i in 1 .. total  loop
            dbms_output.put_line (y(i));                   --E
      end loop;
   end;
   /
```

Output of Listing 25.2 is given as follows:

```
   15
   30
   25
   18
   10

   PL/SQL procedure successfully completed
```

The following points explain the output of Listing 25.2:

- The statement A declares `vmarktype` as a table of integer. Here no upper bound is specified.
- The statement B declares variable `Y` of the type `vmarktype`.
- The statement C is the constructor method, which is used to initialize the nested table. The name of the constructor method is same as the data type.

- The statement D is used to count number of elements in the collection.
- The statement E prints the values in the elements of the nested table.

Let's learn about declaring and initializing collections in the next section.

Declaring Collections

The varray is declared as shown in the following syntax:

```
type < varray type name> is
varray (upper bound) of < element type> [not null];
```

The nested table is declared as shown in the following syntax:

```
type < nested table type name> is table of <element type> [not null];
```

You can observe the following points in the preceding syntax:

- The type name can be any valid type name.
- The element type can be of any PL/SQL data type, such as `NUMBER` and `DATE`, except `BOOLEAN`, `NCHAR`, `NCLOB`, `NVARCHAR2`, object types with `TABLE` or `VARRAY` attributes, `REF CURSOR`, `TABLE`, and `VARRAY`.

For `VARRAY`, the upper bound has to be declared using integer. The `NOT NULL` is optional. If it is defined, then the elements in the collection cannot have null values.

If the element type is record type, then every field in record type must be scale type, such as number, date, or object type. You can use `%TYPE` or `%ROWTYPE` declaration to specify the element type. The examples of sample declarations are as follows:

```
type monthdate is varray(31) of date;
type marktype is table of number (5,2);
type studentlist is table of enrollment%rowtype;
cursor cl is select fname, sname from enquiry;
type namelist is varray (50) of cl%rowtype;
type addressrec is record
   (plotr varchar2(10),
   street varchar2(30),
   city varchar2(30));
type adr_tab is table of addressrec;
```

The collection types can also be stored in database, as shown in the following syntax:

```
create type namelist as table of varchar2 (30);
/
create type  manager as object ( managername varchar2(30), empnames namelist);
/
```

The identifier `empnames` represents a nested table. Each element stores the list of employees.

You can see the code for type representing the number of course of college student

Listing 25.3: Representing the Number of Courses of a College Student

```
create type course as
object(coursecode number(2), coursename varchar2(30));
/
create type courselist as varray(10) of course;
/
create table student (sname varchar2 (30), course courselist);
```

You can also use a variable name to define the type for another variable, as shown in the following code snippet:

```
Declare
   Type courselist As TABLE of varchar2(30);
   X   courselist;
   Y   X%type;
   ............
```

You can pass nested table or VARRAY to the procedure as a parameter, which is shown in the following code snippet:

```
CREATE  PACKAGE  student AS TYPE courselist IS
TABLE OF VARCHAR2(30);
procedure calc_marks (course In courselist);
..............
```

You can also use collections to return the value of function, as shown in the following code snippet:

```
Function min_marks (rollno integer)
RETURN courselist IS  .......
```

Initializing Collections

Initially collections are automatically `NULL`. They are initialized using the constructor method, either in the `declare` section or in the body of program. The constructor method has the same name as the type of collection. Suppose your declarations are shown in the following syntax:

```
declare
   type studentmarks as table of integer;
   x studentmarks;
```

You can assign values to `x` by using the constructor method shown in the following syntax:

```
x:= studentmarks (15, 30, 48, 88);
```

You can also assign null values to elements; if `NOT NULL` constraint is not imposed:

```
x:= studentmarks (15, 30, null, 48, null, 68);
```

If the collection is a VARRAY, then it is not necessary to assign all the elements of VARRAY for the following declarations:

```
declare
   type studentmarks as varray(10) of  integer;
   x studentmarks;
begin
   x:= studentmarks (10, 30, 40);
```

You can initialize a collection in the `declare` section, as shown in the following syntax:

```
x  studentmarks : = studentmarks(10, 30, 40);
```

If a constructor is used without any argument, then empty, but not null value, is assigned to a collection:

```
Declare
   TYPE studentmarks As Varray(10) of  integer;
   X studentmarks;
begin
   X := studentmarks( );
   If X is NOT NULL then
        ................                    --Condition yields true value
```

NOTE

It is best to initialize collections in the declarations itself.

Suppose your declarations are as shown in the following code snippet:

```
create type namelist as table of varchar2(30);
/
create type manager as object(managername varchar2(30), empnames namelist);
/
x namelist;
y manager;
```

Then `X` is initialized as shown in the following code snippet:

```
x := namelist ( 'Anil','Sunil','Ashok');
```

Y is initialized as shown in the following code snippet:

```
y := manager ('Ajay', namelist ('Anil',' Sunil', 'Ashok');
```

The constructor method is allowed where function calls are allowed. For example, you have created the table student, as shown in Listing 25.4:

Listing 25.4: Creating the tcourse type

```
create or replace type tcourse as object (coursecode number(2),
coursename varchar2 (30))
/
```

Output of Listing 25.4 is given as follows:

```
Type created
```

Listing 25.5: creating the type courselist

```
create or replace type courselist as varray(10) of tcourse
/
```

Output of Listing 25.5 is given as follows:

```
Type created
```

Following program initialize collection and prints content in the collection.

```
declare
 x course;
 y course;
 z courselist;
begin
 x:=tcourse(12,'oracle');
 y:=tcourse(14,'java');
 dbms_output.put_line(' values '||to_char(x.coursecode)||' '||x.coursename);
 z:=courselist();
 z.extend;
 z(1):=x;
 z.extend;
 z(2):=y;
 for i in 1..z.count loop
  dbms_output.put_line(' in varray '||to_char(z(i).coursecode));
 end loop;
end;
/
```

Creating table student

```
create table student(sname varchar2(30), course courselist)
/
```

Result:

```
Table created
```

Listing 25.6: Inserting Data in the Table

```
insert into student values ('ajay', courselist( tcourse (15, 'pascal'),
tcourse (10,'ada'), tcourse (30, 'java'), tcourse (40,'oracle')))
/
```

Output of Listing 25.6 is given as follows:

```
1 row created
```

courselist is the constructor of VARRAY, while Course is the constructor of object course. The following program prints all courses of Ajay.

```
declare
 x courselist;
 y course;
begin
  select course
  into x
  from student
  where sname='Ajay';
  for i in 1..x.count loop
   dbms_output.put_line(x(i).coursecode||' '||x(i).coursename);
  end loop;
end;
/
```

Listing 25.7: Creating VARRAY from VARRAY

```
create or replace type twodim_courselist as varray(10) of courselist
/
```

Output of Listing 25.7 is given as follows:

```
Type created
```

Listing 25.8: Creating a Table from VARRAY

```
create or replace type tab_twodim_courselist as table of courselist
/
```

Output of Listing 25.8 is given as follows:

```
Type created
```

Listing 25.9: Initializing collections

```
declare
  x courselist;
  y twodim_courselist;
begin
  x := courselist(tcourse(10,'oracle'));
  y :=twodim_courselist(x);
end;
/
```

Output of Listing 25.9 is given as follows:

```
PL/SQL procedure successfully completed
```

Referencing Collection Elements

Collection elements are referred as given in the following syntax:

```
collection name (subscript)
```

The valid subscripts for nested table is 1...2147483647. For VARRAY the maximum limit is 1. Suppose your declaration is shown in the following syntax:

```
declare
  type studentmarks is varray(10) of integer;
  x studentmarks;
begin
  x := studentmarks (10, 53, 61);
  dbms_output.put_line (x(2));                    --prints 53
end;
/
```

Output of the preceding syntax is given as follows:

```
53

PL/SQL procedure successfully completed
```

You can call the procedure with an element as a parameter. This is shown in the following syntax:

```
Calcmarks ( X(i), rollno);
```

In the preceding syntax, `calcmarks` is the procedure with an element.

When a function returns collection, the subscript is used to refer the element of collection returned by the function. Suppose, the function declaration is shown in the following code snippet:

```
Function passmarks (rollno..)
   return studentmarks Is
begin
   ..............
end;
```

Further, assume that you have referred the function, as shown in the following code snippet:

```
Y := passmarks (10)(2);
```

In the preceding code snippet, the function returns the collection of type `studentmarks`. The second element of the collection is assigned to `y`, as shown in Listing 25.10:

Listing 25.10: Assigning the Element of Collection to Y

```
declare
   type studentmarks is varray(10) of integer;
   x studentmarks;
   function doublemarks(x in studentmarks)
   return studentmarks is
   y studentmarks;
begin
   y := x;
   for i in 1..x.count loop
          y(i) := 2 * y(i);
   end loop;
   return y;
end;
begin
   x := studentmarks(10, 20, 30);
   dbms_output.put_line(doublemarks(x)(2));
end;
/
```

Output of Listing 25.10 is given as follows:

```
40

PL/SQL procedure successfully completed
```

Assignment Operation

One collection can be assigned to another collection by using the `INSERT`, `UPDATE`, `FETCH`, `SELECT` statement; Assignment statement; and subprogram call. For the assignment operation both the collections should not only have the same element type but also the same datatype name. Suppose your code for assignment operation procedure is:

Listing 25.11: Assignment Operation using the procedure

```
declare
   type phonearray is varray(5) of  varchar2(20);
   type stdarray is varray(5) of  varchar2(20);
   x phonearray := phonearray ( 10, 20 );
   y phonearray := phonearray ( 10, 20 );
   z stdarray := stdarray ( 30, 40 );
begin
   x := y;                                         --legal A
   -- y := z;                                      --illegal B
end;
/
```

Output of Listing 25.11 is given as follows:

```
PL/SQL procedure successfully completed
```

The following points explain the Listing 25.11:

- The statement A is legal because x and y both have the same datatype that is phonearray.
- The statement B is illegal because y and z contain the same element type but their datatype is not same.

If a null collection is assigned to another collection, then the another collection becomes null. Suppose in the example given in Listing 25.11, the variables x and y are declared.

Listing 25.12: Assigning the NULL Collection

```
declare
   type phonearray is varray(5) of  varchar2(20);
   type stdarray is varray(5) of  varchar2(20);
   x phonearray := phonearray (10, 20);
   y phonearray := phonearray ();
   z stdarray := stdarray (30, 40);
begin
   x := y;                                         --x becomes null
end;
/
```

Output of Listing 25.12 is given as follows:

```
PL/SQL procedure successfully completed
```

In Listing 25.12, x automatically becomes NULL. Therefore, when you assign a NULL value to a collection, it automatically becomes null. The values to collection elements are assigned by using the following syntax:

```
Collection(subscript) := expression;
```

In the preceding syntax, the expression should return value of the same datatype as collection element. If the subscript is not a valid integer (if it is either NULL or not convertible to integer), the exception VALUE_ERROR is raised. If the collection is automatically NULL, then the exception COLLECTION_IS_NULL is raised. Listing 25.13 shows an example of raising an exception:

Listing 25.13: Raising an Exception

```
declare
   type studentmarks is
   table of integer;
   x  studentmarks := studentmarks (53, 73, 60, 80);
begin
   x(1) := x(2) + 0.5 *  x(3);
   x(2) := round(100/x(1));
   x ('c') := 5;                      --RAISES EXCEPTION VALUE_ERROR
   x(0) := 10;                        --RAISES EXCEPTION
                                      --SUBSCRIPT_OUTSIDE_LIMIT
```

```
    x(8) := 20;                              --RAISES EXCEPTION
                                             --SUBSCRIPT_BEYOUND_COUNT
  end;
  /
```

Output of Listing 25.13 is given as follows:

```
ERROR at line 1:
ORA-06502: PL/SQL: numeric or value error: character to number conversion error
ORA-06512: at line 8
---------------------------------------------------
```

An exception is raised when the code given in Listing 25.13 is run. This is the first exception, the second exception is raised on:

```
If   " X ('C') := 5;
as:
ERROR at line 1:
ORA-06532: Subscript outside of limit
ORA-06512: at line 9
-----------------------------------------------------
```

It raises an exception VALUE_ERROR. A third exception is raised on:

```
If both ('C') := 5;
and
X(0) := 10;      -- Raises exception are commented
as:
ERROR at line 1:
ORA-06533: Subscript beyond count
ORA-06512: at line 11
It raises an exception VALUE_ERROR.
```

Comparing Collections

Collections can only be compared against null value based variables. If a collection is NULL, then IS NULL condition returns TRUE. Listing 25.14 shows how to use the IS NULL condition for a collection:

Listing 25.14: Using the IS NULL Condition

```
declare
  type studentmarks is table of integer;
  x studentmarks;
  y studentmarks;
begin
  if x is null then                     --CONDITION YIELDS TRUE
       dbms_output.put_line('true');
    end if;
end;
/
```

Output of Listing 25.14 is given as follows:

```
true

PL/SQL procedure successfully completed
```

Collections cannot be compared for equality or inequality. Therefore, the compiler returns an error, if you write the following code snippet:

```
if (X=Y)
```

Equality implies implicit equality comparison. Therefore, collections cannot be used in ORDER BY, GROUP BY, and DISTINCT clauses.

Operation on Whole Collections

You can perform operations on collections as a whole. You can insert, update, or delete collections by using the SQL DML statement. You can reference a collection by using the `SELECT ... INTO` statement. You can declare a whole collection by using the code given in Listing 25.15:

Listing 25.15: Declaring a Whole Collection

```
create type tab_course as
object (coursecode number(2), coursename varchar2(30))
/
```

Result:

```
Type created
```

Declaring a table

```
create type  tab_courselist as
table of tab_course
/
```

Result:

```
Type created
```

Declaring a nested table

```
create table tab_student (sname varchar2(30),
courses tab_courselist)
nested table  courses store as c_tab                    --a
/
```

Result:

```
Table created
```

The nested table clause is required to create a nested table. The table has a column, known as courses, with nested table data type using them.

INSERT *Operations*

You can perform insert operation using the constructor method as shown below:

Listing 25.16: Inserting Data

```
insert into tab_student values( 'anil',
tab_courselist( tab_course (10,'oracle'),
tab_course (20, 'pascal')));
insert into tab_student values( 'sunil',
tab_courselist (tab_course (10,'oracle'),
tab_course (25,'c'), tab_course (30,'fortran')));
```

In Listing 25.16, we are using the constructor method to inserting data.

UPDATE *Statement*

You can update collections by using the `UPDATE` clause. You can use the constructor method to set new values, as shown in Listing 25.17:

Listing 25.17: Assigning New Course Values to Anil

```
update tab_student
set courses = tab_courselist(tab_course (10, 'oracle'),
tab_course (25,'c')) where sname = 'Anil'
/
```

Output of Listing 25.17 is given as follows:

```
1 row updated
```

You can assign new values to Anil by using variables shown in Listing 25.18:

Listing 25.18: Using Variables to Assign Values

```
declare
   x tab_courselist;
begin
   x := tab_courselist (tab_course( 10, 'oracle'), tab_course(25,'c'));
   update tab_student
   set courses = x
   where sname = 'Anil';
end;
/
```

Output of Listing 25.18 is given as follows:

```
PL/SQL procedure successfully completed
```

DELETE Statement

The delete statement is used to delete rows that have collections. This is shown in Listing 25.19:

Listing 25.19: Using the delete Statement

```
delete tab_student
where sname = 'Anil'
/
```

Output of Listing 25.19 is given as follows:

```
1 row deleted
```

SELECT.....INTO Statement

You can retrieve data in a collection by using the `SELECT.....INTO` statement, as shown in Listing 25.20:

Listing 25.20: Taking a Collection in the Variable x

```
declare
   x tab_courselist;
begin
   select courses
   into x
   from tab_student
   where sname = 'Sunil' ;
end;
/
```

Output of Listing 25.20 is given as follows:

```
PL/SQL procedure successfully completed
```

NOTE

Assuming that the data for student Anil exists in the table else the error No data found is displayed.

Operations on **VARRAY**

The operations performed on the nested tables can also be done on `VARRAY`. Suppose your declarations are shown in the following code snippet:

```
create or replace type tcourse1 as
object (coursecode number(2), coursename varchar2 (30))
/
```

The output of preceding code snippet is given as follows:

```
Type created
```

The following code snippet shows another declaration:

```
create or replace type
courselist2 as varray(10) of tcourse1
/
```

The output of the preceding code snippet is given as follows:

```
Type created
```

The following code snippet shows another declaration:

```
create table
student4(sname varchar2(30),course courselist2)
/
```

The output of the preceding code snippet is given as follows:

```
Table created
```

You can perform the following operations on VARRAY:

- Inserting
- Updating
- Deleting
- Selecting

Let's learn about each of these in the next section.

INSERT Statement

You can insert values in a table by using the insert statement, as shown in Listing 25.21:

Listing 25.21: Inserting Values in a Table

```
insert into student4 values ('ajay', courselist2( tcourse1 (15, 'pascal'),
tcourse1 (10,'ada'),     tcourse1 (30, 'java'), tcourse1 (40,'oracle')))
/
```

Output of Listing 25.21 is given as follows:

```
1 row created
```

You can insert a maximum of `10` elements in course.

UPDATE Statement

You can update a collection by using the constructor method, as shown in Listing 25.22:

Listing 25.22: Updating the Existing Collection

```
update student4
set course = courselist2 (tcourse1 (10,'oracle'),
tcourse1 (20,'pascal'), tcourse1 (30, 'c')) where sname = 'ajay';
```

Output of Listing 25.22 is given as follows:

```
1 row updated
```

Listing 25.23: Using a Variable in the UPDATE statement

```
declare
  x courselist2;
begin
  x := courselist2 (tcourse1 (10,'oracle'),
  tcourse1 (20,'pascal'), tcourse1 (30,'c'));
  update student4 set course = x where sname = 'Ajay';
end;
/
```

Output of Listing 25.23 is given as follows:

```
PL/SQL procedure successfully completed
```

DELETE Statement

You can delete rows by using the delete statement, as shown in Listing 25.24:

Listing 25.24: Deleting rows having collections using simple DELETE statement

```
delete student4 where sname = 'Ajay';
```

Output of Listing 25.24 is given as follows:

```
1 row deleted
```

SELECT..... INTO Statement

Listing 25.25: Putting the value of collection into variable of the same datatype

```
declare
  x courselist2;
begin
  select course
  into x
  from student4
  where sname= 'Ajay';
  dbms_output.put_line(x(1).coursename);
                                      --prints oracle
end;
/
```

Output of Listing 25.25 is given as follows:

```
PL/SQL procedure successfully completed
```

NOTE

We assume that the details for the student Ajay exist in the student table otherwise no data found error is displayed.

Manipulating Individual Element in the Nested Table

You can manipulate individual element in a nested table by using the `INSERT`, `UPDATE`, or `DELETE` statement. The required nested table is identified by using `THE` operator.

INSERT Statement

You can insert an additional element in the nested table of student Ajay by using the insert statement:

Listing 25.26: Inserting an Additional Element in the Nested Table of Student Ajay

```
insert into the ( select courses from tab_student where sname= 'Ajay')
values (40,'ada')
/
```

Output of Listing 25.26 is given as follows:

```
1 row is inserted
```

NOTE

If there is no data for Ajay in the table tab_student, the following error can occur:
ORA-22908: reference to NULL table value.

The sub-query with the `THE operator` identifies the nested table on which you want to perform data manipulations.

UPDATE Statement

The update operation can be performed similarly by using THE operator, as shown in Listing 25.27:

Listing 25.27: Manipulating the nested table of Ajay

```
update the ( select courses from tab_student where sname = 'ajay')
set coursename = 'oracle 8.0' where  coursecode= 10
/
```

Output of Listing 25.27 is given as follows:

```
1 row is updated
```

NOTE

If there is no data for `Ajay` in the table tab_student, the following error can occur:
ORA-22908: reference to NULL table value.

DELETE Statement

You can delete rows from a nested table by using the delete statement. The query of THE identifies the nested table on which data manipulation has to be performed. Listing 25.28 shows the code snippet to delete a row from the nested table of Ajay:

Listing 25.28: Deleting a Row from the Nested Table of Ajay

```
delete the (select courses from tab_student where sname = 'Ajay')
where coursecode = 20
/
```

Output of Listing 25.28 is given as follows:

```
1 row deleted
```

NOTE

This will result in error stating:
If there is no data for Ajay in the table tab_student, the following error can occur:
ORA-22908: reference to NULL table value

SELECT.....INTO Statement

You can retrieve data from the nested table by using the SELECT.....INTO statement:

Listing 25.29: Retrieving Data from the Nested Table

```
declare
  x varchar2(30);
begin
  select  coursename
  into x
  from the (select courses
  from tab_student
  where sname = 'sunil')
  where coursecode = 10;
  dbms_output.put_line(x);                    --prints oracle
end;
/
```

Output of Listing 25.29 is given as follows:

```
Oracle

PL/SQL procedure successfully completed
```

NOTE

We assume that the details for the student Sunil exists in the table tab_student, otherwise no data found error is displayed.

The query which is written after `THE` must return maximum one row, otherwise Oracle returns error.

Manipulating Individual Elements in **VARRAY**

You can manipulate individual element in `VARRAY by` using procedural elements. The `THE` operator is not available in `VARRAY; therefore,` you have to use collection methods to manipulate individual element.

INSERT *Operation*

This section explains the insert operation, which is performed to insert data in a table by using the collection method. This is explained with the help of an example. Suppose the data in table Anil is shown as follows:

Anil	10	Oracle
	20	C

Now assume that you want to insert data in VARRAY so that it appears like the following table:

Anil	10	Oracle
	20	C
	30	Pascal (←element inserted at the last position)

To insert data in VARRAY, you need to set data in the local variable, manipulate it, and use the update statement to update the data in the table, as shown in Listing 25.30:

Listing 25.30: Setting data in the local variable, manipulating the local variable, and using update statement update the data in table

```
create or replace procedure insstudent (studentname in varchar2, ccode in
  number, cname in varchar2) as
  x  courselist2;
  c number;
    i number;
begin
  select  course
  into x
  from student4
  where sname = studentname;
  x.extend;--  it extends array to add new element
       x(x.last):=tcoursel(ccode, cname);
                                   --put new values into local variable x
  update student4
  set course = x
  where sname = studentname;     --put updated  value back to table
end;
/
```

Output of Listing 25.30 is given as follows:

```
Procedure created
```

Now, you need to call the insstudent procedure to complete the procedure of inserting data in the table. This is shown in Listing 25.31:

Listing 25.31: Calling the Method

```
begin
  insstudent ( 'Anil', 30, 'Pascal');
end;
/
```

Output of Listing 25.31 is given as follows:

```
PL/SQL procedure successfully completed
```

UPDATE Statement

You can retrieve and update data in the local variable with the help of `update` statement. Let's understand this with the help of an example. Suppose you want to change the name of coursecode 10 of VARRAY. You can do this with the help of the code snippet shown in Listing 25.32:

Listing 25.32: Changing the Name of coursecode 10 of VARRAY of Anil

```
create or replace procedure updstudent ( studentname varchar2, ccode number,
  cname varchar2) as
  x courselist2;
  i number;
  cnt number;
begin
  select course
  into x
  from student4
  where sname = studentname;
  cnt := x.last;
  for i in 1 .. cnt loop
        if x(i).coursecode = ccode then
               x(i).coursename := cname;
        end if;
  End loop;
  update student4
  Set course = x
  where sname = studentname;
end;
/
```

Output of Listing 25.32 is given as follows:

```
Procedure created
```

The `FOR.....LOOP.....END LOOP` scans the array and updates the `coursename` for the given `coursecode`. The last `UPDATE` statement updates the row of specified student name with the new value of `x`. After that, you need to call the method with the help of code shown in Listing 25.33:

Listing 25.33: Calling the Method

```
begin
  updstudent ( 'Anil', 30, 'Pascal6.0');
end;
/
```

Output of Listing 25.33 is given as follows:

```
PL/SQL procedure successfully completed
```

DELETE Statement

You cannot delete the element of `VARRAY` using the `DELETE` method. You can put `NULL` value in that index using the procedure.

Listing 25.34: Removing the Elements having coursecode 10

```
create or replace procedure delstudent (studentname varchar2,ccode number) as
X courselist2;
cnt number;
i number;
begin
   select course
   into x from student4
   where sname = studentname;
   cnt := x.last;
   For i in 1 .. cnt loop
         if x(i).coursecode = ccode then
                 x(i).coursecode := null;
                 x(i).coursename := null;
         end if;
   end loop;
   update student4
   set course = x where sname = studentname;
end;
/
```

Output of Listing 25.34 is given as follows:

```
Procedure created
```

Listing 25.35: Calling the Procedure

```
begin
   delstudent('Anil',10);
end;
/
```

Another method to delete the elements having coursecode 10 is to copy the elements of `X`, excluding code into some other variable `Y`, and then assign `Y` to courses in the `UPDATE` statement.

Retrieving Elements

You can retrieve elements simply by using the `SELECT.....INTO` statement. The individual elements are available in the specified variable (In the above example, it is `x`). Each element can be accessed using subscripts.

Collection Methods

Collection methods are used to provide information and manipulation of collection. The methods are built-in functions and procedure. The built-in functions are `EXISTS`, `COUNT`, `LIMIT`, `FIRST`, `LAST`, `PRIOR` and `NEXT`. The built in procedures are `EXTEND`, `TRIM` and `DELETE`. The methods `EXISTS`, `PRIOR`, `NEXT`, `TRIM`, `EXTEND` and `DELETE` take parameters as integers. The methods are used as:

```
collectionname.method (parameters)
```

Suppose you have created a datatype as shown in the following syntax:

```
create type vmarks as table of integer;
/
```

Now, you want to use variables as shown in the following syntax:

```
x vmarks;
```

After that, you can use the method shown in the following syntax:

```
x.exists(2)
```

Let's now discuss the following built-in functions and procedures of collections methods:

- EXISTS (n) Function
- COUNT Function

- LIMIT Function
- FIRST Function
- LAST Function
- PRIOR(n) Function
- NEXT(n) Function
- EXTEND(n,i) Procedure
- TRIM(n) Procedure
- DELETE(m, n) Procedure

EXISTS (n) Function

The EXISTS (n) function refers to a function, which returns TRUE, if n[th] element of the collection is in existence, otherwise it returns FALSE. In other words, when n is out of range, it returns FALSE, and does not raise an exception

```
SUBSCRIPT_OUTSIDE_LIMIT
```

It is used before referencing an element, especially in sparse nested table (nested table in which some middle elements are not in existence). The typical code of EXISTS is as follows:

```
if x.exists(i) then
   y := x(i);
end if;
```

Therefore, before assigning a value to Y, it checks whether the given element is in existence.

COUNT Function

The COUNT function returns the number of elements, which are currently in existence. It is used when a number of elements in the collection are unknown. Let's consider the following code snippet:

```
type  vmarks is table of integer;
x vmarks;
x := vmarks (30, 40, 50);
dbms_output.put_line ( x.count);          --Returns value 3
```

In the preceding code snippet, COUNT returns the number of elements for collection nested table or VARRAY. It can be used anywhere, where integer value is expected. Therefore, the following FOR.....LOOP.....END LOOP is valid:

```
For i in 1 .. X.count loop
  .............
end loop;
```

This function is used especially to retrieve collection from a database table.

LIMIT Function

The LIMIT function returns value of upper bound, in case of VARRAY. In case of nested table, it returns NULL value. Let's look at the declarations shown in the following code snippet:

```
type vmarks is varray (10) of integer;
type tmarks is table of integer;
x vmarks;
y tmarks;
begin
   dbms_output.put_line (to_char(x.limit));             -- returns value 10
   dbms_output.put_line (to_char(y.limit));             -- returns NULL value
```

The LIMIT function can be used whenever an integer value is expected.

***FIRST* Function**

The function FIRST returns the smallest subscript in the collection. If the collection is empty, then FIRST returns NULL value. For VARRAY, FIRST always returns 1. For nested table, FIRST normally returns 1. If you delete the initial elements from the nested table, then FIRST returns more than 1. Look at the following code to understand it better:

```
...........
X vmarks : = vmarks (10, 20);
...........
Y Tmarks := Tmarks (10, 20, 30);
dbms_output.put_line (To_char (X.FIRST));          --Returns 1
Y.delete (1);                                  --deletes first element from Y
dbms_output.put_line (To_char(Y.FIRST));           --Returns 2
```

***LAST* Function**

The function LAST returns the last subscript in the collection. For VARRAY, LAST always equals COUNT, i.e. upper bound. For nested table LAST normally equals COUNT. But, if middle elements are deleted, then the value of LAST is more than COUNT. IF the collection is empty, then it returns NULL. Look at the following code to understand it better:

```
x tmarks;
x := tmarks ( 10,20,30);
dbms_output.put_line (to_char(x.count));         -- prints 3
dbms_output.put_line (to_char(x last));          -- prints 3
x.delete(2);
dbms_output.put_line (to_char( x.count));            -- prints 2
dbms_output.put_line (to_char (x.last);          -- prints 3
```

***PRIOR(n)* Function**

It returns the subscript of element, which precedes index n of a collection. If n has no predecessor, then PRIOR returns NULL. Thus, the following function always returns NULL:

```
X. PRIOR (X .FIRST)
```

PRIOR ignores the deleted elements in the sparse nested table. Suppose your code is:

```
X := Tmarks (10,20,30);
X.delete (2);
i := X.PRIOR(3);                   --i gets value 1 instead of 2
```

***NEXT(n)* Function**

It returns the subscript of element which follows the index n of a collection. NEXT ignores the deleted elements in the collection. NEXT after the last element always returns NULL. Thus, the following function returns NULL:

```
X.NEXT (X.LAST)
```

Look at the following code:

```
X := Tmarks (10, 20, 30);
X.delete(2);
i := X.NEXT(1);                    --i gets value 3 instead of 2
```

The PRIOR and NEXT functions are used to traverse the collection in forward and reverse direction, as shown in the following code snippet:

```
                                   -- Loop in forward direction
i := X.FIRST;
While i is not NULL loop
  .............
  i := X.NEXT(i);
  ...........
```

```
end loop;
                                        -- Loop in reverse direction
i := X LAST;
While i is NOT NULL loop
   i := X.PRIOR(i);
end loop;
```

Listing 25.36: Using the DELETE() Collection Method

```
declare
   type mark_var is varray(10) of integer;
   type mark_tab is table  of integer;
   x mark_var;
   y mark_tab;
begin
   x := mark_var(10,20,30);
   y := mark_tab(10,20,30);
   dbms_output.put_line('var count '||x.count||' first '||x.first||' last
   '||x.last);
   dbms_output.put_line('tab count '||y.count||' first '||y.first||' last
   '||y.last);
                                              -- x.delete(1); error
   y.delete(1);
   dbms_output.put_line('tab count '||y.count||' first '||y.first||' last
   '||y.last);
   y.delete(3);
   dbms_output.put_line('tab count '||y.count||' first '||y.first||' last
   '||y.last);
end;
/
```

Output of Listing 25.36 is given as follows:

```
VAR COUNT 3 FIRST 1 LAST 3
TAB COUNT 3 FIRST 1 LAST 3
TAB COUNT 2 FIRST 2 LAST 3
TAB COUNT 1 FIRST 2 LAST 2

PL/SQL procedure successfully completed
```

After discussing about functions, let's now discuss about the procedures available in the collection methods.

EXTEND(n,i) Procedure

The EXTEND (n,i) procedure refers to a procedure , which extends the size of a collection. It cannot be used for an automatic `NULL` collection. It appends one element to the collection without using the parameter. The extend collection method uses two parameters, such as `n` and `i`. When both the parameters of this function are given, it copies the ith element of the collection n number of times. When a collection has the `NOT NULL` constraint, the null element cannot be appended in a collection. Look at the following code snippet to understand it in a better way:

```
X Tmarks;
X := Tmarks (10,20,30);
X.EXTEND;                    -- Adds null element at the element of collection
X.EXTEND (3,2);              -- Adds element having value 20 three times at the
                             end of collection.
```

`EXTEND` operates on the internal size of the collection. Therefore, if any deleted element is encountered, it takes that element into account. Suppose the code is:

```
X Tmarks;
X := Tmarks (10,20,30);
X.DELETE (3);              -- Deletes third element in the collection
X.EXTEND;                  -- Appends element at fourth position not on third position
X(4) : = 50;               -- It is legal it will not raise exception SUBSCRIPT_OUTSIDE_LIMIT

                           --OR SUBSCRIPT_BEYOND_COUNT
```

In the preceding code snippet, the internal size of the table includes deleted elements also. Suppose you initialize tables with six elements and delete elements 2 and 6, as shown in the following code snippet:

```
Internal size = 6
Value of LAST = 5                -- Trailing deleted elements are ignored
Value of COUNT = 4               -- All deleted elements are ignored.
```

Listing 25.37: Using the EXTEND() Collection Method

```
declare
   type mark_var is varray(10) of integer;
   type mark_tab is table  of integer;
   x mark_var;
   y mark_tab;
   procedure print_var(px mark_var) is
begin
   for i in 1..px.count loop
         dbms_output.put_line('the elements in varray are '||px(i));
   end loop;
end;
procedure print_tab(px mark_tab) is
begin
   for i in px.first..px.last loop
         if(px.exists(i)) then
                 dbms_output.put_line('the elements in varray are '||px(i));
         end if;
   end loop;
end;

begin
   x := mark_var(10,20,30);
   y := mark_tab(10,20,30);
   dbms_output.put_line('tab count '||y.count||' first '||y.first||' last
   '||y.last);
   print_tab(y);
   dbms_output.put_line('tab count '||y.count||' first '||y.first||' last
   '||y.last);
   y.extend(2,3);--extending third element two times
   dbms_output.put_line('tab count '||y.count||' first '||y.first||' last
   '||y.last);
   print_tab(y);
end;
/
```

Output of Listing 25.37 is given as follows:

```
tab count 3 first 1 last 3
the elements in varray are 10
the elements in varray are 20
the elements in varray are 30
tab count 3 first 1 last 3
```

```
tab count 5 first 1 last 5
the elements in varray are 10
the elements in varray are 20
the elements in varray are 30
the elements in varray are 30
the elements in varray are 30

PL/SQL procedure successfully completed
```

TRIM(n) Function

It is a procedure, which deletes n elements from the end of collection. If called without parameter, it deletes one element from the collection. If n is more than count then it raises an exception:

```
SUBSCRIPT_BEYOND_COUNT
```

Let us understand this in the following code:

```
X  Tmarks;
.........
X := Tmarks (10,15,30,80);
X.TRIM;                    --Trims last element of collection count returns 3
X.TRIM(2);                 --Trims last two elements of collection count returns 1.
```

TRIM takes the internal size into consideration. It decreases the internal size of collection. So if it encounters deleted elements, they are considered. Let us understand the following code:

```
X  Tmarks;
X := Tmarks (10,20,30,40);
X.delete (4);                      --4th element is deleted.
X.TRIM (2);                        --It trims last 2 elements so if the deleted 4th
                                   --element is also considered. The internal size of
                                   --collection is 2 initially it was 4. The function
                                   --COUNT returns value2
```

Oracle recommends using nested table as fixed size array and deletes elements using DELETE. Otherwise, it recommends treatment of nested table as list and uses TRIM and EXTEND. The interaction of TRIM and DELETE is not recommended. Oracle removes placeholder for trimmed element, so referencing them generates an exception. Therefore, in the previous code referencing X(4) generates an exception.

DELETE(m, n) Procedure

The DELETE procedure is used to remove elements from the range m to n in a nested table. However, in the following cases it does nothing:

- m > n
- m is null
- n is null

If m is not specified, then it removes nth element in the collection. In the absence of any parameter, it removes all elements from the collection. DELETE cannot be applied for VARRAY. If the deleted element is not in existence, then delete does nothing. When element is deleted, the occupied memory is made free. Delete does not decrease the internal size of collection. So the deleted element can be assigned a new value.

Listing 25.38: Using DELETE

```
x tmarks;
x := t marks (10,20,30,40,50,60);
x.delete (2);              -- deletes element2
x.delete (3,6);            -- deletes elements from 3 to 6
x(2) := 35;                -- Reassigns value to deleted element
```

Listing 25.39: Using Collection Functions – Delete(), Trim() and Extend()

```
declare
   type mark_var is varray(10) of integer;
   type mark_tab is table  of integer;
   x mark_var;
   y mark_tab;
procedure print_var(px mark_var) is
begin
   for i in 1..px.count loop
        dbms_output.put_line('the elements in varray are '||px(i));
   end loop;
end;
procedure print_tab(px mark_tab) is
begin
   for i in px.first..px.last loop
        if(px.exists(i)) then
                dbms_output.put_line('the elements in varray are '||px(i));
        end if;
   end loop;
end;
begin
   x := mark_var(10,20,30);
   y := mark_tab(10,20,30);
   dbms_output.put_line('tab count '||y.count||' first '||y.first||' last
   '||y.last);
   print_tab(y);
   dbms_output.put_line('tab count '||y.count||' first '||y.first||' last
   '||y.last);
   y.extend(2,3);--extending third element two times
   dbms_output.put_line('tab count '||y.count||' first '||y.first||' last
   '||y.last);
   print_tab(y);
   y.delete(3);
   dbms_output.put_line('tab count '||y.count||' first '||y.first||' last
   '||y.last);
   print_tab(y);
   y.trim(2);
   dbms_output.put_line('tab count '||y.count||' first '||y.first||' last
   '||y.last);
   print_tab(y);
end;
/
```

The output of Listing 25.39 is given as follows:

```
tab count 3 first 1 last 3
the elements in varray are 10
the elements in varray are 20
the elements in varray are 30
tab count 3 first 1 last 3
tab count 5 first 1 last 5
the elements in varray are 10
the elements in varray are 20
the elements in varray are 30
the elements in varray are 30
the elements in varray are 30
tab count 4 first 1 last 5
the elements in varray are 10
the elements in varray are 20
the elements in varray are 30
the elements in varray are 30
```

```
tab count 2 first 1 last 2
the elements in varray are 10
the elements in varray are 20

PL/SQL procedure successfully completed
```

Use of Methods to Parameters

You can use methods, such as FIRST, LAST, and EXTENT, with the parameters within the body of a subprogram. Therefore, methods can be used with the formal parameters, as shown in the following code snippet:

```
create procedure insstudent ( X Tmarks ....)
  if  X.LAST < 10 then
      ................
  end if;
end;
```

For the LIMIT function, the value is always derived by using the TYPE parameter.

Built-in Exceptions

PL/SQL has provided built-in exceptions for handling abnormal situations, while handling collections. The exceptions are as follows:

- COLLECTION_IS_NULL—It is raised when collection is not initialized or is automatically NULL.
- NO_DATA_FOUND—It is raised when the deleted element is referred.
- SUBSCRIPT_BEYOUND_COUNT—It is raised when subscript exceeds the internal size of collection.
- SUBSCRIPT_OUTSIDE_LIMIT—It is raised when the subscript is outside the legal range.
- VALUE_ERROR—It is raised when the subscript is NULL or not convertible to integer value.

Suppose the declarations are:

```
Type tmarks is TABLE OF INTEGER;
X   tmarks;
Begin
  X(1) := 50;                    -- Raises exception COLLECTION_IS_NULL
  X := tmarks (10,20,30);
  Y(. null) := 50;               -- Raises VALUE_ERROR
  X('A') := 50;                  -- Raises VALUE_ERROR
  X(0) := 30;                    -- It  raises exception
                                 --SUBSCRIPT_OUTSIDE_LIMIT
  X(4) := 50;                    -- It raises exception
                                 --SUBSCRIPT_BEYOUND_COUNT
  X.delete (2);
  Y := X(2);                     -- It raises exception NO_DATA_FOUND
```

The DELETE(n) does not raise exception under the following conditions:

- null subscript
- -ve subscript
- Deleting already deleted elements

Records

Records are used to represent logical related information, which is not necessarily of the same type. In arrays, the elements are of the same type, while in the record the elements may not have the same type. Records are used to organize information having different type into one logical unit. The type %ROWTYPE is also used to define record, however, all the properties of records are inherited from table or cursor.

Record Definition

Suppose you want to represent information about an address. The best way is to declare the record. The syntax of record datatype is as follows:

```
Type <recname> is RECORD
 ( fieldname1  fieldspecification,
 fieldname2  field specification, ......) ;
```

In the preceding syntax, you can observe the following points:

- `recname` is the type specifier of the record.
- `Fieldname1` is the name of the field.
- Field specification is the type specifier of the field. It can be any PL/SQL data type, except `REF CURSOR`.
- The `NOT NULL` restriction on the record is optional.

The code to declare a record is shown in Listing 25.40:

Listing 25.40: Declaring a Record

```
type adr_rec is record
(plot varchar2(10),
street varchar2(20),
city varchar2( 20) not null
default  'nagpur');
```

You can initialize the field with some value using the `DEFAULT` expression. It can also be written as shown in the following syntax:

```
city varchar2(20) := 'NAGPUR'
```

In the datatype, you can use `%Type` or `%ROWTYPE` to build a composite record. Each field within the record should be unique. In PL/SQL, a record can contain objects, which cannot have attributes of type record. Some sample declarations of records are as follows:

```
type adr_rec is record
(plot varchar2(10),
street varchar2(20),
city varchar2(20));

type student_rec is record
(rollno number(3),
address adr_rec);

type vendor_type is record
(vendor_info  vendor%rowtype,
address  adr_rec );
```

You can use `VARRAY` or `NESTED` table as datatype of a field. You can define the variables of the record type, as shown in the following syntax:

```
x adr_rec;
y student_rec;
```

You can also pass record datatype as datatype to formal parameters, as shown in the following code snippet:

```
Procedure calcamount ( Student_info student_rec);
```

You can assign a default value to a record in the field definition, as shown in the following code snippet:

```
type student_rec is record
(plot varchar2(10),
street varchar2(20),
city  varchar2(20) := ' NAGPUR);
```

You can impose `NOT NULL` constraint in the field type definition. The fields with `NOT NULL` constraint must be initialized, as shown in the following code snippet:

```
Type student_rec IS RECORD
(plot varchar2(10),
street varchar2(20),
city varchar2(20) NOT NULL := 'NAGPUR');
```

Accessing Fields in the Record

You can access the fields in the record by using the following syntax:

```
record variablename.fieldname
```

Suppose you have declared a variable, as shown in the following syntax:

```
x adr_rec;
```

Then, you can access the fields in the record, as shown in the following syntax:

```
x.plot, x.street and x.city:
```

For example, if you want to assign some values to the fields in the record, you can do so with the help of the following syntax:

```
x.plot := 10;
x.street := ' MGROAD';
x.city := ' NAGPUr';
```

You can refer `X.plot` as any ordinary `VARCHAR2(10)` variable without any difference. If the function returns record datatype, then you can refer the fields in return values as:

```
function_name( parameters ).fieldname
```

Suppose you have written a function, as shown in the following code snippet:

```
Function  count_city ( ...... )
  RETURN  student_rec AS
  ...............
begin
  ...............
end;
```

In the following code snippet, you can refer fields returned by the function:

```
rlno := count_city( ... ).Roll no;
plotnol := count_city ( ... ).address.plot no.
```

In the preceding code snippet, the function returns record of the `student_rec`, type, which has two fields, such as `rollno` and `address`. The dot (.) notation is extended to refer `plotno.` in the address record. If the function is parameter less, then empty brackets are used, as shown in the following code snippet:

```
rlno := count_city( ).rollno;
```

You can also extend the dot (.) notation to refer the attribute of an object, which is the part of a record. Suppose you declare a record, as shown in the following code snippet:

```
type student_rec is record
(rollno number(2),
courses course,
address adr_rec);
x student_rec;
```

In the preceding code snippet, `COURSE` is the object type having attributes `coursecode` and `coursename`. You can write the following statement to refer these attributes:

```
X.courses.coursecode = 10;
```

Operations on Records

You can assign values to fields by using the following syntax:

```
recordvarname.fieldname := expression;
```

Therefore, if you declare a variable shown in the following syntax:

```
X adr_rec;
```

Then, you can assign the values to fields, as shown in the following syntax:

```
X.plot := '10';
X.street := ' MGROAD';
X.city := 'NAGPUR';
```

The behavior of a field depends upon its data types. Therefore, `x.plot` will have the same behavior as ordinary `VARCHAR2(10)` data type. You can use any expression, which returns compatible data types in the assignment statement. Therefore, the following is a legal statement:

```
x.city = initcap( x.city);
```

You can assign one record to another, provided both are having the same datatype name; only matching datatype is not sufficient. Suppose you have a declaration, as shown in the following syntax:

```
type student_rec is record
(rollno number(2),
address adr_rec);
type scholar_rec is record
(rollno number (2),
address adr_rec);
x student_ rec;
y scholar_rec;
begin
   x.plot := 10;
   x := y ;                        --it is illegal because though x and y are
                                   --having compatible datatype name is
                                   --different
   x.address := y.address;         --It is legal because both X.address and
                                   --Y.address refers same record data type
```

When a record variable is used in the `SELECT.....INTO` statement, the columns mentioned in the `SELECT` clause should have data types, which are compatible with the record. This is shown in Listing 25.41:

Listing 25.41: Put a Value in the Variable of the adr_rec Data type

```
x adr_rec;
select vendor.plotno,vendor.street,vendor.city
into x from vendor
where vendorcode = 10;
```

In Listing 25.41, `vender.plotno`, `street`, and `city` should have compatible data types, such as `x.plotno`, `x.street`, and `x.city`. You cannot use the record to insert in a database table. It is illegal to use individual fields in the `INSERT` statement, as shown in the following syntax:

```
insert into vendor (plotno, street, city) values (x);    -- illegal
```

However, it is correct to write the individual fields, as shown in the following syntax:

```
insert into vendor ( plotno, street, city)
values (x.plotno, x.street, x.city);
```

Similarly, you cannot assign multiple values to a record in one statement. Therefore, the following statement is not valid:

```
x := (10, ' MGROAD', 'NAGPUR');
```

Record Comparison

Two records cannot be tested for equality, inequality, or for any relational operator. Similarly, a record cannot be tested for nullity. Suppose, the code is:

```
x adr_rec;
y adr_rec;
```

In that case the following statement is illegal:

```
if  X is null then
   ............
   if (x = y) then
          ............
```

Record Manipulations

Records can be easily manipulated because a set of information can be treated as a single unit. Let's understand this with the help of the following code snippet, which is used to create a record, `enqrec`:

```
Type enqrec IS RECORD
(enqno enqiry.enqno%type,
fname enquiry.fname% type);
cursor c1 is
select enqno, fname
from enquiry;
X enqrec;
begin
   open c1;
   fetch c1 into X;
   While c1% NOT FOUND Loop
          ................
          ................
   end loop;
end;
```

In the preceding code snippet, you can see that data of a table can be retrieved in records and manipulated.

Using Collections as Input and Output

You can transform data between a table and collections as it is useful in the Internet programming where you can get multiple rows in a single Oracle call.

Listing 25.42: Putting table data in collection

```
create or replace type deptobj as
object(deptno number, deptname varchar2(30))
/
```

Output of Listing 25.42 is given as follows:

```
Type created
```

Listing 25.43: Using deptobj Type

```
create or replace  type deptcol as table of deptobj
/
```

Output of Listing 25.43 is given as follows:

```
Type created
```

Listing 25.44: Creating putdeptcol procedure

```
create or replace procedure putdeptcol( x  out deptcol) as
cursor c1 is select deptno,deptname from dept;
y deptobj;
begin
   x := deptcol();
   for z in c1 loop
          x.extend;
          y := deptobj(z.deptno,z.deptname);
          x(x.last):=y;
   end loop;
end;
/
```

Output of Listing 25.44 is given as follows:

```
PL/SQL procedure successfully completed
```

NOTE

For this procedure to work you need to have dept table.

You can use procedure as shown in the following code snippet:

```
declare
   y deptcol;
begin
   y:= deptcol();
   putdeptcol(y);
   dbms_output.put_line(y.last);
   for i in 1..y.last loop
          dbms_output.put_line(y(i).deptno);
   end loop;
end;
/
```

Output of preceding code snippet is given as follows:

```
4
10
20
30
40

PL/SQL procedure successfully completed
```

NOTE

You need to have table dept with proper data in it.

Listing 25.45: Putting data in collection using the ref cursor

```
create or replace type zempobj as
object(empno number, ename varchar2(30), salary number)
/
```

Output of Listing 25.45 is given as follows:

```
Type created
```

Listing 25.46: creating type zempcol

```
create or replace  type zempcol as table of zempobj
/
```

Output of Listing 25.46 is given as follows:

```
Type created
```

Creating procedure

```
create or replace procedure putempcol( x  out zempcol) as
type type_c1 is ref cursor ;
c1 type_c1;
z emp%rowtype;
y zempobj;
begin
   open c1 for select empno,ename,salary from emp;
   x := zempcol();
   fetch c1 into z;
   while c1%found loop
```

```
          x.extend;
          y := zempobj(z.empno,z.ename,z.salary);
          x(x.last):=y;
          fetch c1 into z;
     end loop;
end;
/
```

Output of Listing 25.45 is given as follows:

```
Procedure created
```

Creating procedure

```
create or replace procedure putempcolsal( sal1 in number,sal2 in number,
x out zempcol) as
cursor c1 is
select empno,ename,salary from emp
where salary between sal1 and sal2;
y zempobj;
begin
   x := zempcol();
   for z in c1 loop
          x.extend;
          y := zempobj(z.empno,z.ename,z.salary);
          x(x.last):=y;
   end loop;
end;
/
```

Output of Listing 25.45 is given as follows:

```
Procedure created
```

You can use procedures as:

```
declare
   y zempcol;
begin
   y:= zempcol();
   putempcolsal (2000,3000,y);
   dbms_output.put_line(y.last);
   for i in 1..y.last loop
          dbms_output.put_line(to_char(y(i).empno)||' '||y(i).ename||' '
          ||to_char(y(i).salary));
   end loop;
end;
/
```

Output of Listing 25.45 is given as follows:

```
5
7566 JONES 2975
7698 BLAKE 2850
7782 CLARK 2450
7788 SCOTT 3000
7902 FORD 3000

PL/SQL procedure successfully complete
```

Use the Table Function

You can use the table() function to convert a collection into a series of rows. Suppose you have the student_c table with the following description and data:

```
desc student_c;
```

..Output of preceding code snippet is given as follows

```
 Name                                      Null?    Type
 ----------------------------------------- -------- ----------------------------
 SNAME                                              VARCHAR2(30)
 COURSE                                             COURSELIST

select * from student_c;

SNAME
------------------------------
COURSE(COURSECODE, COURSENAME)
--------------------------------------------------------------------------------
VIJAY
COURSELIST(TCOURSE(1, 'JSP'), TCOURSE(2, 'XML'))

AJAY
COURSELIST(TCOURSE(15, 'PASCAL'), TCOURSE(10, 'ADA'), TCOURSE(30, 'JAVA'), TCOUR
SE(40, 'ORACLE'))
```

The collection `COURSELIST` is the `VARRAY` of object `TCOURSE`. You can convert data of `VARRAY` into series of rows and perform operations on rows, as shown in the following code snippet:

```
select b.*
from student_c a,table(a.course) b
/
```

Output of preceding code snippet is given as follows

```
COURSECODE COURSENAME
---------- ------------------------------
         1 JSP
         2 XML
        15 Pascal
        10 Ada
        30 Java
        40 Oracle

6 rows selected.


select b.coursecode
 from student_c a,table(a.course) b
 where b.coursename='JSP';

COURSECODE
------
     1
```

PL/SQL Table or Associative Array

In the old versions, the PL/SQL table was used to store large number of elements. It was similar to a dynamic array. The usage of PL/SQL table is explained in Listing 25.47:

Listing 25.47: Using the PL/SQL Table

```
declare
   TYPE plstab IS TABLE OF number
      INDEX BY BINARY_INTEGER;
   x plstab;
begin
   x(1) := 54;
   x(2) := 65;
   dbms_output.put_line(x(1));
end;
/
```

Output of Listing 25.47 is given as follows:

```
54

PL/SQL procedure successfully completed
```

Bulk Operations

The concept of bulk operation is explained in detail in the following points:

PL/SQL block processes the procedural statements, and sends the SQL statements to the SQL engine, for execution in some cases, it sends data to the PL/SQL engine.

- Each context switch between the PL/SQL and SQL engines which adds to overhead. Therefore, if many switches are required, then performance degrades.
- This usually happens when the SQL statement executes inside a loop using index-by table or nested table VARRAY as bind variables.

Listing 25.48: Sending the following statement to the SQL engine for each iteration of the FOR loop

```
create table emp (empno number,ename varchar2(20),salary number);
declare
   type emp_id is varray(10) of number;
   id emp_id := emp_id(10001,10010,10013,10018);
begin
   for i in id.first..id.last loop
          delete from emp where empno = id(i);
   end loop;
end;
/
```

Output of Listing 25.48 is given as follows:

```
PL/SQL procedure successfully completed
```

Hence, if the SQL statement affects 4 or more rows in the database, then bulk binds are useful to improve the performance. The assigning of values to PL/SQL variables in SQL statements is called binding.

The binding of the entire collection at once is called as bulk binding.

Bulk binds improve the performance by reducing the number of context switch. For example, the `DELETE` statement, in the preceding code, will be sent only once to the SQL engine as a collection.

Use of the **FORALL** Statement

Listing 25.49: Using Bulk Binds to Insert Rows into the emp_table Table

```
create table emp_table(num number,names varchar2(15));
```

The output of Listing 25.49 is given as follows:

```
Table created
```

NOTE

You can use the FORALL statement to bulk-bind input collections. In addition, you can bulk-bind output collections by using the BULK COLLECT clause.

```
declare
   type numid is table of number(5) index by binary_integer;
   type nameid is table of varchar2(15) index by binary_integer;
   nums  numid;
   names nameid;
   t1 number(5);
   t2 number(5);
   t3 number(5);

procedure gettime (t out number) is
begin select to_char(sysdate,'sssss') into t from dual;
end;
begin
   for j in 1..5000 loop
        nums(j) := j;
        names(j) := 'emp no ' || to_char(j);
        end loop;
        gettime(t1);
        for i in 1..5000 loop          --using  for  loop
        insert into emp_table values (nums(i), names(i));
        end loop;
        gettime(t2);
        forall i in 1..5000                   --a
               insert into emp_table values (nums(i), names(i));
        gettime(t3);
        dbms_output.put_line('the execution time');
        dbms_output.put_line('-----------------');
        dbms_output.put_line('for loop: ' || to_char(t2 - t1));
        dbms_output.put_line('forall:   ' || to_char(t3 - t2));
     forall i in 1..5000                      --b
               insert into emp_table values (nums(i), names(i));
end;
/
```

Result:

```
The Execution Time
-----------------
FOR loop: 4
FORALL:   0  -- If the time is less than 1/100th of second Oracle returns 0
```

NOTE

The FOR.....LOOP.....END LOOP returns 0, if the time is less than 1/100th of second, Oracle returns 0.

You can observe the following points from the output:

- The keyword `FORALL` instructs the PL/SQL engine to bulk-bind the input collection before sending it to the SQL engine.
- The SQL engine executes the SQL statement once for each index number in the range.
- The SQL statement can reference more than one collection.
- PL/SQL engine bulk binds only the subscripted collections.

FORALL *Statement for Object Tables*

You can use the FORALL statement for the object tables, as shown in Listing 25.50:

Listing 25.50: Using FORALL for Object Tables

```
create type obj as object(x number);
/
```

The output of Listing 25.50 is given as follows:

```
Type created
```

You can create a table by using the following syntax:

```
create table objtable of obj;
```

The output of the preceding syntax is given as follows:

```
Table created
```

You can also modify values in a table with the help of following code snippet:

```
declare
   type obj1 is table of obj;
   z obj1:=obj1(obj(1),obj(2),obj(3),obj(4));
   type obj2 is varray(5) of integer;
   x obj2:=obj2(1,2,3);
begin
   forall i in z.first..z.last
   insert into objtable values(z(i));             --Inserts the values in table
                                                  --of objects objtable.

   forall i in x.first..x.last
   insert into emp_table values(x(i),'amit');     --Inserts the values in
                                                  --emp_table
   forall i1 in x.first..x.last
   delete emp_table where num=x(i1);              --Deletes all the records of
                                                  --emp_table
   if sql%bulk_rowcount(2)=0
   then
         dbms_output.put_line('value does not exist');
   else
         dbms_output.put_line('value exist'|| sql%bulk_rowcount(2));
   end if;
   forall i2 in x.first..x.last
   update emp_table set num=x(i2) where num=x(i2);

   if sql%bulk_rowcount(2)=0
   then                                           --A
         dbms_output.put_line('value does not exist');
   end if;
end;
/
```

The output of the preceding code snippet is given as follows:

```
PL/SQL procedure successfully completed
```

You can note the following points in the preceding code snippet:

- If any statement in the `FORALL` clause raises an unhandled exception, then all the database changes made during the previous execution are rolled back.
- However, if the exception is handled, then changes are rolled back to an implicit save point marked before each execution of the SQL statement. The changes made during the previous executions are not rolled back.

Use of %BULK_ROWCOUNT

The use of % BULK_ROWCOUNT is given as follows:

- SQL engine creates an implicit cursor named SQL to process SQL data manipulation statements.
- The SQL cursor has the attribute `%BULK_ROWCOUNT` to be used with the `FORALL` clause.
- Its `i`th element stores the number of rows processed by the `i'th` execution of an `UPDATE` or `DELETE` statement.
- If the `i`th execution affects no rows, `%BULK_ROWCOUNT(i)` returns zero.
- `%BULK_ROWCOUNT` is not maintained for bulk inserts because that would be redundant. If used after insert, it will raise the uninitialized collection exception.
- The `FORALL` statement and `%BULK_ROWCOUNT` attribute use the same subscripts. For example, if `FORALL` uses the range 5.....10, so does `%BULK_ROWCOUNT`.
- `FORALL` statements can only be used for the server side programs.
- The `insert`, `update`, and `delete` statement must reference at least one collection.
- The collection elements in the specified range must exist, otherwise an exception is raised.
- The input collection of the composite values cannot be bounded to the database columns.
- The cursor attribute `%BULK_ROWCOUNT` is neither assigned to other collections nor passed as a parameter to subprograms.
- The keyword `BULK COLLECT` tells the SQL engine to bulk-bind output collection before returning them to the PL/SQL engine.
- You can use this keyword in the `RETURN INTO`, `SELECT INTO`, `FETCH INTO` clauses.

Listing 25.51 shows the usage of %BULK_ROWCOUNT:

Listing 25.51: Using %BULK_ROWCOUNT

```
create table emp_tab4(empno number, ename varchar2(20),salary number)
/
insert into emp_tab4 values(1,'anil',1000)
/
insert into emp_tab4 values(2,'sunil',2000)
/
insert into emp_tab4 values(3,'amit',3000)
/
insert into emp_tab4 values(4,'ajay',4000)
/
insert into emp_tab4 values(5,'vijay',5000)
/
insert into emp_tab4 values(6,'ravi',6000)
/
insert into emp_tab4 values(7,'yogesh',8000)
/
insert into emp_tab4 values(8,'sunil',5000)
```

```
/
declare
   type eno is table of number;
   type ename is table of varchar2(20);
   x eno;
   y ename;
   cursor c1 is select empno,ename from emp_tab4 where salary > 1000;
   rows natural:=2;
   cnt number:=0;
begin
   select empno,ename bulk collect into x , y from emp_tab4;--a
   open c1;
   fetch c1  bulk collect into x , y;
   for i in x.first..x.last loop
         dbms_output.put_line(x(i)||'  '||y(i));
   end loop;
   close c1;
   open c1;
   fetch c1  bulk collect into x , y limit rows; --b
   dbms_output.put_line('limits the no of rows');
   for i in x.first..x.last loop
         dbms_output.put_line(x(i)||'  '||y(i));
   end loop;
   close c1;
   delete emp_tab4 where ename='sunil'                      --c
   returning empno  bulk collect into x;
   for i in x.first..x.last loop
         cnt:=cnt+1;
   end loop;
   dbms_output.put_line('the no of rows affected'||' '|| cnt);
end;
/
```

The output of Listing 25.51 is given as follows:

```
PL/SQL procedure successfully completed
```

You can observe the following points in Listing 25.51:

- In statement A, the SQL engine bulk-binds all collections referenced in the INTO list.
- The SQL engine loads the entire `empno` and `ename` columns into nested tables, before returning them to PL/SQL engine.
- The SQL engine initializes and extends the collection automatically.
- You can limit the number of rows returned by the SQL engine, for example if the `emp_tab4` table has `1000` rows, then you can take only the first, say `100` rows, using the pseudocolumn `ROWNUM`, such as:

```
select  empno,ename BULK COLLECT into x , y from emp_tab4
where ROWNUM<100;
```

Therefore, your target collection will be having only 100 entries.

- You can also bulk-fetch from a cursor into one or more collections.
- In statement B, the `LIMIT` clause limits the number of rows fetched from the database. It is applicable to bulk-fetch statements only. The syntax to apply the LIMIT clause is as follows:

```
FETCH -- BULK COLLECT INTO-- [LIMIT rows];
```

Therefore, rows can be a variable or expression but that must result into an integer.

- In the preceding example, the number of rows fetched from the cursor `c1` is limited to `2` only.

- In the statement C, you can also use the `BULK COLLECT` in the `RETURN INTO` clause of the `insert`, `update`, or `delete` statement.

If there are two or more employees with the name `sunil`, then their employee numbers are collected in `x`.

- The `BULK COLLECT` clause can be used only in server-side programs. All targets in a `BULK COLLECT INTO` clause must be collections.
- You cannot bulk-fetch from a cursor into a collection of records, as shown in the following code snippet:

```
declare
  type type1 is table of emp%rowtype;
  x type1;
  cursor c1 is select empno,ename from emp WHERE sal > 1000;
begin
  open c1;
  fetch c1 BULK COLLECT into x; --illegal
  close c1;
end;
/
```

The output of the preceding code snippet is given as follows:

```
ERROR at line 8:
ORA-06550: line 8, column 10:
PLS-00394: wrong number of values in the INTO list of a FETCH statement
ORA-06550: line 8, column 10:
PL/SQL: SQL Statement ignored
```

Fetching into Multiple Collections

You can perform the bulk-fetching operation into multiple collections by using the code shown in Listing 25.52:

Listing 25.52: Bulk-fetching from a Cursor into One or More Collections

```
declare
    type name is table of emp_tab4.ename%type;
    type sal is table of emp_tab4.salary%type;
    cursor c1 is select ename, salary from emp_tab4 where salary > 1000;
    names name;
    sals  salary;
 begin
    open c1;
    fetch c1 bulk collect into names, sals;
    close c1;
 end;
 /
```

The output of Listing 25.52 is given as follows:

```
PL/SQL procedure successfully completed
```

Listing 25.53: Showing how you can bulk-fetch from a cursor into a collection of records

```
declare
        type emp_rec is table of emp%rowtype;
        rec emp_rec;
        cursor c1 is
        select empno, ename, salary from emp where salary > 1000;
begin
        open c1;
        fetch c1 bulk collect into rec;
```

```
        close c1;
end;
/
```

The output of Listing 25.53 is given as follows:

```
PL/SQL procedure successfully completed
```

You can observe the following points with Listing 25.53:

- You cannot use composite targets, such as objects in the returning clause. Else you will get the error-unsupported feature with returning clause.
- You can combine the `BULK COLLECT` clause with FORALL in which the SQL engine bulk binds the column values incrementally.
- In the following example, if collection `emp_no` has two elements, each of which causes two rows to be deleted, then the collection `ENUM` has four elements when the statement completes.

NOTE

The column values returned by each execution are added to the values returned previously. , The previous values are overwritten with a FOR loop.

```
declare
   type emp_tab4_no is table of number;
   x emp_tab4_no:=emp_tab4_no(1,2);
   enum emp_tab4_no;
begin
   forall i in x.first..x.last
   delete from emp_tab4 where empno = x(i)
   returning empno bulk collect into enum;
end;
/
```

Result:

```
PL/SQL procedure successfully completed
```

You can observe the following points with the preceding code snippet:

- You cannot use the `select.....BULK COLLECT` statement in a `FORALL` statement. You cannot use `SELECT`, `BULK COLLECT`, and `FORALL` together.
- Client side programs can use the anonymous PL/SQL blocks to bulk-bind the input and output host arrays. Host arrays are declared in the host environment, such as OCI or pro*C program, and must be prefixed with a colon (:) to distinguish them from PL/SQL collections.

Cast and Multiset Operators

You can use the cast and multiset operators to convert the output of query into a collection, as shown in Listing 25.54:

Listing 25.54: Creating a Table and Inserting Data

```
create or replace type complex as object(rl number, im number);
/
```

The output of Listing 25.54 is given as follows:

```
Type created
```

You can create the table COMPLEXTAB by using the following syntax:

```
create or replace type complextab as table of complex;
/
```

The output of the preceding syntax is given as follows:

```
Type created
```

You can create the table CSAMPLE by using the following syntax:

```
create table csample(sn number,c1 complextab,c2 complextab)
nested table c1 store as nc1, nested table c2 store as nc2;
```

The output of the preceding syntax is given as follows:

```
Table created
```

You can insert data in CSAMPLE by using the following code snippet:

```
insert into csample values(1,complextab(complex(2,3),
complex(4,5)),complextab(complex(2,7),complex(4,5)));
```

The output of the preceding syntax is given as follows:

```
1 row created
```

You can insert more data in CSAMPLE by using the following code snippet:

```
insert into csample
values(2,complextab(complex(12,3),
complex(4,5)),complextab(complex(2,9),complex(4,5)));
```

The output of the preceding syntax is given as follows:

```
1 row created
```

You can create the table TCOMPLEX by using the following syntax:

```
create table tcomplex(arl number,aim number);
```

The output of the preceding code snippet is given as follows:

```
Table created
```

You can insert data into table TCOMPLEX by using the following syntax:

```
insert into tcomplex values(2,5);
```

The output of the preceding syntax is given as follows:

```
1 row created
```

You can insert more data in TCOMPLEX by using the following syntax:

```
insert into tcomplex values(5,9);
```

The output of the preceding syntax is given as follows:

```
1 row created
```

Listing 25.55: Using the CAST Operator to Put Data from CSAMPLE to the Nested Table in Collection

```
update csample
set c1=cast(multiset(select arl,aim from tcomplex) as complextab) where sn=1
/
```

The output of Listing 25.55 is given as follows:

```
1 row updated
```

You can display the data of CSAMPLE by using the following syntax:

```
select * from csample where sn=1;
```

The output of the preceding syntax is given as follows:

```
        SN
----------
C1(RL, IM)
----------------------------------------------
C2(RL, IM)
----------------------------------------------
         1

COMPLEXTAB(COMPLEX(2, 5), COMPLEX(5, 9))
COMPLEXTAB(COMPLEX(2, 7), COMPLEX(4, 5))
```

NOTE

The underlined data indicates the values from table.

Multiset operations are a set operations made on collections. These are similar to union, intersect and minus operations. You can use the multiset operations by using the code shown in Listing 25.56:

Listing 25.56: Using the Multiset Operation

```
select * from csample;
```

The output of Listing 25.56 is given as follows:

```
        SN
----------
C1(RL, IM)
---------------------------------------------------------------------------
C2(RL, IM)
---------------------------------------------------------------------------
         1
COMPLEXTAB(COMPLEX(2, 5), COMPLEX(5, 9))
COMPLEXTAB(COMPLEX(2, 7), COMPLEX(4, 5))

         2
COMPLEXTAB(COMPLEX(12, 3), COMPLEX(4, 5))
COMPLEXTAB(COMPLEX(2, 9), COMPLEX(4, 5))

        SN
----------
C1(RL, IM)
-----------------
C2(RL, IM)
-----------------
```

The `multiset except` returns elements of first collection, which are not in the second collection. The underlined data in the preceding result indicates row collections with element `(4,5)` common in both sets. However, in a `multiset except` it is removed. Listing 25.57 shows you the usage of multiset except:

Listing 25.57: Using multiset except

```
select sn, c1 multiset except c2 as c1_c2 from csample;
```

The output of Listing 25.57 is given as follows:

```
        SN
----------
C1_C2(RL, IM)
---------------------------------------------------------------------------
         1
COMPLEXTAB(COMPLEX(2, 5)) , COMPLEX(5, 9))

         2
COMPLEXTAB(COMPLEX(12, 3))
```

The `multiset intersect` returns elements, which are common in both sets. You can use multiset intersect by using the code shown in Listing 25.58:

Listing 25.58: Using multiset intersect

```
select sn, c1 multiset intersect c2 as c1_and_c2  from csample;
```

Output of Listing 25.58 is given as follows:

```
        SN
----------
C1_AND_C2(RL, IM)
---------------------------------------------------------------------------
         1
COMPLEXTAB()
         2
COMPLEXTAB(COMPLEX(4, 5))
```

The `multiset union` returns elements, which, in both sets, are similar to union all.

You can use the MULTISET UNION with the help of code shown in Listing 25.59:

Listing 25.59: Using MULTISET UNION

```
select sn, c1 multiset union  c2 as c1_or_c2  from csample;
```

Output of Listing 25.59 is given as follows:

```
        SN
----------
C1_OR_C2(RL, IM)
---------------------------------------------------------------------------
         1
COMPLEXTAB(COMPLEX(2, 5), COMPLEX(5, 9), COMPLEX(2, 7), COMPLEX(4, 5))
         2
COMPLEXTAB(COMPLEX(12, 3), COMPLEX(4, 5), COMPLEX(2, 9), COMPLEX(4, 5))
```

If you use distinct then duplicates are removed.

Listing 25.60: Using MULTISET UNION DISTINCT

```
select sn, c1 multiset union distinct  c2 as c1_or_c2  from csample;
```

The output of Listing 25.60 is given as follows:

```
        SN
----------
C1_OR_C2(RL, IM)
------------------------------------------------------------------------------
         1
COMPLEXTAB(COMPLEX(2, 5), COMPLEX(5, 9), COMPLEX(2, 7) , COMPLEX(4, 5))

         2
COMPLEXTAB(COMPLEX(12, 3), COMPLEX(4, 5), COMPLEX(2, 9))
```

Summary

In this chapter, you have learned about the collections and records. You have also learned about the Collection Methods, PL/SQL Table or Associative Array, and Bulk Operations. In the next chapter, you will learn about the LOB data types.

Exercise

1. Write a program to declare the collections.
2. Write a program to use collections as Input and Output.
3. Write a program to compare collections using the IS NULL Condition.
4. Write program for each built-in functions and procedures of collections methods.

26

LOB, BFILE, and DBMS_LOB

LOBs are used to store and process very large data. The data can be character data such as very large text or binary data such as sound files or video files. The LOB data can be stored in row and for processing variables are used. The data is processed using DBMS_LOB package.

New Data types (**LOB**)

Oracle uses the `LOB(Large Object)` datatype for storing large data up to four gigabytes in size. Oracle recommends using the `LOB` datatype over the `LONG` datatype. The difference between the `LONG` datatype and `LOB` datatype is given in Table 26. 1:

Table 26.1: Difference between LOB and LONG

LOB	LONG
Allows you to store maximum of 4 GB of data	Allows you to store maximum of 2 GB of data
Supports random access	Supports sequential access
Allows you to use it as an attribute of user-defined object	Does not allow you to use it as an attribute of user-defined object
Allows you to explicitly specify the storage characteristics. LOB can be stored: • inline (within a table) • out_of_line (within a tablespace) • in external file (BFILE datatype)	Allows only inline storage.

`LOB` can be used for storing text, graphic images, video clips, and sound. `LOB` has the following categories:

- BLOB
- BFILE

Let's discuss these in detail.

*The **BLOB** Datatype*

BLOB is used to store unstructured binary data in the database. It can store up to 4 GB of data. It can be manipulated by the `DBMS_LOB` package in PL/SQL and can participate in transactions.

CLOB** and **NCLOB

`CLOB` stores single byte character data, while `NCLOB` stores data of multibyte character set. They can be manipulated by the `DBMS_LOB` package, PL/SQL, and participate fully in transactions. You cannot create an object type with `NCLOB` datatype but `NCLOB` can be specified as a parameter in a method for object type.

BFILE

BFILE stores unstructured binary data in external operating systems file. It can store up to 4GB of data. The BFILE column actually stores the location of the file containing data. This is read-only, and Oracle processes should have read permission for the file pointed by BFILE. This datatype cannot participate in transactions.

Creating **LOB**

You can create table using LOB columns. If you insert any data in the table then LOB object is created.

Listing 21.6 shows the code to create a table with the LOB column:

Listing 26.1: Creating table with LOB Column

```
create table employee
 (empname char (30),
  empid number (6),
  empinfo clob,
  emppicture bfile)
  lob(empinfo) store as
  (tablespace users storage (initial 10k next 10k))
/
```

The output of Listing 26.1 is as follows:

```
Table created
```

Separate storage parameters can be created for `LOB`. To populate `LOB`, first initialize `LOB` to empty using the `INSERT` statement. Then, populate it using the `DBMS_LOB` package.

*Inserting **LOB** Columns*

The `LOB` column can be set to `NULL`, `EMPTY`, or some other value using the `INSERT` or `UPDATE` statement. Before writing a `LOB` value using the `DBMS_LOB` package, the `LOB` column must be made `NOT NULL`. You can make the LOB column NOT NULL by using the `EMPTY_LOB` function. You can initialize the `BFILE` column by using the `BFILENAME` function. When creating BFILE directory object should be in existence. If it is not present then directory object has to be created. Listing 26.2 shows the code to initialize LOB:

Listing 26.2: Using the INSERT statement to Initialize LOBs (for creating a directory, you need to have the permission for creating one)

```
create directory test as 'c:\lobdoc'
/
```

```
insert into employee values
('anil', 101, empty_clob( ), bfilename('test','a.txt'))
/
```

The output of Listing 26.2 is as follows:

```
1 row created
```

Using update statement to change value of LOB

```
update employee set empinfo='aaaa' where empname='Anil';
```

You have to create a directory before using the files in the directory. You have to use a logical name of the directory in `BFILE` functions. In Listing 26.2, `TEST` is a logical name, and `C:\LOBDOC` is the physical location of the directory.

Copying **LOB**s

You can copy a LOB value from one table to another. Listing 26.3 shows how to create a table by copying LOB values:

Listing 26.3: Creating a Table and Copying a LOB Value

```
create table  emphistory (empname, empid, emppicture, empinfo)
as
Select empname, empid, emppicture, empinfo
from employee
where empid = '101'
/
```

The output of Listing 26.3 is as follows:

```
Table created
```

LOB Locator

LOB values are not stored with the other row data. Along with the LOB row, a locator is stored. This implies that LOB has two attributes, LOB locator and LOB value. In the BFILE column, the actual path of file is stored. LOB locator is a pointer to the actual location of LOB value.

Reading a LOB Value

The LOB column can be used in the SELECT statement. Unlike other columns, SELECT does not return the value of LOB column, but it returns the locator of LOB. After getting the LOB locator, you can obtain the value of LOB object using the DBMS_LOB package procedure, as shown in the following code snippet:

```
declare
  info1 clob;
begin
  select empinfo
  into info1
  from employee
  where empid = '101';
  dbms_output.put_line ( 'size of column is  '|| dbms_lob.getlength(info1));
end;
/
```

The output of the preceding code snippet is as follows:

```
Size of column is 0

PL/SQL procedure successfully completed
```

Deleting LOB

You can delete LOB values by using the DELETE statement or DDL statements, such as DROP TABLE, TRUNCATE TABLE, and DROP TABLESPACE. When you drop LOB, LOB locator and LOB value are also dropped. In case of BFILE, only the locator is deleted. In case of copying LOB, two distinct values of LOB locator and two distinct locators are created.

Updating LOB

You can update a LOB value by using the SELECT FOR UPDATE statement. Before updating a LOB value, you must lock the LOB row. The LOB object in the database can be locked using SELECT…FOR UPDATE statement. If you update a LOB value without locking an error will occur. Listing 26.4 shows how to update a LOB value:

Listing 26.4: Updating a LOB Value

```
declare
  clob_lock clob;
  write_amt  integer;
  write_offset  integer;
  buffer varchar2( 40) := 'employeed in cc';
begin
  select empinfo
  into clob_lock
  from employee
  where empid = 101
  for update;
  write_amt := 6;
  write_offset := 10;
  dbms_lob.write( clob_lock, write_amt, write_offset, buffer);
end;
```

The output of Listing 26.4 is as follows:

```
PL/SQL procedure successfully completed
```

Read Consistency in a **LOB** Locator

When information is obtained in a locator, it remains attached to the locator even though it is updated through the other locator. A locator contains the snapshot of the environment of `LOB`, regardless of the existence of the `FOR UPDATE` clause. For example, if a `LOB` value is read in locator `M` and updated through another locator `N`, then `M` will not see updates of `N`, though `N` commits the changes. Listing 26.5 shows the code to read consistent behaviors of a LOB locator:

Listing 26.5: Reading Consistent Behaviors of a LOB Locator (if value aaaa is stored in LOB, then executing and setting value to aaaaaabb)

```
declare
   clob_s clob;
   clob_u  clob;
   read_amt integer;
   read_oft  integer;
   write_amt integer;
   write_oft integer;
   buffer varchar2(20);
begin
   select empinfo
   into clob_s
   from employee
   Where empid = '101';
   Select empinfo
   into clob_u
   from employee
   where empid = '101'
   for update;
   read_amt := 10;
   read_oft := 1;
   dbms_lob. read (clob_s, read_amt, read_oft, buffer);
   dbms_output.put_line (' value ' || buffer);    -- displays aaaa
   read_amt := 10;
   dbms_lob.read(clob_u, read_amt, read_oft, buffer);
   dbms_output.put_line ('value ' || buffer );    -- displays aaaa
   write_amt := 4;
   write_oft := 5;
   buffer := 'aabb';
   dbms_lob.write(clob_u, write_amt, write_oft, buffer);
   read_amt := 10;
   dbms_lob.read (clob_s, read_amt, read_oft, buffer);
   dbms_output.put_line(' value ' || buffer);-- still displays aaaa
   read_amt := 10;
         dbms_lob.read (clob_u, read_amt, read_oft, buffer);
   dbms_output.put_line(' value ' || buffer);-- aaaaaabb
end;
```

The output of Listing 26.5 is as follows:

```
value          aaaa
value          aaaa
value          aaaa
```

```
value                    aaaaaabb

PL/SQL procedure successfully completed
```

Updating a **LOB** Locator

When an update operation is performed through a locator, it is termed as an updated locator. Any changes made in LOB are visible through the locator only when the locator is refreshed. Updating the LOB value through the DBMS_LOB package is similar to updating value of LOB and reselecting it. If a LOB is updated using the SQL_UPDATE statement, the reselecting of LOB locator makes the changes visible. Listing 26.6 shows how to update a LOB locator:

Listing 26.6: Updating a LOB Locator

```
declare
   clob_u clob;
   read_amt integer;
   read_oft integer;
   buffer varchar2(50);
begin
   select empinfo
   into clob_u
   from employee
   where empid = 101;
   read_amt := 10;
   read_oft := 1;
   dbms_lob.read (clob_u, read_amt, read_oft, buffer);
   dbms_output.put_line(buffer);
   /*  if initial value of empinfo is aaaa, displays aaaa */
   update employee
   set empinfo = empty_clob( )
   where empid = 101;
   read_amt := 10;
   dbms_lob.read (clob_u, read_amt, read_oft, buffer);
   dbms_output.put_line( buffer);
   /* still displays aaaa the old value */
   Select empinfo into clob_u
   from employee
   where empid = 101;
   /* Refreshing locator */
   dbms_lob.read (clob_u, read_amt, read_oft, buffer);
   /* ERROR no Data found */
end;
```

The output of Listing 26.6 is as follows:

```
aaaa
aaaa
declare
*
ERROR at line 1:
ORA-01403: no data found
ORA-06512: at "SYS.DBMS_LOB", line 759
ORA-06512: at line 27
```

Updating the Current LOB Value

When a locator is used as a source to update another LOB, the snapshot environment of the source locator is used to determine the value to be updated. If the source locator is read consistent locator, the SELECT statement determines the value to be updated. If the source locator is an updated locator, the value associated with snapshot environment can be used for updating. Listing 26.7 shows how to update the current LOB values of the specified locator using the source locator as an updated locator:

Listing 26.7: Using the Source Locator as an Updated Locator

```
declare
  clob_u clob;
  clob_c clob;
  clob_s clob;
  read_amt integer;
  read_oft integer;
  write_amt  integer;
  write_oft  integer;
  buffer  varchar2(20);
begin
  select empinfo
  into clob_u
  from employee
  where empid = 101
  for update;
  clob_c := clob_u;
  read_amt := 10;
  read_oft := 1;
  dbms_lob.read ( clob_c, read_amt, read_oft, buffer);
  dbms_output.put_line(buffer);
  /* print 'aaaa' if the initial value is aaaa */
  write_amt := 4;
  buffer := 'bbbb';
  write_oft := 5;
  dbms_lob.write (clob_u, write_amt, write_oft, buffer);
 read_amt := 10;
  dbms_lob.read (clob_u, read_amt , read_oft, buffer);
  dbms_output.put_line (buffer);
  /* displays aaaabbbb*/
  read_amt := 10;
  dbms_lob.read ( clob_c, read_amt, read_oft, buffer);
  dbms_output.put_line( buffer);
  /* displays 'aaaa' */
  insert into employee (empid, empinfo)
  values ( 104, clob_c);
  Select empinfo
  into clob_s
  from employee
  where empid = 104;
       read_amt :=10;
  dbms_lob.read ( clob_s, read_amt, read_oft, buffer);
  dbms_output.put_line (buffer);
  /* display aaaa */
 end;
 /
```

The output of Listing 26.7 is as follows:

```
aaaa
aaaabbbb
aaaa
aaaa

PL/SQL procedure successfully completed
```

LOB Locators across Transactions (For Read Operation)

If you update a LOB locator in one transaction and refer it in another transaction, then reference will not generate an error for a read operation. Listing 26.8 shows how to use LOB locators for a read operation:

Listing 26.8: Using LOB Locators for a Read Operation

```
declare
   clob_u clob;
   read_amt integer;
   read_oft integer;
   write_amt integer;
   write_oft integer;
   buffer varchar2(20);
begin
   select empinfo
   into clob_u
   from employee
   where empid = 101
   for update;
   read_amt := 10;
   read_oft :=1;
   dbms_lob.read ( clob_u, read_amt, read_oft, buffer);
   dbms_output.put_line( buffer);
   /* assumming initial value 'aaaa' displays 'aaaa' */
   write_amt := 4;
   write_oft := 5;
   buffer := 'bbbb';
   dbms_lob.write (clob_u, write_amt, write_oft, buffer);
   commit;
   read_amt := 10;
   dbms_lob.read (clob_u, read_amt, read_oft, buffer);
   /* displays error ORA-22990 : LOB locator cannot span transaction in
   the earlier versions */
end;
```

The output of Listing 26.8 is as follows:

```
bbbb e

PL/SQL procedure successfully completed
```

LOB Locators Across Transactions (For Write Operation)

If you update a LOB locator in one transaction and refer to it in another transaction, then it will generate an error for a write operation. Listing 26.9 shows how to use LOB locators for a write operation:

Listing 26.9: Using LOB Locators for a Write Operation through SELECT.....FROM.....FOR UPDATE

```
declare
   clob_u clob;
   read_amt integer;
   read_oft integer;
   write_amt integer;
   write_oft integer;
   buffer varchar2(20);
begin
   select empinfo
   into clob_u
   from employee
   where empid = 101
   for update;
   read_amt := 10;
   read_oft :=1;
   dbms_lob.read ( clob_u, read_amt, read_oft, buffer);
   dbms_output.put_line( buffer);
   /* assumming initial value 'aaaa' displays 'aaaa' */
   write_amt := 4;
   write_oft := 5;
   buffer := 'bbbb';
   dbms_lob.write (clob_u, write_amt, write_oft, buffer);
   commit;
   read_amt := 10;
         dbms_lob.write (clob_u, write_amt, write_oft, buffer);
   /* displays error ORA-22990 : LOB locator cannot span transaction */
end;
/
```

The output of Listing 26.9 is as follows:

```
aaaa
declare
*
ERROR at line 1:
ORA-22990: LOB locators cannot span transactions
ORA-06512: at "SYS.DBMS_LOB", line 819
ORA-06512: at line 25
```

Listing 26.10 shows generation of error in the write operation when locator of previous transaction is used.

Listing 26.10: Shows generation of error in write operation.

```
declare
   clob_u clob;
   read_amt integer;
   read_oft integer;
   write_amt integer;
   write_oft integer;
   buffer varchar2(20);
begin
   update employee
         set empid=empid;
   select empinfo
   into clob_u
   from employee
```

```
    where empid = 101;
    read_amt := 10;
    read_oft :=1;
    dbms_lob.read ( clob_u, read_amt, read_oft, buffer);
    dbms_output.put_line( buffer);
    /* assumming initial value 'aaaa' displays 'aaaa' */
    commit;
    write_amt := 4;
    write_oft := 5;
    buffer := 'bbbb';
    dbms_lob.write (clob_u, write_amt, write_oft, buffer);
    commit;
    /* displays error ORA-22990 : LOB locator cannot span transaction */
end;
```

The output of Listing 26.10 is as follows:

```
ERROR at line 1:
ORA-22990: LOB locators cannot span transactions
ORA-06512: at "SYS.DBMS_LOB", line 819
ORA-06512: at line 24
```

EMPTY_BLOB and **EMPTY_CLOB** Functions

Before writing data in the `LOB` column, the `LOB` column must be made `NOT NULL`. This implies that the LOB column should contain a locator, pointing to empty or populated `LOB`. The value pointed by locator can be set to empty using the `EMPTY_BLOB()` and `EMPTY_CLOB()` functions. These functions are used only in the SQL `INSERT....VALUES` statement or in the `SET` clause of `UPDATE` statement; otherwise, an exception is raised. Listing 26.11 shows the use of the EMPTY_CLOB() function:

Listing 26.11: Using the EMPTY_CLOB() Function

```
INSERT INTO employee Values
('Anil', 101, EMPTY_CLOB(), BFILENAME('TEST','A.TXT'))
/
```

The output of Listing 26.11 is as follows:

```
1 row created
```

BFILE Operations

`BFILE` supports read only access to large files present on the database server. The files may be present in the hard disk or CDROM. It requires the operating system to support a stream mode access to the files in `BLOB` or `CLOB`. The value which indicates path of BFILE object is stored in tablespace, so when a row is copied to another row, a distinct copy of `LOB` is made. A locator of both rows has distinct copies. In case of `BFILE`, each `LOB` column has its own locator that points to a file which resides on the disk as an operating system file. Therefore, the `BFILE` column of two rows may point to the same file. The integrity and durability of a file is the responsibility of the underlying operating system. Oracle does not provide any transaction support to `BFILE`s.

*Creating **BFILE***

You can create a `BFILE` column by using the `BFILENAME()` function in the `INSERT` statement. Listing 26.12 shows how to create a BFILE column using BFILENAME() in the INSERT statement:

Listing 26.12: Creating a BFILE Column Using BFILENAME()

```
insert into employee values
('anil', 101, empty_clob(), bfilename('test','a.txt'))
/
```

The output of Listing 26.12 is as follows:

```
1 row created
```

Updating BFILE

You can update a BFILE column just as the other column by using the update statement. Listing 26.13 shows how to update a BFILE column:

Listing 26.13: Updating a BFILE Column

```
update employee
set emppicture = BFILENAME('TEST','B.txt') where empid = 101
/
```

The output of Listing 26.13 is as follows:

```
3 rows updated
```

Deleting BFILE

When a row containing a BFILE column is deleted, only the locator is deleted not the file. You can delete the file by using the operating system command.

Scope of a BFILE Locator

The BFILE locator acts similar to a file descriptor. All the operations, such as opening and closing the file, should be done in the same program block. The multiple locators can point to the same file on the disk. It can be passed as a parameter to the procedure or function, but it is recommended that opening and closing of file should be done in the same program block.

You cannot open unlimited number of BFILEs in one session. The maximum number of BFILEs, which can be opened at the same time are limited by the SESSION_MAX_OPEN_FILES initialization parameter, is defined in the INIT.ORA file. You should close the file that is opened during PL/SQL program normal termination or abnormal termination. Therefore, the FILECLOSE call has to be included in the PL/SQL block before normal exit and exception handler. To close all open files, FILECLOSEAll is used.

Directory Object

A directory object is used to specify the logical name to a physical path of directory. You can use the logical directory name in the BFILENAME function. You can create a directory, as shown in the following code snippet:

```
create directory my_dir as ' /u/ student1 '; --linux machine
create directory my_dir as ' C:\lobdoc\student1'; --windows machine
```

You can use the directory, as shown in the following code snippet:

```
BFILENAME ( 'my_dir','Anil.gif ');
```

If the files are moved from one physical directory, then only the logical directory is changed. The program code remains unchanged to create, drop, or alter the directory, you should have the CREATE DIRECTORY, DROP DIRECTORY, or ALTER DIRECTORY system privilege. To allow access to other users, you can grant the READ permission on the directory. Though the READ privilege is available to you, it is the DBA's responsibility to grant operating system privilege. The operating system READ permission should be available to Oracle server process.

Information about Directories

The information about directories is available by selecting the following views:

```
ALL_DIRECTORIES(OWNER, DIRECTORY_NAME, DIRECTORY_PATH)
DBA_DIRECTORIES (OWNER, DIRECTORY_ NAME, DIRECTORY_PATH);
```

Guidelines for Using DIRECTORY

DBA should follow the guidelines for managing a DIRECTORY object. The DIRECTORY object should not point to the location of a directory, which contains datafiles, control files, log files, and system files. You should remember the following points while granting permissions to other users on these files:

- Grant the CREATE ANY DIRECTORY privilege very carefully
- Grant privileges on the DIRECTORY object very carefully
- Grant privileges with the GRANT option very carefully
- If a DIRECTORY object is dropped or altered or its privilege is revoked, n the access of the associated files using DBMS_LOB package or OCI operations will not be available. If the files are opened, the FILECLOSE call will fail and the user has to terminate the session or use the FILECLOSEALL () call.

NOTE

It is recommended that:

DBA should use the commands like CREATE DIRECTORY when applications are not running

DBA should create directory objects and give the READ permission to specific database users.

The **BFILENAME()** Function—Use of Directory Object

The directory object is specified in the BFILENAME function, as shown in the following code snippet:

```
BFILENAME (dirname, filename)
BFILENAME ('my_dir', 'Anil.gif ')
```

The availability and access of the actual file is checked only when the file is accessed using a locator. If the file is not accessed, DBMS_LOB routines or OCI routines generate errors. The BFILENAME() returns BFILE locator, which can be used in various DBMS_LOB routines. Listing 26.14 shows the use of the BFILENAME() function:

Listing 26.14: Using the BFILENAME() Function

```
declare
   fd1 bfile;
         fd2 bfile;
   status integer;
begin
   fd1 := bfilename ( 'test', 'a.txt');
   fd2 := bfilename ( 'test', 'b.txt');
   dbms_lob.fileopen(fd1);
   dbms_lob.fileopen(fd2);
   status := dbms_lob.compare (fd1,fd2,5,1,1);
   if (status != 0) then
         dbms_output.put_line ( 'files are different');
   else
         dbms_output.put_line ('files are same');
   end if;
   dbms_lob.fileclose(fd1);
   dbms_lob.fileclose(fd2);
end;
/
```

The output of Listing 26.14 is as follows:

```
PL/SQL procedure successfully completed
```

The directory names are case sensitive.

The **DBMS_LOB** Package

In the DBMS_LOB package, various types of routines are used to manipulate LOB objects. All the routines work using LOB locators. The LOB object is manipulated by selecting the LOB locator in a PL/SQL LOB variable. The LOB routines are as follows:

- The routines that read LOB values, such as COMPARE, GETLENGTH, INSTR, READ, and SUBSTR
- The routines that modify BLOB, CLOB, and NCLOB, such as APPEND, COPY, ERASE, TRIM, WRITE, LOADFROMFILE, LOADBLOBFROMFILE, LOADCLOBFROMFILE, CREATETEMPORARY, FREETEMPORARY, and ISTEMPORARY
- The routines for BFILE, such as FILECLOSE, FILECLOSEALL, FILEEXISTS, FILEGETNAME, FILEISOPEN, and FILEOPEN

The DBMS_LOB package does not define any new datatype. The existing datatypes that are used are as follows:

- BLOB
- RAW
- CLOB
- VARCHAR2
- INTEGER

It defines the following constants:

- lobmaxsize 4294967295 (4GB)
- file_readonly 0

NOTE

The limit of RAW and VARCHAR2 is 32767 bytes.

Exceptions

Table 26.2 describes the exceptions defined in the DBMS_LOB package:

Exception	Description
INVALID_ARGVAL	Occurs when the argument to runtime is invalid, null, or out of range. The code of the INVALID_ARGVAL exception is 21560.
ACCESS_ERROR	Occurs when an attempt is made to read/write beyond maximum LOB size.
NO_DATA_FOUND	Occurs when an attempt is made to read empty LOB or read after end of LOB has occurred. The code of NO_DATA_FOUND is 1403.
VALUE_ERROR	Occurs when an invalid value is passed as a parameter. The code of VALUE_ERROR is 6502. The exceptions which may occur during access to LOB are as follows: • NOEXIST_DIRECTORY—Occurs when a directory does not exist. Its code is 22285. • NOPRIV_DIRECTORY—Occurs when there is insufficient privilege on a directory. Its code is 22286. • INVALID_OPERATION—Occurs when an operation fails. Its code is 22288. • UNOPENED_FILE—Occurs when an operation is performed on an unopened file. Its code is 22289. • OPEN_TOO_MANY—Occurs when maximum limit is reached on number of opened files. Its code is 22290.

Procedures/Functions

The DBMS_LOB provides various procedures and functions to process data of LOB objects. The procedures and functions are described as follows.

The **APPEND** Function

The APPEND function appends source LOB to destination LOB. If the source is NULL, it raises the VALUE_ERROR exception. The following code snippet shows how to define the APPEND function:

```
Procedure Append (dest In OUT BLOB, Src In BLOB);
Procedure Append (dest IN OUT CLOB CHARACTER SET,
src IN CLOB CHARACTER SET);
```

Listing 26.15 shows the code to use append LOB routine to manipulate an LOB object:

Listing 26.15: Using Append LOB Routine to Manipulate LOB Object

```
declare
  dest clob;
        src clob;
        buffer varchar2(30);
        read_amt integer := 20;
        read_oft integer := 1;
begin
  select empinfo
  into dest from employee
  where empid = 101
  for update;
  select empinfo
  into src from employee
  where empid= 104;
  dbms_lob.append(dest, src);
        dbms_lob.read(dest,read_amt,read_oft,buffer);
        dbms_output.put_line(buffer);
end;
```

The output of Listing 26.15 is as follows:

```
aabb e    aabb e

PL/SQL procedure successfully completed
```

You cannot directly load LOB values into the database. This limitation is overcome by the DBMS_LOB package that includes the LOADFROMFILE procedure, which transfers the BFILE data into an internal LOB column. This procedure does not perform any character-set translation. It converts the BFILE data into a CLOB column, only if the character-set used in the BFILE file is same as that used for the CLOB column. Listing 26.16 shows how to transfer data from BFILE to LOB

Listing 26.16: Transferring Data from BFILE to LOB

```
DECLARE
  x bfile;
  y clob;
  z binary_integer;
begin
  x := bfilename('test','a.txt');
  if dbms_lob.fileexists(x) =1 then
         z := dbms_lob.getlength(x);
         dbms_lob.fileopen(x);
```

```
            insert into empl(empid,empinfo) values(1,empty_clob()) returning
            empinfo into y;
            dbms_lob.loadfromfile(y,x,z);
            dbms_lob.fileclose(x);
    else
            dbms_output.put_line('specified file does not exist.');
    end if;
end;
```

The output of Listing 26.16 is as follows:

```
PL/SQL procedure successfully completed
```

The **COMPARE** Function

The COMPARE function is used to compare data of two LOB objects. For CLOB objects it acts like comparing two strings.

The following code snippet shows how to use the COMPARE function:

```
function compare (lob1 in tp, lob2 in tp, amt in integer, oft1 in integer,
oft2 in integer)
return integer
```

In the preceding code snippet:

- `tp` is any `LOB` datatype, such as `BLOB`, `CLOB`, and `BFILE`
- `amt` is the number of bytes or characters to be compared (maximum value is `4294967295`)
- `oft1` is the starting point of comparison of destination LOB
- `oft2` is the starting point of comparison of source LOB

The COMPARE function returns:

- zero, if the source and destination match
- non-zero, if the source and destination does not match
- `NULL`, if `amt` (amount) is less than `1`
- `NULL`, if `amt` is more than `LOBMAXSIZE`
- NULL, if oft1 (offset) or oft2 < 1
- NULL, if oft1 or oft2 > LOBMAXSIZE

Listing 26.17 shows how to compare data for a specified amount and offset:

Listing 26.17: Comparing Data for a Specified Amount and Offset

```
DBMS_LOB.compare ( bfl1, bfl2,100,150,250);
```

In Listing 26.17, `100` bytes of files described by `bfl1` and `bfl2` are compared. For the first file, the origin is `150` bytes and for the second file, its `250` bytes.

The **COPY** Procedure

The COPY procedure copies the specified number of bytes from the source location to the destination location. It raises the `VALUE_ERROR` exception, if any of the input parameters are `NULL` or valid. The procedure raises the `INVALID_ARGVAL` exception, if

- Source offset or destination offset<1
- Source offset or destination offset>LOBMAXSIZE
- amount < 1 or amount > LOBMAXSIZE

The syntax of the COPY procedure is as follows:

```
procedure copy (dest_lob in out blob,
src_lob in blob, amount in number(38),
dest_offset in number(38) default,
src_offset in number(38) default);
```

The following code snippet shows how to define the COPY procedure:

```
procedure copy (dest in out tp
src in tp,
amt in out integer,
doft in integer,
soft in integer);
```

In the preceding code snippet:

- `tp` refers to `BLOB` or `CLOB`
- `amt` is amount of bytes or characters to be copied
- `soft` is the source object, for which the default value is 1
- `doft` is the destination offset , for which the default value is 1

Listing 26.18 shows how to use the copy procedure in sample program:

Listing 26.18: Using the Copy procedure in Sample Program

```
declare
  dlob CLOB;
  slob CLOB;
  amt integer;
  buffer varchar2(30);
  read_amt integer := 20;
  read_oft integer := 1;
begin
  select empinfo
  into dlob
  from employee
  where empid = 101
  for update;
  Select empinfo
  into slob
  from employee
  where empid = 104;
  dbms_lob.copy(dlob, slob, 10, 1, 1);
  dbms_lob.read(dlob,read_amt,read_oft,buffer);
  dbms_output.put_line(buffer);
  commit;
end;
```

The output of Listing 26.18 is as follows:

```
aabb employ    a

PL/SQL procedure successfully completed
```

In Listing 26.18, the copy procedure copies 100 bytes from destination to source.

The **ERASE** Procedure

The ERASE procedure is used to erase data in the LOB object.

The syntax of the ERASE procedure is as follows:

```
procedure erase (lob in out tp, amt in out integer, oft in integer := 1);
```

In the preceding syntax:

- `tp` refers to `BLOB` or `CLOB`
- `amt` is the amount of bytes or characters which are to be erased
- `oft` is offset from which bytes or characters are to be erased

If the number of bytes erased is in the middle of the LOB object, then the space is filled with zero byte fillers. When the end of the LOB value is reached before erasing the specified number, the actual number of bytes or characters erased differs from the number you specified in the amount (`amt`) parameter.

The ERASE procedure may raise the following exceptions:

- `VALUE_ERROR`, if any parameter is `NULL`
- `INVALID_ARGVAL`, if (`amount < 1` or `amount > LOBMAXIZE`) or (`offset < 1` or `offset > LOBMAXSIZE`)

Listing 26.19 shows how to use the ERASE procedure:

Listing 26.19: Using the ERASE Procedure

```
amt := 100;
dbms_lob.erase (dlob, amt, 200);
```

In Listing 26.19, the ERASE procedure erases 100 bytes from the location, 200.

The **TRIM** Procedure

The TRIM procedure trims the data in `LOB` to the specified length. The syntax of the TRIM procedure is as follows:

```
procedure TRIM(lob in tp, len IN integer)
```

In the preceding syntax:

- `tp` refers to `BLOB` or `CLOB`
- `len` is the new trimmed length of `LOB` in bytes or characters

The TRIM procedure may raise the following exceptions:

- `VALUE_ERROR`, if any of the argument is `NULL`.
- `VALUE_ERROR`, if len is less than `0` or more than `LOBMAXSIZE`

Listing 26.20 shows the use of the TRIM procedure:

Listing 26.20: Using the TRIM Procedure

```
declare
  dlob clob;
  slob clob;
  amt integer;
  buffer varchar2(30);
  read_amt integer := 20;
  read_oft integer := 1;
begin
  select empinfo
  into dlob
  from employee
  where empid = 101
  for update;
```

```
    dbms_lob.trim(dlob,10);
    dbms_lob.read(dlob,read_amt,read_oft,buffer);
    dbms_output.put_line(buffer);
    commit;
end;
```

The output of Listing 26.20 is as follows:

```
aabb e

PL/SQL procedure successfully completed
```

The WRITE Procedure

The WRITE procedure is used to modify data in the LOB object.

The syntax of the WRITE procedure is as follows:

```
procedure WRITE(lob IN OUT tp
amt IN OUT BINARY_INTEGER
oft IN INTEGER,
buffer IN btp);
```

In the preceding syntax:

- `tp` refers to `BLOB` or `CLOB`
- `amt` is the amount of data to be written in bytes or characters
- `oft` is the offset from where writing of data starts
- `buffer` is the variable of which data is written
- `btp` can be `RAW` (for `BLOB`) or `VARCHAR2` (`CLOB`)

The WRITE procedure may raise the following exceptions:

- `VALUE_ERROR`, if input parameters are NULL
- `INVALID_ARGVAL`, if `amount<1` or `amount > MAXBUFSIZE` and `OFFSET < 1` or `OFFSET > LOBMAXSIZE`

Listing 26.21 shows the use of the Write procedure:

Listing 26.21: Using the WRITE Procedure

```
declare
    dlob clob;
    slob clob;
    amt binary_integer;
    v_buffer raw(2000);
begin
    select empinfo
    into dlob
    from employee
    where empid = 101
    for update;
    select empinfo
    into slob
    from employee
    where empid = 104;
    amt:=1000;
    dbms_lob.read(dlob,amt , 500 ,v_buffer);
    dbms_lob.write(slob ,amt , 1200 ,v_buffer);
    commit;
end;
```

The output of Listing 26.21 is as follows:

```
PL/SQL procedure successfully completed
```

The LOADFROMFILE Procedure

The LOADFROMFILE procedure is used to load data of BFILE into CLOB or BLOB. The syntax of this procedure is as follows:

```
DBMS_LOB.LOADFROMFILE(DEST_LOB  IN OUT CLOB,
SRC_BFILE  IN BFILE,
AMOUNT  IN NUMBER,
DEST_OFFSET IN  NUMBER,
SRC_OFFSET IN NUMBER)
```

The following code snippet shows the use of the LOADFROMFILE procedure:

```
declare
x clob;
b bfile;
v varchar2(30);
amt number:=20;
begin
b:=bfilename('scotttmp','sample.txt');
x:='                                        ';
if (dbms_lob.fileexists(b)=1) then
dbms_output.put_line('file in existance');
dbms_lob.fileopen(b);
dbms_lob.loadfromfile(x,b,amt);  --a
dbms_lob.fileclose(b);
dbms_lob.read(x,amt,1,v);
dbms_output.put_line(v);
end if;
end;
```

The output of the preceding code snippet is as follows:

```
FILE IN EXISTANCE
```

This is sample file (Contents of sample file.)

Before executing the preceding program, create the directory, as shown in the following code snippet:

```
CREATE DIRECTORY SCOTTTEMP AS 'C:\TEMP'
```

In the preceding code snippet, Statement A loads data from the sample.txt file in the X LOB object.

The LOADCLOBFROMFILE Procedure

The LOADCLOBFROMFILE procedure loads data from BFILE into CLOB. It is more efficient than LOADFROMFILE as no data conversion is done at the time of loading. The syntax of the LOADCLOBFROMFILE procedure is as follows:

```
dbms_lob.loadclobfromfile
(dest_clob in out clob,
src_bfile in bfile,
amt in number,
dest_offset in out number,
src_offset in out number,
src_charset_id in number,
lang_context in out number,
warning out number)
src_charset_id : source character set identifier
lang_context : language context of source
```

In the preceding syntax, Warning is message that occurs if there is problem with load. Typically this problem occurs if there is problem from converting data of BFILE char set to CLOB char set.

The following code snippet shows how to load data from BFILE to CLOB:

```
declare
x clob;
b bfile;
v varchar2(30);
amt number:=20;
dest_offset number:=1;
src_offset number:=1;
warning number;
src_csid number:=dbms_lob.default_csid;
lang_context number:=dbms_lob.default_lang_ctx;
begin
b:=bfilename('scotttmp','sample.txt');
x:='                                            ';
if (dbms_lob.fileexists(b)=1) then
dbms_output.put_line('file in existance');
dbms_lob.fileopen(b);
dbms_lob.loadclobfromfile(x,b,amt,dest_offset,src_offset,src_csid,lang_context,warning);
dbms_lob.fileclose(b);
dbms_lob.read(x,amt,1,v);
dbms_output.put_line(v);
end if;
end;
```

You can use the DBMS_LOB.LOADBLOBFROMFILE procedure to load data into BLOB.

The CREATETEMPORARY Procedure

The CREATETEMPORARY procedure is used to create LOB objects in temporary tablespace. This procedure is provided with two supporting subprograms FREETEMPORARY and ISTEMPORAY. The FREETEMPORARY procedure frees the storage allocated for LOB objects. The ISTEMPORARY function checks whether the specified LOB is temporary or not. The syntax of CREATETEMPORARY is as follows:

```
DBMS_LOB.CREATETEMPORARY(LOB_OBJ IN OUT  CLOB, CACHE IN BOOLEAN)
```

In the preceding syntax, cache indicates whether the object can be read in memory buffer. The first parameters can be also of the type BLOB. The following code snippet shows the use of the CREATETEMPORARY procedure:

```
declare
x clob;
b bfile;
v varchar2(30);
amt number:=20;
flag integer;
csize number;
begin
b:=bfilename('scotttmp','sample.txt');
dbms_lob.createtemporary(x,true);
if (dbms_lob.fileexists(b)=1) then
dbms_output.put_line('file in existance');
dbms_lob.fileopen(b);
dbms_lob.loadfromfile(x,b,amt);
dbms_lob.fileclose(b);
```

```
dbms_lob.read(x,amt,1,v);
dbms_output.put_line(v);
end if;
flag:=dbms_lob.istemporary(x);
dbms_output.put_line(flag);
csize := dbms_lob.getchunksize(x);
dbms_output.put_line('chunk size '||csize);
dbms_lob.freetemporary(x);
end;
```

The output of the preceding code snippet is as follows:

```
FILE IN EXISTANCE
```

This is sample file.

```
1
CHUNK SIZE 8132
```

The GETCHUNKSIZE function returns number of bytes read or written by LOB data.

The **GETLENGTH** Function

The GETLENGTH function returns the number of bytes or characters in an integer. It returns NULL, in case of BFILE, if LOB is null, or file could not be accessed. The syntax of the GETLENGTH function is as follows:

```
Function GETLENGTH (lob IN tp )
RETURN INTEGER;
```

In the preceding syntax, `tp` refers to `BLOB`, `CLOB`, or `BFILE`.

Listing 26.22 shows the use of the GETLENGTH function:

Listing 26.22: Using the GETLENGTH Function

```
declare
  dlob CLOB;
  slob CLOB;
  amt integer;
  buffer varchar2(30);
  read_amt integer := 20;
  read_oft integer := 1;
begin
  Select empinfo
  into dlob
  from employee
  where empid = 101;
  dbms_output.put_line(dbms_lob.getlength(dlob));
  dbms_lob.read(dlob,read_amt,read_oft,buffer);
  dbms_output.put_line(buffer);
  commit;
end;
/
```

The output of Listing 26.22 is as follows:

```
aabb e

PL/SQL procedure successfully completed
```

The **INSTR** Function

The INSTR function returns the matching position of nth occurrence of pattern. It returns NULL in the following cases:

- if any of the argument is `NULL`
- `oft < 1`
- `oft > LOBMAXSIZE`
- `num < 1`
- `num > LOBMAXSIZE`

The syntax of the INSTR function is as follows:

```
Function INSTR (lob In tp, pattern IN ptp, oft IN INTEGER, num IN INTEGER)
RETURN INTEGER;
```

In the preceding syntax:

- `tp` refers to `BLOB`, `CLOB`, or `BFILE`
- `pattern` is `RAW`, in case of `BLOB` or `BFILE`; `VARCHAR2`, in case of `CLOB`
- `oft` refers to offset
- `num` is the `n`th occurrence of the pattern

NOTE

If the file pointed by BFILE object could not be accessed, it raises an exception.

Listing 26.23 shows how to use the INSTR function:

Listing 26.23: Using the INSTR Function

```
create or replace procedure instr_ex is
  loc                   bfile;
  pattern          raw(32);
  position         integer;
begin
      select  tab.ad_pic into loc from abc tab
  where pmtab.prod_id = 1101 and tab.ad_id = 11002;
  dbms_lob.open(loc, dbms_lob.lob_readonly);
  position := dbms_lob.instr(loc, pattern, 1, 2);
  dbms_lob.close(loc);
end;
```

The output of Listing 26.23 is as follows:

```
PL/SQL procedure successfully completed
```

The **SUBSTR** Function

The SUBSTR function returns substring starting from offset and the length equal to the amount of bytes. It returns `NULL`, if:

- any of the input parameters is `NULL`
- `amt < 1`
- `amt > 32767`
- `oft < 1`
- `oft > LOBMAXSIZE`

The syntax of the SUBSTR function is as follows:

```
Function SUBSTR(lob IN tp, amt IN INTEGER, oft In INTEGER)
RETURN   rtp;
```

In the preceding syntax:

- `tp` refers to `BLOB`, `CLOB`, or `VARCHAR2`
- `amt` is amount of bytes

- `oft` refers to offset beginning from origin
- `rtp` is `RAW` for `BFILE` and `BLOB`; `VARCHAR2` for `CLOB`.

NOTE

If the access is not available in case of BFILE, it returns an exception.

File Related Procedure—The **FILECLOSE** Procedure

The FILECLOSE procedure closes the opened file. If the file could not be accessed, it raises an exception. The syntax of the FILECLOSE procedure is as follows:

```
procedure fileclose(loc in out bfile);
```

File Related Procedure—The **FILECLOSEALL** Procedure

The FILECLOSEALL procedure closes all the opened files. Generally, it is written to close all the files when there is an abnormal exit from the PL/SQL code. The syntax of the FILECLOSEALL procedure is as follows:

```
Procedure FILECLOSEALL;
```

File Related Function—The **FILEEXISTS** Function

The FILEEXISTS function checks whether the file is in existence or not. It returns `1`, if the file exists; and `0` if the file does not exist. It returns `NULL`, if `LOC` is null or the file does not have OS privileges or necessary directory. It may raise the following exceptions:

- `NOEXIST_DIRECTORY`
- `NOPRIV_DIRECTORY`
- `INVALID_DIRECTORY`

The syntax of the FILEEXISTS function is as follows:

```
Function FILEEXISTS (loc IN BFILE)
Return Integer;
```

Listing 26.24 shows the use of the FILEEXISTS function:

Listing 26.24: Using the FILEEXISTS Function

```
declare
   loc BFILE;
begin
   Select emppicture
   into loc
   from employee
   where empid = 101;
   if ( DBMS_LOB.FILEEXISTS( loc )=1) then
                 DBMS_OUTPUT.PUT_LINE ( ' File in existance ' ) ;
   else
        DBMS_OUTPUT.PUT_LINE ( ' File does not exist ' );
   end if;
end;
/
```

The output of Listing 26.24 is as follows:

```
PL/SQL procedure successfully completed
```

File Related Procedure—**FILEGETNAME**

The FILEGETNAME procedure returns the name of file (fname) and directory (dir) in variables. The syntax of the FILEGETNAME procedure is as follows:

```
procedure FILEGETNAME (loc IN BFILE, dir OUT VARCHAR2, fname OUT VARCHAR2);
where
```

In the preceding syntax:

- loc is a BFILE locator
- dir refers to the directory name
- fname is the name of BFILE

The FILEGETNAME procedure raises the following exceptions:

- VALUE_ERROR, if any input parameter is NULL
- INVALID_ARGVAL, if dir or fname is NULL

File Related Function—FILEISOPEN

The FILEISOPEN function returns a non-zero value, if the file of the given locator is open. It raises an exception, if the file is not accessed due to some reason. The syntax of the FILEISOPEN function is as follows:

```
function FILEISOPEN(loc IN BFILE)
RETURN INTEGER;
```

Listing 26.25 shows the use of the FILEISOPEN function:

Listing 26.25: Using the FILEISOPEN Function

```
declare
   loc   bfile;
begin
   select emppicture
   into loc
   from employee
   where empid = 104;
   dbms_lob.fileopen(loc);
   if ( dbms_lob.fileisopen(loc)=1)  then
          dbms_output.put_line ( ' file is open' );
   end if ;
end;
```

In Listing 26.25, the FILEISOPEN function displays the data of the file, if the file contains data, else an error gets displayed.

File Related Procedure—FILEOPEN

The FILEOPEN function opens the file of a given locator. The syntax of the FILEOPEN function is as follows:

```
Procedure FILEOPEN (loc IN OUT BFILE,
mode IN BINARY-INTEGER := FILE_READONLY);
```

The FILEOPEN function may raise the following exceptions:

- The FILEOPEN raises an exception, if the file is not opened due to some reason
- VALUE_ERROR, if any argument is NULL
- INVALID_ARGVAL, if the mode is other than READONLY
- OPEN_TOOMANY, if the number of files opened exceeds SESSION_MAX_OPENFILES

Using the DBMS_LOB Package

Summary of DBMS_LOB package

- The number of bytes or characters, which are read or written, depends upon the limit of RAW or VARCHAR2 datatype

- The character set of `VARCHAR2` buffer should be same as the character set of `CLOB` or `NCLOB`
- Only positive values are to be specified for an amount or offset parameters
- To perform any DML operation using `WRITE` and `TRIM`
- The string functions, such as `INSTR and COMPARE` do not support regular expressions.
- The file need not be opened for functions, such as `FILEEXIST`, `FILEGETNAME`, and `GETLENGTH`.
- When a session is terminated, the files are closed
- It is better to close the file for PL/SQL program normal termination and abnormal termination (exception handler)
- If you are not sure about closing the file, you can call `FILECLOSEALL` in a suitable routine
- The `DIRECTORY` privilege should be granted very carefully

Now that you are familiar with LOB datatypes

Summary

In this chapter, you have learned about LOB and its types BLOB and Bfile. You have also learned about the creating LOB and inserting LOBs values. In the next chapter, you will learn about object and its types.

Exercise

Suppose two files are a.txt and b.txt stored in folder c:\temp are having following lines of text

a. txt

This is sample file.

b. txt

This is test file.

1. Write a program to print data of file a.txt in uppercase.
2. Write a program to calculate number of words in a.txt
3. Write a program to compare data of the two files.

27

Objects and Object Types

Objects are entities that are used to provide more realistic representation of data in real life. Due to increase in popularity of object oriented programming using C++ and Java, Oracle also introduced object programming features in PL/SQL.

Concept of Object

Object is a tool that is used to design object-oriented database in Oracle. The concept of an object is similar to a class. To use an object, a user has to create an object type. A user can create composite as well as simple types from an object type.

In Oracle, the data is stored in an object in natural form, very close to real life data. For objects, the user has to specify both the structure of data and the ways for operating it. Objects make it easier to work with other types of data, such as images, audio, and video.

Let's now see how we can define a bill using an object. A bill consists of information, such as customer code, customer name, address, bill items, date, and billno.

Listing 27.1 shows the code to create various object types:

Listing 27.1: Creating Object Type address

```
create or replace type address as object
(plot varchar2(10),
street varchar2(30),
city varchar2(30),
pincode varchar2(10))
/
```

The output of Listing 27.1 is as follows:

```
Type created
```

Creating object type customer

```
create or replace type customer as object
(ccode number(4),
cname varchar2 (30),
adr address)
/
```

Result:

```
Type created
```

Creating object type billitems

```
create or replace type billitems as object
(itemname varchar2(30),
city number(10, 2),
rate number (10, 2))
/
```

Result:

```
Type created
```

Creating type billitemtable

```
create or replace type billitemtable as
table of billitems
/
```

Result:

```
Type created
```

Creating object type bill

```
create or replace type bill as object
(billno number,
```

```
billdate date,
cust customer,
billitems billitemtable,
member function
billvalue return  number)
/
```

Result:

```
Type created
```

Defining datatypes does not involve any storage allocation. In SQL statement, the datatypes are used in a similar way as other types, such as VARRAY and nested table.

Methods

Method in PL/SQL is a subprogram that returns a value. In the preceding example of the bill, the billvalue is the method. Suppose X is the PL/SQL variable having the type bill. In that case, you can write the code shown in the following code snippet:

```
n := x.billvalue( ) ;
```

In the preceding code snippet, n will have the value of bill. It is not necessary to pass any argument in the method. The billvalue function takes the current value of bill. Suppose you assign the return value of the billvalue method to the z variable, as shown in the following code snippet:

```
z : = y.billvalue( );
```

In the preceding code snippet, the value of the bill is the value calculated using the current attribute, which is y. This type of method invocation is called as selfish style of method invocation.

The Constructor Method

The constructor method is a function. It returns a new object as its value. Every object type has a system defined constructor method. The name of the constructor method is the same as the object type. Consider the following code snippet:

```
Address ( '71',' MGRoad',' Nagpur','440010');
```

The preceding code snippet represents the address object with some values.

The Comparison Method

The objects can be compared in two ways:

- Using Map method
- Using Order method

Using the Map Method

The map method is a function whose value depends upon the value of attributes, for example bill amount of a bill. If two objects x and y have the bill type, then the relationship between these two objects depend on the value of the bill amount.

Using the Order Method

The order method has its own internal logic of comparing two objects. For example, if x and y are two objects of type address, then the LESS THAN relationship may depend upon their value of the zip code.

If two objects lack a comparison method, then the less than or greater than relationship has to be defined. The equal or not equal relationship is defined using their attribute values. The objects can have one of the following two methods, i.e. map or order.

The following are some examples of the comparison method:

Listing 27.2: Declaring Complex1 as Object Type with the map member Function

```
create or replace type complex1 as
object(rl number,
im number,
member procedure  print,
member function add1(x complex1) return complex1,
map member function val return number)
/
```

The output of Listing 27.2 is as follows:

```
Type created
```

Listing 27.3: Defining the Body for the Complex1 Type

```
create or replace type body complex1 as
member function add1 (x complex1) return complex1 is
begin
   return complex1(self.rl + x.rl, self.im + x.im);
end add1;
member procedure print is
begin
   dbms_output.put_line('real part '||rl||' imag part '||im);
end print;
map member function val return number is
begin
   return (sqrt(rl*rl+im*im));
end val;
end;
```

The output of Listing 27.3 is as follows:

```
Type body created
```

Listing 27.4: Adding Two Objects Using the ADD1 Method

```
declare
   x complex1;
   y complex1;
   z complex1;
begin
   x := complex1(3, 4);
   y := complex1(5, 6);
   x.print;
   y.print;
   z := x.add1(y);
   z.print;
end;
/
```

The output of Listing 27.4 is as follows:

```
PL/SQL procedure successfully completed
```

Listing 27.5: Comparing Two Objects Using the Map Method

```
declare
   x complex1;
   y complex1;
   z complex1;
begin
```

```
    x := complex1(3, 4);
    y := complex1(5, 6);
    x.print;
    y.print;
    if(x > y ) then -- call x.val > y.val
          x.print;
    else
          y.print;
    end if;
end;
```

The output of Listing 27.5 is as follows:

```
PL/SQL procedure successfully completed
```

You can create static methods which can be called without creating objects. The method has to be declared static in the type declaration as well as in the body of program.

Listing 27.6: Declaring Complex2 as Object Type with the order member Function

```
create or replace type complex2 as
object(rl number,
im number,
member procedure  print,
static function add1(x complex2, y complex2) return complex2,
order member function val(x complex2) return number)
/
```

The output of Listing 27.6 is as follows:

```
Type created
```

Listing 27.7: Defining the Body for the Complex2 Type

```
create or replace type body complex2 as
static function add1 (x complex2,y complex2) return complex2 is
begin
       --dbms_output.put_line('real part '||rl||' imag part '||im);
       --error
  return complex2(x.rl + y.rl, x.im + y.im);
end add1;
member procedure print is
begin
  dbms_output.put_line('real part '||rl||' imag part '||im);
end print;
order member function val(x complex2) return number is
begin
  if(sqrt(self.rl*self.rl+self.im*self.im)>sqrt(x.rl*x.rl+x.im*x.im))
  then
                  return(1);
     else
        return(-1);
  end if;
end val;
end;
```

The output of Listing 27.7 is as follows:

```
Type body created
```

Listing 27.8: Comparing Two Objects Using the Order Method

```
declare
  x complex2;
```

```
    y complex2;
    z complex2;
  begin
    x := complex2(3, 4);
    y := complex2(5, 6);
    x.print;
    y.print;
    if(x > y ) then         --call x.val(y) > 0 then
                            --x is more otherwise y more
          x.print;
    else
          y.print;
    end if;
  end;
```

The output of Listing 27.8 is as follows:

```
  PL/SQL procedure successfully completed
```

You cannot specify, map, or order a method in subtype, if it is not defined in supertype.

Using Static Methods

Static methods can be used without creating objects as shown in the following code snippet:

```
  declare
    x complex2;
    y complex2;
    z complex2;
  begin
    x := complex2(3, 4);
    y := complex2(5, 6);
    x.print;
    y.print;
    z := complex2.add1(x, y); -- A
    z.print;
  end;
```

The output of the following code snippet is as follows:

```
  PL/SQL procedure successfully completed
```

The A statement has a calling method as classname.methodname `complex2.add1()` and the method is static.

Inheritance in PL/SQL

You can create objects from the existing base objects. The base objects should be declared as `NOT FINAL` (DEFAULT IS FINAL) to allow inheritance. In the following example, `COMPLEX1` is a base object, while `COMPLEX3` is an inherited object. In the `COMPLEX3` additional method, `SUB1` is added. So, `Complex3` has inherited attributes `rl` and `im`, with three inherited methods.

The following are some examples of inheritance in PL/ SQL:

Listing 27.9: Declaring the Base Type Complex1

```
  create or replace type complex1 as
  object(rl number,
  im number,
  member procedure  print,
  member function add1(x complex1) return complex1,
  map member function val return number) not final
  /
```

The output of Listing 27.9 is as follows:

```
Type created
```

Listing 27.10: Defining Body of Base Type Complex1

```
create or replace type body complex1 as
member function add1 (x complex1) return complex1 is
begin
  return complex1(rl + x.rl, im + x.im);
end add1;
member procedure print is
begin
  dbms_output.put_line('real part '||rl||' imag part '||im);
end print;
map member function val return number is
begin
  return (sqrt(rl*rl+im*im));
end val;
end;
/
```

The output of Listing 27.10 is as follows:

```
Type body created
```

Listing 27.11: Declaring Complex3 as an Inherited Type from Complex1

```
create or replace type complex3 under complex1
(
  member function sub1(x complex3) return complex3
)
/
```

The output of Listing 27.11 is as follows:

```
Type created
```

Listing 27.12: Defining Body of Type Complex3

```
create or replace type body complex3 as
member function sub1 (x complex3) return complex3 is
begin
  return complex3(rl - x.rl, im - x.im);
end sub1;
end;
/
```

The output of Listing 27.12 is as follows:

```
Type body created
```

Listing 27.13: Finding the Use of Class Complex3

```
declare
  x complex3;
  y complex3;
  z complex3;
begin
  x := complex3(3, 4);
  y := complex3(5, 6);
  x.print;                                --inherited method
  y.print;
  z := y.sub1(x);
```

```
  z.print;
end;
/
```

The output of Listing 27.13 is as follows:

```
PL/SQL procedure successfully completed
```

Object Functions

You can use object functions to define processing related with object.

The IS OF() Function

The IS OF() function returns TRUE if the object is an instance of the specified type or its supertype. If the object is an instance of COMPLEX3, then the function will also return TRUE for the argument that equals to COMPLEX1 because COMPLEX1 is the supertype of COMPLEX3.

The following code snippet shows the use of the IS OF() function:

```
declare
x complex3;
flag1 boolean;
flag2 boolean;
begin
x := complex3(3,4);
flag1:= x is of (complex1);
if(flag1) then
 dbms_output.put_line(' x is of type complex1');
end if;
flag2:= x is of (complex3);
if(flag1) then
 dbms_output.put_line(' x is of type complex3');
end if;
end;
```

The output of the preceding code snippet is as follows:

- x IS OF TYPE COMPLEX1
- x IS OF TYPE COMPLEX3

The TREAT() Function

The TREAT() function returns object of a super type, if the sub type object is passed as an argument.

The following code snippet shows the use of the TREAT() function:

```
declare
x complex3;
y complex1;
begin
x := complex3(3,4);
y := complex1(5,6);
y:=treat(x as complex1);
y.print;
end;
```

The output of the preceding code snippet is as follows:

```
real part 3 imaginary part 4
```

The SYS_TYPEID() Function

The SYS_TYPEID() function returns the object identifier of the specified object. The object identifier can also be retrieved from the USER_TYPES view.

The following code snippet shows the use of the SYS_TYPEID() function:

```
declare
y complex1;
oid varchar2(20);
oid1 varchar2(20);
tname varchar2(30);
begin
y := complex1(5,6);
select sys_typeid(y)
into oid
from dual;
dbms_output.put_line(' sys_typeid(y) '||oid);
select typeid,type_name
into oid1,tname
from user_types
where typeid=oid;
dbms_output.put_line(oid1||'    '||tname);

end;
```

The output of the preceding code snippet is as follows:

- SYS_TYPEID(Y) 01
- COMPLEX1

Method Overriding

You can declare a method having the same signature as the supertype method. The method has the same name, same argument, and same return type. The following are some examples of method overriding:

Listing 27.14: Declaring a Type Complex2, with a Procedure Named Print which has 2 Member Functions–add1 and val

```
create or replace type complex2 as
object(rl number, im number,
not final member procedure  print,
static function add1(x complex2, y complex2) return complex2,
order member function val(x complex2) return number) not final
/
```

The output of Listing 27.14 is as follows:

```
Type created
```

Listing 27.15: Defining the Type Complex2

```
create or replace type body complex2 as
static function add1 (x complex2, y complex2) return complex2 is
begin
   return complex2(x.rl + y.rl, x.im + y.im);
end add1;
member procedure print is
begin
   dbms_output.put_line('real part '||rl||' imag part '||im);
end print;
```

```
order member function val(x complex2) return number is
begin
  if(sqrt(self.rl*self.rl+self.im*self.im)>sqrt(x.rl*x.rl+x.im*x.im))then
        return(1);
  else
        return(-1);
  end if;
end val;
end;
```

The output of Listing 27.15 is as follows:

```
Type body created
```

Listing 27.16: Inheriting Complex4 from Complex2

```
create or replace type complex4 under complex2
(
       overriding member procedure print
)
/
```

The output of Listing 27.16 is as follows:

```
Type created
```

Listing 27.17: Defining the Type Complex4 to Override the print Method

```
create or replace type body complex4 as
overriding member procedure print is
begin
  dbms_output.put_line(' the real part is '||rl||' the imaginary part
  '||im);
end print;
end;
```

The output of Listing 27.17 is as follows:

```
Type body created
```

Listing 27.18: Using Dynamic Method Dispatch (Polymorphism)

```
declare
  x complex2;
  y complex2;
  z complex4;
begin
  x := complex2(3, 4);
  y := complex2(5, 6);
  x.print;                          --use method complex2.print
  y.print;
  z := complex4(8, 9);
  z.print;
  x := z;                           --you can assign supertype to subtype
  x.print;                          --use method complex4.print
                                    --z:=x; error condition
end;
```

The output of Listing 27.18 is as follows:

```
PL/SQL procedure successfully completed
```

The method to be overridden should be declared as `NOT FINAL`, so that it can be overridden by the subtype (`PRINT` method in `Complex2`). In the subtype, the method should be declared as overriding. If the method is final, then it cannot be overridden. You can assign subtype to supertype reference. Therefore, the methods used by the supertype reference are those that are available by the subtype (in case of overriding methods).

The NOT INSTANTIABLE Clause

When the supertype is NOT INSTANTIABLE, you cannot use the object as it is. You have to create a subtype to use the functionality of the object. In the subtype, you have to implement that method which is NOT INSTANTIABLE.

The following are some examples of using the NOT INSTANTIABLE clause:

Listing 27.19: Making Complex5 as not instantiable Object

```
create or replace type complex5 as
object( rl number, im number,
not instantiable not final member procedure  print)
not instantiable not final
/
```

The output of Listing 27.19 is as follows:

```
Type created
```

Listing 27.20: Inheriting Complex6 from Complex5

```
create or replace type complex6 under complex5
(
    overriding member procedure  print
  )
/
```

The output of Listing 27.20 is as follows:

```
Type created
```

Listing 27.21: Creating Type Body—Defining Type Complex6

```
create or replace type body complex6 as
overriding member procedure  print is
begin
  dbms_output.put_line('method  is implemented '||rl||' '||im);
end;
end;
```

The output of Listing 27.21 is as follows:

```
Type body created
```

Listing 27.22: Using Subtype

```
declare
  x complex6;
  y complex6;
  z complex5;
begin
  x := complex6(3, 4);
  y := complex6(5, 6);
                                  --z:=complex5(5, 7);
                                  --Error cannot instantiate object
  x.print;
  y.print;
  z := x;                         --no error. You can assign object reference
                                  --of subtype to supertype
  z.print;
end;
```

The output of Listing 27.22 is as follows:

```
PL/SQL procedure successfully completed
```

Object Table

The object table holds objects and provides a relational view of the object, as shown in the following code snippet:

```
create table address_table of address;
```

An object table can be viewed using the following ways:

- A single column table where each row is an address object
- A multicolumn table where columns are plot, street, city, and pincode

The data can be inserted in a table using ordinary `Insert` statements, such as:

```
insert into address_table
values (' 701', 'MGRoad', ' Nagpur', '440010');
```

Listing 27.23 shows how to select an object as a single column table:

Listing 27.23: Selecting an Object as a Single Column Table

```
select value (a)
from address_table a
where a.pincode = '440010';
```

The output of Listing 27.23 is as follows:

```
VALUE(A)(PLOT, STREET, CITY, PINCODE)
-----------------------------------------------------------
ADDRESS(' 701', 'MGRoad', ' Nagpur', '440010')
```

The objects, which appear as a row of table are called row objects. The object, which appears as an attribute of another object is called as the column object.

Listing 27.24: Create the dept1 Table

```
create table dept1 (deptno number PRIMARY KEY, deptname  char(20))
/
```

The output of Listing 27.24 is as follows:

```
Table created
```

Listing 27.25: Creating empobj as an Object Type

```
create or replace type empobj as object (
empid            number,
name             varchar2(30),
address          varchar2(30),
deptno number)
/
```

The output of Listing 27.25 is as follows:

```
Type created
```

Listing 27.26: Creating a Table from a Defined Object Type

```
create table empobjtab of empobj(constraint pkemp primary key(empid),
constraint fk_dept  foreign key(deptno) references dept1(deptno))
/
```

The output of Listing 27.26 is as follows:

```
Table created
```

Listing 27.27: Creating the empcoltab Table

```
create table empcoltab (orgno number, emp empobj,
constraint pkemp1 primary key(emp.empid),
constraint fk_dept1  foreign key(emp.deptno) references dept1(deptno))
/
```

The output of Listing 27.27 is as follows:

```
Table created
```

You can create a table of objects (row object) and define constraints, such as normal table. You can also define some columns as objects, such as table `empobjtab (column object)`. You can also refer the column as objectname.attributename.

Listing 27.28: Inserting Data into the dept1 Table

```
insert into dept1 values
(1,'workshop')
/
```

The output of Listing 27.28 is as follows:

```
1 row created
```

Listing 27.29: Inserting Data into empobjtab

```
insert into empobjtab values
(1,'Anil','Nagpur',1)
/
```

The output of Listing 27.29 is as follows:

```
1 row created
```

Listing 27.30: Inserting Data into empobjtab

```
insert into empobjtab values
(2,'sunil','delhi',1)
/
```

The output of Listing 27.30 is as follows:

```
1 row created
```

Listing 27.31: Inserting Data into empcoltab which has Nested Objects

```
insert into empcoltab values
(1,empobj(1,'anil','nagpur',1))
/
```

The output of Listing 27.31 is as follows:

```
1 row created
```

Listing 27.32: Retrieving Data

```
select empid, name from empobjtab;
```

The output of Listing 27.32 is as follows:

```
 EMPID NAME
------ ------------------------------
     1 anil
     2 sunil
```

Listing 27.33: Setting Alias, p, to Refer Individual Attributes of a Column

```
select p.orgno,p.emp.name from empcoltab p
/
```

The output of Listing 27.33 is as follows:

```
    ORGNO EMP.NAME
--------- ------------------------------
        1 anil
```

REF Datatype

Each row object is identified by a unique, non-changeable identifier, which is generated by Oracle. You can refer an object quickly by using identifiers. The identifier is 16 byte long and can refer 2^128 objects. The system size may be 42–46 bytes. The identifier can be referred using the REF operator. The following code snippet shows the syntax of the REF declaration:

```
< varname > REF < object type name >
```

In the preceding code snippet, the object type reference is called as target of the reference.

Listing 27.34: Using the Ref Operator

```
declare
   x ref empobj;
   y empobj;
begin
   select ref(p)
   into x
   from empobjtab p
   where p.empid=1;
   select deref(x)
   into y
   from dual;
   dbms_output.put_line(y.name);
end;
/
```

The output of Listing 27.34 is as follows:

```
anil

PL/SQL procedure successfully completed
```

In this case, the SELECT statement returns a table with a single column. The REF operator then takes the table as an argument and returns a REF value of the row object. When the REF is declared in PL/SQL for type, which is not an object, an error is generated.

Creating Table of **REF**

The table column can be defined to store reference of the object as explained in the following example.

Listing 27.35 shows the code to create a table:

Listing 27.35: Creating Table of Column of the Ref Type

```
CREATE TABLE emp_ref (orgno number, emp REF empobj);
```

The output of Listing 27.35 is as follows:

```
Table created
```

Listing 27.36 shows the code to insert data into a table:

Listing 27.36: Inserting Data into the Table

```
declare
   x ref empobj;
   cursor c1 is
   select ref(p) refp
   from empobjtab p;
begin
   for z in c1 loop
         insert into emp_ref values(1, z.refp);
   end loop;
end;
/
```

The output of Listing 27.36 is as follows:

```
PL/SQL procedure successfully completed
```

DEREF Operator

The `DEREF operator` takes an object identifier as an argument and returns value of the object.

Listing 27.37 shows the code of using the DEREF operator:

Listing 27.37: Using the DEREF Operator

```
declare
   x  empobj;
   cursor c1 is
   select deref(p.emp) derefp
   from emp_ref p;
begin
   for z in c1 loop
           x := z.derefp;
           dbms_output.put_line(x.name);
   end loop;
end;
/
```

The output of Listing 27.37 is as follows:

```
anil
sunil

PL/SQL procedure successfully completed
```

Dangling **REF**s

If some variable is holding a value of `REF` of an object, and if the target object is deleted, then `REF` becomes a dangling `reference,` i.e. it will refer to an object which is not in existence.

Listing 27.38 shows the code to delete the target object:

Listing 27.38: Deleting the Target Object

```
delete from empobjtab where empid=2;
```

The output of Listing 27.38 is as follows:

```
1 row deleted
```

Listing 27.39 shows the code to display dangling Ref:

Listing 27.39: Showing Dangling Ref

```
declare
   x  empobj;
   cursor c1 is
   select deref(p.emp) derefp
   from emp_ref p;
begin
   for z in c1 loop
   x := z.derefp;
   if x is null then
          dbms_output.put_line('dangling ref');
   else
          dbms_output.put_line(x.name);
   end if;
   end loop;
end;
/
```

The output of Listing 27.39 is as follows:

```
anil
dangling ref

PL/SQL procedure successfully completed
```

The **IS NULL** Operator

The object can have a value NULL, if it is not initialized or has been assigned a value of the object, which is NULL. The null value of the object can be tested using the IS NULL operator.

The SQL **INSERT** Statement

You can insert data in a table using the insert statement by giving values or using the constructor method. Listing 27.40 shows the code to insert data:

Listing 27.40: Inserting Data

```
insert into empobjtab values
(3,'ajay','delhi',1)
/
```

The output of Listing 27.40 is as follows:

```
1 row created
```

Listing 27.41 shows the code to insert values in a nested object:

Listing 27.41: Inserting Value in a Nested Object

```
insert into empcoltab values
(1,empobj(2,'sunil','delhi',1))
/
```

The output of Listing 27.41 is as follows:

```
1 row created
```

If the object is nested/column object, then you cannot use the REF clause. Suppose emp_ref1 is a table having the single REF column, then you cannot write the code shown in the following code snippet:

```
create table emp_ref1(emp ref empobj)
/
```

The output of the preceding code snippet is as follows:

```
Table created
```

The statement shown in the following code snippet generates an error:

```
insert into emp_ref1
select ref(p.emp)
from empcoltab p
/
```

The output of the preceding code snippet is as follows:

```
ERROR at line 2:
ORA-00904: "P"."EMP": invalid identifier
```

Since empcoltab is a nested table, you cannot use the REF clause. You can use the VALUE function in the select statement for manipulating object.

The statement shown in the following code snippet does not generate an error:

```
insert into emp_ref1
select ref(p)
from empobjtab p
/
```

The output of the preceding code snippet is as follows:

```
3 rows created
```

Listing 27.42 shows the how to use the Value function:

Listing 27.42: Using the VALUE Function

```
declare
   x empobj;
begin
   select emp
   into x
   from empcoltab p
   where p.emp.empid=1;
   dbms_output.put_line(x.name);
   select value(p) -- use of value function
   into x
   from empobjtab p
   where p.empid=1;
   dbms_output.put_line(x.name);
end;
```

The output of Listing 27.42 is as follows:

```
anil
anil

PL/SQL procedure successfully completed
```

Listing 27.43 shows the code to create a table similar to another table:

Listing 27.43: Creating table emp2, a Table Similar to the empobjtab Table

```
create table emp2 as(select * from empobjtab)
/
```

The output of Listing 27.43 is as follows:

```
Table created
```

Listing 27.44 shows the code to insert values into the emp2 table

Listing 27.44: Inserting Value of an object into the emp2 Table

```
insert into emp2
select value(p)
from empobjtab p
/
```

The output of Listing 27.44 is as follows:

```
3 rows created
```

The UPDATE Statement

The table containing objects can be modified using the `UPDATE` statement in two ways—as a normal UPDATE statement or using the constructor method.

Listing 27.45 shows the code to modify a table containing objects by using the Update statement:

Listing 27.45: Using the Update Statement is One Way to Modify the Table Containing Object

```
update empobjtab
set address = 'cal'
where empid=1
/
```

The output of Listing 27.45 is as follows:

```
1 row updated
```

The row containing the object can be modified using the constructor method.

Listing 27.46 shows the use of the Update Statement:

Listing 27.46: Using the Update Statement to Modify a Table Using the Constructor Method

```
update empobjtab p
set p = empobj(1,'anil','cal',1)
where p.empid=1
/
```

The output of Listing 27.46 is as follows:

```
1 row updated
```

The first statement uses an object just as a row, while the second statement uses the constructor method.

The **DELETE** Statement

The row containing an object can be deleted using the DELETE statement.

Listing 27.47 shows the code to delete rows from an object table:

Listing 27.47: Deleting One or More Rows from an Object Table Using the DELETE Statement

```
delete empobjtab p
where p.empid=1
/
```

The output of Listing 27.47 is as follows:

```
1 row deleted
```

The **SELECT** Statement

When the data is returned using the `VALUE` function, the `SELECT` statement returns a row of unnamed type having a single column whose type is the object type.

Listing 27.48 shows the code to use the value function in the SELECT statement:

Listing 27.48: Using the value Function in the SELECT Statement

```
declare
   x empobj;
begin
   select emp
   into x
   from empcoltab p
   where p.emp.empid=1;
   dbms_output.put_line(x.name);
   select value(p) -- use of value function
   into x
   from empobjtab p
   where p.empid=1;
   dbms_output.put_line(x.name);
end;
/
```

The output of Listing 27.48 is as follows:

```
anil
ajay

PL/SQL procedure successfully completed
```

Listing 27.49 shows the code to insert values into the empobjtab table:

Listing 27.49: Inserting Value into the empobjtab table:

```
insert into empobjtab
values
(1,'abc','123abc',1);
```

The output of Listing 27.49 is as follows:

```
1 row created
```

NOTE

A record with the empid as 1 must exist in the empobjtab table for the INSERT command to work.

Retrieving **REF** Using the **SELECT** Statement

Reference can be retrieved using the REF clause. Suppose emp_ref is a table that stores references.

Listing 27.50 shows how to insert data into the table:

Listing 27.50: Inserting Data into the Table

```
insert into emp_ref values (3,
 (select REF(p)
from empobjtab  p
where p.empid = 1));
```

The output of Listing 27.50 is as follows:

```
1 row created
```

Listing 27.51 shows the code to collect single reference in the PL/SQL variable:

Listing 27.51: Collecting Single Reference in the PL/SQL Variable

```
declare
   x ref empobj;
   cursor c1 is
   select ref(p) refp
   from empobjtab p;
begin
   for z in c1 loop
          insert into emp_ref values(1,z.refp);
   end loop;
end;
/
```

The output of Listing 27.51 is as follows:

```
PL/SQL procedure successfully completed
```

Listing 27.52 shows the code to insert a value of the object using the DEREF clause:

Listing 27.52: Inserting a Value of the Object Using the DEREF Clause

```
update empobjtab p
set p = deref (ref(p))
where p.empid = 1;
```

The output of Listing 27.52 is as follows:

```
1 row updated
```

Referring to Nested Attributes

You need to use a dot (.) notation to refer a nested object within an object.

Listing 27.53 shows the code to retrieve a plot of customer using the . notation

Listing 27.53: Retrieving a Plot of Customer

```
select p.emp.name
from empcoltab  p;
```

The output of Listing 27.53 is as follows:

```
EMP.NAME
----------------------------
anil
sunil
```

The following code snippet shows how to insert data in the empcoltab table:

```
insert into empcoltab
values ( 3, empobj (3, 'Anil', ' Nagpur', 1));
```

The output of the following code snippet is as follows:

```
1 row created
```

Null Values in Object

The object can be `NULL` or its attributes can be `NULL`. If the object is `NULL`, then it is called as atomic null. Consider the following code snippet:

```
declare
  empl address;
begin
  If empl is NULL Then                        --A
     If empl.empid is NULL Then               --B
```

In the preceding code snippet, both `A` and `B` conditions are true. Since `empl` is `NULL`, its attributes are also `NULL`. If an attempt is made to assign values to attributes of the `NULL` object, then an exception is raised. Listing 27.54 shows how to raise an exception:

Listing 27.54: Raising an Exception

```
empl.empid := 1;
```

If an object is initialized as:

```
Empl := empobj( ..);
```

then you can assign values in the object as:

```
empl.plot := 1;
```

NOTE

A primary object in object table cannot be NULL.

Name Resolution

Name resolution indicates rules to resolve names when expressed using (.) notation.

Suppose a name is used as `C1.C2.C3 ....Cn`. In that case, it is resolved according to the following rules:

- Determine the rightmost name, `Cn`, as column name using the SQL rule.
- If there are any names, which are on the right side of `Cn`, then treat the names as attributes.

Consider the following code snippet:

```
select *
from empobjtab
where empid
in
(select p.emp.empid
from empcoltab p
where p.emp.name = 'anil'
and p.emp.empid= 3) ;
```

The output of the preceding code snippet is as follows:

```
  EMPID NAME                           ADDRESS
------- ------------------------------ ------------------------
      3 ajay                           delhi
```

To resolve `p.emp.empid`, Oracle first tries to determine whether `empid` is the column of table `empcoltab`. If `empid` is not a column of address, then it tries to resolve `emp` as the column name of `empcoltab`, and `empid` as attribute of the object. Suppose `empid` is not a column of `empcoltab`. In that case, it determines `emp` as a column of `empcoltab`. Suppose, later on, `empid` is added in the table `empcoltab`. Then `empcoltab.empid` is resolved as the column of `empcoltab`. This type of method for resolving names is called as the outer capture.

In the outer capture, addition of a column in the outer table captures a qualified reference, which originally refers to a column of the inner table. To remove such type of ambiguity, it is recommended to use alias in query.

Listing 27.55 shows how to refer Address as column of customer:

Listing 27.55: Referring Address as Column of Customer

```
select *
from address a
where a.plot
in
(select c.plot
from customer c
where c.address.code = '701');
```

The output of Listing 27.55 is as follows:

```
No rows selected
```

The method that uses aliases to qualify all column references is called as capture avoidance rule.

Table Function

Table functions are used to treat collections as tables that can be queried or assigned to other collections. Suppose there is a function which returns a collection, then you can use it in the SQL statement, as shown in the following code snippet:

```
create or replace type pcmobj as
object(rn number,
p number,
c number,
m number,
name varchar2(30));
/
```

The output of the preceding code snippet is as follows:

```
Type created
```

The following code snippet shows how to create object types:

```
create or replace type tablepcm as table of pcmobj;
/
```

The output of the preceding code snippet is as follows:

```
Type created
```

The following code snippet shows how to create functions:

```
create or replace function getpcm return tablepcm as
cursor c1 is
select rollno, physics, chemistry, maths, name from pcm;
t tablepcm;
begin
   t := new tablepcm();
   for z in c1 loop
         t.extend;
         t(t.last) := pcmobj(z. rollno,z. physics,z. chemistry,z.
         maths,z.name);
   end loop;
   return(t);
end;
```

The output of the preceding code snippet is as follows:

```
Function created
```

For successful creation of this function, the following table (PCM) must exist. To test this function, you can insert following data in the table.

```
select * from pcm;
```

The output of the preceding code snippet is as follows:

```
ROLLNO                NAME             PHYSICS    CHEMISTRY    MATHS
---------- -------------------- ---------- ----------  ----------
         1           anil              67          89          76
         2           sunil             89          65          99
         3           ajay              77          95          94
         4           sushil            75          92          91
```

You can also use it using the TABLE function:

```
select f.rn, f.p from table(getpcm) f;
```

Result:

```
        RN          P
---------- ----------
         1         67
         2         89
         3         77
         4         75
```

The output of the table function can be pipelined or parallelized, and used for improving performance. Pipelining means that rows can be taken to the next stage, instead of completing the execution of the complete set.

Listing 27.56 shows the code to create a pipelined function:

Listing 27.56: Creating a Pipelined Function

```
create or replace function getpcmpipe return tablepcm pipelined as
cursor c1 is
select rollno,physics,chemistry,maths,name from pcm;
t tablepcm;
begin
```

```
    for z in c1 loop
           pipe row (pcmobj(z.rollno,z.physics,z.chemistry,z.maths,z.name));
    end loop;
    return;
  end;
  /
```

The output of Listing 27.56 is as follows:

```
Function created
```

It can be used in the same way as:

```
select f.rn,f.p from table(getpcmpipe) f;
```

Result:

```
        RN          P
---------- ----------
         1         67
         2         89
         3         77
         4         75
```

The function can be created by passing the `ref` cursor as variable. The table function cannot be used as target to DML operation.

Pragma Restrict References

When a function does another task in addition to returning a value, then it is called as side effect. When a function performs DML operation or updates some package variable, then it is said to be having a side effect. Functions having side effect is a poor programming practice because the programmer, while using the function, may not take the side effect into account. The extent of side effect is measured using the purity level.

Suppose a function `calcbatchamt` returns the total collection of batch and updates the `summerycollection` table. Now the programmer who is using the function might be unaware that the function is also updating the table. To minimize side effects, the following rules are applied on the function code:

- Function should not perform DML operation on table
- Function should not update packaged variable, if it is executing in parallel or remotely
- It should not update packaged variables, if it is called from `SELECT`, `VALUES`, and `SET` clause
- It should not call other subprogram, which violates these rules

To impose these rules, the user has to use compiler directive (pragma) `RESTRICT_REFERENCES`. The syntax of `RESTRICT_REFERENCES` is as follows:

```
RESTRICT_REFERENCE(method name, Restrictions);
```

If the word `DEFAULT` is used, then the restriction applies to all methods. The pragma is used as follows:

```
Create type student AS OBJECT
(Name Varchar2(30),
marks number (512),
.......
MAP MEMBER FUNCTION calcmarks RETURN real;
PRAGMA RESTRICT_REFERENCES (calcmarks,RNDS,WNDS,RNPS,WNPS);
......
);
```

The restrictions are as follows:

- `RNDS` – Reads no database state
- `WNDS` – Writes no database state
- `RNPS` – Reads no package state
- `WNPS` – Writes no package state

These constraints can be specified in any order and are optional. To call the method in parallel queries, all four constraints should be specified.

Summary

This chapter dealt with objects and object types. It also described methods to compare two objects and inheritance in the objects. The next two chapters will concentrate on some sample programs using the concept which we are familiar with.

Exercise

1. Represent point object in the Cartesian coordinate system.
2. Using the point object, define the LINE object with the methods that calculate the length and slope of a line.
3. Using the LINE object, define the POLYGON object.

28

Sample Programs-I

Listing 28.1: Displaying Contents of course

```
declare
  cursor c1 is
  select *
  from course;
begin
   for z in c1 loop
        dbms_output.put_line(z.coursecode||' '||z.coursename||' '||
               z.syllabus||'  '||z.lastno);
  end loop;
end;
```

Listing 28.2: Displaying Contents of batch

```
declare
  cursor c1 is
  select *
  from batch;
begin
  for z in c1 loop
        dbms_output.put_line(z.batchcode||' '||z.coursecode||'  '||
        z.startingdate||' '||z.coursefees||' '||z.netincome||' '||
        z.expectedincome||' '||z.lastno);
  end loop;
end;
```

Listing 28.3: Displaying Contents of a batch for a Particular Course

```
declare
  cursor c1(ccode number) is
  select *
  from batch
  where coursecode = ccode;
 begin
  for z in c1(10) loop
              dbms_output.put_line(z.batchcode||' '||z.coursecode||' '||
              z.startingdate||' '||z.coursefees||' '||z.netincome||' '||
              z.expectedincome||' '||z.lastno);
  end loop;
 end;
```

Listing 28.4: Displaying Contents of batch, which Starts from a Particular Date

```
declare
  cursor c1( d1 date) is
  select *
  from batch
  where startingdate = d1;
begin
  for z in c1('25-JAN-99') loop
        dbms_output.put_line(z.batchcode||' '||z.coursecode||' '||
        z.startingdate||' '||z.coursefees||' '||z.netincome||' '||
        z.expectedincome||' '||z.lastno);
  end loop;
end;
```

Listing 28.5: Displaying the batchcode from Batch Having netincome More than 5000

```
declare
  cursor c1 is
  select batchcode
  from batch
```

```
    where netincome > 5000;
  begin
    for z in c1 loop
          dbms_output.put_line(z.batchcode);
    end loop;
  end;
```

Listing 28.6: Displaying the batchcode from Batch Having expectedincome More than netincome by 2000

```
  declare
    cursor c1 is
    select batchcode
    from batch
    where expectedincome > (netincome + 2000);
  begin
    for z in c1 loop
          dbms_output.put_line(z.batchcode);
    end loop;
  end;
```

Listing 28.7: Displaying the enquiryno of a Course

```
  declare
    cursor c1 (zcname varchar2) is
    select enquiryno from enquiry e,course c  where c.coursename = zcname
    and c.coursecode = e.coursecode;
  begin
    for z in c1('ORACLE') loop
          dbms_output.put_line(z.enquiryno);
    end loop;
  end;
```

Listing 28.8: Displaying the Names of Persons Having city as Nagpur

```
  declare
    cursor c1 is
    select fname
    from enquiry
    where city = 'NAGPUR';
  begin
    for z in c1 loop
          dbms_output.put_line(z.fname);
    end loop;
  end;
```

Listing 28.9: Displaying the Advertisement Dates

```
  declare
    cursor c1 is
    select advdate
    from advertisement;
  begin
    for z in c1 loop
          dbms_output.put_line(z.advdate);
    end loop;
  end;
```

Listing 28.10: Displaying rollno of a Particular Batch

```
  declare
    cursor c1 (bcode number) is
    select rollno
    from enrollment
    where batchcode = bcode;
```

```
begin
  for z in c1(10003) loop
              dbms_output.put_line(z.rollno);
  end loop;
end;
```

Listing 28.11: Displaying all Expenditure Codes

```
declare
  cursor c1 is
  select expcode
  from expenditure;
begin
  for z in c1 loop
        dbms_output.put_line(z.expcode);
  end loop;
end;
```

Listing 28.12: Displaying the Name of a Person Enquired for a Particular Course

```
declare
  cursor c1(coursenm varchar2) is
  select e.fname
  from enquiry e,course course
  where course.coursename = coursenm
  and course.coursecode = e.coursecode;
 begin
  for z in c1('ORACLE') loop
              dbms_output.put_line (z.fname);
  end loop;
 end;
```

Listing 28.13: Displaying the Details of enrollment

```
declare
  cursor c1 is
  select *
  from enrollment;
begin
  for z in c1 loop
        dbms_output.put_line(z.rollno|| ' '||z.enquiryno|| ' '||
              z.batchcode|| ' '||z.enrollmentdate);
  end loop;
end;
```

Listing 28.14: Displaying the Contents of Expenditure

```
declare
  cursor c1 is
  select *
  from expenditure;
begin
  for z in c1 loop
        dbms_output.put_line(z.expcode|| ' '||z.amount|| ' '||z.expdate|| '
  '|| z.bankname|| ' '||z.remark|| ' '||z.batchcode);
  end loop;
end;
```

Listing 28.15: Displaying the Installment Having Status is N

```
declare
  cursor c1 is
  select *
  from installment
```

```
    where installmentstatus = 'N';
  begin
    for z in c1 loop
          dbms_output.put_line(z.rollno||' '||z.installmentdate||'
          '||z.amount);
    end loop;
  end;
```

Listing 28.16: Displaying the Syllabus for a Particular Course

```
declare
  cursor c1 (cname varchar2) is
  select syllabus
  from course
  where coursename = cname;
 begin
  for z in c1('ORACLE') loop
               dbms_output.put_line(z.syllabus);
  end loop;
 end;
```

Listing 28.17: Displaying the Contents of Expenditure Master (expmaster)

```
declare
  cursor c1 is
  select *
  from expmaster;
begin
  for z in c1 loop
               dbms_output.put_line(z.expcode||' '||z.expname||' '||z.exptype||'
               '|| z.netexp);
  end loop;
end;
```

Listing 28.18: Displaying all Details of Expaudit

```
create table expaudit
  (expcode number(5),
  username varchar2(30),
  expdate date);

/*This table stores information of the user who has entered information in
  expenditure and at which datetime the information is entered */

declare
  cursor c1 is
  select *
  from expaudit;
begin
  for z in c1 loop
       dbms_output.put_line(to_char(z.expcode)||'
       '||to_char(z.expdate)||' '||z.username );
  end loop;
end;
```

Listing 28.19: Displaying coursename and startingdate of all Batches

```
declare
  cursor c1 is
  select crs.coursename,bat.startingdate
  from course crs,batch bat
  where bat.coursecode = crs.coursecode;
begin
```

```
    for z in c1 loop
           dbms_output.put_line(z.coursename||' '||z.startingdate);
    end loop;
  end;
```

Listing 28.20: Displaying coursename and startingdate for a Particular Batch

```
declare
  cursor c1(bcode number) is
  select crs.coursename,bat.startingdate
  from course crs,batch bat
  where bat.batchcode = bcode
  and bat.coursecode = crs.coursecode;
begin
  for z in c1(20002) loop
                 dbms_output.put_line(z.coursename|| ' '||z.startingdate);
  end loop;
end;
```

Listing 28.21: Displaying medianame and Date of Advertisement for a Specified Course

```
declare
  cursor c1(crs varchar2) is
  select medianame,advdate
  from advertisement a,course c,enquiry e
  where c.coursename = crs
  and c.coursecode = e.coursecode
  and e.refcode = a.refcode;
begin
  for z in c1('ORACLE') loop
                 dbms_output.put_line(z.medianame|| ' '||z.advdate);
  end loop;
end;
```

NOTE

Here enquiry table is used because ref code is present in enquiry table only.

Listing 28.22: Displaying rollno and Names of Students for a Particular Batch

```
declare
  cursor c1(bcode number) is
  select rollno,fname
  from enrollment,enquiry
  where enrollment.batchcode = bcode
  and enrollment.enquiryno = enquiry.enquiryno;
begin
  for z in c1(10001) loop
        dbms_output.put_line(z.rollno||','||z.fname);
  end loop;
end;
```

Listing 28.23: Displaying rollno and address of Student in a Specified Batch

```
declare
  cursor c1(bcode number) is
  select rollno,fname,plotno,street,city
  from enrollment,enquiry
  where enrollment.batchcode = bcode
  and enrollment.enquiryno = enquiry.enquiryno;
begin
  for z in c1(10001) loop
```

```
        dbms_output.put_line(z.rollno|| ' '||z.fname|| ' '||z.plotno|| '
        '|| z.street|| ' '||z.city);
    end loop;
 end;
```

Listing 28.24: Displaying rollno, name, and feespaid for a Particular Batch

```
 declare
   cursor c1(bcode number) is
   select fp.rollno,fname,sum(amount) sumamt
   from feespaid fp,enrollment en,enquiry eq
   where en.batchcode = bcode
   and en.rollno = fp.rollno
   and en.enquiryno = eq.enquiryno
   group by fp.rollno,fname;
 begin
   for z in c1(20002) loop
               dbms_output.put_line(z.rollno|| ' '||z.fname|| ' '||z.sumamt);
   end loop;
  end;
```

Listing 28.25: Displaying rollno, name, installmentdate, and amount for a Particular Batch

```
 declare
   cursor c1(bcode number) is
   select ins.rollno,fname,installmentdate,amount
   from installment ins,enrollment en,enquiry eq
   where en.batchcode = bcode
   and en.rollno = ins.rollno
   and en.enquiryno = eq.enquiryno;
 begin
   for z in c1(20002) loop
        dbms_output.put_line(z.rollno|| '    '||z.fname|| '
   '||z.installmentdate|| '    '||z.amount);
   end loop;
 end;
```

Listing 28.26: Displaying coursename and Details of All Batches

```
 declare
   cursor c1 is
   select coursename,batchcode,startingdate,duration,coursefees,
   netincome,expectedincome,batch.lastno
   from course,batch
   where course.coursecode=batch.coursecode;
 begin
   for z in c1 loop
        dbms_output.put_line(z.coursename||'   '||z.batchcode||'   '||
               z.startingdate||'   '||z.duration||'   '||z.coursefees||'   '||
               z.netincome||'   '||z.expectedincome||'   '||z.lastno);
   end loop;
 end;
```

Listing 28.27: Displaying Expenditure Details for a Particular Expenditure Type

```
 declare
   cursor c1(exptp varchar2) is
   select e.expcode,e.expdate,e.amount,e.bankname,e.remark
   from expenditure e,expmaster ex
   here ex.exptype = exptp
   and ex.expcode = e.expcode;
 begin
   for z in c1('Xerox') loop
```

```
                dbms_output.put_line(z.expcode||' '||z.expdate||' '||z.amount||'
                '|| z.bankname||' '||z.remark);
    end loop;
  end;
```

Listing 28.28: Displaying rollno and the Name of Student who Paid Fees More than 5000 at a Time

```
declare
  cursor c1 is
  select fp.rollno,fname
  from feespaid fp,enrollment en,enquiry eq
  where fp.rollno = en.rollno
  and en.enquiryno = eq.enquiryno
  and fp.amount > 5000;
begin
  for z in c1 loop
        dbms_output.put_line(z.rollno|| ' '||z.fname);
  end loop;
end;
```

Listing 28.29: Displaying Code of Batches Having netincome More than the Specified batch

```
declare
  cursor c1(bcode number) is
  select b2.batchcode
  from batch b1,batch b2
  where b1.batchcode = bcode
  and b2.netincome > b1.netincome;
begin
  for z in c1(10001) loop
               dbms_output.put_line(z.batchcode);
  end loop;
 end;
```

Listing 28.30: Displaying Names of Persons Having Address in the Same City, where a specifiedperson is Living

```
declare
  cursor c1(name varchar2) is
  select e2.fname
  from enquiry e1,enquiry e2
  where e1.fname = name
  and e2.city = e1.city;
begin
  for z in c1('ANIL') loop
        dbms_output.put_line(z.fname);
  end loop;
end;
```

Listing 28.31: Displaying the batchcode of Batches Having expectedincome More than Any Specified Batch (all the Batches should be of the Same Course)

```
declare
  cursor c1(bcode number) is
  select b2.batchcode
  from batch b1,batch b2
  where b1.batchcode = bcode
  and b2.expectedincome > b1.expectedincome
  and substr(to_char(b2.batchcode),1,2) =substr(to_char(b1.batchcode),1,2);
begin
  for z in c1(10001) loop
```

```
        dbms_output.put_line(z.batchcode);
    end loop;
end;
```

Listing 28.32: Displaying the Names of Students who are in the Same Batch in which Anil is Enrolled

```
declare
    cursor c1 is
    select e2.fname
    from enquiry e2,enrollment enr2
    where enr2.enquiryno = e2.enquiryno
    and enr2.batchcode
    in
    (select enr1.batchcode
    from enquiry e1,enrollment enr1
    where e1.fname = 'ANIL'
    and e1.enquiryno = enr1.enquiryno);
begin
    for z in c1 loop
        dbms_output.put_line(z.fname);
    end loop;
end;
```

Listing 28.33: Displaying the Names of Students who are Enrolled in the Same Course as Anil Enrolled

```
declare
    cursor c1 is
    select e2.fname
    from enquiry e1,enquiry e2
    where e1.fname = 'ANIL'
    and e1.coursecode = e2.coursecode
    and e2.en_st = 'Y';
begin
    for z in c1 loop
              dbms_output.put_line(z.fname);
    end loop;
 end;
```

Listing 28.34: Displaying the Names of Students Living in the Same City where Anil is Living

```
declare
    cursor c1 is
    select e2.fname
    from enquiry e1,enquiry e2
    where e1.fname = 'ANIL'
    and e1.city = e2.city;
begin
    for z in c1 loop
        dbms_output.put_line(z.fname);
    end loop;
end;
```

Listing 28.35: Displaying the Names of Persons Having Same Batch as Anil and Sunil

```
declare
    cursor c1 is
    select e2.fname
    from enquiry e2,enrollment enr2
    where enr2.enquiryno = e2.enquiryno
    and enr2.batchcode
    in
    (select enr1.batchcode
```

```
   from enquiry e1,enquiry e2,
   enrollment enr1,enrollment enr2
   where e1.fname = 'ANIL'
   and e2.fname = 'SUNIL'
   and enr1.batchcode = enr2.batchcode);
begin
   for z in c1 loop
         dbms_output.put_line(z.fname);
   end loop;
end;
```

Listing 28.36: Displaying the Names of Persons Having Same Batch as Anil or Sunil

```
declare
   cursor c1 is
   select e2.fname
   from enquiry e2,enrollment enr2
   where enr2.enquiryno = e2.enquiryno
   and enr2.batchcode
   in
   (select enr1.batchcode
   from enquiry e1, enquiry e2,enrollment enr1
   where e1.fname = 'ANIL'
   and e2.fname = 'SUNIL');
begin
   for z in c1 loop
         dbms_output.put_line(z.fname);
   end loop;
end;
```

Listing 28.37: Displaying Details of Installment of a Specified rollno

```
declare
   cursor c1(insrollno number) is
   select *
   from installment
   where rollno = insrollno;
begin
   for z in c1(20002001) loop
                dbms_output.put_line(z.installmentdate||z.amount||z.
         installmentstatus);
   end loop;
 end;
```

Listing 28.38: Deleting All the Rows from the course Table

```
create or replace procedure delete_course as
begin
   delete course;
end;
```

Listing 28.39: Deleting All the Rows from Batch Having the Specified batchcode

```
create or replace procedure delete_spbatch(bcode in number) as
begin
   delete batch where batchcode = bcode;
end delete_spbatch;
```

Listing 28.40: Deleting the Rows from batch, which is Not Having Any expectedincome

```
create or replace procedure del_nullexpbatch as
begin
   delete batch
```

```
      where expectedincome = 0;
   end del_nullexpbatch;
```

Listing 28.41: Deleting Rows from enquiry for a Specified coursename

```
   create or replace procedure del_enq_crs(coursenm in varchar2) as
   begin
      delete enquiry
      where coursecode
      in
      (select coursecode
      from course
    where coursename = coursenm);
   end del_enq_crs;
```

Listing 28.42: Deleting Rows from enquiry, which are 6 Months before System Date, and Not Having Enrollment

```
   create or replace procedure delete_oldenq as
   begin
      delete enquiry
      where enquirydate < add_months(sysdate,-6)
      and en_st = 'N';
   end delete_oldenq;
```

Listing 28.43: Updating batch and Setting netincome According to feespaid

```
   create or replace procedure update_netincome as
      cursor c1 is
      select batchcode,netincome
      from batch;
      cursor c2 is
      select sum(amount) samt,substr(to_char(rollno),1,5) bcode
      from feespaid
      group by substr(to_char(rollno),1,5);
   begin
      for z1 in c1 loop
                  for z2 in c2 loop
                         if(to_char(z1.batchcode)= z2.bcode) then
                                update batch
                                set netincome = z2.samt
                                where batchcode = z1.batchcode;
                         end if;
                  end loop;
      end loop;
    end update_netincome;
```

Listing 28.44: Updating batch and Setting the expectedincome from installment

```
   create or replace procedure update_expincome as
      cursor c1 is
      select batchcode,expectedincome
      from batch;
      cursor c2 is
      select sum(amount) samt,substr(to_char(rollno),1,5) bcode
      from installment
      group by substr(to_char(rollno),1,5);
   begin
      for z1 in c1 loop
           for z2 in c2 loop
       if(to_char(z1.batchcode)= z2.bcode) then
        update batch
        set expectedincome = z2.samt
```

```
      where batchcode = z1.batchcode;
     end if;
       end loop;
   end loop;
 end update_expincome;
```

Listing 28.45: Updating lastno of course Having Data from batch

```
create or replace procedure update_lastno_crs as
  cursor c1 is
  select lastno,coursecode
  from course;
  cursor c2 is
  select sum(lastno) slastno,
         substr(to_char(batchcode),1,2) ccode
  from batch
  group by substr(to_char(batchcode),1,2);
begin
  for z1 in c1 loop
     for z2 in c2 loop
        if(to_char(z1.coursecode)=z2.ccode) then
                update course
                set course.lastno = z2.slastno
                where coursecode = z1.coursecode;
        end if;
      end loop;
  end loop;
end update_lastno_crs;
```

Listing 28.46: Deleting Duplicate Rows from enquiry

```
create or replace procedure delete_duplicate_enq as
  cursor c1 is
  select *
  from enquiry;
begin
  for z in c1 loop
                delete enquiry
                where enquiry.enquiryno = z.enquiryno
                and rowid > any
                (select rowid
                from enquiry
                where enquiry.enquiryno = z.enquiryno);
  end loop;
 end delete_duplicate_enq;
```

29

Sample Programs-II

Listing 29.1: Displaying the Names of Persons Enrolled in a Batch Having Code 10 and 20

```
declare
  cursor c1 is
  select enq.fname
  from enrollment enr,enquiry enq
  where substr(to_char(batchcode),1,2) = 10
  and enr.enquiryno = enq.enquiryno
  intersect
  select enq.fname
  from enrollment enr,enquiry enq
  where substr(to_char(batchcode),1,2) = 20
  and enr.enquiryno = enq.enquiryno;
begin
  for z in c1 loop
        dbms_output.put_line(z.fname);
  end loop;
end;
/
```

Listing 29.2: Displaying the Names of Persons Enrolled in batch Having Code 10 or 20

```
declare
  cursor c1 is
  select enq.fname
  from enrollment enr,enquiry enq
  where substr(to_char(batchcode),1,2) = 10
  and enr.enquiryno = enq.enquiryno
  union
  select enq.fname
  from enrollment enr,enquiry enq
  where substr(to_char(batchcode),1,2) = 20
  and enr.enquiryno = enq.enquiryno;
begin
  for z in c1 loop
        dbms_output.put_line(z.fname);
  end loop;
end;
/
```

Listing 29.3: Displaying the Names of Persons Enrolled in batch Having Code 10, but Not Enrolled in Batch Having Code 20

```
declare
        cursor c1 is
        select enq.fname
        from enrollment enr,enquiry enq
        where substr(to_char(batchcode),1,2) = 10
        and enr.enquiryno = enq.enquiryno
        minus
        select enq.fname
        from enrollment enr,enquiry enq
        where substr(to_char(batchcode),1,2) = 20
        and enr.enquiryno = enq.enquiryno;
begin
        for z in c1 loop
        dbms_output.put_line(z.fname);
```

```
        end loop;
end;
/
```

Listing 29.4: Displaying the Names of Persons Enrolled in Three Batches Having Codes 10, 20, 30

```
declare
  cursor c1 is
  select enq.fname
  from enrollment enr,enquiry enq
  where substr(to_char(batchcode),1,2) = 10
  and enr.enquiryno = enq.enquiryno
  intersect
  select enq.fname
  from enrollment enr,enquiry enq
  where substr(to_char(batchcode),1,2) = 20
  and enr.enquiryno = enq.enquiryno
  intersect
  select enq.fname
  from enrollment enr,enquiry enq
  where substr(to_char(batchcode),1,2) = 30
  and enr.enquiryno = enq.enquiryno;
begin
  for z in c1 loop
        dbms_output.put_line(z.fname);
  end loop;
end;
/
```

Listing 29.5: Displaying the Names of Persons Enrolled in coursecode 10 and coursecode 20

```
declare
  cursor c1 is
  select enq.fname
  from enquiry enq
  where coursecode = 10
  and enq.en_st = 'Y'
  intersect
  select enq.fname
  from enquiry enq
  where coursecode = 20
  and enq.en_st = 'Y';
begin
  for z in c1 loop
        dbms_output.put_line(z.fname);
  end loop;
end;
/
```

Listing 29.6: Displaying the Names of Persons Enrolled in coursecode 10, but Not 20

```
declare
  cursor c1 is
  select enq.fname
  from enquiry enq
  where coursecode = 10
  and enq.en_st = 'Y'
  minus
```

```
    select enq.fname
    from enquiry enq
    where coursecode = 20
    and enq.en_st = 'Y';
  begin
    for z in c1 loop
          dbms_output.put_line(z.fname);
    end loop;
  end;
  /
```

Listing 29.7: Displaying the Names of Persons Enrolled in coursecode 10 or 20

```
  declare
    cursor c1 is
    select enq.fname
    from enquiry enq
    where coursecode = 10
    and enq.en_st = 'Y'
    union
    select enq.fname
    from enquiry enq
    where coursecode = 20
    and enq.en_st = 'Y';
  begin
    for z in c1 loop
          dbms_output.put_line(z.fname);
    end loop;
  end;
  /
```

Listing 29.8: Displaying the Names of Batches Along with their Course Name Having netincome More than 50,000

```
  declare
    cursor c1 is
    select coursename,batchcode
    from batch,course
    where netincome > 50000
    and batch.coursecode = course.coursecode;
  begin
    for z in c1 loop
          dbms_output.put_line(z.coursename||'   '||z.batchcode);
    end loop;
  end;
  /
```

Listing 29.9: Displaying the Names of Expenditures of Expenditure Type T1 and Expenditure Type T2

```
  declare
    cursor c1 is
    select expname
    from expmaster
    where exptype = 'T1'
    union
    select expname
    from expmaster
    where exptype = 'T2';
```

```
begin
  for z in c1 loop
        dbms_output.put_line(z.expname);
  end loop;
end;
/
```

Listing 29.10: Displaying the Names of Persons who have not Paid Fees

```
declare
        cursor c1 is
        select distinct fname
        from enquiry enq,enrollment enr,installment ins
        where ins.installmentstatus = 'N'
        and ins.installmentdate < sysdate
        and ins.rollno = enr.rollno
        and enr.enquiryno = enq.enquiryno;
 begin
        for z in c1 loop
        dbms_output.put_line(z.fname);
        end loop;
end;
/
```

Listing 29.11: Displaying the Details of Batches Having a Specified coursename

```
declare
  cursor c1 (crs varchar2)is
  select *
  from batch
  where coursecode
  in
  (select coursecode
        from course
        where coursename = crs);
begin
        for z in c1 ('ORACLE') loop
        dbms_output.put_line(z.batchcode||'    '||
            z.coursecode||'    '||z.startingdate
            ||'    '||z.duration||'    '||z.coursefees
            ||'    '||z.netincome||'    '||z.expectedincome
            ||'    '||z.lastno);
        end loop;
end;
/
```

Listing 29.12: Displaying the Names of Persons Enrolled in a Specified Batch

```
declare
        cursor c1(bcode number) is
        select fname
        from enquiry
        where enquiryno
        in
        (select enr.enquiryno
        from enrollment enr,enquiry enq
        where batchcode = bcode
        and enr.enquiryno = enq.enquiryno );
```

```
begin
        for z in c1(10001) loop
        dbms_output.put_line(z.fname);
        end loop;
end;
/
```

Listing 29.13: Displaying the Names of Persons Enrolled in a Specified Course

```
declare
        cursor c1 (crsname varchar2)is
        select distinct fname
        from enquiry
        where en_st = 'Y'
        and coursecode
        in
        (select coursecode
        from course
        where coursename = crsname);
begin
        for z in c1('ORACLE') loop
        dbms_output.put_line(z.fname);
        end loop;
end;
/
```

Listing 29.14: Displaying the Amounts of Expenditure Having the Specified Expenditure Type

```
declare
  cursor c1 (exptp varchar2)is
  select sum(exp.amount) samt from expenditure exp, expmaster exm
  where exp.expcode=exm.expcode and exptype='CASH';
begin
        for z in c1(10) loop
        dbms_output.put_line(z.samt);
        end loop;
end;
/
```

Listing 29.15: Assuming that One Person is Enrolled in Multiple Courses, Display the Names of Persons

```
declare
        cursor c1 is
        select fname
        from enquiry enq  where
  enq.enquiryno in (select enquiryno from enrollment enr
        where enq.enquiryno = enr.enquiryno)
  group by fname
        having count (enq.coursecode) > 1;
begin
  for z in c1 loop
                dbms_output.put_line(z.fname);
        end loop;
end;
/
```

Listing 29.16: Displaying the Names of Students who have Not Paid Any Fees

```
declare
        cursor c1 is
        select distinct fname
        from enquiry enq,enrollment enr
        where enq.enquiryno = enr.enquiryno
        and enr.rollno
        not in
        (select rollno
        from feespaid);
begin
        for z in c1 loop
        dbms_output.put_line(z.fname);
        end loop;
end;
/
```

Listing 29.17: Displaying the Names of Persons Enrolled in Batch Having startingdate More than the Specified Date

```
declare
        cursor c1 (d1 date) is
        select fname, en.batchcode
        from enquiry eq, enrollment en
        where
  eq.enquiryno=en.enquiryno and
  en.batchcode
        in
        (select batchcode
        from batch
        where startingdate > d1);
begin
        for z in c1 ('20-FEB-99') loop
        dbms_output.put_line(z.fname ||' '|| z.batchcode );
        end loop;
end;
/
```

Listing 29.18: Displaying the Names of Students Living in NAGPUR and Enrolled in coursecode 10

```
declare
        cursor c1 is
        select distinct fname
        from enquiry
        where city = 'NAGPUR'
        and en_st = 'Y'
        and coursecode = 10;
begin
        for z in c1 loop
        dbms_output.put_line(z.fname);
        end loop;
end;
/
```

Listing 29.19: Displaying the Names of Students Having Enrollment Date More than Specified Date

```
declare
        cursor c1 (d1 date) is
        select distinct fname
        from enquiry
        where enquiry.enquiryno
        in
        (select enquiryno
        from enrollment
  where enrollmentdate > d1);
 begin
        for z in c1 ('20-JAN-99') loop
        dbms_output.put_line(z.fname);
        end loop;
end;
/
```

30

Error Handling

PL/SQL provides a feature of exception handling, which is used to handle to errors, occurs during the execution of PL/SQL statement. With exception handling, we can debug the code and provide a possible solution for error in the code.

In this chapter, you learn about exceptions and their use. Next, you learn about built-in and user-defined exceptions. Further, you learn about pragma EXCEPTION_INIT and the RAISE_APPLICATION_ERROR procedure. The chapter also explains how to raise, propagate, reraise, and handle exceptions. You also learn how to handle exceptions raised in declarations. In addition, you learn about the SQLCODE and SQLERRM functions. In the end, you learn about unhandled exceptions and guidelines for handling exceptions.

Exceptions

Oracle offers various ways to handle runtime errors or exceptions. The errors occur due to various reasons, such as incorrect coding, hardware failure, and memory faults. Oracle provides exceptions to handle the errors according to the users' way, functions which are used to generate error messages, and replaces default error messages. Listing 30.1 shows how to handle exceptions:

Listing 30.1: Handling Build-in Exceptions

```
declare
  firstname varchar2(30);
begin
  select fname
  into firstname
  from enquiry
  where enquiryno=10;
  dbms_output.put_line('The name is ' || firstname);
  exception
  when no_data_found then
  dbms_output.put_line('The required name is not present');
  when others then
  dbms_output.put_line('Error is generated');
end;
/
```

The output of Listing 30.1 is as follows:

```
The required name is not present
PL/SQL procedure successfully completed
```

In Listing 30.1, we have printed the name of the person having enquiry number `10`. If the required row (having enquiry number 10) is not present, the program raises the `NO_DATA_FOUND` exception. The code for handling this exception is written at the end of the PL/SQL block. It is called an exception handler. You can write any PL/SQL code in exception handler. When an exception is raised, the control transfers to the exception handler, the exception handler is executed, and the block that raised the exception terminates. The control returns to the enclosing block. If there is no enclosing block, the control returns to the host environment.

If any exception is raised for which the exception handler is not written, the control is transferred to the exception handler of `OTHERS`. Therefore, if there are two rows for enquiry number 10, the `TOO_MANY_ROWS` exception is raised. There is no exception handler for this exception, so the exception handler for `OTHERS` is executed.

The `NO_DATA_FOUND` or `TOO_MANY_ROWS` exceptions are called built-in exceptions. You can also define your own abnormal conditions and handle such conditions using exceptions. Listing 30.2 shows how to use user-defined exceptions:

Listing 30.2: Using User-defined Exceptions

```
declare
  edate date;
  enqno number:= 110002;
```

```
    invalid_date exception;
begin
    select enquirydate into edate
    from enquiry
    where enquiryno=enqno;
    if edate > SYSDATE then
            raise invalid_date;
    end if;
    exception
    When invalid_date then
    dbms_output.put_line('The enquiry date is not proper');
end;
/
```

The output of Listing 30.2 is as follows:

```
PL/SQL procedure successfully completed
```

The built-in exceptions are raised automatically; whereas, the user-defined exceptions has to be raised explicitly. The user-defined exceptions are declared in the declaration part. You can also raise a predefined exception by using the `RAISE` statement.

Utility of Exceptions

Exceptions are used to handle abnormal situations or error conditions. In the absence of an exception, the error conditions are handled by the language. For example, in Pascal, the program terminates when `the division by zero` condition occurs. When the `ZERO_DIVIDE` exception is raised in PL/SQL, the user-defined code is executed rather than merely terminating the PL/SQL program. Without exception, the error handling routine cannot be separated from error processing. The following code snippet shows how to handle errors:

```
BEGIN
   SELECT...
   if error condition then..
         SELECT..
   if error condition then..
END
```

If you do not write an error handling routine, the error goes undetected and may generate unrelated errors. The following code snippet shows how to handle errors using exceptions:

```
Select..
Select..
Exception
When NO_DATA_FOUND THEN
....
```

Using an exception, you can write a single code for handling multiple similar errors. The code becomes more readable because of error handling routine. Exception has a property of propagation, that is, if it is not handled in the current block, it propagates to the enclosing block. This property is used to standardize methods for error handling.

Built-in Exceptions

PL/SQL generates an error or warning when a program crosses a system dependent limit or violates certain Oracle rules. In Oracle, for every error there is an error number and error message. The predefined Oracle package, `STANDARD`, has defined exceptions for certain common errors. These exceptions are handled using names, and not error numbers. The errors, which are not handled using built-in exceptions, can be handled using the `OTHERS` exception. You can use the `SQLCODE` and `SQLERRM` functions to set actual error numbers. Alternatively, you can use `EXCEPTION_INIT` to associate exception with Oracle error number. Table 30.1 describes some built-in exceptions:

Exception	Oracle error	SQLCODE value	Description
ACCESS_INTO_NULL	ORA-06530	-6530	Occurs when an attempt is made to automatically assign a value to a null object.
COLLECTION_IS_NULL	ORA-06531	-6531	Occurs when any collection method, other than EXISTS, is applied to null collection. It is also raised when an element of null collection is referred.
CURSOR_ALREADY_OPEN	ORA-06511	-6511	Occurs when an attempt is made to open an already opened cursor. The cursor FOR.....LOOP.....END LOOP already opens the cursor so when an attempt is made to open a cursor inside the cursor FOR.....LOOP.....END LOOP, an exception is raised.
DUP_VAL_ON_INDEX	ORA-00001	-1	Occurs when an attempt is made to insert duplicate value in unique index. It is also raised when you try to insert duplicate values in primary key columns or unique key columns.
INVALID_CURSOR	ORA-01001	-1001	Occurs when a cursor operation is done on closed or not opened cursor.

INVALID_NUMBER	ORA-01722	-1722	Occurs only in SQL when conversion from character string to number fails due to improper format, as shown in the following code snippet:
			`n number;`
			`c char(4);`
			`..`
			`c := 'AB';`
			`n := to_number(C);`
			`--Raise Exception`

LOGIN_DENIED	ORA-01017	-1017	Occurs when login is denied.
NO_DATA_FOUND	ORA-01403	+100	Occurs when the SELECT...INTO statement fails to write any row; or any deleted element in nested table is referred; or any uninitialized index by table element is referred. It is not raised when the SELECT...INTO statement, which calls group of function, such as AVG or SUM, returns NULL value. It is also not raised when the FETCH statement does not return any value.
NOT_LOGGED_ON	ORA-01012	-1012	Occurs when you issue database call without being connected to Oracle.
PROGRAM_ERROR	ORA-06501	-6501	Occurs when a PL/SQL program fails to execute due to an internal problem.
ROWTYPE_MISMATCH	ORA-06504	-6504	Occurs when a cursor FETCH statement stores a value in a variable having incompatible datatype.
STORAGE_ERROR	ORA-06500	-6500	Occurs when there is memory error.
SUBSCRIPT_BEYOND_COUNT	ORA-06533	-6533	Occurs when a subscript is referred to the element of collection having out of range value.
SUBSCRIPT_OUTSIDE_LIMIT	ORA-06532	-6532	Occurs when valid subscript is not mentioned.

Exception	Oracle error	SQLCODE value	Description
TIMEOUT_ON_RESOURCE	ORA-00051	-51	Occurs when Oracle is waiting for the resource and the resource is busy for a long time, which exceeds time out limit.
TOO_MANY_ROWS	ORA-01422	-1422	Occurs when the SELECT...INTO statement returns more than one row.

VALUE_ERROR	ORA-06502	-6502	Occurs where there is failure in arithmetic, conversion, and truncation expressions. It also occurs due to size constraint. For example:
			`select fname`
			`into  X`
			`.....`
			If fname is varchar2(30) and X is varchar2(10), PL/SQL raises VALUE_ERROR. If conversion from character string to number fails, VALUE_ERROR is raised, while in SQL INVALID_NUMBER is raised.

ZERO_DIVIDE	ORA-01476	-1476	Occurs when the expression has division by zero.

Let's now learn about user-defined exceptions.

User-defined Exceptions

User-defined exceptions are used to handle the abnormal conditions which are application-specific. Such conditions can be treated as exceptions. Listing 30.3 shows how to raise user-defined exceptions:

Listing 30.3: Inserting an Amount in the feespaid Table and Raising a User-defined Exception for High Amount

```
create or replace procedure insamt (rollno in number, fdate in date,
amt in number) as
highamt exception;
begin
   if (amt > 10000) then
        raise highamt;
   else
                insert into feespaid(rollno, feespaiddate, amount) values (rollno,
                fdate, amt);
   end if;
end;
/
```

The output of Listing 30.3 is as follows:

```
Procedure created
```

The following code is used to run the above procedure. This code raises an exception and it is handled by exception OTHERS

```
begin
   insamt(1234,'12-jun-2003',67000);
      exception
   when others then
   dbms_output.put_line('very high amount specified');

end;
/
```

The output of the preceding code snippet is as follows:

```
very high amount specified

PL/SQL procedure successfully completed
```

Declaring an Exception

Before using a user-defined exception, you should first declare it in the `DECLARE` section. You can declare an exception, as shown in the following code snippet:

```
exceptionname exception;
```

Exceptions are declared similar to variables and have the same scope rules as the variables have.

Scope Rules

You cannot declare the same exception twice in the same block. When an exception is declared in the block, it has its scope in that block and in all the blocks which are enclosed by that block, as shown in the following code snippet:

```
declare
   x exception;                              --block a
begin
   declare                                   --block b
         y exception;
   begin
exception
   when x then
         .....
   end;                                      --end of b
end;                                         --end of a
```

In the preceding code snippet, the `x` exception has scope in block a as well as in block b. In block a, it is considered as local; whereas, it is considered as global in block b. The `y` exception is declared in block b and it has scope only in that block. You cannot use this exception in block a.

If the same exception is defined in the enclosing block, the local declaration is considered. In such a case, to use a global exception, you can use the following syntax:

```
block name.exception_name
```

Consider the following code snippet:

```
<<main>>
declare
   Z exception;   -- C
begin
   declare
         z exception;    -- B
   begin
         ........
         raise z;        -- A
Exception
   when Z then
         ........
   end;
end;
```

In the preceding code snippet, the A statement refers to an exception, which is declared in the local block, that is, at statement B. Suppose you want to start the exception at statement C. Then, you can modify the statement at A, as shown in the following code snippet:

```
raise main.z;
```

If you have not handled exception Z in the inner block, it would not be handled in the enclosing block, though both exceptions have the same name. To handle the Z exception, which is raised in the outer block, you have to remove its declaration from the inner block or write a handler for the OTHERS exception in the outer block. If an exception, other than the defined exception, is encountered then the OTHERS exception is raised. Listing 30.4 shows how to write a handler for the OTHERS exception:

Listing 30.4: Writing a Handler for the OTHERS Exception

```
declare
   x exception;                          --A
   n number;
begin
   n := 56;
   declare
               x exception;              --B
   begin
               raise x;                  --handled by others, referring B
   end;                                  --End of inner block B
Exception
   when x then                           --handler referring definition A
   dbms_output.put_line('exception x');
   when others then
   dbms_output.put_line('others');
end;
/
```

The output of Listing 30.4 is as follows:

```
others

PL/SQL procedure successfully completed
```

Pragma **EXCEPTION_INIT**

EXCEPTION_INIT is used to handle internal errors, similar to any other exception. To associate an exception with the error code, the PRAGMA EXCEPTION_INIT is declared. Listing 30.5 shows how to use pragma EXCEPTION_INIT to associate an exception with the error code:

Listing 30.5: Using PRAGMA EXCEPTION_INIT

```
alter table enquiry add constraint pk_enq primary key (enquiryno)
/
declare
   pk_violation exception;
   pragma exception_init(pk_violation, -0001);
begin
   insert into enquiry(enquiryno, enquirydate, fname) values(12345,'12-jul-
   2003','anil');
exception
   when pk_violation then
   dbms_output.put_line('primary key violation');
end;
/
```

The output of Listing 30.5 is as follows:

```
PL/SQL procedure successfully completed
```

In Listing 30.5, the pk_violation exception is attached to the error having code '0001'. When an error is generated for primary key violation, while inserting row in table enquiry, the pk_violation exception is raised. The exception handler then executes the code to handle the exception. The exception has to be declared before using it in pragma.

The **RAISE_APPLICATION_ERROR** Procedure

The `RAISE_APPLICATION_ERROR` procedure is used to generate user-defined errors in the stored program. The `RAISE_APPLICATION_ERROR` procedure has the following syntax:

```
raise_application_error(errorcode, error message, TRUE/FALSE);
```

In the `RAISE_APPLICATION_ERROR` procedure, the valid `errorcode` is within the `20000` to `-20999` range. The message length is maximum `2048` bytes. The optional third parameter `TRUE` indicates that the error is stored in stack. If `FALSE` is mentioned, the error replaces all previous errors. This procedure is defined in the `DBMS_STANDARD` package. Suppose you have to write a procedure to insert a row in the `enquiry` table. If `amt` is more than `1,00,000` an error is raised. Listing 30.6 shows the code to generate an error:

Listing 30.6: Writing a Code for Generating an Error

```
create or replace procedure insert_fees(rlno in number, fdate date, amt number)
  as
begin
  if (amt>100000) then
              raise_application_error(-20110,'Amount is very high');
  else
              insert into feespaid(rollno, feespaiddate, amount)
       values (rlno, fdate, amt);
  end if;
end;
/
```

The output of Listing 30.6 is as follows:

```
Procedure created
```

Listing 30.7 shows how to call the procedure that we have created in Listing 30.6:

Listing 30.7: Calling the insert_fees Procedure

```
begin
  insert_fees(12345,'12-jul-2003',2345555);
end;
/
```

The output of Listing 30.7 is as follows:

```
*
ERROR at line 1:
ORA-20110: Amount is very high
ORA-06512: at "PLSQL.INSERT_FEES", line 4
ORA-06512: at line 2
*/
```

When RAISE_APPLICATION_ERROR is executed, the subprogram ends and the error code and error message return to the calling program. The code and messages in the calling program can be obtained using the `SQLCODE` and `SQLERRM` functions. In the calling program, you can attach an error number to an exception and treat the error as an exception. Listing 30.8 shows how to associate an exception name with an Oracle error number:

Listing 30.8: Using pragma EXCEPTION_INIT to Associate an Exception Name with an Oracle Error Number

```
declare
  x exception;
  pragma exception_init(x,-20110);
begin
  insert_fees(12345,'12-jul-2003',2345555);
```

```
exception
  when x then
  dbms_output.put_line('handling error using exception');
end;
/
```

The output of Listing 30.8 is as follows:

```
handling error using exception

PL/SQL procedure successfully completed
```

When the insert_fees procedure is called and it generates an error in the calling program, the `x` exception is raised and the handler for it is executed. When the same exception is again declared, its original meaning is lost because the local declaration is always given more preference than global declaration. In such a case, to refer a predefined exception, the package name is used. Consider the following code snippet to understand how a built-in exception, `VALUE_ERROR`, is used:

```
declare
  value_error exception;
        x varchar2(2);
begin
  x :='abc'; -- A .generates exception value_error
Exception
  when value_error then
                                        --Handler for local exception
                                        --when STANDARD.value_error then handles
                                        --exception generated at A
                                        --Handler for global exception
  ........
end;
```

Raising an Exception

An exception is raised due to some internal error or when you execute the `RAISE` statement. An exception is also raised when it is impossible to proceed because of abnormal conditions. You can also raise the built-in exception by using the `RAISE` statement.

The following code snippet shows how to raise an exception explicitly:

```
create procedure insfees(rlno IN number,fdate IN date, amt IN number) as
highamt EXCEPTION;
begin
  if amt > 100000 then raise highamt;
  end if;
  if amt < 0 then raise INVALID_NUMBER;
  end if;
Exception
when highamt then
  .........
when invalid_number then
  .........
end;
```

In the preceding code snippet, `INVALID_NUMBER` is a predefined exception, which is raised explicitly.

Propagation of an Exception

When an exception is raised, it is handled in the current block if the handler is present in the current block. The current block terminates its execution and the control goes to the enclosing block. If there is no handler in the current block, the control goes to the outer block, and an exception handler present in that block handles it. If the exception is not handled in any block, the unhandled exception error is returned. In this section, we consider these cases one-by-one.

Case 1: When an exception is handled in the current block, as shown in the following code snippet:

```
declare
  .....                                --Block A
begin
  declare
  .....                                --Block B
  begin
       .....
  Exception
  when VALUE_ERROR then
       ......                          --C
  end;
  ........                             --E
Exception
when VALUE_ERROR then                  --D
  .......
end;
```

In the preceding code snippet, Block A is the outer block and block B is the inner block. If the VALUE_ERROR exception is raised in the inner block, it is handled by the exception handler, which is defined locally at statement C. The current block B is terminated and the control shifts to the outer block at statement E.

Case 2: When an exception is handled in the outer block, as shown in the following code snippet:

```
declare
  .....                                --Block A
begin
  declare
       ....                            --Block B
  begin
                                       -- Raise exception
  end;
                                       ---E
EXCEPTION
  WHEN VALUE_ERROR THEN
       .........
```

In the preceding code snippet, when the VALUE_ERROR exception is raised in block B, the corresponding handler is searched in the current block B. Since no handler is provided in block B; therefore, the current block terminates and the control goes to the outer block at the exception handler section. Since the outer block has a handler, the exception is handled and then the outer block, A, gets terminated.

Case 3: Unhandled exception, as shown in the following code snippet:

```
declare                     --Block A
begin
  declare                   --Block B
  begin

  end;
end;
```

In the preceding code snippet, when an exception is not handled in the current block and any of its outer blocks, then the unhandled exception error is generated. If the VALUE_ERROR exception is raised in block B, exception handler will be searched in block B. If it does not get it there, exception handler will be searched in outer block,

A. In case it does not get it there also, it will search in the outer block which encloses A. If there is no handler for the VALUE_ERROR exception, an unhandled exception error is generated.

Case 4: Propagation of an exception that is not declared, as shown in the following code snippet:

```
declare
   ....                                    --Block A
begin
   ....
   declare
          z exception                      --Block B
   begin
          ....
          raise z;                         --C
   end;
Exception
when others then
   .....
end;
```

In the preceding code snippet, an exception is raised in inner block B at statement C. Since there is no handler in that block, the exception is propagated to the enclosing block. Since exception z is not declared in that block, only the handler for exception OTHERS is executed.

Re-raising an Exception

You can re-raise an exception, if the exception has to be handled globally and locally in different ways, by using the Raise statement without the exception name. The following code snippet shows how to re-raise an exception:

```
DECLARE
   high_amt exception;                     --Block A
BEGIN
   BEGIN
          IF amt > 100000 THEN
                  raise high_amt;
          END IF;
   EXCEPTION
   WHEN high_amt THEN
                                           --handle the error locally
          RAISE;                           --C
   END;
   .....
EXCEPTION
WHEN others THEN
                                   --handle the exception in a different way
END;
```

In the preceding code snippet, we have re-raised an exception in a local handler by giving the RAISE statement without the exception name. The RAISE statement without the exception name re-raises the current exception.

Handling Exceptions

Exceptions are handled using the EXCEPTION HANDLER code, written at the end of the block. The following code snippet shows how to handle exceptions:

```
DECLARE
   .....
BEGIN
```

```
    .....
    A;
    E;
EXCEPTION
WHEN high_amt THEN
    .....
WHEN low_amt THEN
    B;
    C;
WHEN VALUE_ERROR THEN
    .....
WHEN OTHERS THEN
    .....
END;
```

In the preceding code snippet, when an exception is raised, the control goes to the required exception handler and the handler gets executed. After executing the handler, the current block terminates and the control returns to the executing block. For example, statement A raises the `low_amt` exception, and the control goes to the exception handler, and statements B and C are executed.

After executing these statements, the control does not return to statement E, but the block gets terminated. If the exception does not have the handler, the `OTHERS` exception handler `gets` executed. The handler for `OTHERS` should be written at last in the list of exception handlers. Otherwise, other exceptions, such as `high_amt` and `low_amt`, are not handled. It is always recommended that `OTHERS` should be written, so that handling all possible exceptions is guaranteed. One block should have only one handler for each exception.

When the same code has to be executed for one or more exceptions, you can use the `or` clause in the exception handler. You can have the same exception handler for the `high_amt` and `low_amt` exceptions, as shown in the following code snippet:

```
EXCEPTION
WHEN high_amt or low_amt THEN
    ......
```

A simple block can have any number of exception handlers, one for each exception. The scope rules for PL/SQL variables are also applied to exceptions.

The explicit cursor attributes are not available in handler, if the exception is raised inside the `FOR.....LOOP.....END LOOP` cursor. This is because when the control goes out of the `FOR.....LOOP.....END LOOP`, the cursor gets closed. Now you will not be able to refer the attributes of a closed cursor, as shown in the following code snippet:

```
DECLARE
    CURSOR c1 IS
    SELECT *
    FROM enquiry;
    high_amt EXCEPTION;
BEGIN
    FOR  z IN c1 LOOP
            ......
            IF amt > 100000 THEN
                    RAISE high_amt;
            END IF;
    END LOOP;
EXCEPTION
WHEN high_amt THEN
    IF c1%ROWCOUNT THEN
            ....
    END IF;
END;
```

In the preceding code snippet, the `if c1%ROWCOUNT` statement in the handler is illegal because you cannot refer the cursor attributes, `c1%ROWCOUNT`, for a closed cursor. A cursor closes when the control goes out of `For.....Loop.....End Loop`.

Exceptions Raised in Declarations

When an exception is raised in a declaration then it is not handled in the current block, but the control goes to the outer block and the exception gets handled in the outer block. The following code snippet shows how to handle exceptions raised in declarations:

```
DECLARE
  .....
BEGIN
   DECLARE
         X NUMBER(2):=135;
   BEGIN

   EXCEPTION
   WHEN OTHERS THEN
         A;
   END;
   ......
   WHEN OTHERS THEN
   B;
END;
```

In the preceding code snippet, `X` cannot store number `135` because of shorter width. Therefore, an exception is raised. Since the exception cannot be caught in the current block, statement A is not executed. The exception is handled in the enclosed block, and statement B is executed.

Exception Raised in a Handler

When exceptions are raised in the exception handling section, they are not handled in the current block. The control goes to the outer block where these exceptions are handled. The following code snippet shows how to handle exceptions raised in a handler:

```
DECLARE
  ....
BEGIN
   DECLARE
   BEGIN
         .....
   EXCEPTION
   WHEN low_amt THEN
         INSERT INTO ...(..);                --A
   WHEN dup_val_on_index THEN                --B
         ......RAISE EXCEPTION;
   END;
......
WHEN dup_val_on_index THEN                   --C
  .........
END;
```

In the preceding code snippet, if the `low_amt` exception is raised, the control goes to statement A. It inserts data in some table. Now, if exception `dup_val_on_index` is raised by the `INSERT` statement, it is not handled by the exception handler of the current block, but is propagated to the outer block. Therefore, the exception is caught by the exception handler at C of outer block.

*Restriction on Use of the **GOTO** Statement in an Exception Handler*

You cannot branch from an exception handler to any part of the current block. Also, you cannot branch from any part to the exception handler. The following code snippet shows the GOTO statement in Exception handler:

```
DECLARE
  .....
BEGIN
  GOTO S1;                          --A
  <<S2>>
        S2;
EXCEPTION
WHEN NO_DATA_FOUND THEN
<<S1>>
  S3;
GOTO S2;                            --B
END;
```

In the preceding code snippet, statement A is illegal because it is branching to an exception handler. Statement B is illegal, because it is branching from an exception handler to a current block.

The **SQLCODE** and **SQLERRM** Functions

The SQLCODE and SQLERRM functions return error code and error message, respectively, of the recent error. The SQLERRM function returns the error message associated with its error and the SQLCODE function returns the error code associated with the most recently raised error. SQLCODE returns error code as a negative number. Only for the NO_DATA_FOUND exception, it returns positive value, +100 and for user-defined exceptions, it returns +1. The SQLERRM function returns the length of the message which is 512 characters. This message includes code, message, table name, and column name.

If no exception is raised, SQLCODE returns zero and SQLERRM returns ORA-0000: normal, successful, completion.

In case of user-defined exception, SQLERRM returns the following message:

```
'User-defined Exception'
```

Listing 30.9 shows how to use the SQLCODE and SQLERRM functions:

Listing 30.9: Using SQLCODE and SQLERRM

```
declare
  user_exception exception;
  code number;
  msg varchar2(512);
begin
  raise user_exception;
exception
  when user_exception then
  code := sqlcode;
  msg := sqlerrm;
  dbms_output.put_line('code and messages are *'||code||' '||msg);
end;
/
              --code and messages are *1 User-Defined Exception
declare
  x exception;
  code number;
  msg varchar2(512);
```

```
   pragma exception_init(x,-20110);
begin
   insert_fees(12345,'12-jul-2003',2345555);
exception
   when x then
   code := sqlcode;
   msg := sqlerrm;
   dbms_output.put_line('code and messages are'||code||' '||msg);
end;
/
         --code and messages are-20110 ORA-20110: Amount is very high
```

In Listing 30.9, when an exception is associated with an error code using pragma `EXCEPTION_INIT`, the error code and error message are returned.

When some error code is passed to `SQLERRM` as a parameter, it returns a corresponding error message. If a positive value is passed, it always returns fixed message, `user_defined_exception`.

If the value 100 is passed, it returns the following message:

```
ORA-01403: no data found
```

When zero is passed, it returns the following message:

```
ORA-0000: normal successful completion
```

The following code snippet prints the error message:

```
errmsg := SQLERRM (ercode);
dbms_output.put_line(errmsg);
```

You cannot use the `SQLCODE` and `SQLERRM` functions directly in a SQL statement. To use their values, you have to store their values in local variables and then use these local variables. The following code snippet shows how to store recent errors in an error table:

```
ercode := SQLCODE;
ermsg  := SQLERRM; (errcode, ermsg)
Insert into errortable values
```

The `SQLCODE` and `SQLERRM` functions are used specially in exception handler for `OTHERS`, because they help you to find an internal error (if occurred).

Unhandled Exceptions

If the PL/SQL block results in an unhandled exception, then the actual outcome depends upon the actual outermost environment. If the stored program fails due to unhandled exceptions, the changes made by it are not rolled back. If an unhandled exception occurs in P the L/SQL block in the precompiler environment, then all the changes made by the block are rolled back. If subprograms fail due to an unhandled exception, then PL/SQL does not assign values to the `OUT` parameter.

Guidelines for Handling Errors

It is always recommended to handle exceptions explicitly in the block. If the block does not have an exception handler, it is terminated. Therefore, you should anticipate type of exceptions that may be raised in the block. You should include an exception handler `OTHERS` to provide a path for normal exit from the block. In the next section, you learn some techniques for handling errors in certain conditions.

Continuing after an Error has Occurred

Suppose you want to continue after an error has occurred or an exception is raised. In such a case, you can enclose the statement which is prone to errors in the PLSQL block and write an exception handler in the block. Listing 30.10 shows statement A and B which may generate error

Listing 30.10: Writing a Simple Code which may generate error

```
declare
   x number(2);
   bcode number(8);
begin
   bcode := 100010;
   select expectedincome/nvl(netincome,0)
   into x
   from batch
   where batchcode = bcode;          -- a
   insert into batchanalysis(batchcode, value)
   values(bcode,x);                  -- b
end;
/
```

The output of Listing 30.10 is as follows:

```
PL/SQL procedure successfully completed
```

In Listing 30.11, if the A statement has null `netincome`, it will raise an error, `ZERO-DIVIDE`, and the block gets terminated. Listing 30.11 shows how to handle the divide by zero exception:

Listing 30.11: Handling the Divide by Zero Exception

```
declare                                                   --block a
      x number(3);
      bcode batch.batchcode % type;
   begin
      bcode := 100010;
      begin                                      --block b
             select expectedincome/nvl(netincome,0)
             into x
             from batch
             where batchcode = bcode;
      exception
      when zero_divide then
             x :=0;
      end;
      insert into batchanalysis(batchcode,value)
      values (bcode, x);
   end;
 /
```

The output of Listing 30.11 is as follows:

```
PL/SQL procedure successfully completed
```

In Listing 30.11,

- The statement is written in the inner block B.
- If the statement raises an unhandled exception, `ZERO_DIVIDE`, the exception handler for it is executed, which makes the value of `X` as `Zero` and the procedure continues inserting values into the `batchanalysis` table, i.e. the execution will not stop after the exception is raised, rather the exception is handled and the procedure continues. After that, block B is terminated, and the next statement in block A is executed, that is, it stores value `0` in the table.

Using a Locator Variable

If multiple statements in the block raise the same exception, then the same exception handler is executed. There is no built-in facility to provide information regarding which statement has raised an exception. The following code snippet shows use of locator variable

```
DECLARE
BEGIN
   INSERT INTO BATCH ...(,.);                              --A
   .......
   INSERT INTO COURSE ...(..);                             --B
   .......
   INSERT INTO .... ;                                      --C
EXCEPTION
WHEN DUP_VAL_ON_INDEX THEN
.....
END;
```

In the preceding code snippet, if the statements A, B, or C raises the same exception `DUL_VAL_ON_INDEX`, then the same action is taken in all the cases. However, if you want to perform different actions, you can use a locator variable. The current value of locator variable gives information about the statement that raised the exception. The following code snippet shows the use of the locator variable:

```
declare
   loc_var number(2);
begin
   loc_var := 1;
   insert into batch....;                                  --A
   loc-var := 2;
   insert into course...;                                  --B
   loc_var := 3;
   insert into ....;                                       --C
Exception
when DUP_VAL_ON_INDEX then
   if loc_var = 1 then
         -- Action A;
   end if;
   if loc_var = 2 then
         -- Action B;
   end if;
   if loc_var = 3 then
         -- Action C
   end if;
end;
```

In the preceding code snippet, if statement B has raised an exception, then `loc_var` will have value 2. You can take an action according to the current value of variable in the exception handler.

Retrying Transactions

Suppose you want to retry a transaction. In that case, you can issue the savepoint before issuing the statement. If an error occurs, you can rollback to savepoint and retry again. You can also loop for limiting the number of attempts. Listing 30.12 shows how to retry transactions:

Listing 30.12: Using Savepoint for Retrying a Transaction

```
create or replace procedure insenquiry (penquiryno in number, pfname in        varchar2,
   penqdate in date) as enqno number;
begin
   enqno := penquiryno;
                                        --some more work a
   loop
            begin   --block b
               savepoint startpt;
```

```
                        --some more work b
            insert into enquiry(enquiryno, fname, enquirydate) values
            (enqno, pfname, penqdate);
            exit;
        exception
            when dup_val_on_index then
            enqno := enqno+1;
                rollback to startpt;
        end;
    end loop;
end;
/
```

The output of Listing 30.12 is as follows:

```
Procedure created
```

In Listing 30.12, after inserting value into the `enquiry` table if it sees that the primary key is being violated, then the transaction is rolled back upto a savepoint. Listing 30.13 shows how to insert values in the enquiry table:

Listing 30.13: Calling the insenquiry Procedure for Inserting Values into the enquiry Table

```
begin
   insenquiry(12345,'SUNIL','12-JUL-2003');
end;
/
```

The output of Listing 30.13 is as follows:

```
PL/SQL procedure successfully completed
```

In Listing 30.13, the `INSERT` statement is enclosed in the block B. If the row with `12345` already exists, it will insert `12346`. When an exception is raised, the handler restores the state before the actual operation. In the handler, we are increasing enquiry number so that for the next attempt, the same exception may not be generated.

Summary

In this chapter, you have learned about exception, which is a very powerful tool for handling errors. Using exceptions, you can handle errors in user defined way. You have also learned about the built in exception and user-defined exceptions. The next chapter will focus on subprograms

Exercise

1. What is the difference between built in exception and user defined exception.
2. Name important built in exceptions.
3. Explain importance of pragma EXCEPTION_INIT.

31

Subprograms in PL/SQL

Subprograms are used to provide modularity and encapsulate a sequence of statements. While developing an application, subprograms work as small building blocks. These building blocks have mutually isolated operations, and are therefore easy to construct and maintain.

Subprograms also provide reusability. After a subprogram is built and validated, it can be used in a number of applications. If the definition of a subprogram changes, it affects that particular program only. This makes the maintenance of subprograms easy.

Subprograms also provide abstraction, which means a user of a subprogram should only know what the subprogram does and not bother about the implementation details of the subprogram.

NOTE

You can break a large program into small manageable modules, which are easy to construct. This type of method of program design is called a top-down design.

Describing a Subprogram

Subprograms are first constructed and then used. Let's now explore some examples that illustrate the use of subprograms.

Listing 31.1: Finding the Name of a Person with a Specified Enquiry Number

```
create or replace Procedure  findname (enqno1 IN number, fname1 out varchar2) is
fname2 varchar2(30);                                          --A
begin
   select fname
   into fname2
   from enquiry
   where enquiryno = enqno1;                                  --B
   fname1:= fname2;                                           --C
Exception
   when no_data_found then
   raise_application_error (-20100,
   'The given enquiry number is not present');                --D
end;
/
```

The output of Listing 31.1 is as follows:

```
Procedure created
```

Listing 31.2: Calling a Procedure in a PL/SQL Block

```
declare
   enqno2  number(5);
   fname2  varchar2(30);
begin
   enqno2:= 12345;
   findname(enqno2,fname2);                         --call to subprogram
   dbms_output.put_line(fname2);
end;
/
```

The output of Listing 31.2 is as follows:

```
Smith

PL/SQL procedure successfully completed
```

Listing 31.3: Writing a Function to Retrieve an Employee Name with a Specified Enquiry Number

```
Create or replace function getname(enqno1 number) return varchar2 as
fname1 varchar2(30);
begin
   select   fname
   into  fname1
   from enquiry
   where enquiryno = enqno1;
   return (fname1);
Exception
   when no_data_found then
   raise_application_error(-20110,'The enquiry number is not present');
end;
/
```

The output of Listing 31.3 is as follows:

```
Function created
```

Listing 31.4: Calling a Function in PL/SQL

```
declare
   fname2 varchar2(30);
   enqno2 number(5);
begin
   enqno2 := 12345;
   fname2 := getname(enqno2);
   dbms_output.put_line(fname2);
end;
/
```

The output of Listing 31.4 is as follows:

```
Smith

PL/SQL procedure successfully completed
```

Subprograms provide extensibility. In other words, they allow you to use PL/SQL according to your requirements. After writing a procedure or function, you can use it similar to a built-in procedure or function in the language.

Let's now learn about procedures and functions.

Procedure

Procedures are written for performing a specific action. The syntax of procedure is as follows:

```
PROCEDURE <Procedure name> (Parameter name1 [IN/OUT/IN OUT]
   Parameter type 1, Parameter name2,...)
IS
   local declarations;
BEGIN
   PL/SQL executable statements;
   ....
EXCEPTION
   exception handlers;
END <procedure name>;
```

A procedure has two parts, specification and body. Specification consists of the name of the procedure and parameter declaration. Parameter declaration is optional. A procedure without parameters does not need parentheses.

Suppose you want to use a procedure to update the data of a batch. You can do so by writing it as a procedure as shown in the following code snippet:

```
Procedure updatebatch is ....
```

In the preceding code snippet, each parameter can be declared by using the following syntax:

```
Parameter-name [IN/OUT/IN OUT] parameter-datatype;
```

You can declare a parameter by using the following syntax:

```
enqno1 IN number;
frame1 OUT number;
```

You can supply the default value to a parameter by using the `DEFAULT` clause or the := operator. For example, if you want to use the default value `100, you` can write it as shown in the following code snippet:

```
enqno1 IN number := 100;
```

or:

```
enqno1 IN number DEFAULT 100;
```

You cannot impose the `NOT NULL` constraint on parameters. Similarly, parameter declarations should be unconstrained. Therefore, the following declaration is illegal:

```
enqno1 IN number(5)
```

The body of a procedure consists of local declarations, the executable part, and the exception handling part. In Listing 31.1, for example, statement A is a part of the local declaration. You can declare a number of such local variables. Here you do not have to write the `DECLARE` keyword like PLSQL block.

The executable part can have any number of PL/SQL executable statements but at least one PL/SQL executable statement should be present. You can use the NULL statement if you do not want to execute any statement.

The exception block in the procedure body is optional. A user can write any number of exception handlers in the exception block.

Functions

A function computes a value. However, structurally, functions have a `RETURN` clause. The syntax for using a function is as follows:

```
FUNCTION (function name>
  (parametername1 [IN/OUT/IN OUT] parameterdatatype1,
  parametername2 ([IN/OUT/IN OUT]...)
  RETURN return_datatype IS
BEGIN
  PL/SQL executable statements;
EXCEPTION
  exception handlers;
END;
```

A function, similar to a procedure, has two parts, specification and body. The specification part contains the name of the function, parameter declarations, and the return datatype. Parameter declarations are optional, and if parameters are not present, then you need not use parentheses. For example, you can write a function as shown in the following code snippet:

```
Function maxbatch return NUMBER IS..
```

If the parameter mode is not given (like `IN`, `OUT`, ...), the `IN` mode is assumed by default. For example, in the `getname` function (Listing 31.4), the parameter `enqno` has the `IN` mode.

The body of a function contains three parts:

- The declarative part: Contains local declarations. The keyword DECLARE is not used in this part.
- The executable part: Contains PL/SQL executable statements. It should have one or more return statements with an expression, i.e. in the form RETURN(expr). The expression should return the value of the datatype mentioned in the return datatype.
- The exception handling part: used for writing exceptions. A user function should be written for a specified purpose and the function should not have side effects.

The function should have at least one RETURN statement. When this statement is executed, the execution of the subprogram terminates, and the control returns to the caller routine. The RETURN statement need not be the last statement in the program, but if the RETURN statement is executed, then further statements are not executed. Therefore, the following code snippet is perfectly legal:

```
Create Function check_amt(amt number)
  Return varchar2 is
begin
  if amt > 100000 then
        return ('HIGH');
  else
        return('LOW');
  end if;
end;
/
```

The output of the preceding code snippet is as follows:

```
Function created
```

A subprogram can have multiple RETURN statements, but such practice should generally be avoided.

Listing 31.5 shows a program with less number of return statements:

Listing 31.5: Writing a Program with less Number of return Statements

```
Create or replace Function check_amt(amt  number)
  return varchar2 is
  X varchar2 (10);
begin
  if amt > 100000 then
        X :='HIGH';
  else
        X:='LOW';
  end if;
  RETURN (X);
END;
/
```

The output of Listing 31.5 is as follows:

```
Function created
```

In a function, the RETURN statement must have an expression. The expression should have the same datatype, such as RETURN. You can write a complex expression with the RETURN statement, as shown in the following code snippet:

```
RETURN (A*B/C);
```

If a function is terminated without executing the RETURN statement, a PROGRAM ERROR exception is generated in the calling program. A procedure can also have a RETURN statement, but this is not mandatory. The RETURN statement in a procedure should not have any expression. The statement, in this case, is written in the procedure, as shown in the following code snippet:

```
RETURN;
```

When a `RETURN` statement is executed, the procedure is terminated and the control returns to the caller routine.

Subprogram Declaration

You can declare subprograms in a PL/SQL block, subprogram, or package. However, you should declare a subprogram only after declaring its variables. The following syntax is used to declare a subprogram in a PL/SQL block:

```
declare
   localvariable declarations;
   subprogram    declarations;
begin
   ..........
end;
Thus following declarations is illegal
declare
   procedure findname ...
...
   end findname;
   x varchar2(30);
begin
   ......
end;
```

Forward Declaration

If you want to use one subprogram in another subprogram, then the process has to be defined in a proper order. For example, if procedure `X` is calling procedure `Y`, then `Y` should be declared before `X`. Therefore, the order shown in the following code snippet is not valid:

```
Declare
   ....
   procedure X(..) is
begin
   y(..);                                    --illegal call
end;
procedure y(..) is
begin
end;
```

To solve such problems, PL/SQL provides the facility of forward declaration. When using forward declaration, you have to write the specification of the procedure before its definition. Therefore, you can write the procedure in the order shown in the following code snippet:

```
declare
   procedure Y(..);                          --forward declaration
   procedure X(...) is
   begin
         Y(..);
   end;
   procedure Y(..)is
   begin
         ....
   end;
begin
   ......
end;
```

In forward declaration, you have to write the procedure name and its parameter specification, i.e. specification of the subprogram. In a function, you have to specify the RETURN datatype as well. Using forward declarations, you can write subprograms in alphabetical order; define mutually recursive programs; and group subprograms into packages. The subprograms can be written anywhere after forward declaration but should appear in the same program unit.

Subprogram Declaration in a Package

You can group related subprograms in a package. A package consists of two parts, package specification and package body. The package specification part contains subprogram specification, while the package body part you write the implementation of those subprograms. For example, the following code snippet shows you how to implement a package, used to store subprograms related with an enquiry:

```
CREATE PACKAGE  enquiry_analysis AS
function calc_enq_month (monthno number)
RETURN Number;
procedure calc_enq_date(edate IN date, enqnumber OUT number);
...
end enquiry-analysis;

CREATE PACKAGE BODY enquiry_analysis AS
FUNCTION calc_enq_-month(monthno NUMBER)
  RETURN number IS
  .....
begin
end calc_enq_month;
PROCEDURE calc_enq_date(edate IN DATE, enqnumber OUT Number) IS
begin
  .....
end calc-enq-date;
end enquiry-analysis;
```

You can also define additional subprograms in the body of the package, but such subprograms can be available or accessed only in the body of the package.

Stored Subprograms

Subprograms can be stored in a database so that they can be accessible from all the products of Oracle as well the products which can interact with Oracle, such as Visual Basic.

Listing 31.16 shows you how to create a stored procedure in a subprogram:

Listing 31.6: Creating the calc_enq_month Stored Procedure (field names as per enquiry table given in Appendix)

```
CREATE or replace PROCEDURE calc_enq_month(monthno IN number, cnt OUT number) As
BEGIN
  Select Count(enquiryno) into cnt from enquiry
  where to_number(to_char(enquirydate,'mm')) = monthno;
END;
/
```

The output of Listing 31.16 is as follows:

```
Procedure created
```

When a subprogram is created, the word AS is used instead of IS. Stored subprograms are used the same way as other subprograms.

Parameters

Information to a subprogram is passed through parameters. The parameters used in the implementation or definition of a subprogram are called formal parameters. The parameters used to call subprograms are called actual parameters.

Listing 31.7 shows the use of formal parameters:

Listing 31.7: Using Formal Parameters

```
declare
   A number;
   B number;
   C number;
   procedure sum (X IN number,Y IN number, Z OUT number) is
   begin
           Z := X+Y;
   end;
begin
   A:=5;
   B:=10;
   sum(A,B,C);   --A
   dbms_output.put_line (to_char(C));     -- prints value 15
end;
/
```

The output of Listing 31.17 is as follows:

```
15

PL/SQL procedure successfully completed
```

In Listing 31.17, X, Y, and Z are called formal parameters. The parameters A, B, and C, used in the call as mentioned in statement A are called actual parameters. Though you can use the same names for actual and formal parameters, such practice is not recommended. In the call, the actual parameter is substituted for the formal parameter. Therefore, A is substituted for X; B for Y; and C for Z. Before assigning value to a formal parameter, the datatype of the value of the actual parameter is converted so that it matches the datatype of the formal parameter. Therefore, the call in the following code snippet is legal:

```
sum ('10', '20', C);
```

Though implicit conversion is possible, explicit conversion is recommended by using conversion functions, such as to_number. When conversion is not possible, the PL/SQL exception VALUE_ERROR is raised. Therefore, the call shown in the following code snippet generates an error:

```
sum('$10', '$20', C);
```

The error is generated because it is not possible to convert value $10 into a valid number.

Methods for Passing Actual Parameters

You can pass actual parameters by the following three methods:

- Using positional notation
- Using named notation
- Using mixed notation

Let's discuss these methods in the following sections.

Positional Notation

You can call a procedure as:

```
sum (A, B, C);
```

Here:

- First actual parameter A is substituted in place of the first formal parameter X
- Second actual parameter B is substituted with second formal parameter Y, and so on.

Thus, A is substituted for S, B for Y, and C for Z

Named Notation

In this method, the actual parameter is associated with the formal parameter by using => arrow symbol. Therefore a call to procedure using named notation is as follows:

```
sum(X=>A, Y=>B, Z=>C);
```

Here:

- A is associated with X
- B is associated with Y
- C is associated with Z.

It is not necessary to maintain the order of actual parameter. Therefore, the following statement has the same effect:

```
sum(Y=>B, X=>A, Z=>C);
```

Mixed Notation

In the mixed notation method, you can use both notations in a procedure call. However, the positional notation must precede the named notation. Therefore the call in the following code snippet is legal:

```
sum(A,B,Z=>C);                    --legal
```

However, the following statement is not legal:

```
sum( X=>A,B,C);                   --illegal
```

Mode of Passing Parameters

You can pass parameters in three modes: IN, OUT, and IN OUT. In a legal statement, A and B are passed as IN parameters and C is passed as the OUT parameter. If no mode is specified, then the IN mode is taken by default. In the case of functions, it is recommended that parameters be passed in the IN parameter because a function is expected to return a single value. Making functions return multiple values is considered good programming practice. If all the parameters are IN parameters, then the function is free from side effects, i.e. they cannot change the values of variables that are not local. Let's now understand the modes in detail.

The IN Mode

The IN mode is used to pass values to a subprogram. Inside the subprogram, IN acts as a constant, and any attempt to change its value causes a compilation error. Consider the following code snippet:

```
Procedure sum ( X  IN number, Y IN number, Z out  number) is
begin
   Z := X + Y;                        -- A
   X := X + 1;                        -- B
   Y := Y + 1;                        -- C
end;
```

In the preceding code snippet, statements B and C cause compilation errors, because an attempt is made to change the value of the IN parameter. The actual parameters corresponding to the IN parameter can be initialized to variables, constants, literals, or expressions. Therefore, you can call the procedure sum as shown in the following code snippet:

```
sum(A,B,C);                  --Actual parameters are initialized variables.
sum(10,B,C);                 --Actual parameter is literal 10 for X.
sum(10,10+15,C);               --Actual parameter is literal expression 10+15 for Y.
```

```
declare
   K constant:= 10;
   ....
   sum(A,K,C);                              -- Actual parameter is constant K for Y.
```

The OUT Mode

The `OUT` mode is used to return a value to the calling routine.

Listing 31.8 shows you how to use the OUT Parameter

Listing 31.8: Using the OUT Parameter

```
declare
   A number;
   B number;
   C number;
   procedure sum (X IN number, Y IN number, Z OUT number) is
   begin
               Z := Z+10;                      --Null Values
               Z := X+10;                      -- Z is initialized
         Z := X+Y+Z;
   end;
begin
   A:=5;
   B:=10;
         C:=12;
   sum(A,B,C);
   dbms_output.put_line (to_char(C));
end;
/
```

The output of Listing 31.8 is as follows:

```
30

PL/SQL procedure successfully completed
```

In the preceding output, the parameter `Z` is the OUT parameter in the procedure `sum`. In a subprogram, the OUT parameter acts as an uninitialized variable. Any attempt to refer the value of this parameter results in a null value.

The actual parameter for the OUT mode must be a variable; otherwise, a syntax error is displayed.

Therefore, the call shown in the following code snippet is not legal:

```
Sum (A, B, C+1);                              -- illegal call
```

If the actual parameter has certain values, then it will be lost after the call. The following code snippet will help you understand this better:

```
C := 10;
sum (10,15,C);
dbms_output.put_line(TO_CHAR(C));                  -- prints value 45
```

When a subprogram is called, the actual parameter for the OUT mode is initialized to `NULL`. If a subprogram terminates abnormally, then the value of the actual parameter remains `NULL`.

The IN OUT Mode

The `IN OUT` mode is used to pass values to a subprogram and for taking the value out of a subprogram. Consider the following code snippet to write a procedure for squaring a number:

```
Create procedure sqr (X IN OUT number) is
begin
  X:= X * X;
end;
/
```

In the preceding code snippet, the `IN OUT` parameters act similar to initialized variables. Therefore, you can refer the value of a variable or assign it some other value. The actual parameter used must be a variable and not a constant or expression. Therefore, the calls in the following code snippet are not legal:

```
sqr(A+1);                                   -- illegal
sqr(50);                            -- illegal
```

The `IN OUT` parameter is used to pass a value to a subprogram, and gets updated values from the subprogram.

Default Values

`The Default` clause is used when you want to initialize the `IN` parameter with some other value. When the actual parameter is not passed, the default value is assumed. Consider the following code snippet:

```
Create or replace procedure sum (X number default 10,
Y number default 20, Z OUT number) is
begin
  Z := X + Y;
end;
/
```

The output of the preceding code snippet is as follows:

```
Procedure created
```

Now, suppose you want to declare a bind variable at the SQL prompt, as shown in the following code snippet:

```
variable c number;
```

Now, call the procedure as shown in the following code snippet:

```
exec sum(z=>:C);
```

The output of the preceding code snippet is as follows:

```
PL/SQL procedure successfully completed
```

Displaying value of variable C as follows:

```
print c;
```

Result:

```
C
--------
30
```

In the above case, the values for the formal parameters `X` and `Y` are not given. Therefore, the default values `10` and `20` are taken. If you call the procedure shown in the following code snippet:

```
exec sum(3,4,:C);
```

The output of the preceding code snippet is as follows:

```
PL/SQL procedure successfully completed
```

Displaying value

```
Print c;
```

Result:

```
C
----
7
```

Procedure puts the value 7 in C, i.e. if parameter values are supplied, then the default values do not have any effect. Suppose you want to supply the value of Y, but not X. In that case, you have to use a named notation, as shown in the following code snippet:

```
exec sum(Y=>15, Z=>:C);
```

The output of the preceding code snippet is as follows:

```
PL/SQL procedure successfully completed
```

Displaying value as follows:

```
print c;
```

Result:

```
C
----
25
```

This sum procedure will take the value for X as 10. Therefore, call in the following code snippet is illegal:

```
exec sum ( ,10,:C);
```

If a null value is to be passed to initialize formal parameters, then it should be passed explicitly, as shown in the following code snippet:

```
exec Sum (X=>0, Y=>10, Z=>:C);
```

You cannot use a bind variable as a default value. Therefore, the following declaration is also illegal:

```
sum(X number default :var, Y ...)
```

One advantage of using default values is that you can add formal parameters without changing the calling routines.

Aliasing

Aliasing occurs when a global variable is referred in a call and is also passed as a parameter to a subprogram. In case of aliasing, the result is indeterminate and depends on the type of parameter passing method being used by the compiler.

The parameters are passed by using two methods, by value and by reference. When a parameter is passed by value, a copy of the parameter is passed to a subprogram. If the parameter is passed by reference, only the address of the object is passed. This is done for large objects, such as composite objects or arrays. This is because the copy of a large object requires a lot of time to be passed. In case of aliasing, the result depends on the method of parameter being passed.

Listing 31.9 shows the use of Aliasing:

Listing 31.9: Using Aliasing

```
declare
   Xglobal number(2);
   procedure sample(X in out number)is
   begin
          X := 10;
          Xglobal:= 20;
   end;
begin
   Xglobal := 5;
   sample(Xglobal);
   dbms_output.put_line (to_char(Xglobal));
   -- prints 10 if parameter is passed by value--result
   -- prints 20 if parameter is passed by reference
end;
/
```

The output of Listing 31.9 is as follows:

```
10

PL/SQL procedure successfully completed
```

In the preceding output:

- If the parameter is passed by value, then X and Xglobal are two separate copies of the same object. Therefore, changing one does not affect the other.
- If the parameter is passed by reference, then X and Xglobal are the two names of the same object. Therefore, changing the object by using one name changes the value of the object as well.

Overloading

Subprograms differ in their formal parameter with respect to number, order, or datatype family. Overloading means the use of the same subprogram name to call different subprograms.

Listing 31.10 shows the use of overloading:

Listing 31.10: Overloading Two Functions

```
declare
x number;
y number;
function findenqno (fname1 varchar2) return number is --function 1
enqno1 number (5);
begin
  select enquiryno
  into enqno1
  from enquiry
  where fname = fname1;
  return(enqno1);
end;
function findenqno (refcode1 number) return number is --function 2
enqno1 number (5);
begin
  select enquiryno
  into enqno1
  from enquiry
  where refcode = refcode1;
  return (enqno1);
end;
begin
                                    -- You call the function as:
  X := findenqno ('Anil');
  dbms_output.put_line('using name '||x);
  Y := findenqno (345);
  dbms_output.put_line('using refcode '||y);
end;
/
```

The output of Listing 31.10 is as follows:

```
using name 5
using refcode 5

PL/SQL procedure successfully completed
```

In the preceding output, the first definition is used in the first function, while for second function, the second definition is used.

Using the same name for a similar type of functionality makes simplifies programming. The two subprograms can be placed in the same block, the same package, or in the same subprogram.

Restrictions While Overloading

Overloading cannot be applied in the following cases:

- Standalone procedures
- Functions with the same name
- Parameters belonging to the same datatype family
- Return types

Let's discus each case separately in the following sections.

Standalone Procedures

Overloading is not allowed in standalone programs. For example: following function cannot be overloaded.

```
create function findenqno (fname1 varchar2) return number is
enqno1 number (5);
begin
  .....
end;
```

Functions Having the Same Name

You cannot overload two subprograms, if they differ only in their parameter names. In other words, you cannot create overloaded functions with the same names, as shown in the following code snippet:

```
create function findenqno (fname1 varchar2) return number is
enqno1 number (5);
begin
  .....
end;
...
create function findenqno(refcode number) return number is
begin
  ......
end;
```

The preceding code snippet generates an error stating that the concerned object already exists.

Parameters Belonging to the Same Datatype Family

Two subprograms cannot be overloaded, if their parameters differ only in datatype, but belong to the same datatype family, i.e. `char` and `varchar2`. Therefore, the two subprograms in the following code snippet are not overloaded:

```
function findenqno(fname1 varchar2) return number is
begin
  ......
end;
function findenqno(fname2 char) return number is
begin
  ......
end;
```

In the preceding code snippet, parameters `fname1` and `fname2` have datatypes `varchar2` and `char`, which belong to the same datatype family.

Return Types

Two functions cannot be overloaded if they differ only in their return datatype. The following functions cannot be overloaded:

```
function findenqno(fname1 varchar2) return number is
begin
   .....
end;
```

```
function findenqno(fname1 varchar2) return varchar2 is
begin
   .....
end;
```

Here functions differ only in their return datatype, so they cannot be overloaded.

Resolving Subprograms Calls

When a subprogram is called, it is resolved according to the following procedure:

- PL/SQL searches for the subprogram in the current scope. If the subprogram is found, it undergoes further processing. Otherwise, the process ends in the current scope and the outer scope is searched.
- When the subprogram is not found in the current or outer scope, a syntax error is generated.
- When a subprogram is found, the actual parameters are matched with the formal parameters. If a match is found for only one definition, then the call is resolved. In case of mismatch or multiple matches, an error is generated. Therefore, while overloading, you must ensure that multiple matches are not present for the same subprogram call.

Built-in Functions

PL/SQL stores built-in functions in a package called `STANDARD`. Re-declaring a function with the same name is error-prone, because local declaration overrides global declaration. Suppose you declare the `length` function, which takes `char` as input, as shown in the following code snippet:

```
declare
   function length (S char) return number as
   begin
         .....
   end;
   n number;
   m number;
   y varchar2(30);
   z varchar2(30);
begin
   n := LENGTH(y);                          -- A
   m := STANDARD.Length(z);                 -- B
end;
```

In the preceding code snippet, the `length` function in statement A refers to the locally declared function. If you want to refer a built-in function, then you have to explicitly specify the package name with the function. Therefore, it is better to use a different name than the built-in function name.

Recursion

Calling the same subprogram within a subprogram is termed as recursion. For example, you can write a recursive function to calculate `N!` (N factorial), as shown in the following code snippet:

```
Create function fact (N number) return number is
begin
  if N = 0 then
        return(1);
  else
        return(N * fact(N-1));
  end if;
end;
/
```

The output of the preceding code snippet is as follows:

```
Function created
```

Procedure using the function `fact`

```
declare
  j number;
begin
  j:=fact(4);
  dbms_output.put_line(j);
end;
/
```

Result of the above program:

```
24

PL/SQL procedure successfully completed
```

Recursive programs are simple to write, but are inherently slow. In recursion, the information for each subprogram call is put in a stack. Therefore, a large stack is required. If a subprogram call is made within the `CURSOR`, `LOOP...END LOOP` or `OPEN CURSOR` and `CLOSE CURSOR` statements, then for each call a new cursor is opened and the cursor limit may exceed the limit of the maximum `OPEN_CURSORS`.

NOTE

Any program that can be written by using recursion can be also written by using interaction. Recursion is not recommended in writing applications related to DBMS.

Let's now look at some examples that make use of procedures and functions:

Listing 31.11: Displaying the Average Amount of Batches

```
create or replace procedure batch_avgamt as
cursor c1 is
select avg(netincome) avgamt,batchcode
from batch
group by batchcode;
begin for z in c1 loop
  dbms_output.put_line(z.batchcode||'    '||z.avgamt);

end loop;
end batch_avgamt;
/
```

The output of Listing 31.11 is as follows:

```
Procedure created
```

Listing 31.12: Displaying the Batch Name that has the Average Amount of More than 10,000

```
create or replace procedure batchname_avgamt_more as
cursor c1 is
select avg(netincome) avgamt,batchcode from batch
group by batchcode
having avg(netincome)>10000;
begin
   for z in c1 loop
                dbms_output.put_line(z.batchcode||'     '||z.avgamt);
   end loop;
end batchname_avgamt_more;
/
```

The output of Listing 31.12 is as follows:

```
Procedure created
```

Listing 31.13: Displaying the Name of the Course with the Maximum Net Income

```
create or replace function crs_maxinc return varchar2 as
name varchar2(15);
begin
   select coursename
          into name
          from batch,course
          where course.coursecode = batch.coursecode
          and netincome =
          (select max(netincome)
          from batch);
          return(name);
end crs_maxinc;
/
```

The output of Listing 31.13 is as follows:

```
Function created
```

Listing 31.14: Finding the Name of the Course with the Maximum Difference in Net Income and Expected Income

```
create or replace procedure crs_maxdiff as
cursor c1 is
select coursename
from batch,course
where course.coursecode = batch.coursecode
and (expectedincome-netincome) =
(select max(expectedincome-netincome)
from batch);
begin
   for z in c1 loop
          dbms_output.put_line(z.coursename);
   end loop;
end crs_maxdiff;
/
```

The output of Listing 31.14 is as follows:

```
Procedure created
```

Listing 31.15: Finding the Total Fee Paid by a Student

```
create or replace function tot_feepaid(name varchar2)return number as
eno number(8);
rno number(8);
samt number;
begin
   select enquiryno
          into eno
          from enquiry
          where fname = name;
          select sum(amount),f.rollno
          into samt,rno
          from feespaid f,enrollment e
          where enquiryno = eno
          and f.rollno = e.rollno
          group by f.rollno;
          return(samt);
end tot_feepaid;
/
```

The output of Listing 31.15 is as follows:

```
Function created
```

Listing 31.16: Displaying the Difference between Expected fee and Total Fee for a rollno

```
create or replace function feediff_rollno (prollno number)
return number is
diff number;
begin
   select max(coursefee)-sum(fee.amount)
   into diff
   from feespaid fee,batch
   where substr(to_char(fee.rollno),1,2)=substr(to_char(batchcode),1,2)
   and rollno = prollno
   group by rollno,batchcode;
   return(diff);
end feediff_rollno;
/
```

The output of Listing 31.16 is as follows:

```
Function created
```

Listing 31.17: Finding Course Wise Income

```
create or replace procedure crs_income as
cursor c1 is
select sum(netincome) sumnet,coursecode
from batch
group by coursecode;
cursor c2 is
select coursecode,coursename
from course;
z1 c1%rowtype;
z2 c2%rowtype;
begin
   for z2 in c2 loop
                 for z1 in c1 loop
```

```
                        if z1.coursecode = z2.coursecode then
                        dbms_output.put_line(z2.coursename||'
                 '||z1.sumnet);
                        end if;
          end loop;
      end loop;
    end crs_income;
    /
```

The output of Listing 31.17 is as follows:

```
    Procedure created
```

Listing 31.18: Displaying the Course with Maximum Income

```
    create or replace function crs_maxinc return varchar2 as
    cname varchar2(30);
    mamt batch.netincome %type;
    ccode number(3);
    begin
      select netincome,coursecode
           into mamt,ccode
           from batch
           where netincome>=
           (select max(netincome)
           from batch);
           select coursename
           into cname
           from course
           where coursecode=ccode;
           return(cname);
    end crs_maxinc;
    /
```

The output of Listing 31.18 is as follows:

```
    Function created
```

The function crs_maxinc be called as follows:

```
    declare
      cname varchar2(30);
    begin
      cname:=crs_maxinc;
      dbms_output.put_line(cname);
    end;
    /
```

Result of the above program:

```
    ORACLE

    PL/SQL procedure successfully completed
```

Listing 31.19: Summing Expenditure According to Expenditure Type

```
    create or replace procedure sumexp_type as
    cursor c1 is
    select exptype,sum(amount) samt
    from expenditure ex,expmaster mast
    where ex.expcode=mast.expcode
    group by exptype;
    begin
```

```
    for z in c1 loop
                dbms_output.put_line(z.exptype||'  '||z.samt);
    end loop;
end sumexp_type;
/
```

The Output of Listing 31.19 is as follows:

```
Procedure created
```

Listing 31.20: Summing Expenditure According to Expenditure Code

```
create or replace procedure sumexp_code as
cursor c1 is
select expcode,sum(amount) samt
from expenditure
group by expcode;
begin
    for z in c1 loop
                dbms_output.put_line(z.expcode||'  '||z.samt);
    end loop;
end sumexp_code;
/
```

Result:

```
Procedure created
```

Listing 31.21: Displaying the Sum of Fee and the Respective rollno for a Specified Course

```
create or replace procedure sumfee_crs(name varchar2) as
cursor c1 is
select rollno,sum(amount) samt from feespaid,course
where coursename = name
and course.coursecode = substr(to_char(rollno),1,2)
group by rollno;
begin
    for z in c1 loop
                dbms_output.put_line(z.rollno||'   '||z.samt);
    end loop;
end sumfee_crs;
/
```

The output of Listing 31.21 is as follows:

```
Procedure created
```

Listing 31.22: Displaying the Difference in the Sum of Fee and the Sum of Expected fee for a Batch

```
create or replace function diff_feexp(bcode number) return number as
rno number(8);
eamt number;
dif number;
begin
    select expectedincome
          into eamt from batch
          where batchcode = bcode;
          select substr(to_char(rollno),1,5),eamt-sum(feespaid.amount)
          into rno,dif
          from feespaid
          where substr(to_char(rollno),1,5) = bcode
          group by substr(to_char(rollno),1,5);
          return (dif);
```

```
end diff_feexp;
/
```

The output of Listing 31.22 is as follows:

```
Function created
```

Listing 31.23: Finding the Total Amount Collected

```
create or replace function totamt return number as
tamt number;
begin
   select sum(amount)
   into tamt
   from feespaid;
   return(tamt);
end totamt;
/
```

The output of Listing 31.23 is as follows:

```
Function created
```

Listing 31.24: Displaying the Number of Enquiries of a Specified Advertisement Code

```
create or replace function totenq_advcode(adv number) return number as
tenq number;
begin
   select count(*)
   into tenq from enquiry
   where refcode = adv;
   return(tenq);
end totenq_advcode;
/
```

The output of Listing 31.24 is as follows:

```
Function created
```

Listing 31.25: Finding the Number of Enquiries for a Specified Course

```
create or replace function totenq_course(name varchar2) return number as
tenq number;
begin
   select count(*)
   into tenq
   from enquiry,course
   where course.coursename=name
   and course.coursecode=enquiry.coursecode;
   return(tenq);
end totenq_course;
/
```

The output of Listing 31.25 is as follows:

```
Function created
```

Listing 31.26: Finding the Sum of Amount Collected Month Wise (here field names are as per old tables)

```
create or replace procedure sumamt_month as
cursor c1 is
select sum(amount) samt,
substr(to_char(feespaiddate,'DD-MON-YY'),4,3) mnth
from feespaid
group by substr(to_char(feespaiddate,'DD-MON-YY'),4,3);
begin
```

```
   for z in c1 loop
                  dbms_output.put_line(z.mnth||'  '||z.samt);
   end loop;
end sumamt_month;
/
```

The output of Listing 31.26 is as follows:

```
Procedure created
```

Listing 31.27: Displaying the Sum of Amount Collected Weekly (here field names are as per old tables)

```
create or replace procedure sumamt_week as
cursor c1 is
select to_char(feespaiddate,'MON') mnt,
to_char(feespaiddate,'W') week,
sum(amount) samt from feespaid
group by to_char(feespaiddate,'MON'),to_char(feespaiddate,'W');
begin
   for z in c1 loop
                  dbms_output.put_line(z.mnt||'    '||z.week  ||'    '||z.samt);
   end loop;
end sumamt_week;
/
```

The output of Listing 31.28 is as follows:

```
Procedure created
```

Listing 31.28: Displaying the rollno and name of the student who has not paid the amount according to the installment date (here field names are as per old tables)

```
create or replace procedure amt_instdate as
cursor c1 is
select enquiryno eno,fname
from enquiry;
cursor c2 is
select enq.enquiryno eno,ins.rollno rno
from installment ins,enquiry enq,enrollment enr
where installmentstatus = 'N'
and installmentdate < sysdate
and ins.rollno = enr.rollno
and enr.enquiryno = enq.enquiryno;
z1 c1%rowtype;
z2 c2%rowtype;
begin
   for z1 in c1 loop
                  for z2 in c2 loop
                            if (z2.eno=z1.eno) then
                            dbms_output.put_line(z2.rno||'    '||z1.fname);
                            end if;
         end loop;
         end loop;
end amt_instdate;
/
```

The output of Listing 31.28 is as follows:

```
Procedure created
```

Listing 31.29: Finding the Date Wise Enrollment for the Previous 15 Days (as per fields of old enrollment table)

```
create or replace procedure enrl_batch_days(bcode number) as
cursor c1 is
select enrollmentdate dt,count(*) cnt
from enrollment,batch
where batch.batchcode=bcode
and batch.batchcode=substr(to_char(rollno),1,5)
and (to_date(sysdate)-enrollmentdate)
between 1 and 15
group by enrollmentdate;
begin
  for z in c1 loop
              dbms_output.put_line(z.dt||'   '||z.cnt);
  end loop;
 end enrl_batch_days;
 /
```

The output of Listing 31.29 is as follows:

```
Procedure created
```

Listing 31.30: Finding the Quarterly Income for a Specified Course (as per fields of old feespaid table)

```
create or replace procedure quartinc_crs(name varchar2) as
cursor c1 is
select to_char(feespaiddate,'Q') qtr,
to_char(feespaiddate,'MON')mnt, sum(amount) samt
from feespaid,course
where course.coursename=name
and course.coursecode=substr(to_char(rollno),1,2)
group by to_char(feespaiddate,'Q'),to_char(feespaiddate,'MON');
begin
  for z in c1 loop
              dbms_output.put_line(z.qtr||'    '||z.mnt    ||'    '||z.samt);
        end loop;
end quartinc_crs;
/
```

The output of Listing 31.30 is as follows:

```
Procedure created
```

Listing 31.31: Displaying Month Wise Expenditure

```
create or replace procedure sumexp_month as
cursor c1 is select sum(amount) samt,
substr(to_char(expdate,'DD-MON-YY'),4,3) mnth
from expenditure
group by substr(to_char(expdate,'DD-MON-YY'),4,3);
begin
  for z in c1 loop
              dbms_output.put_line(z.mnth||'  '||z.samt);
  end loop;
end sumexp_month;
/
```

The output of Listing 31.31 is as follows:

```
Procedure created
```

Listing 31.32: Creating table for recording Monthly Average Income and Average Expenditure

```
create table month_avgincexp
(month varchar2(10),
income number(10,2),
expenditure number(10,2))
/
```

The output of Listing 31.32 is as follows:

```
Table created
```

Listing 31.33: Finding the Monthly Average Income and Average Expenditure

```
create or replace procedure  month_avg_incexp  as cursor c1 is
select avg(amount)amt,to_char(feespaiddate,'MON') paydt from feespaid
group by to_char(feespaiddate,'MON');
cursor c2 is
select avg(amount)amt,to_char(expdate,'MON') expdt from expenditure
group by to_char(expdate,'MON');
x varchar2(6);
y varchar2(6);
indt varchar2(10);
expdt varchar2(10);
begin
  for z1 in c1 loop
               x := z1.paydt;
        select nvl(month,null) into indt from month_avgincexp where
  month=z1.paydt;
               if (indt <> ' ') then
                       update month_avgincexp
                       set income = nvl(income,0)+z1.amt
                       where month_avgincexp.month = x;
        else
                       insert into month_avgincexp (month, income)
                       values(z1.paydt, z1.amt);
               end if;
  end loop;
        for z2 in c2 loop
               y := z2.expdt;
        select nvl(month,null) into expdt from month_avgincexp where
  month=z2.expdt;
               if (expdt <> ' ') then
                       update month_avgincexp
                       set expenditure = nvl(expenditure,0)+z2.amt
                       where month_avgincexp.month = y;
        else
                       insert into month_avgincexp (month, expenditure)
                       values(z2.expdt, z2.amt);
               end if;
  end loop;
end month_avg_incexp;
/
```

The output of Listing 31.33 is as follows:

```
Procedure created
```

Listing 31.34: Calculating the Date Wise Response for an Advertisement

```
create or replace procedure date_resadv(advname varchar2) as
cursor c1 is select enquirydate,count(*) cnt
from enquiry,advertisement adv
where adv.medianame = advname
and adv.refcode = enquiry.refcode
group by enquirydate;
begin
   for z in c1 loop
                 dbms_output.put_line(z.enquirydate||'   '||z.cnt);
   end loop;
end date_resadv;
/
```

The output of Listing 31.34 is as follows:

```
Procedure created
```

Listing 31.35: Displaying the Details of a Person of a Specific Name

```
create or replace procedure person_dlt_as(name varchar2) as
cursor c1 is
select * from enquiry
where fname like name;
begin
   for z in c1 loop
          dbms_output.put_line(z.ENQUIRYNO||'    '||
              z.FNAME||'    '||z.SNAME||'   '||
              z.COURSECODE||'   '||z.PLOTNO||'   '||z.STREET||'   '||
              z.CITY||'   '||z.PINCODE||'   '||z.PHONE||'   '||
              z.ENQUIRYDATE||'   '||z.REFCODE||'   '||z.EN_st);
          end loop;
end person_dlt_as;
/
```

The output of Listing 31.35 is as follows:

```
Procedure created
```

Executing the procedure

```
SQL> Exec person_dlt_as('Anil');
```

Result:

```
5   Anil          345
PL/SQL procedure successfully completed
```

Listing 31.36: Displaying the Number of People Whose Names Start with V

```
create or replace function count_person_asV
return number as cnt number;
begin
   select count(fname)
   into cnt from enquiry
   where fname like 'V%';
   return cnt;
end count_person_asV;
/
```

The output of Listing 31.36 is as follows:

```
Function created
```

Listing 31.37: Replacing all the Names with the First Character Capital, and Others in Lower Case (table fields as per old tables)

```
create or replace procedure initcaps as
begin
   update enquiry
   set fname = initcap(fname), sname = initcap(sname);
end initcaps;
/
```

The output of Listing 31.37 is as follows:

```
Procedure created
```

Listing 31.38: Displaying Amount in the Format Rs. 99,999,99

```
create or replace procedure amt_format as
cursor c1 is
select rollno,to_char(amount,'99,999,99') amt from feespaid;
begin
   for z in c1 loop
         dbms_output.put_line(z.rollno||'      '||z.amt);
   end loop;
end amt_format;
/
```

The output of Listing 31.38 is as follows:

```
Procedure created
```

Producing statistics of fee collected as:

0	1000	0
1001	5000	4
5001	10000	0
10001	15000	0
15001	20000	0

Listing 31.39: Procedure for statistics of fee collected

```
create or replace procedure stat_feecollected as
tmpamt number;
i number;
inc number;
incamt number;
cnt number;
begin
   i := 0;
   tmpamt := 0;
   inc := 1000;
   while i < 20000 loop
         select count(*) into cnt
         from feespaid
         where amount between i and inc;
         dbms_output.put_line(i||'     '||inc||'     '||cnt);
         i := inc+1;
         tmpamt := tmpamt + 5000;
         inc := tmpamt;
```

```
   end loop;
end stat_feecollected;
/
```

The output of Listing 31.39 is as follows:

```
Procedure created
```

Listing 31.40: Finding the Statistics for a Particular Course

```
create or replace procedure stat_feecollected_crs (cname varchar2)as
tmpamt number;
i number;
inc number;
incamt number;
cnt number;
begin
   i := 0;
   tmpamt := 0;
   inc := 1000;
   while i < 20000 loop
         select count(*) into cnt from feespaid,course
         where course.coursename = cname
         and to_char(course.coursecode) = substr(to_char(rollno),1,2)
         and amount between i and inc;
         dbms_output.put_line(i||'    '||inc||'    '||cnt);
         i := inc+1;
         tmpamt := tmpamt + 5000;
         inc := tmpamt;
   end loop;
end stat_feecollected_crs;
/
```

The output of Listing 31.40 is as follows:

```
Procedure created
```

Listing 31.41: Finding the Closing Amount on Each Date (table fields as per old tables)

```
create or replace procedure date_closing_amount as
cursor c1 is
select sum(amount) amt,to_char(feespaiddate,'DD-MON-YY') dt
from feespaid
group by to_char(feespaiddate,'DD-MON-YY');
begin
   for z in c1 loop
              dbms_output.put_line(z.dt||'    '||z.amt);
        end loop;
end date_closing_amount;
/
```

The output of Listing 31.41 is as follows:

```
Procedure created
```

Taking table Fields as per old tables and finding the statistics of enquiries as:

0	5	0
6	5	0
6	10	0

11	15	0
16	20	0
21	25	0
26	30	0

Listing 31.42: Procedure for statistics of enquiries:

```
create or replace procedure stat_enq as
tmpamt number;
i number;
inc number;
incamt number;
cnt number;
begin
   i := 0;
         tmpamt := 0;
         inc := 5;
         while i < 30 loop
         select count(*) into cnt from enquiry
         where to_char(enquirydate,'monyy')=to_char(sysdate,'monyy')
         and to_number(to_char(enquirydate,'dd'))
         between i and inc;
         dbms_output.put_line(i||'    '||inc||'    '||cnt);
         i := inc+1;
         tmpamt := tmpamt + 5;
         inc := tmpamt;
         end loop;
end stat_enq;
/
```

The output of Listing 31.42 is as follows:

```
Procedure created
```

Listing 31.43: Displaying the batchcode with the Fifth Maximum netincome

```
create or replace function batch_5maxinc return number is
cursor c1 is
select batchcode,netincome
from batch
order by netincome desc;
bcode number(5);
cnt number;
begin
   cnt := 0;
   for z in c1 loop
         cnt := cnt + 1;
         if cnt = 5 then
                         bcode := z.batchcode;
         end if;
   end loop;
   return(bcode);
end batch_5maxinc;
/
```

The output of Listing 31.43 is as follows:

```
Function created
```

Listing 31.44: Finding the Monthly Summary of Income and Expenditure

```
create or replace procedure monthlysum as
cursor c1 is
select avg(amount)amt,to_char(feespaiddate,'MON') paydt
from feespaid
group by to_char(feespaiddate,'MON');
cursor c2 is
select avg(amount)amt,to_char(expdate,'MON') expdt
from expenditure
group by to_char(expdate,'MON');
x varchar2(6);
y varchar2(6);
indt varchar2(10);
expdt varchar2(10);
begin
  for z1 in c1 loop
            x := z1.paydt;
       select nvl(month,null) into indt from month_avgincexp where
  month=z1.paydt;
            if (indt <> ' ') then
                  update month_avgincexp
                  set income = nvl(income,0)+z1.amt
                  where month_avgincexp.month = x;
            end if;
  end loop;
       for z2 in c2 loop
            y := z2.expdt;
       select nvl(month,null) into expdt from month_avgincexp where
  month=z2.expdt;
            if (expdt <> ' ') then
                  update month_avgincexp
                  set expenditure = nvl(expenditure,0)+z2.amt
                  where month_avgincexp.month = y;
            end if;
  end loop;
end monthlysum;
/
```

The output of Listing 31.44 is as follows:

```
Procedure created
```

Listing 31.45: Finding the Start and End Date for a Specified Batch (table fields as per old tables)

```
create or replace procedure minmaxdt_batch (bcode in number) as
cursor c1 is
select min(enrollmentdate) min_date,max(enrollmentdate) max_date
from enrollment
where batchcode = bcode;
begin
  for z in c1 loop
       dbms_output.put_line(z.min_date||'    '||z.max_date);
       end loop;
```

```
end minmaxdt_batch;
/
```

Result:

```
Procedure created
SQL> exec minmaxdt_batch(20002);
```

Result:

```
01-JUL-00    11-JUL-00

PL/SQL procedure successfully completed
```

Listing 31.46: Creating view by using the enquiry, feespaid, and enrollment Tables

```
create or replace view vw_adanalysis as
select enq.refcode,enq.enquiryno,enrl.rollno,fee.amount
from enquiry enq,feespaid fee,enrollment enrl
where enq.enquiryno = enrl.enquiryno
and enrl.rollno = fee.rollno;
/
```

The output of Listing 31.46 is as follows:

```
View created
```

Listing 31.47: Displaying the Analysis of an Advertisement

```
create or replace view vw_incforrefcode as
select sum(amount)sumamt,refcode
from vw_adanalysis
group by refcode;
create or replace procedure addanalysis as
cursor c1 is
select medianame,amount expenditure,sumamt income
from advertisement adv,vw_incforrefcode vw
where adv.refcode = vw.refcode(+);
begin
  for z in c1 loop
                dbms_output.put_line(z.medianame||'    '||
           z.expenditure||'    '||z.income);
  end loop;
end addanalysis;
/
```

Result:

```
Procedure created
exec addanalysis;
```

Result:

```
Hindustan Times
Times Of India

PL/SQL procedure successfully completed
```

Listing 31.48: Finding the Month with Maximum Enrollments (here table fields are as per old tables)

```
create or replace view vw_enroll  as
select to_char(enrollmentdate) dt,count(*) cnt
from enrollment
group by to_char(enrollmentdate)
/
```

Result:

```
View created
```

Creating a view and a procedure for Listing 31.48

```
create or replace procedure maxenroll (mnt out varchar2,ecnt out number) as
begin
  select to_char(to_date(dt,'dd-mon-yy'),'mon'),cnt into mnt,ecnt
  from vw_enroll where cnt in
  (select max(cnt) from vw_enroll);
end maxenroll;
/
```

Result:

```
Procedure created
```

Listing 31.49: Finding the Name of the Student with Balance Amount

```
create or replace view vw_enqenrl_student as
select enq.enquiryno,fname,rollno
from enquiry enq,enrollment enrl
where enq.enquiryno = enrl.enquiryno
/
```

Result:

```
View created
```

Creating a view and a procedure for Listing 31.49

```
create or replace procedure bal_left as
cursor c1 is
select fname,sum(amount) sumamt
from installment ins,vw_enqenrl_student vw
where installmentstatus = 'N'
and ins.rollno = vw.rollno
group by fname
order by sum(amount)desc;
begin
  for z in c1 loop
        dbms_output.put_line(z.fname||'    '||z.sumamt);
  end loop;
end bal_left;
/
```

Result:

```
Procedure created
```

Listing 31.50: Displaying the Expenditure for a Particular Batch

```
create or replace function expforbatch (bcode number)
return number is
samt number;
begin
  select sum(amount)
  into samt
  from expenditure
  where batchcode = bcode;
  return(samt);
end expforbatch;
/
```

The output of Listing 31.50 is as follows:

```
Function created
```

Listing 31.51: Finding the Income and Expenditure for a Particular Year

```
create or replace procedure yearlysum(year varchar2)as
   cursor c1 is
   select sum(amount) income,to_char(feespaiddate,'YY') paydt
   from feespaid
   group by to_char(feespaiddate,'YY');
   cursor c2 is
   select sum(amount) expenditure,to_char(expdate,'YY') expdt
   from expenditure
   group by to_char(expdate,'YY');
   paysum number;
   expsum number;
begin
   for z1 in c1 loop
       if z1.paydt = to_char(year) then
          paysum := z1.income;
       end if;
   end loop;
   for z2 in c2 loop
       if z2.expdt = to_char(year) then
          expsum := z2.expenditure;
       end if;
   end loop;
   dbms_output.put_line('year'||'    '||'expenditure'||'    '||'income');
   dbms_output.put_line(to_char(year)||'    '||expsum||'    '||paysum);
end yearlysum;
/
```

The output of Listing 31.51 is as follows:

```
Procedure created
```

Listing 31.52: Finding the Number of Enquiries Not Enrolled Course Wise

```
create or replace view vw_enqcrs_notenroll as
 select coursecode,count(*) notenroll
 from enquiry
 where en_st = 'n'
 group by coursecode
/
```

The output of Listing 31.52 is as follows:

```
View created
```

Creating a view and a procedure for Listing 31.52

```
create or replace procedure noenroll_crs as
cursor c1 is
select unique(crs.coursename) nm,vw.notenroll notenroll
from course crs,vw_enqcrs_notenroll vw
where crs.coursecode = vw.coursecode(+);
begin
  for z in c1 loop
      dbms_output.put_line(z.nm||'    '||z.notenroll);
```

```
  end loop;
end noenroll_crs;
/
```

Result:

```
Procedure created
```

Listing 31.53: Displaying the Statistics of an Advertisement on a Daily Basis

```
create or replace view vw_adv as
 select to_char(advdate,'dy') day,to_char(advdate,'monyy') mnt,
 count(*) cnt
 from advertisement
 group by to_char(advdate,'dy'),to_char(advdate,'monyy');
/
```

Result:

```
View created
```

Creating a view and a procedure for Listing 31.53

```
create or replace procedure advstat as
   cursor c1 is
   select * from vw_adv;
   cursor c2 is
   select to_char(enq.enquirydate,'dy') day,
        to_char(enq.enquirydate,'monyy') mnt,en_st
   from enquiry enq;
   z1 c1 %rowtype;
   z2 c2 %rowtype;
   res number;
 begin
    for z1 in c1 loop
        res := 0;
        for z2 in c2 loop
            if z1.day = z2.day and z1.mnt = z2.mnt then
               res := res + 1;
            end if;
        end loop;
        dbms_output.put_line(z1.day||'   '||
                             z1.mnt||'   '||
                             z1.cnt||'   '||res);
     end loop;
 end advstat;
 /
```

Result:

```
Procedure created
```

Listing 31.54: Finding the Number of Students batch wise that have not Completed the Course

```
create or replace procedure incomplete_crs_batch as
   cursor c1 is
   select substr(to_char(rollno),1,5) batch,count(*) cnt
   from installment ins
   where installmentstatus = 'N'
   and installmentdate < sysdate
   group by substr(to_char(rollno),1,5);
 begin
   for z in c1 loop
```

```
        dbms_output.put_line(z.batch||'    '||z.cnt);
    end loop;
 end incomplete_crs_batch;
 /
```

The output of Listing 31.54 is as follows:

```
Procedure created
```

Listing 31.55: Finding the Number of Students who have not Completed their Course

```
create or replace procedure incomplete_crs_std as
  cursor c1 is
  select fname
  from vw_enqenrl_student vw,installment ins
  where installmentstatus = 'N'
  and installmentdate < sysdate
  and vw. rollno = ins. rollno;
begin
   for z in c1 loop
     dbms_output.put_line(z.fname);
   end loop;
end incomplete_crs_std;
/
```

The output of Listing 31.55 is as follows:

```
Procedure created
```

Listing 31.56: Displaying names of the students having date less than 15 days of batchdate who have not enrolled

```
create or replace procedure std_notenroll as
   cursor c1 is select enq.fname name
   from batch bat,enquiry enq
   where en_st = 'n'
   and substr(to_char(bat.batchcode),1,2)=to_char(enq.coursecode)
   and enq.enquirydate > (bat.startingdate)-15;
begin
   for z in c1 loop
       dbms_output.put_line(z.name);
   end loop;
end std_notenroll;
/
```

The output of Listing 31.56 is as follows:

```
Procedure created
```

Listing 31.57: Displaying the Expenditure details using Expenditure Master

```
create or replace procedure exp_details as
    cursor c1 is
    select * from expmaster;
begin
    for z in c1 loop
        dbms_output.put_line(z.expcode||'   '||z.expname
                    ||'   '||z.exptype||'   '||z.netexp);
    end loop;
end exp_details;
/
```

The output of Listing 31.57 is as follows:

```
    Procedure created
```

This is all there is about subprograms in PL/SQL.

Summary

In this chapter, you have learned about describing a subprogram, declaring the subprogram, aliasing and overloading. The next chapter will focus attention on packages.

Exercise

1. Write a function to calculate value of factorial of a number.
2. Write a procedure to calculate sum of first N numbers.
3. Consider a table as follows:

CAR	REGION	SALE

   a. Write a procedure to print top three regions and in each such region top three cars in terms of sale.
   b. Write a procedure to print average sale in each region.

32

Package

A package in PL/SQL can be described as a single entity, which groups logically related PL/SQL types, items, and subprograms. A package, generally, has two parts, specification and body or definition. In the specification part, a user can declare datatypes, variables, constants, exceptions, and subprogram specifications, whereas in the body part the implementation of subprograms is done. The body may contain additional subprograms, which can be used to implement subprograms provided in the specification.

The following Listing 32.1 package specifications define two variables x and y, procedure add3 and function SQR. The definition or body of the package has implementation of this procedure and function. The body may have additional variable z as defined in statement A and additional functions and procedures, such as add2. The body components, such as z and add2, are visible only inside the body of the package. Since they are not visible outside the body of the package, the user of package cannot have access to these components. At the end of body, the block enclosed by begin and end (statement B to statement C) is called as package initialization part and it is used to initialize package variable, such as x and y and body variables, such as z. This part is executed only once during the session when the package component is used for the first time. You can create the package specification and its definition or body, as shown in the following listings:

Listing 32.1: Creating the Package Specification

```
create or replace package test1 as
x number;
y number:=90;
procedure add3(a in number,b in number,d in number,c out number);
function sqr(a number) return number;
end test1;
/
```

Listing 32.2: Creating the Package Definition or Body

```
create or replace package body test1 as
z number;  --A
function add2(a in number,b in number) return number is
begin
 return(a+b);
end;
procedure add3(a in number,b in number,d in number,c out number) is
e number;
begin
 e := add2(a,b);
 z := add2(e,d);
 c:= z;
end;
function sqr(a number) return number is
begin
 return(a*a);
end;
begin --B
  x :=67;
  y :=80;
  z :=0;
  dbms_output.put_line(' initialization code');
end test1; --C
/
```

Let's take an example of packages. You can create the procedure of the package test1, as shown in Listing 32.3:

Listing 32.3: Creating the Procedure of the Package test1

```
declare
  z number;
begin
  test1.add3(45,89,34,z);
      dbms_output.put_line(z);
 end;
/
```

The output of Listing 32.3 is given as follows:

```
initialization
168
PL/SQL procedure successfully completed
```

Now, take another example of package. The PKGbatchcode package defines two components procedure generate_batchcode and a function validate_batchcode. The body defines implementation of these components. Listing 32.4 shows the code to create the package specification of the PKGbatchcode package:

Listing 32.4: Creating the Package Specification of the PKGbatchcode Package

```
create or replace package PKGbatchcode as
u1 varchar2(30);
date1 date;
procedure generate_batchcode
(ccode IN number,
bcode out number);
function validate_batchcode (bcode IN number) return boolean;
end PKGbatchcode;
/
```

The output of Listing 32.4 is given as follows:

```
Package created
```

Listing 32.5 shows the code to create the package body of the PKGbatchcode package:

Listing 32.5: Creating the Package Body of the PKGbatchcode Package

```
create or replace package Body PKGbatchcode As
procedure retrieve_batchno (ccode in number, batchno out number) ;
function validate_coursecode(ccode  number) return boolean is
cursor c1 is
select 'x'
from course
where coursecode = ccode;
flag boolean;
z c1%rowtype;
begin
  open c1;
  fetch c1 into z;
  if c1%notfound  then
        flag := false;
  else
        flag := true;
  end if;
  close c1;
  return (flag);
end validate_coursecode;
procedure generate_batchcode(ccode in number,bcode out number) is
flag boolean;
```

```
batchno number;
begin
  flag := validate_coursecode(ccode);
  if (flag ) then
        retrieve_batchno(ccode, batchno);
        bcode := ccode * 1000 + batchno;
        update course
        set  lastno = lastno + 1
        where coursecode = ccode;
  else
        raise_application_error(-20110,'invalid-coursecode');
  end if;
end generate_batchcode;
procedure retrieve_batchno (ccode in number, batchno out number) is
begin
  select lastno
  into batchno
  from course
  where coursecode = ccode;
exception
when no_data_found then
  raise_application_error(-20110, 'invalid coursecode');
end retrieve_batchno;
function validate_batchcode (bcode in number) return boolean is
  flag1 boolean;
  ccode number(2);
  flag2 boolean;
begin
  if length(to_char(bcode))=5 then
        ccode := bcode/1000;
        flag1 := validate_coursecode(ccode);
        if flag1 = true then
               flag2 := true;
        else
               flag2 := false;
        end if;
  else
        flag2 := false;
  end if;
  return (flag2);
end validate_batchcode;
begin
  select user
  into u1
  from dual;
  select sysdate
  into date1
  from dual;
   end PKGbatchcode;
/
```

The output of Listing 32.5 is given as follows:

```
Package body created
```

After creating the package body, you need to execute the functions of the PKGbatchcode package, as shown in Listing 32.6:

Listing 32.6: Executing Functions of the PKGbatchcode Package by creating procedure

```
declare
  x boolean;
begin
  x := PKGbatchcode.validate_batchcode(20002);
        --x := PKGbatchcode.validate_coursecode(20); error not accessible
  if(x) then
        dbms_output.put_line('code is valid');
  else
        dbms_output.put_line('code is not valid');
  end if;
end;
/
```

The output of Listing 32.6 is given as follows:

```
code is not valid

PL/SQL procedure successfully completed
```

After getting a general idea of package, let's learn about package specification, package body, advantages of packages, and referencing package element.

Package Specification

The package specifications contain datatypes, variables, exceptions, and subprogram declarations, which are available to the user. The implementation part is defined in the body. A sample package specification is shown in the following code snippet:

```
create or replace package enq_analysis as
type address_rec is record
(plot varchar2(30),
street varchar2(30),
city varchar2(3),
pin number (8));
lastenqno number;
invalid_date exception;
cursor c1 return enquiry%rowtype;
function findname(enqno number) return varchar2;
procedure updateenrollstatus(enqno in number);
end enq_analysis;
/
```

The output of the preceding code snippet is given as follows:

```
Package created
```

In the preceding code snippet, the package specifications define datatype `ADDRESS_RECORD`, variable `LASTENQNO`, exception `INVALID_DATE`, function `FINDNAME`, and procedure `UPDATEENROLLSTATUS`.

Package Body

The package body implements specified subprograms, such as `GENERATE_BATCHCODE` and `VALIDATE_BATCHCODE`. It also has implementation procedure of subprograms, which are required to implement these subprograms, i.e. `VALIDATE_COURSECODE` and `RETRIEVE_BATCHNO`. At the end of the package body, the initialization part is provided which is executed whenever a package element is referenced for the first time. Therefore, when a user refers the package for the first time, the audit record is added in the table.

Advantages of Packages

Packages offer several advantages for application design. Some of the advantages are listed in the following points:

- **Modularity**—Refers to the fact that packages group all logically related items, such as datatypes, variable, and subprograms. The interface between packages is clear and well defined.
- **Information hiding**—Refers to that part of the package, which is hidden from the user. A package has two parts, such as specification and definition, and only the specification part is available to users, while the implementation part is hidden from users. The specification part is called as the public part, while the definition part is called as the private part. The specification of packaged subprograms is accessible and changeable only when it is used in a program. Therefore, any changes done in the definition of subprograms do not affect the calling programs. Suppose you have written a package `math` in which you have written a function `fact, as shown in the following syntax:`

  ```
  x := 4;
  y := math.fact(x);
  ```

  Suppose the definition of function `fact` is changed from recursion to iteration. It would not affect the calling program.
- **Global variables**—Refer to variables (For example cursors), which can be used to pass information from one subprogram to another. Therefore, you can assign a value to a packaged variable in one subprogram and use it in another. This implies that variables declared in packages persist across the session.
- **Building application prototype**—You can build prototype of the application very fast by just making the package specification. You can compile the package specification without its body. You can write other subprograms and compile them without the package body. When the whole application is fully specified, the user can write its actual implementation.
- **Better performance**—When a package is referred for the first time, the whole of the package elements are loaded in the memory so that further reference to a package does not require disk I/O. This property speeds up application execution.

Referencing Package Element

The package elements are referred, as shown in the following syntax:

```
Packagename.element name
```

For example, if you want to declare the variable `mailing_address` in the program, you can write it as shown in the following syntax:

```
mailing_address enq_analysis.address_rec;
```

Suppose you want to use the function `findname,` you can write it as shown in the following syntax:

```
x varchar2(4);
x := enq_analysis.findname(100);
                --It gives name for enquiry number 100
```

The packaged variables of the remote database cannot be accessed directly or indirectly. Therefore, the following procedure of the remote database cannot be used:

```
CREATE PACKAGE enq_analysis As
lastenqno number;
procedure updateenrollstatus(enqno IN number := lastenqno);
.....
end enq_analysis;
```

The packed variable of the database cannot be used remotely, because the package variable `lastenqno` is used for initialization.

Implementing Package Elements

The implementation of package elements given in the package specification is done in the package body. The elements that require implementation are cursor and subprogram. The body can contain additional variables and subprograms, which can be used for implementation of package elements given in the specification. These are called private variables and private subprograms. These are not accessible from outside. The implementation of packaged elements is shown in Listing 32.7:

Listing 32.7: Implementing Elements

```
create package body enq_analysis as
enqdate1 date;
cursor c1 is
select * from enquiry;
function checkenqno(enqno number) return boolean is
begin
end checkenqno;
function findname (enqno number) return varchar2 is
begin
end findname;
procedure updateenrollstateus(enqno number) is
begin
end;
begin                                   --package initialization part
   select max(enquiryno)
   into lastenqno
   from enquiry;
end enq_analysis;
/
```

The variable `enqdate1` is a private variable, which can be used only inside the package body. Similarly, the function `CHECKENQNO` can be used inside the package body. Therefore, the following reference in the program results in an error:

```
enq_analysis.enqdate1
```

The package initialization part is executed when any package element is referred for the first time. The function `checkenqno` is private to the package and cannot be referred outside. It is used to build subprograms defined in the specification.

The variable, `lastenqno`, acts as a global variable and the user can use them to transform information from one program to another. The packaged variables have across the sessions.

Overloading

Overloading can be applied on packaged subprograms. The rules for overloading are same as those for subprograms. You can create package specification using overloaded functions, as shown in Listing 32.8:

Listing 32.8: Creating Package Specification by Using the Overloaded Functions

```
create or replace package enq_analysis as
function finddate (enqno1 number) return date;
function finddate (fname1 varchar2,lname1 varchar2) return date;
end enq_analysis;
/
```

The output of Listing 32.8 is given as follows:

```
Package created
```

You can create the package body enq_analysis by using the code shown in Listing 32.9:

Listing 32.9: Creating the Package Body enq_analysis

```
create or replace package body enq_analysis as
U1 varchar2(20);
date1 date;
function finddate (enqno1 number) return date is
begin
   select enquirydate
   into date1
   from enquiry
   where enquiryno = enqno1;
   return (date1);
end finddate;
function finddate(fname1 varchar2,lname1 varchar2) return date is
begin
   select enquirydate
   into date1
   from enquiry
   where fname=fname1
   and sname=lname1;
   return (date1);
end finddate;
end enq_analysis;
/
```

The output of Listing 32.9 is given as follows:

```
Package body created
```

Overloading is used when two subprograms have the same functionality. You can overload functions or procedures specified in PL/SQL anonymous block, as shown in Listing 32.10:

Listing 32.10: Overloading Functions or Procedures in Anonymous Block

```
declare
   xcname varchar2(10);
   xsal number;
   function getsal(pename in varchar2) return number is           --a
   lsal number;
begin
   select salary
   into lsal
   from emp_company
   where ename=pename;
   return lsal;
exception
   when too_many_rows then
         return(-1);
   when no_data_found then
         return(-1);
end;
function getavgsal(pcname in varchar2) return number is                 --b
lsal number;
begin
   select avg(salary)
   into lsal
```

```
    from emp_company
    where cname=pcname;
    return lsal;
end;
function getavgsal(pdate1 in date,pdate2 in date) return number is     --c
lsal number;
begin
    select avg(salary)
    into lsal
    from emp_company
    where jdate between pdate1 and pdate2;
    return lsal;
end;
procedure getpsal(pename in varchar2,osal out number)  is
lsal number;
begin
    select salary
    into lsal
    from emp_company
    where ename=pename;
    osal := lsal;
end;
begin
    xsal:= getavgsal('07-jun-91','01-jan-98'); --calling c
                          --xsal:= getsal('shankar');
                          --xsal:= getavgsal('acc');
    dbms_output.put_line('avg  sal is '||to_char(xsal));
end;
/
```

The output of Listing 32.10 is given as follows:

```
PL/SQL procedure successfully completed
```

Serially Reusable Packages

When a package is required for only a single call to the server then it can be marked as serially reusable. When a package is marked as serially reusable, then the memory allocated to the package is in a small pool. Normally, the memory for packages is allocated in User Global Area (UGA). When a package's work is over, the memory is made free and can be used by another user.

You can mark the package as serially reusable, as shown in Listing 32.11:

Creating the enquiry and batchaudit Table

```
create table enquiry
(ENQUIRYNO                NUMBER(8),
FNAME                     VARCHAR2(30),
Sname                     Varchar2(30),
COURSECODE                NUMBER(2),
PLOTNO                    VARCHAR2(30),
STREET                    VARCHAR2(30),
CITY                      VARCHAR2(30),
PINCODE                   NUMBER(6),
PHONE                     NUMBER(6),
ENQUIRYDATE               DATE,
```

```
REFCODE                    NUMBER(5),
EN_ST                      CHAR(1));
create table batchaudit(uname varchar2(30), udate date);
```

Listing 32.11: You can create the package specification as serially reusable, as shown in the following syntax:

```
Create or replace package enq_analysis as
PRAGMA SERIALLY_REUSABLE;
u1 varchar2(30);
date1 date;
function finddate (enqno1 number) return date;
function finddate (fname1 varchar2) return date;
end enq_analysis;
/
```

The output of the preceding syntax is as follows:

```
Package created
```

You can also create the package body, as shown in the following syntax:

```
create or replace package body enq_analysis as
PRAGMA SERIALLY_REUSABLE;
u1 varchar2(30);
date1 date;
function finddate (enqno1 number) return date is
date1 date;
begin
  select enquirydate
  into date1
  from enquiry
  where enquiryno = enqno1;
  Return (date1);
end finddate;
function finddate(fname1 varchar2) return date is
date1 date;
begin
  select enquirydate
  into date1
  from enquiry
  where fname=fname1;
  return (date1);
end finddate;
begin
  select USER
  into u1
  from dual;
  select sysdate
  into date1
  from dual;
  insert into batchaudit values(u1, date1);

end enq_analysis;
/
```

The output of the preceding syntax is as follows:

```
Package body created
```

You can insert a value in into the enquiry table, as shown in the following syntax:

Listing 32.12: Inserting a Value into the enquiry Table

```
insert into enquiry values(1,'anil',' ',1,1,'mgroad','mumbai',4456,789,'12-
  jun-2006',1,1);
edit p4                             -- write following program in file P4
declare
  x date;
begin
  x := enq_analysis.finddate(1);
  dbms_output.put_line(x);
end;
/
@p4
```

The output of Listing 32.12 is given as follows:

```
12-JUN-06
PL/SQL procedure successfully completed
```

You can retrieve the data from the batchaudit table, as shown in Listing 32.13:

Listing 32.13: Retrieving the Data from the batchaudit Table

```
select * from batchaudit;
```

The output of Listing 32.13 is given as follows:

```
UNAME                          UDATE
------------------------------ ---------
SCOTT                          29-JUL-09
```

The number of times you use the package is the number of times it is given a place in memory, as it is serially reusable. Therefore, `scott` is displayed the same number of times, as shown in the following syntax:

```
@p4
```

The output of the preceding syntax is given as follows:

```
12-JUN-06
PL/SQL procedure successfully completed
```

Listing 32.14 shows how to retrieve data from table without using the pragma serially reusable

Listing 32.14: Retrieving Data from the batchaudit Table without pragma serially reusable

```
select * from batchaudit;
```

The output of Listing 32.14 is given as follows:

```
UNAME                          UDATE
------------------------------ ---------
SCOTT                          29-JUL-09
SCOTT                          29-JUL-09

@p4
```

Result:

```
PL/SQL procedure successfully completed
```

You can retrieve data from the batchaudit Table, as shown in Listing 32.15:

Listing 32.15: Retrieving Data from the batchaudit Table

```
select * from batchaudit;
```

The output of Listing 32.15 is given as follows:

```
UNAME                          UDATE
------------------------------ ---------
SCOTT                          29-JUL-09

@p4
```

Result:

```
PL/SQL procedure successfully completed.
```

You can retrieve data from the batchaudit table, as shown in Listing 32.16:

Listing 32.16: Retrieving Data from the batchaudit Table

```
select * from batchaudit;
```

The output of Listing 32.16 is given as follows:

```
UNAME                          UDATE
------------------------------ ---------
SCOTT                          29-JUL-09
```

You can execute `P4` many times to check that one record is added in the table `batchaudit` (because the package is serially reusable). The record is added in the initialization part and it is executed each time you execute the package element. It would not happen this way if the package is not serially reusable (only one record is added).

NOTE

P4 is a SQL file that can be called any number of times

Built-in Packages in Oracle

Oracle provides the following packages to for a good programming environment:

- `STANDARD`—Defines the datatypes, exceptions, and subprograms, which are available to every PL/SQL program. For example, the exception `NO_DATA_FOUND` is defined in this package. The functions, such as `SUBSTR` and `TO_CHAR`, are specified in this package. Most of the subprograms, such as `TO_CHAR`, `TO_NUMBER` are overloaded. PL/SQL resolves the call by matching the number of arguments and their datatypes. If a user has defined subprograms having the same name, then the original subprograms can be called using the package name `STANDARD`, such as `STANDARD.SUBSTR`. The package `STANDARD` is available in precompilers, forms, reports, and various other Oracle products.
- `DBMS_PIPE`—Transmits information from one session to another. The information is transmitted using messages. You can also send information by using `send_message` and `pack_message` procedures. The procedures, such as `receive_message` and `unpack_message`, are used to receive information. Named pipes are used for precompilers.
- `UTL_FILE`—Processes the operating system text files. The operations are normal file operations. To open the file, the function `fopen` is used, to read the file the procedure `get_line` is used, to write the file the procedure `put_line` is used and to close the file function `fclose` is used. The facilities are available on the client-side as well as server-side. On server-side, the file access is restricted to directories listed in the accessible directories list, which is specified in the initialization parameter file.
- `UTL_HTTP`—Retrieves data from the Internet by contacting the specified site. The entry point in package accepts the URL, contacts specified site, and returns the requested data. The requested data is in the HTML format.
- `DBMS_SQL`—Executes SQL, DDL, and DML statements dynamically at runtime.
- `DBMS_ALERT`—Alerts the application when a specific database value is changed. It operates independently of any timing mechanism.

When a package is written, it is better to put only the required objects in the package. The changes in package specifications require that only objects, which reference the package elements, should be recompiled. However, changes made in packages body do not require compilation of dependent objects.

Summary

In this chapter, you have learned about the packages and defining packages specification. You have also learned about the defining packages with overloading, understanding the package element and using the Serially Reusable Packages.

Let's move on to the next chapter that deals with database triggers.

Exercise

1. Creating the Package Specification
2. Write a package specification for Overloading Functions.
3. Create the package specification as serially reusable.
4. Retrieve Data from a table without pragma serially reusable

33

Trigger (Database)

Triggers are stored programs that may be configured to automatically execute or fire when certain events take place. A trigger is a code, which is executed for certain database event, such as DML operation on a table. A user can write triggers on a table or view.

Triggers are used to implement complex validation, security and auditing, and replication of data. The code of trigger is fired when the corresponding DML operation is performed on the table to which the trigger is attached. The DML operation can be carried out from any terminal, from any product.

Sample Trigger

You can create a sample trigger to check the validity of a batchcode before inserting a row in the batch table, as shown in Listing 33.1:

Listing 33.1: Trigger to check the validity of a batchcode

```
create or replace trigger batch_ins_trg1                                    --A
before insert on batch                                                      --B
for each row                                                                --C
declare                                                                     --G
ccode number(2);

begin                                                                       --H
   If (length(:new.batchcode)!=5 )                                          --D
   then
          raise_application_error(-20110,'Invalid length');
   end if;
   ccode:= :new.batchcode/1000;
   if not(pkgbatchcode.validate_batchcode(:new.batchcode)) then             --F
          raise_application_error(-20111,'invalid batchcode') ;
   end if ;
end;
/
insert into batch values (10,10,'12-jul-2003',50,3000,12000,15000,1)
```

The output of Listing 33.1 is given as follows:

```
Trigger created
ERROR at line 1:
ORA-20110: Invalid length
ORA-06512: at "PLSQL.BATCH_INS_TRG1", line 7
ORA-04088: error during execution of trigger 'PLSQL.BATCH_INS_TRG1'Description
```

You can observe the following points from Listing 33.1:

- The statement A indicates the trigger name, which should be unique for the user.

NOTE

Generally, the trigger name should indicate the table name, operation, and type of trigger, that is row trigger or statement trigger.

If the clause FOR EACH ROW is present in the trigger, then the trigger is known as row trigger otherwise it is known as statement trigger.

- The statement B indicates the operations, such as insert, delete, or update for which the trigger is fired. It should also indicate as to when the trigger code is to be executed that is before or after the operation; and the table name to which the trigger code is attached, such as batch.
- Validation and security is implemented in the before trigger, while auditing and replication is done in the after trigger.

- The statement C indicates whether the trigger is row trigger or the statement trigger. Row trigger fires each time for each affected row, while the statement trigger fires once for each statement submitted. This is shown in the following example:

```
update batch
set last no= last no+1
where ccode=10;
```

This code updates 10 rows—the statement trigger fires only once, but the row trigger fires ten times.

- The statement G indicates the declare section of the trigger code. Each trigger in PL/SQL block has a declarative section and body. You can declare any variable in the declare section which can be used in the body of the trigger.
- The statement H indicates the beginning of the body of PL/SQL block.
- In the body, you can refer values to be inserted using `:new` at the beginning of the column. In the statement D, you can refer value of batchcode of the row, which is to be inserted `by using`: new batchcode is used.
- The statement F checks valid batchcode using function `pkgbatchcode.validate_batchcode`. It is assumed that the function is written in the package. The procedure stops processing after `raise_appliction_error` procedure is invoked.

*Referring the **:new** and **:old** Values*

You can refer new and old values for various statements, such as `INSERT`, `DELETE`, and `UPDATE`.

- The `INSERT statement`—Use `:new` because values are new. For example, `:new.batchcode`.
- The `DELETE statement`—Use `:old` because values are from an existing row. For example, `:old.batchcode`.
- The `UPDATE statement`—Use `:new` and `:old` because the row will have both the old and new values. For example, `:new.batchcode` and `:old.batchcode`.

Triggers are used to implement complex validations, complex security, auditing, and replication of data. Before triggers are used for validations and security, whereas after triggers are used for auditing and replication.

Listing 33.2: Trigger to check the validity of coursecode (should be of 2 digits—less than 10 and greater than 99) before a row is inserted in the course table

```
create or replace trigger ins_course
before insert on course
for each row
declare
begin
  if (:new.coursecode <10) or (:new.coursecode>99) then
       raise_application_error (-20110,' invalid length') ;
  end if;
end;
/
```

The output of Listing 33.2 is given as follows:

```
Trigger created
```

Listing 33.3: Create a trigger, which does not allow any DML operation over the enquiry table, if the user is STUDENT1

```
create or replace trigger enquirytrgl
before insert or update or delete  on enquiry
declare
  uname varchar(30);
begin
  select user into uname
```

```
   from dual;
   If uname='STUDENT1'                                         --caps
   then
        raise_application_error(-20110,'Invalid insertion');
   end if;
end;
/
```

The output of Listing 33.3 is given as follows:

```
Trigger created
```

Listing 33.4: Creating a trigger that allows no DML operation on the enquiry table to be performed on any weekday, but allows only insertion on Sunday

```
create trigger enquiry1_sunday
before insert or update or delete on enquiry
declare
  uname varchar2(20);
begin
  select user into uname from dual;
  if inserting  then
        if (to_char(sysdate,'Day') != 'Sunday')
        then
                  raise_application_error(-20111,'Insertion is not allowed
                 on other days');
        end if;
  end if;
  if updating or deleting then
        raise_application_error(-20112,'Updation and Deletion is not
  allowed ');
  end if;
end;
/
```

The output of Listing 33.4 is given as follows:

```
Trigger created
```

Listing 33.5: Changing Listing 33.4 and not allowing insertion operation for coursecode 10 only

```
create trigger enquiry_type1
before insert or update or delete on enquiry
for each row
when (new.coursecode=10)
declare
  uname varchar2(20);
begin
  select user into uname from dual;
  if INSERTING  then
        if (to_char(sysdate,'Day') != 'Sunday')
        then
                 raise_application_error(-20111,'Insertion is not allowed on
        other days');
        end if;
  end if;
  if updating or deleting then
        raise_application_error(-20112,'Updation and Deletion is not
  allowed ');
  end if;
end;
/
```

The output of Listing 33.5 is given as follows:

```
Trigger created
```

NOTE

The trigger code is executed only when the specified WHEN condition is true. This condition should be a simple expression and not a subquery.

Trigger Concept

If a DML statement fires a trigger or sequence of triggers and an error is generated during the execution of any of these triggers, then the whole effect produced by the DML statement and the trigger code is completely undone. The state of the system is moved to the state just prior to the statement, which has fired the trigger. Look at the following code snippet:

```
insert into enrollment                                      --C
update enquiry                                              --D
set cnt=cnt+1
when refcode=101;
....
```

Suppose the update trigger has to update 10 rows, and before updating these rows, the row trigger is already written for each row. If an error is generated during the updation of the 7th row, all the updation of the first six rows are undone. Now the user will return to the same state, which was present after the statement C shown in the preceding code snippet.

Statement-Level Atomicity

Statement-level atomicity is the process to ensure that the effect of the statement is either full or null. It gives 100% guarantee to the user about the outcome of the statement. Therefore, when an error is generated, the effect generated by the statement directly or indirectly via trigger is undone. If the error is generated during execution of the statement then all the partial effects done by the statement are undone and the state is restored to point prior to the execution of statement. Therefore, it will not undo the effect of the statement C, but undo the effect of the statement D. Statement-level atomicity is provided only for database object. It is not provided for package variables and sequences. If the package variable or sequence is updated during trigger execution and there is a trigger failure, then the updated value is retained. Suppose that the trigger code for a certain trigger is as follows:

```
Insert into enqanalysis(..);
batchanalysis.lastno=batchanalysis.lastno+1;
```

The `batchanalysis.lastno` has value 10 before execution of trigger and the trigger code is executed. If the trigger code generates an error after the first two updations are done, then `batchanalysis.lastno` will have value 12. This implies that the effect of trigger failure is not undone. The effect of insertion of rows in `enqanalysis` is undone.

The error, which causes trigger failure, may be an Oracle error or user-defined error or execution of raise-application error. The failure may be in the direct triggers or indirect triggers. For example, before an update trigger `T1` is written on `enquiry` (which inserts rows into `enqanalysis`), there is a before insert trigger `T2` on `enqanalysis`. Updation of `enquiry` causes `T1` to fire which, in turn, causes `T2` to fire. Therefore, `T1` is a direct trigger, while `T2` is an indirect trigger. This is also called cascade of triggers.

Savepoint

Statement-level atomicity is implemented using savepoint to undo some recent effects of transaction (partial effect of transaction). Rollback cannot be used to undo partial effects because rollback undo's total effect of transaction. Suppose a code snippet is written as follows:

```
commit;                                          --C
Analysis of sales for all regions;               --A
SAVEPOINT Z;                                     --B
detail analysis of region  X;
If data is not proper then
   Rollback to Z;
end if;
```

In the preceding code, savepoint saves the state at B. If a rollback is done up to savepoint, then the effect of statement A is not undo. In case of full rollback, the state is restored to point C, and the effect of statement A is also is undo. Savepoint is a property of transaction. When a transaction ends, savepoints are deleted.

If rollback is done to a certain savepoint, then all the prior savepoints are retained, while the next savepoint, after that savepoint is deleted.

Let's consider the following code snippet:

```
commit              commit
S1                  S1
Savepoint A;                  Savepoint A
S3                  S3
Savepoint B;                  savepoint B;
S4                  S4
S5                  S5
Rollback to A;      Rollback to B;
Rollback to B;      Rollback to A;
```

In the preceding code snippet, rollback to A, in the first case, causes deletion of savepoint B. In the second case, rollback to B, does not delete savepoint A. When the DML statement is submitted for execution, Oracle creates implicit savepoint before processing the statement. The typical sequence of statement execution is as follows:

```
savepoint;
1) Fire before statement trigger;
2) for each row affected
   2.1 fire before row trigger constraint checking;
   2.2 Row processing i.e. insertion, deletion, updation
   2.3 fire after row trigger
   end for;
3) Fire after statement trigger.
```

Restriction on Trigger Code

There are some restrictions on PL/SQL code, which has to be written in the trigger. The restrictions are listed in the following points:

- You cannot write any transaction control statement, such as `COMMIT`, `ROLLBACK`, and `SAVEPOINT`. Inside the trigger code, no DDL statement can be executed directly or indirectly (via procedures). This is done to support the statement level atomicity. Suppose the `Commit` statement is allowed inside the trigger body. In that case, it may record partial effect of the statement. For example, a statement intends to update 10 rows and after updating each row, the `Commit` statement is issued. Now, if after two rows, there occurs a problem in the third row, then the user gets a partial effect of the statement.
- If the row trigger is not properly written then it generates the effect, which depends on the order in which rows are processed. Since the user cannot control the order in which rows are processed, such triggers may generate unexpected data. A user has to take care that the trigger code should generate effect, which is independent of the order in which rows are evaluated.

Row Evaluation Order

The effect of trigger may depend on the order in which rows are evaluated. In such cases, the trigger code may generate unexpected results. Therefore, one should always avoid writing such code. Let's understand this with the help of an example, shown in the following code snippets.

Create table `tempfeespaid,` as shown in the following code snippet:

```
create table tempfeespaid(amt number)
/
```

Create table `feesanalysis`, as shown in the following code snippet:

```
create table feesanalysis(amt number)
/
```

Create table `feesaudit`, as shown in the following code snippet:

```
create table feesaudit(amt number)
/
```

Insert data into table `tempfeespaid`, as shown in the following code snippet:

```
insert into tempfeespaid values(100);

insert into tempfeespaid values(200);

insert into tempfeespaid values(300);
```

Listing 33.6: Setting a Trigger `t1` on a Table

```
create or replace trigger t1
before update on tempfeespaid
for each row
declare
  x number;
begin
  insert into feesanalysis
  values (:old.amt);
  select avg(amt)
  into x
  from feesanalysis;
  if  x > 200 then
        insert into feesaudit values (x);
  end if;
end;
/
```

The output of Listing 33.6 is given as follows:

```
Trigger created
  AMT
1 100    R1
2 200    R2
3 300    R3
```

If rows are updated in the order `R1`, `R2`, and `R3`, then no rows are inserted in the table feesaudit. If rows are updated in the order `R3`, `R2`, and `R1`, then two rows are inserted in the table `feesaudit`.

Since relational database does not guarantee the order of evaluation of rows, a user should avoid writing such triggers. In case of modification of global variables in row triggers, the modification depends upon the order in which the rows are evaluated.

The updation of global variables should always be avoided in row triggers. It is better to initialize global variables in before statement trigger. For example:

Listing 33.7: Initializing global variables in before statement trigger

Case 1:

```
select * from tempfeespaid;
```

Result:

```
       AMT
----------
       100
       200
       300

update tempfeespaid set amt = amt +0;
```

Result:

```
3 rows updated
```

```
select * from feesaudit;
```

Result:

```
no rows selected
```

In the case 1, you can observe the following points:

- Prior to updating `tempfeespaid`, the old value of amount is entered in `feesanalysis` table
- Moreover, when the average value is greater than 200, the row would be inserted in the feesaudit table. In this case, when the data is 100, 200, 300 …, the average of first row is 100, which is less than 200, so no row is inserted in `feesaudit`.
- Average of first and second row is 150, which is less than 200. So again no row is inserted in `feesaudit`
- Similarly, average of first 3 rows is 200, so no rows are inserted in `feesaudit`.

First truncate both `tempfeespaid` and `feesanalysis` tables and then insert this data:

```
truncate table tempfeespaid;

truncate table feesanalysis;

insert into tempfeespaid values(300);

insert into tempfeespaid values(200);

insert into tempfeespaid values(100);
```

Therefore, we first truncate the values in both tables and re-insert them in reverse manner.

Case 2:

```
select * from tempfeespaid;
```

Result:

```
       AMT
----------
       300
       200
       100
```

Therefore, when `tempfeespaid` is updated, the trigger `t1` is called, which does the following:

- Average of first row is 300, which is greater than 200. So this row is inserted in `feesaudit` table
- Average of first and second row is 250, which is again greater than 200. So another row is inserted in `feesaudit`
- However, when the average of all three rows are calculated, it equals 200 and not greater than 200. So this row is not inserted in `feesaudit` table.

```
update tempfeespaid set amt=amt+0;
```

Result:

```
3 rows updated
```

Displaying data

```
select * from feesaudit;
```

Result:

```
       AMT
----------
       300
       250
```

Therefore, we are updating table `tempfeespaid`, but displaying the records of another table. This is because, whenever `tempfeespaid table` is updated, it calls the trigger `t1`.

Mutating and Constraining Table

Oracle enforces certain restrictions on row trigger to have a consistent view of data during the execution of triggers. This restriction is defined in terms of mutating and constraining table.

Mutating Table

A mutating table is the table, which is affected directly by DML statement or indirectly because of `ON_DELETE_CASCADE` clause in referential integrity constraint. The error will not occur for `INSERT INTO TABLE ..... VALUES` statement, because it inserts only one row at a time. If the trigger is written as follows:

```
create trigger t1
before insert on feespaid
for each row
.........
```

In the preceding code snippet, the table `feespaid` is mutating table for the trigger `t1`. You can create a mutation table by using the syntax shown in Listing 33.8:

Listing 33.8: Creating a Mutation Table

```
create table t(a number);
```

The output of 33.8 is given as follows:

```
Table created
```

After creating the mutation table, you can insert value in *t*, as shown in the following syntax:

```
insert into t values (1);
```

The output of the preceding syntax is as follows:

```
1 row created
```

Now, you can commit the operation by using the following command:

```
commit;
```

Let's take another example. You can also create trigger `TRG`, which increments the value of `A` in the table `T` before any insertion is done, as shown in the following code snippet:

```
create or replace trigger trg
before insert on t
for each row
declare
   x number;
begin
   select max(a) into x from t;
   :new.a:=x+1;
end;
/
```

Now, you can insert a value in the table `t,` as shown in the following code snippet:

```
insert into t values(2);                        --Here there is no error
```

The output of the preceding code snippet is as follows:

```
1 row created
```

Creating table

```
create table s as select * from t;
```

Result:

```
Table created
```

Displaying data

```
select * from s;
```

Result:

```
         A
----------
         1
         2
```

Inserting data

```
insert into t select a from s;   --This will cause error
```

Result:

```
insert into t select a from s
            *
ERROR at line 1:
ORA-04091: table SCOTT.T is mutating, trigger/function may not see it
ORA-06512: at "SCOTT.TRG", line 4
ORA-04088: error during execution of trigger 'SCOTT.TRG'
```

Constraining Table

A constraining table is the table, which directly reads by the SQL statement in the trigger or indirectly because of the foreign key constraint.

NOTE

This error has been removed from 8i.

Suppose the trigger code is as follows:

```
create trigger t1
before insert on feespaid
for each row
...........
select amt
into x
from expenditure;
.............
```

You can observe in the preceding trigger code that the table `expenditure` is a constraining table. The constraints on row trigger are defined as:

- The row trigger should not read from or modify mutating table.
- The row trigger should not change `PRIMARY`, `FOREIGN`, or `UNIQUE KEY` column of constraining table. There is one exception to this rule. The `BEFORE ROW` trigger, which inserts a single row in a foreign key table, can modify any column in the primary key table.

> **NOTE**
> *This constraint was present in the earlier versions; not from 9i.*

These rules minimize the affect, which depends on the row evaluation order.

Case Studies

Generating a Primary Key Based on Max Value of Column

Suppose, `A` is a primary key and when you insert a row, the value of `A` becomes `1+MAXVALUE`. You cannot use only row trigger because reading `max` value generates a mutating error. The solution to this problem is to read `MAX` value in a package variable in statement trigger and use this value in row trigger, as shown in Listing 33.9:

Listing 33.9: Reading Value in a Package Variable in Statement Trigger and using this Value in Row Trigger

```
create table t(a number primary key,b number)
/
insert into t values(1, 8)
/
insert into t values(5, 9)
/
insert into t values(7, 10)
/
select * from t;
```

The output of Listing 33.9 is given as follows:

```
       A          B
   -------    ------
       1          8
       5          9
       7         10
```

```
create table s(a number, b number);
insert into s values(1, 10)
/
insert into t values(2, 15)
/
select * from s;
```

Result:

```
         A          B
---------- ----------
         1         10
```

```
create package cnt_pkg as
cnt number;
end cnt_pkg;
/
```

Listing 33.10: Creating trigger SETMAXTRG to select the maximum value of `A` from table T and put the selected value into cnt variable of package cnt_pkg

```
create or replace trigger setmaxtrg before insert on t
begin
   select nvl(max(a),0) into cnt_pkg.cnt from t;
end;
/
```

The statement trigger in which the value of package variable `cnt` is read is shown in the following code snippet:

```
create or replace trigger inserttrg before insert on t for each row
begin
   :new.a := cnt_pkg.cnt+1;
   cnt_pkg.cnt:=cnt_pkg.cnt+1;
end;
/
insert into t( select * from s);
select * from t;
```

The output of the preceding code snippet is given as follows:

```
         A          B
---------- ----------
         1          8
         5          9
         7         10

         2         15
         8         10
5 rows selected.
```

This is the row trigger in which the value of package variable `cnt` is being used.

Implementing Update Cascade Functionality Using Trigger

Update cascade refers that if you update a parent row, corresponding foreign key columns in the child rows are also updated. A trigger can be used to implement updates cascade functionality, as shown in Listing 33.11:

Listing 33.11: Using trigger to implement update cascade functionality

```
create table parent(a int primary key, b int)
/
```

The output of Listing 33.11 is given as follows:

```
Table created
```

You can also insert data

```
insert into parent values (1, 2)
/
```

Result:

```
1 row created
```

You can insert more data….., as shown in the following syntax:

```
insert into parent values(2, 4)
/
```

The output of the preceding syntax is given as follows:

```
1 row created
```

After that, you can commit a transaction, as shown in the following syntax:

```
commit
/
```

The output of the preceding syntax is given as follows:

```
Commit complete
```

Creating table

```
create table child(a int references parent(a),c int)
/
```

Result:

```
Table created
```

Inserting data

```
insert into child values(1,8)
/
```

Result:

```
1 row created
```

Inserting data

```
insert into child values(1,10)
/

1 row created

insert into child values(2,7)
/
```

Result:

```
1 row created
```

Committing a transaction

```
commit
/
```

Result:

```
Commit complete
```

Creating a trigger

```
create trigger update_cascade after update on parent for each row
begin
  update child set a = :new.a where a =:old.a;
end;
/
```

Result:

```
Trigger created
```

Displaying data

```
select * from parent
/
```

Result:

```
         A          B
---------- ----------
         1          2
         2          4
```

Displaying data

```
select * from child
/
```

Result:

```
      A          C
------- ----------
      1          8
      1         10
      2          7
```

Updating table

```
update parent set a = 3 where a = 1
/
```

Result:

```
1 row updated
```

Displaying data

```
select * from child
/
```

Result:

```
     A          C
----- ----------
     3          8
     3         10
     2          7
```

Using rollback

```
ROLLBACK
/
```

Result:

```
Rollback complete
```

Reversing Update

In case of reverse update, if you update a child row, the corresponding primary key of parent row is also updated. This is shown in Listing 33.12:

Listing 33.12: Creating Trigger to use Reverse Update

```
create or replace trigger rev_update_cascade before update on child for each row
begin
    update parent set a =:new.a where a =:old.a;
end;
/
select * from parent;
```

The output of Listing 33.12 is given as follows:

```
Trigger created
         A          B
---------- ----------
         1          2
         2          4
```

Now, you can display data of the child table, as shown in the following statement

```
select * from child;
```

The output of the preceding code snippet is given as follows:

```
         A          C
---------- ----------
         1          8
         1         10
         2          7
```

You can update the value of A in child table, as shown in the following SQL Statement:

```
update child set a = 10 where a = 1;
```

The output of the preceding code snippet is given as follows:

```
2 rows updated
```

After updating the child table, you can display the data, as shown in the following SQL statement:

```
select * from parent;
```

The output of the preceding code snippet is given as follows:

```
         A          B
---------- ----------
        10          2
         2          4
```

Deleting Cascade

The deleting cascade refers to the fact that if you delete parent rows then the corresponding child rows are also deleted. This can be explained with the help of Listing 33.13:

Listing 33.13: Using Delete Cascade

Retrieve rows from `parent` table:

```
select * from parent;
```

Result:

```
         A          B
---------- ----------
        10          2
         2          4
```

Retrieving rows from `child` table:

```
select * from child;
```

Result:

```
         A          C
---------- ----------
        10          8
        10         10
         2          7
```

Creating trigger:

```
create or replace trigger delete_cascade before delete on parent for each row
begin
    delete child where a = :old.a ;
end;
/
```

Result:

```
Trigger created
```

Deleting from `Parent` table (the corresponding child table entry also gets deleted because of the trigger):

```
delete parent where a = 10;
```

Result:

```
1 row deleted
```

Retrieve rows from `Child`:

```
select * from child;
```

Result:

```
         A          C
---------- ----------
         2          7
```

Retrieve rows from `Parent`:

```
select * from parent;
```

Result:

```
         A          B
---------- ----------
         2          4
```

Altering Trigger

After creating a trigger, it cannot be altered. If a user wants to change a trigger then he can do it by dropping the trigger and then recreating it. In addition, you can change a trigger if it is created by using the `CREATE` or `REPLACE` command, which is shown in following code snippet:

```
DROP TRIGGER t1
  or
CREATE OR REPLACE TRIGGER t1
...................
```

Enabling and Disabling Trigger

You can temporarily disable a trigger in the following cases:

- Referenced objects are not available
- Large data is loaded in the table

The trigger is disabled using the `ALTER TRIGGER` command.

You disable a trigger by using the disable clause, as shown in Listing 33.14:

Listing 33.14: Disabling a Trigger

```
alter trigger trg1 disable;
```

The output of Listing 33.14 is given as follows:

```
Trigger altered
```

You can disable all triggers for table T1 by using the disable clause:

Listing 33.15: Disabling all Triggers for Table **T1**

```
alter table t1
disable all triggers;
```

The output of Listing 33.15 is given as follows:

```
Table altered
```

In addition, you can enable a trigger by using the Enable clause, as shown in Listing 33.16:

Listing 33.16: Enabling a Trigger

```
alter trigger trg1 enable;
```

The output of Listing 33.16 is given as follows:

```
Trigger altered
```

You can enable all triggers of table T1 by using the Enable clause, as shown in Listing 33.17:

Listing 33.17: Enabling all Triggers of Table T1

```
alter table t1
enable all triggers;
```

The output of Listing 33.17 is given as follows:

```
Table altered
```

Information on Triggers

You can get all information about the triggers from the following views:

- USER_TRIGGERS
- ALL_TRIGGERS
- DBA_TRIGGERS

These views give you the information related to the owner of the trigger, trigger name, its type, the triggering event, and the table owner.

Summary

In this chapter, we discussed triggers, their basic concepts, how they can be enabled, disabled, used for deletion, row order evaluation.

In the next chapter, we will discuss the concept of autonomous triggers and their use.

Exercise

1. Write a trigger to check the email address in the database.
2. Creating a Mutation Table.
3. Creating Trigger to use Reverse Update.
4. Write a statement to Alter a Trigger.

34

Autonomous Transaction

Concept of Autonomous Transaction

An autonomous transaction is an independent transaction started by another transaction (also called as the parent transaction). Autonomous transaction allows you to suspend the parent transaction, perform some SQL operations, commit or rollback and then resumes the parent transaction. Once an autonomous transaction starts, it is fully independent, i.e. it shares no locks or resources or commit dependencies with the main transaction. Using autonomous transactions, you can build modular and reusable software components. For example, you can start and finish an autonomous transaction in the stored procedure itself. A calling application does not need to know about the autonomous operations a procedure, and the procedure need not know about the transaction context of an application. Autonomous transactions have all the functionality of regular transactions, such as distributed processing. They also allow parallel queries and also support all transaction control statements, including `SET TRANSACTION`.

Listing 34.1 shows the code to create table `Z` to create an autonomous procedure:

Listing 34.1: Creating Table Z

```
create table z (a number, b number);
```

The output of Listing 34.1 is as follows:

```
Table created
```

The following code snippet shows the code to create an autonomous procedure, `auto2`:

```
                                        --The procedure auto2 is marked as
                                        --autonomous
create or replace procedure auto2 as
pragma autonomous_transaction;
procedure local is
begin
  insert into z values(1,5);
end local;
begin
  local;
  commit;
end auto2;
/
```

The output of the preceding code snippet is as follows:

```
Procedure created
```

The following code snippet shows the code to call the autonomous procedure, `auto2`:

```
declare
begin
    insert into z values(10,10);        --Starts the main(Parent
                                        --transaction).
  auto2;                                --Suspends the main transaction.
  insert into z values(1,1);            --Again starts the main transaction.
  insert into z values(1,'asd');        --Main transaction that causes
                                        --error.
end;                                    --End of main transaction.
/
```

The output of preceding code snippet is as follows:

```
declare
*
ERROR at line 1:
ORA-01722: invalid number
ORA-06512: at line 5
```

The following code snippet shows the code to use the `SELECT` statement:

```
select * from z;
```

In the preceding code snippet, if the main transaction causes error resulting in a rollback, the autonomous transaction is still able to insert data, since it is independent of the main transaction. You can also mark the PL/SQL block as autonomous.

The output of the preceding code snippet is as follows:

```
   A          B
---- ----------
   1          5
```

Listing 34.2 shows the code to mark the database trigger as autonomous:

Listing 34.2: Marking the Database Trigger as Autonomous

```
create table z_copy(a number , b number);
/
create or replace trigger autotrigger
before insert on  z for each row
declare
  pragma autonomous_transaction;
begin
  insert into z_copy values(:new.A,:new.B);
  commit;
end;
/
```

The output of Listing 34.2 is as follows:

```
Trigger created
```

The following code snippet shows the code to display the inserted data:

```
insert into z values(1,1);
/
```

The output of the preceding code snippet is as follows:

```
1 row created
```

The following code snippet shows the code to commit a transaction:

```
commit;
```

The output of preceding code snippet is as follows:

```
Commit Complete
```

The following code snippet shows the code to select the z_copy table:

```
select * from z_copy;
```

The output of the preceding code snippet is as follows:

```
   A          B
---- ----------
   1          1
```

You can neither mark all the subprograms in the package as autonomous, nor methods in the object types as autonomous, as shown in the following code snippet:

```
create package autopack as
pragma autonomous_transaction;                    --Illegal
/
```

The output of the preceding code snippet is as follows:

```
Warning: Package created with compilation errors
```

Only the individual routines can be marked as autonomous. Although an autonomous transaction starts in another transaction, it cannot be called a nested transaction since it does not depend on the main transaction, i.e. if the main transaction rollbacks, the nested transaction also rollbacks while the autonomous transaction does not. Exceptions raised in an autonomous transaction can cause a transaction-level rollback, but not a statement-level rollback. The main transaction shares its context with the nested routine and not with the autonomous transaction. But, if the autonomous transaction calls another non-autonomous routine then they share the same transaction context.

The changes made by the autonomous transaction are visible to the main transaction when autonomous transaction commits and the isolation level is READ_COMMITED. This statement says that when the isolation level is READ_COMMITED and the autonomous transaction commits, only then autonomous transaction will be visible to the main transaction.

Behavior of the **SERIALIZABLE** Transaction

If the isolation level is SERIALIZABLE, then the changes made by the autonomous transaction will not be seen by the main transaction, when it resumes.

Listing 34.3 shows the Serializable isolation level:

Listing 34.3: Showing Serializable Isolation Level

```
commit;
/
```

The output of Listing 34.3 is as follows:

```
Commit complete
```

The following code snippet shows the code to truncate a table:

```
truncate table z;
/
```

The output of the preceding code snippet is as follows:

```
Table truncated
```

The following code snippet shows the code to verify the effect of serializability:

```
declare
  x number;
begin
  set transaction isolation level serializable;
              --main transaction isolation level set to serializable
              --therefore it will not see the effect   made by
              --autonomous transaction

  auto2;      ---inserts a row a=1 and b=5 in z
  select a into x from z where b =5;
              --main transaction resumes and throws an exception
exception
       when no_data_found then
```

```
    dbms_output.put_line('main isolation level is serializable ');
end;
/
```

The output of the preceding code snippet is as follows:

```
MAIN ISOLATION LEVEL IS   SERIALIZABLE
PL/SQL procedure successfully completed
```

To control the autonomous transaction, use the following statements, which are applicable to the current transaction as well:

- `COMMIT`—Ends the current transaction and makes changes permanent to the database.
- `ROLLBACK TO SAVEPOINT_NAME`—Ends the current transaction and undoes the changes made to the database.
- `SAVEPOINT SAVEPOINT_NAME`—Records the state of the database.
- `SET TRANSACTION`—Sets transaction properties such as read/write access and isolation level. The transaction properties set by the main transaction are applicable to it only; the setting will not be applicable to autonomous transaction.

When you execute the autonomous routine, the main transaction suspends. When you exit the autonomous routine, the main transaction resumes. `COMMIT` and `ROLLBACK` ends the active transaction but does not end the autonomous transaction. The SQL statement following the commit or rollback begins another transaction.

Listing 34.4 shows the procedure using SAVEPOINT:

Listing 34.4: Procedure using SAVEPOINT

```
declare
pragma autonomous_transaction;
begin
   insert into z values(0,0);
   commit;                              --end of autonomous transaction 1
   insert into z values(0,0);           --2nd autonomous transaction begins
   savepoint save1;
   insert into z_copy values(3,6);
   rollback to save1;
   commit;
end;
/
```

The output of Listing 34.4 is as follows:

```
PL/SQL procedure successfully completed
```

The scope of the `SAVEPOINT` is up to the transaction in which it is defined, i.e. the savepoint defined in the main transaction is not related with the savepoint defined in the autonomous transaction. Both the transactions can use the same savepoint names.

NOTE

If the autonomous transaction attempts to access the resource of the main transaction, then a deadlock can occur. In that case, Oracle raises an exception in the autonomous transaction.

Oracle initialization parameter, TRANSACTIONS, specifies the maximum number of concurrent transactions, which may exceed if more autonomous transactions are opened (since autonomous transactions execute concurrently with the main transaction).

You cannot exit the active autonomous transaction without COMMIT or Rollback.

Next, let's learn about autonomous triggers.

Autonomous Triggers

You can use database triggers to log events transparently, e.g. tracking all the inserts in a particular table even those that Rollback.

Suppose you have a table T2 and use the trigger to insert the rows into the table. Because the trigger is autonomous, it can COMMIT to insert in table T2, even if the main table, T1, commits or rollbacks.

Listing 34.5 shows the code to Use autonomous triggers:

Listing 34.5: Using Autonomous Triggers

```
create table t1 (a number, b number)
/
```

The output of Listing 34.5 is as follows:

```
Table created
```

The following code snippet shows the code to create table T2:

```
CREATE TABLE T2 (A NUMBER, B NUMBER)
/
```

The output of the preceding code snippet is as follows:

```
Table created
```

The following code snippet shows the code to create trigger, trace_trigger:

```
create or replace  trigger trace_trigger
before insert on T1 for each row
declare
pragma autonomous_transaction;
begin
   insert into T2 values(:new.A,:new.B);
           commit;
end;
/
```

The output of the preceding code snippet is as follows:

```
Trigger created
```

The following code snippet shows the code to inserting data in table T1:

```
insert into T1 values(1,12) --insert statement is committed.
/
```

The output of the preceding code snippet is as follows:

```
1 row created
```

The following code snippet shows the code to commit a transaction:

```
commit
/
```

The output of the preceding code snippet is as follows

```
Commit complete
```

The following code snippet shows the code to use rollback:

```
rollback
/
```

The output of the preceding code snippet is as follows:

```
Rollback complete
```

Unlike regular triggers, autonomous triggers can execute the DDL statements using native dynamic SQL. The following code snippet shows the drop_table trigger, where the table `T2` is dropped after updating table `T1`:

```
create trigger drop_table
after update on T1
declare
pragma autonomous_transaction;
begin
   execute immediate 'drop table T2';
end;
/
```

The output of the preceding code snippet is as follows:

```
Trigger created
```

Let's learn about how to call autonomous functions from SQL.

Calling Autonomous Functions from SQL

A function called from SQL must obey certain rules meant to control side effects. To check for violations of the rules, you can use the pragma, `RESTRICT_REFERENCES`. The pragma asserts that a function does not read and/or write database tables and/or package variables. Autonomous routines never violate the rules, Read No Database State (RNDS) and Write No Database State (WNDS) no matter what they do.

Listing 34.6 shows the code to create the debug table:

Listing 34.6: Creating the debug Table

```
create table debug (msg varchar2(100))
/
```

The output of Listing 34.6 is as follows:

```
Table created
```

The following code snippet shows the code to call autonomous function from SQL:

```
create or replace function send_msg(msg varchar2)return varchar2
is
pragma autonomous_transaction;
begin
   insert into debug values(msg);
   commit;
   return msg;
end;
/
```

The output of preceding code snippet is as follows:

```
Function created
```

The following code snippet shows the code to call the `SEND_MSG` function:

```
declare
x varchar2(100);
begin
   select send_msg('calling function from sql') into x from dual;
                                  --even if you roll back in this scope, the insert
                                  --into 'debug' remains committed because
                          --it is part of an autonomous transaction
   dbms_output.put_line(x);
```

```
   rollback;
end;
/
```

The output of preceding code snippet is as follows:

```
CALLING FUNCTION FROM SQL
PL/SQL procedure successfully completed
```

The following code snippet shows the code to display records to see whether the data is inserted:

```
select * from debug;
```

The output of preceding code snippet is as follows:

```
MSG
--------------------------------
CALLING FUNCTION FROM SQL
```

Summary

This chapter dealt with autonomous transactions in depth. The next chapter will get you acquainted with some important PL/SQL packages.

Exercise

1. Explain the concept of autonomous transaction.
2. What is the effect of serializability on autonomous transaction?

35

Important PL/SQL Packages

Oracle has supplied PL/SQL packages for some important functionality in programming. Here are some important packages.

The **DBMS_SQL** Package

The DBMS_SQL package is used mainly to execute Data Definition Language (DDL) statements in a PL/SQL program as well as to execute SQL statements which are constructed at runtime. For example, you can use the `DBMS_SQL` package to decide a table name at runtime. Listing 35.1 creates a table to demonstrate to fetch data using DBMS_SQL:

Listing 35.1: Creating Table EMP1 to Demonstrate Fetching Data Using DBMS_SQL

```
create table emp1(empno number,ename varchar2(20),salary number)
/
```

The output of Listing 35.1 is as follows:

```
Table created
```

Inserting values into table

```
insert into emp1 values(1,'AMIT',1000)
/
```

Result:

```
1 row created
```

Inserting values into table

```
insert into emp1 values(2,'SUNIL',2000)
/
```

Result:

```
1 row created
```

Inserting values into table

```
insert into emp1 values(3,'LALIT',2000)
/
```

Result:

```
1 row created
```

Inserting values into table

```
insert into emp1 values(4,'AJAY',3000)
/
```

Result:

```
1 row created
```

Inserting values into table

```
insert into emp1 values(5,'RAVI',4000)
/
```

Result:

```
1 row created
```

Inserting values into table

```
insert into emp1 values(6,'ABHAY',4000)
/
```

Result:

```
1 row created
```

Listing 35.2 shows how to use procedure to execute SQL statements at runtime:

Listing 35.2: Use of DBMS_SQL package to execute sql statement constructed at runtime

```
declare
  str varchar2(200);
  cursor_c1 int;
```

```
    no_of_rows int;
    name varchar2(10);
    id int;
    wherestr varchar2(50) := ' and  salary < 5000';
begin
                            --open cursor and get cursor pointer
    cursor_c1 := dbms_sql.open_cursor;
                            --construct dynamic string
    str := 'select empno, ename from empl where   salary > :sal' || wherestr;
                            --a. first phase parse the statement
    dbms_sql.parse(cursor_c1, str, dbms_sql.native);
                            --b. bind variable like :sal should be given values
    dbms_sql.bind_variable(cursor_c1, 'sal', 3000);
                            --c. define variable where values from rows are kept
    dbms_sql.define_column(cursor_c1, 1, id);
    dbms_sql.define_column(cursor_c1, 2, name,10);
                                    -- d. execute phase
    no_of_rows := dbms_sql.execute(cursor_c1);
                            -- execute return value only for dml statement
    loop
                            -- e. fetch a row
          if dbms_sql.fetch_rows(cursor_c1) > 0 then
                            -- fetch columns from the row
                 dbms_sql.column_value(cursor_c1, 1, id);
                 dbms_sql.column_value(cursor_c1, 2, name);
                 dbms_output.put_line(id||'   '||name);
          else
                            exit;
          end if;
    end loop;
    dbms_sql.close_cursor(cursor_c1);
                            -- f. close cursor
end;
/
```

The output of Listing 35.2 is as follows:

```
5  RAVI
6  ABHAY
PL/SQL procedure successfully completed
```

From Listing 35.2, the following points are clear:

- Dynamic SQL is a programming technique that lets you build SQL statements dynamically at runtime. For example, dynamic SQL lets you create a procedure that operates on a table whose name is not known until runtime.
- From Oracle8i, the only way to implement dynamic SQL was using the `DBMS_SQL` package. Oracle8i introduced native dynamic SQL, an alternative to the `DBMS_SQL` package.
- Dynamic SQL also lets you execute DDL statements.
- You can use the `EXECUTE IMMEDIATE` statement to invoke anonymous PL/SQL blocks. The ability to invoke dynamic PL/SQL blocks can be useful for application extension and customization where the module to be executed is determined dynamically at runtime.
- To execute the `EXECUTE IMMEDIATE` statement you have to follow steps A, B, C, D, E, and F as given in the form of comments in Listing 35.2.

Deciding Procedure Execution at Runtime

You can decide the procedure that you want to call at runtime by using the dynamic SQL facility. Listing 35.5 shows how to call procedure using the IF statement. You can achieve the same functionality by constructing procedure name at runtime and calling same using EXECUTE IMMEDIATE, as given in listing 35.6. Let's create a procedure first to add two numbers, as shown in Listing 35.3:

Listing 35.3: Creating a Procedure to Add Two Numbers

```
create or replace procedure compute1(a number, b number)
as
c number;
begin
   c:=a+b;
   dbms_output.put_line('Adds the two nos'||' '||'a+b ='||''||c);
end;
/
```

The output of Listing 35.3 is as follows:

```
Procedure created
```

After creating the procedure, you need to execute it, as shown in the following code snippet:

```
exec compute1(1,2);
```

The output of the preceding code snippet is as follows:

```
Adds the two nos a+b =3

PL/SQL procedure successfully completed
```

Let's create another procedure to compute subtraction of two numbers, as shown in Listing 35.4:

Listing 35.4: Creating a Procedure to Compute Subtraction of Two Numbers

```
create or replace procedure compute2(a number,b number)
as
c number;
begin
   c:=a-b;
   dbms_output.put_line('Substract the two nos'||' '||'a-b        ='||''||c);
end;
/
```

The output of Listing 35.4 is as follows:

```
Procedure created
```

Now execute the procedure, as shown in the following code snippet:

```
exec compute2(1,2);
```

The output of the preceding code snippet is as follows:

```
Substract the two nos a-b  =-1

PL/SQL procedure successfully completed
```

Listing 35.5: Creating a procedure to Compute Addition or Subtraction of Two Numbers (a, b) Using the If Statement

```
create or replace procedure cal(a number,b number,operation number)
as
begin
   if(operation = 1 ) then
          compute1(a,b);
   elsif(operation = 2) then
          compute2(a,b);
```

```
    end if;
end;
/
```

The output of Listing 35.5 is as follows:

```
Procedure created
```

After creating the procedure, invoking it to compute addition of numbers, as shown in the following code snippet:

```
begin cal(12,3,1); end;
/
```

The output of the preceding code snippet is as follows:

```
Adds the two nos a+b =15
PL/SQL procedure successfully completed.
```

Invoke the procedure to compute subtraction of numbers, as shown in the following code snippet:

```
begin CAL(12,3,2); end;
/
```

The output of the preceding code snippet is as follows:

```
Adds the two nos a+b =15

PL/SQL procedure successfully completed
```

In Listing 35.5, if `operation = 1`, the procedure `CAL` calls `COMPUTE1`. If `operation = 2`, the procedure CAL calls `COMPUTE2`. The preceding code is not extensible since the procedure `CAL` needs to be updated every time a new operation is added.

Listing 35.6: Creating the CAL Procedure Using Dynamic SQL

```
create or replace procedure cal(a number,b number,operation number)
as
begin
  execute immediate
  'begin
        compute' || to_char(operation)||'(:1,:2);
  end;'
  using a,b;
end;
/
```

The output of Listing 35.6 is as follows:

```
Procedure Created
```

Now, execute the procedure, as shown in the following code snippet:

```
exec cal(1,2,1);
```

The output of the preceding code snippet is as follows:

```
Adds the two nos a+b =3

PL/SQL procedure successfully completed
```

In Listing 35.6, the `EXECUTE IMMEDIATE statement` is used for executing dynamic SQL. It is called native dynamic SQL and is more readable than the `DBMS_SQL` package. It prepares a string and executes it immediately. The string is enclosed within quotes.

DML operations using Dynamic SQL

You can use dynamic sql to execute Data Manipulation Language (DML) statements. In the following example UPDATE statement is dynamically constructed at runtime and executed.

Listing 35.7: Creating Department table

```
create table department(empno number, dept varchar2(20));
```

Result:

```
Table created
```

Inserting values

```
insert into department values(1,'account');
```

Result:

```
1 row created
```

Inserting values

```
insert into department values(2,'account');
```

Result:

```
1 row created
```

Inserting values

```
insert into department values(3,'management');
```

Result:

```
1 row created
```

Inserting values

```
INSERT INTO DEPARTMENT VALUES(4,'MANAGEMENT');
```

Result:

```
1 row created
```

Inserting values

```
insert into department values(5,'personnel');
```

Result:

```
1 row created
```

Inserting values

```
insert into department values(6,'personnel');
```

Result:

```
1 row created
```

Listing 35.8 shows how to create or replace a procedure:

Listing 35.8: Creating or Replacing the salary_raise Procedure

```
create or replace procedure salary_raise (incr number)   is    type
  dept_array_type is table of number
       index by binary_integer;
            str varchar2(200);
            dep_array dept_array_type;
            eno1 number;
      begin
          select empno bulk collect into dep_array
          from department where dept ='account';
       for i in dep_array.first..dep_array.last loop
         eno1:=dep_array(i);
          str :='update emp1  set salary = salary +:incr'||' '
          || ' where empno =:eno1';
          execute immediate str using incr,eno1;

      end loop;
   end;
     /
```

The output of Listing 35.8 is as follows:

```
Procedure created
```

Listing 35.9 shows how to execute a procedure:

Listing 35.9: Executing the Procedure

```
execute salary_raise(100);
```

The output of Listing 35.9 is as follows:

```
PL/SQL procedure successfully completed
```

Listing 35.8 increments the salary of employees of Account Department by 100 rupees. The increment as well as the `EMPNO` of the `Account` department is unknown until runtime (Listing 35.9).

Using DDL in a PL/SQL Program

`You can also use the EXECUTE IMMEDIATE` statement to perform DDL operations in a PL/SQL program. Let's understand this by creating a table inside a procedure, as shown in Listing 35.10:

Listing 35.10: Creating the EMP_DETAILS Table

```
create or replace procedure ddl_add_table is
begin
   execute immediate
   'create table emp_detail
   (
   ename   varchar2(10),
   city    varchar2(20)
)';
end;
/
```

The output of Listing 35.10 is as follows:

```
Procedure created
```

Now, execute the procedure, as shown in the following code snippet:

```
exec ddl_add_table;
```

The output of the preceding code snippet is as follows:

```
PL/SQL procedure successfully completed
```

Checking the success of the procedure by viewing the table that has been created by this procedure

```
desc emp_detail;
```

The output of the preceding code snippet is as follows:

```
Name                                    Null?    Type
-------------------------------      -------- ---------------------
ENAME                                           VARCHAR2(10)
CITY                                            VARCHAR2(20)
```

Dynamic Single Row Query

You can use the SELECT……INTO statement to get single row value. The statement is dynamically constructed and fired using EXECUTE IMMEDIATE. Let's understand this by creating a function to retrieve single value, as shown in Listing 35.11:

Listing 35.11: Creating a Function to Retrieve the Number of Employees of a Department

```
create or replace function get_employees (dept varchar2)
return number is
str varchar2(300);
num_of_employees number;
begin
```

```
   str := 'select count(*) from
   department where dept = :dept';
   execute immediate str
   into num_of_employees
   using dept;
   return num_of_employees;
end;
/
```

The output of Listing 35.11 is as follows:

```
Function created
```

After creating the function, you need to call it, as shown in the following code snippet:

```
declare
   x number;
begin
   x:= get_employees('ACCOUNT');
   dbms_output.put_line('The no. of emp are:'||' '||x);
end;
/
```

The output of the preceding code snippet is as follows:

```
The no. of emp are: 2

PL/SQL procedure successfully completed
```

Dynamic Multiple Row Query

You can use a cursor to fetch multiple rows using dynamic SQL. The query is constructed in string and cursor is opened using that string. Listing 35.12 shows to fetch multiple rows dynamically:

Listing 35.12: Using a Procedure to List Employee Id and Name Using Multiple Row Query

```
create or replace procedure list_employees(dept1 varchar2) is
type curtype is ref cursor;
c1          curtype;
str      varchar2(300);
name     varchar2(20);
id       number;
begin
   str:='select e.empno,e.ename from emp1 e where
   exists(select * from department d where
   d.dept = :dept1
   and
   e.empno = d.empno)';
   open c1 for str using dept1;
   loop
         fetch c1 into id,name;
         exit when c1%notfound;
         dbms_output.put_line('id:'||' '||id);
         dbms_output.put_line('name:'||' '||name);
   end loop;
   close c1;
end;
/
```

The output of Listing 35.12 is as follows:

```
Procedure created
```

After creating the procedure, you need to call it, as shown in the following code snippet:

```
begin
   list_employees('ACCOUNT');
end;
/
```

The output of the preceding code snippet is as follows:

```
ID: 1
NAME: AMIT
ID: 2
NAME: SUNIL

PL/SQL procedure successfully completed
```

*Native Dynamic SQL and **DBMS_SQL** Packages*

Native dynamic SQL enables you to place dynamic SQL statements directly into the PL/SQL code. These dynamic statements include DML statements, PL/SQL blocks, DDL statements, and transaction control statements. To process native dynamic SQL statements, you can use the `EXECUTE IMMEDIATE` statement. However, to process a multi-row query (`SELECT` statement), you can use the `OPEN-FOR`, `FETCH`, and `CLOSE` statements.

The `DBMS_SQL` package is a PL/SQL library that offers a programmatic API to execute SQL statements dynamically. The `DBMS_SQL` package has programmatic interfaces to open a cursor, parse a cursor, and supply binds. Let's now distinguish between the native dynamic SQL and `DBMS_SQL` packages, as shown in Table 35.1:

Table 35.1: Difference between Native Dynamic SQL and the `DBMS_SQL` Package

Native dynamic SQL	DBMS_SQL
Native dynamic SQL is much simpler to use than the `DBMS_SQL` package. Since it is integrated with SQL, you can use it in the same way that you use static SQL within PL/SQL code.	The `DBMS_SQL` package is not as easy to use as native dynamic SQL. Many procedures and functions must be used in a strict sequence.
Native dynamic SQL is comparable with static SQL because the PL/SQL interpreter has built-in support for native dynamic SQL. Therefore, the performance of the programs using native dynamic SQL is much better than the programs that use the `DBMS_SQL` package.	`The DBMS_SQL` package is based on a procedural API and therefore there are large procedure calls and data copy overhead. For example, when you bind a variable, `DBMS_SQL` copies the bounded variable into its space for later use. Similarly, when `FETCH` executes, the data is copied into the space managed by the `DBMS_SQL` package and then the fetched data is copied one column at a time. Whereas native dynamic SQL bundles the statement preparation, binding and execution steps into a single operation, which minimizes the data copying and procedure call overhead and improves performance.
Native dynamic SQL provides support for `user_defined` types, such as `user_defined` objects, collections, and `REF`.	The `DBMS_SQL` package does not support these `user_defined` types.
Native dynamic SQL and static SQL both support fetching records.	`DBMS_SQL` package does not support fetching records.

Table 35.1: Difference between Native Dynamic SQL and the DBMS_SQL Package

Native dynamic SQL	DBMS_SQL
Native dynamic SQL is not supported in client-side programs.	Currently, the DBMS_SQL package is supported in client-side programs. Every call to the DBMS_SQL package from the client-side program translates to a PL/SQL remote procedure call, these calls occur when you need to bind a variable, define a variable, or execute a statement.
Native dynamic SQL does not have the DESCRIBE facility.	The DESCRIBE_COLUMNS procedure in the DBMS_SQL package can be used to describe the columns for a cursor opened and parsed through DBMS_SQL.
Native dynamic SQL only supports a RETURNING clause if a single row is returned.	The DBMS_SQL package supports statements with a RETURNING clause that update or delete multiple rows.
Native dynamic SQL does not support SQL statements greater than 32 KB.	DBMS_SQL supports SQL statements greater than 32 KB.

Listing 35.13 shows how to create a procedure using native dynamic SQL to insert values into a table:

Listing 35.13: Procedure Using Native Dynamic SQL to Insert Values into a Table

```
create or replace procedure insert_into_table (
table_name  varchar2,
empno             number,
name      varchar2,
sal       number) is
str       varchar2(200);
begin
  str := 'insert into ' ||
  table_name || ' values
  (:empno, :name, :sal)';
  execute immediate str
  using
  empno,name,sal;
end;
/
```

The output of Listing 35.13 is as follows:

```
Procedure created
```

After creating the procedure, you need to call the procedure, as shown in the following code snippet:

```
begin
  insert_into_table('EMP1',6,'SUMIT',1200);
end;
/
```

The output of the preceding code snippet is as follows:

```
PL/SQL procedure successfully completed
```

Now, execute the select command to check whether the value has been inserted in the table or not, as shown in the following code snippet:

```
Select * from emp1;
```

The output of the preceding code snippet is as follows:

```
  EMPNO ENAME                    SALARY
------- -------------------- ----------
      1 AMIT                       1100
```

```
        2 SUNIL                    2100
        3 LALIT                    2000
        4 AJAY                     4000
        5 RAVI                     3000
        6 ABHAY                    4000
        6 SUMIT                    1200
```

NOTE

Whether you use native dynamic SQL or DBMS_SQL, you can improve performance by using bind variables, because bind variables allow Oracle to share single cursor for multiple SQL statements. The parse procedure parses the SQL statement only once. Therefore, the statement can be used multiple times with different binding variables.

Listing 35.14 shows the code to create ARRAY_TYPE in DBMS_SQL:

Listing 35.14: Creating ARRAY_TYPE in the DBMS_SQL Package

```
create type array_type is
varray(100) of varchar2(50);
/
```

The output of Listing 35.14 is as follows:

```
Type created
```

Creating table Table1 for storing sample data

```
create table table1(ename varchar2(20));
```

The output of the preceding code snippet is as follows:

```
Table created
```

```
insert into table1 values('a')
/
insert into table1 values('b')
/
```

Creating table Table2

```
create table table2(ename varchar2(20));
```

The output of the preceding code snippet is as follows:

```
Table created
```

```
create or replace procedure copy_ename
(table1 varchar2,
enamecol out array_type) as
begin
  execute immediate
  'begin
        select ename bulk collect into :tab
        from ' || table1 || '; ok
  end;'
  using out enamecol;
end;
/
```

The output of the preceding code snippet is as follows:

```
Procedure created
```

Listing 35.15 shows how to use a procedure to copy the column of one table into another table:

Listing 35.15: Using the copy_ename1 Procedure to Copy the data from one table to another

```
                                --insert the 'ename' column into another
                                --table table2
create or replace procedure copy_ename1
(table1 varchar2, table2 varchar2) is
```

```
enamecol  array_type;
begin
        copy_ename(table1,enamecol);
  execute immediate
  'begin
        forall i in :first .. :last
         insert into ' || table2 || ' values (:tab(i));
  end;'
  using enamecol.first, enamecol.last, enamecol;
end;
/
```

The output of Listing 35.15 is as follows:

```
Procedure created
```

The following code snippet shows the code to execute the copy_ename1 procedure:

```
begin
copy_ename1('table1','table2');
end;
/
```

The output of the preceding code snippet is as follows:

```
PL/SQL procedure successfully completed
```

Listing 35.16 shows how to insert a row in a table using a procedure:

Listing 35.16: Inserting a Row in the Department Table Using a Procedure

```
create or replace procedure insert_dbms_sql(empnumber number,deptname varchar2)
as
str varchar2(200);
cursor1 number;
rows_processed number;
begin
  str := 'insert into department values (:empno, :dname)';
    cursor1 := dbms_sql.open_cursor;
  dbms_sql.parse(cursor1, str, dbms_sql.native);
  dbms_sql.bind_variable
  (cursor1, ':empno', empnumber);
  dbms_sql.bind_variable
  (cursor1, ':dname', deptname);
  rows_processed := dbms_sql.execute(cursor1); -- execute
  dbms_sql.close_cursor(cursor1); -- close
end;
/
```

The output of Listing 35.16 is as follows:

```
Procedure created
```

Now, execute the `INSERT_DBMS_SQL` procedure, as shown in the following code snippet:

```
exec insert_dbms_sql(12,'PERSONNEL');
```

The output of the preceding code snippet is as follows:

```
PL/SQL procedure successfully completed
```

Now, execute the select command to check the success of the procedure, that is, whether the value has been inserted into the `department` table, as shown in the following code snippet:

```
select * from department;
```

The output of the preceding code snippet is as follows:

```
     EMPNO DEPT
---------- --------------------
         1 ACCOUNT
```

```
         2 ACCOUNT
         3 MANAGEMENT
         4 MANAGEMENT
         5 PERSONNEL
         6 PERSONNEL
        12 PERSONNEL

7 rows selected
```

The last row has been entered through the procedure.

Let's now learn how to update a table using a procedure, as shown in Listing 35.17:

Listing 35.17: Updating the Department Table, Setting dept=Personnel and Returning the Number of Rows Updated

```
create or replace procedure update_dbms_sql(deptname varchar2) as
empid_array dbms_sql.number_table;
cursor1 number;
str varchar2(200);
rows_processed number;
begin
  str := 'update department
    set dept = :newdept
  returning empno into :id';
  cursor1 := dbms_sql.open_cursor;
  dbms_sql.parse
  (cursor1, str, dbms_sql.native);
                                --supply binds
  dbms_sql.bind_variable
  (cursor1, ':newdept', deptname);
  dbms_sql.bind_array
  (cursor1, ':id', empid_array);
                                --execute cursor
  rows_processed := dbms_sql.execute(cursor1);
                                --get returning column into out bind array
  dbms_sql.variable_value
  (cursor1, ':id', empid_array);
                                --display the empoyee id
  for i in empid_array.first..empid_array.last loop
  dbms_output.put_line('the empid of updated department
  is'||empid_array(i));
  end loop;
  dbms_output.put_line('the number of rows processed are:' ||
  rows_processed);
  dbms_sql.close_cursor(cursor1);
end;
/
```

The output of Listing 35.17 is as follows:

```
Procedure created
```

Now, execute the procedure, as shown in the following code snippet:

```
exec update_dbms_sql('personnel');
```

The output of the preceding code snippet is as follows:

```
The EmpId of updated department     is1
The EmpId of updated department     is2
The EmpId of updated department     is3
The EmpId of updated department     is4
The EmpId of updated department     is5
```

```
The EmpId of updated department      is6
The EmpId of updated department      is12
The number of rows processed are:7

PL/SQL procedure successfully completed
```

The **DBMS_SESSION** Package

The DBMS_SESSION package provides access to SQL alter session and sets role statements.

The DBMS_SESSION package provides various procedures and functions, which are described in the next section.

The **DBMS_SESSION.SET_ROLE** Procedure

The DBMS_SESSION.SET_ROLE procedure enables or disables roles. It is equivalent to `SET_ROLE SQL` statement. The syntax of the DBMS_SESSION.SET_ROLE procedure is as follows:

```
dbms_session.set_role(rolename varchar2);
```

The **DBMS_SESSION.SET_SQL_TRACE** Procedure

The DBMS_SESSION.SET_SQL_TRACE procedure turns the tracing on or off. The syntax of the DBMS_SESSION.SET_SQL_TRACE procedure is as follows:

```
dbms_session.set_sql_trace (tracesql boolean);
```

The **DBMS_SESSION.SET_NLS** Procedure

The DBMS_SESSION.SET_NLS procedure sets up your national language support. The syntax of the DBMS_SESSION.SET_NLS procedure is as follows:

```
dbms_session.set_nls
(parameter varchar2,              --the parameter name must begin with nls
parameter_value varchar2);
```

The **DBMS_SESSION.CLOSE_DATABASE_LINK** Procedure

The DBMS_SESSION.CLOSE_DATABASE_LINK procedure closes the database link (`dblink`). The syntax of the DBMS_SESSION.CLOSE_DATABASE_LINK procedure is as follows:

```
dbms_session.close_database_link (dblink varchar2);
```

The **DBMS_SESSION.RESET_PACKAGE** Procedure

The DBMS_SESSION.RESET_PACKAGE procedure frees the memory used by functions, packages, and procedures, which run in the session. In packages, memory holds the current state of package variables. Using the `RESET_PACKAGE` procedure, the memory held by these variables is made free. This procedure is used to reliably restart a program that failed in the session. It ensures that all package variables are reset to their initial values. This procedure frees the memory only when the PL/SQL call that made the invocation has finished running. The syntax of the DBMS_SESSION.RESET_PACKAGE procedure is as follows:

```
DBMS_SESSION.RESET_PACKAGE;
```

The **DBMS_SESSION.UNIQUE_SESSION_ID** Function

The DBMS_SESSION.UNIQUE_SESSION_ID function returns an identifier that is unique to all the sessions, which are currently connected to the database. The syntax of the DBMS_SESSION.UNIQUE_SESSION_ID function is as follows:

```
dbms_session.unique_session_id
return varchar2;
```

It returns id up to `24` bytes.

The **DBMS_SESSION.IS_ROLE_ENABLED** Function

The DBMS_SESSION.IS_ROLE_ENABLED function returns TRUE if the specified role is enabled in the session. The syntax of the DBMS_SESSION.IS_ROLE_ENABLED function is as follows:

```
dbms_session.is_role_enabled (role_name varchar2)
return boolean;
```

The **DBMS_SESSION.IS_SESSION_ALIVE** Function

The DBMS_SESSION.IS_SESSION_ALIVE function returns TRUE if the specified session is alive. The syntax of the DBMS_SESSION.IS_SESSION_ALIVE function is as follows:

```
dbms_session.is_session_alive (unique_session_id varchar2)
return boolean;
```

The **DBMS_SESSION.SET_CLOSE_CACHED_OPEN_CURSORS** Procedure

The DBMS_SESSION.SET_CLOSE_CACHED_OPEN_CURSORS procedure turns `closed_cached_open_cursors` ON or OFF. The syntax of the DBMS_SESSION.SET_CLOSE_CACHED_OPEN_CURSORS procedure is as follows:

```
CLOSE_CACHED_OPEN_CURSORS.
DBMS_SESSION.SET_CLOSE_CACHED_OPEN_CURSORS (closecursors BOOLEAN);
```

The **DBMS_SESSION.FREE_UNUSED_USER_MEMORY** Procedure

The DBMS_SESSION.FREE_UNUSED_USER_MEMORY procedure reclaims the unused memory after performing the operations that required large memory for processing. You can monitor the user memory by tracking the statistics session UGA (User Global Area) memory and session PGA (Private Global Area) memory in the `v$sesstat` or `v$statname` fixed views. The syntax of the DBMS_SESSION.FREE_UNUSED_USER_MEMORY procedure is as follows:

```
DBMS_SESSION.FREE_UNUSED_USER_MEMORY;
```

In dedicated servers, it returns the unused PGA and session memory to the operating system. Session memory is allocated from the PGA. In MTS (Multithreaded Server) server, it returns the unused session memory to `shared_pool`. The session memory is allocated from the `shared_pool`.

When memory is allocated for some operation, for example, to scan a table or to do some sort operations, then only that type of operation can reuse the allocated memory. Therefore, if the operation is complete and memory is no longer in use, you can call this procedure to free the unused memory.

Memory is allocated implicitly for index tables. As the number of elements in table increases, more memory is allocated by the database. The time period for which these tables acquire memory, depends on how they are declared. Indexed tables declared in a package are globally declared. These tables are allocated memory from session memory and remain in use as long as the user logs in. Indexed tables declared in PL/SQL blocks, procedures, and functions allocate memory from PGA.

This memory is in use when the user is running the procedure or function. After the procedure or function has finished running, this memory becomes available for other locally declared indexed tables. This procedure is useful especially for globally declared index tables.

The **DBMS_SESSION.SET_CONTEXT** Procedure

The DBMS_SESSION.SET_CONTEXT procedure sets or resets the value of the context attribute. Listing 35.18 shows the use of the DBMS_SESSION.SET_CONTEXT procedure:

Listing 35.18: Writing Header for the SET_CONTEXT Procedure in DBMS_SESSION Package

```
procedure dbms_session.set_context (namespace varchar2,
                                   --(30 bytes)name of the namespace to use in
                                   --app.context
attribute_name varchar2,           --(30 bytes)name of attribute to set
value varchar2);                   --value of the attribute(256 bytes)
                                   -- following code sets date format
```

Following is sample code for using DBMS_SESSION package.

To execute `DBMS_SESSION.SET_NLS` procedure

```
begin
dbms_session.set_nls('nls_date_format','''dd-month-yyyy''');
dbms_output.put_line(to_char(sysdate));
end;
/
```

The output of the preceding code snippet is as follows:

```
30-AUGUST-2006

PL/SQL procedure successfully completed
```

Displaying system date

```
select sysdate from dual;
```

The output of the preceding code snippet is as follows:

```
SYSDATE
-----------------
30-AUGUST-2006
```

The **DBMS_PIPE** Package

The `DBMS_PIPE` package is used to communicate between sessions. The message is sent using the send_message procedure and it is received by using the receive_message procedure. Before sending the message, it is packed in queue. After receiving the message, it is unpacked. Listing 35.19 shows the use of the `DBMS_PIPE` package:

Listing 35.19: Creating the SendMessage Procedure

```
--this is done from terminal 1
create or replace procedure sendmessage(msg varchar2) as
status_id  number;
begin
   dbms_pipe.pack_message(length(msg));
   dbms_pipe.pack_message(msg);
   status_id := dbms_pipe.send_message('send_message');
   if status_id != 0
   then
         raise_application_error(-20099, 'send error');
   end if;
end sendmessage;
/
```

The output of Listing 35.19 is as follows:

```
Procedure created
```

Now, execute the procedure, as shown in the following code snippet:

```
exec sendmessage('hello');
```

The output of the preceding code snippet is as follows:

```
PL/SQL procedure successfully completed
```

In Listing 35.19, we have created a procedure named `sendmessage`, which sends the message when it is executed.

NOTE

You should be granted privilege to execute on DBMS_PIPE by user sys.

Listing 35.20 shows how to receive messages:

Listing 35.20: Receiving Message by PL/SQL blocks

```
--This is done from terminal 2

declare
len number;
str varchar2(100);
status number;
begin
   status:=dbms_pipe.receive_message('send_message',1);
   IF status = 0
   THEN
          DBMS_PIPE.UNPACK_MESSAGE(len);
          DBMS_PIPE.UNPACK_MESSAGE(str);
          dbms_output.put_line(str);
   END IF;
   if status != 0
   then
          dbms_output.put_line('No Message Available'||'  '||'status is'||'
          '||status);
   end if;
end;
/
```

The output of Listing 35.20 is as follows:

```
hello

PL/SQL procedure successfully completed
```

`DBMS_PIPE` is used to communicate between two sessions. Therefore, to show the working of `DBMS_PIPE`, we have to execute the same procedure in two different sessions.

TERMINAL 1:

```
exec sendmessage('this is test');
```

Result:

```
PL/SQL procedure successfully completed
```

TERMINAL 2:

```
-- Execute program Listing 35.20
```

You should remember the following points about DBMS_PIPE:

- When two or more sessions in the same instance wants to communicate with each other, the `DBMS_PIPE` package is used.
- Information sent through Oracle pipes is buffered in SGA. All the information in the pipes is lost when the instance is shutdown.
- Pipes are independent of transactions.
- Public pipes can be created either implicitly or explicitly.
- The implicit public pipes are created when they are first referenced, and destroyed when they contain no data. You can create an explicit pipe by using the `CREATE_PIPE` function with the private flag set to `false, as shown in the following code snippet:`

```
declare
x number;
begin
   x:=dbms_pipe.create_pipe('pipe_msg',8192,false);
```

```
   dbms_output.put_line(x);
end;
/
```

The output of the preceding code snippet is as follows:

```
0

PL/SQL procedure successfully completed
```

You can deallocate the explicitly created pipes using the `remove_pipe` function. The domain of the public pipe is the schema in which it is created. The following code snippet shows how to deallocate an explicitly created pipe:

```
declare
x number;
begin
   x:=dbms_pipe.remove_pipe('pipe_msg');
   dbms_output.put_line(x);
end;
/
```

The output of the preceding code snippet is as follows:

```
0

PL/SQL procedure successfully completed
```

Writing and Reading Pipes

You should remember the following points to write and read pipes:

- Public pipes are asynchronous. Any schema object can write the pipe, if they have the `execute` privilege and know the name of the pipe.
- Once you have read the buffer, information is emptied from the buffer and becomes unavailable to the readers of the same pipe.
- The sending session uses the `PACK_MESSAGE` procedure to build a message. This procedure adds the message to the session's local message buffer. The information in this buffer is sent by calling the `SEND_MESSAGE` function along with the pipe name to be used to send the message.
- The process, which has to receive the message, calls the `RECEIVE_MESSAGE` function. It then receives the message along with the pipe name from which it has to receive the message.
- The process, which called the `RECEIVE_MESSAGE` function, calls the `UNPACK_MESSAGE` function to access each of the items in the message.

Private Pipes

- The `CREATE_PIPE` function can explicitly create private pipes. Once created, these pipes reside in the shared memory and you have to explicitly deallocate them using the `REMOVE_PIPE` function, when you do not need them.
- Private pipes are accessed by the user who creates it, as well as the users connected as `SYSDBA` or `INTERNAL`.

Uses of Pipes

Some of the uses of pipes are as follows:

- You can communicate with the user written services that are external to RDBMS. The requestor of the service does not need to block a waiting reply. The requestor can check the response at a later time. The service can be written in any language that Oracle supports.

- Triggers and stored procedures can send debugging information to a pipe. Another session can keep reading out of the pipe and display it on the screen or write it to a file.

DBMS_PIPE Procedures and Functions

DBMS_PIPE has various procedures and functions. All these functions are described in the next section.

The **DBMS_PIPE.CREATE_PIPE** Function

The DBMS_PIPE.CREATE_PIPE function explicitly creates a public or private pipe. The syntax of the DBMS_PIPE.CREATE_PIPE function is as follows:

```
dbms_pipe.create_pipe (
pipe_name    in varchar2,
max_pipe_size in integer default 8192,
private_public
in boolean default true) return integer;
```

While using the DBMS_PIPE.CREATE_PIPE function, remember the following points:

- The pipe name should not be greater than 128 bytes.
- Private/Public in CREATE_PIPE specifies the type. If true, it creates a private pipe.

*The **CREATE_PIPE** Function returns:*

- 0, if the pipe already exists and the user creating it is authorized to do.
- ORA-23322 error, indicating a naming conflict error, if a pipe with the same name exists and is created by a different user.

The **DBMS_PIPE.PACK_MESSAGE** Procedure

The DBMS_PIPE.PACK_MESSAGE procedure builds your message into local message buffer. To send a message, first make one or more calls to PACK_MESSAGE. Then call SEND_MESSAGE to send the message in the local buffer on the named pipe. The syntax of the DBMS_PIPE.PACK_MESSAGE procedure is as follows:

```
dbms_pipe.pack_message (item  in  data_type);
```

In the preceding syntax, data_type can be date, nchar, number, raw, or rowid.

The **DBMS_PIPE.SEND_MESSAGE** Function

The DBMS_PIPE.SEND_MESSAGE function is used to send messages to the specified pipe. The syntax of the DBMS_PIPE.SEND_MESSAGE function is as follows:

```
dbms_pipe.send_message (
pipe_name in varchar2,
timeout in integer default maxwait,
max_pipe_size in integer default 8192)
return integer;
```

The SEND_MESSAGE function returns:

- 0, if the pipe exists and the user creating it is authorized to do it.
- 1, if it cannot get a lock on the pipe, or because the pipe is too full to be used.
- 3, if an interrupt occurs. It means the pipe is implicitly created and is empty.

The **DBMS_PIPE.RECEIVE_MESSAGE** Function

The DBMS_PIPE.RECEIVE_MESSAGE function receives the message into local message buffer. When you receive a message it is removed from the pipe, that is, the message can only be received once. If the pipe you specify, when you call RECEIVE_MESSAGE, does not exist, Oracle implicitly creates the pipe and waits to receive the message. If the message does not arrive within a timeout interval, then the call returns and the pipe is removed. The syntax of the DBMS_PIPE.RECEIVE_MESSAGE function is as follows:

```
dbms_pipe.receive_message (
pipe_name in varchar2,
max_time_out in integer default max_wait)
return integer;
```

The RECEIVE_MESSAGE function returns:

- **0**—Success
- **1**—Time out
- **2**—Record in the pipe is too large for the buffer
- **3**—An interrupt occurred

The **DBMS_PIPE.NEXT_ITEM_TYPE** Function

The DBMS_PIPE.NEXT_ITEM_TYPE function determines the next item type in the buffer. The syntax of the DBMS_PIPE.NEXT_ITEM_TYPE function is as follows:

```
dbms_pipe.next_item_type
return integer;
```

The NEXT_ITEM_TYPE function returns integer according to type of data. The number and corresponding type is described as follows.

- **0**—No more items
- **6**—Number
- **9**—Varchar2
- **11**—Rowid
- **12**—Date
- **23**—Raw

The **DBMS_PIPE.UNPACK_MESSAGE** Procedure

The DBMS_PIPE.UNPACK_MESSAGE procedure is used to retrieve the items from the buffer. The syntax of the DBMS_PIPE.UNPACK_MESSAGE procedure is as follows:

```
dbms_pipe.unpack_message (item out data_type);
```

In the preceding syntax:

- `data_type` may be any of the `varchar2`, `nchar`, `date`, `raw`, and `rowid`
- `Item` is an argument to receive the next unpacked item from the local message buffer

The **DBMS_PIPE.PURGE** Procedure

The DBMS_PIPE.PURGE procedure clears the content of the specified pipe. An empty implicitly created pipe is deallocated by SGA using the LRU (Least recently used) policy. Therefore, the `PURGE` procedure can be used to free the memory used by the pipe. When `PURGE` calls `RECEIVE_MESSAGE`, the local buffer might be overwritten with messages as they are purged from the pipe.

The **DBMS_PIPE.RESET_BUFFER** Procedure

The DBMS_PIPE.RESET_BUFFER procedure resets the `PACKED_MESSAGE` and `UNPACKED_MESSAGE` indicators to `0`. As all pipes share a single buffer, you might find it useful to reset the buffer before using a new pipe.

The **DBMS_PIPE.UNIQUE_SESSION_NAME** Function

The DBMS_PIPE.UNIQUE_SESSION_NAME function receives a name that is unique among all the sessions connected to the database. Multiple calls to this function from the same session returns the same value. The syntax of the DBMS_PIPE.UNIQUE_SESSION_NAME function is as follows:

```
dbms_pipe.unique_session_name
return varchar2;
```

The **DBMS_ALERT** Package

`DBMS_ALERT` is used to give signals to other sessions. When there is any DML operation on `emp1` table, the following trigger fires and sends a message to the `ALERTTEST` procedure. Before this trigger is created, you must grant permission over the `DBMS_ALERT` package. For this, first you must connect to the database, as shown in the following code snippet:

```
connect sys/<password> as sysdba;
```

The output of the preceding code snippet is as follows:

```
Connected
```

After connecting to the database, you can grant the permission, as shown in the following code snippet:

```
grant execute on dbms_package  to scott;
```

The output of the preceding code snippet is as follows:

```
Grant succeeded
```

Now, connect to `scott` and then create the trigger, as shown in Listing 35.21:

Listing 35.21: Creating the alerttrigger1 Trigger

```
create or replace trigger alerttrigger1 after insert or update or                    delete on
  scott.emp
begin
  dbms_alert.signal('alert_demo', 'this is a test');
end;
/
```

The output of Listing 35.21 is as follows:

```
Trigger created
```

Listing 35.22 shows how to create a procedure:

Listing 35.22: Creating procedure ALERTTEST to receive alert

```
create or replace procedure alerttest
as
x number;
y varchar2(100);
begin
  dbms_alert.register('alert_demo');
  dbms_alert.waitone('alert_demo',y , x,1);
  if x=1 then
         dbms_output.put_line(x);
  else
         dbms_output.put_line('the alert occurred '||x||y);
  end if;
end;
/
```

The output of Listing 35.22 is as follows:

```
Procedure created
```

Now, execute the procedure, as shown in the following code snippet:

```
exec alerttest;
```

The output of the preceding code snippet is as follows:

```
1

PL/SQL procedure successfully completed
```

Listing 35.23 shows how to insert values into emp1:

Listing 35.23: Inserting Values into emp1 to fire trigger created in listing 35.21

```
insert into emp1 values (2,'sunil',4000)
/
```

The output of Listing 35.23 is as follows:

```
1 row created
```

Now, commit a transaction, as shown in the following code snippet:

```
commit
/
```

The output of the preceding code snippet is as follows:

```
Commit complete
```

After committing the transaction, executing the `alerttest` procedure, as shown in the following code snippet:

```
                                        --From other terminal
begin alerttest;
end;
/
```

The output of the preceding code snippet is as follows:

```
1

PL/SQL procedure successfully completed
```

Some of the points to remember while using the DBMS_ALERT package are as follows:

- The package provides an asynchronous notification of an application when a database event occurs.
- When this package is used along with a trigger, an application can cause itself to be notified, whenever values of interest in the database are changed.
- Alerts are transaction based, that is, the waiting session does not get notified until the transaction calling the alert `COMMITS`.
- The application can register multiple events and then wait for any one of them to be notified, using the `WAITANY` procedure. An optional parameter `TIMEOUT` can be given to the `WAITONE /WAITANY` procedure. The signalling session can send the message to the waiting session.
- Old alerts are discarded when the alerts are signalled more often than the corresponding application wait calls. The application always gets the latest alert based on the transaction commit times.
- If the application does not require transaction based alerts, then `DBMS_PIPE` may be useful.
- If the transaction is rolled back after the call to signal, then no alert occurs. Oracle is event driven, that is, there are no pooling loops. However, they can occur in the following cases:
  - If the database is running in shared mode, then pooling loop is required to check for alerts from another instance.
  - When you are using the `WAITANY` procedure and if the session does a signal but does not commit within one second of the signal, then a pooling loop is required so that the uncommitted alert does not camouflage other alerts.

NOTE

Alert name begins with ORA$ and they must be of 30 bytes or less. Alert name is case sensitive.

The DBMS_ALERT package provides various procedures, which are as follows:

- DBMS_ALERT.REGISTER
- DBMS_ALERT.REMOVE
- DBMS_ALERT.REMOVEALL

- DBMS_ALERT.SET_DEFAULTS
- DBMS_ALERT.SIGNAL
- DBMS_ALERT.WAITANY
- DBMS_ALERT.WAITONE

Let's discuss these in detail.

The **DBMS_ALERT.REGISTER** Procedure

The DBMS_ALERT.REGISTER procedure registers the named alert for the session. The name of the alert is the IN parameter. The session can register any number of alerts. The syntax of the DBMS_ALERT.REGISTER procedure is as follows:

```
dbms_alert.register(name in varchar2);
```

The **DBMS_ALERT.REMOVE** Procedure

The DBMS_ALERT.REMOVE procedure is used to deregister alerts. The syntax of the DBMS_ALERT.REMOVE procedure is as follows:

```
dbms_alert.remove(name in varchar2);
```

The **DBMS_ALERT.REMOVEALL** Procedure

The DBMS_ALERT.REMOVEALL procedure removes all the alerts for a session from the registration list. The syntax of the DBMS_ALERT.REMOVEALL procedure is as follows:

```
dbms_alert.removeall;
```

This procedure is automatically called when the DBMS_ALERT package is referenced first in the session. This procedure always performs a COMMIT.

The **DBMS_ALERT.SET_DEFAULTS** Procedure

The DBMS_ALERT.SET_DEFAULTS procedure is used to set the pooling interval in case the pooling loop is required. The syntax of the DBMS_ALERT.SET_DEFAULTS procedure is as follows:

```
dbms_alert.set_default(interval in number);
```

In the preceding syntax, interval is the time in seconds to sleep between pools. The default time interval is 5 seconds.

The **DBMS_ALERT.SIGNAL** Procedure

The DBMS_ALERT.SIGNAL procedure signals the alert. The effect of signal occurs only when the transaction, in which it is called, commits. All the sessions that have registered this alert are notified. If the sessions are currently waiting, then they are notified. If they are not, then they are notified the next time they do a wait call. Multiple sessions can concurrently perform signals on the same alert.

Each session, as it signals alert, blocks the other session until it commits, an effect of serializing the transaction. The syntax of the DBMS_ALERT.SIGNAL procedure is as follows:

```
dbms_alert.signal (
name in varchar2,
message in varchar2);           --message can be up to 1800 bytes
```

The **DBMS_ALERT.WAITANY** Procedure

The DBMS_ALERT.WAITANY procedure waits for an alert to occur for any of the alerts for which the current session is registered. The same session that waits for the alert may also signal the alert. You must commit transaction after the signal and before the wait; otherwise, DBMS_LOCK.REQUEST, which is called by DBMS_ALERT, returns status 4. The syntax of the DBMS_ALERT.WAITANY procedure is as follows:

```
dbms_alert.waitany (
name      out  varchar2,
message   out  varchar2,
status    out  integer,
max_time   in   number default maxwait);
```

This message received is provided by a signal call.

The WAITANY procedure returns:

- 0, if alert occurs
- 1, if time-out occurs
- MAX_TIME, maximum time for alert to occur. If no alert occurs before MAX_TIME, then this returns status 1

The **DBMS_ALERT.WAITONE** Procedure

The DBMS_ALERT.WAITONE procedure waits for the specific alert to occur. The syntax of the DBMS_ALERT.WAITONE procedure is as follows:

```
dbms_alert.waitone (
name      out  varchar2,         //--name of the alert to wait for.
message   out  varchar2,
status    out  integer,
max_time   in   number default maxwait);
```

The **DBMS_JOB** Package

The DBMS_JOB package subprograms schedule and manages jobs in the job queue. Listing 35.24 shows the use of the DBMS_JOB package:

Listing 35.24: Using the DBMS_JOB Package

```
declare
jobno number;
begin
  dbms_job.submit(jobno,
     'insert into empl(empno,salary)
     values(1,2000);',sysdate,'sysdate+1/24');
     commit;
     dbms_output.put_line(jobno);
end;
/
```

The output of Listing 35.24 is as follows:

```
49 - jobno generated by procedure submit

PL/SQL procedure successfully completed
```

The DBMS_JOB package provides various procedures, which are as follows:

- DBMS_JOB.SUBMIT
- DBMS_JOB.REMOVE(jobno)
- DBMS_JOB.NEXT_DATE(jobno,date)
- DBMS_JOB.RUN(jobno)
- DBMS_JOB.BROKEN(jobno,flag boolean,date)
- DBMS_JOB.INTERVAL

Let's discuss these in detail.

The **DBMS_JOB.SUBMIT** Procedure

The DBMS_JOB.SUBMIT procedure submits the new job. It selects the job number from the sys.jobseq sequence.

The **DBMS_JOB.REMOVE(jobno)** Procedure

The DBMS_JOB.REMOVE(jobno) procedure removes the job from the job queue. For example, the following code snippet shows how to remove job having number 3:

```
execute dbms_job.remove(3);
```

The **DBMS_JOB.NEXT_DATE(jobno,date)** Procedure

The DBMS_JOB.NEXT_DATE(jobno,date) procedure changes time when the existing job next runs. The syntax of the DBMS_JOB.NEXT_DATE(jobno,date) procedure is as follows:

```
begin
  dbms_job.next_date(3,sysdate);
end;
```

The **DBMS_JOB.RUN(jobno)** Procedure

The DBMS_JOB.RUN(jobno) procedure runs the specified job. The syntax of the DBMS_JOB.RUN(jobno) procedure is as follows:

```
execute dbms_job.run(3);
```

The **DBMS_JOB.BROKEN(jobno,flag boolean,date)** Procedure

The DBMS_JOB.BROKEN(jobno,flag boolean,date) procedure sets the broken flag. The broken jobs are never run. If the flag is having value FALSE then job can be scheduled again. The syntax of the DBMS_JOB.BROKEN(jobno,flag boolean,date) procedure is as follows:

```
execute dbms_job.broken(3,true, sysdate+2 );
```

The **DBMS_JOB.INTERVAL** Procedure

The DBMS_JOB.INTERVAL procedure changes the interval when a job runs. The syntax of the DBMS_JOB.INTERVAL procedure is as follows:

```
dbms_job.interval (
    job        in  integer,
    interval   in  varchar2);
```

The **UTL_FILE** Package

You can read or write operating system files similar to files scripted in any other language by using the UTL_FILE package. You can use normal operating system calls while doing this operation, such as FOPEN, FCLOSE, PUT, or PUT_LINE for writing; and GET or GETLINE for reading files. The file pointer has to be given the UTL_FILE type for opening a file, as shown in the following code snippet:

```
file1 utl_file.file_type;
```

You have to give the location of the file in terms of directory and name of file. Also, you need to give the mode in which the file should be opened. Modes can be read, write, or append. The name of directory should be mentioned using initialization parameter, UTL_FILE_DIR; otherwise, FOPEN raises an exception. After opening the file, you can read or write it using the GET and PUT procedures. Once the entire file is read, the next read generates an exception, NO_DATA_FOUND. After reading or writing process is over, you can close the file. Listing 35.25 shows how to create UTL_FILE:

Listing 35.25: Creating UTL_FILE

```
declare
   file1 utl_file.file_type;
   samstr varchar2(100);
   errstr varchar2(1000);
       DIR_TEMP VARCHAR2(30)='C:\TEMP';
begin
                                        --utl_file_dir=/home/oracle8i/tmp
                                        -- utl_file_dir=C:\temp\,C:\TEMP1

   file1 := utl_file.fopen(DIR_TEMP,'sample.txt','r');
   begin
                 loop
                          utl_file.get_line(file1,samstr);
                          dbms_output.put_line('the sample output '||samstr);
                 end loop;
                 exception
                 when no_data_found then
                 dbms_output.put_line('the sample output is complete');
           end;
                                        --dbms_output.put_line('the sample output
                                        --'||samstr);
   utl_file.fclose(file1);
   file1 := utl_file.fopen(DIR_TEMP,'sample.txt','a');
   utl_file.put_line(file1,'The test is passed');
   utl_file.fclose(file1);
   exception
   when others then
   errstr :=sqlerrm;
   dbms_output.put_line(errstr);
end;
/
```

The output of Listing 35.25 is as follows:

```
PL/SQL procedure successfully completed
```

NOTE

To execute this procedure successfully, you need to set parameter UTL_FILE_DIR = c:\temp and put file sample.txt in C:\temp.

Summary

In this chapter, you have learned about the important packages such as DBMS_SQL Package, DBMS_SESSION Package, DBMS_PIPE Package, DBMS_ALERT Package, DBMS_JOB Package, and UTL_FILE Package. In the next chapter, you will learn about object views.

Exercise

1. Give one example of dynamic SQL statement.
2. Write a procedure which counts number of rows in any specified table.
3. How will you read or write operating system file?

36

Object Views

The object views are provided to convert relational designs to object designs. The ordinary view is constructed using conventional tables. The object view has one or more columns with the object type. In the object view, each row has `REF` to access data. The object view can be defined on normal and object tables as well as on normal and object views.

The object identifier has to be constructed on a set of key attributes. These key attributes uniquely identify each row in the base table. If an object is identified from the row identifier (primary key) of the base table, then it is called a Primary Key-based Object Identifier (PKOID). The object identifier has to be specified in the `CREATE VIEW` command.

Listing 36.1 shows the code to create type as an object in the object view:

Listing 36.1: Creating type as an object to be used in the object view

Following type is used to demonstrate concept of object view.

```
create or replace type cust_type as
object (cust_code number(5),
cust_name  varchar2(30),
city varchar2(30),
member function getname return varchar2)
/
```

The output of Listing 36.1 is as follows:

```
Type created
```

The following code snippet shows the code to create type body:

```
create or replace type body cust_type as
member function getname return varchar2 is
begin
return(upper(cust_name));
end;
end;
/
```

The output of the preceding code snippet is given as follows:

```
Type body created
```

The following code snippet shows the code to create the Cust_table table with cust_code, cust_name, and city columns:

```
create table cust_table
(cust_code  number(5),
cust_name varchar2(30),
city  varchar2(30))
/
```

The output of the preceding code snippet is given as follows:

```
Table created
```

The following code snippet shows the code to create a view:

```
create or replace view cust_nagpur of cust_type
with object oid (cust_code) as
select cust_code, cust_name, city
from cust_table
where city = 'NAGPUR'
/
```

The output of the preceding code snippet is given as follows:

```
View created
```

The following code snippet shows the code to insert values into the Cust_table table:

```
insert into cust_table values(1,'ANIL','NAGPUR')
/
```

The output of the preceding code snippet is given as follows:

```
1 row created
```

The following code snippet shows the code to commit the transaction:

```
commit
/
```

The output of the preceding code snippet is given as follows:

```
Commit complete
```

The following code snippet shows the code to retrieve values from the cust_nagpur view:

```
select * from cust_nagpur
/
```

The output of the preceding code snippet is given as follows:

```
CUST_CODE            CUST_NAME           CITY
---------            ----------------    --------------
        1            Anil              Nagpur
```

Listing 36.2 shows the code to use REF with object view

Listing 36.2: Using REF with Object View

```
declare
  x ref cust_type;
  y cust_type;
begin
  select ref(p)
  into x
  from  cust_nagpur p
  where cust_code=1;
  select deref(x)
  into y
  from dual;
  dbms_output.put_line('name is '||y.cust_name);
  dbms_output.put_line('name is '||y.getname);
end;
/
```

In Listing 36.2, object view `cust_nagpur` of object `cust_type` is created. The object identifier is `cust_code`.

`REF` can be used to represent an instance in the object view. Such `REF` is called as primary key-based REF (PKREF). The object can be manipulated through PKREF. The PKREF should not be stored directly in the base table as `REF` attribute of the object column. It is because PKREF contains the foreign key value and it could be large, if composite foreign key is large. If the `WITH OBJECT ID` clause is omitted, then the object identifier of underlying object table is used.

The output of Listing 36.2 is given as follows:

```
name is Anil
name is ANIL

PL/SQL procedure successfully completed
```

Next, let's learn about column types in view.

Column Types in View

Apart from the conventional views, object views support the following column types:

- Object datatype
- Nested table datatype
- REF datatype
- VARRAY datatype
- LOB datatype

Object Datatype

The object datatype can be created using the default constructor of a user-defined type. The view is created in the following code snippet:

```
create or replace view cust_nagpur (cust_nagpur_col)
as
select cust_type (cust_code, cust_name, city)
from cust_table
where city = 'NAGPUR';
```

In the preceding code snippet, the object is of the type, cust_type. The object column is inherently updateable.

The output of the preceding code snippet is given as follows:

```
View created
```

A view is updateable in the following cases:

- The view consists of only one base table
- The constructor is the default constructor
- Every attribute in the constructor is either a simple column or, if it is a nested object then, an updateable default constructor expression
- If the SELECT statement consists of JOIN, GROUP BY, ORDER BY, SET operations, and DISTINCT, then the view is not updateable
- Every attribute of view should be uniquely mapped to the base table column
- If a view is not updateable, then DML operations can be done using INSTEAD OF trigger

Object Expression

You can use object expression while creating views, which are not updateable. Suppose you have created a function, as shown in the following code snippet:

```
CREATE OR REPLACE FUNCTION
new type( cust_code IN NUMBER(5),cust_name IN VARCHAR2(30),city IN VARCHAR2(30))
IS
BEGIN
   .............
   ................
END;
If you create view as

CREATE VIEW  new_view (view_col) As
SELECT  new_type (cust_code, cust_name, city)
From Cust_table;
```

In the preceding code snippet, the view is not updateable, since it is not based on the default constructor.

Views on Object Column

Views can be based on single column of base table, as shown in the following code snippet:

```
CREATE VIEW cust_view (code_col)
AS
SELECT cust_code
FROM cust_table
/
```

In the preceding code snippet, the `FROM` clause can mention the view or base table. The object column can never have `NULL` values because the default constructor always returns an object even if attributes are null.

The output of the preceding code snippet is given as follows:

```
View created
```

Next, let's learn about nested table datatype.

Nested Table Datatype

Nested table is used in cases where one in one row multiple values are stored. The nested table can be constructed using the `CAST` operator to cast the result of a subquery.

Listing 36.3 shows the code to use the cast operator to show one to many relationship between product and customer tables:

Listing 36.3: Using the cast Operator

```
drop table product
/
```

The following code snippet shows the code to create the `product` table:

```
create table product
(productcode number(2) primary key,
 productname varchar2(30))
/
```

The output of the preceding code snippet is given as follows:

```
Table created
```

The following code snippet shows the code to create type, `Cust_type`:

```
create or replace type cust_type as
object (cust_code number(5),
cust_name  varchar2(30),
city varchar2(30),
member function getname return varchar2)
/
```

The output of the preceding code snippet is given as follows:

```
Type created
```

The following code snippet shows the code to create `type_body`:

```
create or replace type body cust_type as
member function getname return varchar2 is
begin
  return(upper(cust_name));
end;
end;
/
```

The output of the preceding code snippet is given as follows:

```
Type body created
```

The following code snippet shows the code to drop the cust_table table:

```
drop table cust_table
/
```

The output of the preceding code snippet is given as follows:

```
Table dropped
```

The following code snippet shows the code to create the `Cust_table table with` cust_code, cust_name, city, and productcode:

```
create table cust_table
(cust_code number(5),
cust_name varchar2(30),
city varchar2(30),
productcode number(2))
/
```

The output of the preceding code snippet is given as follows:

```
Table created
```

The following code snippet shows the code to create view, `cust_nagpur`:

```
create or replace view cust_nagpur of cust_type
with object oid (cust_code) as
select cust_type (cust_code, cust_name, city)
from cust_table
where city = 'nagpur'
/
```

The output of the preceding code snippet is given as follows:

```
View created
```

The following code snippet shows the code to create type, `cust_list`:

```
create or replace type cust_list as table of cust_type
/
```

The output of preceding code snippet is as follows:

```
Type created
```

The following code snippet shows the code to create type, `productobj`:

```
create or replace type productobj as
object (productcode number(2),
productname varchar2(30),
customers cust_list )
/
```

The output of the preceding code snippet is given as follows:

```
Type created
```

The following code snippet shows the code to create view, `productview`:

```
create or replace view productview of productobj
with object oid (productcode) as
select productcode,productname,cast(multiset(select cust_code,cust_name,city
from cust_table c where c.productcode=d.productcode)as cust_list)
from product d
/
```

The output of the preceding code snippet is given as follows:

```
View created
```

The following code snippet shows the code to create insert data:

```
insert into product values(10,'pen')
/
```

The output of the preceding code snippet is given as follows:

```
1 row created
```

The following code snippet shows the code to insert data in the cust_table table:

```
insert into cust_table values(1,'ANIL','NAGPUR',10)
/
```

The output of the preceding code snippet is given as follows:

```
1 row created
```

The result of the subquery is cast to type `ALL_CUST_TAB`. The object view of nested table is not updateable. The nested table column in object view can be obtained from the following points:

- PL/SQL function returning nested table
- Array column
- Nested table column of a table or view
- Nested table attribute of an object

REF Datatype

You can map reverse relationship between a customer and product using `REF` datatype. The `REF` view column represents a reference to an object residing in a table or a view.

Listing 36.4 shows the code to use REF datatype:

Listing 36.4: Using the REF Datatype

```
create type cust_t as object
(
  cust_code  number,
  cust_name  varchar2(20),
  city           varchar2(30),
  productref ref productobj
)
/
```

The output of Listing 36.4 is as follows:

```
Type created
```

The following code snippet shows the code to create view, `cust_view1`:

```
create view cust_view1 of cust_t with object identifier(cust_code)
as select c.cust_code,c.cust_name,c.city,
make_ref(productview, c.productcode)
from cust_table c
/
```

In the preceding code snippet, the function MAKE_REF prepares for the REF view column. The first argument is the name of the object view and second is the foreign key column (productcode in cust_table). The number of foreign key columns must be its object SID in the referred object view productview. To create a view having the REF column, a referential relationship or foreign key should exist in the respective underlying columns.

The output of the preceding code snippet is given as follows:

```
View created
```

You can create the `REF` view column using a function, which returns a `REF` datatype, as shown in the following code snippet:

```
CREATE or REPLACE FUNCTION f_REF (custcode IN NUMBER)
RETURN REF cust_nagpur IS
BEGIN
   .............
   .............
```

```
END;
/
CREATE VIEW f_view (f_col) As
SELECT f_REF (cust_code)
FROM cust_table;
```

The view in the preceding code snippet is not inherently updateable. You can create a view in query, which has the following types:

- REF columns of a table
- REF column at a view
- REF attribute of table
- REF attribute of a view

The REF view column can be null, if the REF column is NULL. If a column has its source from MAKE_REF function, then it cannot be null.

VARRAY *Datatype*

VARRAY is used to represent multiple value attributes of an entity. If we have to store phone numbers of many customers, then a VARRAY is created for representing phone numbers.

Listing 36.5 shows the code to use VARRAY datatype:

Listing 36.5: Using VARRAY Datatype

```
create type phone AS object
(phoneno number (6),
location varchar2 (30));
/
```

The output of Listing 36.5 is as follows:

```
Type created
```

The following code snippet shows the code to create type, cust_type1:

```
create type cust_type1 as object
(custcode number(5),
cust_name varchar2(30),
cust_phone phone);
/
```

The output of the preceding code snippet is given as follows:

```
Type created
```

The following code snippet shows the code to create type, phone_array:

```
create type phone_array as
varray(5) of phone;
/
```

The output of the preceding code snippet is given as follows:

```
Type created
```

The following code snippet shows the code to create table, cust_income:

```
Create table cust_income
(cust_code Number(5),
income Number(10,2));
/
```

The output of the preceding code snippet is given as follows:

```
Table created
```

The following code snippet shows the code to create type, all_cust:

```
Create type all_cust as object
(cust_code Number(5),
income Number(10,2),
cust_phone phone_array);
/
```

The output of the preceding code snippet is given as follows:

```
Type created
```

The following code snippet shows the code to create type, phone_table:

```
Create type phone_table As
table of phone;
/
```

The output of the preceding code snippet is given as follows:

```
Type created
```

The following code snippet shows the code to create table, Cust_table with cust_code, cust_name, city, and cust_phone columns:

```
create table cust_table
(cust_code number(5),
cust_name varchar2(30),
city  varchar2(30),
cust_phone phone_array)
/
```

The output of the preceding code snippet is given as follows:

```
Table created
```

The following code snippet shows the code to create view, cust_view:

```
create or replace view cust_view of all_cust with object identifier(cust_code)
as
select cust_code, income, cast(( select cust_phone from cust_table
where cust_table.cust_code = cust_income.cust_code)as phone_array)
from cust_income;
/
```

In the preceding code snippet, phone_numbers are stored in VARRAY. If this query returns more than 5 values, then an error is returned. Array view columns are not updateable. These columns can be updated using the INSTEAD OF trigger.

The output of the preceding code snippet is given as follows:

```
View created
```

The following is function, column, and attribute from where an array view column can be taken:

- PL/SQL function, which returns a array
- Array column of a table or view
- Array attribute of an object column of a table

Updation Using Views

You can use normal DML statement for updating the underlying base table. If the view is not updateable, then the tables can be updated using `INSTEAD OF` trigger, which is different from an ordinary trigger. In `INSTEAD OF` trigger, the actual DML statements are not executed, but the code of the `INSTEAD OF` trigger is executed. The `INSTEAD OF` trigger is executed for each row. It can be used for a relational view as well as for an object view.

Listing 36.6 shows the code to use Instead of trigger:

Listing 36.6: Using the Instead of Trigger

```
create table parent(a number(2),
                    b number(2),
```

```
constraint pk_parent primary key(a))
/
```

The output of Listing36.6 is as follows:

```
Table created
```

The following code snippet shows the code to create table, child:

```
create table child(a number(2),
                   c number(2),
constraint fk_child foreign key(a)
references parent(a))
/
```

The output of the preceding code snippet is given as follows:

```
Table created
```

The following code snippet shows the code to create view, parent_child:

```
create or replace view parent_child as select p.a,p.b, q.c from parent p,
child q
/
```

The output of the preceding code snippet is given as follows:

```
View created
```

The following code snippet shows the code to create trigger, parent_ins:

```
create or replace trigger parent_ins
instead of insert on parent_child
for each row
declare
  x number;
begin
  select max(a)
  into x
  from parent;
  x := x+1;
  insert into parent values(x,:new.b);
end;
/
```

The output of the preceding code snippet is given as follows:

```
Trigger created
```

NOTE

The LOB datatype has already been discussed in Chapter 26 in detail.

Summary

In this chapter, you got familiar with object views; let us now proceed to understand transaction processing in the next chapter.

Exercise

1. Explain object views with the help of an example.
2. What is the use of NESTED datatype?

37

Transaction Processing in Oracle

Introduction

A transaction is used to simulate a logical unit of work inside a computer. When you computerize a real system, then one logical unit of work may be implemented as multiple units of work inside the computer (multiple DML statements in Oracle). For example, if you want to transfer Rs.100 from account number 1000 to account number 2000(single logical unit of work), you have to write two update statements, as shown in the following code snippet:

Listing 37.1: Updating an Account (initial value is taken as Rs.1000 as amount for both the accounts)

```
update account
set amt = amt-100
where account_no=1000;
                                              --A
update account
set amt = amt+100
where account_no=2000;
                                              --B
commit;
                                              --C
```

The output of Listing 37.1 is as follows:

```
I     1000           1000  initial value
A      900           1000 value at State A
B      900           1100 value at State B
```

From Listing 37.1, it is clear that:

- To implement one logical unit of work, you may have to execute multiple jobs in the system, such as multiple DML statements.
- After executing multiple units, the system state moves from one consistent state to another. In the output of Listing 37.1, I and B are consistent states.
- While going from one consistent state to another, a system generates some states that have inconsistent data. For example, state A.
- If due to some problem, such as a power failure, the system is left in a state in which there is inconsistent data, then that data may not match the data in real life and such a system will not be useful.
- To avoid such problems, all multiple units are grouped under one logical unit called transaction.
- Practically, a transaction refers to a set of DML and `SELECT` statements representing one logical unit of work.
- In Oracle, a transaction is a set of statements (DML and `SELECT`) between two successive commits.

Properties of a Transaction (ACID)

The essential properties of a transaction are commonly termed as ACID, an abbreviation that can be expanded as follows:

- A – Atomicity
- C – Consistency
- I – Isolation
- D – Durability

Let's discuss these properties one by one in the following sections.

ATOMICITY

Atomicity means that the effect of the transaction is either full or null. It is assumed that a system always starts from a consistent state and moves to another consistent state after executing a complete transaction. In Listing 37.1, we get either state I or state B as a consistent state of the transaction.

CONSISTENCY

Consistency means that a transaction should generate consistent data defined by application logic and inconsistency should not be generated due to the nature of the system, such as job scheduling or slow disk I/O.

ISOLATION

Isolation indicates the level of interference in one transaction due to the other transaction. A strict isolation level is the basic condition for executing of a transaction as if it is lonely executed.

DURABILITY

The effect of a transaction should be durable, irrespective of the nature of storage, such as volatile, nonvolatile memory.

Transactions in Oracle

A set of multiple DML statements and `SELECT` statements between two successive commits make one transaction in Oracle.

Transaction States

During execution, a transaction can have the following states:

```
Active -End request-- transaction→Partially committed→Committed -- End
  |                        |
Abort request            Failed→Abort
```

The following is a brief description of the preceding diagram

- Active state means that the transaction is in progress. In Oracle, you can get information about an active transaction from the view `V$` transaction).
- When a user issues the end request, i.e. `COMMIT`, all deferred constraints in the transaction are checked. The transaction is also checked for consistent data. Only after the checking is successful, the transaction is allowed to move to the commit state.
- In the commit state, the effect of the transaction is written to stable storage, which satisfies the property of durability.
- If there is a failure in partially committing data, then the transaction moves to a failed state.
- A transaction can move to a failed state even if the user makes abort request i.e. (ROLLBACK in Oracle).
- From the failed state, the transaction moves to abort state in which some undo operations are performed, such as the releasing of a few resources.
- In Oracle, rollback to SAVEPOINT does not change the state of a transaction. It remains in the active state.

Durability of a Transaction

The durability property of a transaction ensures that the effect of the transaction will be the same even after system has failed because of a problem and after it has recovered from the problem. For example, if a power failure occurs during transaction `C`, then, when the power is restored, you should get the value 900, 1100. Similarly, if the power fails at transaction B, you should get the value 1000, 1000.

Problems in Providing Durability

Nature of the System

Any changes on disk blocks are done in memory by bringing these blocks to the memory.

The transaction first makes changes in main memory of the system and then data from main memory is written on the disk. Here B1 and B2 are two blocks brought from disk to memory.

```
Transaction→memory→disk
               B1     B1
               B2     B2
```

The following points explain how a system works:

- A computer system has 3 components: a processor, which executes the transaction; memory, which is fast, volatile storage for keeping data temporarily; and a slow, non-volatile disk, which provides durability in case of power failure.
- The processor does not write directly on the disk; instead, a block on the disk is copied to memory and changes are done in the memory. The area of memory that is reserved for holding disk blocks is called a data buffer or file buffer.
- Data is therefore represented at two places, data buffers and the disk.
- There is a difference between the data in a memory image and the data in a disk image, if updations are done in the memory.
- Writing from memory to disk may not be done immediately because it may lead to multiple disk writes, which slows down the performance of the system. Suppose you have a disk, block `B1`, in which you want to make three changes. Writing the disk block after every change involves three disk writes. Instead of doing this, you can make the three changes and then write the block, which involves only one disk write.
- The efficiency of a system depends on when the decision to write the buffers after making changes in them (dirty buffers) on the disk is made. This decision is made on statistical information based on the pattern of block references, and, generally, the Least Recently Used (LRU) policy is used to make the decision.
- In the LRU policy, it is assumed that the buffer or block, which is recently referred, has more probability of reference, so it is not written immediately.
- If a block has not been referenced for quite some time, say a block that has been least used, then this block has more probability of replacement.

Here's an example for you.

Reference string	2	3	2	1	5	2	4	5	3	2	5	2
Frame 1	2	2	2	2	2	2	2	2	3	3	3	3
Frame 2		3	3	3	5	5	5	5	5	5	5	5
Frame 3				1	1	1	4	4	4	2	2	2
					F1		F2		F3	F4		

In the preceding diagram the blocks/pages are referenced in some sequence as follows:

2 3 2 1 5 2 4 5 3 2 5 2

Figure indicates how the blocks are allocated memory buffers assuming three buffers are allocated which are referred as page frames.

- Frame 1
- Frame 2
- Frame 3

In addition, Figure shows the following page faults:

- F1
- F2
- F3
- F4

A page fault occurs when a page in a frame is replaced by a new page in the series. Initially, when the three frames have pages in them and a new page is referred in the series, then a fault takes place. In the preceding example, when page 5 is referred, frames 1, 2, and 3 already have pages in them, and therefore one of the existing pages in the frames is to be replaced. This is the point where the first page fault takes place.

F1 is the first page fault and page 3 in the series is the page that has not been referenced for the longest period and it is replaced by page 5, i.e. page 5 appears in Frame 2. You can check this by looking at the numbers to the left of page 5. Among 1, 2, and 3, you can clearly see that page 3 has not been referenced for the longest period as compared to 1 and 2. Therefore, page 3 is replaced with page 5.

The next page fault occurs when page 4 comes in the series. Again, check the pages to the left of page 4 in the series. Clearly, among the pages 2, 5, and 1, you can see that page 1 was not referenced for the longest period as compared to pages 2 and 5. Therefore, page 1 is replaced by page 4, and page 4 appears in Frame 3.

Similarly, for the page faults F3 and F4, the least used pages are replaced.

Size of Volatile Storage

Since the size of memory or allocated memory to disk blocks is small compared to the number of disk blocks, it is not possible to keep every disk block in memory. For example, in a normal system you may have something like 100,000 disk blocks and 2000 buffers. When a transaction is executed, depending on the requirements, blocks of disks are brought to the buffer area and eventually, all the buffers are used. As there are no free buffers for new requests, the existing buffers are replaced to accommodate new incoming buffers. Therefore, a replacement policy is generally used to decide which buffer is to be replaced. For example, replacing a frequently used buffer will result in an increase in the number of disk reads and the reduce the efficiency of system. For example, there are five buffers in the request pattern 1 2 3 1 4 5 1. Now, every time you replace buffer 1 will result in a lot of disk reads. A good replacement policy means that the system is kept efficient. Generally, a replacement policy is based on LRU or a variant of LRU.

Note that the replacement policy itself should not use too much information, which will take a lot of time to analyze the information and thereby makes the system inefficient.

General Buffer Management

To create an efficient replacement and writing policy, you should maintain the status of buffers. The status of a buffer is categorized as follows:

- **Free buffer**—Refers to a buffer that can be immediately replaced without writing, i.e. the disk image and memory image of a block is the same.
- **Dirty buffer**—Refers to the buffer in which a block is brought to the main memory and modified, i.e. the image of the block on the disk and in the memory does not match. When such a buffer is replaced, it is written on the disk first and then replaced.
- **Pinned buffer**—Refers to the buffer that is currently in use or one that cannot be replaced for some reason.

Buffers are arranged in multiple lists, generally by using the `mod n` function. This allows you to quickly check whether a block is present in the block area or not. For example, if `n = 4`, it means there are 4 lists. If the block number is 19, then the block is searched in `19 MOD 4`, i.e. the 3rd list.

To help in the replacement of a buffer, the buffer is also kept in LRU list. If the buffer is recently accessed, then it will be put in the most recently used (MRU) end of the list. With time, due to aging, the buffer moves towards the LRU end. Generally, two processes operate on the buffer. The first process, known as Oracle Server Process, requests for the buffer; this process may also be used to read the buffer or write in it. In the case of Oracle, Server

Process is responsible for executing SQL statements. The second process writes dirty buffers from buffer area to the disk. In Oracle, this process is called Database Writer (DBWR)

Buffer Management from View of the Servers

- When a server process requires a free buffer, it scans the LRU list from the LRU end. If the server finds a free buffer by scanning the list below the scan threshold value, it replaces the buffer and puts the buffer into the MRU end.
- If a server process scans the threshold number of buffers but does not find a free buffer, it waits and signals DBWR to write buffers on the disk from the LRU end. After finishing writing DBWR, signals server process to resume.

Buffer Management from DBWR Point of View

DBWR writes dirty buffers on the disk. There are two important issues involved in writing:

- When to write
- How much to write

A high frequency of writing means an increased number of disk writing and the same buffer is written multiple times in small intervals.

A low frequency of writing may increase the waiting time for the server process because of an increase in the number of dirty buffers.

Writing of DBWR

DBWR process writes buffers as follows

- By default, DBWR is a suspended process.
- When a server process scans the LRU list up to some threshold value and the (DB_BLOCK_MAX_SCAN_CNT) parameter does not get a free buffer, it signals DBWR to write dirty buffers. The number of buffers to be written is decided by an internal parameter, such as (DB_BLOCK_WRITE_BATCH).
- If the number of dirty buffers goes beyond a certain threshold value, the server process signals to DBWR, which scans threshold buffer values from the LRU end and writes a predefined number of buffers, such as like 2*(DB_BLOCK_WRITE_BATCH).
- If DBWR does not wake up due to the preceding two events, it then wakes up after a timeout of 3 seconds and writes the number of buffers, similar to the second event.

Thus, we require buffer management, which works independently without interference from other factors such as frequency of user commits.

Solution of Durability or Implementation of Commit

Let's consider a transaction involving the transfer of an amount. We assume that the data of the account number 1000 is in disk block B1, and data of the account number 2000 is in disk block B2.

	B1m	B2m	B1d	B2d
0	1000	1000	1000	1000
u1	900	1000	1000	1000
u2	900	1100	1000	1000
w1	900	1100	900	1000
w2	900	1100	900	1100

NOTE

m indicates memory image and d indicates disk image. u1 and u2 are two update operations and w1 and w2 are two write operations.

Solution 1

Makes the changes of the transaction in a buffer and when the user issues `COMMIT`, writes all the changes on the disk and then issues the message stating that the transaction is committed, i.e. the message will be given only after the completion of `w2`.

Disadvantages

- If there is a failure after `w1`, then a partial effect remains on the disk and there is no information of `undo`.
- It disturbs the buffer management policy because it does not compulsorily describe which buffer should not be replaced, and which should be written.
- If several transactions start but are not committed, then it means that the buffers may be full and new buffers cannot be brought in the memory.

Solution 2

The solution should be such that it will provide the following:

- Durability
- Consistent recovery in case of failure
- No interference or least interference in buffer management. This is provided by using the concept of log file.

Concept of Log File

A log file is a sequential file that records the history of transactions. It records the effect of a transaction as it comes, so that the individual steps of the transaction can be interleaved in recording. The following code snippet shows sample entries in a log file:

```
<Ti start>
<Ti, A1000, 1000, 900>
<Tj, start>
<Ti, A2000, 1000, 1100>
<Tj, A1200, 3400, 5600>
<Ti commit>
```

When a transaction starts, the start record is added in a log file. When a data item is changed in the transaction, the changed record is added in the log file in the form of `<transaction id, data item, old value, new value>` and if the transaction commits, the commit record is added in the log file.

In the log file, the changes in a transaction are first written in a log buffer and then transferred to the disk by the LGWR process. The log buffer does not require a complex buffer management policy because the log buffer is sequentially written. There is no reading or reference from the log buffer. When a server process makes the changes, it generates three entries for:

- The database buffer
- The log buffer
- The rollback segment (to provide read consistency, which is explained later)

When a user commits, the log buffers are written on the disk and a commit record is recorded in a log file on the disk and the user gets the commit message. Database buffers may or may not be written on the disk when user commits transaction, but are written according to the buffer management policy.

Database buffers are not written on the disk, unless its corresponding log records are not written on it. Such buffers get pinned status.

A user will get a commit message only after the commit record is written on the disk in log file.

Transaction Recovery using a Log File

Transaction are recovered in the following steps

- During the recovery process, a log file is scanned from start to end.
- Transactions that have start and commit records are redone by applying the REDO (Ti) operation. In redo, a new value is written in the database, irrespective of the existing value.
- An undo operation is applied on transactions that have the start record but not the commit record. The old value of data item is written, irrespective of the existing value.

Two Modes of using Log Files

The log file is used in two ways, known as deferred update and immediate update.

Deferred Update

In deferred update, the modifications are done not on the database buffer but on a copy of the database buffer. Changes are applied to database buffer only after issuance of commit. The changes are written in the log buffer immediately after the `COMMIT` and log buffers are written on the disk. This ensures that the log file contains commit record. No changes are made on the database side before commit.

The disadvantage of this kind of update is that a separate buffer is required and thus it influences buffer management policy. The deferred update method is suitable only for small transactions. In Oracle, its variation is given by using the PL/SQL packaged procedure `DBMS-TRANSACTION.BEGIN_DISCRETE_TRANSACTION`. The procedure should be executed at the beginning of a transaction.

Immediate Update

In the immediate update method, no separate copy of the database buffer is maintained and changes are made in database buffers themselves. This method is used in Oracle. The database buffer is written according to the buffer management policy, and recovery requires both the redo and undo operations. Immediate update clause gives independence in terms of allocation of space in buffer management. In Oracle this method is used.

How a Log File Decreases Disk Writes

Database changes are written at two places, on database files and on log files. Therefore, ideally the number of disk writes should increase, whereas the fact is that the number reduces. This is because the transactions by several users make effect in various data blocks, but in log file, these changes are written sequentially; therefore, even if a transaction makes changes in 100 blocks, its effect is written only in one block of log file. When the transaction commits, the number of data block writes are decreased, i.e. instead of writing 100 blocks, only one block write is required, that is, of the log file.

With time, transactions make changes in one block multiple times. But in the buffer management policy, it will write the changes at the last so that only one data block write is required.

For example, suppose there are N numbers of transactions, which make 10 changes in each of the 100 blocks. One log block can accommodate 200 changes. So, effectively five block writes are required during the running of a system. In the absence of a log file to record 1000 changes, 1000 disk block writes are required. However, in the presence of a log file, you will require only five log writes. A log file serializes the effect of the transaction, which is randomly distributed across multiple blocks. To provide durability of the transaction only the log block writes are required. Log file writing also depends on the frequency of commit. To reduce log file writing, the concept of GROUP COMMIT is used. When a user issues commit in a group commit, the commit record is not written immediately to a log file. Instead, Oracle waits some time and then writes the commit record on the disk. During this interval, if another COMMIT is issued from any other transaction, then that commit is also written.

Therefore, a log file provides durability, atomicity, recovery of transaction, and independence of buffer management.

Isolation Level

Isolation level indicates the degree of interference of a transaction on another transaction. For example, you read total deposit using `SELECT` statement and, in the same transaction, you issue the same `SELECT` after sometime. You may get the same value or different values, depending on the isolation level. Isolation levels are defined by using different types of reads:

- **Dirty read**—This means one transaction reads uncommitted data of another transaction.
- **Non Repeatable read**—If the same transaction reads the same value two times, then the values are different due to updates in other transaction.
- **Phantom read**—If the same transaction reads the same value two times, then the values are different because of inserts or deletes in other transactions.

The following are the different isolation levels:

- Read uncommitted (1, 2, 3)
- Read committed (2, 3)
- Repeatable Read (3) (Phantom read)
- Serializable ( )

The numbers in bracket indicate operations that are allowed in these isolation levels.

Oracle supports two isolation levels, read committed and serializable. You can set the default setting by using the `INIT.ORA` parameter or the `ALTER SESSION` command, as shown in the following syntax:

```
set transaction isolation level serializable;
```

In addition to this, Oracle also has the read only transaction, which is similar to the serializable transaction but does not have the DML statement.

- **Read committed**—Supports committed reads and phantom reads, but not dirty reads.

Similarly, the updating of the same data items from multiple transactions is not allowed. The changes made in one transaction are visible in that transaction and not for other transactions. Suppose a query is fired to read a large number of rows, say 200. The query reads the rows one by one. As soon as the first 100 rows are read, suppose that another transaction updates the last rows and commits them. In this case, for the first query, the old values and not the committed values are read. This means that read committed is provided, according to read consistency.

Read consistency means providing data present at a certain point of time. For example, if a transaction begins execution at 3 p.m., it will supply all the data at 3 p.m., irrespective of the time when this data is actually fetched. It is implemented by using ROLLBACK segments in versions before Oracle 8i, and the UNDO tablespace in Oracle 9i (10g). This type of implementation is called the multiversion timestamp protocol.

Write Consistency

Write Consistency implies following rules

- It indicates that a transaction should not update the uncommitted data of another transaction
- One transaction should not view the committed data of another transaction during its execution. It means that the update should be on the data which is present at a certain point of time.
- Two transactions should not do concurrent updation on the same data without committing it.

Write consistency is implemented using locks.

- When a transaction wants to update some row(s), it places share lock on the items which are hierarchically at the upper level, i.e. table and tablespaces. It means if one transaction updates a row, then the other transaction should not drop the table.
- When a transaction wants to update or change an item, the item should be locked exclusively. The exclusive lock is also called as write lock.
- If a transaction wants to alter the table, it should place exclusive lock on the table.

- More than one transaction can put share lock or read lock on the same data item.
- The transaction can put exclusive lock on an item only if there is no `LOCK` already on that item.
- Locks are released only if transaction commits or transaction makes full rollback.
- In case of rollback to savepoint, locks are retained.
- In case of multiple rows updation, a transaction starts locking rows in the order as they are fetched. If it can't lock a certain row, then it will wait for that row but does not release locks of earlier rows.
- If a row is locked when 'for update no wait' is fired, the query gets cancelled. This way the user can check whether the rows are already locked.
- When a transaction waits for a certain row, it keeps the information of that row
- When another transaction releases the lock on that row, it checks whether its claim for that row is valid or not.

For example, the other transaction may change items in the row such that the row should not be locked according to the `WHERE` condition of the first transaction. If the claim is valid, it locks the row. If the claim is not valid, it relinquishes the claim, and requires the data to put locks on rows.

Listing 37.2: Opening Three Different instances of an Oracle Application for Term T1, T2, and T3:

Case 1: Procedure to delete child table

```
begin
  delete child;
end;
/
```

Result:

```
PL/SQL procedure successfully completed
```

Listing 37.3: Inserting Values into the Child Table

```
insert into child values(1,1)
/
```

Result:

```
 1 row created
```

Inserting values into `Child` table

```
insert into child values(2,2)
/
```

Result:

```
 1 row created
```

Inserting values into `Child` table

```
insert into child values(3,3)
/
```

Result:

```
 1 row created
```

Listing 37.4: Updating the Child Table in Terminal T1

```
Term T1
update child set c=4 where c=2;
```

The output of Listing 37.5 is as follows:

```
1 row updated
```

Listing 37.5: Updating the Child Table in Terminal T2

```
Term T2
update child set c=6 where c=2;
                               --hang
```

Listing 37.6: Updating `Child` table in Terminal T3

```
Term T3
update child set c=2 where c in (1,3);
```

Result:

```
2 rows updated
```

Listing 37.7: Committing transaction in Terminal T3

```
commit;
```

Result:

```
Commit complete
```

Listing 37.8: Committing transaction

```
Term T1
commit;
```

Result:

```
Commit complete
```

Updating `child`

```
Term T2
--lockset gets changed so re-query
update child set c=6 where c=2;
```

Result:

```
0 rows updated
```

After the `COMMIT` in the Oracle application, instances for Term `T1` and `T3`, both locks will be removed and the `update` SQL command, which previously hanged, gets executed automatically.

Committing transaction

```
commit;
```

Result:

```
Commit complete
```

Listing 37.9: Selecting values from Child table

```
select * from child;
```

Result:

```
         A          C
---------- ----------
         1          6
         2          4
         3          6
```

Case 2: Selecting values in `Child` table

```
Term T1
select * from child;
```

Result:

```
         A          C
  --------   --------
         1          2
         2          4
         3          2
```

Updating `Child` table

```
update child set c=4 where c=2;
```

Result:

```
1 row updated
```

Updating Child table

```
Term T2
update child set c=6 where c=2;
                                            --hang
```

Updating Child table

```
Term T3
update child set c=2 where c in (1,3);
```

Result:

```
2 rows updated
```

Listing 37.10: Committing a transaction

```
commit;
```

Result:

```
Commit complete
```

Listing 37.11: Rolling back a transaction

```
Term T1
rollback;
```

Result:

```
Rollback complete
```

Updating Child table

```
Term T2
update child set c=6 where c=2;  --no lockset change no re-query
```

Result:

```
1 row updated
```

Listing 37.12: Selecting values from Child table

```
select * from child;
```

Result:

```
         A          C
---------- ----------
         1          2
         2          6
         3          2
```

Locking row using PL/SQL

Transaction can lock the row using following PL/SQL code

Listing 37.13: Using the UPDATE NOWAIT Clause

```
declare
  cursor cl is
  select ename from emp
  where cname='acc'
  for update
  nowait;
begin
  open cl;
  close cl;
end;
/
```

The output of Listing 37.13 is as follows:

```
PL/SQL procedure successfully completed
```

Isolation Level Serializable

A sequence of statement execution of individual terminal is called as schedule. There are three types of schedules:

- Serial schedule
- Non-serial schedule
- The serializable schedule

Serial Schedule

A serial schedule is when the second transaction does not start before the completion of the first transaction. In real life, all schedules are serial schedules and always generate consistent data. Practically, they are very inefficient because they impose a lot of waiting time for other transactions.

Non-Serial Schedules

In a non-serial schedule, transactions statements execute in an interleaved fashion.

Serializable

A schedule is serializable when its effect is the same as that of the serial schedule.

Let's look at some of the examples of schedules:

A and B are data items , WA and WB are write operations which changes values of A and B from 100,100 to 120 ,150.

Observing serial schedule S1:

```
A=100 B=100 WA=120 WB=150
T1
R(A)
W(A)

T2
R(B)
W(B)
```

Here, `T1` and `T2` are transactions.

Observing schedule S2, which is a non-serial schedule, i.e. Serializable:

```
S2
T1          R(A)
T2 R(B)
T2 W(B)
T1 W(A)
```

NOTE

Non-serial schedules are also called serializable schedules, because they are non-seriable schedules that produce the same result as serial schedules.

Observing non-serializable:

```
A = 50          T1        RA
                T2        RA
                T2        WA(A=100)
                T1        WA(A=200)
```

This schedule is non-serializable because it is not equivalent to any schedule `T1-T2` or `T2-T1`.

For serial schedule `T1` and `T2`

- T1 reads 50 and writes A=200
- T2 reads 200 and writes A=100

For serial schedule T2 and T1

- T2 reads 50 writes A=100
- T1 reads 100 writes A=200

Say, the given schedule, S4, is as follows:

```
S4: A = 50
          T1        RA
          T2        RA
          T2        WA(A=100)
          T1        WA(A=200)
```

Here, S4 is not serializable because its effect is not equivalent to any of the serial schedule T1-T2 or T2-T1.

Observing Serializable S5

```
S5: A = 50
          T1        RA
          T2        RA
          T1        WA(A=200)
```

Here, S5 is serializable because its effect is same as schedule T2-T1.

Determining Whether a Schedule is Serializable

The serializiblity of schedule is determined using following steps.

- For each transaction put a node in the graph.
- If T1 reads the data item and then T2 writes the same data item, put link from T1 to T2.
- If T1 writes the data item and then T2 writes the same data item, put the link from T1 to T2.

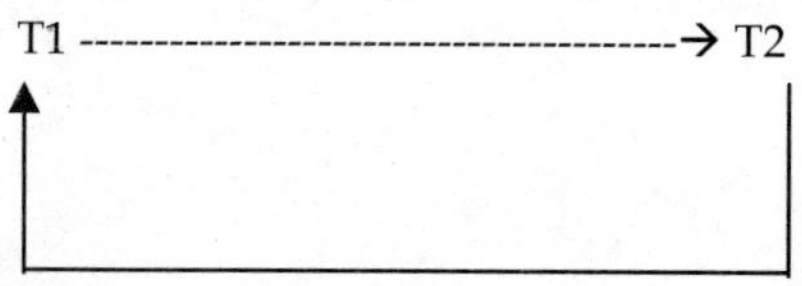

- If the graph is cyclical, then the schedule is not serializable, as shown in the following:

```
T1 <----> T2
```

If the graph does not have any cycle, then it is a serializable schedule and is called conflict serializable. The other type of serializable schedule is view serializable. In case of view serializable, the link is not put when two transactions write the same data item because it is assumed that the transaction does not make read option, while writing data only. The end effect of the transaction is checked. For example, consider the update state shown in the following code snippet:

```
update T set A = 10;
```

In the preceding cod snippet there is no read operation, while writing and such writes are called blind writes. Oracle implements conflict serializability.

You can set isolation level serializable as follows

Listing 37.14: Setting the isolation level for entire session

```
TERM T1
SET TRANSACTION ISOLATION LEVEL SERIALIZABLE;
```

Result:

```
Transaction set
```

Retrieving values from Child table of Terminal T1

```
select * from child;
```

Result:

```
         A          C
---------- ----------
         1          6
         1         25
         2         61
         1         97
         1         97
```

Retrieving values from `Child` table of Terminal T2

```
TERM T2
select * from child;
```

Result:

```
         A          C
---------- ----------
         1          6
         1         25
         2         61
         1         97
         1         97
```

Updating the `Child` table from Terminal T2

```
update child set c=29 where c=6;
```

Result:

```
1 row updated
```

Committing transaction

```
commit;
```

Result:

```
Commit complete
```

Retrieving values from `Child` table of Terminal `T1`

```
TERM T1
select * from child;
```

Result:

```
         A          C
---------- ----------
         1         29
         1         25
         2         61
         1         97
         1         97
```

Updating the `Child` table from Terminal `T1`

```
update child set c=31 where c=29;
```

Result:

```
1 row updated
```

Selecting values from `child` table

```
select * from child;
```

Result:

```
         A          C
---------- ----------
         1         31
         1         25
```

```
            2           61
            1           97
            1           97
```

Updating `child` table

```
update child set c=35 where c=25;
```

Result:

```
UPDATE CHILD SET C=35 WHERE C=25
       *
ERROR at line 1:
ORA-08177: can't serialize access for this transaction
```

Committing the transaction

```
commit;
```

Practically, a serializable transaction is a transaction that does not see the affect of another transaction or make changes according to the changes of the other transaction.

The Read Only Transaction

You can mark a transaction as read only for querying the data. You can use directive set transaction read only at the beginning of transaction. Dirty reads, non-repeatable reads, and phantom reads are not supported in a read only transaction. Suppose you issue the following statement at the beginning of a transaction:

```
select * from emp;
set transaction read only;
```

Now, if you issue the same statement after some time, the output gives the same set of rows, irrespective of whether between the statement, the table is updated and committed by the other transaction.

Discrete Transaction

A small transaction can be marked as discrete by using the `DBMS_TRANSACTION.BEGIN_DISCRETE_TRANSACTION` Procedure.

Let's now look at some examples that illustrate the use of discrete transactions:

Listing 37.15: Using the DBMS_TRANSACTION.BEGIN_DISCRETE_TRANSACTION Procedure before a Commit

```
begin
  dbms_transaction.begin_discrete_transaction;
  update child set c=56 where c=29;
  commit;
end;
/
```

The output of Listing 37.15 is as follows:

```
BEGIN
*
ERROR at line 1:
ORA-08175: discrete transaction restriction violated (psdbot: transaction
already started)
ORA-06512: at line 2
```

Now at SQL prompt give the `COMMIT` command

```
commit;
```

Result:

```
Commit complete
```

Running the above procedure

```
begin
  dbms_transaction.begin_discrete_transaction;
  update child set c=56 where c=29;
  commit;
end;
/
```

Result:

```
PL/SQL procedure successfully completed
```

In case of a discrete transaction, durability is implemented by using the deferred update method. This means that changes are not applied to the database until the transaction is committed. During recovery, only the redo option is required. Using `DBMS_TRANSACTION`, you can do all functions that are possible by using SQL commands.

Listing 37.16: Using DBMS_TRANSACTION to Retrieve the Unique Identifier of a Transaction

```
declare
  x varchar2(30);
begin
  x :=dbms_transaction.local_transaction_id (true);
  dbms_output.put_line(x);
end;
/
```

The output of Listing 37.16 is as follows:

```
 3.41.2533

PL/SQL procedure successfully completed
```

Setting the transaction read only

```
begin
  dbms_transaction.read_only;
end;
 /
```

Result:

```
PL/SQL procedure successfully completed
```

Setting read write transaction

```
begin
  dbms_transaction.read_write;
end;
/
```

Result:

```
PL/SQL procedure successfully completed
```

Performing rollback transaction

```
begin
  dbms_transaction.rollback;
end;
/
```

Result:

```
PL/SQL procedure successfully completed
```

Performing rollback to savepoint

```
dbms_transaction.rollback_savepoint(savept in varchar2);
```

Creating savepoint

```
dbms_transaction.savepoint (savept in varchar2);
```

Forcing transaction using specified rollback segment

```
dbms_transaction.use_rollback_segment (rb_name in varchar2);
```

NOTE

These statements are not complete procedures. They are part of a procedure and therefore no result will be displayed.

Summary

In this chapter, you have learned about the concepts of transaction processing in Oracle. You also come across the DBMS_TRANSACTION procedure. In the next chapter, you will learn about locking.

Exercise

1. How COMMIT is implemented in Oracle?
2. How will you set isolation level serializable in transaction?

38

Locking in Oracle

Introduction to Locking

When the Data Manipulation Language (DML) operation is done on a table, Oracle locks the row which is going to be affected by the DML statement, so that during the period of operation that particular row cannot be updated by any other transaction. This concept of locking rows, which makes them available to only one operation at a time, is called row lock.

Before locking a row, it also locks the corresponding table so that the table cannot be altered or dropped by other transactions. There are 5 types of locks on a table:

- RS (row share)
- RX (row exclusive)
- S (share)
- SRX (share row exclusive)
- X (exclusive)

These locks restrict table operations in an increasing order, that is, an exclusive lock can restrict most of the operations in the lock table. Table 1 summarizes various locks and the types of permissions associated with different kinds of SQL statements:

SQL Statement	Mode of Table Lock	Lock Modes Permitted?				
		RS	RX	S	SRX	X
`SELECT...FROM table...`	none	Y	Y	Y	Y	Y
`INSERT INTO table ...`	RX	Y	Y	N	N	N
`UPDATE table ...`	RX	Y*	Y*	N	N	N
`DELETE FROM table ...`	RX	Y*	Y*	N	N	N
`SELECT ... FROM table FOR UPDATE OF ...`	RS	Y*	Y*	Y*	Y*	N
`LOCK TABLE table IN ROW SHARE MODE`	RS	Y	Y	Y	Y	N
`LOCK TABLE table IN ROW EXCLUSIVE MODE`	RX	Y	Y	N	N	N
`LOCK TABLE table IN SHARE MODE`	S	Y	N	Y	N	N
`LOCK TABLE table IN SHARE ROW EXCLUSIVE MODE`	SRX	Y	N	N	N	N
`LOCK TABLE table IN EXCLUSIVE MODE`	X	N	N	N	N	N
** If no conflicting row locks are held by another transaction. Otherwise, waits occur.*						

The Mode of Table Lock column indicates the lock acquired by the transaction. The Locks Modes Permitted column indicates lock, which is acquired or which can be acquired by another transaction.

Following two examples describe how the locking is done.

Example 1

If user executes update statements then he acquires RX lock on the table. Other transactions can acquire any type of lock given by the Lock Modes Permitted column. The other transaction can put RS lock, and RX on the table, but not S, SRX, and exclusive (X) lock.

Example 2

Select from table for update.

When a user fires the SELECT statement, the transaction acquires RS lock. The other transaction can acquire RS lock, RX lock, S lock and SRX lock, but it cannot acquire X lock. Y* indicates that the locks acquired on the rows, which are not locked by other transactions, by default insert, update and delete statement puts RX lock. If you want to use a different lock, then the command is `lock table <lock mode>`.

These locks are used for various other purposes as well. Suppose you want to read data from the table in a SQL statement a number of times. In this case, if you do not want to allow other transactions to change the data, then you can lock the table in shared mode. The locks in shared mode are released after commit or full rollback. You can use lock statements in PL/SQL programs as it is.

Deadlock

Locks are not released until the user commits or makes full rollbacks. Users can also try to acquire locks directly or indirectly, while holding another lock. If most of the locks are exclusive (only one transaction can acquire lock), there can be a situation of deadlock, that is both transactions have to wait for each other to release the lock.

For example, transaction T1 locks row A, while transaction T2 locks row B. Then T1 requests for B and T2 requests for A. Now both the transactions will wait for the resource to be released by the other transaction. Therefore, a situation of deadlock arises. Oracle automatically detects deadlock and cancels waiting in a transaction, so that the transaction can commit or rollback.

Listing 38.1 shows the code of a deadlock:

Listing 38.1: Showing a deadlock (this will run on terminal 1)

```
select * from child;
```

The output of Listing 38.1 is as follows:

```
         A          C
---------- ----------
         1          2
         2          6
         3          2
```

NOTE

Term1 refers to terminal 1. We will be working on 2 different instances, Term1 being the first instance and Term2 being the second instance

Updating the Child table

```
update child set c=10 where a=1;
```

Result:

```
1 row updated
```

Displaying data of the Child table (this will run on terminal 2)

```
select * from child;
```

Result:

```
         A          C
---------- ----------
         1          2
         2          6
         3          2
```

Updating the Child table and setting the value of c=20 where a=2

```
update child set c=20 where a=2;
```

Result:

```
1 row updated
```

Updating the `Child` table and setting value `c=25` where `a=1` (this will run on terminal 2)

```
update child set c=25 where a=1;
```

Result:

```
Session gets suspended
        *
ERROR at line 1:
ORA-00060: deadlock detected while waiting for resource
```

Updating the `Child` table and setting value `c=25` where `a=2` (this will run on terminal 1)

```
update child set c=25 where a=2;
```

Result:

```
Session suspended
        *
ERROR at line 1:
ORA-00060: deadlock detected while waiting for resource
```

You will see that it hangs while waiting for a locked row (this will run on terminal 2).

```
update child set c=25 where a=1;
```

Result:

```
update child set c=25 where a=1
        *
ERROR at line 1:
ORA-00060: deadlock detected while waiting for resource
```

This conveys that there is deadlock.

Listing 38.2 shows the code for displaying values of the Child table:

Listing 38.2: Displaying values of the Child table

```
select * from child;
```

The output of Listing 38.2 is as follows:

```
         A          C
---------- ----------
         1          2
         2         20
         3          2
```

Committing the transaction:

```
commit;
```

Result:

```
Commit complete
Term 1
1 row updated
```

Displaying all records:

```
select * from child;
```

Result:

```
         A          C
---------- ----------
         1         10
         2         25
         3          2
```

Detecting Blocking Transactions

You can detect lock contention or blocking sessions using the V$LOCK and V$LOCKED_OBJECT views.

Listing 38.3 shows the code to detect blocked transactions:

Listing 38.3: Detecting Blocked Transactions

```
Term 1(By user plsql)
select * from child;
```

The output of Listing 38.3 is as follows:

```
         A          C
---------- ----------
         1         10
         2         25
         3          2
```

Updating child table and setting c=15, where a=1

```
update child set c=15 where a=1;
```

Result:

```
1 row updated
```

Listing 38.4 shows the code to give access of a table:

Listing 38.4: Giving access of table to the user Scott

```
Grant update on child to scott;
```

The output of Listing 38.4 is as follows:

```
Grant succeeded
```

User scott updating the Child table

```
Term2 (by user scott)
update plsql.child set c=20 where a=2;
```

Result:

```
1 row updated
```

Listing 38.5 shows the code to display locked object of each user:

Listing 38.5: Displaying locked object of each user

```
set linesize 1000
select s.username, decode( l.type,'tm','table lock','tx','row lock',null) "lock
  level", o.owner, o.object_name,o.object_type
from v$session s, v$lock l,dba_objects o
where
s.sid = l.sid
and o.object_id = l.id1
and s.username is not null
/
```

The output of Listing 38.5 is as follows:

```
USERNAME         LOCKLEVEL        OWNER            OBJECT_NAME
-----------      ------------     ------------     ------------
PLSQL            TABLE            LOCK PLSQL               CHILD
SCOTT            TABLE            LOCK PLSQL               CHILD
```

The result shows which user has locked which object.

Listing 38.6 shows the code to update same row

Listing 38.6: Assuming that Term 2 requests for locking the same row as Term 1

```
Term 2
update plsql.child set c=30 where a=1;
                                    --it will wait for release of lock
```

The output of Listing 38.6 is as follows:

```
1 row updated
```

You can detect users involved in locking by using `V$LOCKED_OBJECT`. It displays all the locks currently held by every user on the system.

Listing 38.7 shows the code to find the user holding the blocking lock:

Listing 38.7: Finding the user who holds the blocking lock

```
select lpad( ' ' ,decode(lobj.xidusn,0,3,0)) || lobj.oracle_username "username",
 o.owner,o.object_name,o.object_type
 from
 v$locked_object lobj,dba_objects o
 where
 lobj.object_id = o.object_id
 order by o.object_id,1 desc
/
```

The output of Listing 38.7 is as follows:

```
USERNAME          LOCKLEVEL       OWNER           OBJECT_NAME
-----------       ----------      ------------    ------------
PLSQL              TABLE          LOCK PLSQL              CHILD
SCOTT              TABLE          LOCK PLSQL              CHILD
```

Listing 38.8 shows the code to find the session id and serial number of a particular user

Listing 38.8: Finding the session id and serial number of a particular user

```
SELECT sid, serial# FROM V$SESSION where username = 'SCOTT'
/
```

The output of Listing 38.8 is as follows:

```
       SID    SERIAL#
---------- ----------
         8         30
```

Listing 38.9 shows the code to kill a session:

Listing 38.9: Killing a session

```
alter system kill session '8,30';
```

The output of Listing 38.9 is as follows:

```
System altered
```

Using Package **DBMS_LOCK**

If you want user-defined locking, then you can use the `dbms_lock` package. Using this package, you can acquire lock, process data, and then release it. Suppose you want that the code specified in statement C should be executed exclusively. Then, before processing, you should acquire lock, process the code, and then release it. Here a large processing is simulated using procedure the `dbms_lock.sleep(10)`

Listing 38.10 shows how to use the DBMS_LOCK package:

Listing 38.10: Using the DBMS_LOCK package

```
                                              --lock1
declare
  x varchar2(100);
```

```
   y number;
begin
   dbms_lock.allocate_unique('a',x);              --A
   dbms_output.put_line(x);
   y := dbms_lock.request(x);                     --B
   dbms_output.put_line(y);
   dbms_lock.sleep(10);                           --C
   y := dbms_lock.release(x);                     --D
   dbms_output.put_line(y);
end;
/
```

The output of Listing 38.10 is as follows:

```
10737418241073741824147
0
0
PL/SQL procedure successfully completed
```

In Listing 38.10:

- Statement A indicates that you want to use a lock named a. Internally, Oracle allocates one number, called as lock handle to identify it.
- Statement B requests lock before processing data. The signature is shown in the following code snippet:

```
dbms_lock.request(
   id                     in  integer ||
   lockhandle             in  varchar2,
   lockmode               in  integer default x_mode,
   timeout                in  integer default maxwait,
   release_on_commit      in  boolean default false)
   return integer;
```

In this case:

- You can use id or lockhandle for identifying a lock. The lockmode is the default exclusive(x_mode). The other modes are:
  - nl_mode
  - ss_mode
  - sx_mode
  - ssx_mode
- These modes have similar meaning as table locks.
- Timeout indicates how much time the process waits for fulfilling a request.
- RELEASE_ON_COMMIT indicates that the lock is released after commit.
- The return value of function is as follows:
  - 0 (success)
  - 1 (timeout)
  - 2 (deadlock)
  - 3 (parameter error)
  - 4 (already own lock)
  - 5 (illegal lock handle)
- Statement C indicates that the process is sleeping for 10 seconds.
- Statement D indicates the release of lock. The return value is as follows:

- 0 (success)
- 3 (parameter error)
- 4 (does not own lock)
- 5 (illegal lock handle)

Listing 38.11 shows the code to execute lock2 from another terminal:

Listing 38.11: Executing lock2 from another terminal by running code listed in 38.10

```
                                    --lock2 executed from another terminal
declare
   x varchar2(100);
   y number;
begin
   dbms_lock.allocate_unique('a',x);
   dbms_output.put_line(x);
   y := dbms_lock.request(x,dbms_lock.x_mode,1);
   dbms_output.put_line(y);
   dbms_lock.sleep(1);
   y := dbms_lock.release(x);
   dbms_output.put_line(y);
end;
/
```

The output of Listing38.11 is as follows:

```
PL/SQL procedure successfully completed
```

Summary

Now that you are comfortable with locking concepts, let's move to the next chapter that deals with rollback segments.

Exercise

1. Which lock is used if user wants to print very large report?
2. How you will find out which tables are locked by which user?

39

Rollback Segments

What is Rollback Segment?

A rollback segment is used to store undo information of a transaction. Suppose a transaction changes value of A from 10 to 30. In that case, the data segment stores value 30 and the old value is stored in the rollback segment.

The block in data segment, which carries a new value, indicates where the old value is stored. When the same transaction, which has updated the value, tries to read the value of A, it will read the new value. When any other transaction tries to read the value of A, it checks whether A is modified by other transaction and whether that transaction is committed or not.

If a transaction is committed then it will read the new value. If the transaction is not committed then the other transaction will read the information from rollback segment of that transaction. In other words, if a transaction (say `X`) has been committed, then any other transaction (`Y`), after the commit statement, will be able to read the new value. However, if the transaction is not committed, then the next transaction (`Y`) will pick up data from the rollback segment. The rollback segment has the original data, the data that was there before the transaction `X`.

The information about a transaction and the location of a block in the rollback segment of that transaction is stored in `INITRANS` entry or transaction entry in the block and the row, which is updated, carries that entry number, such as 1, 2, and 3. The number of `INITRANS` entries is a parameter of the table and it can be specified at the time of table creation. The number of `INITRANS` entries controls the maximum number of concurrent accesses of the block by the transactions. Therefore, when the other transaction reads the updated row, it will get `INITRANS` entry number, say it is 2. From 2, it will read the transaction entry number 2 where it will get the transaction and the location of that block in the rollback segment. From there it will read the old value of the row.

Therefore, a rollback segment is used to implement two important properties of a transaction. First, the transaction will not read uncommitted data of other transaction; and second, if the changes are made in a transaction then they are visible in the same transaction, irrespective of whether they are committed. The rollback segment also implements the concept of read consistency. Read consistency means it allows a transaction to read committed data, which is present at a particular point of time. Let's understand it with the help of an example.

Suppose there are two transactions `T1` and `T2`.

- `T1` is supposed to read 10000 rows of a table and it is fired at 3 p.m.
- When `T1` has read 100 rows, `T2` is also fired.
- `T2` updates the last 100 rows and also commits changes.
- `T1` resumes after `T2`, and starts reading rows.

What data will transaction read at the last? Old data that was present at the time 3 p.m. or the data, which is updated by `T2`.

Suppose `T1` reads the updated data. Then the effect of transaction depends on scheduling policy of the system, i.e. we allow `T2` to be executed before `T1` is finished. Since scheduling policy depends on the operating system, we may get data, which varies from one system to another.

Instead of it, we allow reading the data that is present at 3 p.m. (the time when `SELECT` statement begins its execution) though the row is actually fetched at 3:15 p.m. In that way, we always get consistent results irrespective of operating system.

Implementation of Read Consistency

Implementation of read consistency suggests that you have to store old values of the changes in the rollback segments even if the transaction is committed. Theoretically, it requires infinite storage of rollback segment, which is not possible practically. In Oracle, changes are preserved in rollback segment for a longer period of time to provide read consistent view of data. When Oracle is unable to submit read consistent data, it returns an error '`snapshot too old`' rather than providing erroneous data.

Operations related with Rollback Segment

How Oracle Preserves Data for a Longer Time

When the server process changes in a row, it generates three entries—one for data files; second for rollback segments; and third for log files. The transaction writes the previous value, i.e. value before the transaction is saved temporarily in the rollback segments, which is allocated to it at the beginning. The system has multiple rollback segments and, by default, they are allocated in round robin fashion.

Getting information about rollback segment

The information about rollback segment is obtained by querying view V$ROLLSTAT.

The `V$ROLLSTAT` dynamic performance view can be queried to monitor rollback segment statistics, as shown in Listing 39.1:

Listing 39.1: Viewing Statistics of Rollback Segment

```
select * from v$rollstat;
```

The output of Listing 39.1 is given as follows:

```
       USN      LATCH    EXTENTS     RSSIZE     WRITES      XACTS       GETS
---------- ---------- ---------- ---------- ---------- ---------- ----------
     WAITS    OPTSIZE    HWMSIZE    SHRINKS      WRAPS    EXTENDS AVESHRINK
---------- ---------- ---------- ---------- ---------- ---------- ----------
 AVEACTIVE STATUS                   CUREXT     CURBLK
---------- --------------- ---------- ----------
         0          0          6     385024       7500          0        107
         0                385024          0          0          0          0
         0 ONLINE                        4          6

         1          1         16    6938624     307900          0        816
         0               6938624          0          0          0          0
         0 ONLINE                       14        110

         2          2         20    9166848     312408          0        926
         0               9166848          0          0          0          0
         0 ONLINE                       19         84

         3          0         17    7987200     384066          0       1223
         0               7987200          0          0          0          0

         0 ONLINE                       15        118

         4          1          7     450560       4756          0         76
         0                450560          0          1          0          0
      6553 ONLINE                        3          0

         5          2         26    7593984     346996          0       2803


         0               7593984          0          0          0          0
         0 ONLINE                       22        107

         6          0         77   12902400      51466          0        392
         0              12902400          1          1          2      65536
      6553 ONLINE                       74          7
```

```
        7         1       120  27516928     1726650         0     24360
        0          27516928          0           10        10         0
   179071 ONLINE                   108           26

        8         2        50   8183808       62586         0       215
        0           8183808          0            0         0         0
        0 ONLINE                    49          100

        9         0        12    778240           0         0        59
        0            778240          0            0         0         0
        0 ONLINE                    10            3

       10         1         2    122880           0         0        59
        0            122880          0            0         0         0

        0 ONLINE                     0            0

11 rows selected
```

You can observe the following points in the output of Listing 39.1:

- USN is the rollback segment number. If this view is joined with the V$ROLLNAME view, the rollback segment name can be determined.
- LATCH is the latch for the rollback segment.
- EXTENTS is the number of extents in the rollback segment.
- RSSIZE is the size (in bytes) of the rollback segment. This value differs by the number of bytes in one database block from the value of the BYTES column of the ALL/DBA/USER_SEGMENTS views.
- WRITES is the number of bytes of entries written to the rollback segment.
- XACTS is the number of active transactions.
- GETS is the number of rollback segment header requests.
- WAITS is the number of rollback segment header requests that result in waits.
- OPTSIZE is the value of the optimal parameter for the rollback segment.
- HWMSIZE is the highest value (high water mark), in bytes, of the rollback segment size reached during usage.
- SHRINKS is the number of shrinks that the rollback segment has had to perform to stay at the optimal size.
- WRAPS is the number of times a rollback segment entry has wrapped from one extent to another.
- EXTENDS is the number of times that the rollback segment had to acquire a new extent.
- AVESHRINK is the average number of bytes freed during a shrink.
- AVEACTIVE is the average number of bytes in active extents in the rollback segment, measured over time.
- STATUS denotes the rollback segment status, which can be one of the following:
  - ONLINE
  - PENDING OFFLINE
  - OFFLINE
  - FULL
- CUREXT is the current extent.
- CURBLK is the current block.

Listing 39.2: Viewing the Names of Online Rollback Segments

```
select * from v$rollname;
```

The output of Listing 39.2 is given as follows:

```
       USN NAME
---------- -------------------------
         0 SYSTEM
         1 _SYSSMU1$
         2 _SYSSMU2$
         3 _SYSSMU3$
         4 _SYSSMU4$
         5 _SYSSMU5$
         6 _SYSSMU6$
         7 _SYSSMU7$
         8 _SYSSMU8$
         9 _SYSSMU9$
        10 _SYSSMU10$

11 rows selected
```

`V$ROLLSTAT` and `V$ROLLNAME` are joined to map `USN` with name of the rollback segment.

Rollback Segment States

The number of rollback segments, which are acquired by Oracle instance, depends on two parameters—transactions and transaction per rollback. Therefore, if a transaction equals to 20 and the transaction per rollback equals to 5, then the number of rollback segments acquired by an instance are 4.

If the instance cannot acquire the rollback segment then it will not open. For a single instance of Oracle, all the rollback segments are public; but for a parallel server, there can be public and private rollback segments. Public segments are acquired by using these two parameters, and private instances or private rollback segments are allocated using the initializing parameter of rollback segments.

When you create a rollback segment, it has status offline. You can explicitly make it online by giving the command:

```
ALTER ROLLBACK SEGMENT ONLINE
```

The rollback segment can have the following status:

- Online
- Offline
- Invalid
- Needs recovery
- Partly available

Online status means that the user can use the rollback segment. It can be made offline using the following command:

```
ALTER ROLLBACK SEGMENT OFFLINE
```

If the rollback segment has active entries then it cannot be made offline immediately. Instead, it will get the status pending offline. When a transaction is committed, the active extents are released and the rollback segment is made offline. When users drop the rollback segment, it gets the invalid status. When the block in the rollback segment is corrupted and Oracle cannot write in that rollback segment, then it will get the needs recovery status.

Take the case of a distributed transaction, in which, in a single transaction, data is updated on multiple sites. If there is a problem in transaction say `commit due to communication failure`, then the rollback segment gets the partly available status. This is because there is no guarantee when a transaction is resolved, since it can be resolved only when the communication link to a server is established. In such a case, the rollback segment carries active entries and there is no guarantee when such a transaction is committed. In this case, the rollback segment will just grow in size, so that the administrator has to make such rollback segment offline.

The administrator has to create sufficient rollback segments and adjust the parameters and transactions per rollback so that these segments can be acquired during startup, otherwise after startup they are made online using the `ALTER ROLLBACK` command. In addition, the administrator has to make rollback segment offline, if failure in distributed transaction is detected. You can view the current status of online rollback segments, as shown in Listing 39.3:

Listing 39.3: Viewing the current status of online rollback

```
select segment_name, tablespace_name, status
from sys.dba_rollback_segs;
```

The output of Listing 39.3 is given as follows:

```
SEGMENT_NAME                   TABLESPACE_NAME                STATUS
------------------------------ ------------------------------ ----------------
SYSTEM                         SYSTEM                         ONLINE
_SYSSMU1$                      UNDOTBS1                       ONLINE
_SYSSMU2$                      UNDOTBS1                       ONLINE
_SYSSMU3$                      UNDOTBS1                       ONLINE
_SYSSMU4$                      UNDOTBS1                       ONLINE
_SYSSMU5$                      UNDOTBS1                       ONLINE
_SYSSMU6$                      UNDOTBS1                       ONLINE
_SYSSMU7$                      UNDOTBS1                       ONLINE
_SYSSMU8$                      UNDOTBS1                       ONLINE
_SYSSMU9$                      UNDOTBS1                       ONLINE
_SYSSMU10$                     UNDOTBS1                       ONLINE
_SYSSMU11$                     UNDOTBS1                       OFFLINE
_SYSSMU12$                     UNDOTBS1                       OFFLINE
_SYSSMU13$                     UNDOTBS1                       OFFLINE
_SYSSMU14$                     UNDOTBS1                       OFFLINE
_SYSSMU15$                     UNDOTBS1                       OFFLINE
_SYSSMU16$                     UNDOTBS1                       OFFLINE
_SYSSMU17$                     UNDOTBS1                       OFFLINE
_SYSSMU18$                     UNDOTBS1                       OFFLINE

19 rows selected
```

Space Allocation in Rollback Segments

The location of the rollback segments is normally in the tablespace, which is used only for keeping rollback information. Since Oracle handles various types of data, a user can divide this data logically using a tablespace. Tables, indexes, package code, or procedure code is attached to one of the tablespaces. Generally, the following tablespaces are created after Oracle is installed:

- **System**—Refers to the tablespace that is used to keep a data dictionary and code of stored subprograms.
- **User tablespace**—Refers to the tablespace that is used by user objects, such as employee table or department table. It is better to have a separate tablespace for each application, such as payroll and marketing.
- **Rollback tablespace**—Refers to the tablespace that is used to keep rollback information.
- **Temporary tablespace**—Refers to the tablespace that is used to keep temporary data. For example, sorting option (ORDER BY) requires temporary space.

The data is actually stored in files, which are called data files. One table can have multiple data files, but one data file can be present in only one tablespace. Oracle internally maintains the information of data files and tablespaces and their relationships.

One tablespace is logically divided into a number of segments and one segment can have multiple extents. An extent is a set of logical contiguous blocks. For example, if a set of 5 blocks can be formed of values 23, 24, 25, 26, and 27 and a table can have normally one segment, the storage hierarchy is as follows:

Tablespace → segment → extent → blocks → bytes

In Oracle, allocation is done using extents. For example, a table can have the extents shown in Figure 39.1:

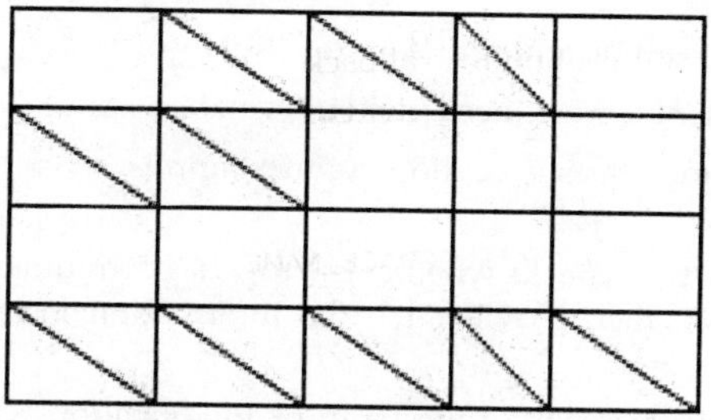

Figure 39.1: Extents in data segment

Therefore, the table has been given three extents, such as 3, 4, and 5.

How Oracle Allocates Space to Rollback Segments

The following procedure is adopted to allocate space to rollback segments:

- When a transaction issues the first DML statement, a rollback segment is allocated to that transaction to keep the undo information.
- One transaction can have at most one rollback segment. However, one rollback segment can have multiple transactions associated with it.
- Multiple transactions can write their rollback information in the same extent, but not in the same block. For example, if there are four rollback segments, such as `RBS1`, `RBS2`, `RBS3`, and `RBS4`, then for transaction `T1`, `RBS1` is allocated; for `T2`, `RBS2`; and so on. After allocating all the four rollback segments, `RBS1` may be allocated for transaction `T5`.
- The transaction starts writing in the extent in a cyclic manner, such as `E1`, `E2`, `E3`, and then again `E1`. This is shown in Figure 39.2:

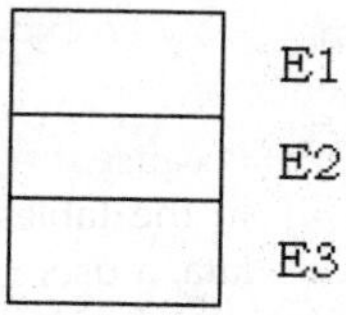

Figure 39.2: Extents of rollback segment

- When a transaction commits, it makes the used block as free block so that it can be used by other transaction. A free block data is not immediately overwritten.
- An extent which has all free blocks is called as free extent.
- An extent having entries of uncommitted transactions is called as active extent.
- In case of circular writing, when it encounters active extent, Oracle allocates a new extent and temporarily attaches that extent to the rollback segment. For example, if the transaction has written `E3`, it requests for `E1`; if it is active then it allocates a new extent `E4` and starts writing it.
- Allocation in this manner, along with cyclic writing, keeps undo information for a longer time even if the transaction commits.

Implementing Read Consistency using Rollback Segment

Read consistency rules are implemented using rollback segment as follows

- When a row is modified, then the following information is also recorded:
  - Transaction identifier
  - Time stamp of modification
  - Status of row—committed or not committed
  - Location in rollback segment, where there is old information about row
- When a query is submitted and starts execution, a timestamp is given to the query indicating the starting time of execution.
- When the query fetches the row, it checks whether the row has committed or uncommitted information. If it does not have commit status, then it will fetch the information from rollback segment where the old information is guaranteed to exist.
- If the status is committed, it checks the timestamp of modification with the timestamp of query. If the timestamp of modification is less than query timestamp, it will read from the row. If not, it will read from the rollback segment. It means, even if a transaction is committed and blocks in rollback segment are declared as free blocks, the information in a block is not overwritten at that time; only the status is changed. The information is overwritten only according to circular writing. If it fails to return read consistent information from rollback segment, then it will issue an error `snapshot to old`.

The tracking of rollback information is managed by one special entry in block, called transactional entry. When you create a table at that time, you can mention the number of transaction entries, `INITRANS`. The concurrent accesses of blocks are controlled by `INITRANS`, if it's value is 2 then it is guaranteed that at least two transactions concurrently access the block. The maximum number of such entries in a block is controlled by the parameter `MAXTRANS`. If `MAXTRANS = 5`, it means that at the most five transactions can concurrently access the block.

Administrative Aspects in a Rollback Segment

Following administrative functions are related with rollback segment

- If you are getting an error `snapshot to old`, it means that the time duration of keeping rollback information is less. It means, you should have longer rollback segments. This is done by increasing the value of parameter to optimal.
- If the rollback segment has less size, then there may be extra overheads of allocating extents at runtime that will slow down the speed of update statements.
- You cannot keep a very large rollback segment because it will unnecessarily occupy space on the disk.
- Oracle allocates extents at runtime to increase the size of rollback segment according to the requirement.

Following code indicates how the Rollback segments are administered.

Listing 39.4: Creating a Rollback Segment

```
create rollback segment rbs1 tablespace
rollback_segment1;
```

The output of Listing 39.4 is given as follows:

```
Rollback segment created
```

Listing 39.5: Creating a Rollback Segment with Storage Parameters

```
create public rollback segment rbs7
tablespace rbs
storage (
  initial 100k
        next 100k
        optimal 4m
```

```
            minextents 10
            maxextents 100);
```

The output of Listing 39.5 is given as follows:

```
Rollback segment created
```

You can alter a rollback segment as online, which is shown in the following syntax:

```
alter rollback segment rbs7 online;
```

The output of preceding syntax is given as follows:

```
Rollback segment altered
```

You can also alter the storage parameter of a rollback segment, as shown in the following syntax:

```
alter rollback segment rbs7 storage (maxextents 120);
```

The output of preceding syntax is given as follows:

```
Rollback segment altered
```

In addition, you can shrink a rollback segment, as shown in the following syntax:

```
alter rollback segment rbs7 shrink to 100k;
```

The output of preceding syntax is given as follows:

```
Rollback segment altered
```

After shrinking a rollback segment, let's learn to set a transaction to use a specifically named for a rollback segment. This can be done by using the code given in the following syntax:

```
set transaction use rollback segment rbs7;
```

The output of preceding syntax is given as follows:

```
Transaction set
```

You cannot make a tablespace offline, which contains active rollback segment. Therefore, you need to change the property of `USER` tablespace to offline, as shown in the following syntax:

```
alter tablespace users offline;
```

The output of the preceding syntax is given as follows:

```
ALTER TABLESPACE USERS OFFLINE
*
ERROR at line 1:
ORA-01539: tablespace 'USERS' is not online
```

You cannot drop a rollback segment because the current transactions are using it. Therefore, you have to first make it `OFFLINE` and then drop it, as shown in Listing 39.6:

Listing 39.6: Altering a Rollback Segment as Offline

```
alter rollback segment rbs8 offline;
```

The output of Listing 39.6 is given as follows:

```
Rollback segment altered
```

Listing 39.7 shows you the code to drop a rollback segment:

Listing 39.7: Dropping a Rollback Segment

```
drop rollback segment rbs8;
```

The output of Listing 39.7 is given as follows:

```
Rollback segment dropped
```

*The Role of the **OPTIMAL** Parameter in the **Rollback** Segment*

The optimal value can be decided by reading view V$ROLLSTAT

- If you plot the rollback segment requirement over a period of time, then you get Figure 39.3, which shows that the high requirement is only for a small period of time:

Graph of Requirement (in bytes) with Time

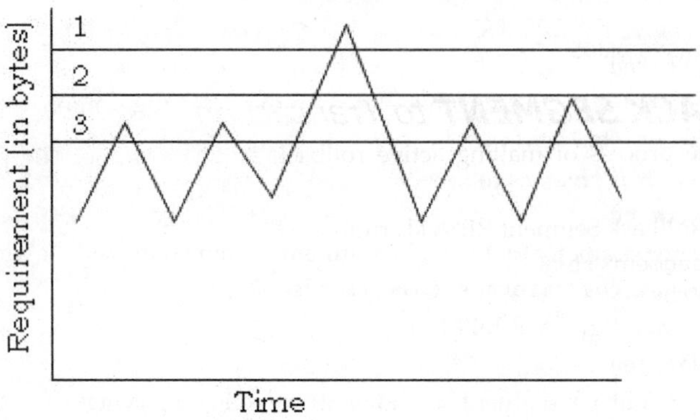

Figure 39.3: Requirement of rollback tablespace

- Suppose you put optimal at line 3 then there are a large number of shrinks.
- If you put optimal at line 1, then the number of shrinks is less, but your optimal is more than what is required.

The correct value of optimal is given by line 2, where the number of shrinks and the size of the rollback segment is less. It is indicated by less number of shrinks and high value of average size of shrink. The number of shrinks and average size of a shrink can be obtained from the `V$Rollstat` view. In addition, the `V$Rollstat` view shows the maximum rollback segment requirement reached over a period of time. It is indicated by the HWM (High Water Mark) size.

Finding Rollback Segments Allocated to transaction

You can find out which rollback segment is currently allocated to a transaction. Suppose a transaction is as follows:

```
create table emp(EMPNO NUMBER(8));
```

The output of this transaction is given as follows:

```
Table Created
```

You can insert values in the `emp` table, as shown in the following syntax:

```
insert into emp values(546);
```

The output of the preceding syntax is given as follows:

```
 1 row created
```

Listing 39.8: Viewing rollback segment information

```
select z.usn "rsegment_no",z.name "rsegment_name", z1.username ,z.status from
(select v1.usn usn,v1.name name,v2.status status from v$rollname v1,v$rollstat
  v2 where v1.usn = v2.usn and xacts>0)z,
(select v.username username, v1.xidusn usn from v$session v,v$transaction v1
where v.saddr = v1.ses_addr) z1
where
z.usn = z1.usn ;
or
select v2.usn"rsegment_no",v3.name "rsegment_name",v.username ,v2.status from
  v$session v,v$transaction v1,v$rollstat v2,v$rollname v3
where v.saddr = v1.ses_addr
and v1.xidusn = v2.usn
and v2.usn = v3.usn
/
```

The output of Listing 39.8 is given as follows:

```
RSEGMENT_NO      RSEGMENT_NAME          USERNAME              STATUS
----------- --------------------- --------------- --------
5                _SYSSMU5$              SYS                   ONLINE
```

Allocating ROLLBACK SEGMENT to Transaction

This section explains the process of making active rollback segment offline. The process starts by creating a rollback segment:

Listing 39.9: Creating a Rollback Segment RBS8 (Terminal1)

```
create rollback segment rbs8
      tablespace rbs
      storage (
      initial 100k
      next 100k
      optimal 4m
      minextents 2
      maxextents 10);
```

The output of Listing 39.9 is given as follows:

```
Rollback segment created
```

Listing 39.10: Altering RBS Rollback Segment to Online

```
alter rollback segment rbs8 online;
```

The output of Listing 39.10 is given as follows:

```
Rollback segment altered
```

Listing 39.11: Setting transaction to use a specifically named rollback segment

```
set transaction use rollback segment rbs8;
```

The output of Listing 39.11 is given as follows:

```
Transaction set
```

It is recommended that for long and large transactions, you should allocate large rollback segments; and for small transactions, you should allocate small rollback segments. This is to avoid runtime allocation for large transactions and for small transactions. In addition, you can fit the total rollback segment into the main memory. Therefore, it avoids disk writes.

Dropping Rollback segment

To drop rollback segment, the rollback segment is made offline. If rollback segment is having uncommitted entries of transaction then it is not made offline immediately. After transaction committed the status of rollback segment is made offline. This is explained using following example. INSERT statement given in listing 39.12 uses rollback segment RBS8.

--FROM TERMINAL 1

Setting transaction to use a specifically named rollback segment

```
set transaction use rollback segment rbs8;
```

Result:

```
Transaction set
```

Listing 39.12: Inserting Data into the emp Table

```
insert into emp(empno) values(546);
```

The output of Listing 39.12 is given as follows:

```
1 row created
```

Listing 39.13: Altering Rollback Segment Offline (Terminal 2)

```
alter rollback segment rbs8 offline;
```

The output of Listing 39.13 is given as follows:

```
Rollback segment altered
```

Viewing rollback segment information (Still you get status as ONLINE)

```
select v2.usn"rsegment_no",v3.name "rsegment_name",v.username ,v2.status
   from v$session v,v$transaction v1,v$rollstat v2,v$rollname v3
          where v.saddr = v1.ses_addr
          and v1.xidusn = v2.usn
          and v2.usn = v3.usn
/
```

Result:

```
RSEGMENT_NO                RSEGMENT_NAME            USERNAME                STATUS
-----------                -----------------        -----------------       --------
5                          _SYSSMU5$                SYS                     ONLINE
```

After committing transaction having statement given in Listing 39.12

Committing transaction (Terminal1)

```
commit;
```

Result:

```
Commit Complete
```

Dropping the rollback segment

```
drop rollback segment rbs8;
```

Result:

```
Rollback segment dropped
```

Viewing description of the rollback segment (RBS8 is not listed)

```
select * from dba_rollback_segs;
```

Result:

```
SEGMENT_NAME                         OWNER  TABLESPACE_NAME                SEGMENT_ID
   FILE_ID   BLOCK_ID INITIAL_EXTENT NEXT_EXTENT MIN_EXTENTS MAX_EXTENTS PCT_INC
REASE STATUS            INSTANCE_NUM                                  RELATIVE_FNO
------------------------------ ------ ------------------------------ ----------
---------- ---------- -------------- ----------- ----------- ----------- -------
----- ---------------- ---------------------------------------- ------------
SYSTEM                               SYS    SYSTEM                                  0
         1        128         114688       57344           1       32765
      ONLINE                                                                1
_SYSSMU1_1518548437$                 PUBLIC UNDOTBS1                                1
         3        128         131072       65536           2       32765
      ONLINE                                                                3
_SYSSMU2_2082490410$                 PUBLIC UNDOTBS1                                2
         3        144         131072       65536           2       32765
      ONLINE                                                                3
_SYSSMU3_991555123$                  PUBLIC UNDOTBS1                                3
         3        160         131072       65536           2       32765
      ONLINE                                                                3
_SYSSMU4_2369290268$                 PUBLIC UNDOTBS1                                4
         3        176         131072       65536           2       32765
      ONLINE                                                                3
_SYSSMU5_1018230376$                 PUBLIC UNDOTBS1                                5
```

```
         3          192          131072          65536             2         32765
       ONLINE                                                                           3
_SYSSMU6_1834113595$                  PUBLIC UNDOTBS1                                     6
         3          208          131072          65536             2         32765
       ONLINE                                                                           3
_SYSSMU7_137577888$                   PUBLIC UNDOTBS1                                     7
         3          224          131072          65536             2         32765
       ONLINE                                                                           3
_SYSSMU8_1557854099$                  PUBLIC UNDOTBS1                                     8
         3          240          131072          65536             2         32765
       ONLINE                                                                           3
_SYSSMU9_1126410412$                  PUBLIC UNDOTBS1                                     9
         3          256          131072          65536             2         32765
       ONLINE                                                                           3
_SYSSMU10_3176102001$                 PUBLIC UNDOTBS1                                    10
         3          272          131072          65536             2         32765
       ONLINE                                                                           3
```

NOTE

Oracle recommends that there should not be more than 50 rollback segments per database.

Summary

In this chapter, you have learned about the concept of rollback segments. You also learned how to create and allocate rollback segments. In the next chapter, you will deal with the `UNDO` tablespace.

Exercise

1. How to view information of rollback segment?
2. How to create rollback segment and allocate rollback segment to transaction?

40

UNDO Tablespace

An UNDO segment is used to keep the old value (UNDO data) when a process alter the data in the database. It stores the location of the data and the data as it existed before being modified. The header of the UNDO segment contains the transaction table where the information about the current transactions using the UNDO segments is stored. A serial transaction uses only one UNDO segment to store all of its UNDO data. The following are the features of the UNDO tablespace:

- UNDO tablespaces are special tablespaces used only to store the UNDO information. In the UNDO tablespace you cannot create any other type of segment.
- One database can have zero or more UNDO tablespaces. The UNDO data is managed within the UNDO tablespace using UNDO segments, which are created and maintained by Oracle.
- UNDO tablespaces are locally managed, i.e. their extent status is managed in bitmaps. At any time, an extent is either allocated or used by a transaction table, or it is free.
- The UNDO tablespace is useful for:
  - Transaction recovery
  - Read consistency
  - Transaction rollback
- The UNDO management is done in either of the following two ways:
  - `Rollback segments` (Manual mode)
  - `Undo tablespace management` (Automatic mode)

You cannot use both methods in the same database instance. If you use the rollback segment method of managing the UNDO space, you are said to be operating in the manual UNDO management mode. If you are managing UNDO using UNDO_TABLESPACE, you are said to be operating in the AUTO UNDO management mode.

Manual Mode

In the manual mode, a non-system UNDO segment, which is created by the database administrator, can be used for changes made to the objects in any NON-SYSTEM tablespace. There are three types of non-system UNDO segments:

- **Private**—Refers to the UNDO segments that are brought online by the instance because they are listed in the parameter file. You can explicitly bring them online using the following command:

```
ALTER ROLLBACK SEGMENT <name> ONLINE;
```

- **Public**—Refers to the UNDO segments that form a pool of UNDO segments available in the database. They are normally used with RAC.
- **Deferred**—Refers to the UNDO segments that are created when the tablespace is brought OFFLINE. They are used to rollback the transactions when the tablespace is brought back ONLINE. They are dropped automatically when they are not needed.

Auto **UNDO** Management (AUM)

Data is managed using an UNDO tablespace. Each Oracle instance is assigned one and only one UNDO tablespace. Oracle automatically maintains the UNDO data within the UNDO tablespace.

Configuration

The following two INIT parameters need to be configured:

- `UNDO_management`—It can have two values—AUTO or MANUAL
- `UNDO_tablespace`—It is the name of the tablespace

If only one UNDO tablespace exists in the database and UNDO_MANAGEMENT is set to AUTO, then UNDO_TABLESPACE parameter is optional, that is Oracle will automatically choose the UNDO tablespace.

In the manual mode (DEFAULT), you can create and manage the UNDO segments when needed:

- The UNDO_management parameter cannot be modified dynamically
- The UNDO_tablespace parameter can be changed dynamically

The following code snippet shows how to dynamically redirect to UNDO tablespaces:

```
ALTER SYSTEM SET UNDO_TABLESPACE  '<NAME>';
```

Management of the ***UNDO*** Tablespace

Listing 40.1 shows how to view the parameters of Undo_management:

Listing 40.1: Viewing the Parameters of Undo_management

```
show parameter Undo_management;
```

The output of Listing 40.1 is as follows:

```
NAME                            TYPE                VALUE
------------------------        -----------         ---------------
Undo_management                 string              AUTO
```

When the first DML operation is executed within a transaction, the transaction is bound to an UNDO segment in the current UNDO tablespace. If the instance does not have a designated UNDO tablespace, the transaction binds to the system UNDO segment.

Types of **UNDO** Segments

- **System**—It is used for objects in the SYSTEM tablespace
- **Non-system**—It is used for objects in other tablespaces

The system UNDO segment is created in the SYSTEM tablespace, when a database is created. This UNDO management can only be used for changes made to objects in the SYSTEM tablespace. It exists and works the same way in both manual and auto modes.

The database that has multiple tablespaces needs atleast one non-system UNDO segment for the manual mode or one UNDO tablespace for the AUTO mode.

Listing 40.2 shows the code to view information about system rollback segment from DBA_EXTENTS:

Listing 40.2: Viewing Information about System Rollback Segment from DBA_EXTENTS

```
select tablespace_name, segment_name, segment_type, sum(bytes),         count(extent_id)
from dba_extents
where segment_type = 'ROLLBACK'
group by tablespace_name,
segment_name,segment_type;
```

The output of Listing 40.2 is as follows:

```
TABLESPACE_NAME
------------------------------
SEGMENT_NAME
--------------------------------------------------------------------------------
SEGMENT_TYPE       SUM(BYTES) COUNT(EXTENT_ID)
------------------ ---------- ----------------
SYSTEM
SYSTEM
ROLLBACK               393216                6
```

Listing 40.3 shows the code to view information using UNDO segments:

Listing 40.3: Viewing Information of UNDO Segments

```
select tablespace_name, segment_name, segment_type, sum(bytes),          count(extent_id)
from dba_extents
where segment_type = 'TYPE2 UNDO' group by tablespace_name,
   segment_name,segment_type;
```

The output displays 20 rows; therefore, we have not included it here.

You can select a segment information from `dba_segments, as:`

```
select * from dba_segments where segment_type='TYPE2 UNDO';
```

The output displays 20 rows; therefore, we have not included it here.

Creating the **UNDO** Tablespace

There are two methods of creating an `UNDO` tablespace:

- Using the `CREATE DATABASE` statement. This method is used when you are creating a new database, and the instance is started in automatic `UNDO` management mode (`UNDO_MANAGEMENT = AUTO`).
- Using the `CREATE UNDO TABLESPACE` statement.

*Using the **CREATE DATABASE Statement***

If you do not specify the `UNDO TABLESPACE` clause in the `CREATE DATABASE` statement, then Oracle will create the `UNDO` tablespace with the `SYSTEM_UNDOTBS` name, size `10M`, and the filename as `dbu1<sid>.dbf`, `as shown in the following code snippet:`

```
CREATE DATABASE rbdb1
     CONTROLFILE REUSE
...
     UNDO TABLESPACE UNDOtbs_01 DATAFILE 'D:\UNDOTBS01.dbf'
```

*Using the **CREATE UNDO TABLESPACE Statement***

The UNDO tablespace is created using the CREATE UNDO TABLESPACE command as follows:

```
create undo tablespace undotbs_01 datafile
' d:\undotbs01.dbf '
size 2m reuse autoextend on;
```

The result of the preceding code snippet is as follows:

```
Tablespace created
```

Listing 40.4 shows how to initialize an undo tablespace:

Listing 40.4: Initializing an Undo Tablespace by Setting the UNDO_tablespace Name

```
UNDO_TABLESPACE=<name>;
```

Altering the **UNDO** Tablespace

Listing 40.5 shows how to alter an UNDO tablespace:

Listing 40.5: Altering an UNDO Tablespace

```
alter tablespace undotbs_01 add datafile
'd:\undo03.dbf'
size 2m
autoextend on;
```

The output of Listing 40.5 is as follows:

```
Tablespace altered
```

The options to alter an UNDO tablespace are as follows:

- ADD DATAFILE (used in Listing 40.5)
- RENAME
- DATAFILE[ONLINE/OFFLINE]
- BEGIN BACKUP
- END BACKUP

Switching the **UNDO** Tablespace

The UNDO tablespace is used by Oracle by switching to created UNDO tablespace using the following command:

```
alter system set undo_tablespace ='<name>';
```

The switch operation is ONLINE. This operation does not wait for transactions in the old UNDO tablespace to commit. If there is any pending transaction in the old UNDO tablespace, then the old UNDO tablespace enters into a PENDING OFFLINE mode. In this mode, all existing transactions can continue to execute, but UNDO records for the new user transactions cannot be stored in this UNDO tablespace.

In the PENDING OFFLINE mode, the UNDO tablespace cannot be assigned to another instance nor can it be dropped. After all the transactions are complete, this tablespace displays the status OFFLINE.

In the OFFLINE mode, the UNDO tablespace can be either dropped or assigned to another instance.

If UNDO_TABLESPACE is set to '' (2 single Quotes), then the current UNDO tablespace will be switched out without switching to another UNDO tablespace. This is required if you want to revert to manual UNDO management mode.

Listing 40.6 shows how to alter a system specific UNDO_Tablespace:

Listing 40.6: Altering System to a Specific UNDO_Tablespace

```
alter system set UNDO_Tablespace = '';
```

The output of Listing 40.6 is as follows:

```
System altered
```

Connecting to Oracle as user Scott and inserting a row into the emp table

```
connect scott/tiger@orcl
insert into emp(empno) values(2);
```

Result:

```
insert into emp(empno) values(2)
            *
ERROR at line 1:
ORA-12096: error in
materialized view log on "SCOTT"."EMP"
ORA-01552: cannot use system rollback segment for non-system tablespace 'USERS'
```

Dropping the **UNDO** Tablespace

Listing 40.7 shows the syntax for dropping the UNDO tablespace:

Listing 40.7: Syntax for Dropping the UNDO Tablespace

```
DROP TABLESPACE <UNDO_ts_name>;
```

The UNDO tablespace can only be dropped if it is currently not in use by any other instance. To drop a UNDO tablespace, first switch to new UNDO tablespace. Drop the tablespace only after all the current transactions are complete.

Listing 40.8 shows the code to view active transactions:

Listing 40.8: Viewing Active Transactions

```
select name, xacts "active transactions"
    from v$rollname, v$rollstat
    where v$rollname.usn = v$rollstat.usn;
```

The output of Listing 40.8 is as follows:

```
NAME                           ACTIVE TRANSACTIONS
------------------------------ -------------------
SYSTEM                                           0
```

The UNDO Retention

The UNDO retention indicates how much time the UNDO information is guaranteed to be retained after a transaction commits. It is specified in seconds, as shown in the following code snippet:

```
SHOW PARAMETER UNDO_retention;
```

The output of the preceding code snippet is as follows:

```
NAME                                 TYPE    VALUE
------------------------------------ ------- ------------------------------
UNDO_retention                       integer  900
```

The UNDO_RETENTION parameter value can also be changed dynamically at any time using the ALTER SYSTEM command.

Listing 40.9 shows how to change the UNDO_retention parameter dynamically:

Listing 40.9: Dynamically Changing the UNDO_retention Parameter

```
alter system set UNDO_retention = 5;
```

The output of Listing 40.9 is as follows:

```
System altered
```

If an application requires that a version of the database be available reflecting its content 12 hours (12*60*60 seconds), then the UNDO_retention must be set to 43200. The amount of the UNDO space required to satisfy the UNDO retention requirement can be estimated using the following formula:

```
UNDOSpace = UR * UPS + overhead
```

In this formula:

- UNDOSpace is the number of UNDO blocks
- UR is UNDO_retention in seconds
- UPS is the UNDO blocks for each second
- overhead is the small overhead for metadata (transaction tables, bitmaps, and so forth)

For example, if UNDO_retention is set to 2 hours, and the transaction rate (UPS) is 200 UNDO blocks for each second, with a 4 K block size, the required UNDO space is computed as follows:

```
(2 * 3600 * 200 + 4K) = 5.8 GB
```

UNDO_suppress_errors

This enables users to suppress the errors while executing manual UNDO management mode operations (for example ALTER ROLLBACK SEGMENT ONLINE) in automatic UNDO management mode. Setting this parameter enables users to use the UNDO tablespace feature before all application programs and scripts are converted to automatic UNDO management mode. For example, if you have an application that uses SET TRANSACTION USE ROLLBACK SEGMENT statement, you can add the statement:

```
alter session set undo_suppress_errors = true;
```

Performance Views

The performance of UNDO tablespace can be analyzed using the following views:

- The V$UNDOSTAT view
- The V$ROLLSTAT view
- The V$TRANSACTION view
- The DBA_UNDO_EXTENTS view
- Dictionary managed tablespaces

The *V$UNDOSTAT* View

The V$UNDOSTAT view helps to estimate the amount of the UNDO space required for the current workload. It is available in 2 modes—manual undo management mode and automatic undo management mode.

Column	Description
UNDOTSN	Specifies the last active UNDO tablespace number in this duration.
UNDOBLKS	Specify the total numbers of UNDO blocks consumed. To obtain the consumption rate of UNDO blocks you can use this column, and thereby estimate the size of UNDO tablespace.
MAXQUERYLEN	Detects the length of the longest query (in number of seconds) executed in the instance during the period. To estimate the proper setting of the UNDO_RETENTION parameter you can use this statistic.
UNXPSTEALCNT	Gives the number of attempts to obtain UNDO space by stealing unexpired extents from other transactions.

Listing 40.10 shows how to view statistics of undospace consumption:

Listing 40.10: Viewing Statistics of undospace Consumption

```
select undotsn, undoblks, maxquerylen, unxpstealcnt
from v$undostat;
```

The output of Listing 40.10 is as follows:

```
  UNDOTSN   UNDOBLKS   MAXQUERYLEN   UNXPSTEALCNT
---------- ---------- -----------   ------------
        1         18           0              0
        1        126           0              0
```

The *V$ROLLSTAT* View

For automatic UNDO management mode, information reflects the behavior of the UNDO segments in the UNDO tablespace.

The *V$TRANSACTION* View

The V$TRANSACTION view contains UNDO segment information, as shown in the following code snippet:

```
select sum(used_ublk) from v$transaction;
```

This tells you how much UNDO is being used by the current transactions.

The **DBA_UNDO_EXTENTS** View

It shows the commit time for each extent in the `UNDO` tablespace. Suspendable statements work best with an `UNDO` tablespace. If rollback segments are located in the dictionary managed tablespaces, then space allocation for rollback segments is not resumable. However, space allocation for user objects (tables, indexes, and the likes) would still be resumable. To workaround this limitation, we recommend using automatic `UNDO` management or placing the rollback segments in locally managed tablespaces.

Dictionary Managed Tablespaces

A DDL operation, such as `CREATE TABLE` or `CREATE INDEX`, is executed with an explicit `MAXEXTENTS` (parameter which decides the maximum size of a table) setting which causes an out of space error during its execution. So the operation will not be suspended. Instead, it will be aborted. This error is treated as non-repairable because the properties of an object (for example, `MAXEXTENTS`) cannot be altered before the operation is complete.

However, if a DML operation causes an already existing table or index to reach the `MAXEXTENTS` limit, it will be suspended and can be resumed later. This restriction can be overcome either by setting the `MAXEXTENTS` clause to `UNLIMITED` or by using locally managed tablespaces.

Why **UNDO** Tablespaces

There are special cases that may result in an `ORA-01555 (snapshot too old)`, a rollback segment created with the `OPTIMAL` clause. It may cause a query to return `ORA-01555`, if it has shrunk during the life of the query causing rollback segment information required to generate consistent read versions of blocks to be lost. In `AUTO UNDO`, you just have to set the size of `UNDO` tablespace using the formula that avoids the possibility of a 'snapshot too old' error.

Let's now discuss some cases which describe advantages of the `UNDO` tablespace. The first case indicates conventional rollback segment while the second case indicates the UNDO segment. One of the advantages of the UNDO tablespace is the resumable session.

Case1: Using Dictionary Managed **Roll Back Segment**

The basic steps to use dictionary managed roll back segment are as follows:

- Create a 256 K tablespace (local) `MY_LMT`
- Create a 1 MB tablespace tablespace (dictionary) `MY_RBS`
- Create a rollback segment `rbs10` on `MY_RBS`
- Create a table `TEST` on `MY_LMT` as an empty copy of `DBA_SOURCE`
- Set the transaction to use `rbs10`
- Insert value in test table as selected from `dba_source`

Listing 40.11 shows how to create a tablespace:

Listing 40.11: Creating a Data Tablespace

```
create tablespace MY_LMT datafile                              'd:\my_lmt01.dbf' size 256K;
```

The output of Listing 40.11 is as follows:

```
Tablespace created
```

Creating dictionary managed tablespace

```
create tablespace my_rbs datafile '                        d:\my_rbs01.dbf' size 1m extent
  management                dictionary;
```

Result:

```
Tablespace created
```

Creating rollback segment for `my_rbs tablespace`

```
create rollback segment rbs10 tablespace MY_RBS;
```

Result:

```
Rollback segment created
```

Altering the rollback segment to online

```
alter rollback segment rbs10 online;
```

Result:

```
Rollback segment altered
```

Creating a table named `test` in `my_lmt tablespace`

```
create table test(owner varchar2(30),name   varchar2(30),type            varchar2(12),line
   number,text varchar2(4000)) tablespace my_lmt;
```

Result:

```
Table created
```

Enabling resumable space allocation for the session

```
alter session enable resumable;
```

Result:

```
Session altered
```

Assigning the current transaction to `rbs10` rollback segment.

```
set transaction use rollback segment rbs10;
```

Result:

```
Transaction set
```

Inserting value in `test` as selected from `DBA_SOURCE`

```
insert into test(select * from dba_source);
```

Result:

```
*
ERROR at line 1:
ORA-01562: failed to extend rollback segment number 11
ORA-01650: unable to extend rollback segment RBS10 by 5 in tablespace MY_RBS
In the Alertlog file:
Mon Jan 01 19:03:11 2001
Statement in resumable session 'User SYSTEM(5), Session 7, Instance 1' was      suspended
due to
ORA-01653: unable to extend table SYSTEM.TEST by 16 in tablespace MY_LMT.
Mon Jan 01 19:10:47 2001
FULL status of rollback segment 11 set.
Statement in resumable session 'User SYSTEM(5), Session 7, Instance 1' was      aborted.
```

It shows that if a transaction is using dictionary managed rollback segments, then the operation is aborted rather than suspended.

Case2: Using UNDO Segment in ***UNDO*** *Tablespace*

The basic steps to use undo segment in an UNDO tablespace are as follows:

- Create `UNDO` tablespace `my_lmt_rs` of size `2 M`
- Check for `UNDO` parameters
- Check whether we can create rollback segments in `UNDO` tablespace

- Switch to new UNDO tablespace
- Check parameters for new changes
- Make session resumable
- Fire insert statement which requires large space than which is not available

Listing 40.12 shows how to create an undo tablespace:

Listing 40.12: Creating an undo Tablespace

```
create undo tablespace my_lmt_rs datafile 'my_lmt_rs01'
    size 2m
/
```

The output of Listing 40.12 is as follows:

```
Tablespace created
```

Displaying information about the initialization parameters for the current session

```
select * from v$parameter where name like '%UNDO%';
```

Result:

```
NUM     NAME                     TYPE      VALUE
------  ----------------------  ---------  --------
370     UNDO_management           2        AUTO
371     UNDO_tablespace           2        UNDOTBS
375     UNDO_suppress_errors      1        FALSE
379     UNDO_retention            3        900
```

Creating a rollback segment in my_lmt_rs tablespace

```
create rollback segment my_lmt_rs_rbs01 tablespace  my_lmt_rs;
```

Result:

```
Rollback segment created
```

Dynamically redirecting to MY_LMT_RS undo tablespaces

```
alter system
set undo_tablespace = 'my_lmt_rs';
```

Result:

```
System altered
```

Displaying information about the initialization parameters for the current session

```
select * from v$parameter where name like '%UNDO%';
```

Result:

```
NUM           NAME                        TYPE             VALUE
-------   --------------------------   -----------     ------------
370             UNDO_management               2                  AUTO
371       UNDO_tablespace            2             MY_LMT_RS
375             UNDO_suppress_errors          1                  FALSE
379             UNDO_retention                3                  900
```

In the alert file, you can see that the old UNDO segments are switched offline and new segments are made online. The alert file is located in this directory $ORACLE_HOME/admin/bdump/.

Creating a rollback segment in my_lmt_rs tablespace

```
create rollback segment my_lmt_rs_rbs01 tablespace my_lmt_rs;
```

Result:

```
Rollback segment created.
Sat Aug 16 16:33:13 2003
ORA-30019 signalled during: CREATE ROLLBACK SEGMENT MY_LMT_RS_RBS01
  TABLESPACE...
Sat Aug 16 16:33:46 2003
UNDO Segment 13 Onlined
UNDO Segment 14 Onlined
UNDO Segment 15 Onlined
UNDO Segment 16 Onlined
UNDO Segment 17 Onlined
UNDO Segment 18 Onlined
UNDO Segment 19 Onlined
Successfully onlined UNDO Tablespace 12. where 12 IS THE "MY_LMT_RS" TABLESPACE
  NUMBER
UNDO Segment 1 Offlined
UNDO Segment 2 Offlined
UNDO Segment 3 Offlined
UNDO Segment 4 Offlined
UNDO Segment 5 Offlined
UNDO Segment 6 Offlined
UNDO Segment 7 Offlined
UNDO Segment 8 Offlined
UNDO Segment 9 Offlined
UNDO Segment 10 Offlined
UNDO Tablespace 1 successfully switched out.
```

Dynamically redirecting undo tablespaces with memory scope

```
alter system set undo_tablespace='my_lmt_rs' scope=memory;
```

Result:

```
System altered
```

Connecting as user `Anil` and creating a table `test1`:

```
schema : anil
create table test1 as select * from dba_source where 1 = 0;
```

Result:

```
Table created
```

Altering session to enable the session mode

```
alter session enable resumable;
```

Result:

```
Session altered
```

Inserting data into `test1` as selecting data from `dba_source`

```
                  --if this statement is not fired then the transaction is
                  --aborted instead of suspend if the error occurs.
insert into test (select * from dba_source);
```

NOTE

Session remains suspended

Result:

```
Alert file

Sat Aug 16 16:50:28 2003
```

```
statement in resumable session 'User ANIL1(102), Session 9, Instance 1' was
   suspended due to
ORA-30036: unable to extend segment by 16 in UNDO tablespace 'MY_LMT_RS'
```

The `SELECT` statement has 1447429 rows, so the code here may come across an `OUT-OF-SPACE` error during insertion. However, we have enabled resumable space in the code above (`ALTER SESSION ENABLE`). This feature allows the operation to be suspended and later resumes automatically from the point of interruption, as soon the error condition is fixed.

You will see that the size of the new `UNDO` tablespace remains unchanged. Oracle cannot grow the `UNDO` segment, since the size of tablespace does not allow any more extension. However, the transactions do not fail. So Oracle tries to find space. If there is no way to get the `UNDO` space, it reuses the space. In case the datafile has enough space or it is autoextensible, it will not reuse the space.

Listing 40.13 shows how to view datafiles of a tablespace:

Listing 40.13: Viewing Datafiles of a Tablespace

```
select * from dba_data_files where tablespace_name = 'MY_LMT_RS';
```

The output of Listing 40.13 is as follows:

```
FILE_NAME        C:\APP\ADMINISTRATOR\PRODUCT\11.2.0\DBHOME_1\DATABASE\MY_LMT_RS01
FILE_ID           9 MY_LMT_RS
TABLESPACE_NAME     2097152
BYTES               256
BLOCKS STATUS       AVAILABLE
RELATIVE_FNO        9 NO
AUT                 0
MAXBYTES            0
MAXBLOCKS           0
INCREMENT_BY        1048576
USER_BYTES          128
USER_BLOCKS
ONLINE_             ONLINE
```

If the `UNDO` tablespace is offlined or otherwise made unavailable, Oracle will use the normal copy for the `UNDO` information into the system rollback segments, so that we can rollback any outstanding transactions upon re-onlining or recovering that tablespace.

DDL Statements on Dictionary/Locally Managed Tablespaces

If you fire a DDL statement in dictionary managed tablespace with resumable session, the space management is not resumable and the statement creation will fail, whereas in locally managed tablespaces the create statement is resumable.

Listing 40.14 shows how to create a tablespace:

Listing 40.14: Creating Tablespace

```
create tablespace data datafile ‘ my_lmt’ size  256k extent management          local;
```

The output of Listing 40.14 is as follows:

```
Tablespace created
```

Connecting as user `Anil` and altering session to enable the session mode

```
schema : anil1
alter session enable resumable;
```

Result:

```
Session Altered
```

Creating table in `My_lmt` table space

```
create table resume_create( a number) tablespace my_lmt  storage( initial
   0k next 300k);
```

NOTE

The session waits for sometime.

Result:

```
In Alert log file
Sat Aug 16 19:30:29 2003
Statement in resumable session 'User ANIL1(102), Session 11, Instance 1' was
   suspended due to ORA-01658: unable to create INITIAL extent for segment in
   tablespace MY_LMT.
```

Tracking Changes in Database Using Triggers

You can track changes in the database, such as creating table, dropping table, suspending a transaction using triggers. These triggers are written on various events.

Listing 40.15 shows how to create a trigger to raise an error if a user drops any object:

Listing 40.15: Creating Trigger to Raise an Error if the User SCOTT Drops any Object

```
create or replace trigger drop_trg
before drop on scott.schema
begin
   raise_application_error(-20012,'can not drop object');
end;
```

NOTE

The trigger should be created by DBA.

The output of Listing 40.15 is as follows:

```
Trigger created
```

Dropping table when connected as `Scott`, to check the functionality of the above trigger

```
drop table t;
```

Result:

```
drop table t
*
ERROR at line 1:
ORA-00604: error occurred at recursive SQL level 1
ORA-20012: can not drop object
ORA-06512: at line 2
```

Creating a trigger that uses various system variables to get information about an event when an object is dropped

```
                                          --dbtrg2
create or replace trigger drop_trg
before drop on scott.schema
begin
       dbms_output.put_line(ora_sysevent);
   dbms_output.put_line(ora_login_user);
   dbms_output.put_line(ora_instance_num);
   dbms_output.put_line(ora_database_name);
   dbms_output.put_line(ora_dict_obj_type);
```

```
    dbms_output.put_line(ora_dict_obj_name);
    dbms_output.put_line(ora_dict_obj_owner);
end;
```

Result:

```
Trigger created
```

Dropping table zpcm (the code is executed by user Scott)

```
drop table zpcm;
```

We have created a trigger that will show various system variables when any object is dropped by user SCOTT. In this case, when we try to drop the table zpcm, the output displays the following variables (the result given below these variables will clarify the concept):

- DROP—System event
- SCOTT—Name of login user
- 1—Database instance name
- ORCL10—Database name
- TABLE—Database type
- ZPCM—Object name
- SCOTT—Owner of object

Result:

```
DROP
SCOTT
1
ORCL
TABLE
zpcm
SCOTT
DROP
SCOTT
1
ORCL
TABLE
zpcm
SCOTT

Table dropped
```

Other than BEFORE DROP, you can also write trigger for the following events:

AFTER DROP	BEFORE ALTER
AFTER ALTER	BEFORE ANALYZE
AFTER ANALYZE	BEFORE ASSOCIATE STATISTICS
AFTER ASSOCIATE STATISTICS	BEFORE AUDIT
AFTER AUDIT	BEFORE COMMENT
ADD COMMENT	BEFORE CREATE
AFTER CREATE	BEFORE DDL

AFTER DDL	BEFORE LOGOFF
AFTER LOGON	BEFORE RENAME
AFTER RENAME	BEFORE REVOKE
AFTER REVOKE	AFTER SUSPEND
BEFORE TRUNCATE	AFTER TRUNCATE
BEFORE GRANT	AFTER GRANT
ALTER USER	CREATE USER

You can also use appropriate additional variables:

```
ora_server_error
ora_is_servererror
space_error_info
ora_revokee
ora_privileges
ora_grantee
ora_with_grant_option
ora_privileges
ora_des_encrypted_password
(for ALTER USER events)
ora_is_alter_column, ora_is_
drop_column (for ALTER TABLE
events)
```

Listing 40.16 shows how to write a trigger on database events:

Listing 40.16: Writing a Trigger on Database Events

```
create or replace trigger db_trg
after servererror on database
declare
  l_sql_text ora_name_list_t;
  l_n number;
begin
  if (is_servererror(2345))
  then
  insert into t values ('ora_server_error = ' || ora_server_error(1));
         l_n := ora_sql_txt( l_sql_text );
         for i in 1 .. l_n
         loop
              insert into t values ( 'l_sql_text(' || i || ') = ' ||
              l_sql_text(i) );
         end loop;
     end if;
   end;
/
```

The output of Listing 40.16 is as follows:

```
Trigger created
```

- Apart from AFTER SERVERERROR, you can also have the following events:
- AFTER STARTUP
- BEFORE SHUTDOWN

Summary

This chapter dealt with UNDO tablespaces. The next chapter will deal with invoker rights and the NOCOPY clause.

Exercise

1. Explain the concept of UNDO tablespaces.
2. Write down the statement to create, alter and drop UNDO tablespaces

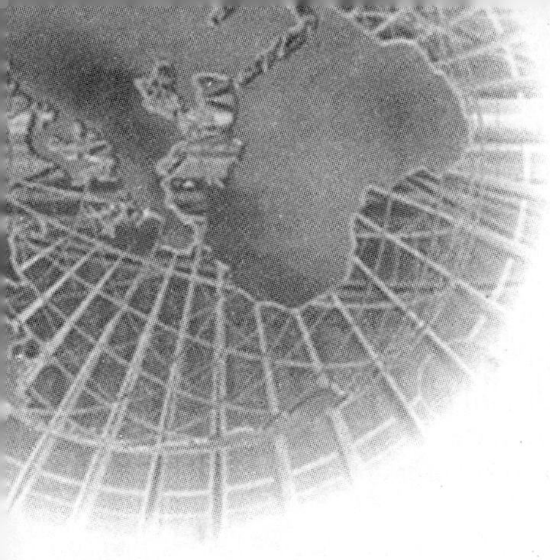

41

Invoker Rights and NOCOPY Clause

If you need an Information on: *See page:*

Since Oracle 10g there are two features in stored procedures, first is invoker right and second is NOCOPY clause in parameter specification. Invoker right enables to use same procedure for multiple users to process their data. NOCOPY clause in parameter specification allows user to pass very large data to procedure without increasing memory overheads.

Understanding Invoker Rights

When a stored procedure is created, then by default, the objects referred in the procedure are accessible according to definer rights. For example, suppose you have created a procedure `emp_proc1` in which you are referring the `emp_temp` object. Granting permission of `emp_proc1` to another user does not mean that the user will have permission on `emp_temp`.

This is explained using the concept of security domain. Security domain refers to a set of objects that are accessible to a user. When a user is executing the program, it will run under the security domain of that user. However, when the user calls another user's stored procedure, then that stored procedure will be executed under the security domain of the definer (The user who created stored procedure). This implies that there is a shift of security domain so that the call of `emp_proc1` refers to the table `emp_temp`. It refers to the `emp_temp` of user who has created that stored procedure.

If you want to run the procedure without shifting the security domain, that is, you want to execute the procedure of another user, but want that the procedure should refer your object then you can use the `AUTHID CURRENT USER` clause. In this case, the referred object refers to objects of the user who will invoke the procedure. Listing 41.1 shows the working of invoker rights:

Listing 41.1: Demonstrating the Working of Invoker Rights

```
                              --invoke1 create table and procedure using
                              --invoker right.It is created by user U1
create table emp_temp(empno number,ename varchar2(20))
/
```

The output of Listing 41.1 is as follows:

```
Table created
```

Listing 41.2 shows the code to create a procedure:

Listing 41.2: Creating procedure emp_proc

```
create or replace procedure emp_proc(myempno1 number)
authid current_user as
myename varchar2(15);
begin
  select ename into myename from emp_temp where empno = myempno1;
  dbms_output.put_line('ename is '||myename);
end;
/
```

The output of Listing 41.2 is as follows:

```
Procedure created
```

Listing 41.3 shows how to grant the execute permission to another user on the procedure:

Listing 41.3: Granting the Execute Permission to User scott

```
grant execute on emp_proc to scott;
```

The output of Listing 41.3 is as follows:

```
Grant succeeded
```

Listing 41.4 shows how scott executes the procedure that we have created in Listing 41.2:

Listing 41.4: User scott executing the procedure

```
execute U1.emp_proc(1);
BEGIN
U1.emp_proc(1);
END;
```

The output of Listing 41.4 is as follows:

```
*
ERROR at line 1:
ORA-00942: table or view does not exist
ORA-06512: at "U1.EMP_PROC", line 5
ORA-06512: at line 1
                                -- the table emp_temp is not in existence
```

Listing 41.5 shows the code to create the emp_temp table used for demonstration:

Listing 41.5: Creating table emp_temp

```
create table emp_temp (empno number,ename varchar2(20));
```

The output of Listing 41.5 is as follows:

```
Table created
```

Listing 41.6 shows how to insert records into the emp_temp table:

Listing 41.6: Inserting Records into emp_temp

```
insert into emp_temp values(1,'Anil');
```

The output of Listing 41.6 is as follows:

```
1 row created
```

Now, commit the transaction, as shown in the following code snippet:

```
commit;
```

The output of the preceding code snippet is as follows:

```
Commit complete
```

Listing 41.7: Execution of the emp_proc Procedure by User U1

```
set serveroutput on
execute U1.emp_proc(1);
```

The output of Listing 41.7 is as follows:

```
ename is Anil
PL/SQL procedure successfully completed
```

In Listing 41.7, `set serveroutput on` displays the content of the output buffer on screen. In other words, it helps to display the output of a procedure on a screen.

Listing 41.8: Insert value into emp_temp if it not present

```
insert into emp_temp values(1,'Sunil');
```

The output of Listing 41.8 is as follows:

```
1 row created
```

Now, commit the transaction, as shown in the following code snippet:

```
commit;
```

The output of the preceding code snippet is as follows:

```
Commit complete
```

After committing the transaction, execute the `emp_proc` procedure, as shown in the following code snippet:

```
set serveroutput on
execute emp_proc(1);
```

The output of the preceding code snippet is as follows:

```
ename is Sunil
PL/SQL procedure successfully completed
```

Listing 41.9 shows the working of definer rights:

Listing 41.9: Demonstrating the Working of Definer Rights by Creating a Procedure

```
create or replace procedure emp_proc1(myempno1 number) as
myename varchar2(15);
begin
  select ename into myename from emp_temp where empno = myempno1;
```

```
    dbms_output.put_line('ename is '||myename);
  end;
  /
```

The output of Listing 41.9 is as follows:

```
Procedure created
```

Granting the execute permission on the procedure to user `scott,` as shown in the following code snippet:

```
grant execute on emp_proc1 to scott;
```

The output of the preceding code snippet is as follows:

```
Grant succeeded
```

Listing 41.10 shows the code how scott executes the procedure:

Listing 41.10: User scott Executing the Procedure

```
execute U1.emp_proc1(1);
```

The output of Listing 41.10 is as follows:

```
ename is Sunil
PL/SQL procedure successfully completed
```

From Listing 41.10, it is clear that:

- The execution of `emp_proc` procedure by `scott` shows that the invoker table `emp_temp of scott` is used.
- The execution of procedures `emp_proc1` by `scott` shows that the definer table `emp_temp of owner of procedure` is used.

The **NOCOPY** Clause

The `NOCOPY` clause is used for the out argument or the out parameter. Oracle implements out parameter using copy. When you call a procedure by passing a variable and when the procedure is executed, it puts the output in a local variable internally and when the procedure ends, it copies the value from the internal local variable to the actual output variable.

If the out parameter is a large object, then there are a lot of memory overheads. The memory overhead results due to two spaces because there are two spaces where values are stored—first is local space and second is the space occupied by variable which is given as target for output. For example, observe the `y` variable in the following example:

When `NOCOPY` is used, `out` is implemented using reference. Therefore, `NOCOPY` is similar to call by reference. When a procedure is called, reference of `y` is passed and modifications are done in `y`. In this way, it saves the memory space by storing the data one place. Listing 41.11 shows the use of the NOCOPY clause:

Listing 41.11: Using the NOCOPY Clause

```
                                        --nocopy
declare
  y number;
  procedure test(x out nocopy number) is
  excp1 exception;
begin
  x := 5+50;
  raise excp1;
end;
begin
  y := 45;
  test(y);
  dbms_output.put_line(y);
  exception
  when others then
  dbms_output.put_line(y);
```

```
end;
/
```

The output of Listing 41.11 is as follows:

```
55
PL/SQL procedure successfully completed
```

NOTE

NOCOPY is used for saving memory when large objects are passed as Out parameter.

Listing 41.12 shows how to retain the Changes in NOCOPY parameter, even in case of EXCEPTION

Listing 41.12: Retaining the Changes in NOCOPY parameter, even in case of EXCEPTION

```
                                        --NOCOPY
create procedure test(a in number,b in number,c out nocopy number) as
begin
  c:= a+b;
end;
/
```

The output of Listing 41.12 is as follows:

```
Procedure created
```

Now, create a procedure that references and executes the `test` procedure, as shown in the following code snippet:

```
declare
  z number;
begin
  test(4,5,z);
  dbms_output.put_line (z);
end;
/
```

The output of the preceding code snippet is as follows:

```
9
PL/SQL procedure successfully completed
```

Now let's create a procedure in the SQL file using the `NOCOPY` clause, as shown in the following code snippet:

```
edit nocopy
declare
  y number;
  procedure test(x out nocopy number) is
  excp1 exception;
begin
  x := 5+50;
  raise excp1;
end;                                        --end of test
begin
  y := 45;
  test(y);
  dbms_output.put_line(y);
  exception
  when others then
  dbms_output.put_line(y);
end;
/
```

The output of the preceding code snippet is as follows:

```
55

PL/SQL procedure successfully completed
```

In the preceding code snippet:

- The edit NOCOPY statement opens the editor window
- The code is then written in the editor window and saved
- The @NOCOPY command is used to execute this procedure

Execute the code in SQL file, NOCOPY, as shown in the following code snippet:

```
@nocopy
```

The output of the preceding code snippet is as follows:

```
55
```

Now, let's create a procedure in SQL file without using NOCOPY, as shown in the following code snippet:

```
edit normal                                         --NORMAL
declare
   y number;
   procedure test(x out  number) is
   excp1 exception;
begin
   x := 5+50;
   raise excp1;
end;
begin
   y := 45;
   test(y);
   dbms_output.put_line(y);
   exception
   when others then
   dbms_output.put_line(y);
end;
/
```

The output of the preceding code snippet is as follows:

```
45
PL/SQL procedure successfully completed
```

In the preceding code snippet:

- The edit normal statement opens the editor window
- The code is then written in the editor window and is saved
- This code is then executed by the @NORMAL command at the SQL prompt

Execute the code in SQL file, @NORMAL, as shown in the following code snippet:

```
@normal
```

The output of the preceding code snippet is as follows:

```
45
```

Summary

This chapter dealt with invoker rights. The next chapter will focus on dependency tracking in Oracle.

Exercise

1. Explain the difference between invoker right and detıner right.
2. What is the advantage of NOCOPY clause?

42

Dependency Tracking in Oracle

If you need an Information on:	*See page:*

Oracle provides the dependency tracking mechanism to keep account of dependant objects as well as referred objects. Suppose the stored procedure `proc1` refers to the table `pls_test`. In such a case, the `pls_test` table is called as the referred object and `proc1` is called the dependant object. When a procedure is created, the validity of the referred objects in the procedure is checked. If the procedure is compiled successfully, it gets a valid status, which means that the procedure can now be successfully executed. Therefore, whenever the procedure is called, it does not check the validity of the referred objects. In addition, the execution of the procedure is fast. However, if a referred object is altered or dropped from the procedure, then the procedure is always successfully executed. In such a case, the procedure gets the invalid status, which means that it has to be recompiled. If there is a call to procedure having invalid status, the procedure is recompiled and if the recompilation is successful, it gets a valid status and is executed. However, if the recompilation is not successful, a runtime error is generated, which may halt the application. So the runtime compilations should always be avoided. When objects are modified, the dependency tracking mechanism helps you to find the dependant objects that are directly or indirectly dependant on referred object. You can then recompile those objects by using the `recompile` command.

Using the dependency tracking utility in Oracle, you can use to get a list of dependant objects. The utility creates a table, `deptree_temptab`, to store the dependant objects. In addition, it provides the `deptree_fill` procedure to fill the table with dependant objects, for a specified referred object. It gives two views, `deptree` and `ideptree`, which give the output so that a user can conveniently interpret dependencies. Suppose you want to find the dependency object for the table `pls_test`. In this case, you can call the `deptree_fill` method with the arguments as type of object; name of user; name of object; and after executing this you give the following command which gives a list of dependant objects:

```
select * from ideptree;
```

Understanding Scripts for Dependency Tracking

Run the `utldtree` script stored in rdbms/admin directory to create a table, procedures, and views required for dependency tracking. Following procedure is used to demonstrate dependency tracking mechanism.

Listing 42.1: Creating the pls_test Table

```
create table pls_test(a number,b number)
/
```

The output of Listing 42.1 is as follows:

```
Table created
```

Listing 42.2: Creating the proc1 Procedure

```
create or replace procedure proc1 as
x number;
begin
   select count(1)
   into x
   from pls_test;
   dbms_output.put_line(x);
end;
/
```

The output of Listing 42.2 is as follows:

```
Procedure created
```

Listing 42.3: Checking the Status of Objects

```
select object_name, status from user_objects where object_name
   in('pls_test','proc1');
```

The output of Listing 42.3 is as follows:

```
OBJECT_NAME       STATUS
-----------       ---------
PROC1                 VALID
PLS_TEST              VALID
```

Listing 42.4: Modifying the Referred Object

```
alter table  pls_test  modify (a not null);
```

The Output of Listing 42.4 is as follows:

```
Table altered
```

Listing 42.5: Finding Dependant Objects and Removing Existing Data

```
--suppose deptree_temptab stores dependency information
delete deptree_temptab;
```

The output of Listing 42.5 is as follows:

```
2 rows deleted
```

Listing 42.6: Filling and Viewing Dependency Information in the Table

```
begin
   deptree_fill('table','plsql','pls_test');
                     --DEPTREE_FILL(objecttype,owner,objectname)
                                --fills dependency information in table deptree_temptab
end;
/
select * from ideptree;
                    --view ideptree operates on base table deptree_temptab to
                    produce information of referred objects and dependant
            objects in tree structured form
```

The output of Listing 42.6 is as follows

```
dependencies
table plsql.pls_test
    procedure plsql.proc1
```

The output shows the dependent object in a tree form (displaced by certain spaces).

Listing 42.7: Checking the Status of Dependent Objects

```
select object_name, status from user_objects where object_name
   in('pls_test','proc1');
```

The output of Listing 42.7 is as follows:

```
OBJECT_NAME               STATUS
------------              --------
PROC1                 INVALID
PLS_TEST              VALID
```

Listing 42.8: Compiling Dependent Object Explicitly

```
alter procedure proc1 compile;


select object_name, status from user_objects where object_name
   in('pls_test','proc1');
```

The output of Listing 42.8 is as follows:

```
Procedure altered
PROC1                         VALID
PLS_TEST                      VALID
```

Before executing above steps following points should be considered:

- The script for creating objects for dependency tracking is given in the `UTLDTREE.SQL` file provided by Oracle.
- It is better to remove the existing data from table `deptree_temptab`.

NOTE

It is recommended that you compile procedures and packages explicitly when the load on the system is less to avoid runtime errors.

Summary

Now that you are acquainted with dependency tracking and its concepts, let us move ahead to the next chapter on flashback queries.

Exercise

1. What is the advantage of compiled procedure?
2. How dependency tracking utility is used?

43

FlashBack Queries

In this chapter, you learn about flashback queries and flashback tables. You also learn about FLASHBACK_ARCHIVE. In the end, you learn how to use Recycle Bin to recover the deleted data.

Use of Flashback Queries

By default, any operation on a database uses the most recent committed data available. Sometimes you are interested in the data which existed in the past (historical database) then you can retrieve that data using flashback queries.

Suppose a user accidentally deleted some important rows from a table and wanted to recover the deleted rows. To achieve this, you have to make incomplete media recovery prior to 9i. Using Flashback queries user can recover data due to his past mistakes.

Concept of Flashback Queries

Flashback queries let you view and repair historical data. It queries the database by `TIME` or user specified System Change Number (SCN). Every Data Manipulation Language (DML) statement has SCN attached to it. It uses Oracle's multiversion read-consistency capabilities to restore data by applying `UNDO` as needed.

You can configure `UNDO` retention by simply specifying how long `UNDO` should be kept in the database. Flashback queries do not perform an undo operation. You can take the output from a flashback query and perform an `UNDO` yourself. It does not tell you what has UNDO. You can get the undo content by using `LOGMINER package of Oracle`.

Flashback query does not work with data definition language (DDL) operations that modify columns and dropped or truncated tables.

Advantages of Flashback Queries

You can query the past data using the flashback mode, without making inconvenience to other users. You can mention time or SCN for querying the data and storing it in some convenient form like text file. You have to set proper `UNDO` interval to get an appropriate past data. Listing 43.1 shows the use of flashback queries:

Listing 43.1: Creating table to Use a flashback query

```
create table child
 (
 a number
 ,b number);
```

The output of Listing 43.1 is as follows:

```
Table created
```

After creating a table, let's display the structure of the `Child` table, as shown in the following code snippet:

```
desc child;
```

The output of the preceding code snippet is as follows:

```
Name                                      Null?    Type
----------------------------------------- -------- ----------------------------
A                                                   NUMBER
B                                                   NUMBER
```

Let's now create a procedure to insert values into the child table, as shown in the following code snippet:

```
begin
   for i in 1..100 loop
   insert into child values(1,i);
   end loop;
end;
/
```

The output of the preceding code snippet is as follows:

```
PL/SQL procedure successfully completed
```

Now, commit the transaction, as shown in the following code snippet:

```
commit;
```

The output of the preceding code snippet is as follows:

```
Commit complete
```

Display the number of rows in the `Child` table using the select statement, as shown in the following code snippet:

```
select count(*) from child;
```

The output of the preceding code snippet is as follows:

```
COUNT(*)
----------
100
```

Now, after some time, say 10 minutes, delete the inserted rows from the child table, as shown in the following code snippet:

```
delete from child;
```

The output of the preceding code snippet is as follows:

```
100 rows deleted
```

Now, commit the transaction, as shown in the following code snippet:

```
commit;
```

The output of the preceding code snippet is as follows:

```
Commit complete
```

Display the records after transaction, as shown in the following code snippet:

```
select count(*) from child;
```

The output of the preceding code snippet is as follows:

```
COUNT(*)
----------
0
```

Let's now learn how to set time of flashback and retrieve data, as shown in Listing 43.2:

Listing 43.2: Setting the time of flashback and retrieving data before 5 minutes, i.e. 5/1440(1440 is number of minutes in a day)

```
execute dbms_flashback.enable_at_time(sysdate - 5/1440);
```

The output of Listing 43.2 is as follows:

```
PL/SQL procedure successfully completed
```

Now you will get all data, which was in existence before 5 minutes. After this code, all data that was existed before 5 minutes can be retrieved.

After the flashback state has been enabled, you again need to check the number of rows in the `Child` table, as shown in Listing 43.3:

Listing 43.3: Using the select statement to display the number of rows in the Child table

```
select count(*) from child;
```

The output of listing 43.3 is as follows:

```
COUNT(*)
----------
100
```

Since the flashback is enabled, it retrieves the records that have been entered 10 minutes before even when the records have been deleted.

You cannot insert values in the `Child` table in the flashback mode, as shown in the following code snippet:

```
insert into child values(2,11);
```

The output of the preceding code snippet is as follows:

```
INSERT INTO CHILD VALUES(2, 11)
          *
ERROR at line 1:
ORA-08182: operation not supported while in Flashback mode
```

Now, disable the `DBMS_FLASHBACK` package, as shown in the following code snippet:

```
execute dbms_flashback.disable;
```

The output of the preceding code snippet is as follows:

```
PL/SQL procedure successfully completed
```

After disabling the DBMS_FLASHBACK package, you can insert records in the child table, as shown in the following code snippet:

```
insert into child values(2, 11);
```

The output of the preceding code snippet is as follows:

```
1 row created
```

Setting of an UNDO tablespace

You can set an UNDO tablespace to use FLASHBACK feature using following steps if it is not already set.

Listing 43.4 shows how to create the undo tablespace:

Listing 43.4: Creating the UNDO tablespace (already created in 9i or higher version by default)

```
create undo tablespace undodata1 datafile 'undotbs001.dbf' size 10m;
```

The output of listing 43.4 is as follows:

```
Tablespace created
```

Since the undo tablespace can be created only by a sys user; therefore, you need to use the statement shown in the following code snippet to connect to sys:

```
Connect to sys
```

Listing 43.5: Checking the values of UNDO_MANAGEMENT parameter to check whether UNDO management is in auto mode.

```
show parameter undo_management;
```

The output of listing 43.5 is as follows:

```
NAME                                 TYPE        VALUE
------------------------------------ ----------- ------------------------------
undo_management                      string      AUTO
```

Checking the value of `undo_retention` parameter

```
show parameter undo_retention;
```

The output of the preceding code snippet is as follows:

```
NAME                                 TYPE        VALUE
------------------------------------ ----------- ------------------------------
undo_retention                       integer     900
```

NOTE

The undo retention time is given in seconds and should be given more than the time of flashback.

Checking the value of `UNDO_TABLESPACE` parameter

```
show parameter undo_tablespace;
```

The output of the preceding code snippet is as follows:

```
NAME                                   TYPE        VALUE
------------------------------------ ----------- ------------------------------
undo_tablespace                        string      UNDOTBS1
```

Setting flashback state using SCN

You can set flashback state using following code as follows

Now, create a table, as shown in the following code snippet:

```
create table scn_table(a number,time_ins date,scn number);
```

The output of the preceding code snippet is as follows:

```
Table created
```

Insert the data into scn_table, as shown in the following code snippet:

```
insert into scn_table values(1,sysdate,
dbms_flashback.get_system_change_number)
/
```

The DBMS_FLASHBACK.GET_SYSTEM_CHANGE_NUMBER property gives SCN

The output of the preceding code snippet is as follows:

```
1 row created
```

Commit the transaction, as shown in the following code snippet:

```
commit
/
```

The output of the preceding code snippet is as follows:

```
Commit complete
```

Inserting value in `scn_table`

```
insert into scn_table values(2,sysdate,dbms_flashback.get_system_change_number)
/
```

Result:

```
1 row created
```

Committing transaction

```
commit
/
```

Result:

```
Commit complete
```

Inserting value into `scn_table`

```
insert into scn_table values(3,sysdate,dbms_flashback.get_system_change_number)
/
```

Result:

```
1 row created
```

Committing transaction

```
commit
/
```

Result:

```
Commit complete
```

Inserting value in to scn_table

```
insert into scn_table values(4,sysdate,dbms_flashback.get_system_change_number)
/
```

Result:

```
1 row created
```

Committing transaction

```
commit
/
```

Result:

```
Commit complete
```

Inserting value in `scn_table`

```
insert into scn_table values(5,sysdate,dbms_flashback.get_system_change_number)
/
```

Result:

```
1 row created
```

Committing transaction

```
commit
/
```

Result:

```
Commit complete
```

Inserting value in scn_table

```
insert into scn_table values(6,sysdate,dbms_flashback.get_system_change_number)
/
```

Result:

```
1 row created
```

Committing transaction

```
commit
/
```

Result:

```
Commit complete
```

Retrieve the entered values in scn_table, as shown in the following code snippet:

```
select * from scn_table;
```

The output of the preceding code snippet is as follows:

```
         A TIME_INS         SCN
---------- --------- ----------
         1 04-AUG-06    3997971
         2 04-AUG-06    3997973
         3 04-AUG-06    3997975
         4 04-AUG-06    3997977
         5 04-AUG-06    3997979
         6 04-AUG-06    3997981
6 rows selected
```

You need to enable the flashback mode to view the historical data, as shown in Listing 43.6:

Listing 43.6: Enabling the flashback mode to view the historical data

```
begin
  dbms_flashback.enable_at_system_change_number(3997981);
end;
/
```

The output of Listing 43.6 is as follows:

```
PL/SQL procedure successfully completed
```

You can view the data by using the select command, as shown in the following code snippet:

```
select * from scn_table;
```

The output of the preceding code snippet is as follows:

```
         A TIME_INS         SCN
---------- --------- ----------
         1 04-AUG-06    3997971
         2 04-AUG-06    3997973
         3 04-AUG-06    3997975
         4 04-AUG-06    3997977
         5 04-AUG-06    3997979
5 rows selected
```

Here the data prior to SCN 3997981 is shown.

After retrieving the data, you can disable the flashback mode, as shown in Listing 43.7:

Listing 43.7: Disabling the flashback mode

```
begin
  dbms_flashback.disable;
end;
/
```

The output of listing 43.7 is as follows:

```
PL/SQL procedure successfully completed
```

Let's now learn about the flashback table.

Flashback Table

From Oracle 10g, you can use the concept of flashback tables, instead of putting all the system in flashback mode. You can define past time either in terms of interval or timestamp. You have to enable the row movement to use the flashback feature, let's understand the concept of flashback tables by first creating a table and inserting rows in it, as shown in Listing 43.8:

Listing 43.8: Creating the fabc table and inserting rows into it

```
create table fabc(a number, b number, c timestamp);
```

The output of listing 43.8 is as follows:

```
Table created
```

Enable the row movement by altering the table, as shown in the following code snippet:

```
alter table fabc enable row movement;
```

The output of the preceding code snippet is as follows:

```
Table altered
```

Inserting values

```
insert into fabc values(41,41,systimestamp);
```

Result:

```
1 row created
```

Inserting values

```
insert into fabc values(21,2,systimestamp);
```

Result:

```
1 row created
```

Inserting values

```
insert into fabc values(31,3,systimestamp);
```

Result:

```
1 row created
```

Inserting values

```
insert into fabc values(41,4,systimestamp);
```

Result:

```
1 row created
```

Inserting values

```
insert into fabc values(51,5,systimestamp);
```

Result:

```
1 row created
```

Inserting values

```
insert into fabc values(61,6,systimestamp);
```

Result:

```
1 row created
```

Inserting values

```
insert into fabc values(410,41,systimestamp);
```

Result:

```
1 row created
```

Inserting values

```
insert into fabc values(201,2,systimestamp);
```

Result:

```
1 row created
```

Inserting values

```
insert into fabc values(301,3,systimestamp);
```

Result:

```
1 row created
```

Inserting values

```
insert into fabc values(401,4,systimestamp);
```

Result:

```
1 row created
```

Inserting values

```
insert into fabc values(501,5,systimestamp);
```

Result:

```
1 row created
```

Inserting values

```
insert into fabc values(601,6,systimestamp);
```

Result:

```
1 row created
```

after inserting values in the table, you can display the values, as shown in Listing 43.9:

Listing 43.9: Displaying values of table

```
select * from fabc;
```

The output of Listing 43.9 is as follows:

```
         A          B  C
---------- ---------- ----------------------------------------
        41         41  04-AUG-06 12.05.06.765000 PM
```

```
        21          2    04-AUG-06 12.05.06.781000 PM

        31          3    04-AUG-06 12.05.06.812000 PM

        41          4    04-AUG-06 12.05.06.828000 PM

        51          5    04-AUG-06 12.05.06.859000 PM

        61          6    04-AUG-06 12.05.06.875000 PM
       410         41    04-AUG-06 12.05.06.906000 PM

       201          2    04-AUG-06 12.05.06.921000 PM

       301          3    04-AUG-06 12.05.06.953000 PM

       401          4    04-AUG-06 12.05.06.968000 PM

       501          5    04-AUG-06 12.05.07.000000 PM

       601          6    04-AUG-06 12.05.07.546000 PM

12 rows selected
```

You need to create a flashback table to retrieve the historical data, as shown in Listing 43.10:

Listing 43.10: Creating the flashback table

```
flashback table fabc to timestamp (systimestamp - interval '1' minute);
```

The output of Listing 43.10 is as follows:

```
Flashback complete
```

Listing 43.11 shows the code to display the data of the fabc table:

Listing 43.11: Displaying the data of the fabc table

```
select * from fabc;
```

The output of listing 43.11 is as follows:

```
         A          B    C
---------- ----------    ----------------------------

        41         41    04-AUG-06 12.05.06.765000 PM

        21          2    04-AUG-06 12.05.06.781000 PM

        31          3    04-AUG-06 12.05.06.812000 PM

        41          4    04-AUG-06 12.05.06.828000 PM

        51          5    04-AUG-06 12.05.06.859000 PM

        61          6    04-AUG-06 12.05.06.875000 PM

       410         41    04-AUG-06 12.05.06.906000 PM

       201          2    04-AUG-06 12.05.06.921000 PM
```

```
        301          3    04-AUG-06 12.05.06.953000 PM

        401          4    04-AUG-06 12.05.06.968000 PM

        501          5    04-AUG-06 12.05.07.000000 PM
        601          6    04-AUG-06 12.05.07.546000 PM

12 rows selected
```

Listing 43.12 shows the code to insert values in the table:

Listing 43.12: Performing the DML (insert) operation on the table

```
insert into fabc values(56,78,systimestamp);
```

The output of Listing 43.12 is as follows:

```
1 row created
```

Commit the transaction, as shown in the following code snippet:

```
commit;
```

The output of the preceding code snippet is as follows:

```
Commit complete
```

You can define flashback in terms of time, as shown in Listing 43.13:

Listing 43.13: Defining flashback in terms of time

```
flashback table fabc to timestamp (to_timestamp('04-aug-06 12.11.07.546000'))
/
```

The output of Listing 43.13 is as follows:

```
Flashback complete
```

You will get data at the time specified in the query. But, if you alter table then you will not be able to get flashback data.

Listing 43.14: Displaying data without moving the table to past time using the version of table

```
select a,b,c from fabc as of timestamp (systimestamp - interval '3' minute)
  /
```

Result:

```
         A          B   C
---------- ----------  -------------------------------------

        41         41   04-AUG-06 12.05.06.765000 PM

        21          2   04-AUG-06 12.05.06.781000 PM

        31          3   04-AUG-06 12.05.06.812000 PM

        41          4   04-AUG-06 12.05.06.828000 PM

        51          5   04-AUG-06 12.05.06.859000 PM

        61          6   04-AUG-06 12.05.06.875000 PM

       410         41   04-AUG-06 12.05.06.906000 PM

       201          2   04-AUG-06 12.05.06.921000 PM
```

```
       301          3   04-AUG-06 12.05.06.953000 PM

       401          4   04-AUG-06 12.05.06.968000 PM
       501          5   04-AUG-06 12.05.07.000000 PM

       601          6   04-AUG-06 12.05.07.546000 PM

        56         78   04-AUG-06 12.08.42.218000 PM

13 rows selected
```

Listing 43.15 shows the code to retrieve the data on the basis of timestamp:

Listing 43.15: Retrieving data from fabc on the basis of timestamp

```
select a,b,c from fabc as of TIMESTAMP(TO_TIMESTAMP('04-AUG-06
  12.11.07.546000'))
/
```

The output of Listing 43.15 is as follows:

```
         A          B   C
---------- ----------   ----------------------------------------
        41         41   04-AUG-06 12.05.06.765000 PM

        21          2   04-AUG-06 12.05.06.781000 PM

        31          3   04-AUG-06 12.05.06.812000 PM

        41          4   04-AUG-06 12.05.06.828000 PM

        51          5   04-AUG-06 12.05.06.859000 PM

        61          6   04-AUG-06 12.05.06.875000 PM

       410         41   04-AUG-06 12.05.06.906000 PM

       201          2   04-AUG-06 12.05.06.921000 PM

       301          3   04-AUG-06 12.05.06.953000 PM

       401          4   04-AUG-06 12.05.06.968000 PM

       501          5   04-AUG-06 12.05.07.000000 PM

       601          6   04-AUG-06 12.05.07.546000 PM

        56         78   04-AUG-06 12.08.42.218000 PM

13 rows selected
```

You can retrieve data from `fabc` using timestamp with intervals, as shown in the following code snippet:

```
select a,b,c from fabc
  versions between timestamp
    systimestamp - interval '5' minute and
    systimestamp - interval '4' minute
/
```

The output of the preceding code snippet is as follows:

```
         A          B  C
---------- ----------  ------------------------------------
        41         41  04-AUG-06 12.05.06.765000 PM

        21          2  04-AUG-06 12.05.06.781000 PM

        31          3  04-AUG-06 12.05.06.812000 PM

        41          4  04-AUG-06 12.05.06.828000 PM

        51          5  04-AUG-06 12.05.06.859000 PM

        61          6  04-AUG-06 12.05.06.875000 PM

       410         41  04-AUG-06 12.05.06.906000 PM

       201          2  04-AUG-06 12.05.06.921000 PM

       301          3  04-AUG-06 12.05.06.953000 PM

       401          4  04-AUG-06 12.05.06.968000 PM

       501          5  04-AUG-06 12.05.07.000000 PM

       601          6  04-AUG-06 12.05.07.546000 PM

        56         78  04-AUG-06 12.08.42.218000 PM

13 rows selected
```

Now, drop the table, as shown in the following code snippet:

```
Drop table fabc;
```

The output of the preceding code snippet is as follows:

```
Table dropped
```

If you drop the table, you will not get data; instead an error would be displayed. The following code snippet shows the code to retrieve the data from the dropped table:

```
select a,b,c from fabc;
```

The output of the preceding code snippet is as follows:

```
               *
ERROR at line 1:
ORA-00942: table or view does not exist
```

Now, let's learn about FLASHBACK_ARCHIVE.

Using FLASHBACK_ARCHIVE

Oracle 11g has introduced the concept of FLASHBACK ARCHIVE to track changes in a table over a period of time. You can allocate space and specify retention time in for the flashback archive and assign flashback archive to a table.

Creating FLASHBACK_ARCHIVE

You can create flashback archive by using the CREATE FLASHBACK ARCHIVE command. The following code snippet shows how to create flashback archive:

```
create flashback archive arch_pcm
   tablespace users
   quota 5 m
   retention 1 day;
```

The preceding command creates archive named ARCH_PCM in the USERS tablespace. The space 5M is allotted for storing archive data. The retention is guaranteed for 1 day, that is, you can see the state of the data at any time of the past one day. The retention can be specified for months and years.

You must have FLASHBACK ARCHIVE ADMINISTER system privilege to create archive.

Assigning table to archive

You can assign PCM table of scott to archive as

```
alter table scott.pcm flashback archive arch_pcm
```

You can also specify the flash back archive at the time of creating table as follows.

```
create table pcm (name varchar2(30), p number, c number, m timestamp) flashback archive
   arch_pcm;
```

Viewing past data of the table

You can view the past data using different ways, which are as follows:

- Specifying timestamp using interval, as shown in the following code snippet:

```
select * from pcm as of timestamp(systimestamp -interval '10' minute);
```

- Specifying actual TIMESTAMP, as shown in the following code snippet:

```
select * from timestamp as of timestamp to_timestamp('2010-01-11 14:10:00','yyyy-mm-dd
   hh24:mi:ss');
```

- Specifying time window using timestamp, as shown in the following code snippet:

```
select * from pcm versions between timestamp
to_timestamp('2010-01-11 13:10:00','yyyy-mm-dd hh24:mi:ss');
and
to_timestamp('2010-01-11 14:10:00','yyyy-mm-dd hh24:mi:ss);
```

- Using MAXVALUE; you can view changes from past time to recent time, as shown in the following code snippet:

```
select * from pcm versions between timestamp
to_timestamp('2010-01-11 13:10:00','yyyy-mm-dd hh24:mi:ss);
and
maxvalue;
```

- Changing attributes of archive; you can change attributes of archive using the ALTER FLASHBACK ARCHIVE command, as shown in the following code snippet:

```
alter flashback archive modify retention 5 day;
```

Purging data of ARCHIVE

You can purge data of the archive by using time interval. You can also purge all data from archive. The following code snippet shows how to purge data from archive:

```
alter flashback archive arch_pcm purge before
timestamp before timestamp (systimestamp - interval '2' day);
alter flashback archive arch_pcm purge all;
```

Dropping FLASHBACK ARCHIVE

You can drop flashback archive using following command

```
drop flashback archive arch_pcm;
```

Using Recycle Bin

You can recover data from the recycle bin. If you drop a table and want to recover it, you can recover it from the Recycle Bin. This feature is introduced from Oracle 10g. Listing 43.16 shows how to recover data from the Recycle Bin:

Listing 43.16: Recovering data from recycle bin

```
select * from user_recyclebin;
```

The output of listing 43.16 is as follows:

```
rows will be truncated

OBJECT_NAME                       ORIGINAL_NAME                      OPERATION
-------------------------------- -------------------------------- ---------
TYPE                         TS_NAME                          CREATETIME
------------------------- ------------------------------ -------------------
DROPTIME                  DROPSCN PARTITION_NAME                   CAN CAN
------------------- ---------- -------------------------------- --- ---
   RELATED BASE_OBJECT PURGE_OBJECT      SPACE
---------- ----------- ------------ ----------
BIN$MfaBOHdGRdCBOodXq6fYBQ==$0 SCN_TABLE                        DROP
TABLE                        USERS                          2006-07-26:17:09:31
2006-08-04:11:23:08    3997949                                  YES YES
     51361       51361        51361          8

BIN$dUxL6HFpTGSfOydV7NLM7Q==$0 FABC                             DROP
TABLE                        USERS                          2006-07-31:15:03:12
2006-08-04:11:25:05    3998055                                  YES YES
     51618       51618        51618          8
```

Create an SQL file named restore to write following command, as shown in the following code snippet

```
edit restore
```

The output of the preceding code snippet is as follows:

```
Opens the editor window
```

Using flashback to retrieve a table before it is dropped

```
flashback table fabc to before drop
   rename to fabc1;
/
```

Run the SQL spool file, as shown in the following code snippet:

```
@restore
```

The output of the preceding code snippet is as follows:

```
Flashback complete
```

Execute the select command to display records of table `fabc1`, as shown in the following code snippet:

```
select * from fabc1;
```

The output of the preceding code snippet is as follows:

```
         A          B   C
-------------- --------- --------------
        41         41    04-AUG-06 11.25.06.578000 AM
```

```
        21          2    04-AUG-06 11.25.06.609000 AM

        31          3    04-AUG-06 11.25.06.640000 AM

        41          4    04-AUG-06 11.25.06.656000 AM

        51          5    04-AUG-06 11.25.06.687000 AM

        61          6    04-AUG-06 11.25.06.703000 AM

       410         41    04-AUG-06 11.25.06.734000 AM

       201          2    04-AUG-06 11.25.06.750000 AM

       301          3    04-AUG-06 11.25.06.781000 AM

       401          4    04-AUG-06 11.25.06.796000 AM

       501          5    04-AUG-06 11.25.06.828000 AM

       601          6    04-AUG-06 11.25.07.375000 AM

12 rows selected
```

Retrieving data from user_recyclebin to get information about the dropped tables

```
select * from user_recyclebin;
```

The output of the preceding code snippet is as follows:

```
OBJECT_NAME                    ORIGINAL_NAME                    OPERATION
------------------------------ -------------------------------- ---------
TYPE                      TS_NAME                        CREATETIME
------------------------- ------------------------------ -------------------
DROPTIME            DROPSCN PARTITION_NAME                   CAN CAN
------------------- ---------- -------------------------------- --- ---
   RELATED BASE_OBJECT PURGE_OBJECT      SPACE
---------- ----------- ------------ ----------
BIN$MfaBOHdGRdCBOodXq6fYBQ==$0 SCN_TABLE                        DROP
TABLE                     USERS                          2006-07-26:17:09:31
2006-08-04:11:23:08    3997949                                  YES YES
     51361       51361        51361          8

BIN$dUxL6HFpTGSfOydV7NLM7Q==$0 FABC                             DROP
TABLE                     USERS                          2006-07-31:15:03:12
2006-08-04:11:25:05    3998055                                  YES YES
     51618       51618        51618          8

BIN$wAFPXMdwQqavf6WCYIJNGw==$0 FABC1                            DROP
TABLE                     USERS                          2006-07-26:17:35:01
2006-08-04:12:22:19    4005693                                  YES YES
     51364       51364        51364          8
```

Listing 43.17 shows remove objects from the Recycle Bin:

Listing 43.17: Removing all objects from the Recycle Bin

```
Purge user_recyclebin;
```

The output of the preceding code snippet is as follows:

```
Recyclebin purged
```

Listing 43.18 shows how to drop a table having multiple items with the same name and then restore the items one by one:

Listing 43.18: Dropping a table having multiple times with the same name and then restoring it one by one

Displaying the structure of table s

```
desc s;
```

Result:

```
Name                                      Null?    Type
----------------------------------------- -------- ------------------------
A                                                  NUMBER
```

Displaying the structure of table fabc1, as shown in the following code snippet:

```
desc fabc1;
```

The output of the preceding code snippet is as follows

```
Name                                      Null?    Type
----------------------------------------- -------- ------------------------
A                                                  NUMBER
B                                                  NUMBER
C                                                  TIMESTAMP(6)
```

Rename table fabc1, as shown in the following code snippet:

```
rename fabc1 to fabc;
```

The output of the preceding code snippet is as follows:

```
Table renamed
```

Displaying the structure of table s

```
desc fabc;
```

Result:

```
Name                                      Null?    Type
----------------------------------------- -------- ------------------------
A                                                  NUMBER
B                                                  NUMBER
C                                                  TIMESTAMP(6)
```

Displaying the structure of table `fabc`

```
desc s;
```

Result:

```
Name                                      Null?    Type
----------------------------------------- -------- ------------------------
A                                                  NUMBER
```

Drop table fabc, as shown in the following code snippet:

```
drop table fabc;
```

The output of the preceding code snippet is as follows

```
Table dropped
```

Rename table s, as shown in the following code snippet:

```
rename s to fabc;
```

The output of the preceding code snippet is as follows:

```
Table renamed
```

Drop table fabc, as shown in the following code snippet:

```
drop table fabc;
```

The output of the preceding code snippet is as follows:

```
Table dropped
```

Retrieve data from USER_RECYCLEBIN, as shown in the following code snippet:

```
select * from user_recyclebin;
```

The output of the preceding code snippet is as follows:

```
OBJECT_NAME                        ORIGINAL_NAME                    OPERATION
------------------------------ -------------------------------- ---------
TYPE                      TS_NAME                        CREATETIME
------------------------- ------------------------------ -------------------
DROPTIME                 DROPSCN PARTITION_NAME                   CAN CAN
------------------- ---------- -------------------------------- --- ---
   RELATED BASE_OBJECT PURGE_OBJECT      SPACE
---------- ----------- ------------ ----------
BIN$c/zMg2C1TuCjiSxpWDuozw==$0 FABC                             DROP
TABLE                     USERS                          2006-08-04:12:05:06
2006-08-04:12:25:22    4005907                                  YES YES
     51692       51692        51692          8
```

NOTE

The two tables in the recycle bin have the same name.

Opening the SQL file editor

```
edit restore
```

Run the spool file, as shown in the following code snippet:

```
@restore
```

Since nothing has been written in the spool file, this command will not give any output.

Display the structure of table fabc1, as shown in the following code snippet:

```
desc fabc1;
```

The output of the preceding code snippet is as follows:

```
Name                                      Null?    Type
----------------------------------------- -------- ----------------------------
A                                                  NUMBER
```

Run the spool SQL file, as shown in the following code snippet:

```
@restore1
```

The output of the preceding code snippet is as follows:

```
Flashback complete
```

Displaying the structure of table `fabc1`

```
desc fabc2;
```

The output of the preceding code snippet is as follows:

```
Name                                      Null?    Type
----------------------------------------- -------- ------------------
A                                                  NUMBER
B                                                  NUMBER
C                                                  TIMESTAMP(6)
```

Listing 43.19 shows the code to restore a table and give the object name of table:

Listing 43.19: Restoring a specific table and giving the object name of table

```
flashback table "bin$hxskcce7s3cmrxsm3pgfwa==$0" to before drop rename to fabc3
```

The output of listing 43.19 is as follows:

```
Flashback complete
```

When you retrieve a table, the indexes and constraints created in the table are also retrieved.

Summary

By now, you must be familiar with flashback queries and its concepts. In the next chapter, we will deal with sequences.

Exercise

1. Create any table multiple times after dropping it with different structure. Retrieve each version of the table.
2. Explain the various ways of retrieving past data of the table.

44

Sequence

Sequence is used for creating values for primary key generation. Sequence guarantees generation of a new value, irrespective of a session or a user. By default, sequence doesn't give guarantee of order in generating values, e.g. if a sequence is referred from the terminal one, you may get values, such as 1, 2, 3, 4, and if from another terminal, you may get values, such as 11, 12, 13, 14. So, the sequence guarantees uniqueness, not ordering.

Sequence Usage

Values from a sequence can be accessed using any of the two methods—`NEXTVAL` and `CURVAL`. `NEXTVAL` gives current value and increments the sequence, while `CURVAL` only returns the current value. To use `CURVAL`, there should be at least one call to `NEXTVAL`, i.e. you should have invoked `NEXTVAL` previously.

You can create a sequence using the following parameters:

- `INCREMENT BY`—The sequence is incremented by this value.
- `MINVALUE/NOMINVALUE`—This decides the initial value of a sequence.
- `MAXVALUE/NOMAXVALUE`—It is the maximum value of a sequence.
- `CYCLE/NOCYCLE`—If it is cycle parameter then the values generated will be in cyclic order, i.e. after reaching `MAXVALUE` the generation will start from `MINVALUE`.
- `CACHE/NOCACHE`—If it is `cache`, then the call to `NEXTVAL` puts that many values in the session memory. For example, if the cache is 20, then the first call to `NEXTVAL` caches the first 20 values. If there is a sudden shutdown, then these values are lost.

For example, if 20 values are cached but the user has used only the first five values and there is an instant shutdown or system failure, then the remaining 15 values will be lost and the next generated value will be 21.

- `ORDER/NOORDER`—It indicates that the generated values are ordered according to time. It means the value, which is generated at 3:15, is greater than the value generated at 3:14, irrespective of the session.

Listing 44.1 shows how to create a sequence:

Listing 44.1: Creating a Sequence

```
create sequence testseq
      increment by 1
      start with 1
      nomaxvalue
      nocycle
      cache 10
/
```

The output of Listing 44.1 is as follows:

```
Sequence created
```

Listing 44.2 displays the next value of a sequence:

Listing 44.2: Displaying the Next Value of a Sequence Using NEXTVAL

```
select testseq.nextval from dual;
```

The output of Listing 44.2 is as follows:

```
   NEXTVAL
----------
         1
```

Re-execute the previous statement to again find the next value in sequence:

```
/
```

Result:

```
   NEXTVAL
----------
         2
```

Re-execute the statement to find the next value in the sequence:

```
/
```

Result:

```
   NEXTVAL
----------
         3
```

Selecting the current value of the sequence:

```
select testseq.currval from dual
/
```

Result:

```
   CURRVAL
----------
         3
```

Summary

In this chapter, you have learned about sequences and its usages. In the next chapter, you learn about PL/SQL wrapper.

Exercise

1. Write a sequence definition which generates values from 10 to 10000.
2. Write a sequence definition which guarantees ordering according to time.

45

PL/SQL Wrapper

Sometimes the source code in PL/SQL has to be made hidden from the user. The source code developed for procedures, packages and triggers can be hidden using PL/SQL wrapper.

Utility of PL/SQL Wrapper

When you want to hide the source code from a user, you can do so by using the PL/SQL Wrapper utility. When you create a stored procedure or package, the code can be viewed by using the USER_SOURCE view.

Listing 45.1 shows how the source code is visible.

Listing 45.1: Creating the wrap_proc.txt Procedure

```
edit wrap_proc.sql        -- open the editor window
```

The preceding command opens an editor window in which you can write the procedure. You then need to write the code shown in the following code snippet, in the editor window and save:

```
create or replace procedure wrap_proc as
begin
  dbms_output.put_line('wrapping the .sql file');
end;
/
```

No output is displayed for the preceding code snippet. When you close the editor window, the SQL prompt is displayed on the screen.

Wrapping a procedure by using @wrap:

```
@wrap_proc.sql
```

Result:

```
procedure created
```

Displaying wrapper text by using user_source:

```
                                          --Wrap1.txt
select text from user_source
where type='PROCEDURE' and NAME='WRAP_PROC';
```

Result:

```
TEXT
---------------------------------------------------------------------------
procedure wrap_proc as
begin
dbms_output.put_line('wrapping the .sql file');
end;
```

Wrapping Code Using PL/SQL Wrapper

Following steps are required to use PL/SQL wrapper.

Listing 45.2: Encrypting Code by using the PL/SQL Wrapper

```
C:\>wrap iname=wrap_proc.sql oname=ewrapproc.sql
```

The output of Listing 45.2 is as follows:

```
PL/SQL Wrapper: Release 8.1.7.0.0 - Production on Sat Aug 16 15:18:01 2003

Copyright (c) Oracle Corporation 1993, 2000.  All Rights Reserved.

Processing wrap_proc.sql to ewrapproc.sql
```

Listing 45.3: Creating a Procedure by using an Encrypted File

```
@ewrapproc.sql
```

The output of Listing 45.3 is as follows:

```
procedure created
```

NOTE

You cannot view the code of an encrypted procedure.

Listing 45.4: Displaying the Code from an Encrypted Procedure

```
select text from user_source
where type='procedure' and name='wrap_proc';
```

The output of Listing 45.4 is as follows:

```
TEXT
--------------------------------------------------------------------------------
procedure wrap_proc wrapped
a000000
b2
abcd
abcd
abcd
abcd
abcd
abcd
abcd
abcd
abcd
abcd
abcd
abcd
abcd
abcd
abcd
7
52 92
PeF+YdubWdG9BdTX+3INCK4aSe8wg5nnm7+fMr2ywFznKMB04yimwJR21r5ucVUAc1Nxbs/W
hnOEhOHmhNKpVxnG63JchO0OFi0OyoKWTGsU71w1ZFN8gKhigklcTOvs2T1ylez7phk8BEQ=
```

Summary

In this chapter, you have learned about the PL/SQL wrapper.

The next chapter will throw light on the Oracle expression filter.

Exercise

1. Write a stored procedure for addition of two numbers.
2. Write a query to view the code of the above mentioned procedure.
3. Write steps to wrap the above code using PL/SQL wrapper.

46

Oracle Expression Filter

Oracle expression filter allows users to specify selection using conditional expressions. Using Oracle Expression Filter you can avoid writing multiple WHERE conditions. Suppose you want to store information about customers interested in buying property. Property will essentially contain the following attributes:

- Year of construction
- Area of the property
- Price of the property

Take an example of a customer, `Anil`, who is interested in buying property with the following specifications:

- Year of construction of the building more than 2000
- Area more than 1000 sqft.
- Price less than 6 lacs

After storing the preceding information, you want to be able to retrieve the records with the following information:

- Name of customers interested in following properties
- Year of construction of building more than 2002
- Area of property more than 1200 sqft, or price less than 5 lacs

In this case, `Anil` will be part of the result. Without an expression filter, you have to explicitly build all the conditions in the `WHERE` clause. However, expression filters help this in a better way.

Using an Expression Filter

You can use an expression filter by follows these steps:

- Create an object with attributes needed to define the selection criterion. In the preceding example involving Anil, the attributes are `property type`, `year` of building, `price`, and `area`.

Listing 46.1 shows how to create object to represent various properties

Listing 46.1: Creating an Object Type with Property, Type, Year, Price, and Area as Attributes

```
create or replace type property4sale as object
(propertytype   varchar2(20),
year  number,
price  number,
sqft  number);
/
```

The output of Listing 46.1 is as follows:

```
Type created
```

- Create an attribute set using the object.

Listing 46.2 shows you how to create an attribute set for the object:

Listing 46.2: Creating an Attribute Set

```
begin
  dbms_expfil.create_attribute_set(attr_set  => 'property4sale',
  from_type => 'yes');
end;
/
```

The output of Listing 46.2 is as follows:

```
PL/SQL procedure successfully completed
```

- Define the mapping between the attribute set and a column of the table so that Oracle knows that the attribute expressions are stored in that column.

Listing 46.3 shows you how to define the mapping between the attribute set and the table:

Listing 46.3: Defining the Mapping Between an Attribute Set and the column of a Table

```
begin
  dbms_expfil.assign_attribute_set (
                  attr_set => 'property4sale',
               expr_tab => 'consumer',
               expr_col => 'interest',
           force=>'true');
end;
/
```

The output of Listing 46.3 is as follows:

```
PL/SQL procedure successfully completed
```

- Create a table in which you can store the attribute expressions. You can reserve certain columns to store attribute expressions. Here `interest` is the column of the following table which is used for storing attribute expression.

Listing 46.4 shows you how to create a table to store attribute expressions:

Listing 46.4: Create the Consumer table to store Attribute Expressions

```
create table consumer(consumername varchar2(30),
  pincode      number,
  phone        varchar2(12),
  interest     varchar2(200));
```

The output of Listing 46.4 is as follows:

```
Table created
```

- If you want to add customized function using attributes you can create such functions as given in the following listing.

Listing 46.5 shows you how to add customized functions by using attributes:

Listing 46.5: Adding Customized functions by using Attributes

```
create or replace function actprice(year number,price number)
return number is
begin
   return price - (extract(year from sysdate)-year)*0.01*price;
end actprice;
/
```

The output of Listing 46.5 is as follows:

```
Function created
```

- Assign the customized functions to an attribute set.

Listing 46.6 shows you how to assign functions to an attribute set

Listing 46.6: Assigning functions to an attribute set

```
begin
  dbms_expfil.add_functions (attr_set => 'property4sale',
     funcs_name => 'actprice');
end;
/
```

The output of Listing 46.6 is as follows:

```
PL/SQL procedure successfully completed
```

- Insert the attribute expression just as character data. If the expression does have character data, then you have to repeat '(single quote) two times.

Listing 46.7 shows you how to inserting an attribute expression in a table:

Listing 46.7: Inserting an Attribute Expression in the Consumer Table

```
insert into consumer values ('anil', 440010, '222333',
'propertytype=''flat'' and year>1999 and price < 150000 and sqft < 600');
```

Result:

```
1 row created
```

Inserting values

```
insert into consumer values ('sunil', 440011, '777888',
   'propertytype=''house'' and year > 2000 and price < 200000');
```

Result:

```
1 row created
```

Inserting values

```
insert into consumer values ('abhay', 640011, '977888',
   'propertytype=''flat'' and year < 2001 and price < 200000');
```

Result:

```
1 row created
```

Inserting values

```
insert into consumer values ('ajay', 640011, '877888','propertytype=''flat''     and year
   > 2001 and year < 2006 and price < 220000');
```

Result:

```
1 row created
```

Inserting values

```
insert into consumer values ('vijay', 640011, '777888', 'propertytype=''flat'' and year >=
   2000 and price >= 200000 and sqft>= 600');
```

Result:

```
1 row created
```

- Check whether the expression is evaluated to true or not by using the `EVALUATE` condition, as shown in the following code snippet:

```
select * from consumer where
    evaluate (consumer.interest,
              'propertytype=>''flat'', year=>1998,
               price=>140000, sqft=>500') = 1;
```

The output of the preceding code snippet is as follows:

```
CONSUMERNAME              PINCODE          PHONE            INTEREST
----------------          ----------       ---------        ------------
abhay                     640011           877888           propertytype='flat' and
                                                            Year < 2001 and Price <
                                                            200000
```

Experimentation

Create a table and store the following data:

CUSTOMER

CONSUMERNAME	PINCODE	PHONE	INTEREST
abhay	640011	877888	propertytype='flat' and Year < 2001 and Price < 200000
ajay	640011	877888	propertytype='flat' and Year > 2001 and year < 2006 and Price < 220000

CONSUMERNAME	PINCODE	PHONE	INTEREST
anil	440010	222333	propertytype='flat' and year>1999 and Price < 150000 and sqft < 600
sunil	440011	777888	propertytype='house' and Year > 2000 and Price < 200000
vijay	440011	777888	propertytype='flat' and Year >= 2000 and Price >= 200000 and sqft>= 600

Listing 46.8: Firing a query to evaluate a row with the following conditions—having property worth Rs. 140000, area 500 sqft, and year of building 2000

```
select * from consumer where
    evaluate (consumer.interest,
              'propertytype=>''flat'',
              year=>2000,
              price=>140000,
              sqft=>500'
              ) = 1
/
```

The output of Listing 46.8 is as follows:

```
CONSUMERNAME        PINCODE      PHONE       INTEREST
----------------    ----------   ---------   ------------
anil                440010       222333      propertytype='flat' and
                                             year>1999 and Price < 150000
                                             and sqft < 600

abhay               640011       877888      propertytype='flat' and Year
                                             < 2001 and Price < 200000
```

In the query, `anil` and `abhay` are evaluated as true attribute expressions because both of them satisfy the condition, i.e. `anil` requires `flat`, year above 1999, price below `150000`, and sqft area less than `600`.

You can insert rows using the function that you have created.

```
insert into consumer values ('jaya', 640011, '877888',          'propertytype=''flat''
  and year > 2001 and year < 2006 and
  actprice(year,price)<150000');
```

Result:

```
1 row created
```

Suppose you submit a query as:

```
select * from consumer where
    evaluate (consumer.interest,
  'propertytype=>''flat'',
  year=>2002,
  price=>140000,
  sqft=>500'
  ) = 1
/
```

Result:

```
CONSUMERNAME        PINCODE      PHONE       INTEREST
----------------    ----------   ---------   ------------
ajay                640011       877888      propertytype='flat' and Year
                                             > 2001 and year < 2006 and
                                             Price < 220000
```

jaya	640011	877888	propertytype='flat' and Year > 2001 and year < 2006 and actprice(year,price)<150000
anil	440010	222333	propertytype='flat' and year>1999 and Price < 150000 and sqft < 600

Here, jaya along with `anil`, and `abhay` will be displayed in the result, since they all satisfy the condition.

Summary

In this chapter, you got familiar with expression filters. The next chapter will throw light on a server model for a system.

Exercise

1. Create a set of tables to store job profiles and candidate preferences.
2. Write suitable queries using Oracle Expression Filter to retrieve jobs according to candidate preferences.

47

Server Model for Bill Entry System

Designing a server model consists of designing tables, columns, constraints, indexes, storage definitions, packages, and triggers. Here, the programmatic aspects of server model are given. The following definitions are created using the Oracle designer and here it is given to a reader to familiarize how the packages and triggers are written in Oracle.

Table Definition

Customer *Table*

Alias `CUSTOMER`

Display Title: Customer

Description: It stores customer list

User/Help Text: It stores customer list

Column Summary

Col.Seq.	Column	Nulls?	Type
1	CUSTID	NOT NULL	NUMBER()
2	CUSTNAME	NOT NULL	VARCHAR2 (30)
3	CUSTADDRESS	NULL	VARCHAR2 (100)

Primary Key

Name	Column
CUSTOMER_PK	CUSTID

Column Detail

The following additional constraints are provided on the columns:

1 `CUSTID`: It identifies item
Optional ? :No ; Number () ; Uppercase ? :No ; Sequence :`CUSTSEQ` ;

2 `CUSTNAME`: It stores customer name
Optional ? :No ; Varchar2 (30) ; Uppercase ? :No ;

3 `CUSTADDRESS`: It stores customer address
Optional ? :Yes ; Varchar2 (100) ; Uppercase ? :No ;

Items *Table*

Alias `ITEMS`

Display Title: Items

Description: It stores itemlist

User/Help Text: It stores itemlist

Column Summary

Col.Seq.	Column	Nulls?	Type
1	ITEMDESC	NULL	VARCHAR2 (30)
2	ITEMID	NOT NULL	NUMBER()

Primary Key

Name	Column
ITEMS_PK	ITEMID

Column Detail

The following additional constraints are provided on the columns:

1 `ITEMDESC`: It is the name of item.

Optional ? :Yes ; Varchar2 (30) ; Uppercase ? :No ;

2 `ITEMID`: It identifies an item.

Optional ? :No ; Number () ; Uppercase ? : No ; Sequence :ITEMSEQ ;

Billcustomer *Table*

Alias `BILLCUS`

Display Title: Billcustomer

Description: It stores customer information of bill

User/Help Text: It stores customer information of bill

Column Summary

Col.Seq.	Column	Nulls?	Type
1	USERID	NULL	VARCHAR2 (30)
2	BILLNO	NOT NULL	NUMBER (10)
3	AMOUNT	NULL	NUMBER (10, 2)
4	BILLDATE	NOT NULL	DATE
5	PAIDSTATUS	NULL	NUMBER (1)
7	CUSTID	NOT NULL	NUMBER

Primary Key

Name	Column
BILLCUST_PK	BILLNO

Foreign Keys

`BILLCUST_CUSTOMER_FK`

CUSTID references `CUSTOMER.CUSTID`

Transferable ? Yes   Update Rule Restricted

Mandatory ? Yes   Delete Rule Restricted

Index Summary

Name	Seq. Column	Index	Type
BILLCUST_CUSTOMER_FK_I	20	CUSTID	NOT UNIQUE

Column Detail

The following additional constraints are provided on the columns:

1 `USERID`: It indicates the name of user who entered a bill

Optional ? : Yes ; Varchar2 (30); Uppercase ? :No ;

2 `BILLNO`: It identifies a bill

Optional ? :No ; Number (10); Uppercase ? :No ; Sequence :BILLSEQ ;

3 `AMOUNT`: It is the total amount of bill

Optional ? :Yes ; Number (10, 2); Uppercase ? :No ;

4 `BILLDATE`: It is the date at which bills are made

Optional ? :No ; Date; Uppercase ? :No ;

5 `PAIDSTATUS`: It indicates whether bill is paid or not. if 1 then paid, if 2 then it is not paid

Optional ? :Yes ; Number (1); Uppercase ? :No ; Default Value :2 ;

7 `CUSTID`: It identifies a customer

Optional ? :No ; Number (); Uppercase ? :No ;

Billitems *Table*

Alias `BILLITEM`
Display Title: Billitems

Column Summary

Name	Column	Null?	Type
2	ITEMNAME	NULL	VARCHAR2 (30)
3	RATE	NOT NULL	NUMBER (10, 2)
4	ITEMTOTAL	NULL	NUMBER (10, 2)
5	QUANTITY	NOT NULL	NUMBER (10)
7	BILLNO	NOT NULL	NUMBER (10)
9	ITEMID	NOT NULL	NUMBER
19	BILLITEMNO	NULL	NUMBER

Primary Key

Name	Column
BILLITEMS_PK	BILLNO, ITEMID

Foreign Keys

The following additional constraints are provided on the columns:

- `BILLITEMS_BILLCUST_FK`
  BILLNO references `BILLCUSTOMER.BILLNO`
  Transferable Yes Update Rule Restricted
  Mandatory ? Yes Delete Rule Restricted
- `BILLITEMS_ITEMS_FK`
  ITEMID references `ITEMS.ITEMID`
  Transferable Yes Update Rule Restricted
  Mandatory ? Yes Delete Rule Restricted

Index Summary

Name	Seq.	Column	Index Type
BILLITEMS_BILLCUST_FK_I	20	BILLNO	NOT UNIQUE
BILLITEMS_ITEMS_FK_I	20	ITEMID	NOT UNIQUE

Column Detail

The following additional constraints are provided on the columns:

2 ITEMNAME

Optional ? :Yes ; Varchar2 (30) ; Uppercase ? :No ;

3 RATE

Optional ? :No ; Number (10, 2) ; Uppercase ? :No ;

4 ITEMTOTAL

Optional ? :Yes ; Number (10, 2) ; Uppercase ? :No ; Derivation RATE * QUANTITY

5 QUANTITY

Optional ? :No ; Number (10) ; Uppercase ? :No ;

7 BILLNO: It identifies bill

Optional ? :No ; Number (10) ; Uppercase ? :No ;

9 ITEMID: It identifies item

Optional ? :No ; Number () ; Uppercase ? :No ;

19 BILLITEMNO

Optional ? :Yes ; Number () ; Uppercase ? :No ;

Table Scripting

Creating Table ***BILLITEMS—BILL.tab***

The following code snippet shows how to create the `BILLITEMS` table:

```
PROMPT Creating Table 'BILLITEMS'
CREATE TABLE BILLITEMS
 (ITEMNAME  VARCHAR2(30)
 ,RATE  NUMBER(10,2) NOT NULL
 ,ITEMTOTAL  NUMBER(10,2)
 ,QUANTITY  NUMBER(10) NOT NULL
 ,BILLNO  NUMBER(10) NOT NULL
 ,ITEMID  NUMBER NOT NULL
 ,BILLITEMNO  NUMBER
 )
/
```

The output of the preceding code snippet is as follows:

```
Table created
```

The following code snippet shows how to create the `CUSTOMER table`:

```
PROMPT Creating Table 'CUSTOMER'
CREATE TABLE CUSTOMER
 (CUSTID  NUMBER NOT NULL
 ,CUSTNAME  VARCHAR2(30) NOT NULL
 ,CUSTADDRESS  VARCHAR2(100)
 )
/
```

The output of the preceding code snippet is as follows:

```
Table created
```

The following code snippet shows how to create the `ITEMS` table:

```
PROMPT Creating Table 'ITEMS'
CREATE TABLE ITEMS
 (ITEMDESC  VARCHAR2(30)
 ,ITEMID  NUMBER NOT NULL
 )
/
```

The output of the preceding code snippet is as follows:

```
Table created
```

The following code snippet shows how to create the `BILLCUSTOMER` table:

```
PROMPT Creating Table 'BILLCUSTOMER'
CREATE TABLE BILLCUSTOMER
 (USERID  VARCHAR2(30)
 ,BILLNO  NUMBER(10) NOT NULL
 ,AMOUNT  NUMBER(10,2)
 ,BILLDATE  DATE NOT NULL
 ,PAIDSTATUS  NUMBER(1) DEFAULT 2
 ,CUSTID  NUMBER NOT NULL
 )
/
```

The output of the preceding code snippet is as follows:

```
Table created
```

*Creating Primary Key on **BILLITEMS—BILL.con***

The following code snippet shows how to create primary key on `BILLITEMS`:

```
PROMPT Creating Primary Key on 'BILLITEMS'
ALTER TABLE BILLITEMS ADD (CONSTRAINT
 BILLITEMS_PK PRIMARY KEY
  (BILLNO
  ,ITEMID))
/
```

The output of the preceding code snippet is as follows:

```
Table altered
```

The following code snippet shows how to create a primary key on `CUSTOMER`:

```
PROMPT Creating Primary Key on 'CUSTOMER'
ALTER TABLE CUSTOMER ADD (CONSTRAINT
 CUSTOMER_PK PRIMARY KEY
  (CUSTID))
/
```

The output of the preceding code snippet is as follows:

```
Table altered
```

The following code snippet shows how to create a primary key on `ITEMS`:

```
PROMPT Creating Primary Key on 'ITEMS'
ALTER TABLE ITEMS ADD (CONSTRAINT
 ITEMS_PK PRIMARY KEY
  (ITEMID))
/
```

The output of the preceding code snippet is as follows:

```
Table altered
```

The following code snippet shows how to create primary key on `BILLCUSTOMER`:

```
PROMPT Creating Primary Key on 'BILLCUSTOMER'
ALTER TABLE BILLCUSTOMER ADD (CONSTRAINT
 BILLCUST_PK PRIMARY KEY
  (BILLNO))
/
```

The output of the preceding code snippet is as follows:

```
Table altered
```

Functionality

The tables provide the following functionalities:

- `Customer` table
  - Generates primary key using sequence and implement in trigger.
- `Items` table
  - Generates primary key using sequence and implement in trigger.
- `BillCustomer` table
  - Generates primary key using sequence and implements trigger.
  - Assigns system date to billdate.
  - Assigns userid of the user who enters bill in the column `USERID`.
  - Amount is derived as total amount of items. It is called aggregating child value into parent.
- `BillItems` table
  - `ITEMNAME` is a denormalised column having same name as `itemdesc`.
  - `ITEMTOTAL` is calculated as `rate * quantity`.
  - `BILLITEMNO` gets the value according to items entered in the bill. For the first item it will be `1`, for second it will be `2`. This is called as sequence within parent.

Apart from the above functionality, you can implement other functionalities, such as update cascade and table auditing.

Sample Scripts

The functionality related with the `billcustomer` is implemented in the following scripts:

- `billcust.pks`
- `billcust.pkb`
- `billcust.trg`

The scripts also generate provision of other functionalities, such as update cascade and delete cascade. You can scan the code and check how this functionality is implemented.

*Package Specification for the **BILLCUSTOMER—Billcust.pks** Table*

```
PROMPT Creating API Package Specification for Table 'BILLCUSTOMER'
--+++++++++++++++++++++++++++++++++++++++++++++++++++++++++++++++++++++++--
-- Name:         cg$BILLCUSTOMER
-- Description: BILLCUSTOMER table API package declarations
--+++++++++++++++++++++++++++++++++++++++++++++++++++++++++++++++++++++++--
CREATE OR REPLACE PACKAGE cg$BILLCUSTOMER IS

called_from_package BOOLEAN := FALSE;

--  Repository User-Defined Error Messages
BILLCUST_PK CONSTANT VARCHAR2(240) := '';
BILLCUST_CUSTOMER_FK CONSTANT VARCHAR2(240) := '';

--  Column default prompts. Format PSEQNO_COL
P1USERID CONSTANT VARCHAR2(240) := 'Userid';
P2BILLNO CONSTANT VARCHAR2(240) := 'Billno';
P3AMOUNT CONSTANT VARCHAR2(240) := 'Amount';
P4BILLDATE CONSTANT VARCHAR2(240) := 'Billdate';
P5PAIDSTATUS CONSTANT VARCHAR2(240) := 'Paidstatus';
P7CUSTID CONSTANT VARCHAR2(240) := 'Custid';

cg$row BILLCUSTOMER%ROWTYPE;

--  BILLCUSTOMER row type variable
TYPE cg$row_type IS RECORD
(USERID cg$row.USERID%TYPE
,BILLNO cg$row.BILLNO%TYPE
,AMOUNT cg$row.AMOUNT%TYPE
,BILLDATE cg$row.BILLDATE%TYPE
,PAIDSTATUS cg$row.PAIDSTATUS%TYPE
,CUSTID cg$row.CUSTID%TYPE
,the_rowid ROWID
,JN_NOTES VARCHAR2(240));

--  BILLCUSTOMER indicator type variable
TYPE cg$ind_type IS RECORD
(USERID BOOLEAN DEFAULT FALSE
,BILLNO BOOLEAN DEFAULT FALSE
,AMOUNT BOOLEAN DEFAULT FALSE
,BILLDATE BOOLEAN DEFAULT FALSE
,PAIDSTATUS BOOLEAN DEFAULT FALSE
,CUSTID BOOLEAN DEFAULT FALSE);

--  BILLCUSTOMER primary key type variable
TYPE cg$pk_type IS RECORD
(BILLNO cg$row.BILLNO%TYPE
,the_rowid ROWID
,JN_NOTES VARCHAR2(240));
```

```
--  PL/SQL Table Type variable for triggers
TYPE cg$table_type IS TABLE OF BILLCUSTOMER%ROWTYPE
     INDEX BY BINARY_INTEGER;
cg$table cg$table_type;

TYPE cg$tableind_type IS TABLE OF cg$ind_type
     INDEX BY BINARY_INTEGER;
cg$tableind cg$tableind_type;
idx BINARY_INTEGER := 1;

PROCEDURE   ins(cg$rec IN OUT cg$row_type, cg$ind IN OUT cg$ind_type,
                do_ins IN BOOLEAN DEFAULT TRUE);
PROCEDURE   upd(cg$rec IN OUT cg$row_type, cg$ind IN OUT cg$ind_type,
                do_upd IN BOOLEAN DEFAULT TRUE);
PROCEDURE   del(cg$pk  IN cg$pk_type, do_del IN BOOLEAN DEFAULT TRUE);
PROCEDURE   lck(cg$old_rec  IN cg$row_type, cg$old_ind  IN cg$ind_type,
                nowait_flag IN BOOLEAN DEFAULT TRUE);
PROCEDURE   slct(cg$sel_rec IN OUT cg$row_type);

PROCEDURE   validate_arc(cg$rec IN OUT cg$row_type);
PROCEDURE   validate_domain(cg$rec IN OUT cg$row_type);
PROCEDURE   validate_foreign_keys_ins(cg$rec IN cg$row_type);
PROCEDURE validate_foreign_keys_upd( cg$rec IN cg$row_type,
                cg$old_rec IN cg$row_type, cg$ind IN cg$ind_type);
PROCEDURE   validate_foreign_keys_del(cg$rec IN cg$row_type);
PROCEDURE   cascade_update(cg$new_rec IN OUT cg$row_type,
                cg$old_rec IN cg$row_type );
PROCEDURE   cascade_delete(cg$old_rec IN OUT cg$row_type);
PROCEDURE   domain_cascade_delete(cg$old_rec IN OUT cg$row_type);
PROCEDURE   upd_denorm2( cg$rec IN cg$row_type,cg$ind IN cg$ind_type );
PROCEDURE   upd_oper_denorm2( cg$rec IN cg$row_type,
                 cg$old_rec IN cg$row_type,cg$ind IN cg$ind_type,
                 operation IN VARCHAR2 DEFAULT 'UPD');

END cg$BILLCUSTOMER;
/
```

The output of the preceding code snippet is as follows:

```
Package created
```

*Package Body for the **BILLCUSTOMER—Billcust.pkb** Table*

The `cg$errors` package needs to exist on the system on which the following package body is to be created:

```
PROMPT Creating API Package Body for Table 'BILLCUSTOMER'
--+++++++++++++++++++++++++++++++++++++++++++++++++++++++++++++++++++++++--
-- Name:         cg$BILLCUSTOMER
-- Description: BILLCUSTOMER table API package definitions
--+++++++++++++++++++++++++++++++++++++++++++++++++++++++++++++++++++++++--
CREATE OR REPLACE PACKAGE BODY cg$BILLCUSTOMER IS

PROCEDURE   validate_mandatory(cg$val_rec IN cg$row_type,
                               loc        IN VARCHAR2 DEFAULT '');
PROCEDURE   up_autogen_columns(cg$rec    IN OUT cg$row_type,
```

```
                              cg$ind    IN OUT cg$ind_type,
                              operation IN VARCHAR2 DEFAULT 'INS',
                              do_denorm IN BOOLEAN DEFAULT TRUE);
PROCEDURE   err_msg(msg  IN VARCHAR2,
                    type IN INTEGER, loc  IN VARCHAR2 DEFAULT '');
PROCEDURE   uk_key_updateable(uk IN VARCHAR2);
PROCEDURE   fk_key_transferable(fk IN VARCHAR2);
```

```
--+++++++++++++++++++++++++++++++++++++++++++++++++++++++++++++++++++++++--
-- Name:        uk_key_updateable
--
-- Description: Raise appropriate error when unique key updated
--
-- Parameters:  none
--+++++++++++++++++++++++++++++++++++++++++++++++++++++++++++++++++++++++--
PROCEDURE uk_key_updateable(uk IN VARCHAR2) IS
BEGIN
      cg$errors.push(cg$errors.MsgGetText(cg$errors.API_UNIQUE_KEY_UPDATE,
  cg$errors.ERR_UK_UPDATE, uk),
                 'E',
                 'API',
                 cg$errors.API_UNIQUE_KEY_UPDATE,
                 'cg$err.uk_key_updateable');
                 cg$errors.raise_failure;
END uk_key_updateable;
```

```
--+++++++++++++++++++++++++++++++++++++++++++++++++++++++++++++++++++++++--
-- Name:        fk_key_transferable
--
-- Description: Raise appropriate error when foreign key updated
--
-- Parameters:  none
--+++++++++++++++++++++++++++++++++++++++++++++++++++++++++++++++++++++++--
PROCEDURE fk_key_transferable(fk IN VARCHAR2) IS
BEGIN
      cg$errors.push(cg$errors.MsgGetText(cg$errors.API_FOREIGN_KEY_TRANS,
  cg$errors.ERR_FK_TRANS, fk), 'E', 'API', cg$errors.API_FOREIGN_KEY_TRANS,
          'cg$err.fk_key_transferable');
      cg$errors.raise_failure;
END fk_key_transferable;
```

```
--+++++++++++++++++++++++++++++++++++++++++++++++++++++++++++++++++++++++--
-- Name:        up_autogen_columns
--
-- Description: Specific autogeneration of column values and conversion to
--              uppercase
--
-- Parameters:  cg$rec    Record of row to be manipulated
--              cg$ind    Indicators for row
--              operation Procedure where this procedure was called
--+++++++++++++++++++++++++++++++++++++++++++++++++++++++++++++++++++++++--
PROCEDURE up_autogen_columns(cg$rec IN OUT cg$row_type,
                             cg$ind IN OUT cg$ind_type,
                             operation IN VARCHAR2 DEFAULT 'INS',
```

```
                              do_denorm IN BOOLEAN DEFAULT TRUE) IS
BEGIN
    IF (operation = 'INS') THEN

            cg$rec.USERID := user;

        cg$rec.USERID := user;
        BEGIN
            SELECT BILLSEQ.nextval
            INTO   cg$rec.BILLNO
            FROM   DUAL;
            cg$ind.BILLNO := TRUE;
        EXCEPTION WHEN OTHERS THEN
            cg$errors.push(SQLERRM, 'E',  'ORA',  SQLCODE,
                           'cg$BILLCUSTOMER.up_autogen.BILLNO.others');
            cg$errors.raise_failure;
        END;

        cg$rec.BILLDATE := trunc(sysdate);

        NULL;
    ELSE
        NULL;
    END IF;

    IF NOT (called_from_package) THEN
        BEGIN
            IF(cg$rec.BILLNO IS NULL)
            THEN
                cg$rec.AMOUNT := NULL;
            ELSE
                SELECT SUM(ITEMTOTAL)
                INTO   cg$rec.AMOUNT
                FROM   BILLITEMS
                WHERE  BILLNO = cg$rec.BILLNO;
            END IF;
        END;
    END IF;

EXCEPTION
    WHEN no_data_found THEN
        NULL;
    WHEN OTHERS THEN
        cg$errors.push(SQLERRM,'E', 'ORA',SQLCODE,
                       'cg$BILLCUSTOMER.up_autogen_columns.denorm');
        cg$errors.raise_failure;

END up_autogen_columns;
```

```
--+++++++++++++++++++++++++++++++++++++++++++++++++++++++++++++++++++++++++++--
-- Name:        validate_mandatory
--
-- Description: Checks all mandatory columns are not null and raises appropriate
--              error if not satisfied
```

```
--
-- Parameters:  cg$val_rec Record of row to be checked
--              loc        Place where this procedure was called for error
--                         trapping
--++++++++++++++++++++++++++++++++++++++++++++++++++++++++++++++++++++++++++++--
PROCEDURE validate_mandatory(cg$val_rec IN cg$row_type,
                             loc IN VARCHAR2 DEFAULT '') IS
BEGIN
    IF (cg$val_rec.BILLNO IS NULL) THEN
       cg$errors.push(cg$errors.MsgGetText(cg$errors.API_MAND_COLUMN_ISNULL,
    cg$errors.VAL_MAND, P2BILLNO), 'E', 'API',
                       cg$errors.API_MAND_COLUMN_ISNULL, loc);
    END IF;
    IF (cg$val_rec.BILLDATE IS NULL) THEN
       cg$errors.push(cg$errors.MsgGetText(cg$errors.API_MAND_COLUMN_ISNULL,
    cg$errors.VAL_MAND, P4BILLDATE),'E', 'API',
                       cg$errors.API_MAND_COLUMN_ISNULL, loc);
    END IF;
    IF (cg$val_rec.CUSTID IS NULL) THEN
        cg$errors.push(cg$errors.MsgGetText(cg$errors.API_MAND_COLUMN_ISNULL,
      cg$errors.VAL_MAND, P7CUSTID), 'E', 'API',
                       cg$errors.API_MAND_COLUMN_ISNULL, loc);
    END IF;
    NULL;
END validate_mandatory;
```

```
--++++++++++++++++++++++++++++++++++++++++++++++++++++++++++++++++++++++++++++--
-- Name:        validate_foreign_keys
--
-- Description: Checks all mandatory columns are not null and raises appropriate
--              error if not satisfied
--
-- Parameters:  cg$rec Record of row to be checked
--++++++++++++++++++++++++++++++++++++++++++++++++++++++++++++++++++++++++++++--
PROCEDURE validate_foreign_keys_ins(cg$rec IN cg$row_type) IS
    fk_check INTEGER;
BEGIN
   NULL;
END;

PROCEDURE validate_foreign_keys_upd( cg$rec IN cg$row_type,
                                     cg$old_rec IN cg$row_type,
                                     cg$ind IN cg$ind_type) IS
         fk_check INTEGER;
BEGIN
   NULL;
END;

PROCEDURE validate_foreign_keys_del(cg$rec IN cg$row_type) IS
         fk_check INTEGER;
BEGIN
   NULL;
END;
```

```
--+++++++++++++++++++++++++++++++++++++++++++++++++++++++++++++++++++++++++++--
-- Name:         slct
--
-- Description: Selects into the given parameter all the attributes for the row
--              given by the primary key
--
-- Parameters:  cg$sel_rec  Record of row to be selected into using its PK
--+++++++++++++++++++++++++++++++++++++++++++++++++++++++++++++++++++++++++++--
PROCEDURE slct(cg$sel_rec IN OUT cg$row_type) IS

BEGIN

    IF cg$sel_rec.the_rowid is null THEN
       SELECT    USERID
       ,         BILLNO
       ,         AMOUNT
       ,         BILLDATE
       ,         PAIDSTATUS
       ,         CUSTID
       , rowid
       INTO      cg$sel_rec.USERID
       ,         cg$sel_rec.BILLNO
       ,         cg$sel_rec.AMOUNT
       ,         cg$sel_rec.BILLDATE
       ,         cg$sel_rec.PAIDSTATUS
       ,         cg$sel_rec.CUSTID
       , cg$sel_rec.the_rowid
       FROM   BILLCUSTOMER
       WHERE  BILLNO = cg$sel_rec.BILLNO;
    ELSE
       SELECT    USERID
       ,         BILLNO
       ,         AMOUNT
       ,         BILLDATE
       ,         PAIDSTATUS
       ,         CUSTID
       , rowid
       INTO      cg$sel_rec.USERID
       ,         cg$sel_rec.BILLNO
       ,         cg$sel_rec.AMOUNT
       ,         cg$sel_rec.BILLDATE
       ,         cg$sel_rec.PAIDSTATUS
       ,         cg$sel_rec.CUSTID
       , cg$sel_rec.the_rowid
       FROM   BILLCUSTOMER
       WHERE  rowid = cg$sel_rec.the_rowid;
    END IF;
EXCEPTION WHEN OTHERS THEN
    cg$errors.push(SQLERRM, 'E', 'ORA',  SQLCODE,
                   'cg$BILLCUSTOMER.slct.others');
    cg$errors.raise_failure;

END slct;
```

```
--+++++++++++++++++++++++++++++++++++++++++++++++++++++++++++++++++++++++++++--
-- Name:        cascade_update
--
-- Description: Updates all child tables affected by a change to BILLCUSTOMER
--
-- Parameters:  cg$rec     Record of BILLCUSTOMER current values
--              cg$old_rec Record of BILLCUSTOMER previous values
--+++++++++++++++++++++++++++++++++++++++++++++++++++++++++++++++++++++++++++--
PROCEDURE cascade_update(cg$new_rec IN OUT cg$row_type,
                         cg$old_rec IN     cg$row_type) IS
BEGIN
    NULL;
END cascade_update;
```

```
--+++++++++++++++++++++++++++++++++++++++++++++++++++++++++++++++++++++++++++++++--
-- Name:        cascade_delete
--
-- Description: Delete all child tables affected by a delete to BILLCUSTOMER
--
-- Parameters:  cg$rec     Record of BILLCUSTOMER current values
--+++++++++++++++++++++++++++++++++++++++++++++++++++++++++++++++++++++++++++--
PROCEDURE cascade_delete(cg$old_rec IN OUT cg$row_type) IS
BEGIN
    NULL;
END cascade_delete;
```

```
--+++++++++++++++++++++++++++++++++++++++++++++++++++++++++++++++++++++++++++--
-- Name:        domain_cascade_delete
--
-- Description: Delete all child tables affected by a delete to BILLCUSTOMER
--
-- Parameters:  cg$rec     Record of BILLCUSTOMER current values
--+++++++++++++++++++++++++++++++++++++++++++++++++++++++++++++++++++++++++++--
PROCEDURE domain_cascade_delete(cg$old_rec IN OUT cg$row_type) IS
BEGIN
    NULL;
END domain_cascade_delete;
```

```
--+++++++++++++++++++++++++++++++++++++++++++++++++++++++++++++++++++++++++++--
-- Name:        validate_arc
--
-- Description: Checks for adherence to arc relationship
--
-- Parameters:  cg$rec     Record of BILLCUSTOMER current values
--+++++++++++++++++++++++++++++++++++++++++++++++++++++++++++++++++++++++++++--
PROCEDURE validate_arc(cg$rec IN OUT cg$row_type) IS
  i NUMBER;
BEGIN
    NULL;
END validate_arc;
```

```
--+++++++++++++++++++++++++++++++++++++++++++++++++++++++++++++++++++++++++++--
-- Name:        validate_domain
--
```

```
-- Description: Checks against reference table for values lying in a domain
--
-- Parameters:  cg$rec     Record of BILLCUSTOMER current values
--+++++++++++++++++++++++++++++++++++++++++++++++++++++++++++++++++++++++++--
PROCEDURE validate_domain(cg$rec IN OUT cg$row_type) IS
   dummy NUMBER;
   no_tabview EXCEPTION;
   PRAGMA EXCEPTION_INIT(no_tabview, -942);
BEGIN

    NULL;

EXCEPTION
    WHEN cg$errors.cg$error THEN
        cg$errors.raise_failure;
    WHEN no_tabview THEN
        cg$errors.push(cg$errors.MsgGetText(cg$errors.API_RV_TAB_NOT_FOUND,
      cg$errors.APIMSG_RV_TAB_NOT_FOUND, 'CG_REF_CODES','BILLCUSTOMER'),
                       'E', 'API', cg$errors.API_RV_TAB_NOT_FOUND,
                       'cg$BILLCUSTOMER.v_domain.no_reftable_found');
        cg$errors.raise_failure;
    WHEN OTHERS THEN
        cg$errors.push(SQLERRM, 'E', 'ORA', SQLCODE,
                       'cg$BILLCUSTOMER.v_domain.others');
        cg$errors.raise_failure;
END validate_domain;
```

```
--+++++++++++++++++++++++++++++++++++++++++++++++++++++++++++++++++++++++++--
-- Name:        err_msg
--
-- Description: Pushes onto stack appropriate user defined error message
--              depending on the rule violated
--
-- Parameters:  msg     Oracle error message
--              type    Type of violation e.g. check_constraint: ERR_CHECK_CON
--              loc     Place where this procedure was called for error
--                      trapping
--+++++++++++++++++++++++++++++++++++++++++++++++++++++++++++++++++++++++++--
PROCEDURE err_msg(msg   IN VARCHAR2,
                        type  IN INTEGER,
                        loc   IN VARCHAR2 DEFAULT '') IS
              con_name VARCHAR2(240);
BEGIN
    con_name := cg$errors.parse_constraint(msg, type);
    IF (con_name = 'BILLCUST_PK') THEN
        cg$errors.push(nvl(BILLCUST_PK
                  ,cg$errors.MsgGetText(cg$errors.API_PK_CON_VIOLATED
              ,cg$errors.APIMSG_PK_VIOLAT
                                  ,'BILLCUST_PK'
                                  ,'BILLCUSTOMER')),
                      'E',
                      'API',
                      cg$errors.API_PK_CON_VIOLATED,
                      loc);
```

```
    ELSIF (con_name = 'BILLITEMS_BILLCUST_FK' AND type =
       cg$errors.ERR_DELETE_RESTRICT) THEN
        cg$errors.push(cg$errors.MsgGetText(cg$errors.API_DEL_RESTRICT,
     cg$errors.ERR_DEL_RESTRICT, 'Billcustomer', 'Billitems'),
                        'E',
                        'API',
                        cg$errors.API_DEL_RESTRICT,
                        loc);

    ELSIF (con_name = 'BILLCUST_CUSTOMER_FK') THEN
        cg$errors.push(nvl(BILLCUST_CUSTOMER_FK
                        ,cg$errors.MsgGetText(cg$errors.API_FK_CON_VIOLATED
                                              ,cg$errors.APIMSG_FK_VIOLAT
                                   ,'BILLCUST_CUSTOMER_FK'
                                   ,'BILLCUSTOMER')),
                        'E',
                        'API',
                        cg$errors.API_FK_CON_VIOLATED,
                        loc);
    ELSE
        cg$errors.push(SQLERRM,
                        'E',
                        'ORA',
                        SQLCODE,
                        loc);
    END IF;
END err_msg;
```

```
--+++++++++++++++++++++++++++++++++++++++++++++++++++++++++++++++++++++++++--
-- Name:        doLobs
--
-- Description: This function is updating lob columns
--
-- Parameters:  cg$rec  Record of row to be inserted
--              cg$ind  Record of columns specifically set
--+++++++++++++++++++++++++++++++++++++++++++++++++++++++++++++++++++++++++--
PROCEDURE doLobs(cg$rec IN OUT cg$row_type,
                 cg$ind IN OUT cg$ind_type) IS
BEGIN
   NULL;
END doLobs;
```

```
--+++++++++++++++++++++++++++++++++++++++++++++++++++++++++++++++++++++++++--
-- Name:        ins
--
-- Description: API insert procedure
--
-- Parameters:  cg$rec  Record of row to be inserted
--              cg$ind  Record of columns specifically set
--              do_ins  Whether we want the actual INSERT to occur
--+++++++++++++++++++++++++++++++++++++++++++++++++++++++++++++++++++++++++--
PROCEDURE ins(cg$rec IN OUT cg$row_type,
              cg$ind IN OUT cg$ind_type,
              do_ins IN BOOLEAN DEFAULT TRUE) IS
          cg$tmp_rec cg$row_type;
```

```
--  Constant default values

D5_PAIDSTATUS CONSTANT BILLCUSTOMER.PAIDSTATUS%TYPE := 2;

BEGIN
--  Application_logic Pre-Insert <<Start>>
--  Application_logic Pre-Insert << End >>

--  Defaulted

    IF NOT (cg$ind.PAIDSTATUS) THEN cg$rec.PAIDSTATUS := D5_PAIDSTATUS; END IF;
--  Auto-generated and uppercased columns

    up_autogen_columns(cg$rec, cg$ind, 'INS', do_ins);

    called_from_package := TRUE;

    IF (do_ins) THEN
        validate_foreign_keys_ins(cg$rec);
        validate_arc(cg$rec);
        validate_domain(cg$rec);

        INSERT INTO BILLCUSTOMER
            (USERID
            ,BILLNO
            ,AMOUNT
            ,BILLDATE
            ,PAIDSTATUS
            ,CUSTID)
        VALUES
            (cg$rec.USERID
            ,cg$rec.BILLNO
            ,cg$rec.AMOUNT
            ,cg$rec.BILLDATE
            ,cg$rec.PAIDSTATUS
            ,cg$rec.CUSTID);
        doLobs(cg$rec, cg$ind);
        slct(cg$rec);

        upd_oper_denorm2(cg$rec, cg$tmp_rec, cg$ind, 'INS');
    END IF;

    called_from_package := FALSE;

    IF NOT (do_ins) THEN
        cg$table(idx).USERID := cg$rec.USERID;
        cg$tableind(idx).USERID := cg$ind.USERID;

        cg$table(idx).BILLNO := cg$rec.BILLNO;
        cg$tableind(idx).BILLNO := cg$ind.BILLNO;

        cg$table(idx).AMOUNT := cg$rec.AMOUNT;
```

```
        cg$tableind(idx).AMOUNT := cg$ind.AMOUNT;

        cg$table(idx).BILLDATE := cg$rec.BILLDATE;
        cg$tableind(idx).BILLDATE := cg$ind.BILLDATE;

        cg$table(idx).PAIDSTATUS := cg$rec.PAIDSTATUS;
        cg$tableind(idx).PAIDSTATUS := cg$ind.PAIDSTATUS;

        cg$table(idx).CUSTID := cg$rec.CUSTID;
        cg$tableind(idx).CUSTID := cg$ind.CUSTID;

        idx := idx + 1;
    END IF;

--  Application logic Post-Insert <<Start>>
--  Application logic Post-Insert << End >>

EXCEPTION
    WHEN cg$errors.cg$error THEN
        called_from_package := FALSE;
        cg$errors.raise_failure;
    WHEN cg$errors.mandatory_missing THEN
        validate_mandatory(cg$rec, 'cg$BILLCUSTOMER.ins.mandatory_missing');
        called_from_package := FALSE;
        cg$errors.raise_failure;
    WHEN cg$errors.check_violation THEN
        err_msg(SQLERRM, cg$errors.ERR_CHECK_CON,
            'cg$BILLCUSTOMER.ins.check_violation');
        called_from_package := FALSE;
        cg$errors.raise_failure;
    WHEN cg$errors.fk_violation THEN
        err_msg(SQLERRM, cg$errors.ERR_FOREIGN_KEY,
    'cg$BILLCUSTOMER.ins.fk_violation');
        called_from_package := FALSE;
        cg$errors.raise_failure;
    WHEN cg$errors.uk_violation THEN
        err_msg(SQLERRM, cg$errors.ERR_UNIQUE_KEY,
     'cg$BILLCUSTOMER.ins.uk_violation');
        called_from_package := FALSE;
        cg$errors.raise_failure;
    WHEN OTHERS THEN
        cg$errors.push(SQLERRM,
                       'E',
                       'ORA',
                       SQLCODE,
                       'cg$BILLCUSTOMER.ins.others');
        called_from_package := FALSE;
        cg$errors.raise_failure;
END ins;
```

```
--+++++++++++++++++++++++++++++++++++++++++++++++++++++++++++++++++++++++++++++--
-- Name:        upd
--
-- Description: API update procedure
```

```
--
-- Parameters:  cg$rec  Record of row to be updated
--              cg$ind  Record of columns specifically set
--              do_upd  Whether we want the actual UPDATE to occur
--++++++++++++++++++++++++++++++++++++++++++++++++++++++++++++++++++++++++--
PROCEDURE upd(cg$rec IN OUT cg$row_type,
              cg$ind IN OUT cg$ind_type,
              do_upd IN BOOLEAN DEFAULT TRUE) IS
cg$upd_rec cg$row_type;
cg$old_rec cg$row_type;
RECORD_LOGGED BOOLEAN := FALSE;

BEGIN
--  Application_logic Pre-Update <<Start>>
--  Application_logic Pre-Update << End >>

    cg$upd_rec.BILLNO := cg$rec.BILLNO;
    cg$old_rec.BILLNO := cg$rec.BILLNO;

    cg$upd_rec.the_rowid := cg$rec.the_rowid;
    cg$old_rec.the_rowid := cg$rec.the_rowid;

    IF (do_upd) THEN
        slct(cg$upd_rec);

    --  Check updates to Primary Key BILLCUST_PK allowed
        IF (cg$ind.BILLNO AND cg$rec.BILLNO != cg$upd_rec.BILLNO) THEN
            uk_key_updateable('BILLCUST_PK');
        END IF;
        IF NOT (cg$ind.USERID) THEN
            cg$rec.USERID := cg$upd_rec.USERID;
        END IF;
        IF NOT (cg$ind.BILLNO) THEN
            cg$rec.BILLNO := cg$upd_rec.BILLNO;
        END IF;
        IF NOT (cg$ind.AMOUNT) THEN
            cg$rec.AMOUNT := cg$upd_rec.AMOUNT;
        END IF;
        IF NOT (cg$ind.BILLDATE) THEN
            cg$rec.BILLDATE := cg$upd_rec.BILLDATE;
        END IF;
        IF NOT (cg$ind.PAIDSTATUS) THEN
            cg$rec.PAIDSTATUS := cg$upd_rec.PAIDSTATUS;
        END IF;
        IF NOT (cg$ind.CUSTID) THEN
            cg$rec.CUSTID := cg$upd_rec.CUSTID;
        END IF;
    ELSE
     -- Perform checks if called from a trigger
     -- Indicators are only set on changed values
     null;
    --  Check updates to Primary Key BILLCUST_PK allowed
        IF (cg$ind.BILLNO ) THEN
```

```
            uk_key_updateable('BILLCUST_PK'); END IF;

    END IF;

--  Auto-generated and uppercased columns

    up_autogen_columns(cg$rec, cg$ind, 'UPD', do_upd);

--  Now do update if updateable columns exist
    IF (do_upd) THEN
        DECLARE
            old_called BOOLEAN;
        BEGIN
            old_called := called_from_package;
            called_from_package := TRUE;

            validate_foreign_keys_upd(cg$rec, cg$old_rec, cg$ind);
            validate_arc(cg$rec);
            validate_domain(cg$rec);

            slct(cg$old_rec);

            IF cg$rec.the_rowid is null THEN
                        UPDATE BILLCUSTOMER
                        SET
                 USERID = cg$rec.USERID
                 ,AMOUNT = cg$rec.AMOUNT
                 ,BILLDATE = cg$rec.BILLDATE
                 ,PAIDSTATUS = cg$rec.PAIDSTATUS
                 ,CUSTID = cg$rec.CUSTID
                 WHERE  BILLNO = cg$rec.BILLNO;
                 null;
            ELSE
                        UPDATE BILLCUSTOMER
                        SET
                 USERID = cg$rec.USERID
                 ,AMOUNT = cg$rec.AMOUNT
                 ,BILLDATE = cg$rec.BILLDATE
                 ,PAIDSTATUS = cg$rec.PAIDSTATUS
                 ,CUSTID = cg$rec.CUSTID
                 WHERE rowid = cg$rec.the_rowid;

                 null;
            END IF;

            slct(cg$rec);

            upd_denorm2(cg$rec, cg$ind);
            upd_oper_denorm2(cg$rec, cg$old_rec, cg$ind, 'UPD');
            cascade_update(cg$rec, cg$old_rec);
            called_from_package := old_called;
        END;
    END IF;
```

```
    IF NOT (do_upd) THEN
        cg$table(idx).USERID := cg$rec.USERID;
        cg$tableind(idx).USERID := cg$ind.USERID;
        cg$table(idx).BILLNO := cg$rec.BILLNO;
        cg$tableind(idx).BILLNO := cg$ind.BILLNO;
        cg$table(idx).AMOUNT := cg$rec.AMOUNT;
        cg$tableind(idx).AMOUNT := cg$ind.AMOUNT;
        cg$table(idx).BILLDATE := cg$rec.BILLDATE;
        cg$tableind(idx).BILLDATE := cg$ind.BILLDATE;
        cg$table(idx).PAIDSTATUS := cg$rec.PAIDSTATUS;
        cg$tableind(idx).PAIDSTATUS := cg$ind.PAIDSTATUS;
        cg$table(idx).CUSTID := cg$rec.CUSTID;
        cg$tableind(idx).CUSTID := cg$ind.CUSTID;
        idx := idx + 1;
    END IF;

--  Application_logic Post-Update <<Start>>
--  Application_logic Post-Update << End >>

EXCEPTION
    WHEN cg$errors.cg$error THEN
        called_from_package := FALSE;
        cg$errors.raise_failure;
    WHEN cg$errors.upd_mandatory_null THEN
        validate_mandatory(cg$rec, 'cg$BILLCUSTOMER.upd.upd_mandatory_null');
        called_from_package := FALSE;
        cg$errors.raise_failure;
    WHEN cg$errors.check_violation THEN
        err_msg(SQLERRM, cg$errors.ERR_CHECK_CON,
            'cg$BILLCUSTOMER.upd.check_violation');
        called_from_package := FALSE;
        cg$errors.raise_failure;
    WHEN cg$errors.fk_violation THEN
        err_msg(SQLERRM, cg$errors.ERR_FOREIGN_KEY,
     'cg$BILLCUSTOMER.upd.fk_violation');
        called_from_package := FALSE;
        cg$errors.raise_failure;
    WHEN cg$errors.uk_violation THEN
        err_msg(SQLERRM, cg$errors.ERR_UNIQUE_KEY,
      'cg$BILLCUSTOMER.upd.uk_violation');
        called_from_package := FALSE;
        cg$errors.raise_failure;
    WHEN OTHERS THEN
        cg$errors.push(SQLERRM,
                       'E',
                       'ORA',
                       SQLCODE,
                       'cg$BILLCUSTOMER.upd.others');
        called_from_package := FALSE;
        cg$errors.raise_failure;
END upd;
```

```
--+++++++++++++++++++++++++++++++++++++++++++++++++++++++++++++++++++++++++--
-- Name:        upd_denorm
--
-- Description: API procedure for simple denormalization
--
-- Parameters:  cg$rec  Record of row to be updated
--              cg$ind  Record of columns specifically set
--              do_upd  Whether we want the actual UPDATE to occur
--+++++++++++++++++++++++++++++++++++++++++++++++++++++++++++++++++++++++++--
PROCEDURE upd_denorm2( cg$rec IN cg$row_type,
                       cg$ind IN cg$ind_type ) IS
BEGIN

  NULL;
END upd_denorm2;
```

```
--+++++++++++++++++++++++++++++++++++++++++++++++++++++++++++++++++++++++++--
-- Name:        upd_oper_denorm
--
-- Description: API procedure for operation denormalization
--
-- Parameters:  cg$rec  Record of row to be updated
--              cg$ind  Record of columns specifically set
--              do_upd  Whether we want the actual UPDATE to occur
--+++++++++++++++++++++++++++++++++++++++++++++++++++++++++++++++++++++++++--
PROCEDURE upd_oper_denorm2(cg$rec IN cg$row_type,
                           cg$old_rec IN cg$row_type, cg$ind IN cg$ind_type,
                           operation IN VARCHAR2 DEFAULT 'UPD') IS
cg$rec_BILLITEMS cg$BILLITEMS.cg$row_type;
cg$rec_BILLITEMS2 cg$BILLITEMS.cg$row_type;
BEGIN
  NULL;
END upd_oper_denorm2;
```

```
--+++++++++++++++++++++++++++++++++++++++++++++++++++++++++++++++++++++++++--
-- Name:        del
--
-- Description: API delete procedure
--
-- Parameters:  cg$pk  Primary key record of row to be deleted
--+++++++++++++++++++++++++++++++++++++++++++++++++++++++++++++++++++++++++--
PROCEDURE del(cg$pk IN cg$pk_type,
              do_del IN BOOLEAN DEFAULT TRUE) IS
BEGIN
--  Application_logic Pre-Delete <<Start>>
--  Application_logic Pre-Delete << End >>

--  Delete the record

    called_from_package := TRUE;

    IF (do_del) THEN
        DECLARE
            cg$rec cg$row_type;
```

```
            cg$old_rec cg$row_type;
            cg$ind cg$ind_type;
         BEGIN
            cg$rec.BILLNO := cg$pk.BILLNO;
            slct(cg$rec);

            validate_foreign_keys_del(cg$rec);
            domain_cascade_delete(cg$rec);

            IF cg$pk.the_rowid is null THEN
               DELETE BILLCUSTOMER
               WHERE  BILLNO = cg$pk.BILLNO;
            ELSE
               DELETE BILLCUSTOMER
               WHERE  rowid = cg$pk.the_rowid;
            END IF;

            upd_oper_denorm2(cg$rec, cg$old_rec, cg$ind, 'DEL');
            cascade_delete(cg$rec);
         END;
     END IF;

     called_from_package := FALSE;

--   Application_logic Post-Delete <<Start>>
--   Application_logic Post-Delete << End >>

EXCEPTION
     WHEN cg$errors.cg$error THEN
         called_from_package := FALSE;
         cg$errors.raise_failure;
     WHEN cg$errors.delete_restrict THEN
         err_msg(SQLERRM, cg$errors.ERR_DELETE_RESTRICT,
     'cg$BILLCUSTOMER.del.delete_restrict');
         called_from_package := FALSE;
         cg$errors.raise_failure;
     WHEN no_data_found THEN
         cg$errors.push(cg$errors.MsgGetText(cg$errors.API_ROW_DEL,
      cg$errors.ROW_DEL),
                         'E',
                         'ORA',
                         SQLCODE,
                         'cg$BILLCUSTOMER.del.no_data_found');
         called_from_package := FALSE;
         cg$errors.raise_failure;
     WHEN OTHERS THEN
         cg$errors.push(SQLERRM,
                         'E',
                         'ORA',
                         SQLCODE,
                         'cg$BILLCUSTOMER.del.others');
         called_from_package := FALSE;
         cg$errors.raise_failure;
END del;
```

```
--+++++++++++++++++++++++++++++++++++++++++++++++++++++++++++++++++++++++++--
-- Name:        lck
--
-- Description: API lock procedure
--
-- Parameters:  cg$old_rec  Calling apps view of record of row to be locked
--              cg$old_ind  Record of columns to raise error if modified
--              nowait_flag TRUE lock with NOWAIT, FALSE don't fail if busy
--+++++++++++++++++++++++++++++++++++++++++++++++++++++++++++++++++++++++++--
PROCEDURE lck(cg$old_rec IN cg$row_type,
              cg$old_ind IN cg$ind_type,
              nowait_flag IN BOOLEAN DEFAULT TRUE) IS
cg$tmp_rec cg$row_type;
any_modified BOOLEAN := FALSE;

BEGIN
--  Application_logic Pre-Lock <<Start>>
--  Application_logic Pre-Lock << End >>

--  Do the row lock

    BEGIN
        IF (nowait_flag) THEN
            IF cg$old_rec.the_rowid is null THEN
               SELECT       USERID
               ,            BILLNO
               ,            AMOUNT
               ,            BILLDATE
               ,            PAIDSTATUS
               ,            CUSTID
               INTO         cg$tmp_rec.USERID
               ,            cg$tmp_rec.BILLNO
               ,            cg$tmp_rec.AMOUNT
               ,            cg$tmp_rec.BILLDATE
               ,            cg$tmp_rec.PAIDSTATUS
               ,            cg$tmp_rec.CUSTID
               FROM      BILLCUSTOMER
               WHERE     BILLNO = cg$old_rec.BILLNO
               FOR UPDATE NOWAIT;
            ELSE
               SELECT       USERID
               ,            BILLNO
               ,            AMOUNT
               ,            BILLDATE
               ,            PAIDSTATUS
               ,            CUSTID
               INTO         cg$tmp_rec.USERID
               ,            cg$tmp_rec.BILLNO
               ,            cg$tmp_rec.AMOUNT
               ,            cg$tmp_rec.BILLDATE
               ,            cg$tmp_rec.PAIDSTATUS
               ,            cg$tmp_rec.CUSTID
               FROM      BILLCUSTOMER
```

```
            WHERE       rowid = cg$old_rec.the_rowid
            FOR UPDATE NOWAIT;
         END IF;
     ELSE
         IF cg$old_rec.the_rowid is null THEN
            SELECT        USERID
            ,             BILLNO
            ,             AMOUNT
            ,             BILLDATE
            ,             PAIDSTATUS
            ,             CUSTID
            INTO          cg$tmp_rec.USERID
            ,             cg$tmp_rec.BILLNO
            ,             cg$tmp_rec.AMOUNT
            ,             cg$tmp_rec.BILLDATE
            ,             cg$tmp_rec.PAIDSTATUS
            ,             cg$tmp_rec.CUSTID
            FROM      BILLCUSTOMER
            WHERE     BILLNO = cg$old_rec.BILLNO
            FOR UPDATE;
         ELSE
            SELECT        USERID
            ,             BILLNO
            ,             AMOUNT
            ,             BILLDATE
            ,             PAIDSTATUS
            ,             CUSTID
            INTO          cg$tmp_rec.USERID
            ,             cg$tmp_rec.BILLNO
            ,             cg$tmp_rec.AMOUNT
            ,             cg$tmp_rec.BILLDATE
            ,             cg$tmp_rec.PAIDSTATUS
            ,             cg$tmp_rec.CUSTID
            FROM      BILLCUSTOMER
            WHERE     rowid = cg$old_rec.the_rowid
            FOR UPDATE;
         END IF;
     END IF;

EXCEPTION
     WHEN cg$errors.cg$error THEN
         cg$errors.raise_failure;
     WHEN cg$errors.resource_busy THEN
         cg$errors.push(cg$errors.MsgGetText(cg$errors.API_ROW_LCK,
      cg$errors.ROW_LCK),
                         'E',
                         'ORA',
                         SQLCODE,
                         'cg$BILLCUSTOMER.lck.resource_busy');
         cg$errors.raise_failure;
     WHEN no_data_found THEN
         cg$errors.push(cg$errors.MsgGetText(cg$errors.API_ROW_DEL,
      cg$errors.ROW_DEL),
                         'E',
```

```
                        'ORA',
                        SQLCODE,
                        'cg$BILLCUSTOMER.lck.no_data_found');
            cg$errors.raise_failure;
        WHEN OTHERS THEN
            cg$errors.push(SQLERRM,
                        'E',
                        'ORA',
                        SQLCODE,
                        'cg$BILLCUSTOMER.lck.others');
            cg$errors.raise_failure;
    END;

-- Optional Columns

    IF (cg$old_ind.USERID) THEN
        IF (cg$tmp_rec.USERID IS NOT NULL
        AND cg$old_rec.USERID IS NOT NULL) THEN
            IF (cg$tmp_rec.USERID != cg$old_rec.USERID) THEN
                cg$errors.push(cg$errors.MsgGetText(cg$errors.API_ROW_MOD,
            cg$errors.ROW_MOD, P1USERID
                    ),'E', 'API', CG$ERRORS.API_MODIFIED,
                 'cg$BILLCUSTOMER.lck');
                any_modified := TRUE;
            END IF;
        ELSIF (cg$tmp_rec.USERID IS NOT NULL
        OR cg$old_rec.USERID IS NOT NULL) THEN
            cg$errors.push(cg$errors.MsgGetText(cg$errors.API_ROW_MOD,
         cg$errors.ROW_MOD, P1USERID
                ),'E', 'API', CG$ERRORS.API_MODIFIED, 'cg$BILLCUSTOMER.lck');
            any_modified := TRUE;
        END IF;
    END IF;
    IF (cg$old_ind.AMOUNT) THEN
        IF (cg$tmp_rec.AMOUNT IS NOT NULL
        AND cg$old_rec.AMOUNT IS NOT NULL) THEN
            IF (cg$tmp_rec.AMOUNT != cg$old_rec.AMOUNT) THEN
                cg$errors.push(cg$errors.MsgGetText(cg$errors.API_ROW_MOD,
            cg$errors.ROW_MOD, P3AMOUNT
                    ),'E', 'API', CG$ERRORS.API_MODIFIED,
                 'cg$BILLCUSTOMER.lck');
                any_modified := TRUE;
            END IF;
        ELSIF (cg$tmp_rec.AMOUNT IS NOT NULL
        OR cg$old_rec.AMOUNT IS NOT NULL) THEN
            cg$errors.push(cg$errors.MsgGetText(cg$errors.API_ROW_MOD,
         cg$errors.ROW_MOD, P3AMOUNT
                ),'E', 'API', CG$ERRORS.API_MODIFIED, 'cg$BILLCUSTOMER.lck');
            any_modified := TRUE;
        END IF;
    END IF;
    IF (cg$old_ind.PAIDSTATUS) THEN
        IF (cg$tmp_rec.PAIDSTATUS IS NOT NULL
        AND cg$old_rec.PAIDSTATUS IS NOT NULL) THEN
            IF (cg$tmp_rec.PAIDSTATUS != cg$old_rec.PAIDSTATUS) THEN
```

```
                cg$errors.push(cg$errors.MsgGetText(cg$errors.API_ROW_MOD,
            cg$errors.ROW_MOD, P5PAIDSTATUS
                    ),'E', 'API', CG$ERRORS.API_MODIFIED,
                 'cg$BILLCUSTOMER.lck');
                any_modified := TRUE;
            END IF;
        ELSIF (cg$tmp_rec.PAIDSTATUS IS NOT NULL
        OR cg$old_rec.PAIDSTATUS IS NOT NULL) THEN
            cg$errors.push(cg$errors.MsgGetText(cg$errors.API_ROW_MOD,
         cg$errors.ROW_MOD, P5PAIDSTATUS
                ),'E', 'API', CG$ERRORS.API_MODIFIED, 'cg$BILLCUSTOMER.lck');
            any_modified := TRUE;
        END IF;
    END IF;

-- Mandatory Columns

    IF (cg$old_ind.BILLNO) THEN
        IF (cg$tmp_rec.BILLNO != cg$old_rec.BILLNO) THEN
            cg$errors.push(cg$errors.MsgGetText(cg$errors.API_ROW_MOD,
         cg$errors.ROW_MOD, P2BILLNO
                ),'E', 'API', CG$ERRORS.API_MODIFIED, 'cg$BILLCUSTOMER.lck');
            any_modified := TRUE;
        END IF;
    END IF;
    IF (cg$old_ind.BILLDATE) THEN
        IF (cg$tmp_rec.BILLDATE != cg$old_rec.BILLDATE) THEN
            cg$errors.push(cg$errors.MsgGetText(cg$errors.API_ROW_MOD,
         cg$errors.ROW_MOD, P4BILLDATE
                ),'E', 'API', CG$ERRORS.API_MODIFIED, 'cg$BILLCUSTOMER.lck');
            any_modified := TRUE;
        END IF;
    END IF;
    IF (cg$old_ind.CUSTID) THEN
        IF (cg$tmp_rec.CUSTID != cg$old_rec.CUSTID) THEN
            cg$errors.push(cg$errors.MsgGetText(cg$errors.API_ROW_MOD,
         cg$errors.ROW_MOD, P7CUSTID
                ),'E', 'API', CG$ERRORS.API_MODIFIED, 'cg$BILLCUSTOMER.lck');
            any_modified := TRUE;
        END IF;
    END IF;

    IF (any_modified) THEN
        cg$errors.raise_failure;
    END IF;

--  Application_logic Post-Lock <<Start>>
--  Application_logic Post-Lock << End >>

END lck;

END cg$BILLCUSTOMER;
/
```

*Package for Table BILLCUSTOMER—**billcust.trg***

Trigger Logic for Table **BILLCUSTOMER**

```
PROMPT Creating Trigger Logic for Table 'BILLCUSTOMER'
PROMPT Creating Before Insert Statement Trigger on 'BILLCUSTOMER'
CREATE OR REPLACE TRIGGER cg$BIS_BILLCUSTOMER
BEFORE INSERT ON BILLCUSTOMER
BEGIN
--  Application_logic Pre-Before-Insert-statement <<Start>>
--  Application_logic Pre-Before-Insert-statement << End >>

    cg$BILLCUSTOMER.cg$table.DELETE;
    cg$BILLCUSTOMER.cg$tableind.DELETE;
    cg$BILLCUSTOMER.idx := 1;

--  Application_logic Post-Before-Insert-statement <<Start>>
--  Application_logic Post-Before-Insert-statement << End >>
END;
/
```

The output of the preceding code snippet is as follows:

```
Trigger created
```

Before Insert Row Trigger on **BILLCUSTOMER**

```
PROMPT Creating Before Insert Row Trigger on 'BILLCUSTOMER'
CREATE OR REPLACE TRIGGER cg$BIR_BILLCUSTOMER
BEFORE INSERT ON BILLCUSTOMER FOR EACH ROW
DECLARE
    cg$rec cg$BILLCUSTOMER.cg$row_type;
    cg$ind cg$BILLCUSTOMER.cg$ind_type;
BEGIN
--  Application_logic Pre-Before-Insert-row <<Start>>
--  Application_logic Pre-Before-Insert-row << End >>
--  Load cg$rec/cg$ind values from new

    cg$rec.USERID := :new.USERID;
    IF (:new.USERID IS NULL) THEN
        cg$ind.USERID := FALSE;
    ELSE
        cg$ind.USERID := TRUE;
    END IF;
    cg$rec.BILLNO := :new.BILLNO;
    cg$ind.BILLNO := TRUE;
    cg$rec.AMOUNT := :new.AMOUNT;
    IF (:new.AMOUNT IS NULL) THEN
        cg$ind.AMOUNT := FALSE;
    ELSE
        cg$ind.AMOUNT := TRUE;
    END IF;
    cg$rec.BILLDATE := :new.BILLDATE;
    IF (:new.BILLDATE IS NULL) THEN
        cg$ind.BILLDATE := FALSE;
    ELSE
```

```
        cg$ind.BILLDATE := TRUE;
    END IF;
    cg$rec.PAIDSTATUS := :new.PAIDSTATUS;
    cg$ind.PAIDSTATUS := TRUE;
    cg$rec.CUSTID := :new.CUSTID;
    cg$ind.CUSTID := TRUE;

    if not (cg$BILLCUSTOMER.called_from_package) then
        cg$BILLCUSTOMER.validate_arc(cg$rec);
        cg$BILLCUSTOMER.validate_domain(cg$rec);

        cg$BILLCUSTOMER.ins(cg$rec, cg$ind, FALSE);
        cg$BILLCUSTOMER.called_from_package := FALSE;
    end if;

    :new.USERID := cg$rec.USERID;
    :new.BILLNO := cg$rec.BILLNO;
    :new.AMOUNT := cg$rec.AMOUNT;
    :new.BILLDATE := cg$rec.BILLDATE;
    :new.PAIDSTATUS := cg$rec.PAIDSTATUS;
    :new.CUSTID := cg$rec.CUSTID;

--  Application_logic Post-Before-Insert-row <<Start>>
--  Application_logic Post-Before-Insert-row << End >>
END;
/
```

The output of the preceding code snippet is as follows:

```
Trigger created
```

After Insert Row Trigger on **BILLCUSTOMER**

```
PROMPT Creating After Insert Row Trigger on 'BILLCUSTOMER'
CREATE OR REPLACE TRIGGER cg$AIR_BILLCUSTOMER
AFTER INSERT ON BILLCUSTOMER FOR EACH ROW
DECLARE
    cg$rec cg$BILLCUSTOMER.cg$row_type;
    cg$ind cg$BILLCUSTOMER.cg$ind_type;
BEGIN
--  Application_logic Pre-After-Insert-row <<Start>>
--  Application_logic Pre-After-Insert-row << End >>

    cg$rec.USERID := :new.USERID;
    cg$ind.USERID := TRUE;
    cg$rec.BILLNO := :new.BILLNO;
    cg$ind.BILLNO := TRUE;
    cg$rec.AMOUNT := :new.AMOUNT;
    cg$ind.AMOUNT := TRUE;
    cg$rec.BILLDATE := :new.BILLDATE;
    cg$ind.BILLDATE := TRUE;
    cg$rec.PAIDSTATUS := :new.PAIDSTATUS;
    cg$ind.PAIDSTATUS := TRUE;
    cg$rec.CUSTID := :new.CUSTID;
    cg$ind.CUSTID := TRUE;
```

```
--  Application_logic Post-After-Insert-row <<Start>>
--  Application_logic Post-After-Insert-row << End >>
END;
/
```

The output of the preceding code snippet is as follows:

```
Trigger created
```

After Insert Statement Trigger on **BILLCUSTOMER**

```
PROMPT Creating After Insert Statement Trigger on 'BILLCUSTOMER'
CREATE OR REPLACE TRIGGER cg$AIS_BILLCUSTOMER
AFTER INSERT ON BILLCUSTOMER
DECLARE
    idx      BINARY_INTEGER := cg$BILLCUSTOMER.cg$table.FIRST;
    cg$rec   cg$BILLCUSTOMER.cg$row_type;
    cg$old_rec   cg$BILLCUSTOMER.cg$row_type;
    fk_check INTEGER;
BEGIN
--  Application_logic Pre-After-Insert-statement <<Start>>
--  Application_logic Pre-After-Insert-statement << End >>

    IF NOT (cg$BILLCUSTOMER.called_from_package) THEN
        WHILE idx IS NOT NULL LOOP
            cg$rec.USERID := cg$BILLCUSTOMER.cg$table(idx).USERID;
            cg$rec.BILLNO := cg$BILLCUSTOMER.cg$table(idx).BILLNO;
            cg$rec.AMOUNT := cg$BILLCUSTOMER.cg$table(idx).AMOUNT;
            cg$rec.BILLDATE := cg$BILLCUSTOMER.cg$table(idx).BILLDATE;
            cg$rec.PAIDSTATUS := cg$BILLCUSTOMER.cg$table(idx).PAIDSTATUS;
            cg$rec.CUSTID := cg$BILLCUSTOMER.cg$table(idx).CUSTID;

            cg$BILLCUSTOMER.validate_foreign_keys_ins(cg$rec);

            cg$BILLCUSTOMER.upd_oper_denorm2( cg$rec, cg$old_rec,
        cg$BILLCUSTOMER.cg$tableind(idx), 'INS');

            idx := cg$BILLCUSTOMER.cg$table.NEXT(idx);
        END LOOP;
    END IF;

--  Application_logic Post-After-Insert-statement <<Start>>
--  Application_logic Post-After-Insert-statement << End >>

END;
/
```

The output of the preceding code snippet is as follows:

```
Trigger created
```

Before Update Statement Trigger on **BILLCUSTOMER**

```
PROMPT Creating Before Update Statement Trigger on 'BILLCUSTOMER'
CREATE OR REPLACE TRIGGER cg$BUS_BILLCUSTOMER
BEFORE UPDATE ON BILLCUSTOMER
BEGIN
--  Application_logic Pre-Before-Update-statement <<Start>>
--  Application_logic Pre-Before-Update-statement << End >>
```

```
    cg$BILLCUSTOMER.cg$table.DELETE;
    cg$BILLCUSTOMER.cg$tableind.DELETE;
    cg$BILLCUSTOMER.idx := 1;

--  Application_logic Post-Before-Update-statement <<Start>>
--  Application_logic Post-Before-Update-statement << End >>

END;
/
```

The output of the preceding code snippet is as follows:

```
Trigger created
```

Before Update Row Trigger on **BILLCUSTOMER**

```
PROMPT Creating Before Update Row Trigger on 'BILLCUSTOMER'
CREATE OR REPLACE TRIGGER cg$BUR_BILLCUSTOMER
BEFORE UPDATE ON BILLCUSTOMER FOR EACH ROW
DECLARE
    cg$rec cg$BILLCUSTOMER.cg$row_type;
    cg$ind cg$BILLCUSTOMER.cg$ind_type;
BEGIN
--  Application_logic Pre-Before-Update-row <<Start>>
--  Application_logic Pre-Before-Update-row << End >>

--  Load cg$rec/cg$ind values from new

    cg$rec.USERID := :new.USERID;
    cg$ind.USERID :=    (:new.USERID IS NULL AND :old.USERID IS NOT NULL )
                        OR (:new.USERID IS NOT NULL AND :old.USERID IS NULL)
                        OR NOT(:new.USERID = :old.USERID) ;
    cg$rec.BILLNO := :new.BILLNO;
    cg$ind.BILLNO :=    (:new.BILLNO IS NULL AND :old.BILLNO IS NOT NULL )
                        OR (:new.BILLNO IS NOT NULL AND :old.BILLNO IS NULL)
                        OR NOT(:new.BILLNO = :old.BILLNO) ;
    cg$rec.AMOUNT := :new.AMOUNT;
    cg$ind.AMOUNT :=    (:new.AMOUNT IS NULL AND :old.AMOUNT IS NOT NULL )
                        OR (:new.AMOUNT IS NOT NULL AND :old.AMOUNT IS NULL)
                        OR NOT(:new.AMOUNT = :old.AMOUNT) ;
    cg$rec.BILLDATE := :new.BILLDATE;
    cg$ind.BILLDATE := (:new.BILLDATE IS NULL AND :old.BILLDATE IS NOT NULL )
                        OR (:new.BILLDATE IS NOT NULL AND :old.BILLDATE IS NULL)
                        OR NOT(:new.BILLDATE = :old.BILLDATE) ;
    cg$rec.PAIDSTATUS := :new.PAIDSTATUS;
    cg$ind.PAIDSTATUS := (:new.PAIDSTATUS IS NULL AND :old.PAIDSTATUS IS NOT
  NULL )
                        OR (:new.PAIDSTATUS IS NOT NULL AND :old.PAIDSTATUS IS
                        NULL)
                        OR NOT(:new.PAIDSTATUS = :old.PAIDSTATUS) ;
    cg$rec.CUSTID := :new.CUSTID;
    cg$ind.CUSTID :=    (:new.CUSTID IS NULL AND :old.CUSTID IS NOT NULL )
                        OR (:new.CUSTID IS NOT NULL AND :old.CUSTID IS NULL)
                        OR NOT(:new.CUSTID = :old.CUSTID) ;
    cg$BILLCUSTOMER.cg$table(cg$BILLCUSTOMER.idx).USERID := :old.USERID;
    cg$BILLCUSTOMER.cg$table(cg$BILLCUSTOMER.idx).BILLNO := :old.BILLNO;
```

```
    cg$BILLCUSTOMER.cg$table(cg$BILLCUSTOMER.idx).AMOUNT := :old.AMOUNT;
    cg$BILLCUSTOMER.cg$table(cg$BILLCUSTOMER.idx).BILLDATE := :old.BILLDATE;
    cg$BILLCUSTOMER.cg$table(cg$BILLCUSTOMER.idx).PAIDSTATUS := :old.PAIDSTATUS;
    cg$BILLCUSTOMER.cg$table(cg$BILLCUSTOMER.idx).CUSTID := :old.CUSTID;

    cg$BILLCUSTOMER.idx := cg$BILLCUSTOMER.idx + 1;

    if not (cg$BILLCUSTOMER.called_from_package) then
        cg$BILLCUSTOMER.validate_arc(cg$rec);
        cg$BILLCUSTOMER.validate_domain(cg$rec);

        cg$BILLCUSTOMER.upd(cg$rec, cg$ind, FALSE);
        cg$BILLCUSTOMER.called_from_package := FALSE;
    end if;

    :new.USERID := cg$rec.USERID;
    :new.BILLNO := cg$rec.BILLNO;
    :new.AMOUNT := cg$rec.AMOUNT;
    :new.BILLDATE := cg$rec.BILLDATE;
    :new.PAIDSTATUS := cg$rec.PAIDSTATUS;
    :new.CUSTID := cg$rec.CUSTID;

--  Application_logic Post-Before-Update-row <<Start>>
--  Application_logic Post-Before-Update-row << End >>
END;
/
```

The output of the preceding code snippet is as follows:

```
Trigger created
```

After Update Row Trigger on **BILLCUSTOMER**

```
PROMPT Creating After Update Row Trigger on 'BILLCUSTOMER'
CREATE OR REPLACE TRIGGER cg$AUR_BILLCUSTOMER
AFTER UPDATE ON BILLCUSTOMER FOR EACH ROW
BEGIN
--  Application_logic Pre-After-Update-row <<Start>>
--  Application_logic Pre-After-Update-row << End >>

    NULL;

--  Application_logic Post-After-Update-row <<Start>>
--  Application_logic Post-After-Update-row << End >>
END;
/
```

The output of the preceding code snippet is as follows:

```
Trigger created
```

After Update Statement Trigger on **BILLCUSTOMER**

```
PROMPT Creating After Update Statement Trigger on 'BILLCUSTOMER'
CREATE OR REPLACE TRIGGER cg$AUS_BILLCUSTOMER
AFTER UPDATE ON BILLCUSTOMER
DECLARE
    idx        BINARY_INTEGER := cg$BILLCUSTOMER.cg$table.FIRST;
    cg$old_rec cg$BILLCUSTOMER.cg$row_type;
```

```
    cg$rec      cg$BILLCUSTOMER.cg$row_type;
    cg$ind      cg$BILLCUSTOMER.cg$ind_type;
BEGIN
--  Application_logic Pre-After-Update-statement <<Start>>
--  Application_logic Pre-After-Update-statement << End >>

    WHILE idx IS NOT NULL LOOP
        cg$old_rec.USERID := cg$BILLCUSTOMER.cg$table(idx).USERID;
        cg$old_rec.BILLNO := cg$BILLCUSTOMER.cg$table(idx).BILLNO;
        cg$old_rec.AMOUNT := cg$BILLCUSTOMER.cg$table(idx).AMOUNT;
        cg$old_rec.BILLDATE := cg$BILLCUSTOMER.cg$table(idx).BILLDATE;
        cg$old_rec.PAIDSTATUS := cg$BILLCUSTOMER.cg$table(idx).PAIDSTATUS;
        cg$old_rec.CUSTID := cg$BILLCUSTOMER.cg$table(idx).CUSTID;

    IF NOT (cg$BILLCUSTOMER.called_from_package) THEN
        idx := cg$BILLCUSTOMER.cg$table.NEXT(idx);
        cg$rec.USERID := cg$BILLCUSTOMER.cg$table(idx).USERID;
        cg$ind.USERID := updating('USERID');
        cg$rec.BILLNO := cg$BILLCUSTOMER.cg$table(idx).BILLNO;
        cg$ind.BILLNO := updating('BILLNO');
        cg$rec.AMOUNT := cg$BILLCUSTOMER.cg$table(idx).AMOUNT;
        cg$ind.AMOUNT := updating('AMOUNT');
        cg$rec.BILLDATE := cg$BILLCUSTOMER.cg$table(idx).BILLDATE;
        cg$ind.BILLDATE := updating('BILLDATE');
        cg$rec.PAIDSTATUS := cg$BILLCUSTOMER.cg$table(idx).PAIDSTATUS;
        cg$ind.PAIDSTATUS := updating('PAIDSTATUS');
        cg$rec.CUSTID := cg$BILLCUSTOMER.cg$table(idx).CUSTID;
        cg$ind.CUSTID := updating('CUSTID');

        cg$BILLCUSTOMER.validate_foreign_keys_upd(cg$rec, cg$old_rec, cg$ind);

        cg$BILLCUSTOMER.upd_denorm2( cg$rec, cg$BILLCUSTOMER.cg$tableind(idx));
        cg$BILLCUSTOMER.upd_oper_denorm2( cg$rec, cg$old_rec,
                                          cg$BILLCUSTOMER.cg$tableind(idx));
        cg$BILLCUSTOMER.cascade_update(cg$rec, cg$old_rec);
         cg$BILLCUSTOMER.called_from_package := FALSE;
   END IF;
        idx := cg$BILLCUSTOMER.cg$table.NEXT(idx);
    END LOOP;

    cg$BILLCUSTOMER.cg$table.DELETE;

--  Application_logic Post-After-Update-statement <<Start>>
--  Application_logic Post-After-Update-statement << End >>

END;
/
```

The output of the preceding code snippet is as follows:

```
Trigger created
```

Before Delete Statement Trigger on **BILLCUSTOMER**

```
PROMPT Creating Before Delete Statement Trigger on 'BILLCUSTOMER'
CREATE OR REPLACE TRIGGER cg$BDS_BILLCUSTOMER
BEFORE DELETE ON BILLCUSTOMER
BEGIN
--  Application_logic Pre-Before-Delete-statement <<Start>>
--  Application_logic Pre-Before-Delete-statement << End >>

    cg$BILLCUSTOMER.cg$table.DELETE;
    cg$BILLCUSTOMER.cg$tableind.DELETE;
    cg$BILLCUSTOMER.idx := 1;

--  Application_logic Post-Before-Delete-statement <<Start>>
--  Application_logic Post-Before-Delete-statement << End >>
END;
/
```

The output of the preceding code snippet is as follows:

```
Trigger created
```

Before Delete Row Trigger on **BILLCUSTOMER**

```
PROMPT Creating Before Delete Row Trigger on 'BILLCUSTOMER'
CREATE OR REPLACE TRIGGER cg$BDR_BILLCUSTOMER
BEFORE DELETE ON BILLCUSTOMER FOR EACH ROW
DECLARE
    cg$pk cg$BILLCUSTOMER.cg$pk_type;
    cg$rec cg$BILLCUSTOMER.cg$row_type;
    cg$ind cg$BILLCUSTOMER.cg$ind_type;
BEGIN
--  Application_logic Pre-Before-Delete-row <<Start>>
--  Application_logic Pre-Before-Delete-row << End >>

--  Load cg$rec/cg$ind values from new

    cg$pk.BILLNO := :old.BILLNO;
    cg$rec.BILLNO := :old.BILLNO;
    cg$BILLCUSTOMER.cg$table(cg$BILLCUSTOMER.idx).BILLNO := cg$pk.BILLNO;
    cg$rec.CUSTID := :old.CUSTID;
    cg$BILLCUSTOMER.cg$table(cg$BILLCUSTOMER.idx).CUSTID := cg$rec.CUSTID;

    cg$BILLCUSTOMER.idx := cg$BILLCUSTOMER.idx + 1;

    if not (cg$BILLCUSTOMER.called_from_package) then
        cg$BILLCUSTOMER.del(cg$pk, FALSE);
        cg$BILLCUSTOMER.called_from_package := FALSE;
    end if;

--  Application_logic Post-Before-Delete-row <<Start>>
--  Application_logic Post-Before-Delete-row << End >>
END;
/
```

The output of the preceding code snippet is as follows:

```
Trigger created
```

After Delete Row Trigger on **BILLCUSTOMER**

```
PROMPT Creating After Delete Row Trigger on 'BILLCUSTOMER'
PROMPT Creating After Delete Statement Trigger on 'BILLCUSTOMER'
CREATE OR REPLACE TRIGGER cg$ADS_BILLCUSTOMER
AFTER DELETE ON BILLCUSTOMER
DECLARE
    idx        BINARY_INTEGER := cg$BILLCUSTOMER.cg$table.FIRST;
    cg$rec   cg$BILLCUSTOMER.cg$row_type;
    cg$old_rec   cg$BILLCUSTOMER.cg$row_type;
BEGIN
--  Application_logic Pre-After-Delete-statement <<Start>>
--  Application_logic Pre-After-Delete-statement << End >>

    IF NOT (cg$BILLCUSTOMER.called_from_package) THEN
        WHILE idx IS NOT NULL LOOP
            cg$rec.USERID := cg$BILLCUSTOMER.cg$table(idx).USERID;
            cg$BILLCUSTOMER.cg$tableind(idx).USERID := TRUE;
            cg$rec.BILLNO := cg$BILLCUSTOMER.cg$table(idx).BILLNO;
            cg$BILLCUSTOMER.cg$tableind(idx).BILLNO := TRUE;
            cg$rec.AMOUNT := cg$BILLCUSTOMER.cg$table(idx).AMOUNT;
            cg$BILLCUSTOMER.cg$tableind(idx).AMOUNT := TRUE;
            cg$rec.BILLDATE := cg$BILLCUSTOMER.cg$table(idx).BILLDATE;
            cg$BILLCUSTOMER.cg$tableind(idx).BILLDATE := TRUE;
            cg$rec.PAIDSTATUS := cg$BILLCUSTOMER.cg$table(idx).PAIDSTATUS;
            cg$BILLCUSTOMER.cg$tableind(idx).PAIDSTATUS := TRUE;
            cg$rec.CUSTID := cg$BILLCUSTOMER.cg$table(idx).CUSTID;
            cg$BILLCUSTOMER.cg$tableind(idx).CUSTID := TRUE;

            cg$BILLCUSTOMER.validate_foreign_keys_del(cg$rec);
            cg$BILLCUSTOMER.upd_oper_denorm2( cg$rec, cg$old_rec,
        cg$BILLCUSTOMER.cg$tableind(idx), 'DEL');

            cg$BILLCUSTOMER.cascade_delete(cg$rec);

            idx := cg$BILLCUSTOMER.cg$table.NEXT(idx);
        END LOOP;
    END IF;

--  Application_logic Post-After-Delete-statement <<Start>>
--  Application_logic Post-After-Delete-statement << End >>

END;
/
```

The output of the preceding code snippet is as follows:

```
Trigger created
```

Summary

This chapter focused on the procedures in the bill entry system for the server model. The next chapter focuses on security and auditing.

48

Security and Auditing

Oracle uses entities, such as user, role, privileges, and profiles, to manage security. Only the users having a valid account can login to Oracle and perform operations defined by the privileges. The privileges are granted directly or via role to users. The privileges are divided into two categories, system and object.

System privileges are those privileges, which are related with operations, and are not connected with any object. For example, the `create session` privilege is a system privilege because it enables a user to login to Oracle, but is not related with objects.

On the other hand, the object privileges are related with objects. For example, the privilege `insert into table T of user U` is related with object `T`. The role is used to group privileges and implement application-based security. Application-based security means that the user will get only those privileges which are required for running an application.

Profiles are used to restrict the user to consume system resources, such as disk reads and memory.

In this chapter, you learn how to create a user. Next, you learn about external system authentication. The chapter also explains the privileges, roles, and profile in detail. Further, you learn about composite limit. In addition, you learn about setting password parameters and auditing. In the end, you learn about the DBA_STMT_AUDIT_OPTS view.

Let's start by learning to create a user.

Creating a User

Oracle user is created using command CREATE USER as follows.

Listing 48.1 shows how to create a user:

Listing 48.1: Creating a User

```
create user anil                        --A
identified by pwd_anil                  --B
default tablespace users                --C
quota 10M on users
quota unlimited on payroll              --D
profile userprofile                     --E
/
```

The output of Listing 48.1 is as follows:

```
User created
```

In Listing 48.1:

- Statement A indicates username, which is used for login or making a connection to Oracle.
- Statement B indicates password of user. If you use `identified externally` then user is authenticated using operating system. You have to create a user in operating system with that name. If you set parameters `OS_AUTHENT_PREFIX` in parameter file to `XYZ`, then you have to create Oracle user with name `XYZanil`(Where XYZ is prefix in the name of user).
- In statement C, Oracle uses logical entity tablespace to manage disk space. All the objects are related with tablespace rather than data file on disk. The tablespaces are of the following four types:
  - `System`
  - `System auxiliary`
  - `Temporary`
  - `Undo`

The system and system auxiliary tablespaces are used to store metadata or data dictionary. The temporary tablespace is used to store temporary data generated during query execution. The undo tablespace is used to store rollback data. The user tablespaces are used for general user data. Generally, for one application one tablespace is created. If there are applications, such as payroll, production, marketing, then for each application, one separate tablespace is created. You can specify the name of tablespace in which an object is created at the time of creation of object, such as a table. If you do not mention the name of the tablespace, then the default tablespace is used.

- Statement D indicates quota on the assigned tablespace. You can consume only that space which is mentioned in quota. Any statement, which exceeds the space limit, is rejected. Listing 48.1 indicates that the user can consume 10 megabytes in the user tablespace, and unlimited space in the payroll tablespace.

NOTE

It is the name of profile, which is used for controlling resources. The concept of profile is explained later.

You can lock the account of user temporarily, as shown in the following code snippet:

```
alter user scott account lock;
```

You can also unlock the locked account, as shown in the following code snippet:

```
alter user scott account unlock;
```

The password of the user can also be disables, as shown in the following code snippet:

```
alter user scott password expire;
```

Let's now learn about the external system authentication.

External System Authentication

If you want that user should be authenticated externally (using operating system account) then give the command, shown in the following code snippet:

```
create user ops$smith identified externally;
```

The output of the preceding code snippet is as follows:

```
User created
```

In the preceding code snippet, OPS$ is the default value of OS_AUTHENT_PREFIX, but it can be set to any string or null, as shown the following code snippet:

```
OS_AUTHENT_PREFIX=""
```

If a user with an operating system account named SMITH is to connect to an Oracle database and be authenticated by the operating system, Oracle checks that there is a corresponding database user OPS$TSMITH.

If you want to use operating system user authentication with network clients, set the parameter REMOTE_OS_AUTHENT (default is FALSE) to TRUE in the database's initialization parameter file.

License Parameters

Oracle software is purchased with some defined number of licenses. License parameters are set as follows.

Listing 48.2 shows how to set license parameters:

Listing 48.2: Setting License Parameters to Limit the Number of Concurrent Sessions and Users

```
alter system
   set license_max_sessions = 64
   license_sessions_warning = 54;
/
```

The output of Listing 48.2 is as follows:

```
System altered
```

The parameters can be set in a parameter file to have effect on each startup of Oracle instance. To limit the number of users created in a database, set the LICENSE_MAX_USERS parameter in the database's parameter file, as shown in Listing 48.3:

Listing 48.3: Setting the Maximum Number of Users to 200

```
license_max_users = 200

alter system set license_max_users = 200;
```

The output of Listing 48.3 is as follows:

```
System altered
```

You can get statistics of users, as shown in the following code snippet:

```
select sessions_max s_max,
   sessions_warning s_warning,
   sessions_current s_current,
   sessions_highwater s_high,
   users_max
   from v$license
/
```

The output of the preceding code snippet is as follows:

```
     S_MAX  S_WARNING  S_CURRENT     S_HIGH  USERS_MAX
---------- ---------- ---------- ---------- ----------
        64         54         16         17          0
```

In the preceding code snippet, `SESSION_HIGHWATER` indicates the maximum number of sessions created after startup. If the number of sessions exceeds the limit set by the license `warning` parameter, then a warning message appears in an Oracle alert file and the user will be allowed to create a session.

NOTE

When the number of sessions exceeds the limit set by maximum parameter, then a normal user cannot logon to Oracle. Only the DBA is allowed to login.

Privileges

The operations that a user can perform are controlled by privileges. The following examples show how to grant privileges to users:

Listing 48.4: Granting Privileges to a User to Create Sessions

```
grant create session to anil;
```

The output of Listing 48.4 is as follows:

```
Grant succeeded
```

The statement, `grant create session to anil`, implies that the user Anil can login only if he is having this privilege.

Listing 48.5: Granting Privileges with the admin Option

```
grant create session to anil with admin option;
```

The output of Listing 48.5 is as follows:

```
Grant succeeded
```

The `admin` option allows you to grant privilege to other users or revoke privilege from other users.

Listing 48.6: Granting Privilege to Make Insertions into the emp Table of User Scott

```
grant insert
   on scott.emp to anil;
```

The output of Listing 48.6 is as follows:

```
Grant succeeded
```

This is an object privilege and statement grants insertion on table emp owned by SCOTT to ANIL. The syntax for insertion in emp table owned by scott is as follows:

```
insert into scott.emp values(…);
```

The user anil will insert data into table emp.

Listing 48.7: Granting Privilege to Execute Procedure proc of User scott

```
grant execute
    on scott.proc to anil;
```

The output of Listing 48.7 is as follows:

```
Grant succeeded
```

This is an object privilege. The statement grants permission to Anil to execute the proc procedure, which is created by Scott.

In the following statement, the user anil will execute procedure created by SCOTT.

```
execute scott.proc(parameters if any);
```

The preceding code snippet shows that Anil can execute the proc procedure with any parameters.

Listing 48.8: Granting Updation on Table emp

```
grant update
    on scott.emp to anil with grant option;
```

The output of Listing 48.8 is as follows:

```
Grant succeeded
```

This is an object privilege. The statement grants permission to Anil to update the table (object), which is created by Scott.

Listing 48.9: Selective Updation on a Table

```
grant update
    on scott.emp(empno,sal) to anil;
```

The output of Listing 48.8 is as follows:

```
Grant succeeded
```

In Listing 48.9, the GRANT UPDATE statement grants the update permission only on columns empno and sal.

List of Privileges

In this section, we discuss lists of privileges. Table 48.1 lists the privileges related with SQL statement tuning (reference Oracle 10g documentation):

SQL statement privilege	Description
ADVISOR	Allows you to access the advisor framework through PL/SQL packages, such as DBMS_ADVISOR and DBMS_SQLTUNE
ADMINISTER SQL TUNING SET	Allows you to manage an SQL tuning set owned by the grantee using the DBMS_SQLTUNE package
ADMINISTER ANY SQL TUNING SET	Allows you to manage an SQL tuning set owned by any user using the DBMS_SQLTUNE package
CREATE ANY SQL PROFILE	Allows you to create an SQL Profile recommended by the SQL Tuning Advisor
DROP ANY SQL PROFILE	Allows you to drop an existing SQL Profile
ALTER ANY SQL PROFILE	Allows you to alter the attributes of an existing SQL Profile

Clusters are used to store related data of multiple tables that are physically contiguous. Table 48.2 lists cluster related privileges:

Cluster related privilege	Description
CREATE CLUSTER	Allows you to create clusters in your own schema
CREATE ANY CLUSTER	Allows you to create a cluster in any schema
ALTER ANY CLUSTER	Allows you to alter attributes of a cluster
DROP ANY CLUSTER	Allows you to drop clusters in any schema

Table 48.3 lists context privileges:

Context privilege	Description
`CREATE ANY CONTEXT`	Allows you to create a context namespace in any other user's schema
`DROP ANY CONTEXT`	Allows you to drop any context namespace

Table 48.4 lists database privileges:

Database privilege	Description
`ALTER DATABASE`	Allows you to alter the database configuration
`ALTER SYSTEM`	Allows you to `ALTER SYSTEM` statements to change parameters
`AUDIT SYSTEM`	Allows you to `AUDIT` actions of another user

Table 48.5 lists database link privileges:

Database link privilege	Description
`CREATE DATABASE LINK`	Allows you to use database link to interact with other databases
`CREATE PUBLIC DATABASE LINK`	Allows you to create public database links
`DROP PUBLIC DATABASE LINK`	Allows you to drop public database links

Table 48.6 lists debugging privileges:

Debugging privilege	Description
`DEBUG CONNECT SESSION`	Allows you to connect the current session for using a debugger
`DEBUG ANY PROCEDURE`	Allows you to debug all PL/SQL and Java code in any database object

Table 48.7 lists dimension privileges:

Dimension privilege	Description
`CREATE DIMENSION`	Allows you to create dimensions mainly used in data warehousing
`CREATE ANY DIMENSION`	Allows you to create dimensions in any schema
`ALTER ANY DIMENSION`	Allows you to alter dimensions in any schema
`DROP ANY DIMENSION`	Allows you to drop dimensions in any schema

Table 48.8 lists directories privileges:

Directories privilege	Description
CREATE ANY DIRECTORY	Allows you to create directory database objects for bfiles
DROP ANY DIRECTORY	Allows you to drop directory database objects

Table 48.9 lists indextypes privileges:

Indextypes privilege	Description
CREATE INDEXTYPE	Allows you to create an indextype
CREATE ANY INDEXTYPE	Allows you to create an indextype in any schema
ALTER ANY INDEXTYPE	Allows you to modify indextypes in any schema
DROP ANY INDEXTYPE	Allows you to drop an indextype in any schema
EXECUTE ANY INDEXTYPE	Allows you to refer to an indextype in any schema

Table 48.10 lists index privileges:

Index privilege	Description
CREATE ANY INDEX	Allows you to create a domain index or an index on any table in any schema for faster data access
ALTER ANY INDEX	Allows you to alter indexes in any schema
DROP ANY INDEX	Allows you to drop indexes in any schema

Table 48.11 lists scheduler privileges:

Scheduler privilege	Description
JOB SCHEDULER OBJECTS	Allows you to execute procedures or jobs at a particular time
CREATE JOB	Allows you to create jobs, schedules, or programs in the grantee's schema
CREATE ANY JOB	Allows you to create, alter, or drop jobs, schedules, or programs in any schema
EXECUTE ANY PROGRAM	Allows you to execute any program in a job in the grantee's schema
EXECUTE ANY CLASS	Allows you to specify any job class in a job in the grantee's schema
MANAGE SCHEDULER	Allows you to create, alter, or drop any job class, window, or window group

Table 48.12 lists library privileges:

Library privilege	Description
CREATE LIBRARY	Allows you to create external procedure or function libraries in the grantee's schema
CREATE ANY LIBRARY	Allows you to create external procedure or function libraries in any schema
DROP ANY LIBRARY	Allows you to drop external procedure or function libraries in any schema

Materialized views have their own storage and they are refreshed to synchronize with base table data. Table 48.13 lists materialized views:

Materialized view	Description
CREATE MATERIALIZED VIEW	Allows you to create a materialized view in the grantee's schema
CREATE ANY MATERIALIZED VIEW	Allows you to create materialized views in any schema
ALTER ANY MATERIALIZED VIEW	Allows you to alter materialized views in any schema
DROP ANY MATERIALIZED VIEW	Allows you to drop materialized views in any schema
QUERY REWRITE	This privilege is no longer required in recent version.
GLOBAL QUERY REWRITE	Allows you to enable rewrite using a materialized view when that materialized view references tables or views in any schema
ON COMMIT REFRESH	Allows you to create a refresh-on-commit materialized view on any table in the database
FLASHBACK ANY TABLE	Allows you to issue an SQL Flashback Query on any table, view, or materialized view in any schema

Table 48.14 lists operator privileges:

Operator privilege	Description
CREATE OPERATOR	Allows you to create an operator and its bindings in the grantee's schema
CREATE ANY OPERATOR	Allows you to create an operator and its bindings in any schema
ALTER ANY OPERATOR	Allows you to modify an operator in any schema
DROP ANY OPERATOR	Allows you to drop an operator in any schema
EXECUTE ANY OPERATOR	Allows you to refer to an operator in any schema

Table 48.15 lists outline privileges:

Outline privilege	Description
CREATE ANY OUTLINE	Allows you to create public outlines, which can be used in any schema that uses outlines. These are mainly used to plan stability
ALTER ANY OUTLINE	Allows you to modify outlines
DROP ANY OUTLINE	Allows you to drop outlines

Table 48.16 lists procedure privileges:

Procedure privilege	Description
CREATE PROCEDURE	Allows you to create stored procedures, functions, and packages in the grantee's schema
CREATE ANY PROCEDURE	Allows you to create stored procedures, functions, and packages in any schema
ALTER ANY PROCEDURE	Allows you to alter stored procedures, functions, or packages in any schema

Procedure privilege	Description
DROP ANY PROCEDURE	Allows you to drop stored procedures, functions, or packages in any schema
EXECUTE ANY PROCEDURE	Allows you to execute procedures or functions, either standalone or packaged; you can reference public package variables in any schema

Table 48.17 lists profile privileges:

Profile privilege	Description
CREATE PROFILE	Allows you to create profiles to control resources link CPU or memory
ALTER PROFILE	Allows you to alter profiles
DROP PROFILE	Allows you to drop profiles

Table 48.18 lists role privileges:

Role privilege	Description
CREATE ROLE	Allows you to create roles
ALTER ANY ROLE	Allows you to alter any role in a database
DROP ANY ROLE	Allows you to drop roles
GRANT ANY ROLE	Allows you to grant any role in a database

Table 48.19 lists rollback segments privileges:

Rollback segment privilege	Description
CREATE ROLLBACK SEGMENT	Allows you to create rollback segments
ALTER ROLLBACK SEGMENT	Allows you to alter rollback segments
DROP ROLLBACK SEGMENT	Allows you to drop rollback segments

Table 48.20 lists sequence privileges:

Sequence privilege	Description
CREATE SEQUENCE	Allows you to create sequences in the grantee's schema
CREATE ANY SEQUENCE	Allows you to create sequences in any schema
ALTER ANY SEQUENCE	Allows you to alter any sequence in a database
DROP ANY SEQUENCE	Allows you to drop sequences in any schema
SELECT ANY SEQUENCE	Allows you to refer to sequences in any schema

Table 48.21 lists session privileges:

Session privilege	Description
CREATE SESSION	Allows you to connect to a database
ALTER RESOURCE COST	Allows you to set costs for session resources

Session privilege	Description
ALTER SESSION	Allows you to issue ALTER SESSION statements
RESTRICTED SESSION	Allows you to logon after the instance is started using the SQL*Plus STARTUP RESTRICT statement

Table 48.22 lists synonym privileges:

Synonym privilege	Description
CREATE SYNONYM	Allows you to create synonyms in the grantee's schema
CREATE ANY SYNONYM	Allows you to create private synonyms in any schema
CREATE PUBLIC SYNONYM	Allows you to create public synonyms
DROP ANY SYNONYM	Allows you to drop private synonyms in any schema
DROP PUBLIC SYNONYM	Allows you to drop public synonyms

Table 48.23 lists table privileges:

Table privilege	Description
CREATE TABLE	Allows you to create tables in the grantee's schema
CREATE ANY TABLE	Allows you to create tables in any schema; the owner of the schema containing the table must have space quota on the tablespace to contain the table
ALTER ANY TABLE	Allows you to alter any table or view in any schema
BACKUP ANY TABLE	Allows you to use the Export utility to incrementally export objects from the schema of other users
DELETE ANY TABLE	Allows you to delete rows from tables, table partitions, or views in any schema
DROP ANY TABLE	Allows you to drop or truncate tables or table partitions in any schema
INSERT ANY TABLE	Allows you to insert rows into tables and views in any schema
LOCK ANY TABLE	Allows you to lock tables and views in any schema
SELECT ANY TABLE	Allows you to query tables, views, or materialized views in any schema
FLASHBACK ANY TABLE	Allows you to issue an SQL Flashback Query on any table, view, or materialized view in any schema; this privilege is not needed to execute the DBMS_FLASHBACK procedure
UPDATE ANY TABLE	Allows you to update rows in tables and views in any schema

NOTE

The CREATE ANY TABLE, ALTER ANY TABLE, DROP ANY TABLE, and SELECT ANY TABLE privileges are used only for external tables.

Table 48.24 lists tablespace privileges:

Tablespace privilege	Description
`CREATE TABLESPACE`	Allows you to create tablespaces
`ALTER TABLESPACE`	Allows you to alter tablespaces
`DROP TABLESPACE`	Allows you to drop tablespaces
`MANAGE TABLESPACE`	Allows you to take tablespaces offline and online, begin and end tablespace backups
`UNLIMITED TABLESPACE`	Allows you to use an unlimited amount of any tablespace. The effect will be for future operations. The privilege cannot be granted via role

Table 48.25 lists trigger privileges:

Trigger privilege	Description
`CREATE TRIGGER`	Allows you to create a database trigger in the grantee's schema.
`CREATE ANY TRIGGER`	Allows you to create database triggers in any schema.
`ALTER ANY TRIGGER`	Allows you to enable, disable, or compile database triggers in any schema.
`DROP ANY TRIGGER`	Allows you to drop database triggers in any schema.
`ADMINISTER DATABASE TRIGGER`	Allows you to create a trigger on a `DATABASE`. You must also have the `CREATE TRIGGER` or `CREATE ANY TRIGGER` system privilege.

Table 48.26 lists type privileges:

Type privilege	Description
`CREATE TYPE`	Allows you to create object types and object type bodies in the grantee's schema
`CREATE ANY TYPE`	Allows you to create object types and object type bodies in any schema
`ALTER ANY TYPE`	Allows you to alter object types in any schema
`DROP ANY TYPE`	Allows you to drop object types and object type bodies in any schema
`EXECUTE ANY TYPE`	Allows you to use and refer to object types and collection types in any schema.
`UNDER ANY TYPE`	Allows you to create subtypes under any nonfinal object types

Table 48.27 lists user privileges:

User privilege	Description
CREATE USER	Allows you to create users. This privilege also allows assigning off quotas on any tablespace, setting default and temporary tablespaces, and assigning a profile as a part of a CREATE USER statement.
ALTER USER	Allows you to alter any user. This privilege allows: • Changing another user's password or authentication method • Assigning quotas on any tablespace • Setting default and temporary tablespaces • Assigning a profile and default roles
DROP USER	Allows you to drop users.

Table 48.28 lists view privileges:

View privilege	Description
CREATE VIEW	Allows you to create views in the grantee's schema.
CREATE ANY VIEW	Allows you to create views in any schema.
DROP ANY VIEW	Allows you to drop views in any schema.
UNDER ANY VIEW	Allows you to create subviews under any object views.
FLASHBACK ANY TABLE	Allows you to issue an SQL Flashback Query on any table, view, or materialized view in any schema. This privilege is not needed to execute the DBMS_FLASHBACK procedures.

Table 48.29 lists miscellaneous privileges:

Miscellaneous privilege	Description
ANALYZE ANY	Allows you to analyze any table, cluster, or index in any schema
AUDIT ANY	Allows you to audit any object in any schema using AUDIT schema_objects statements
COMMENT ANY TABLE	Allows you to comment on any table, view, or column in any schema
EXEMPT ACCESS POLICY	Allows you to bypass fine-grained access control
FORCE ANY TRANSACTION	Allows you to force the commit or rollback of any in-doubt distributed transaction in the local database
FORCE TRANSACTION	Allows you to force the commit or rollback of the grantee's in-doubt distributed transactions in the local database
GRANT ANY OBJECT PRIVILEGE	Allows you to grant any object privilege
GRANT ANY PRIVILEGE	Allows you to grant any system privilege
RESUMABLE	Allows you to enable resumable space allocation
SELECT ANY DICTIONARY	Allows you to query any data dictionary object in the SYS schema
SYSDBA	Allows you to perform STARTUP and SHUTDOWN operations ALTER DATABASE (open, mount, back up, or change character set) CREATE DATABASE ARCHIVELOG and RECOVERY CREATE SPFILE User can use the RESTRICTED SESSION privilege
SYSOPER	Allows you to perform STARTUP and SHUTDOWN operations ALTER DATABASE (open, mount, or back up) ARCHIVELOG and RECOVERY CREATE SPFILE User can use the RESTRICTED SESSION privilege

Miscellaneous privilege	Description
CONNECT, RESOURCE, and DBA	Roles are used to group multiple privileges. When you install the Oracle certain roles are created. The view DBA_SYS_PRIVS provides privileges attached to roles
DELETE_CATALOG_ROLE EXECUTE_CATALOG_ROLE SELECT_CATALOG_ROLE	Allows you to access data dictionary views and packages
EXP_FULL_DATABASE IMP_FULL_DATABASE	Allows you to import and export database.
AQ_USER_ROLE AQ_ADMINISTRATOR_ROLE	Allows you to use Oracle Advanced Queuing
SNMPAGENT	User can use this role that is used by the Enterprise Manager Intelligent Agent of Oracle
RECOVERY_CATALOG_OWNER	Allows you to create a user who owns a recovery catalog

Apart from these system privileges, the user can grant various object privileges as well. The object privileges are related with some object. Listing 48.10 shows the code to grant the update permission:

Listing 48.10: Granting Update on Table employee to Scott

```
GRANT UPDATE ON EMPLOYEE TO SCOTT;
```

The output of Listing 48.10 is as follows:

```
Grant succeeded
```

Table 48.30 lists the object privileges:

Object privilege	Description
ALTER	Allows you to change the table definition with the ALTER TABLE statement.
DELETE	Allows you to remove rows from the table with the DELETE statement.
DEBUG	Allows you to access, through a debugger: PL/SQL code in the body of any triggers defined on the table Information on SQL statements that reference the table directly
INDEX	Allows you to create an index on the table with the CREATE INDEX statement.
INSERT	Allows you to add new rows to the table with the INSERT statement.
REFERENCES	Allows you to create a constraint that refers to the table. You cannot grant this privilege to a role.
SELECT	Allows you to query the table with the SELECT statement.
UPDATE	Allows you to change data in the table with the UPDATE statement.
EXECUTE	Allows you to use and reference the specified object and invoke its methods. You can execute specified stored subprogram.
UNDER	Allows you to create a subtype under this type.

Let's now learn about roles.

Role

Roles are used to group a number of systems and object privileges and to provide an application-based security. You can create roles and assign them to users. Roles can be created with or without password, and can be assigned to users as default roles, that is, when user connects to Oracle, the role automatically gets enabled. If a role is not a default role, the user has to enable it explicitly. This property of roles allows you to design an application-based security, that is, you can design security such that a user will get only those privileges which are required for running the application.

Suppose there are two users of your application—manager and operator. For running an application manager, the privileges `P1`, `P2`, and `P3` are required. For running an application as operator, the privileges `P4`, `P5`, and `P6` are required. Listing 48.11 shows how to create and use role-based security:

Listing 48.11: Creating and Using Role-based Security

```
create role mgr identified by pwd1;
```

The output of Listing 48.11 is as follows:

```
Role created
```

Creating role opr, as shown in the following code snippet:

```
create role opr identified by pwd2;
```

The output of the preceding code snippet is as follows:

```
Role created
```

Granting privileges to mgr, as shown in the following code snippet:

```
grant p1, p2, p3 to mgr;
```

The output of the preceding code snippet is as follows:

```
Grant succeeded
```

Granting privileges to opr, as shown in the following code snippet:

```
grant p4, p5, p6 to opr;
```

The output of the preceding code snippet is as follows:

```
Grant succeeded
```

When user is working using MGR role then the user gets privileges P1, P2 and P3 while working using role OPR the user gets privileges P4, P5 and P6.

If there are ten managers and hundred operators, then you can grant the roles using the `grant` statement. Some examples of granting and setting roles are as follows:

Listing 48.12: Granting Role to Anil

```
grant mgr to anil;
```

The output of Listing 48.12 is as follows:

```
Grant succeeded
```

Listing 48.13: Granting Role with the admin Option

```
grant mgr to anil with admin option;
```

The output of Listing 48.13 is as follows:

```
Grant succeeded
```

If the role is granted with the `admin` option, the grantee can grant the role to another user, revoke the role from another user, or drop the role.

Listing 48.14: Creating Role student and Assigning it to Various Users

```
create role "student" identified by "s";
```

The output of Listing 48.14 is as follows:

```
Role created
```

Assigning various privileges to students as follows

```
grant create procedure to "student";
```

Result:

```
Grant succeeded
```

Assigning procedure to `student`

```
grant create sequence to "student";
```

Result:

```
Grant succeeded
```

Assigning session to `student`

```
grant create session to "student";
```

Result:

```
Grant succeeded
```

Assigning synonym to `student`

```
grant create synonym to "student";
```

Result:

```
Grant succeeded
```

Assigning table to `student`

```
grant create table to "student";
```

Result:

```
Grant succeeded
```

Assigning trigger to `student`

```
grant create trigger to "student";
```

Result:

```
Grant succeeded
```

Assigning type to `student`

```
GRANT CREATE TYPE TO "STUDENT";
```

Result:

```
Grant succeeded
```

Assigning view to `student`

```
grant create view to "student";
```

Result:

```
Grant succeeded
grant alter on "scott"."emp" to "student";
```

Result:

```
Grant succeeded
grant delete on "scott"."emp" to "student";
```

Result:

```
Grant succeeded
grant insert on "scott"."emp" to "student";
```

Result:

```
Grant succeeded
grant "connect" to "student";
```

Result:

```
Grant succeeded

grant "resource" to "student";
```

Result:

```
Grant succeeded
create user "ouser1" profile "default"
    identified by "o" default tablespace "users"
    temporary tablespace "temp"
    quota 10 m
    on users
    account unlock;
```

Result:

```
User created
grant student to ouser1;
```

Result:

```
Grant succeeded
create user "ouser2" profile "default"
    identified by "o" default tablespace "users"
    temporary tablespace "temp"
    quota 10 m
    on users
    account unlock;
```

Result:

```
User created
grant student to ouser2;
```

Result:

```
Grant succeeded
```

Listing 48.15: Creating a Role and Setting a Password

```
create role r1 identified by r1;
```

The output of Listing 48.15 is as follows:

```
Role created
```

Granting create table permission to role, as shown in the following code snippet:

```
grant create table to r1;
```

The output of the preceding code snippet is as follows:

```
Grant succeeded
```

Creating another role, as shown in the following code snippet:

```
create role r2;
```

The output of the preceding code snippet is as follows:

```
Role created
```

Granting create view permission to the role, as shown in the following code snippet:

```
grant create view to r2;
```

The output of the preceding code snippet is as follows:

```
Grant succeeded
```

Following set of commands demonstrates use of various commands to set roles and privileges available to users after setting roles.

Using `Set role` command

```
                                        --ANIL
SET ROLE R1;
SET ROLE R1
```

Result:

```
*
ERROR at line 1:
ORA-01979: missing or invalid password for role 'R1'
```

Setting role by user

```
                                        --Anil
SET ROLE R2;
```

Result:

```
Role set
```

Viewing all tables in system

```
select * from tab;
```

Result:

```
TNAME                          TABTYPE  CLUSTERID
------------------------------ ------- ----------
BIN$2YsYwlQUSOmEtzkqz2XlVA==$0 TABLE
BIN$QfVG93wITjCoq3w9FXizvg==$0 TABLE
S                              TABLE
T                              TABLE
TEMP                           TABLE
...
```

NOTE

When we execute this statement, around 3340 rows are displayed as result. We are unable to show these here. However a few of them have been displayed as result.

Since CREATE VIEW privilege is available to user via role , user can use this privilege to create view. Creating view for the table `temp`

```
create view vt as select * from temp;
```

Result:

```
View created
```

Selecting data from view

```
select * from vt;
```

Result:

```
No rows selected
```

Since role R1 is created with password, it requires password to set role.

Listing 48.16: Setting Role R1

```
set role r1 identified by r1;
```

The output of Listing 48.16 is as follows:

```
Role set
```

Now, the role `R1` is set.

Listing 48.17: Setting All Roles Using set role all

```
set role all;
```

The output of Listing 48.17 is as follows:

```
Role set
```

Listing 48.18: Setting All Roles Using set role all with Some Roles having a Password

```
set role all;
```

The output of Listing 48.18 is as follows:

```
SET ROLE ALL
*
ERROR at line 1:
ORA-01979: missing or invalid password for role 'R1'
```

In Listing 48.18, you can see that if some role is having a password, then an error is displayed. In such a case, you have to use the `EXCEPT` clause.

Listing 48.19: Setting All Roles Using set role all and except

```
set role all except r1;
```

The output of Listing 48.19 is as follows:

```
Role set
```

In Listing 48, you can see that all roles except for role `R1` are set.

If you set the role as a default role, then you do not have to activate it in the session. It will be automatically available.

Listing 48.20: Setting a Role as a Default Role

```
grant r1, r2 to sunil;
```

The output of Listing 48.20 is as follows:

```
Grant succeeded
```

Setting `R1` and `R2` as default roles for user `Sunil, as shown in the following code snippet:`

```
alter user sunil default role r1, r2;
```

The output of the preceding code snippet is as follows:

```
User altered
```

Connecting to Oracle as user `SUNIL`

```
                                        --SUNIL
CONNECT SUNIL/SUNIL
```

Result:

```
Connected
```

Since role R1 and R2 are given as default roles, user doesn't have to set role to use privileges. Default roles are automatically available to users after connecting to Oracle. Following command demonstrates that privilege CREATE TABLE is automatically available to user.

Creating a table `temp`

```
create table temp(a number);
```

Result:

```
Table created
```

NOTE

Roles can be granted to another user similar to system privileges. If you want to use an object of another user or some system privilege in the stored subprogram, then you have to grant it directly and not via role, because roles may not be active all the time. Same is the case with the References privilege. This privilege cannot be granted using role. It has to be granted explicitly. If you grant any privilege or role to Public, then it will be available to all users.

Listing 48.21 shows how to find roles that are active for users:

Listing 48.21: Finding the Roles that are Active for Users

```
select * from session_roles;
```

The output of Listing 48.21 is as follows:

```
ROLE
----------------
RESOURCE
CONNECT
```

Listing 48.22 shows how to display system privileges granted to a role:

Listing 48.22: Displaying all the System Privileges Granted to the EMPROLE Role

```
grant alter user to emprole;
select * from role_sys_privs where role = 'emprole';
```

The output of Listing 48.22 is as follows:

```
ROLE                           PRIVILEGE                                ADM
------------------------------ ---------------------------------------- ---
EMPROLE                        ALTER USER                               NO
```

Listing 48.23 shows the code to display all the object privileges granted to a role:

Listing 48.23: Displaying all the Object Privileges Granted to the EMPROLE Role

```
grant select, delete on user49.emp to emprole;
   select table_name, privilege from role_tab_privs
   where role = 'emprole';
```

The output of Listing 48.23 is as follows:

```
TABLE_NAME                PRIVILEGE
------------------        ----------
EMP                       DELETE
EMP                       SELECT
```

Listing 48.24 shows to display which role is granted to which user and whether it is the default role or the role is granted with admin option:

Listing 48.24: Displaying which Role is Granted to which User:

```
select * from sys.dba_role_privs;
```

The output of Listing 48.24 is as follows:

```
GRANTEE                        GRANTED_ROLE                    ADM     DEF
------------------------       --------------------------      ---     ---
SYS                            SNMPAGENT                       YES     YES
SYS                            TIMESERIES_DBA                  YES     YES
SYS                            TIMESERIES_DEVELOPER            YES     YES
SYSTEM                         AQ_ADMINISTRATOR_ROLE           YES     YES
SYSTEM                         DBA                             YES     YES
USER49                         ANIL1                           YES     YES
```

Listing 48.5 shows how to set a role in the PL/SQL block:

Listing 48.25: Setting a Role in the PL/SQL Block

```
create or replace procedure setmyrole
authid current_user as
begin
    sys.dbms_session.set_role('emprole');
end;
```

The output of Listing 48.25 is as follows:

```
Procedure created
```

Predefined Oracle Roles

CONNECT—The privileges are specified in the next section.

RESOURCE—

DBA—All privileges required for doing database administration.

After installation, Oracle creates two users, `SYS` and `SYSTEM`. `SYS` owns all data dictionary and is a most powerful user. `SYSTEM` is mainly used for database administration. You can connect as `SYSDBA` or `SYSOPER`, provided these privileges are granted to you. The privileges of `RESOURCE` are mentioned in Table 48.31:

Privilege	With admin option
CREATE CLUSTER	N
CREATE INDEXTYPE	N
CREATE OPERATOR	N
CREATE PROCEDURE	N
CREATE SEQUENCE	N
CREATE TABLE	N
CREATE TRIGGER	N
CREATE TYPE	N

Activation of System Privileges, Object Privileges, and Roles

You also observe that the role `CONNECT` is used. The `CONNECT` role is created at the time of installation and it provides various privileges, which are listed in Table 48.32:

Privilege	With admin option
ALTER SESSION	N
CREATE CLUSTER	N
CREATE DATABASE LINK	N
CREATE SEQUENCE	N
CREATE SESSION	N
CREATE SYNONYM	N
CREATE TABLE	N
CREATE VIEW	N

In the following example you get the information when the roles are activated and revoked.

We are using two terminals for experimentation—one by DBA and the other by `Anil`. The code for each user is as follows:

DBA

Opening SQL editor for spool file named `cruser`, as shown in the following code snippet:

```
edit cruser
                                    --cruser
```

The editor window opens. Write code in the editor window, as shown in the following code snippet:

```
create user anil
  identified by anil
       default tablespace users
       quota unlimited on users
       temporary tablespace temp
       account unlock;
  grant connect to anil;
```

Run the spoon file, as shown in the following code snippet:

```
@cruser
```

The output of the preceding code snippet is as follows:

```
User created

Grant succeeded
```

ANIL

Creating table T

```
create table t(a number);
```

Result:

```
Table created
```

DBA

Revoking permission from a user

```
revoke connect from anil;
```

Result:

```
Revoke succeeded
```

ANIL

Creating table S

```
create table s(a number);
```

Result:

```
Table created
```

A role is enabled even if it is revoked from user in the current session. For the next session, there is an effect of the revoke.

Listing 48.26: Observing the effect of revoke

```
connect anil/anil
```

Result:

```
ERROR:
ORA-01045: user ANIL lacks CREATE SESSION privilege; logon denied
```

DBA

Listing 48.27: Granting system privilege for connecting with Oracle

```
grant create session to anil;
```

Result:

```
Grant succeeded
```

ANIL

Listing 48.28: Granting create session

```
connect anil/anil
```

Result:

```
Connected
```

Listing 48.29: Seeing how a table is not created because of lack of privilege

```
create table temp(a number);
```

Result:

```
create table temp(a number)
*
ERROR at line 1:
ORA-01031: insufficient privileges
```

DBA

Listing 48.30: DBA giving privilege via role

```
grant connect to anil;
```

Result:

```
Grant succeeded
```

ANIL

Listing 48.31: Executing code when user has insufficient privileges

```
create table temp(a number);
```

Result:

```
create table temp(a number)
*
ERROR at line 1:
ORA-01031: insufficient privileges
```

Since the role is not having effect within session, the privilege is not available.

DBA

Listing 48.32: DBA giving the required privilege as system privilege

```
grant create table to anil;
```

Result:

```
Grant succeeded
```

ANIL

Listing 48.33: Creating table temp

```
create table temp(a number);
```

Result:

```
Table created
```

Thus, system privilege is enabled within session.

DBA

Listing 48.34: DBA revoking privilege

```
revoke create table from anil;
```

Result:

```
Revoke succeeded
```

The revoking has immediate effect in session. Thus, granting of privilege has an immediate effect. The user does not have to disconnect and connect to Oracle.

ANIL

```
create table ztemp(a number);
```

Result:

```
create table ztemp(a number)
*
ERROR at line 1:
ORA-01031: insufficient privileges
```

Listing 48.35: Revoking permission of creating a view from user Anil

```
revoke create view from anil;
```

Result:

```
revoke create view from anil
*
ERROR at line 1:
ORA-01952: system privileges not granted to 'ANIL'
```

Listing 48.36: Revoking privilege available within role

```
revoke create view from anil;
```

Result:

```
revoke create view from anil
*
ERROR at line 1:
ORA-01952: system privileges not granted to 'ANIL'
```

If you try to revoke a privilege available within a role, then it cannot be revoked individually.

Listing 48.37: Revoking create session only in a new session

```
revoke create session from anil;
```

Result:

```
Revoke succeeded
```

Effect of Revoking a Privilege and Dropping a User

If the object privilege is granted to user `U1` by another user `U2` and the privilege is revoked from user `U2`, then the privilege will not be available to `U1`. Even if you drop user `U2`, it will have similar effect. Listing 48.33 shows the code to check the effect of revoking a privilege:

Listing 48.38: Checking the Effect of Revoking a Privilege

```
SCOTT <simple bold>
grant select on pcm to anil with grant option;
```

The output of Listing 48.38 is as follows:

```
Grant succeeded
```

Checking which user is connected to Oracle

```
                                  --ANIL
select user from dual;
```

Result:

```
USER
------------------------------
ANIL
```

Using `select` statement to view data of a table in `scott` when connected as `Anil`

```
select * from scott.pcm;
```

Result:

```
        RN          P          C          M    NAME
---------- ---------- ---------- ----------    ---------
         1         67         89         76    anil
         2         89         65         99    sunil
         3         77         95         94    ajay
         4         75         92         91    sushil
```

Granting permission to a user so as to select data of some other user database

```
grant select on scott.pcm to sunil;
```

Result:

```
Grant succeeded
```

Checking which user is connected to Oracle

```
                                       --SUNIL
select user from dual;
```

Result:

```
USER
------------------------------
SUNIL
```

Using `select` statement to view data of a table in `scott` when connected as `Sunil`

```
select * from scott.pcm;
```

Result:

```
        RN          P          C          M    NAME
---------- ---------- ---------- ----------    --------
         1         67         89         76    anil
         2         89         65         99    sunil
         3         77         95         94    ajay
         4         75         92         91    sushil
```

After revoking privilege

```
                                       --SCOTT
revoke select on pcm from anil;
```

Result:

```
Revoke succeeded
```

This command has revoked the `select` permission from `Anil`. To check the effect when connected as `Anil`, select data from a table of user `scott`. This will result in an error.

Connecting as `Anil`

```
                                       --ANIL
select * from scott.pcm;
```

Result:

```
select * from scott.pcm
                    *
ERROR at line 1:
ORA-00942: table or view does not exist
```

Connecting as user `Sunil`

```
                                       --SUNIL
select * from scott.pcm;
```

Result:

```
select * from scott.pcm
                       *

ERROR at line 1:
ORA-00942: table or view does not exist
```

NOTE

If you grant the object privilege to ANIL with or without grant option then the privilege will not be automatically available to SUNIL. You have to grant it again explicitly.

If the system privilege or role is granted to user `U1` by another user `U2` and the privilege is revoked from user `U2`, then the privilege and the role will be available to `U1`.

Listing 48.39: Granting create table permission to user with Administrative options

```
                                        --DBA
grant create table to anil with admin option;
```

Result:

```
Grant succeeded
```

Creating table when connected to Oracle as `Anil`

```
                                        --ANIL
create table t(a number);
```

Result:

```
Table created
```

Granting create table permission to user `Sunil`

```
grant create table to sunil;
```

Result:

```
Grant succeeded
```

Creating a table when connected to Oracle as `Sunil`

```
                                        --SUNIL
create table t(a number);
```

Result:

```
Table created
```

Connecting as DBA and revoking the create table permission from `Anil`

```
                                        --DBA
revoke create table from anil;
```

Result:

```
Revoke succeeded
```

Connecting as user `Anil`, and creating a table

```
                                        --ANIL
create table zt(a number);
```

This code will result in an error because `create table` permission has been revoked by the DBA.

Result:

```
create table zt(a number)
*
ERROR at line 1:
ORA-01031: insufficient privileges
```

Connecting as user `Sunil` and creating a table

```
                                        --SUNIL
create table zt(a number);
```

Result:

```
Table created
```

Profile

Profile is used to control system resources, such as memory, CPU time, and disk reads. Such a control is essential because the user may perform some operations unnecessarily so that other users working may be affected. For example, user `U1` may fire time-consuming queries because of which performance of other users could be affected. Such time-consuming queries may use shared resources, such as memory or CPU time.

Oracle provides the concept of profile to limit such operations. DBA can create profile and specify the limits on resource usage. The profile can be attached to user using the `ALTER USER` command to create profile following parameters are used.

Table 48.33 lists the profile parameters:

Parameter	Description
SESSIONS_PER_USER	Refers to the number of concurrent sessions that a user can create.
CPU_PER_SESSION	Represents the CPU time limit for a session, expressed in hundredth of seconds. If the queries are computational intensive, such as statistical queries, then it will consume more time.
CPU_PER_CALL	Represents the CPU time limit for a call (Single SQL statement fired by user) expressed in hundredths of seconds. The time is calculated for all the three phases, parse, execute, and fetch.
CONNECT_TIME	Refers to the total elapsed time limit for a session, expressed in minutes. It limits the amount of time a user remains connected in one session. If the limit exceeds, the current transaction is rolled back and the session ends. The next statement returns the error.
IDLE_TIME	Represents the permitted period of continuous inactive time during a session, expressed in minutes. Long-running queries and other operations are not subject to this limit. If the limit exceeds, the current transaction is rolled back and the session ends. The next statement returns an error.
LOGICAL_READS_PER_SESSION	Represents the permitted number of data blocks read in a session, including blocks read from memory and disk. If the limit exceeds, the current statement ends, and user has to commit or rollback the transaction, and end the session.
LOGICAL_READS_PER_CALL	Represents the permitted number of data blocks read for a call to process an SQL statement (parse, execute, or fetch). If the query refers to a large table, the number of logical reads is high. If the SQL statement exceeds the limit, the statement is terminated.
PRIVATE_SGA	Represents the amount of private space a session can allocate in the shared pool of the system global area (SGA), expressed in bytes. The limit is applied only for shared server architecture. The limit of private space for a session in the SGA includes private SQL and PL/SQL areas, but not shared SQL and PL/SQL areas.

Creation of Profile

You can create a profile using the `create profile` command or change the existing limits using the `ALTER PROFILE` command. The profile can be attached to a user. Listing 48.40 shows how to create a profile:

Listing 48.40: Creating a Profile

```
create profile userprofile limit
sessions_per_user 5
cpu_per_session unlimited
cpu_per_call 7500
```

```
logical_reads_per_session unlimited
logical_reads_per_call 134
idle_time 30
connect_time 480
private_sga 50k;
```

The output of Listing 48.40 is as follows:

```
Profile created
```

After creating a profile, you can assign it to a user, as shown in Listing 48.41:

Listing 48.41: Assigning a Profile to a User

```
create user anil123
          identified by anil123
          default tablespace users
          quota unlimited on users
          profile userprofile;
```

The output of Listing 48.41 is as follows:

```
User created
```

You must set the initialization parameter, RESOURCE_LIMIT, to true to have the effect of profile, as shown in the following code snippet:

```
alter system
set resource_limit = true;
```

Initially, all limits of the DEFAULT profile are set to UNLIMITED. However, you can alter a profile, as shown in the following code snippet:

Listing 48.42: Altering a Profile

```
alter profile userprofile limit
cpu_per_call default
cpu_per_session 20000;
```

The output of Listing 48.42 is as follows:

```
Profile altered
```

Let's now learn about composite limits.

Composite Limit

Composite limit is used to limit combined resource usage. Following resource usage can be controlled using composite limit.

Syntax for setting composite limit with resources is as follows:

```
CPU_PER_ SESSION
LOGICAL_READS_PER_SESSION
CONNECT_TIME
PRIVATE_SGA
```

The following code snipped shows how to assign cost to each resource:

```
ALTER RESOURCE COST
CPU_PER_SESSION 5
LOGICAL_READS_PER_SESSION 50
PRIVATE_SGA 7
CONNECT_TIME 4;
```

The output of the preceding code snippet is as follows:

```
Resource cost altered
```

The default cost is 0. You can specify the composite limit in a profile, as shown in the following code snippet:

```
alter profile userprofile limit
composite_limit 70000
/
```

Suppose in one session the statistics is given, as shown in the following code snippet:

```
cpu_time 100
logical_reads 1200
private_sga 100
connect_time 10
```

Then, you can calculate composite resource usage, as shown in the following code snippet:

```
    CPU_TIME × RESOURCE_COST + LOGICAL_READS × RESOURCE_COST + PRIVATE_SGA × RESOURCE_COST +
CONNECT_TIME × RESOURCE_COST
    = 100 * 5 + 1200 * 50 + 100 * 7 + 10 * 4
    = 61240
```

NOTE

You cannot issue any statement, which exceeds the limit of 70000.

Let's now learn how to set password parameters.

Setting Password Parameters

You can also set password parameters by using a profile. Listing 48.43 shows how to set password parameters:

Listing 48.43: Setting Password Parameters

```
create profile passwdprofile limit
   failed_login_attempts 3
   password_life_time 100
   password_reuse_time 70
   password_reuse_max 5
   password_verify_function fnpassword
   password_lock_time 1/24
   password_grace_time 10;
/
```

The output of Listing 48.43 is as follows:

```
Profile created
```

The function fnpassword is user defined function which need be created first.

Table 48.34 lists some password parameters:

Parameters	Description
FAILED_LOGIN_ATTEMPTS	Specifies the number of failed attempts to log in to the user account before the account is locked.
PASSWORD_LIFE_TIME	Specifies the life of password in number of days. The actual life time is the total time calculated by adding PASSWORD_GRACE_TIME. The default value of PASSWORD_GRACE_TIME is unlimited. Suppose you set the values of life time and grace time as 100 and 10, respectively, then the user will get a warning after 100 days. If the user does not change the password after 10 days of the warning, then the connection request is rejected.

Parameters	Description
PASSWORD_REUSE_TIME and PASSWORD_REUSE_MAX	Set the time limit for which an existing password can be used. The default value of these parameters is UNLIMITED in the default profile, and if both values are UNLIMITED then they are ignored. If any of the parameters is an integer and the other UNLIMITED, then you cannot use the same password again. If you set PASSWORD_REUSE_TIME as 5, you cannot set the same password within 5 days. If you set PASSWORD_REUSE_MAX as 3, then you require atleast 3 changes in the password before using the same password again. If you set the value to DEFAULT, then Oracle uses the value in the default profile.
PASSWORD_LOCK_TIME	Specifies the number of days an account will remain locked after the specified number of consecutive failed login attempts.
PASSWORD_VERIFY_FUNCTION	Allows you to enforce additional constraint on password.

Following PLSQL code demonstrates how to create user defined function and how to attach it profile.

Listing 48.44: Writing a function to check that the first character of old and new password are same Signature of function

```
passwd_name (
userid_parameter IN VARCHAR(30),
password_parameter IN VARCHAR (30),
old_password_parameter IN VARCHAR (30)
)
RETURN BOOLEAN
```

Function

```
create or replace function fnpassword
( userid varchar2,
 oldpasswd varchar2,
newpasswd varchar2) return boolean as
begin
if (substr(oldpasswd,1,1)=substr(newpasswd,1,1)) then
 return(true);
else
 return(false);
end if;
end;
```

The output of Listing 48.44 is as follows:

```
Function created
```

The function created is attached to profile as follows.

```
alter profile userprofile limit
password_verify_function fnpassword
/
```

The output of the preceding code snippet is as follows:

```
Profile altered
```

The VARIFY_FUNCTION PASSWORD must be owned by SYS. The function is automatically called when the user changes password. If the function returns true, the password is accepted; otherwise, it is rejected.

Auditing

Auditing is used to track the changes in a database. Suppose you are developing software for a bank that tracks changes in the withdrawal table, that is, which user at which time is withdrawing money. In such a case, you can start the auditing operation on a required table. The result of auditing is retrieved from the `DBA_AUDIT_TRAIL` view (based on `SYS.AUD$`). To enable auditing, you have to set the `AUDIT_TRAIL` initialization parameter to value `db`. Another value of parameter is `os, indicating` that the auditing record is added in the OS file. The following code snippet shows how to set the audit_trial parameter:

```
                                    --DBA
                                    --MAKING INITIALIZATION SETTING
alter system set audit_trail=db scope=spfile;
```

The output of the preceding code snippet is as follows:

```
System altered
```

Execute the shutdown command to shut down the database, as shown in the following code snippet:

```
shutdown immediate;
```

The output of the preceding code snippet is as follows:

```
Database closed
Database dismounted
ORACLE instance shut down
```

Execute the startup command to start the database, as shown in the following code snippet:

```
startup
```

The output of the preceding code snippet is as follows:

```
ORACLE instance started.

Total System Global Area  197132288 bytes
Fixed Size                   788108 bytes
Variable Size             145488244 bytes
Database Buffers           50331648 bytes
Redo Buffers                 524288 bytes
Database mounted.
Database opened.
```

Some examples related to auditing are as follows:

Listing 48.45: Showing Initialization Parameter of Audit

```
show parameter audit_trail;
```

The output of Listing 48.45 is as follows:

```
NAME                                 TYPE           VALUE
------------------------------------ -------------  -------------
audit_trail                          string          DB
```

You can start auditing, as shown in the following code snippet:

```
audit select on scott.pcm by access;
```

The output of the preceding code snippet is as follows:

```
Audit succeeded
```

Issue the statement to check auditing result, as shown in the following code snippet:

```
select * from pcm;
```

The output of the preceding code snippet is as follows:

```
ROLLNO     NAME                           PHYSICS    CHEMISTRY  MATHS
---------- ------------------------------ ---------- ---------- ----------
         1 anil                           67         89         76
         2 sunil                          89         65         99
         3 ajay                           77         95         94
         4 sushil                         75         92         91
```

Check the result of auditing, as shown in the following code snippet:

```
--@craudit
column username format a20
column action_name format a20
column obj_name format a20
column ts format a20
set linesize 100
```

Listing 48.46: Selecting Data from dba_audit_trial

```
select username,obj_name,action_name,to_char(timestamp,'dd-mon-yyyy hh:mi:ss')ts
  from dba_audit_trail;
```

The output of Listing 48.46 is as follows:

```
USERNAME             OBJ_NAME             ACTION_NAME          TS
-------------------- -------------------- -------------------- --------------------
SCOTT                PCM                  SELECT               23-MAY-2011 04:09:28
...
```

Listing 48.47: Enabling Auditing by Session

```
audit select on scott.shares  by session;
```

The output of Listing 48.47 is as follows:

```
Audit succeeded
```

If you enable auditing by session, it will add only one record for that session.

Run the spool file, as shown in the following code snippet:

```
@craudit
```

The output of the preceding code snippet is as follows:

```
USERNAME   OBJ_NAME   ACTION_NAME    TS
---------- ---------- -------------- --------------------
SCOTT      PCM        SELECT         23-MAY-2011 04:09:28
SCOTT      SHARES     SESSION REC    23-MAY-2011 04:26:42
SCOTT      PCM        SELECT         23-MAY-2011 04:30:34
SCOTT      PCM        SELECT         23-MAY-2011 04:30:39
```

Here you are querying `SHARES 3` times and `PCM 3` times. For `PCM` auditing is by access so three records are added. While for auditing by session, only one record is added. Timestamp (TS) indicates the time of first record.

There are three main types of auditing, statement level auditing, privilege level auditing, and object level auditing. If you want to disable auditing, you can use the `NOAUDIT` command.

Statement Level Auditing

In the case of statement level auditing, a statement or group of statements, which affects particular object, is audited. Some examples of statement level auditing are as follows:

Listing 48.48: Performing Statement Level Auditing

```
Audit table by scott by access whenever successful;
```

Or

```
audit table by scott;
```

In Listing 48.48, the audit is enabled in a new session of `scott`. The clause `whenever successful` or `unsuccessful` indicates when an audit record is generated.

The output of Listing 48.48 is as follows:

```
Audit succeeded
```

Following example demonstrates how audit records are generated when operations like CREATE TABLE, DROP TABLE are executed.

Scott issuing statement

```
create table t(a number);
```

The output of the preceding code snippet is as follows:

```
Table created
```

Drop a table, as shown in the following code snippet:

```
drop table t;
```

The output of the preceding code snippet is as follows:

```
Table dropped
```

Generate the audit records, as shown in the following code snippet:

```
@craudit
```

The output of the preceding code snippet is as follows:

```
USERNAME   OBJ_NAME   ACTION_NAME    TS
---------- ---------- -------------- --------------------
SCOTT      PCM        SELECT         23-MAY-2011 04:09:28
SCOTT      SHARES     SESSION REC    23-MAY-2011 04:26:42
SCOTT      PCM        SELECT         23-MAY-2011 04:30:34
SCOTT      PCM        SELECT         23-MAY-2011 04:30:39
SCOTT      T          CREATE TABLE   23-MAY-2011 05:00:19
SCOTT      T          DROP TABLE     23-MAY-2011 05:00:49

6 rows selected
```

Listing 48.49: Auditing Logon and Logoff by Enabling Auditing Using create session

```
audit create session by scott by access;
```

The output of Listing 48.49 is as follows:

```
Audit succeeded
```

Run the spool file, as shown in the following code snippet:

```
@craudit
```

The output of the preceding code snippet is as follows:

```
USERNAME   OBJ_NAME   ACTION_NAME    TS
---------- ---------- -------------- --------------------
SCOTT      PCM        SELECT         23-MAY-2011 04:09:28
SCOTT      SHARES     SESSION REC    23-MAY-2011 04:26:42
SCOTT      PCM        SELECT         23-MAY-2011 04:30:34
SCOTT      PCM        SELECT         23-MAY-2011 04:30:39
SCOTT      T          CREATE TABLE   23-MAY-2011 05:00:19
SCOTT      T          DROP TABLE     23-MAY-2011 05:00:49
SCOTT      PCM        CREATE TABLE   23-MAY-2011 05:04:07
SCOTT      SCENARIO   SESSION REC    23-MAY-2011 05:11:34
SCOTT      SAMPLE     SESSION REC    23-MAY-2011 05:18:02
SCOTT                 LOGOFF         23-MAY-2011 09:21:10
```

Listing 48.50: Displaying Statistics of a User after LOGOFF

```
SELECT USERNAME, LOGOFF_TIME, LOGOFF_LREAD, LOGOFF_PREAD,
    LOGOFF_LWRITE, LOGOFF_DLOCK
    FROM DBA_AUDIT_SESSION;
```

The output of Listing 48.50 is as follows:

```
No rows selected
```

Table 48.35 shows statement-auditing options as specified in the Oracle 10g documentation:

Statement Option	SQL Statements and Operations
CLUSTER	CREATE CLUSTER ALTER CLUSTER DROP CLUSTER TRUNCATE CLUSTER
CONTEXT	CREATE CONTEXT DROP CONTEXT
DATABASE LINK	CREATE DATABASE LINK DROP DATABASE LINK
DIMENSION	CREATE DIMENSION ALTER DIMENSION DROP DIMENSION
DIRECTORY	CREATE DIRECTORY DROP DIRECTORY
INDEX	CREATE INDEX ALTER INDEX DROP INDEX
MATERIALIZED VIEW	CREATE MATERIALIZED VIEW ALTER MATERIALIZED VIEW DROP MATERIALIZED VIEW
NOT EXISTS	All SQL statements fail because a specified object does not exist
PROCEDURE	CREATE FUNCTION CREATE LIBRARY CREATE PACKAGE CREATE PACKAGE BODY CREATE PROCEDURE DROP FUNCTION DROP LIBRARY DROP PACKAGE DROP PROCEDURE
PROFILE	CREATE PROFILE

Statement Option	SQL Statements and Operations
	ALTER PROFILE DROP PROFILE
PUBLIC DATABASE LINK	CREATE PUBLIC DATABASE LINK DROP PUBLIC DATABASE LINK
PUBLIC SYNONYM	CREATE PUBLIC SYNONYM DROP PUBLIC SYNONYM
ROLE	CREATE ROLE ALTER ROLE DROP ROLE SET ROLE
ROLLBACK SEGMENT	CREATE ROLLBACK SEGMENT ALTER ROLLBACK SEGMENT DROP ROLLBACK SEGMENT
SEQUENCE	CREATE SEQUENCE DROP SEQUENCE
SESSION	Logons
SYNONYM	CREATE SYNONYM DROP SYNONYM
SYSTEM AUDIT	AUDIT sql_statements NOAUDIT sql_statements
SYSTEM GRANT	GRANT system_privileges_and_roles REVOKE system_privileges_and_roles
TABLE	CREATE TABLE DROP TABLE TRUNCATE TABLE
TABLESPACE	CREATE TABLESPACE ALTER TABLESPACE DROP TABLESPACE
TRIGGER	CREATE TRIGGER ALTER TRIGGER with ENABLE and DISABLE clauses DROP TRIGGER ALTER TABLE with ENABLE ALL TRIGGERS clause and DISABLE ALL TRIGGERS clause

Statement Option	SQL Statements and Operations
TYPE	CREATE TYPE CREATE TYPE BODY ALTER TYPE DROP TYPE DROP TYPE BODY
USER	CREATE USER ALTER USER DROP USER
VIEW	CREATE VIEW DROP VIEW
CLUSTER	CREATE CLUSTER ALTER CLUSTER DROP CLUSTER TRUNCATE CLUSTER
CONTEXT	CREATE CONTEXT DROP CONTEXT

In Table 48.35, the first column indicates the statement group used in audit command, while the second column indicates the statements which cause the generation of audit record.

Suppose you enable the audit table. In that case, it will insert audit record for creating a table, truncating a table, and dropping a table. Apart from the groups, the following audit options are available:

- `ALTER SEQUENCE`
- `ALTER TABLE`
- `COMMENT TABLE`
- `DELETE TABLE`
- `EXECUTE PROCEDURE`
- `GRANT DIRECTORY`
- `GRANT SEQUENCE`
- `GRANT TABLE`
- `GRANT TYPE`
- `INSERT TABLE`
- `LOCK TABLE`
- `SELECT SEQUENCE`
- `SELECT TABLE`
- `UPDATE TABLE`

Privilege Auditing

In case of privilege auditing, whenever you perform any operation using certain privileges then the timing of the operation is stored in the audit table. For example, if you provide the `SELECT ANY TABLE` privilege to `scott`, then the time when `scott` performs any operation using this privilege is recorded. The following code snippet shows how to perform privilege auditing:

```
audit select any table by scott;
```

Listing 48.51 shows how Scott issues a statement for testing privilege auditing:

Listing 48.51: Issuing a Statement

```
select * from emp.scenario;
```

You can generate audit record, as shown in the following code snippet:

```
@craudit
```

The output of the preceding code snippet is as follows:

```
USERNAME   OBJ_NAME   ACTION_NAME    TS
---------- ---------- -------------- --------------------
SCOTT      PCM        SELECT         23-MAY-2011 04:09:28
SCOTT      SHARES     SESSION REC    23-MAY-2011 04:26:42
SCOTT      PCM        SELECT         23-MAY-2011 04:30:34
SCOTT      PCM        SELECT         23-MAY-2011 04:30:39
SCOTT      T          CREATE TABLE   23-MAY-2011 05:00:19
SCOTT      T          DROP TABLE     23-MAY-2011 05:00:49
SCOTT      PCM        CREATE TABLE   23-MAY-2011 05:04:07
SCOTT      SCENARIO   SESSION REC    23-MAY-2011 05:11:34
```

Object Level Auditing

In object level auditing, auditing is done with reference to a fixed object. Suppose you want to record a history of operations, such as `INSERT`, `UPDATE`, `DELETE`, and `ALTER`. In such a case, you can use object level auditing. Listing 48.52 shows the use of object level auditing:

Listing 48.52: Using Object Level Auditing

```
audit insert,update,delete,alter on scott.sample;
```

The output of Listing 48.52 is as follows:

```
Audit succeeded
```

You can issue following statement to test result of auditing

Listing 48.53: Scott issuing a statement

```
insert into sample(sn) values(1);
```

The output of Listing 48.53 is as follows:

```
1 row created
```

Irrespective of whether the transaction is committed or not, the audit record is added, as shown in the following code snippet:

```
@craudit
```

The output of the preceding code snippet is as follows:

```
USERNAME   OBJ_NAME   ACTION_NAME    TS
---------- ---------- -------------- --------------------
SCOTT      PCM        SELECT         23-MAY-2011 04:09:28
SCOTT      SHARES     SESSION REC    23-MAY-2011 04:26:42
SCOTT      PCM        SELECT         23-MAY-2011 04:30:34
SCOTT      PCM        SELECT         23-MAY-2011 04:30:39
SCOTT      T          CREATE TABLE   23-MAY-2011 05:00:19
SCOTT      T          DROP TABLE     23-MAY-2011 05:00:49
SCOTT      PCM        CREATE TABLE   23-MAY-2011 05:04:07
SCOTT      SCENARIO   SESSION REC    23-MAY-2011 05:11:34
SCOTT      SAMPLE     SESSION REC    23-MAY-2011 05:18:02
```

You can use the following audit options appropriately on objects:

- ALTER
- AUDIT
- COMMENT
- DELETE
- EXECUTE
- FLASHBACK
- GRANT
- INDEX
- INSERT
- LOCK
- READ
- RENAME
- SELECT
- UPDATE

NOTE

You cannot use the EXECUTE option on a table.

The types of objects are as follows:

- TABLE
- PROCEDURES
- FUNCTIONS
- PACKAGE
- INDEX
- OBJECTS
- OBJECT TYPES
- VIEWS
- DIRECTORY
- LIBRARY
- VIEWS
- MATERIALIZED VIEWS
- CONTEXT

The DBA_STMT_AUDIT_OPTS View

The DBA_STMT_AUDIT_OPTS view displays current auditing options. Listing 48.54 shows the use of the DBA_STMT_AUDIT_OPTS view:

Listing 48.54: Using the DBA_STMT_AUDIT_OPTS View

```
select * from dba_stmt_audit_opts;
```

The output of Listing 48.54 is as follows:

```
USER_NAME                      PROXY_NAME
------------------------------ ------------------------------
AUDIT_OPTION                             SUCCESS    FAILURE
---------------------------------------- ---------- ----------
SCOTT
```

```
TABLE                                        BY ACCESS   BY ACCESS

SCOTT
SELECT ANY TABLE                             BY SESSION BY SESSION
```

In Listing 48.54, the `DBA_OBJ_AUDIT_OPTS` view displays the current object auditing options.

The output of the preceding code snippet is as follows:

```
USER_NAME.                     PROXY_NAME
------------------------------ ------------------------------
AUDIT_OPTION                             SUCCESS    FAILURE
---------------------------------------- ---------- ----------
SCOTT
TABLE                                    BY ACCESS  BY ACCESS

SCOTT
SELECT ANY TABLE                         BY SESSION BY SESSION
```

Summary

This chapter detailed you all about security and auditing. The next chapter will provide PL/SQL questions.

Exercise

1. Write PLSQL code to create fifty users with prefix STUDENT. For example STUDENT1, STUDENT2.
2. Enable auditing of these users at record login and logoff timings.
3. Enable auditing of these users to record history of CREATE TABLE command.

49

PL/SQL Questions

Datatypes

- ❐ What is the maximum length of `varchar2` datatypes in PL/SQL?
- ❐ What is the use of `ROWID`?
- ❐ What are the components of `ROWID`?
- ❐ Define subtypes? Give two examples.
- ❐ What are the general standards for declaration?

Control Structure

- ❐ What is the alternative to `CASE` statement?
- ❐ What is an infinite loop?
- ❐ How will you specify `GOTO` statement?

Collections

- ❐ What is the difference between `VARRAY` and `TABLE`?
- ❐ What is the SQL support for nested table?
- ❐ What do you mean by inline and out of line storage of a nested table?
- ❐ What are the common exceptions related with collections?
- ❐ Can you declare VARRY of VARRY or VARRY of table?
- ❐ Define the following terms:
    - VARRY of object
    - Table of objects
- ❐ Write the common methods for handling collections?

Interaction with Oracle

- ❐ What is the constraint on `SELECT INTO` statement?
- ❐ What will happen if an aggregate function, such as `MAX`, does not retrieve any row into the `SELECT` statement?
- ❐ Define cursor? Give its attributes?
- ❐ What is a parametric cursor?
- ❐ What will happen if you use cursor attribute `ROWCOUNT` on a closed cursor?
- ❐ Differentiate a weakly defined and a strongly defined cursor?
- ❐ What are the advantages of a strongly defined cursor?
- ❐ How will you reduce method overheads using cursor variable?
- ❐ Can you write a procedure which returns a cursor? How will you write a calling procedure?

Triggers

- ❐ Can you use new and old columns in a statement trigger? If not, why?
- ❐ What do you mean by statement level atomicity? State its importance.
- ❐ How is statement level atomicity implemented in the case of a trigger?
- ❐ Why is `SAVEPOINT` issued only to the parent SQL statement?

- Why is transaction control statement (`COMMIT`, `ROLLBACK`) not allowed in trigger code?

[Hint: If they are allowed, they may result in saving partial effect of DML statement. Unless the statement releases the lock, next rows are not processed]

- How will you bypass mutating error?

[Hint: Take value of statement trigger in packaged variable and use that value in row trigger]

- Why trigger code is not preferred?
- In which phase of a transaction is the deferred constraints checking applied?
- Give one example of trigger generating code, which is dependent on the order in which rows are evaluated.
- Give trigger code for parent or child to implement update cascade, update set to default, update set to null, and delete cascade.
- If there is an error in execution in trigger code, then what is its effect on the modification done by that statement?

[Hint: The `UNDO` effect covers only database change; it does not cover sequence modification and package variable]

Procedures, Packages, and Objects

- What is procedure overloading? Can you overload two stored procedures?
- What is the advantage of stored subprogram?
- Describe the situation in which you will get error `'Existing state of package discarded'`.

[Hint: Session 1: Create package and use package variable in program; Session 2: Alter package and add some attribute; Session 1: Again use package variable. You will get error in this state]

- When will you get an error `'fetching across commit'`?
- What can you use in package specification part? Can you use variable of type `REF` cursor?
- How will you write initialization in the package? Can you have object initialization?
- What is the difference between a package and an object?
- What will happen if you give constraints datatype as formal parameters?
- How will you make your subprogram more scalable? *[Hint: By using variable declaration as `%rowtype` and `%type`]*
- What are the rules of overloading?
- How will you create subtype from supertype? *[Hint: `Under` clause]*
- Define the following methods:
  - Overloading
  - Overriding
  - Polymorphism
- How will you compare two objects? *[Hint: Map or order method]*
- Can you have two triggers of the same type on the same event? *[Hint: Allowed but not preferred]*
- Differentiate between a strongly defined and a weakly defined cursor.

PL/SQL Packages

- How will you execute dynamic SQL statement and DDL statement inside PL/SQL?
- What work is done in Parse?
- For the `SELECT` statement, what is the work done in execute and fetch phase?
- For the DML statement, what is the work done in execute phase and parse phase?

- Why EXECUTE returns 0 in the SELECT statement?
- What is the utility of DBMS_PIPE?
- Suppose you require that the receiving program should wait for the message, how will you write the receive message procedure?
- What is the status returned, if the message is not received in a specific period?
- Write a protocol so that the sender will go ahead after ensuring that the message is received.
- Write a program to insert a maximum 10 rows at a time in a table. The rows are deleted by another program. If the number of rows in the table exceeds more than 10, then the sender will wait. If the number of rows are 0, then the receiver will wait.
- What is the utility of DBMS alert?
- Can you impose waiting for the alert?
- What is the difference between DBMS_PIPE and DBMS_ALERT?
- How will you schedule jobs using DBMS_JOB?
- How will you write DBMS_JOB, if you want to start the job at 3 p.m., and after executing for 2 minutes, stop the execution at 3.10 p.m.?
- How will you write a program that will execute a certain procedure at 3 p.m. everyday, after a 10 minute interval up to 4 p.m.?
- How will you write a program which executes a certain procedure on every Saturday at 12 o'clock?
- How will you get the information about jobs?
- What is the purpose of parameter UTL_FILE_DIR? Give the setting for Windows and Unix OS?
- How will you execute dynamic SQL statement? Describe phases.
- Can you decide procedure call at runtime?
- What is the difference between execute phase and fetch phase in the SELECT and DML statements.

Autonomous Transactions

- How will you define an autonomous procedure or function?
- What is meant by an autonomous transaction?
- What is meant by an autonomous trigger? What is its utility?
- Why an autonomous transaction should end with COMMIT or ROLLBACK?
- What is the effect of ISOLATION LEVEL SERIALIZABLE?
- What will happen if you make parent transactions SERIALIZABLE, which is calling autonomous transactions?

Exception

- What is the difference between exception and normal IF statement?
- What is rule of propagation in exception?
- What are the normal Oracle built-in exceptions? Give their error code and message.
- What is the use of procedure 'RAIS APPLICATION EROR'?
- How will you convert an Oracle error into an exception?
- Why are exceptions generally declared in package?
- What will happen if an exception is generated:
    - In the declaration section

- In exception handler

- ❐ Suppose you declared an exception with the same name as Oracle exception. How will you write the handler for Oracle exception?
- ❐ What is the use of an exception?

Transactions

- ❐ What is atomicity of transaction?
- ❐ Define `ACID` properties of transaction?
- ❐ What is the use of `COMMIT`?
- ❐ How is durability implemented? What is the problem in implementing durability?
- ❐ What are isolation levels?
- ❐ Name the isolation levels that are supported by Oracle?
- ❐ What is conflict serializable and view serializable schedule?
- ❐ What is a serializable schedule?
- ❐ What is the method of detecting serializable schedule?
- ❐ What is the importance of serializable schedule?
- ❐ How does Oracle makes some transaction serializable?
- ❐ What are read-only transactions?

RBS, UNDO

- ❐ What is read consistency?
- ❐ How is read consistency implemented using RBS?
- ❐ Why is there circular writing in rollback segment (RBS)?
- ❐ Describe the situation in which you will get the error "snapshot too old". What will you do on getting this error frequently?
- ❐ What is the meaning of extent?
- ❐ Why are runtime allocations not preferred?
- ❐ Why is there an enlargement and shrink in RBS?
- ❐ How will you avoid frequency of shrinks?
- ❐ How will you set optimal with RBS and `UNDO`?
- ❐ Write the sample command for creating RBS.
- ❐ What will happen if optimal size is given less than the size decided by `MINEXTENT`?
- ❐ How will you allocate RBS to transaction explicitly?
- ❐ Why is it recommended to use large RBS for large trans and small for small trans?
- ❐ What is the main difference between locally managed and dictionary managed tablespace?
- ❐ What kind of tablespace is used for `UNDO` tablespace? *[Hint: Locally managed]*
- ❐ Name the parameters which are related with `UNDO` tablespace.
- ❐ Which errors are reduced in `UNDO` tablespace?
- ❐ What is a resumable session?
- ❐ If a state is suspended in a resumable session where will you get a record?
- ❐ How will you decide the size of the `UNDO` tablespace?

- What is the meaning of parameter `undo_retention`?
- How will you switch from one `UNDO` tablespace to another?
- Where is the location of alert file?
- What is the meaning of parameter `undo-supress` error?

Locks

- Name the modes in which a table can be locked.
- Which lock is requested in case an `ALTER TABLE` is issued?
- Which locks are obtained, if you issue `SELECT FOR UPDATE` and `ACTUAL UPDATE` STATES?

Suppose you want to present a modified data to another user, which minimum lock will you request? *[Hint: Share lock]*

- When will you have a condition of a deadlock?
- How does Oracle handle deadlocks?
- Which view gives the information about locking transaction?
- How will you kill a session?

FLASHBACK, INVOKER RIGHTS, NOCOPY, PL/SQL Wrapper

- What is the utility of flashback query?
- How will you set flashback mode?
- Why is the DML option not permitted in the flashback mode?
- What procedure will you use to set flashback according to SCN?
- What do you mean by definer right and invoker right?
- How will you provide an invoker right? What is its default setting?
- What are the two methods of implementing? *[Hint: `COPY` and `NOCOPY`]*
- What is the advantage of `NOCOPY`?
- How does `NOCOPY` produce side effect?
- How will you specify `NOCOPY` in formal parameter?
- What is the meaning of referred object and dependent object?
- When does the procedure or function get invalid status?
- From which view, can you check the status of an object?
- What is the disadvantage of runtime recompilation? When does Oracle perform runtime recompilation?
- What is dependency tracking?
- In which file, will you get utilities required for dependency tracking?
- Write the steps for tracking dependencies.
- Suppose you have altered some object. Describe the steps that you will perform to avoid runtime compilation.
- What is the utility of sequence?
- Write sample sequence definition.
- What is the meaning of the statement `sequence guarantees uniqueness, not order`?
- What is the utility of PL/SQL wrapper?
- How you will use PL/SQL wrapper?

Security and Auditing

- How will you create a user?
- What is the meaning of the default tablespace?
- How will you use operating system authentication?
- What are system privileges and object privileges?
- What are the uses of roles?
- Why do you create a role using password?
- What is the meaning of the default role?
- In which context are the privileges of roles available?
- Which privileges are available using the role CONNECT?
- Why do you assign privileges of referred objects in subprograms directly rather than using role?
- What will happen to object privileges, if the grantee (the user who granted privilege) is dropped or his/her privileges are revoked?
- What is the use of auditing?
- What are different levels of auditing?
- How is auditing enabled?
- How will you know that auditing is enabled?
- How will you create a log of users who were connected in the past seven days?
- How will you get information about objects for which auditing is enabled?

A

Tables

Company	
cname	**city**
ACC	MUMBAI
TATA	DELHI

employee		
	ename	**city**
1	ANIL	NAGPUR
2	SHANKAR	MUMBAI
3	JAYA	CHENNAI
4	SUNIL	MUMBAI
5	VIJAY	DELHI
6	PRAKASH	KOLKATA
7	AJAY	CHENNAI

emp_company			
ename	**cname**	**salary**	**jdate**
ANIL	ACC	1500.00	1-MAY-89
SHANKAR	TATA	2000.00	10-JUL-90
JAYA	CMC	1800.00	7-JUN-91
SUNIL	CMC	1700.00	1-JAN-88
VIJAY	TATA	5000.00	3-JAN-88
PRAKASH	TATA	3000.00	27-MAY-89

emp_company			
ename	**cname**	**salary**	**jdate**
AJAY	ACC	8000.00	30-APR-95
AMOL	ACC	1000.00	17-MAR-95

company	
cname	**city**
ACC	CHENNAI
TATA	MUMBAI
ACC	NAGPUR
CMC	MUMBAI
CMC	CHENNAI
TATA	DELHI

manager	
ename	**mname**
ANIL	AJAY
SHANKAR	VIJAY
JAYA	–
SUNIL	JAYA
VIJAY	–
PRAKASH	SHANKAR
AJAY	–

emp_shift	
ename	**shift**
ANIL	A
SUNIL	B
VIJAY	B
PRAKASH	C

Student			
	RN	**Name**	**City**
R1	1	Amit	NGP
R2	2	Ajay	BMB
R3	2	Ashok	DLH
R4	3	Abhay	

Student marks			
	RN	**Year**	**Marks**
R5	1	1	85.2
R6	5	1	76
R7	3	1	109
R8	3	2	A

Parent		
A	**B**	**C**
1	2	3
2	5	9

Child			
	A	**B**	**C**
R1	7	2	3
R2	9	5	9
R3	7	NULL	NULL
R4	1	2	NULL
R5	8	NULL	10

sales_data						
PRODID	**CUSTID**	**TIMEID**	**C**	**PROMOID**	**QUANTITY**	**AMOUNT**
94653	7290	01-JAN-98	S	9999	18	1422
46360	22340	01-JAN-98	S	9999	6	114
4105	37280	01-JAN-98	C	9999	7	553
85	180430	01-JAN-98	T	9999	2	236

sales_data						
PRODID	CUSTID	TIMEID	C	PROMOID	QUANTITY	AMOUNT
7145	136490	01-JAN-98	P	9999	3	195
10880	2630	01-JAN-98	I	9999	14	280
2595	16480	01-JAN-98	I	9999	4	196
6315	6910	01-JAN-98	S	9999	2	78
37195	49900	01-JAN-98	T	9999	9	90
4885	6900	01-JAN-98	C	9999	4	752

PCM				
ROLLNO	NAME	PHYSICS	CHEMISTRY	MATHS
1	anil	67	89	76
2	sunil	89	65	99
3	ajay	77	95	94
4	sushil	75	92	91

sales			
Time	Region	Dept	Profit
1996	Central	pen_sales	34000
1996	Central	pen_sales	41000
1996	Central	book_sales	74000
1996	east	pen_sales	89000
1996	east	book_sales	100000
1996	east	book_sales	15000
1996	west	pen_sales	87000
1996	west	book_sales	86000
1997	Central	pen_sales	82000
1997	Central	book_sales	85000
1997	east	pen_sales	101000
1997	east	book_sales	137000
1997	west	pen_sales	96000
1997	west	book_sales	97000

emp_acc		
ENAME	**SALARY**	**JDATE**
ANIL	1500	01-MAY-89
AJAY	8000	30-APR-95

emp_data		
ENAME	**SALARY**	**JDATE**
SHANKAR	2000	10-JUL-90
VIJAY	5000	03-JAN-88
PRAKASH	3000	27-MAY-89

product		
Product	**DEMAND_RANK**	**SUPPLY_RANK**
A	1	5
B	2	4
C	3	3
D	4	2
E	5	1

product1		
Product	**DEMAND_RANK**	**SUPPLY_RANK**
A	1	1
B	2	2
C	3	3
D	4	4
E	5	5

marks			
Rn	**Phy**	**Che**	**Maths**
1	79	89	90
2	70	80	91
3	65	75	85
4	60	68	98
5	55	57	93

sales_new		
Area	**ZoneA**	**ZoneB**
s	45	59
n	40	43
n	50	47
s	39	51
s	53	39
n	44	49

rainfall		
Rainfall	**Expected**	**Observed**
Y_1990	50	45
Y_1991	35	32
Y_1992	45	40
Y_1993	40	45
Y_1994	33	40

kol_s	
Grade	**Score**
A	30
B	100
A	440
B	500
A	130

mode1	
ID	**Val**
1	10
2	23
3	39
3	32

M_WHITNEY1	
Section	**Strength**
A	35
B	40
A	45
A	50
B	55
A	60
B	65
A	70
A	75
B	80
B	85
A	90
A	95
A	100
B	30
B	105
A	110
B	115
B	120
A	125
B	130
A	135
B	140

MACHINE	
NEW_MAC	**OLD_MAC**
10	12
11	14
12	10
9	11
15	16

MACHINE	
NEW_MAC	OLD_MAC
8	11
20	22
14	16
10	8
13	11
14	15
10	8
7	10
17	16
18	20

ANSWER	
Y_OR_N	Score
Y	50
N	176
Y	100
Y	80
N	95
N	60

scn_table		
A	TIME_INS	SCN
1	04-AUG-06	3997971
2	04-AUG-06	3997973
3	04-AUG-06	3997975
4	04-AUG-06	3997977
5	04-AUG-06	3997979
6	04-AUG-06	3997981

fabc		
A	B	C
41	41	04-AUG-06 12.05.06.765000 PM
21	2	04-AUG-06 12.05.06.781000 PM
31	3	04-AUG-06 12.05.06.812000 PM
41	4	04-AUG-06 12.05.06.828000 PM
51	5	04-AUG-06 12.05.06.859000 PM
61	6	04-AUG-06 12.05.06.875000 PM
410	41	04-AUG-06 12.05.06.906000 PM
201	2	04-AUG-06 12.05.06.921000 PM
301	3	04-AUG-06 12.05.06.953000 PM
401	4	04-AUG-06 12.05.06.968000 PM
501	5	04-AUG-06 12.05.07.000000 PM
601	6	04-AUG-06 12.05.07.546000 PM

fabc1		
A	B	C
41	41	04-AUG-06 11.25.06.578000 AM
21	2	04-AUG-06 11.25.06.609000 AM
31	3	04-AUG-06 11.25.06.640000 AM
41	4	04-AUG-06 11.25.06.656000 AM
51	5	04-AUG-06 11.25.06.687000 AM
61	6	04-AUG-06 11.25.06.703000 AM
410	41	04-AUG-06 11.25.06.734000 AM
201	2	04-AUG-06 11.25.06.750000 AM
301	3	04-AUG-06 11.25.06.781000 AM
401	4	04-AUG-06 11.25.06.796000 AM
501	5	04-AUG-06 11.25.06.828000 AM
601	6	04-AUG-06 11.25.07.375000 AM

Consumer			
Consumername	**Pincode**	**Phone**	**Interest**
abhay	640011	877888	propertytype='flat' and Year < 2001 and Price < 200000
ajay	640011	877888	propertytype='flat' and Year > 2001 and year < 2006 and Price < 220000
anil	440010	222333	propertytype='flat' and year>1999 and Price < 150000 and sqft < 600
sunil	440011	777888	propertytype='house' and Year > 2000 and Price < 200000
vijay	440011	777888	propertytype='flat' and Year >= 2000 and Price >= 200000 and sqft>= 600

Index

V

W